Bankruptcy

ANNE LAWTON

Professor of Law Emerita
Michigan State University College of Law

Third Edition

Acknowledgments

I wish to acknowledge several people who helped make possible this current edition of *Gilbert's on Bankruptcy.*

First, Professor Ned Waxman authored the 2002 edition of *Gilbert's on Bankruptcy.* Much has changed since 2002 with the passage of the Bankruptcy Abuse Prevention and Consumer Protection Act of 2005 and the recently enacted Small Business Reorganization Act of 2019. Nonetheless, this edition retains some text and the basic framework created by Professor Waxman in that earlier edition.

Second, updating the Code to reflect the changes made by the Bankruptcy Abuse Prevention and Consumer Protection Act of 2005 (BAPCPA) would have been a far more arduous task without the Honorable William Houston Brown's (retired) and Lawrence R Ahern III's publication entitled 2005 BANKRUPTCY REFORM LEGISLATION WITH ANALYSIS 2D. This handy guide not only walks the reader through BAPCPA's changes but also reprints the entire Code, as amended, but with BAPCPA's amendments shown in italics.

Third, the Honorable Paul W. Bonapfel, a bankruptcy judge in the Northern District of Georgia, has written *A Guide to the Small Business Reorganization Act of 2019.* It is an invaluable resource on the new subchapter V of Chapter 11.

Fourth, Austin Blessing-Nelson, an MSU law graduate and Associate Counsel at the Michigan Attorney Grievance Commission, provided invaluable research and editing assistance with the 2018 edition of this study guide.

Last, but certainly not least, I want to thank the editors at West Publishing, in particular Jon Harkness and Laura Holle, not only for their editorial assistance but also their patience.

Any errors are mine alone.

Anne Lawton
Professor of Law Emerita
MSU College of Law

Table of Contents

Capsule Summary

I. INTRODUCTION

A. GOALS OF THE FEDERAL BANKRUPTCY LAWS

One of the main purposes of bankruptcy is to relieve an honest debtor of debts, thereby providing an opportunity for a *fresh start.* The bankruptcy laws also benefit creditors by (i) providing a forum for either an orderly liquidation of a debtor's estate or a judicially confirmed plan for full or partial repayment of creditors, (ii) protecting unsecured creditors from preferential or fraudulent transfers of the debtor's property, and (iii) requiring adequate protection of secured creditors' interests in collateral under certain circumstances.

B. LEGISLATIVE HISTORY

Article 1, Section 8 of the United States Constitution empowers Congress to enact uniform laws on bankruptcy. Under this grant of authority, Congress passed the *Bankruptcy Act of 1898* (the "Act"), which the Chandler Act of 1938 substantially amended. The Bankruptcy Reform Act of 1978 repealed the Bankruptcy Act of 1898, and created the *Bankruptcy Code,* which became effective on October 1, 1979. The Code substantially expanded the jurisdiction of the bankruptcy court to enable the bankruptcy judge to hear practically all matters arising in or related to the bankruptcy case, thereby eliminating some of the logistical problems of litigation under the Bankruptcy Act. In 2005, Congress passed the *Bankruptcy Abuse Prevention and Consumer Protection Act* ("BAPCPA"), which made substantial changes to the Bankruptcy Code that affected, among others, individual consumers by erecting an entry barrier to Chapter 7 with the "means test." Recently, Congress enacted the *Small Business Reorganization Act of 2019* ("SBRA"), which created subchapter V of Chapter 11. The SBRA is supposed to streamline the Chapter 11 process for small business debtors, thereby increasing the odds that a small business debtor will emerge from bankruptcy with a confirmed plan.

C. ORGANIZATION OF THE BANKRUPTCY CODE

With the exception of Chapter 12, the Code is organized into *odd-numbered chapters.* Chapters 1, 3, and 5 contain provisions generally applicable to the filing chapters and include definitions, rules on eligibility for relief, provisions on the automatic stay, and what constitutes property of the bankruptcy estate. The filing chapters are 7 (liquidation), 9 (municipalities), 11 (reorganization), 12 (family farmers and family fishermen), 13 (reorganization for individuals only), and 15 (cross-border insolvency). This study guide does not cover Chapters 9 or 15.

D. RULES OF CONSTRUCTION

1. "After Notice and a Hearing"

This statutory language requires notice and an opportunity for a hearing. However, the statutory language authorizes an act without an actual hearing if proper notice is given and: (i) no hearing is requested by a party in interest; or (ii) there is insufficient time for a hearing and the court authorizes the act.

2. **"Order for Relief"**

Entry of an order for relief occurs automatically by the filing of a voluntary petition or upon court determination in an involuntary case that the debtor is generally not paying his debts as they become due. Entry of an order for relief merely means that the case can proceed.

E. TERMINOLOGY

1. Claim

A claim is a right to payment, even if it is unliquidated, unmatured, disputed, or contingent. It also includes the right to an equitable remedy for breach of performance if the breach gives rise to a right to payment. Congress intended a broad definition of "claim."

2. Current Monthly Income

Current monthly income is the debtor's *average monthly income* from all sources during *the six-month period* that ends on the last day of the calendar month immediately before the debtor's bankruptcy filing. The term is used in the Chapter 7 financial eligibility test that Congress created in BAPCPA and also for determining disposable income in Chapter 13 cases.

3. Debt

A debt is a liability on a claim. A *consumer debt* is one incurred by an individual for a personal, family, or household purpose.

4. Entity

This term includes persons, trusts, estates, governmental units, and the United States trustee.

5. Insider

An insider is defined in terms of whether the debtor is an individual, a corporation, or a partnership, and generally includes the debtor's relatives and persons such as directors, officers, control persons, partners, and relatives of such persons.

6. Insolvent

An entity is insolvent when its debts total more than the aggregate value of all of its property, excluding property fraudulently transferred and exempt property.

7. Lien

A *lien* is a charge against or an interest in property to secure payment of a debt or the performance of an obligation. A *judicial lien* is a lien obtained by judgment, levy, sequestration, or other legal or equitable proceeding or process. A *security interest* is a lien that is created by agreement.

8. Person

Individuals, corporations, and partnerships are persons; governmental units are not (with one exception related to eligibility to serve on a Chapter 11 creditors' committee).

9. Transfer

A transfer is any voluntary *or* involuntary disposition of property or interest in property.

F. BANKRUPTCY PETITION PREPARERS

A *bankruptcy petition preparer* is a person, other than the debtor's attorney or an employee under the direct supervision of the debtor's attorney, who prepares for compensation a document, such as the petition, for filing. A bankruptcy petition preparer cannot give a potential debtor legal advice. The Code provides for damages, fines, and injunctive relief against a bankruptcy petition preparer who violates the Code's rules.

II. JURISDICTION AND PROCEDURE

A. BANKRUPTCY COURT

The bankruptcy court in each federal judicial district constitutes a unit of the district court, which refers cases to the bankruptcy judges for the district. Bankruptcy judges are appointed for a judicial district by the United States court of appeals for the circuit in which the district is located. The judge's *term is for 14 years.* The bankruptcy judge may issue any *necessary or appropriate order, process, or judgment* to carry out the Code's provisions. Nothing in the Bankruptcy Code precludes the bankruptcy court from *sua sponte* taking any necessary or appropriate action to enforce its orders or rules, or to prevent an abuse of process. The court also may hold *status conferences* and issue orders to expedite the case. In a *subchapter V* case, the bankruptcy court *must* hold a status conference within *60 days of the order for relief.*

1. Contempt

Most courts have held that the bankruptcy court has the authority to issue *civil* contempt orders to coerce compliance with a court order. The Supreme Court, in *Taggart v. Lorenzen,* held that bankruptcy courts should apply *the fair ground of doubt* standard when deciding whether to hold a creditor in civil contempt for violating the court's discharge order. The courts are split, however, as to *criminal* contempt orders issued to punish the violator.

2. Sanctions

The bankruptcy court may impose sanctions on attorneys, law firms, or parties who sign, file, or submit pleadings or other documents, or advocate for positions that (i) are *not well-grounded in fact or in law* or (ii) are filed for any *improper purpose.*

B. PERSONAL JURISDICTION

The Bankruptcy Rules provide for *nationwide service of process* by first class prepaid mail, except for subpoenas, in adversary proceedings and contested matters. Courts typically do not use the "minimum contacts" test. Service of process on an insured depository institution generally requires certified mail, rather than first class mail.

C. SUBJECT MATTER JURISDICTION

1. District Courts

The United States district courts have *original and exclusive jurisdiction over all cases* under the Bankruptcy Code. The district courts have *original but not exclusive* jurisdiction over *all civil proceedings* arising under, or arising in or related to the bankruptcy case. Finally, the district courts have *exclusive jurisdiction* (i) of all of the *debtor's property*, wherever located, as of the commencement of the bankruptcy case; (ii) of *property of the estate;* and (iii) over *all claims or causes of action* involving construction of or rules relating to disclosure requirements under *§ 327* on employment of professional persons.

2. Referral to Bankruptcy Courts

Each district has its own rule automatically referring all bankruptcy cases and proceedings to the bankruptcy judges in the district.

D. CORE VERSUS NON-CORE PROCEEDINGS

There are three categories of proceedings in a bankruptcy case: proceedings that (i) *arise under* title 11; (ii) *arise in* a bankruptcy case; or (iii) *are related to* a bankruptcy case. Whether the bankruptcy court may enter *final judgments and orders* in a proceeding depends on whether the proceeding is a *statutory core or non-core proceeding* and, if the former, *whether it is a* Stern *claim.*

1. Core Proceedings

Core proceedings are those that *arise under title 11* or *arise in a bankruptcy case.* In a *core proceeding,* the bankruptcy court has the *statutory authority* to enter *final judgments and orders,* subject to regular appellate review. Core proceedings include matters regarding administration of the debtor's estate, allowance or disallowance of property exemptions and creditors' claims, counterclaims by the estate against claimants, the automatic stay, fraudulent transfers, preferences, use or sale or lease of estate property, and other matters listed in 8 U.S.C. § 157(b)(2). In its decision in *Stern v. Marshall,* the Supreme Court made clear that while a bankruptcy court may have *the statutory authority under § 157(b)(2)* to enter a final judgment, it *may not have the constitutional authority* to do so.

2. Non-Core Proceedings

In a *non-core* proceeding that is otherwise related to the bankruptcy case, the bankruptcy court must submit *proposed findings of fact and conclusions of law* to the district court, which enters a final judgment or order, after conducting a *de novo review* on all matters on which a party has timely and specifically objected. If all the parties *consent,* however, the bankruptcy court may enter final judgments and orders, subject to appellate review, in a *non-core* proceeding.

3. Guidelines

- If the proceeding falls into one of the statutory categories of core proceedings and is not a *Stern* claim, then the bankruptcy court may enter a final judgment or order.

- If the proceeding falls into one of the statutory categories of core proceedings and is a *Stern* claim, then the bankruptcy court may enter a final judgment or order only with the parties' consent.

- If the proceeding falls into one of the statutory categories of core proceedings and is a *Stern* claim but the parties do not consent to the bankruptcy court entering a final order or judgment, then the bankruptcy court must submit proposed findings of fact and conclusions of law to the district court to review *de novo.*

- If the proceeding is non-core, then the bankruptcy court may enter a final judgment or order with the parties' consent.

- If the proceeding is non-core but the parties do not consent to the bankruptcy court entering a final order or judgment, then the bankruptcy court must submit proposed findings of fact and conclusions of law to the district court to review *de novo.*

E. JURY TRIALS

The Supreme Court has held that a party is constitutionally entitled to a jury trial of a bankruptcy proceeding if (i) the action would have been brought at law prior to the merger of law and equity courts, (ii) the remedy sought is legal in nature, and (iii) the proceeding involves a private right. In a case in which the right to a jury trial exists, Congress has authorized bankruptcy judges to conduct jury trials if the district court has *specially designated the exercise of this jurisdiction* and *all parties expressly consent.*

F. WITHDRAWAL OF THE REFERENCE

1. Permissive Withdrawal

The district court, *for cause,* may withdraw, in whole or in part, a case or proceeding that has been referred to the bankruptcy court either on its own motion or on the timely motion of a party.

2. Mandatory Withdrawal

On a timely motion, the district court must withdraw a proceeding from the bankruptcy court if *its resolution* requires consideration of *both* the Bankruptcy Code *and* a *nonbankruptcy federal statute* "regulating organizations or activities affecting interstate commerce." While 28 U.S.C. § 157(d) says that withdrawal is mandated when resolution requires consideration of *both* the Code and a non-Code federal statute, the vast majority of courts have interpreted § 157(d) to mandate withdrawal if resolution of the dispute requires "*substantial and material*" consideration of the *non-Code federal statute* and that statute has *more than a de minimis impact* on interstate commerce.

G. ABSTENTION

1. Permissive Abstention

The district court may abstain from hearing a *particular* proceeding arising under the Code or arising in or related to a bankruptcy case when *justice, comity with state courts, or respect for state law* favors resolution of the matter in a state forum.

2. Mandatory Abstention

On a *timely motion,* the district court must abstain from hearing *a particular proceeding* based on a *state law claim or cause of action related to* a bankruptcy case, *but not* arising under the Code or arising in a bankruptcy case if the proceeding: (i) could not have been brought in federal court without bankruptcy jurisdiction; (ii) already has been filed in an appropriate state court; and (iii) is capable of being timely adjudicated in that forum. Proceedings based on personal injury tort and wrongful death claim proceedings are not subject to mandatory abstention.

3. Proceeding Versus Case

It is important to differentiate between the court's abstaining from hearing a *single proceeding* that is only one component of the bankruptcy case and abstaining from hearing the *whole bankruptcy case.* The bankruptcy court may, at any time, abstain from hearing *an entire case* by dismissing it or by suspending all proceedings if it finds that abstention would better serve the interests of creditors and the debtor. Notice and a hearing are required.

4. Appeals of Abstention Orders

With one exception, a bankruptcy court's order to abstain or not abstain, whether permissive or mandatory, from hearing a particular proceeding may be appealed to the district court or bankruptcy appellate panel. An abstention decision by the district court or bankruptcy appellate panel, however, may not be appealed to the court of appeals or the Supreme Court.

H. REMOVAL

1. Claims Related to Bankruptcy Case

A party may remove any claim or cause of action in a civil proceeding from a nonbankruptcy court to the federal district court for the district where the civil action is pending, if there is proper jurisdiction.

Note: Tax court proceedings and civil actions by governmental units to enforce police or regulatory powers are *not* subject to removal.

2. Remand

The court to which a claim or cause of action has been removed has the power, based on the equities, to remand the action to the forum where it was pending. A bankruptcy court's order to remand or not to remand a removed proceeding is reviewable by the district court, but a remand decision by the district court is not reviewable by the court of appeals or the Supreme Court.

I. VENUE

1. Bankruptcy Case

Venue for the filing of a bankruptcy petition is in the federal district where the debtor has maintained her *residence, domicile, or principal place of business or principal assets* in the United States during, or for the longest portion of, the *180 days* immediately prior to filing. Venue is also proper in a district where a bankruptcy case concerning a general partner, partnership, or affiliate of the debtor is pending.

2. Bankruptcy Proceedings

With certain exceptions, for bankruptcy proceedings, venue lies in the district where the case is pending.

a. Exception for Small Debts

With the exception of certain post-petition claims, a bankruptcy trustee must file a proceeding *arising in or related to* the bankruptcy case in the district where the *defendant resides* if the proceeding is to recover (i) a *money judgment or property* worth less than *$1,525;* (ii) *a consumer debt* of less than *$22,700;* or (iii) a *non-consumer debt against a non-insider* of less than *$27,750.*

(i) Exception to Small Debt Exception

The trustee may bring a proceeding *arising under the Code, or arising in or related to* a bankruptcy case based on a claim that arises *post-petition from the operation of the debtor's business* only in the district where the action could have been filed under applicable nonbankruptcy venue law. This rule applies even if the trustee's claim is for a small amount that, otherwise, would qualify for the small debt exception described above.

b. **Post-Petition Claims Against Representative of the Estate**

A proceeding arising under the Code or arising in or related to a bankruptcy case based on a post-petition claim from *operation of the debtor's business* may be brought *against the representative of the estate* either in the district where the case is pending *or* in the district where the action could have been commenced under applicable nonbankruptcy venue law. The trustee is the representative of the estate but the representative of the estate also includes the debtor in possession in a non-subchapter V Chapter 11 case.

c. **Alternative: Trustee as Statutory Successor**

The trustee, as the statutory successor to the debtor or to creditors under Code §§ 541 or 544(b), has the *option* of commencing a proceeding arising in or related to the bankruptcy case in the district where the case is pending *or* in the district where it could have been brought by the debtor or such creditors under applicable nonbankruptcy venue law if the bankruptcy case had not been filed. This provision is subject to the small debt exception.

d. **Personal Injury Tort and Wrongful Death Claims**

The district court in which the bankruptcy case is pending determines whether a claim for personal injury tort or wrongful death is tried in the district court where the *bankruptcy case is pending or* in the district court in the district where the *claim arose*.

3. **Change of Venue**

A district court may transfer a case or proceeding to another district court "in the *interest of justice or for the convenience of the parties.*" The bankruptcy court can order a transfer, because motions to change venue generally are treated as core proceedings.

a. **Improper Venue**

If a case was filed in the wrong district, i.e., venue is improper, the bankruptcy court, upon motion of a party in interest or *sua sponte,* may transfer the case to another district if transfer is in *the interest of justice* or for the *convenience of the parties.* It is unclear whether the court may *dismiss* the case. It also is not clear whether the bankruptcy court may retain the case and not transfer it.

J. APPEALS

1. **Appeals from Bankruptcy Court**

An appeal may be taken from the bankruptcy court to the federal district court or to a bankruptcy appellate panel, if the jurisdiction has such a panel. Under certain limited circumstances, a party may appeal directly to the court of appeals.

a. **District Court**

The appellate jurisdiction of the district court and the bankruptcy appellate panel includes appeals from final orders, judgments, and decrees of the bankruptcy court, and from interlocutory orders extending or shortening the debtor's exclusivity period for filing a plan. For other interlocutory orders, appellate jurisdiction is by leave of the district court or the bankruptcy appellate panel.

b. Bankruptcy Appellate Panels

The judicial council of each circuit must establish a bankruptcy appellate panel, composed of bankruptcy judges from that circuit, to hear appeals **unless** (i) there are **insufficient judicial resources** available in the circuit or (ii) the procedure would cause **undue delay or increased cost** to parties in bankruptcy cases. Each appeal is to be heard by three members of the bankruptcy appellate panel who are not from the district where the appeal arises. Unless the appellant elects at the time of the appeal or any other party elects, no later than **30 days** after service of the appeal notice, to have the district court hear the appeal, the bankruptcy appellate panel will hear the appeal.

(i) Precedential Value

Decisions of the bankruptcy appellate panel bind the parties to the dispute before the court. Whether the panel's decisions are binding on bankruptcy courts within the circuit is unclear.

c. Direct Appeal to Circuit Court

In 2005, Congress provided for a direct appeal to the circuit court, under certain circumstances. The orders from which a direct appeal may be taken are those described in 28 U.S.C. § 158(a): (i) final orders, judgments, and decrees; (ii) interlocutory orders expanding or shortening the exclusivity period under B.C. § 1121; and (iii) with leave of the court, other interlocutory orders and decrees. The process for securing a direct appeal involves several steps.

d. "Clearly Erroneous" Standard

On appeal, the reviewing court must use the "clearly erroneous" standard with regard to the bankruptcy court's findings of fact, but the bankruptcy court's conclusions of law are subject to *de novo* review.

e. Interlocutory Orders

The district court or bankruptcy appellate panel may grant leave to appeal an interlocutory order of the bankruptcy court, but leave to appeal is justified only under **exceptional circumstances.**

f. Time for Appeals

With certain limited exceptions, a party must file a notice of appeal **14 days** after entry of the bankruptcy judge's order, judgment, or decree being appealed.

2. Appeal from District Court or Bankruptcy Appellate Panel

An appeal may be taken to the circuit court from a **final decision, order, or judgment** of (i) the district court, in its **appellate capacity,** or (ii) the bankruptcy appellate panel.

3. District Court as Trial Court

If the district court sits as a trial court, rather than as an appellate court, e.g., in **non-core or Stern-claim** proceedings in which the parties do not consent or in proceedings in which the reference has been **withdrawn,** the normal standard for an appeal to the circuit court of the district court's final decision governs.

4. Automatic Stay Orders

In ***Ritzen Group, Inc. v. Jackson Masonry, LLC,*** the Supreme Court, in a unanimous opinion, held that a bankruptcy court's ruling on a motion for relief from the automatic stay "forms a discrete procedural unit" in the bankruptcy case and "[t]hat unit yields a final, appealable order when the bankruptcy court unreservedly grants or denies relief."

K. SOVEREIGN IMMUNITY

1. Waiver

Bankruptcy Code § 106 waives the sovereign immunity of governmental units with respect to a number of bankruptcy issues. This waiver applies to monetary recoveries, other than punitive damages awards, as well as to declaratory or injunctive relief.

2. Offset Against Governmental Claims

If property of the estate includes a claim against a governmental unit that would be barred by sovereign immunity, the trustee can offset that claim against a claim that the governmental unit holds against the estate, e.g., an unrelated tax claim, but only up to the amount of the government's claim. Section 106(c) applies ***regardless of whether the governmental unit filed a proof of claim.***

3. Compulsory Counterclaims

If a governmental unit has filed a proof of claim in the bankruptcy case, then it is deemed to have waived sovereign immunity with regard to a compulsory counterclaim to its claim that arose out of the same transaction or occurrence.

4. State Sovereign Immunity

The Supreme Court has concluded that the States, by giving Congress the power to make uniform laws on bankruptcy, agreed "not to assert any sovereign immunity defense they might have had in proceedings" created by Congress under the Bankruptcy Clause.

III. COMMENCEMENT AND ADMINISTRATION OF THE CASE

A. ELIGIBILITY: ALL CHAPTERS

1. Person

Only a person (individual, corporation, or partnership) who ***resides*** or has a ***domicile, place of business, or property in the United States*** can be a debtor under the Code. Insolvency is **not** required. The term "corporation" includes business trusts and most companies or associations with corporate attributes. A limited partnership is not a corporation under the Code.

2. When a Debtor May Not File for Relief

In 2005, Congress added a pre-bankruptcy credit counseling requirement for individual debtors. With limited exceptions, an individual may not file for bankruptcy until she has satisfied this credit counseling requirement. An ***individual*** or a ***family farmer*** also is not eligible to file a petition under any chapter of the Bankruptcy Code if she has been a debtor in a case that was ***pending in the preceding 180 days and dismissed,*** either because of the debtor's willful failure to obey court orders or "to appear before the court in proper prosecution of the case," ***or*** because she requested a voluntary dismissal of the case following a party's request for relief from the automatic stay.

B. ELIGIBILITY: CHAPTER-SPECIFIC REQUIREMENTS

1. Chapter 7: "Liquidation"

Chapter 7 relief is available to *any person* that *resides or has a domicile, a place of business, or property in the United States except* (i) individual debtors with primarily consumer debts who fail the "means test"; (ii) railroads; (iii) domestic savings institutions and insurance companies; (iv) certain small business investment companies; (v) foreign insurance companies engaged in such business in the United States; and (vi) foreign banks, savings and loan associations, and other similar financial institutions that have a branch or agency in the United States. Stockbrokers and commodity brokers may be debtors under special provisions of Chapter 7.

2. Chapter 11: "Reorganization"

Only individuals, partnerships, and corporations eligible for Chapter 7 relief can be debtors under Chapter 11. Stockbrokers and commodity brokers cannot be Chapter 11 debtors, but *railroads* are eligible for relief under special provisions of Chapter 11.

a. Business or Consumer Debtors

Designed mainly for business reorganizations, Chapter 11 may also provide relief for consumer debtors. Relief usually entails debtor reorganization by means of a confirmable plan, but the Code also provides for a liquidating plan.

3. Chapter 12: "Family Farmer or Family Fisherman with Regular Annual Income"

A *family farmer or family fisherman* whose *yearly income* is sufficiently *stable and regular* to fund a Chapter 12 plan may file a *voluntary* petition under that chapter. Individuals, individuals and their spouses, corporations, or partnerships may qualify as family farmers or family fishermen.

4. Chapter 13: "Adjustment of Debts of Individuals with Regular Income"

Only *an individual with regular income* who, on the petition date, has noncontingent, liquidated *debts* less than *$2,750,000* is eligible for relief under Chapter 13. An individual with regular income and his spouse may file a joint petition under Chapter 13, provided that their *aggregate* indebtedness is less than *$2,750,000.* This $2.75 million aggregate debt limit is in effect until *June 21, 2024.* Stockbrokers and commodity brokers do not qualify for relief under Chapter 13. A Chapter 13 case may be commenced only by the debtor's *voluntary* petition.

C. VOLUNTARY CASE

1. Filing the Petition

A voluntary case commences upon an eligible debtor's filing of a petition under Chapter 7, 11, 12, or 13. At that time, the filing fee must be paid unless the court has approved installment payments. Commencement of a voluntary case constitutes an *order for relief.*

a. Notice

Notice of the order for relief is sent to all parties in interest.

b. Joint Case

Spouses can file jointly, thereby avoiding another filing fee. The debtors must be legally married; a joint petition may not be filed if they merely cohabitate. After the Supreme Court's decision in **Obergefell v. Hodges,** same-sex couples may legally marry; thus, they are eligible to file a joint bankruptcy petition. Joint filing is available only in a voluntary case.

c. Corporation

State law determines who has authority to file a voluntary bankruptcy petition on behalf of a corporation or a limited liability company. If the person or entity filing the petition lacks authority to do so under state law, then the bankruptcy court must dismiss the petition.

d. Partnership

A petition filed by fewer than all the general partners in a partnership is treated as an involuntary petition.

2. Schedules and Statements

In addition to the petition, a debtor under Chapter 7, 11, 12, or 13 must timely file a list of creditors with their addresses, a schedule of assets and liabilities, a schedule of current income and expenditures, a schedule of executory contracts and unexpired leases, and a statement of the debtor's financial affairs. BAPCPA created a number of new filing obligations for individual debtors, including filing a statement showing compliance with the credit counseling requirement. A debtor's failure to file certain forms or paper work, or to perform certain statutory duties may result in dismissal of the case or lifting of the automatic stay. In addition, there are chapter-specific filing requirements with which the debtor must comply.

3. Automatic Stay

Once a voluntary or involuntary petition is filed, the automatic stay becomes effective against *all entities* to protect the debtor, his property, and property of the estate.

D. INVOLUNTARY CASE

1. Eligibility

An involuntary petition may be filed only under *Chapter 7 or Chapter 11* against a person who qualifies as a debtor under the applicable chapter. An involuntary petition may *not* be filed against (i) a farmer, (ii) a family farmer, or (iii) a nonprofit or charitable corporation.

2. Filing the Petition

If the debtor has *at least 12 creditors holding unsecured, noncontingent, undisputed claims*, then *three or more of these creditors* whose claims aggregate *at least $18,600* may file an involuntary petition against the debtor. If there are *fewer than 12 creditors holding unsecured, noncontingent, undisputed claims,* excluding the debtor's insiders and employees, and transferees of voidable transfers, then *one or more of these creditors* whose claims aggregate *at least $18,600* may file an involuntary petition against the debtor.

3. **Answer**

Only the debtor, or in the case of a partnership debtor a non-petitioning general partner, may file an answer to the involuntary petition. A failure to answer and controvert the petition's allegations will result in the entry of an order for relief.

4. **Entry of an Order for Relief**

The court will enter an order for relief against the debtor if (i) the debtor *fails to timely controvert* the allegations in the petition; (ii) the court finds that the debtor is *generally not paying undisputed debts as they become due;* or (iii) a *custodian* was appointed or took charge of debtor's property within *120 days* before the petition was filed.

5. **Gap Period**

Between the filing of the petition and the entry of an order for relief (the "gap period"), the debtor can remain in possession of her property, continue business operations, and use, acquire, or dispose of assets, unless the court orders otherwise.

   a. **Transfers During Gap Period**

   If the debtor makes a transfer during the gap period, the transfer is not subject to the trustee's avoiding powers *to the extent of post-petition value,* including services, given by the transferee *in exchange for the transfer.*

   b. **Priority for Gap Creditors**

   The Code provides *priority status* for the claims of gap creditors. A gap creditor claim is one that arises in the ordinary course of the debtor's business or financial affairs before the *earlier of* the appointment of a trustee or entry of the order for relief.

   c. **Interim Trustee**

   During the gap period in a Chapter 7 case, on request by a party in interest and after notice to the debtor and a hearing, the court may direct the United States trustee to appoint an interim trustee if the court finds that such an appointment is needed to *preserve property of the estate* or to *avoid loss.*

6. **Dismissal of Involuntary Petition**

If the court dismisses an involuntary petition other than on the consent of all the petitioning entities and the debtor, and if the debtor has not waived her right to damages, then the court may award a judgment to the debtor and against the petitioners for costs and/or reasonable attorneys' fees. If the court dismisses the petition and finds that a petitioning entity filed the petition in *bad faith,* the court may award the debtor damages proximately caused by the involuntary petition, as well as *punitive damages.* BAPCPA added certain protections for *individual debtors* whose involuntary petitions are dismissed, including *sealing all court records* in certain cases and preventing all *consumer reporting agencies* from making a consumer report containing information about the involuntary filing.

7. **Schedules to Be Filed**

If the court enters an order for relief, the debtor must timely file the required lists, schedules, and statements.

E. SECTION 341 MEETING OF CREDITORS

In a *Chapter 7 or Chapter 11* case, within *21 to 40 days after* the order for relief, the United States trustee must convene a meeting of creditors. In a *Chapter 12 case*, the meeting is held within *21 to 35 days after* the order for relief. In a *Chapter 13 case*, the meeting is held within *21 to 50 days after* the order for relief.) In North Carolina and Alabama, the bankruptcy administrator presides. This meeting is called the *§ 341 meeting* of creditors. The debtor must attend the meeting. The United States trustee may also convene a meeting of the debtor's equity security holders.

1. Notice

The clerk of the court provides by mail at least *21 days' notice* of the § 341 meeting to the debtor, the trustee, all creditors, and indenture trustees. If notice by mail is impracticable, the court may order that notice be given by publication. In a reorganization case under Chapter 11, equity security holders must be notified of any § 341 meeting of equity security holders. Official Forms 309A–I provide the § 341 meeting notice and other deadlines in the bankruptcy case.

2. Purpose of Section 341 Meeting

The primary purpose of the § 341 meeting is to afford creditors, any trustee or examiner in the case, any indenture trustee, and the United States trustee or bankruptcy administrator to examine *the debtor under oath.*

F. CONVERSION

Chapters 7, 11, 12, and 13 provide rules for conversion of a case from one chapter to another when the debtor satisfies the eligibility requirements for the succeeding chapter. A court may order conversion of a Chapter 7 or Chapter 11 case to Chapter 12 or Chapter 13 *only upon the debtor's request.* A Chapter 12 or Chapter 13 debtor may convert her case to Chapter 7 at any time.

1. Effects of Conversion

Conversion constitutes an order for relief under the new chapter, but as a general rule does not change the date of the filing of the bankruptcy petition, the commencement of the case, or the order for relief. There are a number of exceptions to this rule, in which the date of conversion is treated as the *date of the order for relief.* Except for administrative expenses, any claims arising in a Chapter 11, 12, or 13 case after the order for relief but before conversion to another chapter are considered pre-petition claims for all purposes.

2. Conversion from Chapter 13: Property of the Estate

If a case is converted from Chapter 13 to another chapter of the Code, property of the estate in the converted case consists of property of the estate *on the date of the Chapter 13 filing* that remains in the debtor's possession or control on the date of conversion. But, if the debtor converts the case in *bad faith,* property of the estate in the converted case consists of estate property *on the date of conversion,* which includes property acquired after the date of the Chapter 13 filing.

3. Conversion from Chapter 13: Secured Claims

Valuations of *property* and of *allowed secured claims* in the Chapter 13 case *only* apply in a case converted to Chapters 11 or 12. The allowed secured claims in Chapters 11 or 12 are *reduced by any amounts paid* under the *Chapter 13* plan.

G. DISMISSAL

The Code provides different rules for dismissal depending on the chapter of the Code under which the debtor filed its petition. Unless the bankruptcy court, for cause orders otherwise, the dismissal of a case is *without prejudice* to the debtor's right to file a subsequent petition, with the *exception of § 109(g)'s 180-day rule*, and obtain a discharge of debts that could have been discharged in the case dismissed. If the court dismisses the case and makes either of the § 109(g) findings, then the dismissal is *with prejudice* as to the debtor's eligibility to refile for bankruptcy within 180 days. If an *individual* in a *voluntary Chapter 7 or Chapter 13 case* fails to file all the information required by § 521(a)(1) *within 45 days* of filing her petition, then her case is *automatically dismissed* on Day 46. While the Code provides for automatic dismissal, it is unclear how that happens, and it is possible, notwithstanding the "automatic dismissal" language that a court order is needed.

IV. OFFICERS OF THE ESTATE

A. TRUSTEE

The trustee is the official representative of the estate and in this capacity can sue or be sued. The trustee has numerous administrative powers and specific duties, which vary according to the chapter under which he is serving.

1. Eligibility

A *disinterested* individual who is competent or a disinterested corporation authorized by its charter or bylaws may serve as trustee. In Chapter 7, 12, or 13 cases, the trustee must *reside or have an office in the judicial district* where the case is pending or in the adjacent district. The Code provides little guidance about the qualifications for a *subchapter V* Chapter 11 trustee, although such person must be disinterested. If necessary, the United States trustee for the district may serve in a Chapter 7, 12, or 13 case or in a subchapter V case, but not in a non-subchapter V Chapter 11 case.

a. "Disinterested Person"

The term *excludes* the debtor's (i) creditors, equity security holders, and insiders; (ii) current directors, officers, and employees; (iii) directors, officers, and employees who served during the two years prior to filing for bankruptcy; and (iv) any person with a *materially adverse* interest to the estate or to any class of creditors or equity security holders.

2. Qualification—Bond

Within seven days after appointment or election, and before beginning service, a trustee must file with the court a *bond,* in favor of the United States, in the amount set by the United States trustee. The United States trustee determines the amount of the bond and must approve the sufficiency of the surety on such bond.

3. Selection of Trustee

a. Chapter 7 Case

All Chapter 7 cases require a trustee chosen from a panel of private trustees maintained by the United States trustee to serve in a particular region. Promptly after entry of the order for relief, the United States trustee appoints a disinterested panel member to serve as the *interim trustee* until the § 341 meeting, at which time the interim trustee will become the permanent trustee unless another person is elected.

b. Non-Subchapter V Chapter 11 Case

In a non-subchapter V Chapter 11 case, the debtor generally remains in possession of property of the estate and continues to manage the business, in an effort to reorganize, *without the necessity of a trustee's appointment.* A party in interest or the United States trustee, however, may move at any time after the filing of the bankruptcy petition but before confirmation of a Chapter 11 plan for appointment of a Chapter 11 trustee. The court may order appointment of a Chapter 11 trustee (i) *for cause;* (ii) if appointment is in the *interests of creditors, any equity security holders,* and other interests of the estate; or (iii) grounds exist to *convert or dismiss* the case, but the court determines that appointment of a trustee is in the *best interests of creditors and the estate.*

(i) When U.S. Trustee Must Act

BAPCPA amended the Code to require the United States trustee to move for the appointment of a Chapter 11 trustee if *reasonable grounds* exist to suspect that current members of the debtor's governing body, debtor's chief executive or chief financial officer, or members of the governing body that selected the chief executive or chief financial officer participated in *actual fraud, dishonesty, or criminal conduct* in *managing the debtor* or the *debtor's public financial reporting.*

c. Subchapter V Chapter 11 Cases

Chapter 11's provisions on appointment and election of a trustee *do not apply* in a *subchapter V* case. Instead, as in Chapter 12 and Chapter 13, a trustee is appointed in a subchapter V case. The Code provides that if the number of cases in a region warrants it, the United States trustee will appoint a *standing trustee* for all *subchapter V Chapter 11 cases* in that region. The Executive Office of the United States Trustees, however, has not yet appointed subchapter V standing trustees. Instead, a subchapter V trustee is appointed on a "case-by-case basis" from a panel or pools of subchapter V trustees created across the country.

d. Chapter 12 and Chapter 13 Cases

If the number of cases in a region warrants it, the United States trustee will appoint *standing trustees* for all Chapter 12 and Chapter 13 cases in the region. If a standing trustee is not appointed, then the United States trustee will appoint a *disinterested person* as the trustee for a particular case, or the United States trustee may serve as the trustee in the case. Notwithstanding the appointment of a trustee, Chapter 12 and 13 debtors remain in possession of property of the estate.

4. Duties of Trustee

a. Chapter 7 Case

The *primary* responsibilities of a Chapter 7 trustee are to *collect and reduce to cash* property of the estate, to *make distributions* to claimants in the order prescribed by the Code, and to *close the estate* as expeditiously as is compatible with best interests of parties in interest. A Chapter 7 trustee also has a number of other important statutory duties, including objecting to allowance of improper claims, objecting to the debtor's discharge, if warranted, and timely filing after the § 341 meeting a statement with the court as to whether the filing of an individual debtor's case creates a presumption of abuse.

b. Non-Subchapter V Chapter 11 Case

A trustee who replaces the debtor in possession in a non-subchapter V case is usually authorized to *operate the debtor's business* and is charged with certain duties of a Chapter 7 trustee, as well as other duties that relate specifically to a Chapter 11 case, such as the advisability of continuing the debtor's business, and filing a Chapter 11 plan.

c. Subchapter V Chapter 11 Case

The debtor remains in possession in a non-subchapter V case. The trustee has a number of the duties of a Chapter 7 trustee, certain duties that relate specifically to subchapter V, such as ensuring that the debtor begins making timely plan payments and facilitating development of a consent plan.

d. Chapter 13

A Chapter 13 trustee must perform certain of the duties of a Chapter 7 trustee, but has a number of other important statutory duties, including: (i) *ensuring that the debtor begins making payments* within 30 days after filing of the plan or the order for relief; (ii) *disbursing payments* to creditors under a confirmed plan; and (iii) if the debtor is engaged in business, *investigating* the debtor's conduct, financial condition, business operations, and the advisability of continuing the business.

e. Chapter 12

A Chapter 12 trustee's duties are similar to those of a Chapter 13 trustee as long as the debtor remains a debtor in possession. If a Chapter 12 debtor is removed as debtor in possession, the trustee is charged with most of the duties of a Chapter 11 trustee, including operation of the debtor's farm or commercial fishing operation.

5. Liability of Trustee

A trustee, as fiduciary of the estate, may be held *personally liable* for breach of her fiduciary duties. Courts differ on whether the trustee is personally liable for only intentional violations or also for negligent violations of fiduciary duty.

6. Powers of Trustee

As the representative of the estate, the trustee is granted many administrative powers, including the power to (i) *file a proof of claim* on behalf of a creditor; (ii) *operate the debtor's business* in a non-subchapter V Chapter 11 case and if in the estate's best interest for a limited time in a Chapter 7 case; (iii) *operate the debtor's business* in a subchapter V or Chapter 12 case in which the court has removed the debtor in possession; (iv) *deposit or invest money;* (v) *employ* professional persons; (vi) *avoid* certain transfers and liens; (vii) *use, sell, or lease property;* (viii) *obtain credit;* (ix) *assume or reject executory contracts or unexpired leases;* (x) demand utility services for the estate; (xi) abandon property; and (xii) waive a debtor corporation's attorney-client privilege.

7. Removal of Trustee

A trustee, other than the United States trustee, or an examiner may be removed by the court *for cause.*

B. EXAMINER

1. Role and Capacity

The Code's provisions on appointment and duties of an examiner *do not apply to subchapter V cases.* In a non-subchapter V Chapter 11 case in which the court does not order the appointment of a trustee, a party in interest or the United States trustee may request, at any time prior to plan confirmation, the appointment of an examiner to conduct an investigation of the debtor, including an investigation of charges of *fraud, dishonesty, incompetence, mismanagement, or irregularity in managing the debtor's affairs* on the part of the debtor's present or former management. The debtor in possession retains her property and continues to operate the business. A disinterested person other than the United States trustee may serve as examiner.

2. Reasons for Appointment

When a party in interest or the United States trustee requests appointment of an examiner, the court, after notice and a hearing, *must order* that an examiner be appointed if the debtor's fixed, liquidated, unsecured debts *exceed $5 million, excluding* debts for goods, services, or taxes, and any debts owed to an insider. The court also must order the appointment of an examiner if such action is in the *best interests of creditors, equity security holders, and the estate.*

3. Duties

An examiner's duties include (i) *investigating* the debtor's conduct, financial condition, and business operations, as well as the *advisability of continuing the business;* (ii) *filing a report* of the investigation; and (iii) any other trustee responsibilities that the court directs the debtor in possession not to perform. An *examiner may not serve as a trustee or professional person* in the same case in which she has served as examiner.

C. PROFESSIONAL PERSONS

A trustee, a debtor in possession, or creditors' or equity security holders' committees in a Chapter 11 case, with court approval, may hire professional persons, e.g., attorneys or accountants, to perform services with respect to the bankruptcy estate. Professional persons must be *disinterested persons* who *do not have an interest adverse* to the estate. Creditors, insiders, and equity security holders are *not* disinterested persons. Neither is any person who is or was an *officer, director, or employee* of the debtor within two years prior to the bankruptcy filing. Court approval *must* be obtained *prior to performing services;* otherwise, the professional's application for compensation may be denied by the court.

1. Special Purpose Attorney

The court may authorize a trustee or a debtor in possession to employ a former attorney of the debtor for a *special purpose,* such as continuing legal expertise in an intricate proceeding, provided that the employment is in the *estate's best interest* and the lawyer does not represent or have an interest adverse to the debtor or to the estate concerning the specific subject matter of the employment. The purpose may *not* be to represent the trustee in administering the bankruptcy case.

2. Creditor's Representative

In a Chapter 7, 11, or 12 case, a professional person is not disqualified from *employment by a trustee solely* because of her employment by or representation of a creditor, unless another creditor or the United States trustee objects and the court finds an ***actual conflict of interest.***

3. Chapter 11 Cases

In a non-subchapter V Chapter 11 case, a person is not disqualified for employment by a debtor in possession *solely* because that person was employed by or represented the debtor prior to the bankruptcy case. In a *subchapter V case*, a person is not disqualified from employment *solely* because of holding a *pre-petition claim of less than $10,000.*

4. Salaried Professionals of the Debtor

A trustee who is authorized to operate the debtor's business may ***retain or replace salaried professionals***, such as attorneys and accountants, who have been ***regularly employed*** by the debtor and are ***necessary to operation*** of the business.

5. Trustee as Professional Person

The court may permit a trustee to also serve as an attorney or accountant for the estate if it is in the estate's best interest.

6. Creditors' Committee May Hire Professional Persons

In a Chapter 11 case, a creditors' committee or an equity security holders' committee may employ attorneys, accountants, or other professionals to perform services for the committee. While representing or in the employ of the committee, the professional person may not represent an entity having an ***adverse interest.*** Representation of a creditor of the same class as the committee represents, however, does not per se constitute representation of an adverse interest. Typically, a creditors' committee is not appointed in a subchapter V Chapter 11 case.

D. OMBUDSMEN

BAPCPA amended the Code to provide, under certain circumstances, for the appointment of a ***consumer privacy ombudsman*** or the appointment of a ***patient care ombudsman.***

1. Consumer Privacy Ombudsman

A bankruptcy court cannot approve a sale of ***personally identifiable information*** that is inconsistent with the debtor's privacy policy unless the court first orders the appointment of a ***consumer privacy ombudsman*** and subsequently holds a hearing, after notice, on the proposed sale. If the court orders the appointment of a consumer privacy ombudsman, then the United States trustee must appoint ***one disinterested person,*** other than the United States trustee, to serve as ombudsman ***no later than 7 days*** before the start of the sale hearing.

2. Patient Care Ombudsmen

If a health care business files for relief under Chapters 7, 9 or 11, then the bankruptcy court must order the appointment, within ***30 days*** of the start of the case, of a ***patient care ombudsman,*** unless the court finds that appointment is not necessary for the protection of patients in a specific case. The job of the patient care ombudsman is to ***monitor the quality of patient care*** and to ***represent*** the ***interests of patients*** of the health care business.

E. COMPENSATION OF OFFICERS

Officers of the estate, including a trustee, an examiner, a Chapter 12 or 13 individual debtor's attorney, a consumer privacy ombudsman, a patient care ombudsman, and any professional person properly employed by a trustee, a debtor in possession, or a creditors' committee may be awarded by the court a ***reasonable fee*** for actual and necessary services, as well as ***reimbursement*** for ***actual and necessary expenses.***

1. Debtor's Attorney

The right of the debtor's attorney to compensation from estate funds varies depending on the chapter of the Code under which the debtor files for relief.

a. Chapter 12 or 13

The Bankruptcy Code expressly provides that the court may award reasonable compensation to the attorney of an individual Chapter 12 or Chapter 13 debtor, based on the ***benefit and necessity of the services*** to the debtor and the criteria outlined below under Fee Applications.

b. Chapter 7

The Supreme Court has held that the ***Code does not authorize payment of compensation*** to the Chapter 7 debtor's lawyer ***from the estate,*** unless the lawyer is hired by the trustee and approved by the bankruptcy court. Because the debtor hires the attorney to file her Chapter 7 case, the attorney representing a Chapter 7 debtor must obtain her fee upfront and not rely on compensation from estate funds.

c. Chapter 11

A Chapter 11 debtor may hire an attorney and so long as the bankruptcy court approves the employment, the attorney is entitled to compensation according to the standards set forth in § 330. In a non-subchapter V Chapter 11 case, however, once the court orders appointment of a Chapter 11 trustee, the debtor's attorney must look to the debtor, not the estate, for compensation for services rendered.

2. Fee Applications

Fee applications must comply with Bankruptcy Rule 2016(a), the procedural guidelines issued by the Executive Office for United States Trustees, and any applicable local rules. The criteria for awarding reasonable compensation include: (i) ***time*** spent; (ii) ***rates*** charged; (iii) ***need*** for the services to administration of the case or ***benefit*** at the time services were rendered toward completion of the case; (iv) the ***reasonableness of the time*** spent considering the complexity and importance of the work; (v) whether the professional person is ***board certified*** or otherwise has shown ***skill and experience*** in the field of bankruptcy; and (vi) ***fees*** charged by ***comparably skilled attorneys*** in non-bankruptcy cases.

3. Limitations on Professionals' Compensation

a. Modification by Court

A trustee, a debtor in possession, or a creditors' or equity security holders' committee may hire a professional person on any reasonable basis, including on a retainer, on an hourly basis, or on a contingent fee basis. However, the compensation ultimately allowed by the court may vary from the agreed-upon terms if those terms prove to be ***improvident in light of later developments*** that could not have been anticipated at the time the fee arrangement was approved.

b. Denial of Compensation

With certain limited exceptions, if, at any time during employment, a professional person is *not disinterested* or *has an interest adverse to the estate* regarding the subject matter of her employment, the court may deny her compensation for services and reimbursement of expenses.

c. Bifurcation of Trustee's Compensation

If a trustee also serves as an attorney or an accountant for the estate, her fee for professional employment may not include compensation for the performance of her duties as trustee. Compensation for services as trustee must be accounted for separately.

4. Interim Compensation

A trustee, examiner, debtor's attorney, or other professional person may apply for interim compensation or reimbursement of expenses *once every 120 days* after the order for relief, or more frequently, if the court allows, instead of waiting until the conclusion of the bankruptcy case to be paid. Any award of interim compensation will cause a reduction, by that amount, in an award of compensation made under § 330. Interim compensation is generally not an issue in Chapter 12 or 13 cases, because bankruptcy courts have standing orders for such cases that provide an allowed standard fee awarded without application or a hearing, and paid as an administrative claim through the plan.

5. Debtor's Transactions with Attorneys

Even if the debtor's attorney does not apply to the court for compensation, she still must file a statement of any fees paid or any fee agreement made within one year before bankruptcy for legal services related to the case. The statement also must indicate the source of payment. If the court determines that the compensation is unreasonable, it may cancel the fee agreement or order that any excessive portion be returned to the estate or to the entity that made the payment.

6. Sharing of Fees Prohibited

A trustee, examiner, attorney, accountant, or other professional person employed in a bankruptcy case and who receives compensation or reimbursement as an administrative expense is prohibited from sharing such compensation or reimbursement with another person. There are *two exceptions.* First, compensation or reimbursement may be shared with another member, partner, or associate of the same professional firm. Second, an attorney representing a creditor who files an involuntary petition is permitted to share her fee with any other attorney who contributes to her services or expenses.

F. UNITED STATES TRUSTEE

For each of the 21 regions throughout the nation, the Attorney General appoints one United States trustee for a five-year term. The judicial districts for Alabama and North Carolina are served by bankruptcy administrators appointed by the United States Courts of Appeals for the Fourth and Eleventh Circuits.

1. Administrative Duties

Under supervision of the Attorney General, the United States trustee functions as an administrator of the bankruptcy system in his region and, as such, has various duties, including (i) establishing a *panel of private trustees for Chapter 7* cases; (ii) appointing *interim trustees in Chapter 7* cases; (iii) appointing a trustee or an examiner, if the court orders, in non-subchapter V Chapter 11 cases; (iv) appointing a *standing trustee in Chapter 12 and 13* cases; (v) convening and presiding at *§ 341 meetings;* (vi) supervising the *administration of bankruptcy cases* and trustees; (vii) monitoring *applications for employment* of professional persons; and (viii) *reviewing fee applications* of trustees, examiners, attorneys, ombudsmen, and other professional persons.

2. Standing

The Code grants a United States trustee standing to appear and be heard as to any issue in a bankruptcy case. However, he cannot file a plan pursuant to § 1121(c).

V. THE BANKRUPTCY ESTATE

A. THE BANKRUPTCY ESTATE

The filing of a petition creates the bankruptcy estate. The estate includes all of the debtor's *legal and equitable interests* in property *at the time the petition is filed.* The Code's definition of property of the estate is expansive and includes insurance policies, income tax refunds based on pre-petition earnings, stock options, liquor licenses, patents, copyrights, and trademarks, and business social media accounts. Property of the estate also includes *community property,* property recovered by the trustee using her *avoiding powers,* certain property acquired *post-petition,* proceeds of estate property, and property acquired by the estate after bankruptcy. In *Chapters 12 and 13*, and *individual Chapter 11* cases (with an exception in subchapter V) *all property* of the kind described in § 541 that the *debtor acquires after bankruptcy* but before the closing, dismissal, or conversion of the case, whichever first occurs, is *property of the estate.* An *individual Chapter 7 debtor's post-petition earnings are not* included in property of the estate.

1. Ipso Facto or "Bankruptcy" Clauses

Even if nonbankruptcy law or a clause in a contract or deed restricts or conditions the debtor's transfer of property, that property becomes property of the estate. [B.C. § 541(c)(1)(A)] A clause in the parties' agreement that provides for possible forfeiture, termination, or modification of the debtor's interest in the property due to (i) the debtor's insolvency, (ii) the debtor's financial condition, (iii) the debtor's filing of a bankruptcy case, or (iv) the appointment of a bankruptcy trustee or a pre-petition nonbankruptcy custodian are unenforceable under the Bankruptcy Code and do not prevent the property from being included in the bankruptcy estate.

Exception: A restriction on the transfer of the debtor's beneficial interest in a trust, if that restriction is enforceable under *applicable nonbankruptcy law,* is *enforceable* in bankruptcy. [B.C. § 541(c)(2)] Congress intended that spendthrift trusts be excluded from estate property to the extent that state law protects the trusts from creditors.

2. Property Excluded from Estate

The Bankruptcy Code *excludes* ten types of interests from the bankruptcy estate. The following items are *not included* in property of the estate: (i) a power that the debtor may exercise *solely for the benefit of an entity other than the debtor;* (ii) a debtor's interest *as a lessee* of an *expired lease* of nonresidential real property; (iii) debtor's eligibility to participate in programs under the Higher Education Act of 1965 or debtor's accreditation status or licensure as an *educational institution;* (iv) debtor's interest in liquid or gaseous hydrocarbons transferred under a *farmout agreement* and certain *production payments from liquid or gaseous hydrocarbon gas and oil producers;* (v) certain funds in an *education IRA;* (vi) funds used to buy tuition credits or certificates or contributions to an account that qualifies as a *State tuition program* pursuant to the Internal Revenue Code; (vii) funds withheld by an employer from employee wages or received by an employer from employees for payment as *contributions* to *certain pension and benefit plans;* (viii) *personal property* that the debtor has *pledged or sold* as collateral for a loan or advance from a *licensed pawnbroker;* (ix) certain proceeds of money orders; and (x) certain funds placed into a *qualified ABLE account.*

3. Distinguish Exemptions

Do not confuse *exclusions* from estate property with *exemptions.* If property is excluded from the estate, it means that the property never comes into the bankruptcy estate. Therefore, there is no need to exempt it.

B. TURNOVER OF PROPERTY TO TRUSTEE

1. Turnover by Entity Other than Custodian

An *entity, other than a custodian*, in possession, custody, or control of property that the trustee may use, sell, or lease under § 363 or that the debtor may exempt under § 522 must deliver the property to the trustee and account for such property or the property's value. The turnover requirement does *not apply* to property of *inconsequential value or benefit to the estate.* The Code defines the word "entity" more broadly than the term "person." Thus, even a governmental unit or a trust is subject to the turnover provisions.

2. Turnover of Property Repossessed Before Bankruptcy

A secured creditor that prior to bankruptcy repossessed collateral but that has not yet sold the collateral to a bona fide purchaser must turn over the collateral to the trustee or the debtor in possession. However, the secured creditor is entitled to adequate protection of its interest.

a. Automatic Stay

The Supreme Court in *City of Chicago v. Fulton* recently held that an entity's mere retention of estate property after the debtor's bankruptcy filing does not violate § 362(a)(3)'s prohibition against "any act . . . *to exercise control over property of the estate."*

3. Payment of Debt That Is Estate Property

An entity that owes a debt that is *property of the estate* and that is matured, payable on demand, or payable on order must pay the trustee the amount of the debt in excess of any setoff permitted the entity under § 553.

4. Exceptions to Turnover

The turnover requirement does *not apply* to property of *inconsequential value or benefit to the estate.* Turnover is not required if an entity, such as a bank, *in good faith* and without either actual notice or knowledge of the bankruptcy petition transfers property of the estate or pays a debt owing to the debtor to an entity other than the trustee.

Note: The Code does *not protect the payee or transferee,* who are subject to the trustee's avoiding power.

5. Turnover of Property by Custodian

A custodian with knowledge of the bankruptcy filing cannot disburse from or take any action to administer (i) any property of the debtor; (ii) any proceeds, rents, profits, products, or offspring of the debtor's property; or (iii) any property of the estate in her possession, custody, or control, except action needed to preserve such property. The custodian must turn over the property to the trustee and file an accounting.

a. "Custodian" Defined

A custodian is: (i) a *receiver or trustee* of the debtor's property appointed in a *nonbankruptcy action;* (ii) an *assignee* under a general *assignment for the benefit of the debtor's creditors;* or (iii) a *trustee or receiver* appointed or authorized to take control of the debtor's property to *enforce a lien or* for the purpose of general administration of such *property* for the benefit of creditors.

b. Exceptions to Custodian's Turnover

After notice and hearing, the bankruptcy court may *excuse* a custodian's duty to turn over property if the interests of creditors and, if the debtor is solvent, the interests of equity security holders are better served by allowing a custodian to remain in possession, custody, or control of the property. After notice and hearing, the bankruptcy court *must excuse* the custodian's obligation to turn over property if the custodian is an assignee for the benefit of creditors who was appointed or took possession of the debtor's property *more than 120 days* before the commencement of the bankruptcy case. If necessary to prevent fraud or injustice, however, the court is not required to excuse the custodian's compliance with the Code's turnover obligations.

c. Compensation or Surcharge

A bankruptcy court may award a custodian reasonable compensation for her services and actual expenses. With the exception of an assignee for the benefit of creditors who was appointed or took possession more than 120 days before bankruptcy, a custodian may be liable for wrongful or excessive disbursements.

6. Turnover of Books and Records

The bankruptcy court, after notice and a hearing, may order, subject to any valid privilege, an attorney, accountant, or other person to turn over to the trustee any books, documents, records, and papers concerning the debtor's finances or property. In the case of a *corporate debtor,* the trustee has the power to waive the corporation's attorney-client privilege concerning *pre-bankruptcy communications* made by former officers and directors to the debtor's attorney. The corporation's attorney may then be required to testify.

a. No Accountant-Client Privilege

Where access to information relating to the debtor's financial condition is needed for complete and accurate disclosure, an accountant or an accounting firm must turn over documents and work papers in its possession. There is no accountant-client privilege under federal law.

C. ABANDONMENT OF ESTATE PROPERTY

After notice and a hearing, the trustee may abandon property that is *burdensome or of inconsequential value and benefit* to the estate. [B.C. § 554(a)] Normally, abandoned property returns to the debtor; it no longer is property of the estate. Abandonment, however, does not affect the validity of any lien on the property. Even though the abandoned property no longer is property of the estate, the automatic stay protects the debtor from actions by a secured creditor to collect on a pre-petition claim or judgment, or to enforce a lien on the debtor's property. At the close of the case, unless the bankruptcy court rules to the contrary, any property that the debtor scheduled that was not administered before case closing is abandoned to the debtor.

1. Exception: Violation of Environmental Laws

The trustee is prohibited from abandoning estate property that is in violation of state or federal environmental laws that are "reasonably designed to protect the public health or safety from identified hazards."

VI. THE TRUSTEE'S AVOIDING POWERS

A. TRUSTEE'S AVOIDING POWERS AS HYPOTHETICAL CREDITOR OR PURCHASER, AND AS SUCCESSOR TO CERTAIN ACTUAL CREDITORS

1. Strong Arm Provision

The Bankruptcy Code grants to the trustee, at the **commencement** of the bankruptcy case, the hypothetical status and the rights and powers of (i) a **judicial lien creditor,** (ii) a creditor with an **unsatisfied execution,** and (iii) a **bona fide purchaser of real property.** Consequently, the trustee is able to avoid any transfer of the debtor's property that any of these entities—**regardless of whether one really exists**—could avoid, "without regard to any knowledge of the trustee or of any creditor."

2. Trustee's Avoiding Power Based on Actual Unsecured Creditors

If at the start of the bankruptcy case, an **actual creditor** exists who possesses an allowable unsecured claim and who has the right, under applicable nonbankruptcy law, to avoid a transfer of the debtor's property, then the trustee can avoid the whole transfer **for the benefit of the estate,** even if its value exceeds the amount of the creditor's claim. The trustee cannot use § 544(b)(1) to avoid the transfer of a charitable contribution not deemed to be a fraudulent transfer under Code § 548(a)(2).

B. TRUSTEE'S AVOIDANCE OF STATUTORY LIENS

1. Liens That Arise Automatically Based on the Debtor's Financial Condition

The trustee may avoid a **statutory lien** that arises **because** of the debtor's bankruptcy, insolvency, or poor financial condition.

2. Liens Not Perfected Against Bona Fide Purchaser

The trustee may avoid a statutory lien that is **not perfected or enforceable against a hypothetical bona fide purchaser** at the time that the bankruptcy petition is filed, **unless** the purchaser is one described under § 6323 of the Internal Revenue Code or any similar provision in State or local law.

3. Liens for Rent

The trustee may avoid statutory liens for **rent or a lien for distress of rent**.

C. TRUSTEE'S POWER TO AVOID PREFERENCES

The bankruptcy trustee may avoid pre-petition preferential transfers, thereby enlarging the estate for the benefit of creditors. This avoiding power discourages a pre-petition rush to the courthouse and ensures the "prime bankruptcy policy of equality of distribution."

1. Elements of Preference

To establish a preference, the trustee must prove a transfer of an **interest of the debtor in property** (i) made **to or for the benefit of a creditor**, (ii) for or on account of *an antecedent debt*, (iii) made at a time when the debtor was *insolvent*, (iv) *within 90 days* prior to filing of the bankruptcy petition or one year if the creditor was an insider, and (v) that *results in the creditor receiving a larger share* than the creditor would have received if the estate had been *liquidated under Chapter 7* and the transfer had *not been made*. If any of the above elements is absent, the trustee may not set aside the transaction as a voidable preference.

a. Presumption of Insolvency

There is a *rebuttable presumption* that the debtor is insolvent during the *90 days* immediately prior to the date on which the petition was filed. Even when the preference period is one year before bankruptcy because the creditor was an insider, the *period during which the presumption of insolvency applies remains the same*—90 days.

b. Secured Creditors

Payments made within 90 days of bankruptcy to a *wholly secured creditor* do not constitute a preference because the creditor does not receive a greater distribution than she would receive in a Chapter 7 case.

2. Exceptions to Preference Rule

The trustee may not avoid any of the following transfers:

a. a transfer that the debtor and creditor *intend as a contemporaneous exchange for new value* and that is, in fact, a *substantially contemporaneous exchange*;

b. a transfer for a debt that was *incurred in the ordinary course of business* or financial affairs of the debtor and the transferee, and that was *made either* (i) in the *ordinary course of business* or financial affairs of the debtor and the transferee or (ii) according to *ordinary business terms*;

c. a *purchase-money security interest* securing new value and perfected no later than 30 days after the debtor takes possession of the collateral;

d. an *extension of new unsecured value* by the creditor subsequent to the transfer;

e. a transfer that creates a perfected security interest in the *debtor's inventory, receivables, or proceeds of inventory or receivables* to the extent that the creditor's position has not improved to the prejudice of the estate during the relevant statutory time period;

f. *statutory liens* that cannot be avoided under § 545;

g. bona fide payment of a *domestic support obligation*;

h. in a case filed by an *individual debtor with primarily consumer debts,* a transfer of property worth less than *$600*;

i. in a case filed by a debtor whose *debts are not primarily consumer debts*, a transfer of property worth less than *$7,575*;

j. a transfer made as part of an *alternative repayment schedule* between the debtor and an approved nonprofit budget and counseling agency; or

k. payments of certain *supplier or rental arrearages,* in any case filed *before December 27, 2022.*

3. Burden of Proof

The trustee has the burden of proving a preference. The creditor has the burden of proving the elements of an applicable exception.

D. TRUSTEE'S POWER TO AVOID FRAUDULENT TRANSFERS

The trustee may avoid a fraudulent transfer of the debtor's interest in property or the fraudulent incurring of an obligation if the transfer was made or the obligation was incurred by the debtor, voluntarily or involuntarily, *within two years* prior to bankruptcy. The trustee also may avoid certain transfers made by the debtor to a *self-settled trust within ten years* prior to bankruptcy.

1. "Fraudulent" Transfer

a. Actual Intent

A trustee may avoid a transfer if there is *actual intent* to hinder, delay, or defraud a creditor. The law has developed certain "badges of fraud" from which *actual intent may be inferred.*

b. Constructive Fraud

The trustee can prove *constructive fraud* by demonstrating that the debtor did not receive something of *reasonably equivalent value* in exchange for the transfer or obligation *and* the debtor (i) was *insolvent* or rendered insolvent by the transfer or obligation, (ii) was *undercapitalized* after the transfer or incurring the obligation, (iii) intended to incur debts *beyond her ability to repay, or* (iv) made the transfer or incurred the obligation to or for the *benefit of an insider under an employment contract* and not in the ordinary course of business. Certain charitable contributions are not treated as transfers for less than reasonably equivalent value.

2. Good Faith Transferee

A *good faith transferee* or obligee for value is entitled to retain, or to receive a lien on, any property conveyed to her or to enforce an obligation incurred, *to the extent of any value given* by the transferee or obligee to the debtor, *unless* the transfer also is subject to the trustee's avoiding power under §§ 544, 545, or 547.

E. POST-PETITION TRANSACTIONS

The trustee may avoid a transfer of estate property occurring *after the filing* of the bankruptcy petition, unless the transfer falls within one of the exceptions described below or is authorized under the Bankruptcy Code or approved by the court.

1. Entity Without Notice or Knowledge

An entity that has *neither actual notice nor knowledge* of the bankruptcy case is protected from liability concerning a post-petition transfer it makes in good faith. The transferee, however, may be subject to the trustee's avoiding power.

2. Exceptions to Trustee's Avoidance

a. Gap Transferee in Involuntary Case

The trustee cannot avoid a transfer made during the gap period *to the extent that the transferee gave value, including services, after the start* of the *bankruptcy case* in exchange for the transfer. This exception does not apply to a transaction that involves the satisfaction or securing of a pre-petition debt.

b. Good Faith Purchaser of Real Property

The trustee cannot avoid a post-petition transfer of real property to a *good faith purchaser* that has *no knowledge* of the bankruptcy case and has paid *present fair equivalent value* if notice of the bankruptcy case has not been filed, prior to perfection of the transfer, in the office where real property transactions are recorded for the county in which the land is located. This exception applies to *voluntary* transfers of real property, not to judicial or tax sales.

F. LIMITATIONS ON TRUSTEE'S AVOIDING POWERS

1. Statute of Limitations for Avoidance, *Except* Post-Petition Transfers

Most of the trustee's avoiding powers are subject to a statute of limitations requiring that the trustee *file an action* to avoid a transfer before the *earlier* of the following time periods:

a. the *later* of (i) *two years* after the entry of the order for relief *or* (ii) *one year* after the appointment or election of the first trustee, if the appointment or election occurs before the two-year period expires; *or*

b. *the time* the case is *closed or dismissed*.

(i) Transfers Affected

This limitations period applies to a trustee's action to avoid: (i) under the strong arm clause; (ii) as successor to certain actual creditors; (iii) a statutory lien; (iv) a preference; (v) a fraudulent transfer; or (vi) a setoff.

2. Statute of Limitations for Avoidance of Post-Petition Transactions

The trustee must file an action to avoid a post-petition transfer before the *earlier* of:

a. two years after the *transfer* was made; *or*

b. the time the case is *closed or dismissed.*

3. Statute of Limitations for *Recovery* of Avoided Transfer

If a transfer is *avoided*, the trustee must commence, an action to *recover* transferred property or, if the court orders, the value of such property *no later than the earlier of:*

a. *one year after avoidance* of the transfer; *or*

b. the time that the case is *closed or dismissed.*

4. Retroactive Perfection and Continuation Statements

The trustee's power to avoid (i) a transfer under the strong arm clause, (ii) as successor to certain actual creditors, (iii) a statutory lien, or (iv) post-petition transactions is subject to any applicable nonbankruptcy law that permits *retroactive perfection* of a security interest, or *filing of a continuation statement,* e.g., under the Uniform Commercial Code. The post-petition retroactive perfection and filing of a continuation statement *are excepted* from the operation of the *automatic stay.*

5. Seller's Reclamation of Goods

The trustee's power to avoid (i) a transfer under the strong arm clause, (ii) a statutory lien, (iii) a preference, or (iv) a post-petition transfer is subject to the right of a seller, under certain circumstances, to *reclaim* goods that it sold to the debtor.

a. Elements Required for Reclamation

The seller has the right to reclaim *goods* from an *insolvent buyer* if the seller satisfies the following requirements: (i) seller sold the *goods* in the *ordinary course* of its business; (ii) debtor *received the goods while insolvent;* (iii) debtor received the goods within *45 days of filing* its bankruptcy case; and (iv) seller made a *written reclamation demand* no later than *45 days* after the debtor received the goods *or 20 days* after the start of the bankruptcy case, if the 45-day period expires after the commencement of the bankruptcy case. The seller's right to reclaim goods is subject to the *prior rights of a creditor with a security interest* in the goods or the proceeds of those goods.

b. Grain Farmers and United States Fishermen

The trustee's power to avoid (i) a transfer under the strong arm clause, (ii) a statutory lien, (iii) a preference, or (iv) a post-petition transfer is subject to any statutory or common law right of a grain farmer or a United States fisherman to *reclaim grain or fish* sold, in the ordinary course of the seller's business, to a grain storage facility or a fish processing facility that is owned or operated by the debtor, if the *debtor received such goods while insolvent.* The grain farmer or U.S. fisherman must make a *written demand for reclamation* no later than *10 days* after the debtor received the grain or fish.

6. Securities Safe Harbor, Repo Agreements, Swap Agreements

The securities safe harbor provides that the trustee cannot avoid a *pre-petition transfer* that is a *margin payment* or a *settlement payment* made by or to or for the benefit of a *commodity broker, forward contract merchant, stockbroker, financial institution, financial participant, or securities clearing agency.* It also provides that the trustee cannot avoid a *pre-petition transfer* made by or to or for the benefit of any of the above-mentioned entities in connection with a *securities contract, commodities contract, or forward contract.*

The trustee also *cannot avoid* (i) a *pre-petition* transfer made by or to or for the benefit of a *repo participant or financial institution* in connection with a *repurchase agreement;* (ii) a *pre-petition* transfer made by or to or for the benefit of a *swap participant or financial participant* under or in connection with any *swap agreement;* or (iii) a *pre-petition* transfer made by or to or for the benefit of a *master netting agreement participant* under or in connection with any *master netting agreement* or individual contract covered thereby.

None of these exceptions to the trustee's avoiding powers apply to transfers made with *actual intent to hinder, delay, or defraud creditors.*

7. Return of Goods

The trustee's power to avoid (i) a transfer under the strong arm clause, (ii) a statutory lien, (iii) a preference, (iv) a post-petition transfer, or (v) a setoff is subject to the right of a Chapter 11 debtor, under certain circumstances, to *return* pre-petition goods. A Chapter 11 debtor, with the creditor's consent and subject to the prior rights of a creditor with a security interest in the goods or the proceeds of such goods, may return goods shipped by the creditor before bankruptcy, and the creditor may offset the purchase price against any pre-petition claim.

8. **Warehouseman's Lien**

   The trustee may not avoid a warehouseman's lien for *storage, transportation, or costs incidental to the storage and handling of goods,* notwithstanding the Code's provisions on avoidance of statutory liens. Courts are to apply the prohibition against avoidance in a manner consistent with U.C.C. § 7–209 or similar state laws.

G. TRANSFEREE'S LIABILITY TO ESTATE FOR AVOIDED TRANSFER

Any transfer that has been avoided or any lien that is void under Bankruptcy Code § 506(d) is automatically preserved for the estate's benefit. By avoiding a transfer, the trustee is entitled to recover *either the property transferred* or, if ordered by the court, *its value.*

1. **From Whom Trustee May Recover**

   The trustee may recover from (i) the initial transferee, (ii) the entity for whose benefit the transfer was made or (iii) any subsequent transferee of the initial transferee. While the trustee may sue any of these entities for recovery, she is entitled to only a *single satisfaction*.

   a. **Exception for Good Faith Future Transferees**

      The trustee may not recover from a *subsequent transferee* who (i) did not know that the transfer was voidable, (ii) took the transfer in *good faith,* and (iii) *gave value* in exchange. A subsequent transferee who gives value, takes in good faith, and lacked knowledge of the voidability of the transfer *shelters* all subsequent *good faith transferees.*

2. **Good Faith Transferee's Lien**

   If the trustee recovers from a good faith transferee, the transferee receives a *lien on the property recovered,* for the purpose of securing *the lesser* of (i) the cost of any *improvements* transferee made after the transfer minus any profits received from the property due to those improvements, *or* (ii) the amount by which such improvements increased the property's value.

3. **Statute of Limitations**

   The trustee must bring any action to recover transferred property or its value under § 550 *before the earlier* of (i) *one year* after the corresponding transfer was avoided, or (ii) the time the case *is closed or dismissed.*

H. POST-PETITION EFFECT OF SECURITY INTEREST

Section 552 of the Bankruptcy Code is not really an avoidance provision. Nonetheless, it operates in a similar fashion by preventing a pre-petition lien from attaching to property acquired post-petition and thereby partially avoiding that lien. An *after-acquired property clause* is a clause in the parties' security agreement that creates a floating lien such that the security interest granted by the debtor to the creditor extends to collateral acquired by the debtor *after* signing the security agreement. With certain exceptions, § 552 of the Bankruptcy Code stops that lien from floating so that the creditor's security interest does not attach to *property acquired after* the filing of the bankruptcy case.

Note: Section 552 applies only to *consensual liens* and, thus, does not apply to federal tax liens, which are statutory.

1. **Exception for Certain Post-Petition Proceeds**

   If the pre-petition security agreement provides that the security interest attaches not only to collateral that the debtor *acquired prior to bankruptcy* but also to the proceeds, profits, products, or offspring of such collateral, then the creditor's security interest attaches to any *traceable post-petition proceeds, products, offspring, or profits* of the collateral acquired pre-petition.

2. **Exception for Certain Post-Petition Rents and Room Revenues**

   If a pre-petition security agreement extends to amounts paid as rent or for charges, fees, accounts, or other payments for hotel, motel, or similar lodgings, then the security interest extends to these post-petition rents, charges, fees, accounts, or other payments.

I. **CREDITOR'S RIGHT OF SETOFF**

   A creditor entitled to a right of setoff under state law may set off a debt he owes to the debtor against a claim he holds against the debtor, if *both the debt and the claim are mutual and arose prior to the filing of the bankruptcy case.* The Bankruptcy Code does not create a right of setoff; it merely preserves whatever right otherwise exists.

   1. **Automatic Stay**

      Once a bankruptcy petition has been filed, the automatic stay enjoins the post-petition setoff of a pre-petition debt owed to the debtor against a creditor's claim. Therefore, a creditor must obtain *relief from the stay* before a setoff may be exercised. In *Citizens Bank v. Strumpf,* the Supreme Court held that a bank's *temporary hold* on a debtor's deposit account up to the amount allegedly subject to setoff, while the bank seeks relief from the automatic stay and the court's determination of its right to a setoff, does not violate the automatic stay. A temporary administrative freeze, pending a judicial determination of the bank's motion to lift the stay, *does not constitute a setoff.*

   2. **Secured Status of Claim Subject to Setoff**

      A claim that may be set off *is deemed secured* to the extent of the amount subject to setoff. Therefore, a creditor holding such a claim is entitled to *adequate protection* unless the court lifts the automatic stay and permits the creditor to exercise her right of setoff.

   3. **Exceptions to Right of Setoff**

      There are several exceptions to a creditor's right of setoff. First, there is no right of setoff to the extent that the court has *disallowed the creditor's claim* against the debtor. Second, there is no right of setoff if an entity other than the debtor *transferred the claim to the creditor* after the filing of the bankruptcy petition or *within 90 days* prior to the bankruptcy petition at a time when the *debtor was insolvent.* Finally, there is no right of setoff if the *creditor incurred the debt* owed to the debtor *within 90 days* prior to the bankruptcy petition, at a time when the *debtor was insolvent,* for the *purpose of using that debt as a setoff.*

   4. **Creditor's Improved Position Due to Pre-Bankruptcy Setoff**

      With certain exceptions, the trustee may avoid and recover for the estate a setoff made by a creditor *within 90 days* prior to the filing of the petition *to the extent* that the creditor (usually a bank) has *improved its position.* The trustee's power to avoid and recover the setoff applies even if the debtor is solvent.

5. Distinguish Recoupment

Setoff should be distinguished from the equitable doctrine of recoupment. The *setoff* of mutual debts between two parties involves independent obligations that usually are derived from *separate transactions. Recoupment*, on the other hand, is used by a creditor to reduce its liability to the debtor because of a right that the creditor has arising out of the *same transaction* or occurrence. Recoupment is basically a defense, e.g., overpayment, to the debtor's claim and not a mutual obligation. Neither the automatic stay nor § 553's limitations on setoffs apply to recoupments.

VII. CLAIMS OF CREDITORS

A. FILING PROOFS OF CLAIMS

1. Claim

Congress intended the "broadest possible definition of the word "claim" to include "all legal obligations of the debtor, no matter how remote or contingent" so as to provide "the broadest possible relief in the bankruptcy court." Thus, the Code defines "claim," in part, as a *"right to payment,* whether or not such right is reduced to judgment, liquidated, unliquidated, fixed, contingent, matured, unmatured, disputed, undisputed, legal, equitable, secured, or unsecured." The second half of the Code's definition of the word "claim" is a *"right to an equitable remedy* for breach of performance if such breach gives rise to a right to payment, whether or not such right to an equitable remedy is reduced to judgment, fixed, contingent, matured, unmatured, disputed, undisputed, secured, or unsecured."

2. Claimants

a. Filing a Proof of Claim or Interest

With certain exceptions, a *creditor,* whether secured or unsecured, must file a proof of claim and an *equity security holder must* file a proof of interest for the claim or interest to be allowed. If a creditor does not timely file a proof of claim, the debtor or trustee may file a proof of claim *in the creditor's name* and a co-debtor, surety, or guarantor may file a proof of claim *for the creditor.*

3. Time to File

The time within which to file a proof of claim or interest depends on the chapter of the Bankruptcy Code governing the particular case.

a. Chapters 7, 12, and 13

Subject to the exceptions below, in a *voluntary case begun in Chapter 7, 12, or 13,* a proof of claim ordinarily must be filed no later than *70 days* after the order for relief. In an *involuntary Chapter 7 case,* a proof of claim is timely filed if it is filed no later than *90 days* after the order for relief.

b. Converted Cases

In a case *converted to Chapter 12 or 13,* a proof of claim is timely filed if it is filed no later than *70 days* after the order of conversion. In a case *converted from Chapter 11, 12, or 13 to Chapter 7,* all claims *actually* filed before conversion of the case are considered automatically filed in the Chapter 7 case. Thus, a second filing is not required. However, a claim must be filed if it was only deemed filed in a case converted from Chapter 11.

c. Chapter 11

In a Chapter 11 case, the court fixes and sends notice of a *bar date,* which operates as a deadline for the filing of proofs of claims or interests. Any claim or interest listed in the debtor's schedules is *deemed filed automatically* for the scheduled amount, *unless* the claim or interest is *scheduled as contingent, unliquidated, or disputed.*

d. Exceptions

The following are *exceptions to the general time periods* for filing proofs of claims.

(i) Governmental Unit Claims

A claim by a *governmental unit* in a Chapter 7, 12 or 13 case is timely if it is filed *no later than 180 days* after the order for relief. A claim by a governmental unit resulting from a *tax return filed under § 1308* is timely if it is filed *no later than 180 days* after the order for relief or *60 days* after the filing of the tax return.

(ii) Infants or Incompetent Persons

In a Chapter 7, 11, 12 or 13 case, the court may extend the time period for filing a proof of claim by an *infant, incompetent person, or the representative* of the infant or incompetent person if extending the time period is in *the interest of justice* and will not *unduly delay administration of the case.*

(iii) Entry of Judgment

In a Chapter 7, 11, 12 or 13 case, an *unsecured claim* arising in favor of an entity or that becomes allowable as a result of the entry of a judgment may be filed *within 30 days after the judgment becomes final if* the judgment is for recovery of money or property from the entity, or denial or avoidance of the entity's interest in property.

(iv) Rejection of Executory Contract or Unexpired Lease

In a Chapter 7, 11, 12 or 13 case, the bankruptcy court may set a time for filing of claims arising from the rejection of executory contracts or unexpired leases.

(v) Chapter 7 "No Asset" Cases

If the Chapter 7 trustee notifies the court that unsecured creditors will receive a dividend in the Chapter 7 case, after creditors have received a notice indicating that no dividend would be paid, the bankruptcy clerk must give *at least 90 days' notice* by mail to creditors of the fact that a dividend will be paid and of the date by which creditors must file a proof of claim.

(vi) Creditor Motion to Extend Time Period

In a Chapter 7, 11, 12, or 13 case, the bankruptcy court, upon motion of a creditor, may extend the time period for filing a proof of claim if the court finds that notice was insufficient under *the circumstances to give the creditor a reasonable time* to file a proof of claim. The court may extend the time period *no more than 60 days* from the order granting the creditor's motion.

(vii) Secured Creditor on Debtor's Principal Residence

In a Chapter 7, 12 or 13 case, a proof of claim filed by the holder of a claim secured by the *debtor's principal residence* is timely filed if (1) the proof of claim and the documents required by the bankruptcy rules are filed *no later than 70 days* after the order for relief *and* (2) any attachments supporting creditor's interest in the property securing the claim, e.g., a copy of the mortgage, and evidence that the creditor's security interest is perfected, are filed as a supplement to the claim *no later than 120 days* after the order for relief.

4. Claims Deemed Pre-Petition

A proof of claim may be filed on the following *post-petition claims* the same as if such claims had arisen *pre-petition:*

a. *a claim for reimbursement or contribution* that becomes fixed after the bankruptcy petition has been filed;

b. *a claim arising in the ordinary course of the debtor's business* or financial affairs during the *gap period* in an *involuntary case*;

c. *a claim arising from the rejection of an executory contract or an unexpired lease* that the trustee or the debtor in possession has not assumed;

d. *a claim for damages* under § 562 for *rejection* of a swap agreement, securities contract, forward contract, commodity contract, repurchase agreement, or master netting agreement;

e. *a claim arising from the recovery of property* under §§ 522, 550, or 553; and

f. *a claim* that does not arise until after the start of the bankruptcy case for a tax *entitled to eighth priority*.

5. Fuel Use Tax

Post-BAPCPA, the Code permits the filing of a single fuel use tax claim to cover fuel use taxes that the debtor owes to various state tax authorities, if the requirements of 49 U.S.C. § 31701 are met.

B. ALLOWANCE OF CLAIMS

Unless a party in interest objects, a claim or interest that has been filed will be allowed by the court and will serve as the basis for distribution. If a party in interest objects to a claim, the court, after notice and a hearing, determines the amount of the claim *as of the date of the filing of the bankruptcy petition,* and allows the claim unless it falls within one of the following recognized exceptions.

1. Exceptions to Allowance

The following claims or portions of a claim are not allowable:

a. a claim that is *unenforceable* because the *debtor has a valid defense;*

b. a claim for *post-petition interest* on an *unsecured claim;*

c. a claim for an *unsecured property tax* in excess of the *debtor's equity* in the property;

d. the portion of a claim for services of an *insider* or *debtor's attorney* that *exceeds the reasonable value* of those services;

e. a claim for a *nondischargeable domestic support obligation* that is *unmatured* as of the bankruptcy filing date;

f. the portion of a *lessor's claim* for damages for a terminated lease of real property that *exceeds* the formula provided by the Code;

g. the portion of an *employee's claim* for *damages* for termination of an employment contract in *excess* of the period provided by the Code;

h. a claim that results from a reduction, due to late payment, in the amount of an otherwise applicable *federal tax credit* available to the debtor in connection with a *state employment tax* on wages, salaries, or commissions earned from the debtor;

i. with certain exceptions, a *tardily filed claim*;

j. any claim of an entity from which property is recoverable under the Code's turnover, recovery of avoidable transfer, or setoff provisions or that is a transferee of an avoidable transfer is not allowable *unless* the entity has paid the amount, or turned over the property, for which it is liable; *and*

k. a claim for reimbursement or contribution by an *entity that is liable with the debtor* or an *entity that secured* the claim of a *creditor if* the creditor's claim is disallowed, the reimbursement or contribution claim is *contingent* at the time of allowance or disallowance, or the entity asserts a *right to subrogation* to the rights of the creditor.

2. Estimation of Claims

If the fixing or liquidation of a *contingent or unliquidated* claim would cause undue delay in the administration of the bankruptcy case, the court must estimate the claim. The bankruptcy court also must estimate a claim for a *right to payment* arising from a *right to an equitable remedy* for breach of performance.

3. Claims Deemed Pre-Petition

For the purpose of allowance or disallowance, certain *post-petition claims* are treated the same as if such claims had arisen pre-petition.

4. Reduction of Claim on Unsecured Consumer Debt

A debtor may move to *reduce by no more than 20%* the amount of a *claim for an unsecured consumer* debt if the following requirements are satisfied:

a. the claim is for a *consumer debt* that is *completely unsecured;*

b. the creditor filing the claim *unreasonably refused to negotiate an alternative repayment schedule* that an approved nonprofit and credit counseling agency proposed on the debtor's behalf;

c. debtor made the offer *at least 60 days* prior to filing of the petition;

d. debtor's offer provided for payment of *at least 60% of the debt* over a period not to exceed the loan's repayment period, or a reasonable extension of that period; and

e. no portion of the debt under the alternative repayment schedule is *nondischargeable.*

The debtor must prove by *clear and convincing evidence* that (i) the creditor unreasonably refused to consider the debtor's proposal *and* (ii) the proposal was made before the expiration of the 60-day period referenced above.

C. SECURED CLAIMS

In bankruptcy, a secured claim is one that has been allowed and is either *secured by a lien* on property of the estate or is subject to *setoff.* The Bankruptcy Code treats a claim as secured *only to the extent of the value of the creditor's collateral* or up to the amount subject to setoff.

1. Undersecured Claims: Bifurcation

An *oversecured creditor* is a creditor with a lien on property worth *more* than the debt owed to that creditor. It is important to distinguish between the *oversecured creditor* and the *secured creditor* whose debt *equals* the value of the property securing the debt. Oversecured creditors are entitled to interest—up to the value of the collateral—in the period between filing of the petition and confirmation of a plan in one of the Code's reorganization chapters.

An *undersecured creditor,* on the other hand, holds a debt in *excess* of the value of the collateral securing that debt. With certain exceptions, if the amount of the creditor's claim exceeds the value of the collateral, the claim is undersecured and is divided into two separate claims: (i) a *secured claim* equal to the value of the collateral, and (ii) an *unsecured claim* equal to the amount by which the claim exceeds the value of the collateral.

2. Undersecured Claims and Bifurcation: Exceptions

a. Debtor's Principal Residence

In a case filed under Chapter 11 or 13, the plan may not modify the rights of a creditor holding a secured claim secured only by the debtor's principal residence.

b. Hanging Paragraph

In a Chapter 13 case, the debtor may not bifurcate the claim of a creditor holding a *purchase-money security interest* (i) in a *motor vehicle* purchased within *910 days of bankruptcy* and acquired for the *debtor's personal use or* (ii) in *any other thing of value,* if the debt was incurred within *one year of the bankruptcy filing.*

c. Section 1111(b) Election

In a Chapter 11 case, if a creditor elects treatment under § 1111(b), the creditor's claim is treated as a secured claim to the extent that the claim is allowed.

3. Valuation of Collateral

In determining the collateral's value, the bankruptcy court must take into account both the *purpose of the valuation* and the *intended disposition or use* of the collateral. In *individual Chapter 7 or 13* cases, the value of *personal property* is its *replacement value,* without deduction for the costs of sale or marketing; the valuation time is the *time of the bankruptcy filing.* If the individual Chapter 7 or 13 debtor acquired the collateral for *personal, family, or household purposes,* then *replacement value for personal property* is *retail value,* based on the *age and condition* of the personal property *at the time value is determined.*

4. Oversecured Claims

If the value of a creditor's collateral exceeds the amount of the claim that it secures, including any surcharges under § 506(c), then the creditor is entitled to *post-petition interest,* regardless of whether the creditor's lien is consensual, e.g., a mortgage or a U.C.C. security interest, or nonconsensual, e.g., a tax lien. To the extent that the claim is oversecured, the creditor also may recover any reasonable fees, e.g., attorneys' fees, costs, or other charges *specified in the agreement* or a *state statute under which the claim arose.*

5. Surcharge Against Collateral

To the extent that a secured creditor *benefits* from the preservation or disposition of the collateral, the trustee or the debtor in possession may be *reimbursed from the collateral* for the necessary and reasonable costs of preserving or disposing of the collateral. This surcharge is *paid ahead of an award of post-petition interest or fees* to an oversecured creditor. In 2005, Congress added the payment of "all ad valorem property taxes with respect to the property" to the expenses that may be charged against a secured creditor's recovery from the collateral.

6. Liens Deemed Void

A valid lien survives bankruptcy even if the secured creditor does not file a proof of claim. In a Chapter 7 case, if the collateral is real property the debtor may not use § 506(d) to strip down the creditor's lien on the real property to the value of the collateral nor may the debtor strip off a junior mortgage if the debt owed on a senior mortgage exceeds the value of the real property.

A lien is *void,* however, to the extent that it secures a claim that is *not an allowed secured claim unless*

a. the claim is *disallowed only* as a *nondischargeable, unmatured domestic support obligation;*

b. the claim is for *reimbursement or contribution* and is *disallowed only under § 502(e);* or

c. the claim is not an allowed secured claim due *only to the failure of the creditor* to *file a proof of claim.*

7. Adequate Protection

A secured creditor has the right to receive adequate protection of her interest in the collateral, and the failure to provide it constitutes cause to grant the creditor relief from the automatic stay.

D. ADMINISTRATIVE EXPENSES

1. Priority

Administration claims are *unsecured, priority* claims. Claims for administrative expenses have the second highest priority, after domestic support obligations, in the distribution of the assets of the estate.

2. Allowable Administrative Expenses

Section 503(b) lists *nine numbered categories* of expenses that qualify for administrative expense status. This list, however, is not exclusive. The following items are allowable as administrative expenses, after notice and a hearing:

a. the *actual and necessary post-petition costs of preserving the bankruptcy estate;*

b. *post-petition taxes* incurred by the estate and *fines or penalties* related to such taxes;

c. compensation and reimbursement to *officers of the estate;*

d. actual and necessary expenses of a creditor who files an *involuntary petition;*

e. actual and necessary expenses of a creditor who, with court approval, *recovers* for the benefit of the *estate* any *property* that the *debtor has either concealed or transferred;*

f. actual and necessary expenses incurred by a creditor in connection with *prosecution of a criminal offense* related to the bankruptcy case or to the debtor's property or business;

g. in a Chapter 11 case, the actual and necessary expenses of certain parties, including an indenture trustee, that make a *substantial contribution;*

h. actual and necessary expenses, as well as compensation, for the services of a pre-petition custodian who has been superseded under § 543;

i. actual and necessary expenses of an official Chapter 11 creditors' or equity security holders' committee;

j. witnesses' fees and mileage expenses;

k. monies due a landlord under a *nonresidential real property lease* that was *first assumed* under § 365 and then *later rejected;*

l. actual, necessary costs and expenses incurred in *closing a health care business;*

m. the value of *goods* sold in the *ordinary course of the debtor's business* and received by the debtor *within 20 days* of the start of the debtor's bankruptcy case; and

n. for cases commenced *before December 27, 2022,* a *temporary* § 503(b)(10) granting administrative expense status to debts incurred under *temporary* § 364(g)(1).

3. Exempt Property

As a general rule, administrative expenses are *not payable* out of *property that the debtor exempts.* However, the debtor's exempt property is liable for the share of administrative expenses related to the trustee's avoidance of a transfer of property or recovery of such property. The share of costs is computed based on the value of the *portion of the property exempted* in relation to the *value of the property recovered.* If the debtor avoids the fixing of a lien under § 522(f) or avoids a transfer of property that the trustee did not attempt to avoid, and then recovers such property for the estate, the exempt property is liable for any costs or expenses associated with the avoidance and recovery actions.

4. Limitations on KERPS

In BAPCPA, Congress added language to the Code that limits a debtor's ability to claim administrative expense priority for *certain post-petition payments made to insiders.* The purpose of this new provision is to place restrictions on Key Employee Retention Plans ("KERPS"). The Code now provides that a payment made or obligation incurred for the *benefit of an insider* to induce the insider to remain with the debtor's business shall not be allowed or paid unless the court makes certain findings based on evidence in the record.

E. PRIORITY CLAIMS

1. Payment Hierarchy

Priority claims are *unsecured claims* but as the name suggest have priority of payment in bankruptcy. There are ten tiers of priority claims, which are *paid in the following order* in a Chapter 7 case:

a. *domestic support obligations,* but there is a payment hierarchy within the first statutory category;

b. *administrative expenses*;

c. *involuntary case gap claims*;

d. wages, salaries, or commissions earned by an *individual* (or corporation with only one employee acting as an independent contractor) within *180 days* before either bankruptcy or "the cessation of the debtor's business," whichever is earlier, but limited to *$15,150*;

e. contributions to an employee benefit plan for services rendered within *180 days* before either bankruptcy or "the cessation of the debtor's business," whichever is earlier, but subject to certain monetary limitations;

f. allowed unsecured claims, subject to a monetary limit, of *grain producers* or United States *fishermen* against a debtor who operates or owns a grain storage facility or against a debtor who operates a fish produce storage or processing facility, respectively;

g. allowed unsecured claims of individuals, limited to *$3,350,* arising from the pre-petition deposit of money with the debtor for the purchase, lease, or rental of property *or* the purchase of services that were not delivered or provided that were intended for the *personal, family, or household* use of the claimant;

h. pre-petition tax claims, including certain income or gross receipts taxes, property taxes, trust fund taxes, employment taxes, excise taxes, custom duties, and penalties on eighth priority tax claims if for compensation for actual pecuniary loss;

i. allowed unsecured claims of a *federal depository institutions regulatory agency* for the amount of any deficiency under the debtor's agreement to maintain the capital of an insured depository institution; and

j. allowed claims for *death or personal injury* resulting from the operation of a *vessel or motor vehicle* if such operation was unlawful because the debtor was *intoxicated* from using alcohol, drugs, or other substances.

2. Exceptions to Equal Treatment of Priority Creditors in a Class

The general rule is that priority creditors *within a class* share equally in any distribution. There are several exceptions, however, to this general rule.

a. Domestic Support Obligations

The trustee, if she administers assets to pay a domestic support obligation, is paid first, then a spouse, former spouse, or child of the debtor with a domestic support obligation claim, and finally, a governmental unit with a domestic support obligation assigned to it by a spouse, former spouse, or child of the debtor.

b. Conversion to Chapter 7

If a case is converted from Chapter 11, 12, or 13 to a case under Chapter 7, the administrative expense claims in the Chapter 7 case *after conversion* have priority over the administrative expenses incurred prior to conversion.

c. Super-Priority: Inadequately Protected Secured Creditor

If the trustee, under §§ 362, 363, or 364, provides adequate protection to a creditor whose claim is secured by a lien on the debtor's property, but the adequate protection ultimately proves to be deficient, the creditor will receive an administrative expense claim with *priority over all other administrative expenses* allowed against the debtor's estate.

d. Super Super-Priority: Post-Petition Credit

If the trustee or the debtor in possession is unable to obtain unsecured post-petition credit by means of an administrative expense priority, the court may approve new credit or the incurring of debt with *priority over all other administrative expense* claims, *including any super-priority claims* arising from the failure of adequate protection.

3. Subrogation

A third party, such as a co-debtor or a surety, who becomes subrogated to the rights of a holder of a claim entitled to a first priority or fourth through ninth priority does *not* become subrogated to the holder's right to priority. Keep in mind that § 507(d) applies *only* to first priority and fourth through ninth priority claims. Thus, an entity subrogated to the rights of (i) a holder of an administrative expense claim (second priority), (ii) a holder of a gap claim in an involuntary case (third priority), or (iii) a holder of a personal injury claim (tenth priority) become subrogated to the respective priorities of such claims.

F. TAX CLAIMS

The bankruptcy court has jurisdiction to determine the amount or legality of any tax, fine, penalty, or addition to tax that has not been contested in and adjudicated by an appropriate judicial or administrative court *prior to bankruptcy.* The court may exercise its power to determine tax liability regardless of whether the tax has been assessed or paid. The bankruptcy court cannot determine the *estate's* right to a tax refund *before the earlier of 120 days* after the trustee properly requests a refund from the appropriate governmental unit, *or* a determination by that governmental unit of the trustee's request. The bankruptcy court *may not* determine the amount or legality of any amount arising in connection with an *ad valorem tax* on the estate's real or personal property if the applicable period for contesting or re-determining that amount under applicable nonbankruptcy law has expired.

1. Tax Liability of Estate

The Code provides a process by which the trustee "can obtain an expedited determination" of the estate's post-petition tax liability. A trustee may request that the appropriate taxing authority determine any unpaid tax liability *of the estate* incurred during the administration of the case by submitting to the governmental unit a tax return accompanied by a request for a determination of the tax. Unless the return is *fraudulent* or contains *material misrepresentations,* the estate, the trustee, and the debtor or a successor to the debtor are discharged from any liability for the tax *upon payment of the tax indicated on the return* if the taxing authority fails to take certain action within the statutory time frames *or upon payment of the tax determined by the taxing authority* or *the court.*

2. **Assessment**

   After the court determines a tax liability, the taxing authority may assess the amount of the tax against the estate, the debtor, or a successor to the debtor, notwithstanding the automatic stay.

3. **Interest on Tax Claims**

   If the Code requires the payment of interest on a *tax claim* or an *administrative expense tax* claim, or the payment of interest to enable a *tax creditor* to receive the *present value* of its claim, then the interest rate is the applicable *rate under nonbankruptcy law.* In the case of taxes paid pursuant to a confirmed plan under Chapter 11, 12, or 13, the date for determining the interest rate is the calendar month in which the plan is confirmed.

4. **Burden of Proof**

   The Supreme Court held that "in the absence of modification in the Bankruptcy Code the burden of proof on a tax claim in bankruptcy remains where the substantive tax law puts it."

G. SUBROGATION CLAIMS

A subrogee is an entity that *has paid* a creditor's claim against the debtor because the entity either had secured the claim or was liable with the debtor on the claim as a co-debtor, co-maker, surety, or guarantor. With certain exceptions, a subrogee *succeeds to the rights of the creditor* whose claim it paid to the extent of the amount paid. A co-debtor's claim, either by way of subrogation or for reimbursement or contribution, will be *subordinated to the principal creditor's claim* until that claim is paid in full, either through distribution under the Bankruptcy Code or by other means.

H. SUBORDINATION OF CLAIMS

A claim in a bankruptcy case may be subordinated to the payment of other claims by a subordination contract enforceable under applicable nonbankruptcy law.

1. **Subordination of Claims for Purchase or Sale of a Security**

   A claim for damages, rescission, or contribution or reimbursement arising from the purchase or sale of a security of the debtor or its affiliate *must be subordinated* to all claims or interests *senior or equal* to that which the security represents.

   a. **Exception: Common Stock**

      If the security is common stock, then the claim will be subordinated to the *same priority as common stock,* not to a lower priority.

2. **Equitable Subordination**

   The court has the equitable power (i) to subordinate all or part of an allowed secured or unsecured claim to another allowed claim, (ii) to subordinate all or part of an allowed interest to another allowed interest, or (iii) to order that any lien securing such a subordinated claim be transferred to the estate. An *essential element* in the equitable subordination of a claim or interest is showing *inequitable conduct* on the claimant's part. Such misconduct falls into one of the following three categories: (i) *fraud, illegality, or breach of fiduciary duties;* (ii) *undercapitalization;* or (iii) the claimant's use of the debtor as a *mere instrumentality or alter ego.*

a. Insiders and Fiduciaries

Courts usually rigorously examine the dealings of insiders and fiduciaries for *good faith and fairness.*

I. DISTRIBUTION OUTSIDE OF BANKRUPTCY CODE

A creditor of a partnership debtor who receives payment on an allowed claim against the partnership from a general partner who is not a debtor in a Chapter 7 case and who has not secured the creditor's claim with a lien on the general partner's own property is prohibited from receiving any payment on the claim until all of the creditors with whom she would have shared equally have received payment equal to the consideration she received from the general partner.

VIII. DEBTOR'S EXEMPTIONS

A. EXEMPTIONS

1. Fresh Start: Exempt Property

Filing of the petition creates the bankruptcy estate which comprises all of the legal and equitable interests of the debtor. An individual debtor, however, does not emerge destitute from bankruptcy, because she is entitled to certain exemptions from property of the estate, either under the Bankruptcy Code or pursuant to applicable state law and nonbankruptcy federal law. These exemptions apply only to individual debtors—not to partnerships or corporations—in cases under Chapters 7, 11, 12, and 13. A waiver by the debtor of an exemption (or exemptions) in favor of an unsecured creditor is unenforceable in bankruptcy. A majority of states have opted out of the federal bankruptcy exemption scheme, thereby restricting debtors domiciled there to the exemptions allowed under their state law and federal nonbankruptcy law. In states that have not opted out, the debtor is free to choose *either* the federal bankruptcy exemptions or those permitted under applicable state and federal nonbankruptcy law.

2. Federal Bankruptcy Exemptions

a. Homestead

The debtor may exempt up to *$27,900 in real or personal property* used by the debtor or a dependent as a *residence,* in a *cooperative that owns property* that the debtor or a dependent uses as a *residence,* or in a *burial plot* for the debtor or a dependent.

b. Motor Vehicle

The debtor may exempt up to *$4,450* in *one motor vehicle.*

c. Household Goods, Clothing, Books, Crops, Animals

The debtor may exempt up to *$14,875 in aggregate value* in household furnishings, household goods, clothing, appliances, books, musical instruments, crops, or animals that are held primarily for the *personal, family, or household use* of the debtor or a dependent.

But note: The debtor may not exempt more than *$700 in any single item* from the list above.

d. Jewelry

The debtor may exempt up to *$1,875* in jewelry held primarily for the personal, family, or household use of the debtor or a dependent.

e. Wildcard Exemption

There is an exemption of up to *$1,475, plus up to $13,950* of any unused portion of the homestead exemption, *in any property.*

f. Tools of the Trade

The debtor may exempt up to *$2,800* in her *professional books* or *tools of the trade* or those of a dependent.

g. Life Insurance

The debtor may exempt any *unmatured* life insurance contract that she owns, except a credit life insurance contract.

h. Loan Value or Accrued Interest of Life Insurance

There is an exemption of up to *$14,875* in the loan value or in accrued interest or dividends of any unmatured life insurance contract that the debtor owns.

i. Health Aids

The debtor may exempt health aids prescribed by a professional for the debtor or a dependent. There is no monetary cap for this exemption.

j. Government Benefits

There is an exemption for the debtor's right to receive social security benefits, veterans' benefits, local public assistance, unemployment benefits or compensation, or disability or illness benefits.

k. Alimony, Support, or Maintenance

The debtor may exempt payments received for *alimony, support, or maintenance,* to the extent that it is reasonably necessary to support the debtor and any dependent.

l. Pension Plan

With certain exceptions, the debtor may exempt payments under a stock bonus, pension, profit sharing, annuity, or similar plan that are based on length of service, age, illness, disability, or death, to the extent that such payment is reasonably necessary to support the debtor and any dependent.

m. Crime Victim Award

The debtor may exempt property or payments received pursuant to an award under a *crime victim's reparation law.*

n. Wrongful Death Award

The debtor may exempt her right to receive payment arising from the wrongful death of an individual of whom the debtor was a dependent, to the extent that the payment is reasonably necessary to support the debtor and any of her dependents.

o. Life Insurance Proceeds

The debtor may exempt a payment under a life insurance contract that insured the life of an individual if debtor was a dependent of that individual on the date of the individual's death. The debtor may exempt the payment only to the extent that the payment is reasonably necessary to support the debtor and any of her dependents.

p.   **Personal Injury Award**

The debtor may exempt payments, up to a *maximum of $27,900,* arising from *personal bodily injury* of the debtor or an individual of whom the debtor is a dependent. This exemption does not include compensation for pain and suffering or compensation for actual pecuniary loss, such as medical expenses.

q.   **Loss of Future Earnings**

The debtor may exempt compensation for the *loss of future earnings* of either the debtor or an individual of whom the debtor was or is a dependent, to the extent that the payment is reasonably necessary to support the debtor and any of her dependents.

r.   **Retirement Funds and IRAs**

The debtor may exempt retirement funds, so long as the monies are in a fund or account that is exempt from taxation under certain provisions of the Internal Revenue Code. The debtor may exempt up to *$1,512,350* of funds in certain individual retirement accounts. The Supreme Court has held that monies in an inherited IRA do not qualify for the exemption under § 522(b)(3)(C).

3.   **State Exemption Law, Federal Limits, and Nonbankruptcy Federal Exemptions**

The exemptions available to the debtor are those allowable under applicable state law and nonbankruptcy federal law, subject to the Bankruptcy Code's domiciliary requirement and to new Code restrictions on state homestead exemptions.

a.   *Which* **State Law Exemptions?**

Subject to the Code's domiciliary requirement and to federal restrictions on state homestead exemptions, the exemptions allowable under state law are those in effect: (i) as of the date the bankruptcy petition was filed and (ii) in the state where the debtor has been domiciled for the *730 days or two years* prior to filing the bankruptcy petition. If the debtor has not been domiciled in a single state for 730 days, then the exemption law of the place where debtor has been domiciled for the *180 days immediately preceding the 730-day period* applies. If the debtor has not been domiciled in a single state for the *180-day period,* then the exemption law of the place where debtor has been domiciled for the *longest portion of the 180-day period* applies. State law exemptions vary widely from state to state.

b.   **Federal Limitations on Homestead Exemptions**

The Bankruptcy Code now contains three limitations on a debtor's right to fully exempt her homestead under state exemption laws. The limitations apply to *real or personal property* that the debtor or a dependent *uses as a residence* or *claims as a homestead,* a *cooperative* that owns property used by the debtor or a dependent as a *residence,* or a *burial plot* for the debtor or a dependent ("the Property").

(i)   **The Fraud Limitation**

The fraud limitation reduces the amount of the debtor's state exemption to the extent that the debtor, *with intent to hinder, delay or defraud creditors,* disposed of *non-exempt property* in the *10-year period* preceding bankruptcy in order to increase the amount of the state-law exemption taken in the Property described above.

(ii) The 1215-Day Limitation

The Bankruptcy Code places a cap of *$189,050* on any interest that the debtor acquires in the Property described above during the *1215-day period* preceding the filing of bankruptcy. This restriction does not apply to the *principal residence of a family farmer.* It also does not apply if the debtor uses the money received from sale of a residence acquired before the 1215-day period to acquire a new residence in the *same state* during the 1215-day period.

(iii) The "Bad Conduct" Limitation

The Bankruptcy Code caps the debtor's exemptible interest at *$189,050* on the Property described above in cases involving certain types of bad conduct by the debtor. The cap does not apply to the extent that the amount of the debtor's interest in the property is *reasonably necessary for the support* of the debtor and any dependents of the debtor.

c. Nonbankruptcy Federal Law

Federal statutes other than the Bankruptcy Code sometimes provide exemptions that may be claimed under § 522(b)(3)(A), such as Social Security payments, veterans' benefits, civil service retirement benefits, or military pension benefits.

d. Tenancy by the Entirety and Joint Tenancy

A debtor who uses the state exemptions also may exempt any interest in property she held, immediately prior to bankruptcy, as a tenant by the entirety or as a joint tenant, to the extent that applicable nonbankruptcy law exempts such interest from process. It is important to recognize that the treatment of property held by the entirety or in a joint tenancy depends on how state law treats such property.

4. Joint Case

In a joint case, *each debtor* is entitled to a separate claim of any allowable exemptions.

a. Federal Exemptions

Joint debtors who elect the federal exemptions may stack their exemptions. But recall that in a joint case, *both debtors* must choose either the federal exemptions or the state exemptions.

b. State Exemptions

The majority of courts have held that state law controls whether debtors in opt-out states may stack state law exemption values.

5. Effect of Exemptions: Not Liable for Debts

The general rule is that, unless the case is dismissed, property exempted by the debtor is not liable *during or after the case* for any pre-petition debt or any debt deemed to have arisen before bankruptcy. The following kinds of debts, however, may be satisfied from the debtor's exempt property:

a. *nondischargeable taxes;*

b. *domestic support obligations;*

c. *a debt secured by a lien* that is not void under § 506(d) and that has not been avoided under certain provisions of the Code;

d. *a debt secured by a tax lien* if notice of the lien was filed properly;

e. *a debt for fraud or defalcation while acting in a fiduciary capacity, embezzlement, or larceny* owed by *an institution-affiliated party of an insured depository institution* to a federal depository institutions regulatory agency acting as the conservator, receiver, or liquidating agent for such institution;

f. *a debt for willful and malicious injury to another entity or its property* owed by *an institution-affiliated party of an insured depository institution* to a federal depository institutions regulatory agency acting as the conservator, receiver, or liquidating agent for such institution; and

g. *a debt in connection with fraud* in obtaining or providing *any financial assistance* for purposes of *financing an education* at an institution of higher learning.

6. Avoidance of Liens That Impair Exemption

Judicial liens, other than a judicial lien securing a debt for a domestic support obligation, and *nonpossessory, nonpurchase-money security interests* in (i) *household goods* and certain other items held *primarily for personal, family, or household use,* (ii) *implements, professional books, or tools of the trade,* and (iii) *professionally prescribed health aids* may be avoided by the debtor when they *impair an exemption* that the debtor could otherwise claim.

7. Property Recovered by Trustee

The debtor may exempt property that the *trustee has recovered* and brought into the estate so long as the debtor, absent the transfer, could have exempted the property under applicable federal or state law, and only if: (i) the debtor *did not voluntarily* transfer the property and did not conceal it; or (ii) the debtor *could have avoided* the transfer under § 522(f)(1)(B).

8. Avoidance by Debtor

If the trustee can avoid a transfer of property or recover a setoff but does not attempt to pursue it, the debtor may *avoid* the transfer or may *recover* the setoff to the extent that she could have exempted the property under § 522(g)(1) if the trustee had used his avoiding powers.

9. Debtor's Recovery and Exemption

A debtor who avoids a transfer of property or recovers a setoff pursuant to §§ 522(f) or 522(h) may *recover* the property or the setoff in accordance with § 550 and may *exempt* it to the extent permitted under the applicable exemption scheme.

10. Administrative Expenses

Subject to certain exceptions, exempt property usually is not liable for the payment of administrative expenses.

B. REDEMPTION: CHAPTER 7 CASES ONLY

1. Tangible Personal Property

In a Chapter 7 case, an *individual debtor* has the right to redeem *tangible personal property* from a lien that secures a dischargeable consumer debt if the property is held mainly for *personal, family, or household use,* and it either has been *exempted* by the debtor or has been *abandoned* by the trustee. The debtor may retain such collateral by paying the secured party the *amount of the allowed secured claim,* which is determined by the collateral's market value.

a. Lump Sum

To redeem collateral, the debtor must make payment in a lump sum and not by installment payments.

2. Changed Intention

A debtor who has filed a statement of intention to reaffirm a secured consumer debt is not bound irrevocably by the decision and still may redeem the collateral, notwithstanding her original statement of intention.

3. No Waiver

A debtor may exercise her right to redeem collateral even if she has waived the right to redeem.

IX. DISCHARGE OF INDEBTEDNESS

A. EXCEPTIONS TO DISCHARGE

Certain debts of an *individual debtor* are not dischargeable and, therefore, survive the bankruptcy of an individual who has received a discharge under Chapter 7, 11, 12, or 13. A creditor who obtains a judicial determination that a particular debt is nondischargeable is free to pursue the debtor and to attempt to recover that debt subsequent to the debtor's discharge. *Distinguish* a determination of nondischargeability under § 523(a), which excepts *a specific debt* from the debtor's discharge, from the complete denial of a debtor's discharge, which allows *all of the debtor's debts* to survive bankruptcy, and thereafter all claimants to compete for satisfaction of their claims.

1. Nondischargeable Debts Under § 523(a)

a. Taxes

Taxes entitled to *third priority (gap period)* and *eighth priority (various unsecured pre-petition claims)* are not dischargeable. Taxes for which a *return was not filed* or for which a *fraudulent return* was filed also are not dischargeable.

Note: Discharge rules for priority taxes differ for a standard Chapter 13 discharge. Chapter 12 also has special discharge rules for unsecured tax claims related to disposition of property used in the debtor's farming operation.

b. Fraud

Debts for money, property, services, or an extension, renewal, or refinancing of credit obtained by *false pretenses, a false representation, or actual fraud,* other than a statement about the financial condition of the debtor or an insider, are not dischargeable if the creditor *justifiably* relies on the fraudulent representation. A debt for money, property, services, or an extension, renewal, or refinancing of credit obtained by the use of a false statement in writing is not dischargeable if (i) the statement was *materially* false; (ii) the statement related to the *financial condition* of the *debtor or an insider;* (iii) the creditor owed the debt *reasonably relied upon* the written statement; *and* (iv) the debtor made the statement with the *intent to deceive.*

Note: While this portion of the capsule summary covers exceptions to discharge for individual debtors, keep in mind that confirmation of a Chapter 11 plan does *not discharge a corporate debtor* from a debt owed to a *domestic governmental unit* that was obtained by *false pretenses, false representation, or actual fraud.* Plan confirmation also does *not discharge a corporate debtor* from a debt owed to a *domestic governmental unit* that was obtained by use of a *false statement in writing* respecting the debtor's *financial condition.*

c.   **Failure to Schedule Debts in Current Case**

Debts involving fraud, misrepresentation, or use of a false written financial statement; larceny, embezzlement, or fraud or defalcation while acting in a fiduciary capacity; or willful and malicious injury are not dischargeable if the debtor's failure to list or schedule the debt in the current case precludes a *creditor without notice or actual knowledge of the bankruptcy case* from timely filing a proof of claim *and* a complaint to determine the dischargeability of the debt. For any other debt, the debt is not dischargeable if the failure to list or schedule it precludes a creditor who has *no notice or actual knowledge of the bankruptcy case* from timely filing a proof of claim.

d.   **Fiduciary Fraud or Defalcation, and Embezzlement or Larceny**

Debts for fraud or defalcation *while acting in a fiduciary capacity* are not dischargeable. Debts arising from *embezzlement or larceny* also are not dischargeable, but there is no requirement that the wrongdoing occur in a fiduciary context.

e.   **Domestic Support Obligations**

Debts owed for *domestic support obligations* are nondischargeable.

f.   **Property Settlements and Other Obligations Arising from Separation Agreements or Divorce Decrees**

Debts that *do not qualify as domestic support obligations* but that are owed to a *spouse, former spouse, or child of the debtor* and that were incurred in the course of a *divorce or separation* or in connection with a separation agreement, divorce decree, other court order, or a governmental unit's determination based on state or territorial law, are nondischargeable.

Note: Such debts are discharged as part of the standard Chapter 13 discharge.

g.   **Willful/Malicious Injury**

Debts for *willful and malicious injury* caused by the debtor to *another entity or its property* are nondischargeable in a *Chapter 7, 11, or 12* case, or in a *Chapter 13* case in which the debtor receives a *hardship discharge.* The standard Chapter 13 discharge excepts from discharge debts for restitution or damages awarded in a *civil action* against the debtor for *willful or malicious injury* resulting in *personal injury or death* of an *individual.*

h.   **Fines, Penalties, and Restitution**

In a case under Chapters 7, 11, or 12, or a hardship discharge case under Chapter 13, a *fine, penalty, or forfeiture* payable *to and for the benefit* of a *governmental unit* is not dischargeable to the extent that it is *not compensation for actual pecuniary loss.*

Note: Debts for *restitution or a criminal fine* that are included in the debtor's sentence for *conviction of a crime* are excepted from the standard Chapter 13 discharge.

i. Restitution for Federal Crimes

The payment of an order of *restitution* for most *federal* crimes is nondischargeable in a Chapter 7, 11, or 12 case, or a Chapter 13 hardship discharge case. *Fines* ordered in connection with certain *federal* crimes are nondischargeable under *all chapters* of the Code, and liens securing them filed in favor of the United States are *not avoidable* in bankruptcy.

Note: The language governing the standard Chapter 13 discharge for debts for restitution is broader than the language of § 523(a)(13), which is limited to restitution orders issued in federal criminal cases.

j. Student Loans

Absent an *undue hardship* on the debtor and her dependents, an educational loan made, insured, or guaranteed by a governmental unit, or extended under a program funded by a governmental unit or a nonprofit institution, or any other educational loan that is a qualified education loan under the Internal Revenue Code is nondischargeable.

k. Operating a Motor Vehicle, Vessel or Aircraft While Intoxicated

Any debt for *death or personal injury* resulting from the debtor's use of a motor vehicle, vessel, or aircraft if such operation was unlawful because debtor was *intoxicated* from using alcohol, drugs, or another substance is nondischargeable.

l. Prior Bankruptcy

A debt that was or could have been listed in a *prior case* in which the debtor *waived discharge* or in which the debtor was *denied discharge* under § 727(a)(2)–(7) is nondischargeable.

Note: Such debts are dischargeable as part of a standard Chapter 13 discharge.

m. Fiduciary Fraud or Defalcation of Officers and Directors of Financial Institutions

Any debt arising from a final judgment or order, or consent order or decree (i) entered by any federal or state court, (ii) issued by a federal depository institutions regulatory agency, or (iii) contained in a settlement agreement with the debtor, resulting from the debtor's *fraud or defalcation* while acting in a *fiduciary capacity* with respect to any *insured depository institution or insured credit union* is nondischargeable.

Note: Such debts are dischargeable as part of a standard Chapter 13 discharge.

n. Failure to Maintain Capital of Insured Depository Institutions

Any debt for *malicious or reckless* failure to maintain the capital of an insured depository institution in breach of a commitment to a federal depository institutions regulatory agency is not dischargeable.

Note: Such debts are dischargeable as part of a standard Chapter 13 discharge.

o. **Debts Incurred to Pay Taxes**

Debts incurred to pay taxes that would be nondischargeable under § 523(a)(1), or fines or penalties imposed under federal election law are nondischargeable.

Note: Such debts are dischargeable as part of a standard Chapter 13 discharge.

p. **Condominium Fees**

Fees or assessments for a condominium, a share in a cooperative housing corporation, or a lot in a homeowners' association that become due and payable *after the order for relief* are nondischargeable for as long as the debtor or the trustee has a legal, equitable, or possessory ownership interest in the condominium, cooperative housing corporation, or lot.

Note: Such debts are dischargeable as part of a standard Chapter 13 discharge.

q. **Courts Costs**

Fees imposed on a prisoner for filing a case, appeal, complaint, or motion, as well as any other costs assessed in connection with the filing are nondischargeable even if the debtor files *in forma pauperis* or has the status of a prisoner.

Note: Such debts are dischargeable as part of a standard Chapter 13 discharge.

r. **Pension Loans**

A debt owed for loans from certain *pension, profit-sharing, stock bonus or other plans* is not dischargeable.

Note: Such debts are dischargeable as part of a standard Chapter 13 discharge.

s. **Securities Law Violations**

A debt owed for violation of *state or federal securities laws,* or for *common law fraud, deceit or misrepresentation* in connection with the *purchase or sale of a security* is nondischargeable if it results from any (i) judgment, order, consent order, or decree entered in any federal or state court, or any administrative proceeding, (ii) settlement agreement entered into by the debtor, or (iii) any court or administrative order for damages, fines, penalties, citations, restitutionary payments, disgorgement payments, attorney fees, costs or any other payment owed by the debtor.

Note: Such debts are dischargeable as part of a standard Chapter 13 discharge.

2. **Certain Long-Term Debts**

Long-term debts, e.g., mortgage, in which the last payment on the debt is due *after* the last payment is due under the debtor's three- or five-year plan, are not part of the Chapter 12 or Chapter 13 discharge, regardless of whether it is a standard or hardship discharge. In a *subchapter V Chapter 11* case in which the plan is *crammed down*, any debt on which the last payment is due after the plan's first three years, or such other time not to exceed five years, is not discharged.

3. **Proof**

The *preponderance-of-the-evidence* standard of proof applies to the exceptions to discharge contained in § 523(a).

B. EFFECTS OF DISCHARGE

1. Relief from Personal Liability

A debtor is relieved of *personal* liability for all debts that are discharged. Thus, while a valid lien that has not been avoided in the bankruptcy case generally survives *in rem* and ultimately may be enforced against the property securing the debt, no action is permitted against the debtor personally for a deficiency if the debt has been discharged.

2. Co-Debtor or Surety—No Discharge

With limited exceptions, the discharge of a debt of the debtor does *not* affect the liability of any other entity, e.g., a co-debtor, surety, or guarantor, or the property of any other entity for that debt.

3. Voluntary Repayment

The Code expressly permits the debtor to voluntarily repay any debt, but in the absence of an enforceable reaffirmation agreement with a creditor, the debtor has no personal *legal* obligation to repay a debt that has been discharged.

C. REAFFIRMATION AGREEMENTS

A reaffirmation agreement is a voluntary contract between the debtor and the holder of a dischargeable claim whereby the debtor promises to repay all or part of the debt after bankruptcy.

1. Requirements for Enforceability

A reaffirmation agreement is enforceable only if all of the following conditions are satisfied:

a. the agreement is *enforceable under nonbankruptcy law;*

b. the agreement is *made before* the granting of the *debtor's discharge;*

c. debtor receives the statutorily mandated *disclosures;*

d. the agreement is filed with the court *no later than 60 days* after the first date set for the § 341 meeting;

e. if the debtor was *not represented by an attorney* during negotiation of the agreement, the court must find that any agreement reaffirming a debt, other than a consumer debt secured by real property, is in the *debtor's best interest* and does not impose an *undue hardship;*

f. debtor does not rescind the agreement before the later of the discharge or *60 days* after the reaffirmation agreement was *filed* with the court; *and*

g. the Code's requirements for a discharge hearing are satisfied.

2. Presumption of Undue Hardship

The Code creates a *presumption of undue hardship* if the scheduled payments on the reaffirmed debt *exceed* the debtor's monthly *income minus expenses.* The presumption applies regardless of whether debtor was represented or not represented by counsel during negotiations for the reaffirmation agreement, but does not apply to reaffirmation agreements in which the creditor is a credit union.

D. PROTECTION AGAINST DISCRIMINATION

In addition to relieving the debtor of personal liability for any debts discharged, the law enhances her fresh start by providing express prohibitions against discriminatory treatment by employers or governmental units. The prohibition applies to discrimination by *governmental units* against a *person*. It prevents a *governmental unit* from (i) terminating an employee; (ii) denying employment; (iii) discriminating with respect to employment; or (iv) denying, revoking, suspending, or declining to renew a license, permit, charter, franchise, or similar privilege for any of these reasons. A private employer may not discriminate with respect to employment against an *individual* or terminate the individual's employment. The prohibition also applies to discrimination by governmental units and lenders engaged in a *guaranteed student loan program*. The Code does not prohibit consideration of an applicant's future financial responsibility or ability if there is no discrimination against bankruptcy debtors.

X. ADMINISTRATIVE POWERS: THE AUTOMATIC STAY

A. THE AUTOMATIC STAY

The automatic stay is "one of the fundamental debtor protections provided by the bankruptcy laws." The stay takes effect *when a bankruptcy petition is filed* and protects the debtor, the property of the estate, and the property of the debtor from certain actions by creditors. Thus, it provides the debtor with a "breathing spell" from collection efforts by her creditors. The stay, however, also benefits creditors because it prevents a rush to the courthouse, thereby ensuring an orderly administration of the bankruptcy case. The automatic stay operates to prohibit a broad range of actions against the *debtor, property of the estate,* or *property of the debtor.* The stay applies to *all entities.*

1. Acts Stayed

a. Proceedings Against Debtor

The commencement or continuation, including the issuance or service of process, of a *judicial, administrative, or other action or proceeding* against the *debtor* is stayed if the action is intended to recover a *pre-petition claim* against the debtor, or if the action was commenced or could have been commenced before the bankruptcy petition was filed.

b. Pre-Petition Judgments

The enforcement against the *debtor* or against *property of the estate* of a pre-petition judgment is stayed.

c. Acts Against Property of the Estate

Any act to *obtain possession* of *property of the estate* or property from the estate, or to *exercise control* over property of the estate is prohibited, regardless of whether the underlying claim arose before or after the filing of the bankruptcy petition.

d. Liens Against Property of the Estate

Any act to *create, perfect, or enforce a lien* against *property of the estate* is stayed. There is a limited exception to the stay that authorizes post-petition perfection in certain circumstances.

e. **Liens Against Debtor's Property**

Any act intended to create, perfect, or enforce a lien against *property of the debtor* is prohibited *to the extent that the lien secures a pre-petition claim.* Property that the trustee has *abandoned* under § 554 reverts to the debtor and is protected by the automatic stay from enforcement of any lien securing a pre-bankruptcy claim. The stay also shields the debtor's *exempt property* and property *acquired post-petition* from a lien securing a pre-petition claim.

f. **Collection Efforts**

Any act to *collect, recover, or assess* a claim against the *debtor* that arose prior to the bankruptcy petition is forbidden.

g. **Setoffs**

The automatic stay also stays the *post-petition setoff of mutual debts.* Thus, the setoff of a pre-petition debt owing to the debtor against a claim asserted against the debtor is prohibited unless the court grants relief from the stay.

h. **Tax Court Proceedings**

The Code stays the *commencement or continuation* of a case in the United States Tax Court concerning the *tax liability* of (i) a *corporate debtor* for a taxable period that the bankruptcy court may determine or (ii) an *individual* for a taxable period ending before the order for relief.

2. **Exceptions to the Automatic Stay**

a. **Criminal Proceedings**

The commencement or continuation of a criminal action against the debtor is not stayed.

b. **Family Law Matters**

A number of family law actions or proceedings do not violate the automatic stay, including the collection of *domestic support obligations,* and the commencement or continuation of proceedings (i) to establish *paternity* or concerning *child custody or visitation,* (ii) regarding *domestic violence,* or (iii) to *dissolve a marriage.*

c. **Certain Acts of Perfection**

The automatic stay does not prohibit the perfection of an interest in property to the extent that perfection occurs within the *30-day grace period* allowed by § 547(e)(2)(A), or to the extent that the trustee's rights and powers are subject to such perfection under § 546(b), such as in the case of *retroactive perfection* of a purchase-money security interest under the Uniform Commercial Code. The filing of a *continuation statement* also is excepted from the automatic stay to the same extent.

d. **Police or Regulatory Powers**

The commencement or continuation of a proceeding by a governmental unit to enforce its police or regulatory power is not stayed. The enforcement of a judgment obtained by a governmental unit in implementing its police or regulatory power is subject to the automatic stay if the judgment is *a money judgment.*

e. **Setoffs and Other Contractual Rights: Commodities and Securities Brokers, Repo, Swap, and Master Netting Agreement Participants**

The automatic stay does not apply to the rights of certain sophisticated financial parties to liquidate, terminate, or accelerate *a securities contract, a commodities contract, a forward contract, a repurchase agreement, a swap agreement or a master netting agreement.* The exception also applies to *setoff* rights under these agreements.

f. **HUD Mortgage Foreclosures**

The *commencement* of certain mortgage or deed of trust foreclosure actions by the Secretary of Housing and Urban Development is excepted from the automatic stay.

g. **Tax Audits and Assessments**

A tax audit, an issuance of a notice of tax deficiency, a demand for tax returns, and an assessment of any tax and issuance of a notice and demand for payment of the assessed tax are excepted from the automatic stay.

h. **Recovery of Property by Certain Lessors**

The automatic stay also does not prohibit any act by a debtor's lessor to obtain possession of nonresidential real property if the lease has *terminated by the expiration of its stated term* prior to the filing of the bankruptcy petition or during the case.

i. **Certain Actions Relating to Negotiable Instruments**

The automatic stay does not stay the presentment of a negotiable instrument, sending notice of dishonor, or protesting dishonor of such instrument.

j. **Certain Actions Against Educational Institutions**

The automatic stay does not apply to any action by an accrediting agency regarding the accreditation status or by a state licensing body concerning the licensure of the debtor as an educational institution. The stay also does not apply to any action by a guaranty agency or the Secretary of Education concerning the debtor's eligibility to participate in programs under the Higher Education Act of 1965.

k. **Repossession of Aircrafts and Vessels**

The automatic stay does not apply in a *Chapter 11 case* to certain actions to foreclose on fleet mortgages or security interests in vessels or fishing facilities by the Secretary of Transportation or the Secretary of Commerce if the action is commenced, continued, or concluded *more than 90 days* after filing of the petition. Congress added these exceptions to the Code for *cases filed after August 1, 1986 and before December 31, 1989,* and has not extended this time period.

l. **Ad Valorem Property Tax Liens and Special Assessments on Real Property**

The automatic stay does not apply to the creation or perfection of a statutory lien for *ad valorem property taxes,* imposed by a governmental unit, that *become due post-petition,* or to *special taxes or special assessments* on real property, regardless of whether ad valorem, imposed by a governmental unit and that *become due post-petition.*

m. Withholding of Income for Pensions

The automatic stay does not apply to the *withholding of income* from a debtor's wages and *collection of those amounts withheld* pursuant to the debtor's agreement authorizing withholding and collection for the benefit of a *pension, profit-sharing, stock bonus or other plan* established under certain sections of the Internal Revenue Code and sponsored by the debtor's employer, or an affiliate, successor, or predecessor of such employer to the extent that the monies withheld and collected are only used to *repay certain loans.*

n. Prior Bankruptcy Cases

The Code contains two exceptions to the stay for actions against *real property* based on what occurred in the debtor's *prior bankruptcy case.*

(i) Scheme to Delay, Hinder, or Defraud

There are *two steps* necessary for this exception to the automatic stay to work. The *first step* requires action by the bankruptcy court under § 362(d)(4) in the debtor's *prior bankruptcy case.* In the prior case, the bankruptcy court had to grant relief from the automatic stay to a creditor whose claim is secured by *real property,* after having found that the debtor's filing for bankruptcy was part of a *scheme to delay, hinder, or defraud* creditors that involved either (1) *the transfer* of part or all of the real property *without the secured creditor's consent* or (2) *multiple bankruptcy filings* affecting such real property. The court's stay relief order remains in effect in any *subsequent bankruptcy case* affecting such real property that is filed within *two years* after entry of the order, if the order is recorded in compliance with applicable state laws for recording real property liens or notices of interest in real property. [B.C. § 362(d)(4)]

The *second step* involves § 362(b)(20), which provides an exception to the automatic stay for any act to *enforce any lien against or security interest in* the *real property* following entry of an order pursuant to *§ 362(d)(4).* In the later bankruptcy case, the debtor may move for relief from such order based on *changed circumstances* or for other *good cause.*

(ii) Ineligible Debtor Based on Prior Bankruptcy Case

The automatic stay does not apply to any act to enforce a lien against or security interest in real property if the debtor is *not eligible to be a debtor* or if the debtor filed the bankruptcy case in *violation of an order in a prior case* prohibiting the debtor from being a debtor in another bankruptcy case.

o. Eviction: Residential Real Property

The Code contains two exceptions to the stay that affect the ability of a lessor to move forward with eviction proceedings, in certain circumstances, without obtaining relief from the automatic stay.

(i) Pre-Petition Judgment for Possession

The automatic stay does not apply to the continuation of any *eviction, unlawful detainer, or similar proceeding* by a lessor of residential real property against a debtor/tenant if the lessor has obtained a *judgment for possession pre-petition.* The exception, however, is subject to § 362(*l*), which keeps the automatic stay in place if the debtor/tenant satisfies certain statutory conditions.

(ii) Property Endangerment or Controlled Substance Use

A lessor of residential real property may commence or continue an eviction action based on *endangerment of the property* or *illegal use of controlled substances on the property* if the lessor files with the court and serves on the debtor a *certification,* under penalty of perjury, that such an *eviction action has been filed* or that the debtor, during the *30 days prior to filing of the certification,* has *endangered* the property or illegally used or allowed the use of a *controlled substance on the property.* The exception, however, is subject to § 362(m), which keeps the automatic stay in place if the debtor/tenant satisfies certain statutory conditions.

p. Non-Avoidable Transfers

The automatic stay does not apply to any transfer that is not avoidable under § 544 and that is not avoidable under § 549.

q. Securities Self-Regulatory Organizations

The automatic stay does not apply to certain conduct by a *securities association* or a *national securities exchange* registered with the Securities Exchange Commission.

r. Setoff Income Tax Refund

The automatic stay does not apply to a governmental unit's setoff, if allowed under nonbankruptcy law, of an *income tax refund for a pre-petition taxable period against a pre-petition tax liability.*

s. Federal Health Care Programs

It is not a violation of the automatic stay for the Secretary of Health and Human Services to exclude the debtor from participating in the Medicare program or any other federal health care program, as defined in the Social Security Act.

t. Amateur Sports

Any action by an *amateur sports organization* to replace a governing body or any action by the *United States Olympic and Paralympic Committee* to revoke the certification of a national governing body does not violate the automatic stay.

u. Small Business Debtor

The automatic stay does not apply to a *small business case* if the debtor files a bankruptcy case (subsequent case) *and*:

(i) *is a debtor in a small business case pending* at the time debtor files its subsequent bankruptcy case;

(ii) *was a debtor in a small business case* that was *dismissed for any reason* by an order that became final in the *two-year period* before the date of the order for relief in the subsequent bankruptcy case;

(iii) *was a debtor in a small business case* in which a *plan was confirmed* in the *two-year period* before the date of the order for relief in the subsequent bankruptcy case; *or*

(iv) is an *entity that acquired substantially all of the assets or business of a small business debtor described above in (i)–(iii),* unless such entity establishes by a preponderance of the evidence that it acquired the assets or business in *good faith and not to evade the Code's restrictions.*

3. **Expiration of the Stay**

   a. **Individual Chapter 7 Debtors and Personal Property**

   In an *individual Chapter 7* case, the automatic stay terminates with respect to *personal property of the estate or of the debtor* that secures a claim or that is subject to a lease, and such property is no longer property of the estate if the debtor fails (i) to *timely file a statement of intention* or to indicate on such statement that it will *surrender or redeem,* the property, *reaffirm the debt* secured by the property, *or assume such unexpired lease;* or (ii) *timely take the action* specified in the statement. The stay does not terminate if the debtor specifies an intention to reaffirm the debt on the original contract terms and the creditor refuses to agree to reaffirmation on those terms.

   b. **General Rules**

   Unless the court grants relief from the automatic stay, the stay of an *act against estate property* is effective until the property no longer constitutes property of the estate. Unless the court grants relief from the automatic stay, the stay of *any other act* enjoined under § 362(a) continues until the case is dismissed, the case is closed, or a discharge in an individual Chapter 7 case or a case under Chapter 11, 12, or 13 is granted or denied, whichever occurs first.

   c. **Serial Filers**

   The Code's provisions on serial filers apply only to *individual debtors,* and only if the debtor's prior case was *dismissed,* but not if the debtor's prior case was dismissed because of the means test.

   (i) **Prior Pending Case: 30-Day Rule**

   If an *individual debtor* files for bankruptcy under Chapter 7, 11, or 13 and if the debtor had a case *pending in the prior year* that was *dismissed,* the Code provides that the stay in debtor's current bankruptcy case expires after *30 days.* The stay expires, however, only as to a debt, property securing that debt, or a lease *with respect to the debtor.* The majority of courts have held that after 30 days, while the automatic stay expires as to *the debtor and property of the debtor,* it remains in place with regard to *property of the estate.* This stay-expiration rule does *not* apply to cases under Chapter 12.

   (ii) **Two or More Prior Pending Cases**

   If an individual debtor files for bankruptcy and there were *two or more bankruptcy cases pending in the prior year* that were *dismissed,* the Code provides that the automatic stay in debtor's current bankruptcy case does not go into effect. The rule seems to apply to all prior bankruptcy filings, including those under Chapter 12.

4. Relief from Stay

Upon request of a party in interest, and after notice and a hearing, the court may grant relief from the automatic stay by *terminating, modifying, annulling, or conditioning* the stay.

a. Grounds for Relief

(i) "Cause"

After notice and a hearing, the bankruptcy court must grant relief from the automatic stay to a party in interest if *cause* exists to lift the stay. The Code does not define the term "cause," but cause may include a *lack of adequate protection* of an entity's interest in property or a *debtor's lack of good faith* in filing the bankruptcy petition.

(ii) Acts Against Property

The bankruptcy court will grant relief from the stay of an act against property if (i) the debtor has *no equity* in the property and (ii) the property is *not necessary for an effective reorganization.*

(iii) Single Asset Real Estate

If a creditor's claim is secured by an interest in single asset real estate, the court must grant relief from the automatic stay if the debtor fails either to (i) *file a plan of reorganization* that has a *reasonable possibility of being confirmed* within a *reasonable time;* or (ii) *start to make monthly payments* in an amount equal to the current nondefault contract rate of interest to each creditor with a claim secured by the real estate, other than creditors with a judgment lien or an unmatured statutory lien.

(iv) Abuse by Debtor: Real Property

The court must provide relief from the stay of any *act against real property* to a creditor with an interest secured by that property if the court finds that filing of the petition was part of a *scheme to delay, hinder, or defraud creditors* that involved either of the following:

(1) the *transfer* of all or a part of the *real property* without the secured creditor's consent or court approval; or

(2) *multiple bankruptcy filings* affecting the real property.

If the stay relief order is *recorded* in such a way as to satisfy applicable state laws on notices of interests or liens on real property, then the order is *binding in any other bankruptcy case* purporting to affect the real property *filed within two years* of the entry of the order. The debtor in the subsequent bankruptcy case, however, may move for relief from the order based on *changed circumstances* or other *good cause* shown, after notice and a hearing. Any governmental unit that accepts notices of interests or liens on real property must accept a certified copy of such a stay relief order for indexing and recording.

b. Procedure for Requesting Relief

(i) Acts Against Estate Property: Hearing

When the relief sought is from the stay of an act against *property of the estate,* the stay terminates, by operation of law with respect to the party in interest making the request for stay relief, *30 days* after the motion is filed unless, after notice and a hearing, the court orders that the stay remain operative until a final hearing is concluded.

(ii) Individual Chapter 7, 11, or 13 Case

In an individual debtor's Chapter 7, 11, or 13 case, the automatic stay terminates, by operation of law, *60 days* after a request for relief is made by a party in interest, *unless* (i) the court renders a *final decision during the 60-day period* starting on the date of the request for stay relief; or (ii) the 60-day period is extended by the *agreement of all parties in interest or* by the court for the time that the court finds is required for good cause.

(iii) Burden of Proof

In any hearing for relief from the stay under § 362(a), the *party seeking relief has* the burden of proof *regarding the debtor's equity* in property. The *party opposing relief* has the burden of proof *on all other issues.*

(iv) Ex Parte Relief

The bankruptcy court may grant *ex parte* relief from the stay as is necessary to prevent *irreparable harm* to an entity's interest in property that will occur before there is time for notice and a hearing.

(v) Appeal

A decision to grant or deny relief from the stay is a final order, which may be appealed. The Supreme Court, in a unanimous opinion, held that a bankruptcy court's ruling on a motion for relief from the automatic stay "forms a discrete procedural unit" in the bankruptcy case and "[t]hat unit yields a final, appealable order when the bankruptcy court unreservedly grants or denies relief."

5. Willful Violation of Stay

An individual who is injured by a *willful* violation of the automatic stay may recover actual damages, costs, attorneys' fees, and, when warranted, punitive damages. If the stay violation is based on an entity's *good faith belief* that the stay has terminated pursuant to § 362(h), then recovery is limited to *actual damages.*

XI. ADMINISTRATIVE POWERS: §§ 363–366 OF THE CODE

A. ADEQUATE PROTECTION

1. Interest in Property

a. Automatic Stay

If an entity's interest in property is subject to the automatic stay and the entity moves to lift the automatic stay because of a lack of adequate protection, the court must grant relief from the stay or require that the entity's interest in the property be adequately protected.

b. Property Used, Sold, or Leased

Upon the request of an entity with an interest in property that the trustee or debtor in possession proposes to use, sell, or lease, the bankruptcy court may condition such use, sale, or lease on the provision of adequate protection of the interest.

c. **Equal or Senior Lien on Property**

If the court authorizes the trustee or the debtor in possession to incur debt or to obtain credit secured by a lien on property of the estate that is equal or senior to a lien held by an entity on the same property, adequate protection of that entity's interest is required.

2. **Methods of Providing Adequate Protection**

The Code provides three non-exclusive methods for providing adequate protection: (i) *cash or periodic cash payments;* (ii) an *additional or replacement lien;* or (iii) the *indubitable equivalent* of the entity's interest in the property. A substantial *equity cushion* may adequately protect a secured creditor's interest in the property.

3. **Valuation of Collateral**

In valuing collateral, courts take account of factors such as the *purpose of the valuation* and the *intended use or disposition of the collateral.*

4. **Failure of Adequate Protection**

If adequate protection is provided to a creditor whose claim is secured by a lien on property of the debtor, but the "adequate protection" eventually is shown to have been deficient, the secured creditor will receive an administrative expense claim with *super-priority,* which means priority over all other administrative expenses allowed in the case.

5. **Chapter 12 Cases**

The adequate protection provisions of § 361 do not apply to a case under Chapter 12. Instead, the trustee may provide adequate protection to a creditor by (a) making *cash or periodic cash payments,* (b) providing an *additional or replacement lien,* (c) paying *reasonable rent* customary in the community *for use of farmland,* or (d) such other relief, other than granting an allowable administrative expense, that will adequately protect the value of the property.

B. **USE, SALE, OR LEASE OF PROPERTY**

1. **Out of Ordinary Course of Business**

After *notice and a hearing,* a trustee or a debtor in possession may use, sell, or lease property of the estate out of the ordinary course of the debtor's business, unless the sale or lease involves *personally identifiable information,* in which case special rules apply. A secured creditor whose lien secures an allowed claim on property sold *outside the ordinary course of business* may "credit bid" at the sale of such property.

2. **Ordinary Course of Business**

A trustee or a debtor in possession who is authorized to operate the debtor's business may use, sell, or lease property of the estate in the ordinary course of business *without notice or a hearing,* unless the court orders otherwise. **Exception:** The trustee or the debtor in possession may use, sell, or lease *cash collateral* in the *ordinary course of business only* if she obtains either *court authorization,* after notice and a hearing, or the *consent* of all entities having an interest in the cash collateral.

3. **Ipso Facto Clauses**

The trustee or debtor in possession may use, sell, or lease property in or out of the ordinary course of business, or the terms of a Chapter 11, 12, or 13 plan may provide for such use, sale, or lease, notwithstanding provisions in a contract, lease, or nonbankruptcy law that otherwise would cause a forfeiture, modification, or termination of the debtor's interest in the property because of (i) the debtor's *insolvency or financial condition;* (ii) the debtor's filing of a *bankruptcy case;* (iii) the appointment of a *bankruptcy trustee or a nonbankruptcy custodian;* or (iv) the *taking possession of property* by a bankruptcy trustee or nonbankruptcy custodian.

4. **Sale Free and Clear**

The trustee or the debtor in possession may sell property of the estate, either in or out of the ordinary course of business, *free and clear* of any interest in the property held by an entity other than the estate *only if one of the following* statutory requirements is satisfied:

a. *applicable state or other nonbankruptcy law allows* a free-and-clear sale of the property;

b. the entity holding the interest *consents to the sale;*

c. *if the interest is a lien,* the *sale price for the property is greater than the total value of all liens* on the property;

d. *there is a bona fide dispute* concerning the entity's interest in the property; *or*

e. *the entity holding the interest could be required to accept a money satisfaction* in a legal or equitable action.

Notwithstanding the conditions for a *free and clear sale,* the trustee or the debtor in possession may sell property free and clear of an entity's *vested or contingent right of dower or curtesy.*

5. **Not Free and Clear: Consumer Credit Transactions**

The sale of any interest in a consumer credit transaction subject to the Truth in Lending Act or any interest in a consumer credit contract is *not free and clear* of any claim or defense related to such consumer credit transaction or consumer credit contract.

6. **Burden of Proof**

In any hearing concerning the use, sale, or lease of property, the trustee or debtor in possession has the burden of proof regarding the question of adequate protection, while the entity claiming an interest in property bears the burden of showing the validity, priority, or extent of that interest.

7. **Appeal: Mootness**

Absent a stay pending appeal, the validity of an authorization to sell or lease property, in or outside the ordinary course of business, is not affected by a reversal or modification on appeal if the purchaser or lessee acted in *good faith,* regardless of the purchaser's or lessee's knowledge of the appeal.

C. OBTAINING CREDIT

1. In Ordinary Course of Business

Unless the court orders otherwise, a trustee or debtor in possession authorized to operate the debtor's business may procure *unsecured credit,* e.g., trade credit, and incur *unsecured debt* in the ordinary course of business without notice or a hearing. Such credit or debt is allowable as an *administrative expense.*

2. Out of Ordinary Course of Business

After *notice and a hearing,* the court may approve the request of a trustee or debtor in possession to obtain unsecured credit or to incur unsecured debt *out of the ordinary course of business* as an *allowable administrative expense.*

3. Priority or Security

If the trustee or debtor in possession is *unable* to obtain unsecured credit allowable as an administrative expense, then the court, after notice and a hearing, may authorize the obtaining of credit or incurring of debt (i) with *super super-priority status;* (ii) secured by a *lien on unencumbered estate property;* or (iii) secured by a *junior lien on encumbered estate property.*

4. Priming Lien

If the debtor has no unencumbered property and the lender will not extend credit or loan money in exchange for administrative expense status or super-super-priority over all other administrative expenses, then the bankruptcy court, after notice and a hearing, may approve new credit or incurring of debt secured by a *senior or equal* lien on property of the estate.

5. Appeal

Absent a stay pending appeal, the validity of the court's order authorizing the debtor to obtain credit or to incur debt, or the validity of any lien or priority granted by the court is not affected by a reversal or modification on appeal, so long as the lender acted in *good faith.* This rule applies even if the lender knew of the appeal.

6. Temporary Change to § 364

For any case begun *before December 27, 2022,* a *temporary COVID-related amendment* to § 364 provides that the bankruptcy court, after notice and a hearing, may authorize a trustee or debtor in possession in a Chapter 11 subchapter V case, or a Chapter 12 or 13 case to obtain a *loan under the Small Business Act.* If the loan is not forgiven pursuant to the provisions of the Small Business Act, then the loan is treated as a debt with *super-super priority.*

D. EXECUTORY CONTRACTS AND UNEXPIRED LEASES

1. General Principles

The debtor in possession or trustee, with the court's approval, may assume or reject an executory contract or an unexpired lease of the debtor.

2. Assumption of Contracts and Leases in Default

If there is a pre- or post-petition *default,* the trustee or debtor in possession may assume an executory contract or an unexpired lease *only* if the trustee or debtor in possession (i) *cures* the default or provides *adequate assurance* that the default will be *cured promptly;* (ii) *compensates* or provides *adequate assurance* of prompt compensation for any *monetary loss* caused by the default; and (iii) furnishes *adequate assurance of future performance* of the executory contract or the unexpired lease.

3. **Assignment**

   The trustee or debtor in possession may assign an executory contract or an unexpired lease *only after assuming* the contract or lease and *providing adequate assurance* of the assignee's *future performance,* regardless of whether there has been a default.

4. **Agreements Not Assumable or Assignable**

   The trustee may not assume or assign certain kinds of executory contracts and unexpired leases, e.g., personal services contracts.

5. **Rejection Constitutes Breach**

   A *rejection* by the trustee or debtor in possession *operates as a breach* of the executory contract or the unexpired lease.

6. **Time Limitations for Assumption or Rejection**

   a. **Chapter 7 Cases**

   The trustee, in a case under Chapter 7, has *60 days* after the order for relief within which to assume or reject an *executory contract* or an unexpired lease of *personal property or residential real property.* Otherwise, the contract or the lease is deemed rejected.

   b. **Chapter 11, 12, and 13 Cases**

   Assumption or rejection of an *executory contract* or unexpired lease of *personal property or residential real property* may occur at any time prior to the confirmation of a plan under Chapter 11, 12, or 13.

   c. **Lease of Nonresidential Real Property**

   If the debtor is a lessee of nonresidential real property, then the trustee or the debtor in possession has until the *earlier of* the date of the entry of a *plan confirmation order or 120 days after the order for relief* within which to assume or reject an unexpired lease of the property, or else the lease is deemed rejected and the property must be immediately surrendered to the lessor.

   Note: For subchapter V cases commenced before *December 27, 2022,* the time period is *210, not 120, days.*

7. **Trustee Obligations Prior to Assumption or Rejection**

   a. **Lease of Nonresidential Real Property**

   The trustee or debtor in possession must timely perform all duties, except those under § 365(b)(2), arising under an unexpired lease of nonresidential real property *after the order for relief* and until assumption or rejection.

   (i) **Subchapter V**

   For cases commenced before *December 27, 2022,* a *temporary COVID-related amendment* provides that if the subchapter V debtor is "experiencing or has experienced a material financial hardship" due to COVID-19, then the bankruptcy court may extend the time for the debtor to perform its lease obligations until the *earlier of* (i) *60 days after* the order for relief, which may be extended for an *additional 60 days* if the debtor continues to experience material financial hardship due to COVID-19 *or* **(ii)** the date on which the lease is *assumed or rejected.*

b. Lease of Commercial Personal Property in Chapter 11

In a Chapter 11 case, the trustee or debtor in possession must timely perform all obligations, except those specified under § 365(b)(2), in a lease of *non-consumer personal property* first arising *from or after 60 days after the order for relief* until the lease is assumed or rejected.

c. Executory Contracts and All Other Leases

The Code does not contain specific rules about the trustee's or debtor in possession's obligations to perform prior to assumption or rejection of executory contracts, or leases of residential property or consumer personal property.

8. Ipso Facto Clauses

With certain exceptions, an executory contract or unexpired lease may not be terminated or modified *after* the filing of a bankruptcy petition solely on account of an *ipso facto* or other bankruptcy termination clause in the contract or lease.

9. Debtor as Lessor of Real Property

If the trustee rejects an unexpired lease of real property under which the *debtor is the lessor,* then the lessee either may consider the lease terminated or, *if the term of the lease has commenced,* retain rights under the lease for the balance of the current term and for any period of renewal or extension enforceable under nonbankruptcy law.

10. Debtor as Seller of Real Property

If the trustee rejects an executory contract to sell real property or a timeshare interest under which the *debtor is the seller,* the buyer, *if in possession,* may treat the contract as terminated or may stay in possession of the real property or timeshare interest.

11. Intellectual Property

If the debtor is the *licensor of a right to intellectual property,* and the trustee or debtor in possession rejects an executory contract under which the license has been granted, the *licensee* may consider the *contract terminated* or *may retain its contractual rights* to the intellectual property, including any right to exclusivity, but excluding any other right to specific performance of the contract, and use the property for the remaining period of the contract and any rightful extension. The Code's definition of intellectual property includes *copyrights, trade secrets, and patents*, but *not trademarks*. But in *Mission Product Holding v. Tempnology, LLC,* the Supreme Court held that a debtor-licensor's rejection of a trademark licensing agreement does not "deprive[ ] the licensee of its rights to use the trademark."

E. UTILITY SERVICE

A utility may not discontinue, alter, or refuse service to, or discriminate against, the trustee or debtor solely because of the filing of a bankruptcy case or because the debtor failed to timely pay a debt owed for utility services furnished prior to the order for relief. But, a utility may discontinue, alter, or refuse service if, within *20 days* after the order for relief, neither the debtor nor the trustee provides *adequate assurance of payment* for post-petition services, such as a deposit or other security. In a *Chapter 11 case,* a utility may alter, refuse, or discontinue service if during the *30-day period* starting with the filing of the petition the debtor or trustee does not provide *adequate assurance of payment* that is *satisfactory to the utility.*

XII. CHAPTER 7: LIQUIDATION

A. INTRODUCTION

1. Eligibility for Relief

Chapter 7 relief is available to *any person* that *resides or has a domicile, a place of business, or property in the United States except* (i) railroads; (ii) domestic savings institutions and insurance companies; (iii) certain small business investment companies; (iv) foreign insurance companies engaged in such business in the United States; and (v) foreign banks, savings and loan associations, and other similar financial institutions that have a branch or agency in the United States. Stockbrokers and commodity brokers may be debtors under special provisions of Chapter 7.

a. Exceptions Based on Financial Situation or Pre-Bankruptcy Conduct

The Code also provides that the following debtors are not eligible for relief under Chapter 7 based on their *current financial situation* or *pre-bankruptcy conduct:*

(i) *an individual or a family farmer* who was a debtor in a case that was *pending in the preceding 180 days* and *dismissed* because of the debtor's willful failure to obey court orders or to appear before the court in proper prosecution of the case, or because the debtor requested and obtained a voluntary dismissal of the case following a party's request for relief from the automatic stay;

(ii) *above-median income individual debtors with primarily consumer debts* who fail the "means test"; *and*

(iii) with certain limited exceptions, an *individual debtor* who has not obtained *credit counseling* during the *180 days* prior to seeking relief under the Bankruptcy Code.

2. Chapter 7 Trustee

Promptly after the order for relief, the United States trustee must appoint a *disinterested member* of the panel of private trustees to serve as the interim trustee in a Chapter 7 case. Then, either a trustee is elected at the § 341 meeting or, as usually occurs, the interim trustee automatically becomes the permanent trustee in the case.

3. Meeting of Creditors

No earlier than 21 and no later than 40 days after the order for relief, the United States trustee convenes and presides at the § 341 meeting.

B. THE MEANS TEST

BAPCPA created a financial eligibility test for *individual Chapter 7 debtors with primarily consumer debts.* The *first step* of this new financial eligibility test is determining whether the individual debtor's income is *above or below the median income* for the debtor's household size in the state in which the debtor resides. The *means test,* which is the second step, only applies to *above-median income debtors.*

1. **The Below-Median Income Debtor**

   The Bankruptcy Code provides that there is no *presumption of abuse* for a *below-median income debtor.* The below median-income debtor's Chapter 7 case still may be dismissed, however, if the court determines that the *petition was filed in bad faith* or *the totality of the debtor's financial situation demonstrates abuse.*

2. **The Above-Median Income Debtor**

   An above-median income debtor must do the *means test* in order to determine whether the debtor's filing for relief under Chapter 7 creates a *presumption of abuse.* If there is no presumption of abuse, then the debtor's case still may be dismissed if it was *filed in bad faith* or if the *totality of the debtor's financial situation demonstrates abuse.*

3. **Above or Below Median?**

   All *individual* debtors must determine their *current monthly income,* because this figure determines the debtor's income status as above or below median. With certain exclusions, *current monthly income* is the debtor's *average monthly income from all sources* that the debtor receives during the *six-month period* prior to filing for bankruptcy. The six-month period *ends on the last day of the calendar month immediately preceding* the filing of the bankruptcy case.

4. **Above-Median Income Debtors and the Chapter 7 Means Test**

   To determine whether there is a presumption of abuse, the above-median income debtor subtracts her *monthly expenses* from her *current monthly income.* The debtor then multiplies the *difference by 60* and compares the *product* with the following numbers.

   a. **$9,075:** If the *product is less than $9,075,* then the debtor's filing for relief under Chapter 7 *does not create* a *presumption of abuse.*

   b. **$15,150:** If the *product is greater than $15,150,* then there is a *presumption of abuse.*

   c. **$9,075 ≥ product ≤ $15,150:** If the *product is greater than or equal to $9,075 but also less than or equal to $15,150,* then the debtor must conduct the *secondary abuse test.*

      (i) **Secondary Abuse Test**

         The *secondary abuse test* requires the debtor to compare the product *with* 25% of the debtor's non-priority unsecured claims. If the product is *equal to or greater than 25%* of the debtor's non-priority unsecured claims, then the presumption of abuse arises. If the product is *less than 25%* of the debtor's non-priority unsecured claims, then the presumption of abuse does not arise.

5. **Means Test Expenses**

   The means test allows the debtor to deduct from current monthly income certain expenses based on *applicable national and local standards,* as well as the *actual amount* that she pays on her *secured debt.* A debtor also may deduct the *actual cost* of *other necessary expenses,* including amounts paid for *federal, state,* and *local taxes, life insurance, alimony, child support,* and *child care.* A debtor's monthly expenses may include *charitable contributions to any qualified religious or charitable entity or organization.*

C. DISTRIBUTION OF PROPERTY OF THE ESTATE

1. Order of Payment

a. Secured Creditors

If the Chapter 7 trustee sells collateral that secures a claim, the secured creditor is paid from the sale proceeds before there is any distribution to priority or general unsecured creditors.

b. Priority Claims

Unsecured claims entitled to priority under § 507 are paid before any distribution to the general unsecured creditors and are paid in the following order of priority provided by the Code:

(i) *administrative expenses of a trustee* to the extent that the trustee administers assets available for payment of *domestic support obligations;*

(ii) *domestic support obligations;*

(iii) *administrative expenses;*

(iv) *involuntary case gap* claims;

(v) *wages, salaries, or commissions;*

(vi) contributions to *employee benefit plans;*

(vii) claims of *grain farmers and United States fishermen;*

(viii) *consumer layaway* claims;

(ix) *unsecured pre-petition taxes;*

(x) *capital requirements of insured depository institutions;* and

(xi) claims for *death or personal injury* resulting from *debtor's unlawful operation of a motor vehicle or vessel due to intoxication.*

c. General Unsecured Claims

After satisfying all priority unsecured claims, the Chapter 7 trustee pays allowed unsecured claims that are *timely filed* and *justifiably late-filed* claims.

d. Unexcused Tardy Claims

Allowed claims filed late without justification are paid after all timely filed and justifiably late-filed claims.

e. Penalty Claims

Next in the order of distribution are allowed unsecured or secured claims for *punitive, exemplary, or multiple damages,* or for *fines, penalties, or forfeitures* that do not constitute compensation for actual pecuniary loss.

f. Interest

If there are sufficient funds to pay all of the allowed claims above, then the Chapter 7 trustee will pay interest, at the legal rate, that accrued from the date that the petition was filed on all priority and general unsecured claims pursuant to § 726(a)(1)–(4).

g. Payment to Debtor

If there is any property of the estate left after payment of post-petition interest on the unsecured claims, it is distributed to the debtor.

2. Pro Rata Payment

The general rule is that priority creditors *within a class* share equally in any distribution.

a. Exceptions to General Rule

(i) Domestic Support Obligations

There is a hierarchy of payment among first priority domestic support obligation claims. The trustee, if she administers assets to pay a domestic support obligation, is paid first, then a spouse, former spouse, or child of the debtor with a domestic support obligation claim, and finally, a governmental unit with a domestic support obligation assigned to it by a spouse, former spouse, or child of the debtor.

(ii) Conversion to Chapter 7

If a case is converted from Chapter 11, 12, or 13 to a case under Chapter 7, the administrative expense claims in the Chapter 7 case *after conversion* have priority over the administrative expenses incurred prior to conversion.

(iii) Super-Priority: Inadequately Protected Secured Creditor

If adequate protection is furnished to a creditor whose claim is secured by a lien on the debtor's property, but the adequate protection ultimately proves to be deficient, the creditor will receive an administrative expense claim with *priority over all other administrative expenses* allowed against the debtor's estate.

(iv) Super Super-Priority: Post-Petition Credit

If the trustee or the debtor in possession is unable to obtain unsecured post-petition credit by means of an administrative expense priority, the court may approve new credit or debt with priority over all other administrative expense claims, *including* any super-priority claims arising from the failure of adequate protection.

D. TREATMENT OF CERTAIN LIENS IN A CHAPTER 7 CASE

1. Avoidance of Liens Securing Penalties

The trustee may *avoid a lien* securing the type of claim described in § 726(a)(4) for a fine, penalty, or forfeiture, or for punitive, multiple, or exemplary damages that do not constitute compensation for actual pecuniary loss.

2. Subordination of Tax Liens

The Code provides for the subordination of certain allowed tax claims that are secured by nonavoidable liens, e.g., a perfected tax lien, on estate property. Before subordinating a tax lien on real or personal property, however, the Chapter 7 trustee must first *exhaust* the estate's *unencumbered assets* and recover from the property securing an allowed secured claim the *reasonable, necessary costs and expenses* of disposing of or preserving the property.

Note: With limited exceptions, the subordination rules do not apply to nonavoidable liens for ad valorem taxes on real or personal property.

E. PARTNERSHIP TRUSTEE'S CLAIM AGAINST GENERAL PARTNERS

If the estate of a Chapter 7 partnership debtor lacks sufficient property to fully satisfy all claims against the partnership, the *trustee* is entitled to a claim for the *deficiency* against any general partner who is personally liable, but only to the extent that the general partner is personally liable under applicable nonbankruptcy law.

F. CHAPTER 7 DISCHARGE

The effect of the discharge is to discharge the debtor's *personal liability* on all debts that arose prior to the order for relief under Chapter 7, as well as from all debts that are treated under the Code as pre-petition debts. The discharge does not include particular debts that are not dischargeable under § 523. It is important to distinguish between a *global denial of the discharge* under § 727 and a determination under § 523 that a *specific debt is nondischargeable.*

1. Grounds for Denial of Discharge

a. Debtor Not an Individual

Under Chapter 7, only an individual may receive a discharge. Therefore, other persons, e.g., corporations and partnerships, are not granted a discharge.

b. Transfer of Property with Intent to Hinder, Delay, or Defraud Creditors

The debtor will be denied a discharge if with the *intent to hinder, delay, or defraud* a creditor or an officer of the estate entitled to possession of the property, she transferred, removed, concealed, mutilated, or destroyed *property of the debtor,* within *one year* before the filing of the petition, or *property of the estate,* after the petition was filed.

c. Destruction or Concealment of Books or Records

The court may deny the debtor a discharge if she concealed, destroyed, mutilated, falsified, or failed to keep or preserve any recorded information, including books, records, documents, and papers from which her business transactions or financial state might be determined, unless the debtor's conduct or failure to act was *justified under the circumstances.*

d. Perjury, Bribery, Extortion, and Other Fraudulent Acts

The bankruptcy court will deny a Chapter 7 debtor a discharge if she *knowingly and fraudulently* in or in connection with the bankruptcy case (i) makes a *false oath* or account; (ii) submits or uses a *false claim;* (iii) gives, offers, receives, or attempts to obtain money, property, or advantage or a promise of money, property or advantage for acting or forbearing to act, i.e., extortion or bribery; or (iv) *withholds any recorded information, including books, records, and papers,* concerning the debtor's property or finances from an officer of the estate who is entitled to possession.

e. Failure to Account for Loss of Assets

Another basis for denial of the debtor's discharge is her failure to adequately explain any *loss of assets* or deficiency of assets to meet her liabilities.

f. Violation of Court Order or Refusal to Respond to Material Question

The court will deny the debtor a discharge if she refuses (i) *to obey a valid court order,* other than one directing the debtor to testify or to answer a material question; (ii) for a reason other than the Fifth Amendment privilege against self-incrimination, to *testify or to answer a material question* that the bankruptcy judge has approved; or (iii) on the basis of the privilege against self-incrimination, to testify or to answer a judicially approved material question *after she has been granted immunity* regarding the matter on which privilege was invoked.

g. **Acts Committed in Insider Case**

The bankruptcy court may deny the Chapter 7 debtor a discharge if the debtor commits any act described in § 727(a)(2)–(6), either during *her bankruptcy case or within one year before the petition* was filed, in connection with a separate *bankruptcy case regarding an insider.*

h. **Prior Discharge Obtained Under Chapter 7 or Chapter 11**

The bankruptcy court will deny a Chapter 7 debtor a discharge in her *current case* if she previously received a discharge in a Chapter 7 or a Chapter 11 case that was *commenced within eight years* before the date that the petition was filed in the current case.

i. **Prior Discharge Obtained Under Chapter 12 or Chapter 13**

Similarly, the bankruptcy court will deny a Chapter 7 debtor a discharge if she previously was granted a discharge in a Chapter 12 or a Chapter 13 case that was *commenced within six years* before the date of the filing of the petition in the *current case,* unless (i) all of the allowed unsecured claims in the earlier case were *paid in full; or* (ii) payments under the plan in the earlier case totaled *at least 70%* of the allowed unsecured claims, and the debtor's plan was *proposed in good faith and represented her best effort.*

j. **Waiver**

The debtor will not receive a discharge if the court approves a *written waiver of discharge* that she executes *after* the Chapter 7 order for relief.

k. **Failure to Complete Instructional Course**

With limited exceptions, the debtor will be denied a discharge if post-petition she fails to complete an instructional course on personal financial management.

2. **Delaying Entry of the Discharge**

The bankruptcy court shall not grant a Chapter 7 debtor a discharge if the court finds, after notice and a hearing held *no more than 10 days* before the entry of the discharge, that *reasonable cause* exists to believe either that *§ 522(q)(1) may apply* to the debtor's case *or* that there is a proceeding pending in which the debtor may be found guilty of a *felony listed in § 522(q)(1)(A)* or liable for a *debt described in § 522(q)(1)(B).* While the new provision is situated in the Code's denial-of-discharge section, the section appears to merely *delay, not deny, the debtor's discharge.*

3. **Revocation of Discharge**

The bankruptcy court, upon request of a creditor, the Chapter 7 trustee, or the United States trustee and after notice and a hearing, must *revoke the debtor's discharge* if the debtor:

a. *obtained the discharge fraudulently,* and the party seeking revocation did not know of the fraud until after the discharge was granted;

b. *acquired property* that is property of the estate *or became entitled to acquire property* that would constitute property of the estate, and she *knowingly and fraudulently* failed to disclose this fact or to turn over the property to the trustee;

c. *committed one of the acts* described in § 727(a)(6); or

d. *failed to satisfactorily explain* (i) *a material misstatement* in an *audit* referred to in 28 U.S.C. § 586(f) *or* (ii) a *failure to make available for inspection* accounts, documents, financial records, papers, files and all other papers, things, or property belonging to the debtor that are requested for *the audit* referred to in 28 U.S.C. § 586(f).

G. CONVERSION

If a Chapter 7 case has not been converted from Chapter 11, 12, or 13, the debtor may convert the case from Chapter 7 to any of such other chapters at any time. The Supreme Court in *Marrama v. Citizens Bank* concluded that a Chapter 7 debtor who engages in fraudulent conduct does not have an absolute right to convert to Chapter 13. Unless the debtor requests or consents to conversion, the court may *not* convert a Chapter 7 case to one under Chapter 12 or 13.

H. DISMISSAL

1. For Cause

Cause to dismiss a Chapter 7 case includes the following:

a. the debtor is responsible for an *unreasonable delay that is prejudicial to creditors;*

b. the debtor has not paid *certain fees or charges;* or

c. the debtor in a voluntary case has *not filed a list of creditors and all schedules and statements* required under § 521(a)(1) within *15 days,* or any extension granted by the court, after the petition was filed.

2. Abuse of Chapter 7

a. Means Test

If an *individual Chapter 7 debtor with primarily consumer debts* fails the "means test," then a presumption of abuse arises. In such a case, after notice and a hearing, the court, on its own motion or a motion by the Chapter 7 trustee, the United States trustee, the Bankruptcy Administrator in North Carolina or Alabama cases, or any party in interest, may dismiss the debtor's case, or, with the debtor's consent, convert the case to Chapter 11 or 13.

b. Bad Faith or Totality of the Circumstances

In determining whether the filing of a Chapter 7 case *by an individual debtor with primarily consumer debts* in which the presumption of abuse either does not arise or is rebutted *nonetheless* constitutes abuse, the court must consider (i) whether the debtor *filed* the petition in *bad faith; or* (ii) whether the *totality of the circumstances of debtor's financial situation* demonstrates abuse.

3. Crime of Violence

The bankruptcy court may dismiss the case of an individual Chapter 7 debtor who has been convicted of a crime of violence or a drug trafficking crime if the victim of such crime moves for dismissal and the court determines that dismissal is in the best interest of the crime victim. The court may not dismiss the case, however, if filing is necessary to satisfy a domestic support obligation.

XIII. CHAPTER 11: REORGANIZATION

A. ELIGIBILITY FOR RELIEF

Relief under Chapter 11 is available to *any person* (individual, corporation, or partnership), who *qualifies to be a debtor under Chapter 7,* except for a stockbroker or a commodity broker. In addition, *railroads are eligible* for relief under special provisions of Chapter 11. An *individual consumer debtor* may file for relief under Chapter 11. As of the writing of this guide, there are *three basic categories* of Chapter 11 debtors: (1) *non-small business debtors*; (2) *small business debtors* that do *not elect subchapter V*; and (3) debtors that *elect subchapter V,* including small business debtors that make the election. An individual debtor may fall into any one of these three categories.

B. ADMINISTRATION OF CHAPTER 11 CASE

1. Creditors' Committees

The Bankruptcy Code provides that shortly after the order for relief, the United States trustee shall appoint a committee of unsecured creditors, usually consisting of those *persons,* willing to serve, that hold the *seven largest unsecured claims* against the debtor. While the Code uses the term "shall," it is not unusual for the United States trustee to be unable to find creditors willing to serve on the unsecured creditors' committee. Unless the bankruptcy court for cause orders otherwise, an official committee of unsecured creditors is *not appointed* in a *small business case or a subchapter V case.*

a. Creditors' Committee Membership

Membership is not limited to individuals. *Governmental units* generally are excluded from the definition of the term "person," but in certain circumstances *may be eligible* to serve on a Chapter 11 creditors' committee.

b. Additional Committees

The bankruptcy court, upon the request of a party in interest, may order the appointment of additional committees of creditors or equity security holders. The United States trustee appoints the committee.

c. Employment of Attorneys or Accountants

A creditors' committee or an equity security holders' committee may hire *attorneys, accountants, or other professionals* to represent or perform services for the committee. The committee's hiring decision must be made at a scheduled meeting attended by a *majority of the committee members* and *court approval* is required.

2. Debtor in Possession

In a non-subchapter V case, unless a trustee is appointed in the case, the *debtor in possession remains in possession* of the property of the estate and has all of the *rights, powers, and duties of a trustee, except* the right to compensation and the duty to investigate the debtor. Unless the court orders otherwise, upon the request of a party in interest and after notice and a hearing, the debtor *continues to operate its business.* While there is a trustee in a subchapter V case, the debtor is still a debtor in possession.

a.   **Employment of Professionals**

Any attorney, accountant, or other professional employed by the debtor in possession must be a ***disinterested*** person and cannot hold or represent any interest that is ***adverse*** to the estate. A person is not disqualified for employment under § 327 by a debtor that ***elects subchapter V solely*** because that person holds a pre-petition ***claim of less than $10,000***.

3.   **Appointment of Trustee**

The rules on appointment of a trustee differ for ***subchapter V versus non-subchapter V*** cases. In subchapter V, a trustee is appointed.

The remainder of this summary on appointment of a trustee applies to ***non-subchapter V*** cases.

Normally, the debtor in possession is considered the most appropriate person to operate its business. Nonetheless, after the filing of the petition and prior to confirmation of a plan, a party in interest or the United States trustee may request and the court may order the appointment of a trustee (i) ***for cause,*** (ii) if the appointment is in the ***interests of creditors,*** equity security holders, and other interests of the estate, or (iii) if the bankruptcy court determines it is in the ***best interests*** of the creditors and the estate to appoint a trustee rather than ***convert or dismiss*** the case. The party requesting appointment of a trustee has the burden of proving grounds for such appointment.

a.   **Mandatory Motion by United States Trustee**

The United States trustee must move for the appointment of a Chapter 11 trustee if there are ***reasonable grounds to suspect*** that current members of the governing body of the debtor, e.g., the board of directors, the chief executive officer, or the chief financial officer, or members of the governing body who selected the CEO or CFO participated in ***actual fraud, dishonesty, or criminal conduct*** in managing the debtor or the debtor's public financial reporting. While the United States trustee must file a motion for appointment under such circumstances, the bankruptcy court is not required to appoint a Chapter 11 trustee.

b.   **Choosing a Trustee**

If the court orders the appointment of a trustee, generally the United States trustee consults with parties in interest and then ***appoints*** a ***disinterested person,*** other than himself, subject to the court's approval. Alternatively, in cases other than railroad reorganizations, the Code provides for ***election*** of the trustee ***if*** a party in interest requests an election within ***30 days after the court orders appointment*** of a trustee.

4.   **Appointment of Examiner**

In a Chapter 11 case in which the court has not ordered the appointment of a trustee, the court sometimes will order the appointment of an examiner, prior to confirmation of a plan, ***to investigate*** any charges of fraud, dishonesty, incompetence, misconduct, mismanagement, or irregularity in managing the debtor's affairs on the part of the debtor's present or former management. The appointment is made by the United States trustee, who selects a ***disinterested person*** other than himself. The debtor in possession, however, retains the estate property and continues to operate the business. The Code's provisions on appointment and duties of an examiner do ***not apply*** in a subchapter V case.

5. Right to Be Heard

The *Securities and Exchange Commission* may raise, and may appear and be heard on, any issue in a Chapter 11 case. While the SEC may not appeal from any judgment, order, or decree entered in the case, it may join or participate in one brought by a true party in interest.

6. Claims and Interests

a. Proofs of Claims or Interests

In a Chapter 11 case, the court fixes and sends notice of a *bar date* that operates as a deadline for filing proofs of claims or interests. A claim or interest that is listed in the schedules filed by the debtor is deemed filed, for the scheduled amount, unless it is scheduled as disputed, contingent, or unliquidated.

b. Secured Claims

In a Chapter 11 case, both recourse and nonrecourse secured claims are treated as recourse claims for the purpose of allowance. A partially secured creditor may elect to have her claim in a Chapter 11 case treated as *secured to the full extent that the claim is allowed,* even though under § 506(a) it otherwise would be considered secured only up to the value of the collateral.

7. Conversion or Dismissal

a. Voluntary Conversion to Chapter 7

The debtor may convert a Chapter 11 case to Chapter 7 so long as (i) the debtor is a debtor in possession; (ii) the case did not begin with the filing of an involuntary Chapter 11 petition; and (iii) the case was not involuntarily converted to Chapter 11, i.e., debtor did not request the conversion to Chapter 11.

b. Mandatory Conversion to Chapter 7 or Dismissal

With certain exceptions, the bankruptcy court, upon request of a party in interest, must dismiss a Chapter 11 case or convert it to Chapter 7, whichever is better for creditors and the estate, if the party in interest *establishes "cause"* for dismissal or conversion. The Code has a non-exhaustive list of *16 reasons* that constitute *cause* for dismissal or conversion, including *substantial or continuing loss to or diminution of the estate* and the absence of a *reasonable likelihood of rehabilitation, gross mismanagement of the estate,* and *failure to comply* with a *court order.*

c. Conversion to Chapter 12 or 13

The court may convert a Chapter 11 case to a Chapter 12 or 13 case *only if* (i) *the debtor requests the conversion;* (ii) the debtor has *not received a Chapter 11 discharge;* and (iii) if the debtor requests *conversion to Chapter 12,* the court finds that conversion is *equitable.*

C. REJECTION OF COLLECTIVE BARGAINING AGREEMENTS

The Code provides detailed rules that the debtor in possession or trustee must satisfy in order to reject a collective bargaining agreement. The rules are those contained at *§ 1113, not § 365,* of the Code. The debtor in possession may not unilaterally terminate or modify any terms of a collective bargaining agreement before compliance with the provisions set forth in § 1113.

D. RETIREE BENEFITS

Section 1114 of the Code provides procedural and substantive protections against a Chapter 11 company's *modification of retiree benefits.* The Code's provisions cover both union and non-union employees.

E. THE DISCLOSURE STATEMENT AND CHAPTER 11 PLAN

1. The Disclosure Statement

After filing of the petition, the debtor or other plan proponent may not solicit acceptances or rejections of the plan unless they first have provided a plan (or plan summary) and a *written court-approved disclosure statement* containing *adequate information* to the holders of the claims or interests whose acceptances or rejections are being sought. Because the purpose of the disclosure statement is to provide information to creditors and equity security holders adequate to evaluate the plan, the Code requires that the disclosure statement contain sufficient information, under the circumstances, to enable a *hypothetical investor* typical of holders of claims or interests of the relevant class to make an *informed decision* to accept or reject the plan.

Note: The Code contains special rules for small business cases. In a subchapter V case, the debtor normally *does not file* a disclosure statement.

2. Filing a Plan

Unless a trustee has been appointed in the case, the *non-small business and non-subchapter V debtor* has the exclusive right to file a plan for the first *120 days after* the order for relief. A small business debtor that does not elect to proceed under subchapter V of Chapter 11 has the exclusive right to file a plan for the first *180 days after* the order for relief. A debtor that elects to proceed under subchapter V of chapter 11 must file a plan within *90 days of the order for relief* unless the bankruptcy court extends that time period based on circumstances for which the debtor "*should not justly be held accountable.*" In a subchapter V case, *only the debtor* may file a plan.

3. Classification of Claims or Interests

With the exception of administrative, gap, and tax claims, the Bankruptcy Code requires that a Chapter 11 plan classify the claims and the equity interests in the case.

a. "Substantially Similar" Claims or Interests

A claim or interest may be placed in a particular class only if it is substantially similar to the other claims or interests included in that class. The Code, however, does *not require* that all substantially similar claims be placed in the same class. While most courts generally allow separate classification of similar claims, there is an important exception: a plan proponent may not separately classify similar claims in an attempt to *gerrymander* the plan confirmation vote.

b. Administrative Convenience Claims

A plan proponent may create a separate class of *unsecured claims* with a value less than or reduced to an amount that the court approves as reasonable and necessary for *administrative convenience.*

c. **Secured Claims**

   Usually, if secured creditors' liens are in different property or are entitled to different priorities in the same property, each secured claim is placed alone in a separate class.

d. **Certain Priority Claims**

   Administrative expenses, involuntary case gap claims, and unsecured, pre-petition tax claims are *excepted* from the requirement of classification because the standards for confirmation require that the plan provide for such claims on an individual, as opposed to a class, basis.

e. **Interests**

   Equity interests in a sole proprietorship, a partnership, or a corporation must be classified separately from creditors' claims. Furthermore, common stock and preferred stock interests should be placed in different classes.

4. **Contents of Plan: Mandatory Provisions**

   All Chapter 11 plans must do the following:

   a. *classify all claims and interests,* other than priority claims for administrative expenses, involuntary case gap claims, or eighth priority taxes;

   b. specify any class that is *not impaired;*

   c. *describe the treatment* to be accorded *any impaired class;*

   d. *treat every claim or interest within a particular class identically,* unless a holder consents to less favorable treatment;

   e. *establish adequate ways to implement the plan;*

   f. *include, in the charter of a corporate debtor or successor,* or any corporation with which debtor *merged or was consolidated, a provision prohibiting the issuance of nonvoting stock,* and complying with certain other requirements concerning voting powers;

   g. *provide for the selection of officers and directors* in a manner consistent with the interests of creditors and equity security holders and that does not violate public policy; and

   h. *with the exception of subchapter V, provide for payment,* in an *individual Chapter 11 case,* of debtor's post-petition earnings or future income *sufficient to execute the plan.*

5. **Contents of Plan: Permissive Provisions**

   In addition to the mandatory items described above, a plan *may:*

   a. *impair or leave unimpaired* any class of claims or interests;

   b. *assume, reject, or assign executory contracts or unexpired leases;*

   c. *settle or adjust any claim or interest* held by the debtor or the estate, or provide for the retention and enforcement of the claim or interest by the debtor, Chapter 11 trustee, or an appointed representative of the estate;

   d. *sell all or substantially all of the estate property,* and distribute the proceeds among claim and interest holders;

   e. *modify the rights of secured creditors or unsecured creditors, unless* the creditor's claim is secured solely by a security interest in real property constituting the ***debtor's principal residence*** (with a variation applicable in subchapter V); and

f. ***include any other appropriate measure*** that is consistent with the provisions of the Bankruptcy Code.

F. CONFIRMATION OF PLAN

1. Requirements for Confirmation of a Consent Plan

a. Plan and Proponent Comply with Code Provisions

The plan must comply with the applicable provisions of the Bankruptcy Code, such as the requirements for classification of claims and the mandatory contents of a Chapter 11 plan. The proponent of the plan also must comply with the applicable provisions of the Code, such as those requiring disclosure of adequate information and solicitation of acceptances.

b. Plan Filed in Good Faith

The plan must be proposed in good faith and not by any means forbidden by law.

c. Payment for Services or Expenses Approved

The court must approve as reasonable all payments made by the plan's proponent, the debtor, or a person issuing securities or receiving property under the plan for services or expenses in or in connection with the Chapter 11 case or related to the plan, e.g., attorneys' fees.

d. Officers, Directors, Insiders Disclosed

The plan must disclose the ***names and affiliations*** of all individuals who, after plan confirmation, will serve as ***officers, directors, or voting trustees*** of the debtor, a successor to the debtor, or a debtor affiliate participating in a joint plan with the debtor. The plan proponent must also disclose the ***names and proposed compensation of all insiders*** who will be employed or retained by the reorganized debtor.

e. Rate Change Approved

If the debtor's rates are regulated by a governmental commission, that commission must approve any rate change proposed by the plan, or the proposed rate change must be expressly conditioned on such approval.

f. "Best Interests of Creditors Test" Met

Each holder of a claim or interest of an ***impaired class*** either must (i) ***accept*** the plan *or* (ii) ***receive*** or retain under the plan property having a ***present value,*** as of the effective date of the plan, of ***not less than the amount*** that the holder would receive in a ***Chapter 7 liquidation.***

g. All Impaired Classes Accept Plan

Each class of claims or interests must have ***accepted*** the plan ***or be unimpaired*** under the plan.

h. Administrative Expenses and Involuntary Gap Claims

The plan must provide for ***payment in full in cash*** on the effective date of the plan for each claim that is entitled to priority as an administrative expense or as an involuntary case gap claim, unless the holder of the claim consents to different treatment.

i. **First, Fourth, Fifth, Sixth, and Seventh Priority Claims**

Unless the holder of a particular claim consents to different treatment, the plan must provide the following treatment to *each holder* of a domestic support obligation claim, wage or commission claim, claim for contributions to an employee benefit plan, claim by a grain farmer or United States fisherman, or a claim for a consumer layaway.

(i) *If the class has accepted the plan,* each claimant is entitled to receive deferred cash payments having a present value, as of the effective date of the plan, equal to the allowed amount of her claim.

(ii) *If the class has rejected the plan,* each claimant must receive total payment of her claim, in cash, on the effective date of the plan.

j. **Eighth Priority Tax Claims**

Unless it consents to different treatment, each tax claimant entitled to eighth priority must receive *regular installment payments in cash:*

(i) having a present value, as of the effective date of the plan, equal to the allowed amount of the claim;

(ii) over a period of time that ends *no later than 5 years from the order for relief;* and

(iii) in a manner *no less favorable* than the plan's treatment—with the exception of a class of creditors under § 1122(b)—of the *most favored non-priority unsecured claim.*

k. **Ninth and Tenth Priority Claims**

The Code provides no special rules for the treatment of ninth or tenth priority claims.

l. **At Least One Impaired Class of Claims Accepts Plan**

If the plan *impairs any class of claims,* then the plan must be accepted by *at least one class of claims* that is impaired, excluding any acceptances by insiders of the consenting class. This requirement *does not* apply to cram down of a *subchapter V plan.*

m. **Plan Is Feasible**

The plan must be feasible, which means that confirmation of the plan is *not likely* to be followed by the *debtor's liquidation* or the need for *further financial reorganization.*

n. **Bankruptcy Fees Paid**

All required bankruptcy fees were paid prior to the confirmation hearing, or the plan must provide that they will be paid on the effective date of the plan.

o. **Retiree Insurance Benefits Protected**

The plan must provide for the continued payment of all retiree benefits at the level originally provided by the debtor unless (i) the debtor or trustee, if one is appointed, and the authorized representative of the recipients agree to a modification or (ii) the court orders the payments to be modified in accordance with § 1114.

p. Domestic Support Obligations

In an individual Chapter 11 case, the debtor must have paid all *post-petition domestic support obligations* required by judicial or administrative order, or by statute. *Distinguish pre-petition domestic support obligations,* which are first-priority claims.

q. Disposable Income Requirement: Individual Cases

If the holder of an *allowed unsecured claim objects* to confirmation of the *individual debtor's* plan, the bankruptcy court cannot confirm the plan unless it provides for either (i) payment of the *present value,* as of the plan's effective date, of such claim; or (ii) payment of the debtor's *projected disposable income* for the *longer* of (a) the five-year period starting when the plan's first payment is due or (b) the period of time during which payments are made under the plan. This requirement does not apply to a *subchapter V case.*

r. Property Transfers

Any transfer of property by a non-profit corporation or trust under the plan must be made in accordance with applicable nonbankruptcy law.

2. Cram down

Section 1129's cram down provisions *do not apply in subchapter V.*

A non-subchapter V plan can be confirmed if all of the above requirements have been satisfied, *except* the requirement that every class of claims or interests accept the plan or be unimpaired under the plan, but the plan must *not unfairly discriminate* and must be *fair and equitable* with respect to any dissenting impaired classes.

a. Unfair Discrimination

The Code does not define "unfair discrimination" and provides no statutory guidance, as it does with the "fair and equitable" requirement. Most courts look at the disparity of treatment proposed in the plan and whether the Code provides a justification for the plan's disparate treatment.

b. Fair and Equitable

(i) Secured Claims

If a class of secured creditors is *impaired and does not accept the plan,* then the plan's treatment of that class *must be fair and equitable.* (Remember that usually each secured claim is classified in a separate class if the liens are in different property or are entitled to different priorities in the same property.) A plan satisfies the "fair and equitable" requirement if it provides for (i) the creditor to *retain her lien* on the collateral for the allowed amount of the secured claim, and to receive payment in deferred *cash installments* that total at least the allowed amount of the secured claim and that have a *present value,* as of the effective date of the plan, of at least the value of the collateral; (ii) the creditor to receive the *indubitable equivalent* of her secured claim; *or* (iii) the collateral to be sold free and clear of the creditor's lien, with the *lien attaching to the proceeds* of the sale.

(ii) Unsecured Claims

A plan satisfies the "fair and equitable" requirement with regard to a class of unsecured creditors if it (i) provides that *each creditor* in the class receives property having a *present value,* as of the effective date of the plan, equal to the allowed amount of her unsecured claim; *or* (ii) satisfies the *absolute priority rule,* which requires that no holder of a claim or an interest that is junior to the impaired unsecured class receive or retain any property on account of the junior claim or interest. The Supreme Court has not decided whether there is a *new value exception* to the absolute priority rule. Courts are divided as to whether Congress has repealed the absolute priority rule for cases involving *individual Chapter 11 debtors.*

(iii) Equity Interests

A plan is "fair and equitable" as to interests if (i) the plan provides that each interest holder *receive or retain property* having a *present value,* as of the effective date of the plan, equal to the allowed amount of any fixed liquidation preference or fixed redemption price to which the holder is entitled, or the value of her equity interest, *whichever is the greatest; or* (ii) no interest holder junior to the class receives or retains any property on account of her junior interest.

G. SMALL BUSINESS DEBTORS

1. Definition of a Small Business Debtor

The *Small Business Reorganization Act of 2019* ("SBRA") amended the Code's definition of a small business debtor. A *small business debtor* is any person *engaged in commercial or business activities,* including any affiliated debtor, whose aggregate *noncontingent liquidated secured and unsecured debts,* on the petition filing date or the date of the order for relief, are *$3,024,725 or less,* excluding debts owed to *affiliates or insiders.* A debtor is *not a small business debtor* if the debtor's *primary activity* is the business of owning *single asset real estate.* To qualify as a small business debtor, at least *50 percent* of the debtor's liabilities must arise from its commercial or business activities. The Code's definition of a *small business debtor does not include:*

a. *any member* of a group of affiliated debtors that has *aggregate noncontingent liquidated secured and unsecured liabilities greater than $3,024,725,* excluding debts owed to insiders and affiliates;

b. any corporate debtor subject to the reporting requirements of *§§ 13 or 15(d) of the Securities Exchange Act of 1934*; or

c. any debtor that is *an affiliate of a corporation* described in clause b above.

2. Official Committee of Unsecured Creditors

Unless the court for cause orders otherwise, an official committee of unsecured creditors is *not appointed* in a small business case.

3. The Small Business Debtor's Disclosure Statement and Plan

a. Disclosure Statement

If the court determines that a disclosure statement must be filed, then it must be filed *no later than 300 days after* the order for relief. The Bankruptcy

Code's disclosure statement requirements are more flexible for small compared with non-small business cases.

(i) The bankruptcy court may determine that a disclosure statement is not needed because the *plan provides adequate information.*

(ii) The bankruptcy court also may approve a disclosure statement submitted on *standard forms.*

(iii) The bankruptcy court may *conditionally approve* the disclosure statement subject to final approval at a hearing after notice, and the debtor may solicit votes on the plan based on a conditionally approved disclosure statement. The court may combine the final hearing on the disclosure statement with the hearing on plan confirmation.

b. Plan Deadlines

Unless the court grants an extension or for cause orders otherwise, the *small business debtor* has the exclusive right to file a plan for the first *180 days after* the order for relief. Unless the court grants an extension, the plan and disclosure statement, if any, must be filed no later than *300 days after* the order for relief. The bankruptcy court must confirm the small business debtor's plan *no later than 45 days after* the plan is filed, unless the time for confirmation is extended.

H. SUBCHAPTER V DEBTORS

1. Definition of a Subchapter V Debtor

The SBRA created *subchapter V of Chapter 11.* A subchapter V debtor is any person *engaged in commercial or business activities,* including any affiliated debtor, whose aggregate *noncontingent liquidated secured and unsecured debts,* on the petition filing date or the date of the order for relief, are *$7,500,000 or less,* excluding debts owed to *affiliates or insiders.* A debtor does not qualify as a subchapter V debtor if its *primary activity* is the business of owning *single asset real estate.* To qualify as a subchapter V debtor, at least *50 percent* of the debtor's liabilities must arise from its *commercial or business activities*.

Subchapter V's definition of *debtor does not include*:

a. *any member* of a group of affiliated debtors that has *aggregate noncontingent liquidated secured and unsecured liabilities greater than $7,500,000,* excluding debts owed to insiders and affiliates;

b. any corporate debtor subject to the reporting requirements of *§§ 13 or 15(d) of the Securities Exchange Act of 1934;* or

c. any debtor that is *an affiliate of a corporation* described in clause b above.

If a *small business debtor elects* to proceed under subchapter V, then the bankruptcy case is *no longer a small business case.* Subchapter V's provisions govern the case. If the small business debtor *does not elect* subchapter V, then chapter 11's rules, including its special provisions for small business cases, govern.

The subchapter V $7.5 million debt limit currently is in effect until *June 21, 2024.*

2. Subchapter V Trustee

A *trustee is appointed* in every subchapter V case. The debtor, however, remains a debtor in possession and continues to manage its business.

3. Official Committee of Unsecured Creditors

Unless the court for cause orders otherwise, an official committee of unsecured creditors is *not appointed* in a subchapter V case.

4. Subchapter V Debtor's Plan and Disclosure Statement

a. Disclosure Statement

Unless the bankruptcy court orders otherwise, the subchapter V debtor *does not file* a disclosure statement. If the court orders the debtor to file a disclosure statement, then the disclosure statement rules applicable to small business cases apply.

b. Plan Contents

Only the subchapter V debtor may file a plan. The debtor must file the plan no later than *90 days after* the order for relief although the bankruptcy court may extend the 90-day period if the extension is *attributable to circumstances* for which the *debtor should not justly be held accountable.*

(i) Mandatory Plan Provisions

The subchapter V plan must satisfy all the requirements applicable to other Chapter 11 plans *except* the rule requiring an individual debtor to provide post-petition personal service earnings sufficient for the plan's execution. The subchapter V plan also must provide: (1) a *brief history* of the debtor's operations; (2) a *liquidation analysis;* (3) *projections* about the debtor's ability to make *plan payments;* (4) for the *submission* of all or such portion of the *debtor's future earnings or income* to the *trustee's supervision and control* as is needed to execute the plan.

(ii) Permissive Plan Provisions

The subchapter V debtor's plan *may* include any of the provisions allowed in other Chapter 11 plans, although subchapter V modifies the rule disallowing the Chapter 11 debtor from modifying a claim secured only by the debtor's principal residence. A subchapter V plan *may* modify a claim secured only by the *debtor's principal residence if new value* received in connection with granting of the security interest (1) was *not used primarily* to acquire the real property; and (2) was *used primarily* in connection with the debtor's *small business.*

c. Plan Confirmation

(i) Consent Plan

The bankruptcy court must confirm a subchapter V plan if it satisfies all the requirements applicable to other Chapter 11 plans *except* the *disposable income requirement for individual debtors.*

(ii) Cram down

Subchapter V has its own cram down provisions. The *absolute priority rule* does not apply in subchapter V. Unlike the cram down rules applicable to other Chapter 11 plans, a subchapter V plan may be confirmed even though *no impaired class* has voted to accept the plan. Subchapter V's cram down provisions require that with regard to *each dissenting impaired class* the plan (1) *does not discriminate unfairly* and (2) is *fair and equitable.* Subchapter V also contains a *special rule* for payment of *administrative and gap creditor claims* in cram down cases.

(1) Not Discriminate Unfairly

The case law on unfair discrimination for other Chapter 11 cases likely applies to subchapter V cases.

(2) Fair and Equitable

There are *three rules of construction* for determining whether a nonconsensual plan is *fair and equitable.* The first is directed specifically to a class of *secured claims* and requires what is required to confirm other Chapter 11 cases when an impaired class of secured creditors votes to reject the plan. The second is a *disposable income* requirement. The third is a *heightened feasibility requirement* coupled, in some cases, with a requirement that the plan contain *appropriate remedies* when the debtor fails to make plan payments.

Important: It is unclear whether the *disposable income* and *heightened feasibility* provisions also apply to a case involving *only* a dissenting class (or classes) of secured creditors.

(3) Administrative and Gap Creditor Claims

In subchapter V, the requirement—applicable to other Chapter 11 plans—that administrative and gap creditor claims be paid in full, in cash on the effective date of the plan *only applies* to a *consent plan.* If the plan is confirmed under subchapter V's *cram down* provisions, then the plan may provide for payment of *administrative and gap creditor claims* over time *through the plan.*

(a) Unexpired Lease of Nonresidential Real Property

In a subchapter V case commenced *before December 27, 2022,* if the court extends the time period for the trustee to perform an obligation of the debtor's under an unexpired lease of nonresidential real property (under the temporary amendment to § 365(d)(3)), then that obligation must be treated as an *administrative expense* for purposes of subchapter V's special rule for payment of administrative and gap claims.

(b) Small Business Act Loans

For cases filed *before December 27, 2022,* a *temporary COVID-related amendment* provides that the subchapter V plan that is crammed down may propose to repay a § 503(b)(10) claim when payment is "due under the terms of the loan giving rise to such claim." *Recall* that § 503(b)(10) is a *temporary amendment* that grants administrative expense status to debts incurred under § 364(g)(1), another *temporary COVID-related amendment* to the Code.

5. Discharge in Subchapter V

a. Consent Plan

If the subchapter V plan is a ***consent plan***, then the debtor, whether an individual or an artificial entity, receives a discharge upon ***plan confirmation.***

b. Cram down

If the plan is confirmed under subchapter V's ***cram down*** provisions, then the debtor does ***not receive a discharge upon plan confirmation***. Instead, the court grants the debtor a discharge ***as soon as practicable*** after the debtor completes all payments due ***within the first three years of the plan*** or such longer period of time, ***not to exceed five years,*** fixed by the bankruptcy court.

If the plan is crammed down, the debtor is ***not discharged*** from any debt (1) of the kind listed in § ***523(a)***; or (2) on which the last payment is due ***after the plan's first three years*** or such longer period, ***not to exceed five years,*** fixed by the court.

I. POST-CONFIRMATION MATTERS

1. Discharge

With certain exceptions noted below, unless the plan or the confirmation order provides otherwise, confirmation discharges the debtor from ***all pre-confirmation debts,*** as well as from debts arising from (i) the rejection of executory contracts or unexpired leases not assumed by the trustee or debtor in possession; (ii) the recovery of property under §§ 522, 550, or 553; and (iii) eighth priority tax claims that occasionally arise post-petition.

a. Corporate and Artificial Entity Debtors

A Chapter 11 discharge is not restricted to individual debtors, as in Chapter 7. Confirmation of a plan does not discharge a corporate debtor from any of the following:

(i) debts for ***fraud*** that are owed to a ***domestic governmental unit;***

(ii) debts owed to a person as a result of an action filed against the United States government under 31 U.S.C. §§ 3721 *et seq.,* or any similar State statute; *or*

(iii) a ***tax or customs duty*** for which the debtor made a ***fraudulent return*** or ***willfully attempted to evade or defeat*** such tax or customs duty.

b. Liquidating Plan

The debtor will not receive a discharge if:

(i) the confirmed plan provides for the liquidation of all or substantially all of the estate property;

(ii) the debtor does not engage in business after the plan is consummated; and

(iii) the debtor would not be granted a discharge under § 727(a) in a Chapter 7 case.

c. Officers and Directors; Co-Debtors

Confirmation of a Chapter 11 plan discharges only the debtor. Discharge of the debtor does not affect the liability of any other entity for such debt.

d. Individual Debtors

In a non-subchapter V case, an individual Chapter 11 debtor does not receive a discharge upon plan confirmation. Instead, the debtor receives a discharge upon *completion of all payments under the plan.* A Chapter 11 discharge for an individual debtor does not include any debts that are *not dischargeable under § 523.*

e. Subchapter V Debtors

Confirmation of a *subchapter V consent plan* discharges the debtor, regardless of whether the debtor is an individual or an artificial entity. If the plan was crammed down, then the debtor is discharged as soon as practicable after the *debtor completes all payments* due within the plan's first *three years*, or such longer period, not to exceed five years, that the court fixes. In the case of *cram down*, the debtor is *not discharged* from any debt of a kind under *§ 523(a) or* on which the last payment is due after the plan's first *three years* or such other time, not to exceed five years, fixed by the court.

2. Revocation of Confirmation Order

Within *180 days* after the entry of the order confirming the Chapter 11 plan, a party in interest may request that the order be revoked, but only on the ground that it was *procured by fraud.*

3. Exemption from Securities Laws

Generally, securities offered or sold by the debtor or its successor under a Chapter 11 plan in exchange for claims against or interests in the debtor or for administrative expense claims are *exempt from the registration requirements* of the 1933 Securities Act and from registration requirements in any state or local securities law.

4. Special Tax Provisions

The issuance, transfer, or exchange of a security *or* the making or delivery of an instrument of transfer under a *confirmed plan* may not be taxed under any law imposing a stamp tax or similar tax. This exemption does not apply to *pre-confirmation transfers.*

J. *MANVILLE*-TYPE TRUST/INJUNCTION

Section 524(g) of the Bankruptcy Code authorizes the bankruptcy court to order the type of trust/injunction used in the *Johns-Manville* case. Section 524(g) applies only to cases in Chapter 11 involving *asbestos-related liabilities* of the debtor when an indeterminable number of substantial future demands for payment necessitate use of the trust in order to deal equitably with claims and future demands.

XIV. CHAPTER 12: FAMILY FARMER OR FAMILY FISHERMAN

A. ELIGIBILITY

Chapter 12 relief is available only to *a family farmer or family fisherman with regular annual income,* and a family farmer or family fisherman with regular annual income is an individual, corporation, or partnership with annual income that is *sufficiently stable and regular* to permit the family farmer or family fisherman to make payments under a Chapter 12 plan. The Code's definition of a family farmer or a family fisherman includes *individuals,* or individuals and their spouses, and *corporations or partnerships.* The Code establishes debt ceilings for eligibility for Chapter 12; the ceiling for a family farmer is significantly higher than that for an individual Chapter 13 debtor.

1. Voluntary Petition

A case under Chapter 12 may be commenced only by the filing of a voluntary bankruptcy petition.

2. 180-Day Bar

A family farmer is *ineligible* for relief under Chapter 12 if the family farmer was a debtor in a case that was dismissed in the preceding 180 days (i) because of the family farmer's intentional failure to obey court orders or to appear before the court, or (ii) as a result of the family farmer's request for a voluntary dismissal of the case following a party's request for relief from the automatic stay.

B. PROPERTY OF THE ESTATE

Estate property is the same in a Chapter 12 case as in a Chapter 13 case. Ordinarily, a Chapter 12 debtor remains in possession of property of the estate unless otherwise directed by (i) a court order removing the debtor from possession, (ii) a provision in a confirmed plan, or (iii) the confirmation order. Furthermore, the Code expressly provides for a *Chapter 12 debtor in possession to continue to operate the farm or commercial fishing operation.*

C. THE PLAN

1. Filing a Plan

The debtor has the *exclusive right* to file a plan, even if the debtor is not a debtor in possession. A Chapter 12 debtor must file a plan *within 90 days* after the order for relief, unless an extension is granted for cause for which the debtor should not justly be held accountable.

2. Plan Duration

With the exception of payments on certain long-term debts, payments under the *Chapter 12* plan may not extend beyond *three years,* unless the court for cause approves a longer time period. The court, however, may not approve a plan period that is longer than *five years.*

3. Mandatory Plan Provisions

With the following two exceptions, the mandatory provisions of a Chapter 12 plan are essentially the same as those under Chapter 13.

a. In a Chapter 12 case, the holder of a particular claim or interest may consent to less favorable treatment than others of the same class.

b. In a Chapter 12 case, the plan must provide for payment of a *claim owed to a governmental unit* that arises out of the *sale, transfer, exchange, or other disposition* of any farm asset used in the *debtor's farming operation.* The claim must be treated as *unsecured* and is not entitled to *priority.*

4. Permissive Plan Provisions

The provisions that may be included in a plan under Chapter 12 differ from those allowable in a Chapter 13 plan, as follows.

a. Modifying Rights

The power of a Chapter 12 debtor to modify the rights of secured or unsecured creditors is not subject to the exception found in Chapter 13 that prohibits modification of a *claim secured solely by a security interest in real property constituting the principal residence of the debtor.*

b. Post-Petition Taxes and Certain Consumer Debts

A Chapter 13 plan may provide for the payment of all or part of a claim for *post-petition taxes* or a *post-petition consumer debt* for property or services needed for the debtor's performance under the plan. Chapter 12 has no comparable provision.

c. Sale or Distribution of Property

A Chapter 12 plan may propose to sell all or any part of estate property or distribute all or any part of estate property among entities having an interest in the property.

d. Payment of Secured Claims

A Chapter 12 plan may provide for secured creditors to be paid over a longer period than the three or five years referred to in § 1222(c). However, any such provision must be in conformity with Chapter 12's confirmation requirements.

5. Confirmation Requirements: Secured Creditors

The court cannot confirm the debtor's plan unless as to each allowed secured claim:

a. *the secured creditor accepts the plan;*

b. *the debtor surrenders the collateral* to the secured creditor; or

c. *the plan preserves the creditor's lien* on the collateral and provides for the distribution of *cash or other property* having a present value, on the effective date of the plan, of at least the amount of the creditor's allowed secured claim.

6. Confirmation Requirements: Unsecured Creditors

a. Best Interests of Creditors

As in a Chapter 13 case, the Chapter 12 plan must provide that *each unsecured creditor* holding an allowed claim will receive property having a *present value,* as of the effective date of the plan, that is not less than the amount he would receive for his claim in a case under Chapter 7 if the estate were liquidated on that date.

b. Best Efforts

If an unsecured creditor or the Chapter 12 trustee objects to confirmation of a plan, the bankruptcy court may not confirm the plan unless *one of the following three conditions* is met.

(i)   The plan provides for *100% payment of the unsecured creditor's claim.*

(ii) The debtor commits all of his *"projected disposable income"* to plan payments for three years or for any longer plan period approved by the court not exceeding five years.

(iii) The plan proposes to distribute *property whose present value* is equal to or greater than the debtor's *projected disposable income* for the relevant plan period.

D. DISCHARGE

A standard discharge under Chapter 12 differs significantly from a standard Chapter 13 discharge, in that ***all debts that are nondischargeable under § 523(a)*** are not discharged in a Chapter 12 case. In Chapter 12, the debts that are nondischargeable under a standard discharge are nondischargeable under a hardship discharge.

If the Chapter 12 plan provides for curing a default within a reasonable time and maintaining payments during the case on any ***secured or unsecured claim*** on which ***the final payment is due after the last plan payment***, then that debt is ***nondischargeable.*** If the plan provides for paying an allowed ***secured claim,*** consistent with the Code's confirmation requirements, over a period in excess of the ***three or five years*** allowed by the Code, then that debt is ***nondischargeable.*** The court may not grant a discharge to an individual Chapter 12 debtor unless it has found ***no reasonable cause to believe*** that (i) ***§ 522(q)(1) may apply*** to the debtor *and* (ii) there is proceeding pending in which the debtor may be found guilty of a felony described in ***§ 522(q)(1)(A)*** or liable for a debt described in ***§ 522(q)(1)(B).*** While not clear, this provision regarding § 522(q) likely merely delays the entry of the discharge order.

E. CONVERSION OR DISMISSAL

The debtor has an absolute right to ***convert the case to Chapter 7,*** and this right cannot be waived. The debtor also has the ***non-waivable right to dismiss the case*** if it has not been converted earlier from Chapter 7 or Chapter 11. On the request of a party in interest, the court may ***dismiss the case for cause.*** The Code provides a non-exhaustive list of reasons that constitute "cause," including ***gross mismanagement or unreasonable delay by the debtor*** that is prejudicial to creditors, failure to ***timely file a plan, continuing loss*** to or ***diminution of*** the Chapter 12 estate and the ***absence of a reasonable probability of rehabilitation,*** and ***material default*** under a confirmed plan.

XV. CHAPTER 13: INDIVIDUAL WITH REGULAR INCOME

A. ELIGIBILITY FOR RELIEF

Chapter 13 relief is available to an ***individual*** (i) who has ***regular income,*** and (ii) whose ***debts*** total less than ***$2,750,000.*** The indebtedness must be noncontingent and liquidated, determined as of the date of the filing of the petition. An individual with regular income is defined as an "individual whose income is sufficiently stable and regular to enable such individual to make payments under a plan under Chapter 13 . . . , other than a stockbroker or a commodity broker." A Chapter 13 case may be commenced only by the filing of a voluntary petition.

The $2.75 million aggregate debt limit is in effect until ***June 21, 2024.***

B. CO-DEBTOR STAY

The filing of a Chapter 13 petition operates not only as a stay of actions against the debtor under § 362, but also as a stay against any civil action or other act by a creditor to collect a ***consumer debt from an individual who secured that debt*** or who is otherwise ***liable on that consumer debt with the debtor.*** The co-debtor stay does not apply if (i) the Chapter 13 case has been ***closed, dismissed, or converted to Chapter 7 or 11;*** or (ii) the co-debtor's liability was incurred in the ***ordinary course*** of ***his*** business.

C. ADMINISTRATION OF CHAPTER 13 CASE

1. Chapter 13 Trustee

In regions where many Chapter 13 cases are filed, the United States trustee ordinarily appoints a qualified individual to serve as a ***standing trustee.***

Otherwise, the United States trustee appoints a disinterested person as the trustee for a particular case, or the United States trustee may serve as the trustee in the case.

2. Rights and Powers of Debtor

In a Chapter 13 case, the *debtor has the exclusive right* to use, sell, or lease estate property under §§ 363(b), (d), (e), (f), or (*l*). A debtor engaged in business is a *self-employed individual* who incurs trade credit in producing income from her business, which she is *entitled to operate unless the court orders otherwise.* A Chapter 13 debtor engaged in business also has the exclusive right to use, sell, or lease property in the ordinary course of business and to obtain credit.

3. Post-Petition Claims

Certain kinds of post-petition claims may be filed in a Chapter 13 case: (i) claims for *taxes* that become due during the pendency of the case, and (ii) claims for *consumer debts* incurred by the debtor after the order for relief for property or services that the debtor needs to carry out the plan.

4. Property of Estate

The Chapter 13 estate consists of (i) all property specified in § 541; (ii) all § 541 property acquired by the debtor post-petition, but before the *earliest* of the closing, dismissal, or conversion of the case; and (iii) all of the debtor's earnings from services performed post-petition, but before the *earliest* of the closing, dismissal, or conversion of the case. The *debtor retains possession* of all property of the Chapter 13 estate *unless a confirmed plan or confirmation order provides otherwise.*

5. Conversion or Dismissal

The debtor has an absolute right to *convert the case to Chapter 7,* and this right cannot be waived. Before a Chapter 13 plan is confirmed, the court, after notice and a hearing, may convert the case to *Chapter 11 or 12* upon a request by a party in interest or the United States trustee. If the *debtor is a farmer,* a Chapter 13 case cannot be converted to Chapter 7, 11, or 12 unless the debtor requests conversion. The debtor also has the nonwaivable right to dismiss the case if it has not been converted earlier from Chapter 7, 11, or 12. There is a long-standing split of authority as to whether the debtor's right to dismiss is absolute or subject to a bad faith or fraud exception.

Upon a request by a party in interest or the United States trustee, the court, *for cause,* may *dismiss the case or convert it to Chapter 7,* whichever is in the *best interests* of creditors and the estate. The Code has a non-exhaustive list of what qualifies as "cause," including *unreasonable delay* by the debtor that *prejudices creditors, failure to timely file a plan, a material default* under a confirmed plan, and *lack of good faith* in filing the Chapter 13 petition.

6. Filing Pre-Petition Tax Returns

If the debtor has not filed *tax returns* for any taxable period ending during the *four years prior to filing of the petition,* the debtor must file those returns with the appropriate tax authorities no later than the day before the *date first scheduled for the § 341 meeting.*

D. CHAPTER 13 PLAN: CONTENTS AND CONFIRMATION

1. Filing a Plan

Only the *debtor* may file a Chapter 13 plan. She must file the plan with the *petition or within 14 days thereafter* (or within 14 days after conversion to Chapter 13), unless the court grants an extension for cause.

2. Requirements for Plan Confirmation

a. Plan Complies with Code Provisions

The plan must comply with the provisions of Chapter 13, as well as with the other applicable provisions of the Code. The plan must include or abide by the following Code requirements.

(i) Sufficient Income to Be Turned over to Trustee

The plan must provide for the *submission* of all or such part of the debtor's *future earnings or other future income* to the supervision and control of the *Chapter 13 trustee* as is needed for implementation of the plan.

(ii) Same Treatment for Claims of a Class

If the plan designates classes of claims, it must provide identical treatment for all claims within any one class.

(iii) Full Payment of Priority Claims

With the exception of certain domestic support obligations, the plan must provide that all priority claims will be *paid fully in deferred cash payments,* unless a particular creditor consents to different treatment. The plan may provide for less than full payment of *domestic support obligations* that as of the filing of the petition had been assigned to a *governmental unit* or were owed directly to or recoverable by a governmental unit so long as the plan provides that all of the *debtor's projected disposable income* is applied to make plan payments for the *five-year period* starting when the first plan payment is due.

(1) Temporary Amendment

For cases commenced *before December 27, 2022,* a *temporary COVID-related amendment* provides that the plan may propose to repay a § 503(b)(10) claim when payment is "due under the terms of the loan giving rise to such claim." *Recall* that § 503(b)(10) is a *temporary amendment* that grants administrative expense status to debts incurred under § 364(g)(1), another *temporary COVID-related amendment* to the Code.

(iv) No Material Alteration of Certain Retirement Fund Loans

The plan may *not materially alter* the terms of a loan taken by the debtor from certain *retirement plans.*

(v) Plan Length

For a *below-median* income debtor, the Code provides for a *three-year* applicable commitment period. For an *above-median* income debtor, the applicable commitment period is *five years.* But the Code also states that the plan may not provide for payments over a period that exceeds *five years.*

b. Fees Paid

All fees, charges, or amounts required to be paid prior to confirmation or by the plan must have been paid.

c. Plan Filed in Good Faith

The *plan* must be proposed in *good faith* and not by any means forbidden by law.

d. Best Interests of the Creditors

Each unsecured creditor must receive *property* whose *present value*, as of the plan's effective date, at least equals what the creditor would receive in a *Chapter 7 liquidation case.*

e. Plan Is Feasible

The plan must be *feasible,* which means that the bankruptcy court must find that the plan has a *reasonable chance of success.*

f. Debtor Filed for Bankruptcy in Good Faith

The debtor must have filed the *Chapter 13 petition in good faith.*

g. Domestic Support Obligations

Debtor must pay all *domestic support obligations* required by judicial or administrative order, or by statute, that came *due after filing* of the petition.

h. Tax Returns

Debtor must have filed all *pre-petition* federal, state, and local *tax returns.*

i. Treatment of Secured Creditors' Claims

The plan must satisfy *one of the following three* requirements for *each allowed secured claim:* (1) the secured creditor *accepted the plan;* (2) the debtor *surrendered the collateral;* or (3) the debtor *complied* with the Code's *cram down requirements.*

(i) Cram down

The debtor may *cram down* a non-consenting secured creditor's claim so long as the plan *preserves the creditor's lien* on the collateral and distributes to the creditor *cash or other property* with a *present value,* on the plan's effective date, of at least the *amount of the creditor's allowed secured claim.*

(ii) Cram down Exception: The Hanging Paragraph

Most courts have held that if the hanging paragraph applies, then the creditor's *secured claim equals the amount that the debtor owes* the secured creditor, regardless of the actual value of the collateral. The hanging paragraph applies if the creditor has a *purchase-money security interest* (1) in a *motor vehicle* that the debtor *acquired for personal use* within *910 days* of filing for bankruptcy; or (2) in *any other thing of value* if the debt was incurred *within one year* of the bankruptcy filing.

(iii) Cram down Exception: Debtor's Principal Residence

A Chapter 13 debtor cannot *strip down* an undersecured mortgage on the debtor's *principal residence* to the fair market value of the home, if the last payment on the secured creditor's claim is due after the final plan payment.

j. Treatment of Unsecured Creditors' Claims

The debtor's plan must satisfy the *best interests of the creditors* test and, if the trustee or an unsecured creditor objects to plan confirmation, the *projected disposable income* test.

(i) Best Interests of Creditors Test

The plan must provide that *each unsecured creditor* holding an allowed claim will receive property having a *present value,* as of the effective date of the plan, of *not less* than the amount he would *receive* for his claim in a *Chapter 7* case on that date, taking into account the exemptions that would be available to the debtor.

(ii) Projected Disposable Income Test

If the *trustee* or an *unsecured creditor* objects to the plan, then the bankruptcy court cannot confirm the plan unless as of the plan's effective date the plan *either* (a) pays the unsecured creditor the *present value of its claim or* (b) provides that the debtor applies all of her *projected disposable income* during the *applicable commitment period* (three or five years), starting on the date of the first plan payment, to making plan payments to her unsecured creditors.

3. Permissive Provisions

The Code contains a number of provisions that the debtor may, but is not required to, include in her plan. The following are some examples.

a. Classification of Claims

The plan may specify various *classes of unsecured claims,* provided that it does not discriminate unfairly against any particular class.

b. Modification of Creditors' Rights

With the exception of the rights of a creditor whose claim is secured *solely* by a security interest in real property constituting the *debtor's principal residence,* the plan may *modify the rights of secured creditors or unsecured creditors,* e.g., by changing the size and timing of installment payments.

c. Long-Term Debts

If the debtor has defaulted on a long-term secured or unsecured debt for which the last payment is due after the final plan payment, the Chapter 13 plan may provide for *curing the default* within a reasonable time and *maintaining payments* while the case is pending.

d. Assumption or Rejection of Executory Contracts or Unexpired Leases

The plan may provide for any previously unrejected executory contract or unexpired lease to be assumed, rejected, or assigned.

4. Modification of Plan

The debtor has the *exclusive right* to modify a plan *prior to confirmation.*

E. PAYMENTS

Unless the court orders otherwise, the debtor must begin making payments under a proposed plan no later than *30 days* after the earlier of the order for relief or the date that the plan is filed. The debtor must remit *plan payments* to the trustee *except* the debtor (i) *directly pays a lessor* for scheduled post-petition payments on a lease of personal property, and (ii) makes *adequate protection* payments directly to a creditor with a *purchase money security interest in personal property* but only with respect to the amount the comes due post-petition.

1. Administrative Expenses

Prior to or concurrent with each payment to creditors under a Chapter 13 plan, the trustee is required to pay any *unpaid administrative expenses or bankruptcy fees or charges,* as well as the percentage fee set for a standing trustee, if one has been appointed.

F. POST-CONFIRMATION MATTERS

1. Effects of Confirmation

A confirmed plan *binds the debtor and every creditor,* regardless of whether a creditor has accepted or rejected the plan or has objected to confirmation of the plan, or whether the creditor's claim is provided for by the plan.

2. Post-Confirmation Modification

The debtor, the trustee, or an unsecured creditor may request a modification of a plan at any time after it has been confirmed but before all payments have been made. Generally, a request for post-confirmation modification of a plan occurs under circumstances in which the income or expenses of the debtor have *changed materially and unexpectedly.*

3. Revocation of Confirmation Order

Within *180 days after an order confirming* a Chapter 13 plan has been entered, a party in interest may request that the order be revoked on the ground that it was *procured by fraud.*

4. Debtor's Failure to Make Payments

If the debtor fails to make all payments under the plan, a party in interest or the United States trustee may move for dismissal of the case or conversion to Chapter 7. Alternatively, the debtor may request a hardship discharge if the circumstances warrant.

G. DISCHARGE

A standard Chapter 13 discharge includes all debts that are provided for by the plan or that have been disallowed by the court. Unless the debtor has executed a court-approved written waiver of discharge subsequent to the order for relief, the debtor will be granted a discharge *after* she has made *all payments* under the plan, and *certified* that she has *paid all domestic support obligations* required by *judicial or administrative order, or by statute* and due prior to the date of the certification.

1. Cases to Which Discharge Does Not Apply

a. Instructional Course

With certain limited exceptions, a Chapter 13 debtor will not receive a discharge if she fails to complete post-petition the *instructional course on personal financial management* mandated by the Code.

b. Prior Bankruptcy Case

The debtor will not receive a discharge in her current Chapter 13 case if she received a discharge in a case filed under *Chapters 7, 11, or 12* during the *four years prior to the filing* of her current Chapter 13 case. The debtor will not receive a discharge in her current Chapter 13 case if she received a discharge in a case filed under **Chapter 13** during the *two years* prior to the filing of her current Chapter 13 case. The time period runs from the *filing date* of the prior case to the *filing date* of the current Chapter 13 case.

c. **Exemption Issue Under § 522(q)**

The bankruptcy court may not grant a discharge unless it has determined, after notice and a hearing held *no more than 10 days* before the discharge order that there is *no reasonable cause to believe* that (i) the Code's limitation on state-law exemption rights pursuant to § 522(q)(1) may apply to the debtor, and (ii) there is a pending proceeding in which the debtor may be found guilty of one of the *felonies listed in § 522(q)(1)(A) or* liable for a *debt described in § 522(q)(1)(B).* This provision of the Code should operate to *delay* rather than *permanently deny* the debtor a discharge.

2. **Nondischargeable Debts**

a. **Long-Term Debts**

If the plan provides for curing any default within a reasonable time and maintaining payments while the case is pending on any debt for which the last payment is due *after* the final plan payment, then that debt is not dischargeable.

b. **Certain Taxes**

The following types of taxes are not dischargeable:

(i) *trust fund taxes*;

(ii) a tax for which a *return, or equivalent report or notice,* if required, was *not filed or given or* was filed or given but *after the date on which it was due and* within the *two year-period prior to filing* of the bankruptcy petition; or

(iii) a tax for which the debtor either made a *fraudulent return or willfully attempted* to *evade or defeat* the tax.

c. **Fraud**

Debts for money, property, services, or an extension, renewal, or refinancing of credit obtained by *fraud, consumer debts* exceeding *$800* incurred within *90 days* of bankruptcy for *luxury goods,* or *cash advances* exceeding *$1,100* obtained within *70 days* of bankruptcy are not dischargeable.

d. **Unscheduled Debts**

Debts that the debtor did not *list or schedule* in time for the creditor to *timely file a proof of claim* are not dischargeable, unless the creditor had *notice or actual knowledge* in time to make a timely filing.

e. **Section 523(a)(2) or (4)**

Debts that are potentially nondischargeable under *§ 523(a)(2) or (4),* and that the debtor neither *listed nor scheduled* in time for the creditor to *timely file a proof of claim* and *timely request a determination of dischargeability* are not dischargeable, unless the creditor had *notice or actual knowledge* in time to make a timely filing.

f. Embezzlement

Debts owed for *embezzlement, larceny,* or *fraud or defalcation in a fiduciary capacity* are not dischargeable.

g. Domestic Support Obligations

Domestic support obligations are not dischargeable. *Debts for support* owed under state law to a *state or municipality* that are enforceable under the Child Support Enforcement Act are not dischargeable.

h. Student Loans

Unless excepting the debt from discharge will constitute an *undue hardship* on the debtor and her dependents, *student loan debt* is not dischargeable. Health Education Assistance Loans are not dischargeable unless the debtor satisfies the three conditions for discharge required by federal nonbankruptcy law.

i. Certain Personal Injury Debts

A debt for *death or personal injury* caused by the debtor's operation of a *motor vehicle, vessel, or aircraft* while *intoxicated* from using *alcohol, drugs, or another substance* is not dischargeable.

j. Restitution

A debt for *restitution,* or a *criminal fine,* that is included in the debtor's sentence for *conviction of a crime* is not dischargeable. A debt for *restitution* or *damages awarded in a civil action* against the debtor as a result of *willful* or *malicious injury* that caused *death or personal injury* also is nondischargeable.

k. Certain Consumer Debts

Post-petition consumer debts for property or services necessary for the debtor to perform the plan are not dischargeable, if the corresponding claims were allowed, and if the trustee's prior approval to incur the debt was practicable but was not obtained.

3. Hardship Discharge

Under certain conditions, the debtor may receive a hardship discharge. A Chapter 13 hardship discharge includes the unsecured debts that discharged under a standard Chapter 13 discharge, *except* the following:

a. debts that are *nondischargeable under § 523(a);*

b. *Health Education Assistance Loans ("HEAL")* not meeting the three conditions for discharge under the applicable federal nonbankruptcy statute;

c. *long-term debts* provided for under *Chapter 13's cure provision;* and

d. *post-petition consumer debts for property or services necessary for the debtor to perform the plan,* if the corresponding claims were allowed, and if the trustee's prior approval to incur the debt was practicable but was not obtained.

4. Revocation of Discharge

The court may revoke a Chapter 13 discharge that was *obtained by the debtor's fraud* if the party in interest seeking the revocation *did not know* of the fraud until *after the discharge* was awarded. The party seeking revocation must make its request for revocation no later than *one year* from the ***date the discharge was granted.***

Approach to Exams

The Bankruptcy Code is a complex statute and its study requires you, the student, to master a number of difficult and detailed provisions. One way to approach an exam question is to isolate the basic subject matter of your professor's question. Does the question involve the Code's administrative powers, e.g., adequate protection, the automatic stay? Does the question ask about the trustee's avoiding powers and, thus, involve property of the estate? Or, is the question more specific and ask whether a debtor may file for relief under a particular chapter of the Code? Use the following questions to guide and organize your thoughts when answering your professor's exam questions.

A. **Chapter 1 of the Code: General Provisions**

   1. Is the debtor *eligible for relief* under a particular chapter of the Bankruptcy Code? [B.C. § 109]

      Remember: In addition to the eligibility requirements under § 109, the above-median income Chapter 7 debtor must pass the "means" test. [B.C. § 707]

   2. If the debtor is an *individual,* has the debtor received counseling from an approved nonprofit budget or credit counseling service in the *180 days prior* to filing for bankruptcy? [B.C. § 109(h)]

   3. If the debtor is an *individual or a family farmer,* was she a debtor in a bankruptcy case pending within *180 days* of the current case that was dismissed? If so, the debtor may not be eligible to file for bankruptcy. [*See* B.C. § 109(g)]

   4. If the case is filed under Chapter 11, is the debtor a *small business debtor*? [B.C. § 101(51D)] Has the debtor elected to proceed under *subchapter V*? [B.C. § 101(51C)]

B. **Chapter 3 of the Code: Case Administration**

   1. Under which chapters of the Code does a *trustee* normally serve? [B.C. § 321]

   2. What must a *professional person* do in order to receive compensation for services rendered in a bankruptcy case? [B.C. §§ 327, 330]

      a. Is the person *disinterested?* Does the person hold *an interest adverse to the estate*?

      b. Is the debtor's attorney paid from estate funds?

   3. What roles do the *consumer privacy ombudsman* and *patient care ombudsman* play in a bankruptcy case? [B.C. §§ 332, 333]

   4. What effect, if any, does *conversion* of a case from one chapter to another have on the date of the order for relief and claims against the estate? [B.C. § 348]

   5. Has a creditor taken any action post-petition that violates the *automatic stay?* [B.C. § 362(a)]

      a. Does the creditor's action fall within one of the *exceptions* to the stay? [B.C. § 362(b)]

      b. Has a secured creditor requested *relief from the automatic stay,* and should such relief be granted?

         i. Is the creditor *adequately protected?* [B.C. §§ 361, 362(d)(1)]

        ii. Does the debtor have *equity* in the collateral, and is the property *necessary for an effective reorganization?* [B.C. § 362(d)(2)]

6. Has *adequate protection* been provided when required by the Code? [B.C. §§ 362(d)(1), 363(e), 364(d)(1)(B)]

    a. What is the connection between a *failure of adequate protection* and *priority claim* status? [B.C. § 507(b)]

7. Does the trustee or debtor in possession plan to *sell, use, or lease* property of the estate? [B.C. § 363]

    a. Is the property *cash collateral*? Has the trustee or debtor in possession obtained *consent* of the party with the interest in the cash collateral or *court authorization* after notice and a hearing? [B.C. § 363(a), (c)]

    b. If the sale or lease involves *personally identifiable information about an individual,* has the trustee or debtor in possession satisfied the Code's requirements for such sale or lease? [B.C. § 363(b)]

    c. Under what circumstances may a trustee or debtor in possession sell property *free and clear* of the interest of any other entity in the property? [B.C. § 363(f)]

    d. What is *credit bidding?* [B.C. § 363(k)]

8. What can the trustee or debtor in possession offer in return for a creditor extending credit or loaning money to the debtor post-petition? [B.C. § 364]

9. Does the debtor have any *unexpired leases or executory contracts*?

    a. Did the trustee or debtor in possession act within the *Code's time frames* to assume or reject any unexpired lease or executory contract? [B.C. § 365(d)]

    b. If the trustee or debtor in possession plans to assume an unexpired lease or executory contract, has the trustee or debtor in possession satisfied the Code's *requirements for assumption,* such as cure of defaults and adequate assurance of future performance? [B.C. § 365(b)]

    c. Is the executory contract or unexpired lease one that the trustee or debtor in possession *cannot assign* if assumed? [B.C. § 365(c)]

    d. Has the trustee or debtor in possession in a Chapter 11 case satisfied the requirements for assuming or rejecting a *collective bargaining agreement*? [B.C. § 1113]

C. Chapter 5 of the Code: Creditors, the Debtor, and the Estate

1. Does the Code impose limitations on the amount of the claim, e.g., damages for long-term leases? [B.C. § 502(b)(6)]

2. Is the creditor's claim *fully secured?* If not, remember that an *undersecured claim* generally is *bifurcated* into two claims: a secured claim up to the value of the collateral and an unsecured claim for the difference between what the debtor owes to the creditor and the collateral's value. [B.C. § 506(a)(1)]

    a. If the debtor is an *individual in a Chapter 7 or Chapter 13* case, be sure to consult the Code's rules for determining the value of a secured claim in *personal property.* [B.C. § 506(a)(2)]

3. What *federal exemptions* are available to an individual debtor? [B.C. § 522(d)] What is an *opt-out state*?

    a.   Has the debtor been domiciled in the state in which she filed her petition for 730 days prior to filing for bankruptcy? If not, which state's exemption law applies to her case? [B.C. § 522(b)(3)]

    b.   In what circumstances can the debtor avoid the fixing of a lien that impairs an exemption to which the debtor otherwise would be entitled? [B.C. § 522(f)]

    c.   Do either of the "mansion loophole" exemption limitations apply to debtor's case? [B.C. § 522(p), (q)]

4.   If the debtor is an ***individual,*** which debts are ***nondischargeable?*** [B.C. § 523(a)] Make sure that you know how the types of nondischargeable debts may vary depending on filing chapter. [B.C. §§ 1141(d), 1192, 1228(a), 1328(a)]

5.   Does the debtor want to ***reaffirm*** any debts? [B.C. § 524]

    a.   What is the ***connection*** between the individual debtor's failure to file or perform her ***intention with regard to debts secured by personal property*** and lifting of the ***automatic stay?*** [B.C. §§ 362(h), 521(a)(2), (6)]

6.   What ***property*** comprises the bankruptcy ***estate?***

    a.   Make sure to consider the different treatment of ***post-petition earnings*** for individual debtors under the various chapters of the Code. [B.C. §§ 1115, 1186, 1207, 1306]

    b.   Can the trustee or debtor in possession ***avoid*** any transactions and ***recover property*** for the benefit of the estate? [B.C. §§ 541(a)(3), 550]

7.   What is a ***floating lien*** and what happens to floating liens when a debtor files for bankruptcy? [B.C. § 552]

8.   What is ***setoff*** and what are the Codes' ***exceptions*** to the right of setoff? [B.C. § 553]

The following questions focus on the Code's various filing chapters. Do not simply memorize the rules. Work toward understanding the differences among the filing chapters. Your professor may ask you to evaluate a debtor's case and recommend the chapter of the Code under which the debtor should file for relief.

D.   Chapter 7: Liquidation

1.   Is the debtor an ***above- or below-median*** income debtor? If an above-median income debtor, does debtor pass the ***"means test"***? [B.C. § 707(b)(2)]

    Remember: If debtor fails the means test, she is not eligible for Chapter 7 unless she can rebut the presumption of abuse.

2.   Are there other grounds, besides the means test, for ***dismissing*** debtor's Chapter 7 case? [B.C. § 707(b)(3)]

3.   What is the ***order of distribution to creditors*** in a Chapter 7 case? [B.C. § 726]

    a.   What is the order of payment of ***priority unsecured claims*** in a Chapter 7 case? [B.C. § 507(a)]

    b.   If your professor provides you with the amount of debtor's non-exempt assets, the amount of all priority claims, and the total of all unsecured claims, you should be able to compute the dividend, if any, that unsecured creditors will receive in the case.

    c.   What are the grounds for a ***global denial of discharge***? [B.C. § 727(a)] How is § 727 different from § 523?

E.   Chapter 11: Reorganization

1.   Must the U.S. trustee appoint an official committee of unsecured creditors? [B.C. § 1102]

2. Is a trustee appointed? If so, under what circumstances? [B.C. §§ 1104, 1183]

3. Has the court approved the *disclosure statement* concerning the proposed plan? [B.C. § 1125] How do the disclosure statement requirements differ for *small business debtors?* [B.C. § 1125(f)] For *subchapter V* debtors? [B.C. § 1181(b)]

4. Who may file a plan? Are there time limits within which the debtor must file a plan? [B.C. §§ 1121, 1189] How do the plan proposal rules differ for *small business debtors* and *subchapter V debtors*?

5. Which provisions *must* the debtor include in its Chapter 11 plan? [B.C. § 1123(a)]

6. How do you determine whether a class of creditors has *accepted* the plan? [B.C. §§ 1124, 1126]

7. What are the grounds for *conversion or dismissal* of a Chapter 11 case? [B.C. § 1112(b)]

8. What are the requirements for *confirmation* of a consent plan? [B.C. § 1129(a)]

   a. Which requirement(s), if any, of § 1129(a) *do not apply* to confirmation of a *subchapter V* consent plan? [B.C. § 1191(a)]

   b. If the debtor is an *individual* and the plan does not propose to pay unsecured creditors in full and an unsecured creditor objects to confirmation, does the plan satisfy the *projected disposable income* test of § 1129(a)(15)?

9. What requirements must the debtor satisfy to confirm a plan using the Code's *cram down* provisions? [B.C. § 1129(b)]

   a. How do the cram down requirements differ for a *subchapter V* plan? [B.C. § 1191(b)–(e)]

   b. If the debtor is an *individual* and must obtain confirmation of her plan under the unsecured cram down provisions of the Code, does she live in a jurisdiction that has adopted the *narrow* or the *broad interpretation of the absolute priority rule?* [B.C. § 1129(b)]

10. When does a Chapter 11 debtor receive its *discharge if* the debtor

   a. is an *individual?* [B.C. § 1141(d)(5)]

   b. elected to proceed under *subchapter V* and the court confirmed a consent plan? [B.C. § 1181]

   c. elected to proceed under *subchapter V* and the plan was crammed down? [B.C. §§ 1191, 1192]

   d. is a *small business debtor* that did not elect subchapter V? [B.C. § 1141(d)]

F. **Chapter 12: Adjustment of Debts of a Family Farmer or Fisherman with Regular Annual Income**

1. How do Chapter 12's rules on *adequate protection* differ from those at § 361? [B.C. § 1205]

2. What are the grounds for *conversion or dismissal* of a Chapter 12 case? [B.C. § 1208]

   a. Does the debtor have an *absolute right* to convert the case to Chapter 7? [B.C. § 1208(a)]

3. Who may file a plan? Are there time limits within which the debtor must file a plan? [B.C. § 1221]

4. What provisions *must* the Chapter 12 plan contain? [B.C. § 1222(a)]

5. Does the plan satisfy the *requirements for confirmation* under § 1225?

    a. If the plan does not propose to pay unsecured creditors in full and an unsecured creditor objects to confirmation, does the plan satisfy the *projected disposable income* test of § 1225(b)?

6. Which debts are *excepted* from the *standard Chapter 12 discharge*? The *hardship discharge*? [B.C. § 1228(a), (b)]

G. Chapter 13: Adjustment of Debts of an Individual with Regular Income

1. What are the grounds for *conversion or dismissal* of a Chapter 13 case? [B.C. § 1307]

    a. Does the debtor have an *absolute right* to convert the case to Chapter 7? [B.C. § 1307(a)]

2. Who may file a plan? Are there time limits within which the debtor must file a plan? [B.C. § 1321]

3. What provisions *must* the Chapter 13 plan contain? [B.C. § 1322(a)]

4. Does the plan satisfy the *requirements for confirmation* under § 1325?

    a. If the plan does not propose to pay unsecured creditors in full and an unsecured creditor objects to confirmation, does the plan satisfy the *projected disposable income* test of § 1325(b)?

    b. Does the *length of debtor's plan* correspond to the debtor's status as an above- or below-median income debtor? [B.C. § 1325(b)(4)]

    c. Does the debtor have any creditors with *"hanging paragraph"* claims? If so, how must the plan treat these creditors' claims? [B.C. § 1325(a)(9) hanging paragraph]

5. Which debts are not *dischargeable* under a *standard Chapter 13 discharge*? The *hardship discharge?* [B.C. § 1328(a), (b)]

    a. How does the standard discharge in Chapter 13 differ from that under Chapter 7?

Introduction

Welcome to the study of bankruptcy law. Congress enacted the Bankruptcy Code in 1978 in a major overhaul of U.S. bankruptcy law. In 2005, Congress made significant changes to the Code with the passage of the Bankruptcy Abuse Prevention and Consumer Protection Act ("BAPCPA"). In 2019, Congress passed the Small Business Reorganization Act ("SBRA"), which created subchapter V of Chapter 11 to streamline the reorganization process for small business entities.

This study guide follows the basic organizational structure of the Code, as amended by BAPCPA and the SBRA. With the exception of Chapter 12, the Code is divided into odd-numbered chapters. With certain limited exceptions, Chapters 1, 3, and 5 of the Bankruptcy Code apply to all filing chapters of the Code. Chapter 1 contains general provisions, such as definitions. Chapter 3 deals with case administration; its provisions range from those on the compensation of professional persons to those on the automatic stay. Chapter 5 provides rules on matters such as creditor claims, property of the estate, and the avoiding powers.

The filing chapters of the Code are Chapters 7, 9, 11, 12, 13, and 15. Chapter 7 is the liquidation chapter. Chapter 9 is for municipal bankruptcies. Chapter 11 is known as the business reorganization chapter, but individual consumer debtors may file for relief under Chapter 11. Chapter 12 is the reorganization chapter for family farmers and family fishermen. Chapter 13 is limited to individuals and is a reorganization chapter in which debtors pay their creditors over either three or five years. Finally, Chapter 15 is the chapter for cross-border insolvency cases. This study guide does not cover Chapters 9 or 15.

The Code is dense and complex, so there are numerous examples throughout the text to help you to understand the concepts. This study guide also includes more than 130 *yes/no* and *true/false* questions, as well as several short-answer essay questions at the end to test your understanding of the material. Bankruptcy is an exciting area of law. I hope that this guide makes your study of the Code more enjoyable.

Bankruptcy

Third Edition

Chapter One

Introduction

CONTENTS	PAGE

Chapter Approach

This Chapter is an introduction to the Bankruptcy Code. The Chapter starts with the basics: the goals of bankruptcy, and the history and evolution of bankruptcy law in the United States. The Chapter then moves onto the organization of the Code and the forms of relief afforded under each of the Code's filing chapters. The Code contains numerous bankruptcy-specific definitions with which you must familiarize yourself. This Chapter provides an introduction to these terms. The final pages of the Chapter describe the various participants in the bankruptcy case and the different roles that they play, e.g., trustee versus United States trustee.

A. Goals of the Federal Bankruptcy Laws

1. Fresh Start

The principal purpose of bankruptcy is to afford the "honest but unfortunate debtor" the opportunity for a financial "fresh start." **Marrama v. Citizens Bank,** 549 U.S. 365 (2007).

e.g. **Example:** Della and Dan are married and struggling financially. Until recently, they both held full-time jobs that allowed them to cover their expenses and save money for a down payment on a house. Eighteen months ago, however, Dan was diagnosed was cancer and had to quit his job because of his illness. Della still works, but without Dan's income the couple struggled to pay bills. They used their credit cards to pay for many ordinary expenses, such as food, gas, and utilities. The couple's health insurance did not cover a significant portion of Dan's medical bills and prescriptions. In an effort to stay afloat financially, Della and Dan depleted their small savings, moved to a smaller apartment and otherwise cut expenses but still were unable to pay down their credit card or medical debt, which totals $300,000. Della and Dan filed for bankruptcy in order to shed their crippling debt. The Bankruptcy Code offers Della and Dan a "fresh start" by discharging the significant unsecured credit card and medical debt that they have accrued. In addition to discharging their debt, the Bankruptcy Code protects Dan and Della from future harassment and collection efforts by creditors. Della and Dan are the typical "honest but unfortunate debtor[s]" that the Code is designed to help. While bankruptcy still affords debtors like Della and Dan the opportunity for a "fresh start," the Bankruptcy Abuse Prevention and Consumer Protection Act of 2005 ("BAPCPA") has made the debtor's decision to file for bankruptcy more complicated than it was prior to BAPCPA's enactment.

2. Forum for Creditors

The bankruptcy process also benefits creditors because it provides a central forum for resolution of creditor claims. Outside bankruptcy, it is a "rush to the courthouse" for creditors. One goal of bankruptcy, however, is equality of distribution. For example, unsecured creditors—with notable exceptions for unsecured priority creditors—share *pro rata* in distributions from the estate. In addition, the Code's avoidance powers protect unsecured creditors by empowering the trustee to "claw back" payments made to certain favored creditors in the run-up to bankruptcy. The Code also provides various protections for secured creditors, such as statutory requirements for adequate protection of the creditor's interest in the collateral during the bankruptcy proceeding.

B. Legislative History

1. Bankruptcy Act

Article 1, Section 8 of the United States Constitution empowers Congress to enact uniform laws on bankruptcy. Under this grant of authority, Congress passed the Bankruptcy Act of 1898 (the "Act"), which the Chandler Act of 1938 substantially amended. [Pub. L. No. 55–541 (1898); Pub. L. No. 75–696 (1938)] Under the Act, the bankruptcy court had *summary jurisdiction,* which meant that it had jurisdiction over the debtor, administration of the estate, and any property in the actual or constructive possession of the court. The Act, however, gave concurrent jurisdiction to the bankruptcy court and state courts for *plenary proceedings,* e.g., disputes about property in the hands of a third party. [H.R. Rep. No. 95–595, at 44 (1977)] Moreover, the bankruptcy court could exercise its jurisdiction over *plenary matters only with consent* of the adverse party. Therefore, the bankruptcy court had no jurisdiction over property in the possession of a third person who had an adverse claim to the property, unless the third party *consented* to the bankruptcy court's jurisdiction. The result was time-consuming litigation about what "constitute[d] adequate possession to give the bankruptcy court jurisdiction and what constitute[d] adequate consent." [H.R. Rep. No. 95–595, at 43 (1977)] The consent requirement also meant that much of the litigation involving property outside of the bankruptcy court's in rem jurisdiction could occur only in the United States district court, under its *plenary jurisdiction,* or in the various state courts. [*See* H.R. Rep. No. 95–595, at 44 (1977) (noting that "a considerable part of a trustee's litigation to recover assets of the estate must be initiated in some court other than the bankruptcy court")] Consequently, the potential number of forums with jurisdiction over issues arising in or related to any single bankruptcy case generally proved to be unduly burdensome and expensive and, as a practical matter, often precluded a trustee's actions to recover property for the benefit of the estate and ultimately for creditors. Moreover, unnecessary and costly litigation regarding which court had proper jurisdiction frequently delayed the efficient administration of bankruptcy cases. [*See* H.R. Rep. No. 95–595, at 45–46 (1977)]

2. Bankruptcy Code

The Bankruptcy Reform Act of 1978 repealed the Bankruptcy Act of 1898, and created the Bankruptcy Code, which became effective on October 1, 1979. [11 U.S.C. §§ 101 *et seq.* (hereafter "B.C.")] The Bankruptcy Code made sweeping substantive changes to the system established under the Bankruptcy Act. The Code substantially expanded the jurisdiction of the bankruptcy court to enable the bankruptcy judge to hear practically all matters arising in or related to the bankruptcy case, thereby eliminating some of the logistical problems of litigation under the Bankruptcy Act. Furthermore, the Code created the United States trustee system to perform the administrative functions previously performed under the Act by bankruptcy judges. Thus, under the Code, bankruptcy judges perform judicial functions while case administration is left to the United States trustees. [*See* H.R. Rep. No. 95–595, at 88–91, 100–102 (1977)]

Note: The laws concerning jurisdiction are contained in title 28 of the United States Code (Judiciary and Judicial Procedure), not in title 11 (Bankruptcy Code).

3. The *Marathon* Case

In 1982, the United States Supreme Court, in a plurality decision, ruled that the grant of jurisdiction to the bankruptcy courts under the Bankruptcy Reform Act of 1978 was unconstitutional. [**Northern Pipeline Construction Co. v. Marathon Pipe Line Co.,** 458 U.S. 50 (1982) (plurality opinion) (finding that the Bankruptcy Reform Act had vested all the

" 'essential attributes' of the judicial power of the United States" in a non-Article III court without the protections of Article III judges, i.e., life-time tenure and a guarantee against diminution of salary); *see id.* (Rehnquist, J., concurring in the judgment) (limiting conclusion to facts of *Marathon* but concurring in judgment because the grant of authority that violated Article III was not "readily severable from the remaining grant of authority to bankruptcy courts under § 1471")] The plurality and concurring Justices in *Marathon* applied the decision prospectively and stayed the judgment until October 4, 1982. *Marathon* thrust the entire bankruptcy system into a state of turmoil, because Congress did not act for another two years. In the interim, a temporary Emergency Rule was adopted in each federal district to refer bankruptcy cases and proceedings to the bankruptcy courts. Under the Emergency Rule, bankruptcy judges could not enter final orders in a *Marathon*-like proceeding.

4. Bankruptcy Amendments and Federal Judgeship Act of 1984

In 1984, Congress enacted the Bankruptcy Amendments and Federal Judgeship Act. [Pub. L. No. 98–353 (1984)] The 1984 Act created a system under which the bankruptcy judge's authority to enter final judgments and orders depended on whether Congress had classified the proceeding as *core versus non-core.* The Supreme Court's decision in *Stern v. Marshall* created a fair bit of confusion about the core versus non-core "fix" that Congress created in 1984. [**Stern v. Marshall,** 564 U.S. 462 (2011)] Two post-*Stern* Supreme Court decisions, however, have provided answers on how bankruptcy courts should proceed when dealing with a *Stern* claim. [*See* Chapter Two for a discussion of the case law.]

5. Congress Creates Family Farmer Chapter and U.S. Trustee Program

Congress again made significant changes to the bankruptcy laws in 1986. It added Chapter 12, which now provides relief for family farmers and family fishermen with regular income. It also made permanent the United States trustee system, which prior to 1986 had operated as a pilot program in some judicial districts. [Pub. L. No. 99–554 (1986)] The United States trustee program now operates in 88 of the 94 United States judicial districts.

Congress also enacted major amendments to the Bankruptcy Code with the Bankruptcy Reform Act of 1994. [Pub. L. No. 103–394 (1994)] In 1990 and in 2000, as part of larger legislative enactments, Congress amended certain sections of the Bankruptcy Code and title 28. [Pub. L. No. 101–508 § 3007 (1990); Pub. L. No. 106–518 §§ 103–105, 208, 209, 501 (2000)]

6. Bankruptcy Abuse Prevention and Consumer Protection Act ("BAPCPA")

In 2005, Congress passed the Bankruptcy Abuse Prevention and Consumer Protection Act ("BAPCPA"), which made substantial changes to the Bankruptcy Code that affected, among others, both individual consumer and small business debtors. [Pub. L. No. 109–8 (2005)] Congress created an entry barrier to Chapter 7 with the "means test." Individual consumer debtors who fail the "means test" may not file for relief under Chapter 7. Congress also made the prior "small business election" mandatory, and created new "drop dead" dates for plan proposal and plan confirmation for small business debtors. BAPCPA changed numerous provisions in the Code, which are discussed throughout this outline.

7. Small Business Reorganization Act of 2019 ("SBRA")

Recently, Congress enacted the Small Business Reorganization Act of 2019 ("SBRA"), which created *subchapter V of Chapter 11.* [Pub. L. No. 116–54 (2019)] The SBRA is supposed to streamline the Chapter 11 process for small business debtors, thereby increasing the odds that a small business debtor will emerge from bankruptcy with a confirmed plan. Subchapter V cases differ from other Chapter 11 cases in some of the following ways: (1) there is a trustee but the debtor is still a debtor in possession; (2) there is no requirement that an official committee of unsecured creditors be appointed; (3) the debtor is not required to file a disclosure statement; (4) only the debtor may file a plan; and (5) the absolute priority rule does not apply.

8. Temporary COVID-Related Changes to the Code

In response to COVID-19, Congress enacted several statutes that temporarily amended provisions of the Bankruptcy Code. On March 27, 2020, President Trump signed the Coronavirus Aid, Relief, and Economic Security Act ("CARES Act") [Pub. L. No. 116–136 (2020)]. The CARES Act *increased the debt limit* for subchapter V, amended the definition of *current monthly income* to exclude certain COVID-19 relief payments, and made several changes to Chapter 13. The CARES Act contained a sunset clause and these changes to the Code expired on *March 27, 2021.*

But in the COVID-19 Bankruptcy Relief Extension Act of 2021 ("COVID Extension Act") [Pub. L. No. 117–5 (2021)], Congress extended the sunset date for certain CARES Act amendments to *two years* from the effective date of the CARES Act or *March 27, 2022.* [COVID Extension Act § 2]

The Consolidated Appropriations Act, 2021 ("CAA") [Pub. L. No. 116–260 (2020)] took effect on December 27, 2020. It made numerous temporary changes to various Bankruptcy Code provisions, e.g., § 364 (obtaining credit), § 365 (executory contracts and unexpired leases), § 547 (preferences), and subchapter V. The sunset periods for these various temporary amendments varied from one to two years from the CAA's effective date. While the CAA's sunset dates have passed, some CAA amendments are still in effect for cases commenced *before December 27, 2022.* [CAA § 320(f)(2)(B), § 1001(f)(2)(B), § 1001(g)(2)(B)]

Thus, the only COVID-related amendments discussed in this study guide are the CAA temporary amendments that apply to cases commenced *before December 27, 2022.*

9. Bankruptcy Threshold Adjustment and Technical Corrections Act ("BTATCA")

The Bankruptcy Threshold Adjustment and Technical Corrections Act ("BTATCA") [Pub. L. 117–151] took effect on *June 21, 2022.* The BTATCA made two important substantive changes to the Bankruptcy Code. First, it *increased the debt limit for subchapter V* cases to $7.5 million. While Congress had increased the limit in the CARES Act, that change was temporary and expired on March 27, 2022. Second, Congress *eliminated the separate secured and unsecured debt limits* for Chapter 13 eligibility. A debtor now may file for relief under Chapter 13 if her debts are less than $2.75 million. These changes to the subchapter V and Chapter 13 debt limits sunset two years from the enactment of the BTATCA or *June 21, 2024.* [BTATCA § 2(i)(1)]

C. Organization of the Bankruptcy Code

1. Chapters 1, 3, and 5

Chapters 1, 3, and 5 of the Bankruptcy Code contain general rules, definitions, and eligibility requirements for bankruptcy relief, as well as provisions about the commencement of a case, the administration of cases, the debtor, the estate and its officers, the trustee's powers to avoid certain transfers and recover property for the estate's benefit, creditors, claims, the automatic stay, adequate protection, and certain administrative powers of a trustee or a debtor in possession. With one small exception for subchapter V cases in Chapter 11, all three chapters apply to cases under Chapters 7, 11, 12, and 13. [B.C. §§ 103(a), 1181(a) (§ 105(d) not applicable in subchapter V)]

2. Chapter 7

The *liquidation* provisions of the Bankruptcy Code are contained in Chapter 7, which contemplates an orderly procedure by which the trustee collects the assets of the debtor's estate, reduces them to cash, and makes distributions to creditors, subject to the debtor's right to retain certain exempt property and the rights of secured parties in their collateral. [B.C. §§ 701 *et seq.*]

3. Chapter 9

Chapter 9 involves the adjustment of debts of a municipality and is beyond the scope of this summary.

4. Chapter 11

Chapter 11 is entitled *"reorganization"* and ordinarily concerns a commercial debtor that desires to continue operating a business and to repay creditors concurrently through an acceptable plan of reorganization confirmed by the court. [B.C. §§ 1101 *et seq.*] *Note:* Some Chapter 11 debtors file liquidating, not reorganization, plans. The Bankruptcy Code permits a Chapter 11 plan to provide for the sale of all or substantially all estate property. [B.C. § 1123(b)(4)] In addition, not all Chapter 11 debtors are commercial entities. The Supreme Court has held that a consumer debtor also may qualify for Chapter 11 relief. [**Toibb v. Radloff,** 501 U.S. 157 (1991)] Congress created the *new subchapter V* of Chapter 11 with the passage of the SBRA, which is covered in more detail in Chapter Thirteen, § H of this study guide. [B.C. §§ 1181–1195] This study guide does not cover subchapter IV of Chapter 11, which provides the rules for railroad reorganizations. [B.C. §§ 1161–1174]

5. Chapter 12

Chapter 12 provides relief for debtors who are *family farmers* or *family fishermen* with regular annual income, allowing them to continue to operate their farms or commercial fishing operations. [B.C. §§ 1201 *et seq.*] Like Chapters 11 and 13, the debtor proposes a plan for repayment of its creditors. Congress created Chapter 12 to provide the family farmer or family fisherman with a speedier, simpler, and less expensive process than under Chapter 11, and with higher debt limitations, in particular for family farmers, than those for Chapter 13. [*Compare* B.C. § 101(18), (19A) *with* § 109(e)]

6. Chapter 13

Chapter 13 provides a method by which an *individual with regular income* may repay all or a portion of her indebtedness over three or five years, under a plan proposed by the debtor and confirmed by the court. [B.C. §§ 1301 *et seq.*]

7. Chapter 15

Congress added Chapter 15 to the Code with the passage of BAPCPA. Chapter 15 is for cases of cross-border insolvency, but is beyond the scope of this study guide. [B.C. §§ 1501 *et seq.*]

D. Rules of Construction

Section 102 provides rules of construction for various terms used throughout the Bankruptcy Code.

1. "After Notice and a Hearing"

The phrase "after notice and a hearing" means notice and an *opportunity for a hearing* appropriate under the particular circumstances. [B.C. § 102(1)(A)] But the Code authorizes an act without an actual hearing if proper notice is given *and* (i) a party in interest fails to timely request a hearing *or* (ii) there is not enough time for a hearing before the act must be done and the court authorizes the act. [B.C. § 102(1)(B)]

2. "Claim Against the Debtor"

The phrase "claim against the debtor" includes a claim against the debtor's property. [B.C. § 102(2)]

3. "Including"

The words "including" or "includes" are not limiting. For example, § 1112(b)(4) enumerates 16 types of conduct that constitute "cause" for conversion or dismissal of a Chapter 11 case but precedes that list with the word "includes." Thus, a bankruptcy court could dismiss or convert a Chapter 11 case based on conduct other than or in addition to the 16 kinds of conduct enumerated. [B.C. § 102(3)]

4. "May Not" and "Or"

The words "may not" prohibit conduct. They are not permissive. [B.C. § 102(4); *see, e.g.,* **Bell v. Bell (*In re* Bell),** 225 F.3d 203 (2d Cir. 2000) (stating that Bankruptcy Rule 2003(a)'s time periods are "strictly enforced" based on Rule 9006(b)(2)—court *may not* enlarge the time—and § 102(4)'s rule of construction that "may not" is prohibitive, not permissive]

The word "or" is not exclusive. [B.C. § 102(5)]

5. "Order for Relief"

"Order for relief" means entry of an order for relief. [B.C. § 102(6)] In a *voluntary case,* the filing of the petition constitutes an order for relief. [B.C. § 301(b)] In an *involuntary case*, the court must enter the order for relief; it does not occur automatically upon the filing of a bankruptcy petition. [B.C. § 303(h)] The order for relief is a term that appears throughout the Code as a point of reference in time and means simply that the bankruptcy case may go forward, unless otherwise ordered by the court.

6. Singular and Plural

The singular includes the plural. [B.C. § 102(7); *see, e.g.,* ***In re*** **Blount,** 624 B.R. 590 (Bankr. D. N.J. 2020) (interpreting the word "payment" in § 522(d)(11)(D) in light of § 102(7) and holding that the Code allows the debtor to exempt the right to receive payment *or* multiple payments on account of personal injury cases so long as the debtor's total exemption does not exceed the statutory cap)]

E. Terminology

1. Introduction

There are a number of terms that appear frequently throughout the Code. Understanding their bankruptcy definitions is helpful.

2. Affiliate

The following categories of *entities or persons* qualify as affiliates:

a. an *entity* that directly or indirectly owns, controls, or holds *20 percent or more* of the *debtor's* outstanding voting stock;

b. a *corporation* in which *20 percent or more* of the outstanding voting stock is directly or indirectly owned, controlled, or held *by the debtor or by an entity* that owns, controls, or holds *20 percent or more* of the *debtor's* outstanding voting stock;

c. a *person* whose *business* the *debtor* operates under a *lease or operating agreement;*

d. a *person substantially all of whose property the debtor* operates under an *operating agreement;* or

e. an *entity* that operates the *debtor's business or substantially all of the debtor's property* under a *lease or operating agreement.* [B.C. § 101(2)]

Example: Carla is the sole shareholder of two corporations—Apex, Inc. and Beta Company—that are currently in Chapter 11. Because Carla owns 20 percent or more of both Apex's and Beta's voting stock, Carla is an affiliate of both companies. (Carla is an entity. *See infra* for definition of entity.) In addition, Apex is an affiliate of Beta, and Beta is an affiliate of Apex. While Apex does not own 20 percent or more of Beta's stock (and vice versa), Apex is a corporation in which 20 percent or more of its voting stock is owned by an entity, Carla, who owns 20 percent or more of the debtor Beta's stock. Therefore, the corporation Apex is an affiliate of the debtor Beta. Similarly, Beta is a corporation in which 20 percent or more of its stock is owned by an entity, Carla, who owns 20 percent or more of debtor Apex's stock. Thus, the corporation Beta is an affiliate of the debtor Apex.

3. Claim

A claim is a *right to payment,* even if it is not reduced to judgment, unliquidated, unmatured, disputed, or contingent. It also includes the "right to an equitable remedy for breach of performance if such breach gives rise to a right to payment." The concept of a claim is significant in determining which debts are discharged and who shares in any distribution from the bankruptcy estate. [B.C. § 101(5)]

Example: Debtor was ordered by a state court to clean up a hazardous waste disposal site. After Debtor failed to comply, the state court appointed a receiver and ordered the receiver to carry out the mandatory injunction while taking possession of Debtor's property, including the disposal site. Debtor then filed a bankruptcy petition. The performance that the receiver sought from Debtor was limited to the payment of money to cover the expense of removal of the wastes. The receiver's *right to payment of money was a claim,* and the liability on that claim was a *debt* capable of being discharged. [**Ohio v. Kovacs,** 469 U.S. 274 (1985)]

a. Comment

The Supreme Court has emphasized the legislative intent to ascribe the broadest possible definition to "claim." [**Pennsylvania Department of Public Welfare v. Davenport,** 495

U.S. 552 (1990) (noting that Congress had "chose[n] expansive language" in the Code's definitions of "claim" and "debt")]

4. Consumer Debt

A consumer debt is one "incurred by an *individual* primarily for a *personal, family, or household* purpose." [B.C. § 101(8)]

5. Current Monthly Income

The term *current monthly income* is used in the new financial eligibility test that Congress added to the Bankruptcy Code with the passage of BAPCPA. The term also is important for determining a debtor's *disposable income* for purposes of payment to the debtor's unsecured creditors in a Chapter 13 case. [B.C. §§ 707(b), 1325(b)] Current monthly income is the *debtor's average monthly income* from all sources *during the six-month period* that ends on the last day of the calendar month immediately before the debtor's bankruptcy filing. [B.C. § 101(10A)]

6. Debt

The word "debt" means "liability on a claim". [B.C. § 101(12)] The debtor receives a "fresh start" because her debts are discharged in bankruptcy.

7. Domestic Support Obligation

A "domestic support obligation" is a debt in the nature of *alimony, maintenance, or support* that is owed to or recoverable by (a) a *spouse, former spouse, or child* of the debtor (including the child's parent, guardian, or responsible relative) or (b) a *governmental unit*. [B.C. § 101(14A)(A), (B)] A domestic support includes *interest* accruing on the debt as provided under nonbankruptcy law. The term covers both pre- and post-petition debt. Domestic support obligations have *priority* status. [B.C. § 507(a)(1)] The plan confirmation and discharge provisions of various chapters of the Code afford special treatment for domestic support obligations. [*See, e.g.,* B.C. §§ 1191(c), (d), 1225(a)(7), 1228(a), 1325(a)(8), 1328(a)]

8. Entity

The term "entity" includes persons, trusts, estates, governmental units, and the United States trustee. [B.C. § 101(15)]

9. Insider

The Code's definition of "insider" varies based on whether the debtor is an individual, a corporation, or a partnership. [B.C. § 101(31)]

a. Individual Debtor

With respect to an individual debtor, the following persons are insiders: relatives of the debtor, a partnership if the debtor is a general partner, and a corporation if the debtor is an officer, a director, or a person in control. [B.C. § 101(31)(A) (insider), 101(9) (corporation), 101(45) (relative)]

b. Corporate Debtor

With respect to a corporate debtor, the following persons are insiders: directors, officers, persons in control of the debtor, general partners of the debtor, a partnership if the debtor is a general partner, and relatives of general partners, directors, officers, or person in control of the debtor. [B.C. § 101(31)(B)]

c. Partnership Debtor

With respect to a partnership debtor, the following persons are insiders: general partners in or of the debtor, persons in control of the debtor, a partnership if the debtor is a general partner, and relatives of general partners in or of the debtor, and of persons in control of the debtor. [B.C. § 101(31)(C)]

d. Affiliates and Managing Directors

The term "insider" also includes the following: (1) an affiliate of the debtor; (2) an insider of an affiliate; or (3) the debtor's managing director. [B.C. § 101(31)(E), (F)]

10. Insolvent

A debtor need not be insolvent to file for relief under Chapters 7, 11, 12, or 13. The definition of insolvent, however, is important in establishing the elements of several of the Code's avoiding powers. With the exception of a partnership, an entity is insolvent if its debts total more than the aggregate value of all of its property, excluding exempt property and property fraudulently transferred. [B.C. § 101(32)(A)] A partnership is insolvent if its debts exceed the total value of (a) all its property, excluding fraudulently transferred property, and (b) the sum of the amounts by which each general partner's personal, non-partnership assets, excluding exempt property and property fraudulently transferred, exceeds each partner's non-partnership debts. [B.C. § 101(32)(B)]

e.g. **Example:** Katya and Levin are general partners of Acme General Partnership. Acme owes $2 million to its creditors. Acme's property is currently valued at $1 million. Katya's non-exempt personal property is valued at $600,000; her personal, non-partnership debts amount to $300,000. Levin's non-exempt property is valued at $500,000; his personal, non-partnership debts equal $200,000. Acme is insolvent because its debts, which are $2 million, exceed $1.6 million, which is the sum of its assets and the net value of its partners' personal, non-partnership assets.

11. Lien

A *lien* is a charge against or an interest in property to secure payment of a debt or the performance of an obligation. [B.C. § 101(37)] A *judicial lien* is a lien obtained by judgment, levy, sequestration, or other legal or equitable proceeding or process. [B.C. § 101(36)] A *security interest* is consensual, i.e., is created by agreement. [B.C. § 101(51)]

12. Person

The term person includes *individuals, corporations, and partnerships.* With a limited exception for purposes of creditors' and equity security holders' committees formed under § 1102, the term person does not include a governmental unit. [B.C. §§ 101(41), 1102]

13. Transfer

A transfer means any of the following: (a) creation of a *lien;* (b) *retention of title* as a security interest; (c) foreclosure of a *debtor's equity of redemption;* or (d) any *direct or indirect, absolute or conditional, voluntary or involuntary* disposition of or parting with property or an interest in property. [B.C. § 101(54)]

F. Participants in the Bankruptcy Case

1. Bankruptcy Administrator

The United States trustee program does not operate in the six judicial districts in Alabama and North Carolina. In those six districts, a ***bankruptcy administrator*** performs many of the same functions in bankruptcy cases as does the United States trustee. Bankruptcy administrators operate under the jurisdiction of the Administrative Office of the United States Courts.

2. Bankruptcy Judge

For many years, under the Bankruptcy Act, the judicial officer in the case was called the "referee"; however, this terminology is now obsolete. Under the Bankruptcy Code, the judicial officer is referred to as the "bankruptcy judge."

3. Debtor

Under the Bankruptcy Act, the bankruptcy case was commenced against the "bankrupt." Under the Bankruptcy Code, the term is "debtor." [B.C. § 101(13)]

4. Debtor in Possession

In a non-subchapter V Chapter 11 case, the debtor is called a "debtor in possession," ***unless a trustee has been appointed.*** [B.C. § 1101(1)] In subchapter V, a trustee is routinely appointed, and the debtor remains a "debtor in possession" unless removed by the bankruptcy court. [B.C. §§ 1182(2), 1185] In Chapter 12, a trustee also is routinely appointed, and the debtor remains a "debtor in possession" unless removed by the bankruptcy court. [B.C. §§ 1203, 1204]

5. Trustee

The trustee is the official representative of the estate and, as such, exercises statutory powers principally for the benefit of the ***unsecured creditors.*** [B.C. § 323(a)] It is important to distinguish a case trustee, e.g., a Chapter 7 or Chapter 13 trustee, from the United States trustee.

6. United States Trustee

The United States trustee assumes many of the administrative responsibilities previously performed by the court, including the ***appointment and supervision of bankruptcy trustees,*** thereby helping to separate the administrative and judicial functions in bankruptcy cases. The United States trustee is appointed for a five-year term by the Attorney General. [28 U.S.C. §§ 581 *et seq.*] The United States trustee's office is a division of the Department of Justice. The program operates in 88 of the 94 judicial districts in the United States. In the remaining six districts in Alabama and North Carolina, bankruptcy administrators oversee the administration of bankruptcy cases.

7. Unsecured Creditor

An unsecured creditor is an entity holding a claim against the debtor that is not secured by collateral. For example, VISA or MasterCard are unsecured creditors, because the holders of such credit cards provide no collateral to secure their promise to pay the balance on their cards.

8. Secured Creditor

A secured creditor is an entity holding a claim against the debtor that is ***secured by a lien*** on property of the estate or that is ***subject to setoff.*** [B.C. § 506(a)(1)] A common type of secured creditor is the bank that finances the purchase of your automobile. You sign a note promising to pay back the money loaned to you by the bank to purchase the car, but the bank also takes a security interest in the vehicle as collateral for your promise to pay. If you fail to pay, the bank has the right to repossess the car.

9. Creditors' Committee

The Bankruptcy Code provides that in a Chapter 11 case, the United States trustee shall appoint a committee of unsecured creditors. The committee usually consists of those persons willing to serve that hold the ***seven largest unsecured claims*** against the debtor. The United States trustee may appoint additional committees of creditors or equity security holders. [B.C. § 1102(a)(1), (b)(1)] In many Chapter 11 cases, there is insufficient creditor interest to allow the United States trustee to form a committee of unsecured creditors. In ***small business cases*** and ***subchapter V cases,*** an official committee of unsecured creditors is ***not formed*** unless the court for cause orders otherwise. [B.C. § 1102(a)(3)]

If a creditors' committee is appointed, the committee may consult with the debtor in possession or with a trustee about administration of the case, investigate the debtor and the operation of its business, and participate in formulating an acceptable plan of reorganization. [B.C. §§ 1102, 1103(c)]

10. Equity Security Holder

An equity security holder is a holder of (a) a share or similar security in a corporation; (b) an interest of a limited partner in a limited partnership; or (c) a holder of a warrant or a right to buy or sell a security or interest in a corporation or limited partnership. [B.C. § 101(16), (17)]

In a Chapter 11 case, the United States trustee may appoint a committee of equity security holders, which ordinarily consists of those persons willing to serve that hold the ***seven largest amounts of the debtor's equity securities.*** [B.C. § 1102(a)(1), (2), (b)(2)]

11. Professional Persons

Professional persons, e.g., attorneys, accountants, appraisers, and auctioneers, often are hired by a trustee, a debtor in possession, or a creditors' or equity security holders' committee. They play an important role in the bankruptcy case, and the bankruptcy court must approve their employment and compensation. [B.C. §§ 327–331]

G. Bankruptcy Petition Preparers

1. Background

Bankruptcy petition preparers are not participants *in* the bankruptcy case. For a fee, they prepare petitions and other bankruptcy documents necessary to file a bankruptcy case. [B.C. § 110] In 1994, Congress added a new section to the Code to address concerns about bankruptcy petition preparers taking "unfair advantage of persons who are ignorant of their rights both inside and outside the bankruptcy system." [H.R. Rep. No. 103–385, at 56 (1994)] In 2005, Congress substantially amended the Code's provisions governing bankruptcy petition preparers.

2. Definitions

A *bankruptcy petition preparer* is a person, other than the debtor's attorney or an employee under the direct supervision of the debtor's attorney, who prepares for compensation a document for filing. [B.C. § 110(a)(1)] A *document for filing* is a petition or any other document prepared for filing by a debtor in the bankruptcy court or a district court in connection with a bankruptcy case. [B.C. § 110(a)(2)]

3. Filing Requirements

Before accepting fees or preparing any documents for filing, the bankruptcy petition preparer must provide the debtor with the notice contained in Official Form 119. [B.C. § 110(b)(2)] The bankruptcy petition preparer signs the form under *penalty of perjury.* [*See* Official Form 119, Part 2]

a. Individual Preparer

If the bankruptcy petition preparer is an *individual,* then she must *sign* and print her *name and address* on the document that she prepares. After her signature, the preparer must place her *social security number* and the social security number of any individual who assisted her in preparing the document for filing. [B.C. § 110(b)(1), (c)]

b. Preparer Not an Individual

If the bankruptcy petition preparer is *not an individual,* then an *officer, principal, responsible person, or partner* of the bankruptcy petition preparer must *sign* and print her *name and address* on the document. [B.C. § 110(b)(1)] The officer, principal, responsible person, or partner of the bankruptcy petition preparer must place her *social security number* after her signature on the document to be filed. [B.C. § 110(c)(2)(B)]

4. Document Copies

For any document that the debtor signs, the bankruptcy petition preparer must provide a copy to the debtor *no later* than the time that the *document is presented to the debtor for her signature.* [B.C. § 110(d)]

5. Prohibited Activities

The Bankruptcy Code prohibits the bankruptcy petition preparer from signing any documents on behalf of the debtor. [B.C. § 110(e)(1)] It *prohibits* a bankruptcy petition preparer from using the word "*legal*" or any similar word in any *advertisements,* and from advertising under any category that includes the word "legal" or any similar term. [B.C. § 110(f)] The Code also provides that the bankruptcy petition preparer cannot receive or collect any payment from the debtor or on behalf of the debtor for *court fees* in association with filing the bankruptcy case. [B.C. § 110(g)] Finally, a bankruptcy petition preparer cannot offer a potential debtor any *legal advice.* [B.C. § 110(e)(2)(A)]

a. What Constitutes Legal Advice?

A bankruptcy petition preparer *cannot advise* a potential debtor

(i) *whether to file* a bankruptcy petition or the *appropriate chapter* of the Code under which to file [B.C. § 110(e)(2)(B)(i)];

(ii) *whether debts will be discharged* in the bankruptcy case [B.C. § 110(e)(2)(B)(ii)];

(iii) whether debtor will be able to *keep her home, car, or other property* after bankruptcy [B.C. § 110(e)(2)(B)(iii)];

(iv) about the *tax consequences* of filing for bankruptcy or the *dischargeability of tax claims* [B.C. § 110(e)(2)(B)(iv)];

(v) whether debtor should promise to repay debts or enter into a *reaffirmation agreement* [B.C. § 110(e)(2)(B)(v)];

(vi) about how to characterize the nature of debtor's interests in property or the debtor's debts [B.C. § 110(e)(2)(B)(vi)]; or

(vii) about *bankruptcy rights and procedures.* [B.C. § 110(e)(2)(B)(vii)]

This is *not an exclusive list* of legal advice; instead, it merely lists some of the types of advice that the Code prevents bankruptcy petition preparers from offering to potential debtors.

Note: Bankruptcy petition preparers also may run afoul of state rules about the unauthorized practice of law. [*See* B.C. § 110(k)]

6. Fees

The Judicial Conference of the United States may establish guidelines for setting *maximum fees* that bankruptcy petition preparers may charge, but has done so yet. [B.C. § 110(h)(1); 2 Collier ¶ 110.08(1)] Some bankruptcy courts, however, have established maximum fees. [*See, e.g.,* Bankruptcy Petition Preparer Guidelines, Bankruptcy Court, Northern District of California (setting maximum fee of $150) *available at https://www.canb.uscourts.gov/ procedure/bankruptcy-petition-preparer-guidelines*] The bankruptcy petition preparer must file with the petition a *disclosure under penalty of perjury* of any *fee received* from or on behalf of the debtor in the *12 months prior* to the bankruptcy filing, as well as *any unpaid fee* charged to the debtor. [B.C. § 110(h)(2); Form 2800]

a. Excessive Fees

The court must *disallow* and order *immediate turnover* to the bankruptcy trustee of any fee found to be in (i) *excess of the value of services rendered* during the 12 months preceding the filing of the petition; or (ii) *violation of any fee rules or guidelines* established by the Supreme Court or the Judicial Conference of the United States. [B.C. § 110(h)(3); *see In re* **Graham,** 2004 WL 1052963 (Bankr. M.D. Ga. 2004), *aff'd,* **Anderson v. West,** 2005 WL 1719934 (M.D. N.C. 2005) (holding that $80 was reasonable value of bankruptcy petition preparer services, and disallowing and ordering turnover to Chapter 7 trustee of $119 of $199 fee charged for such services)] The bankruptcy petition preparer has the burden of proving the reasonableness of any fee she collects. [*In re* **Langford,** 2007 WL 3376664 (Bankr. M.D. N.C. 2007)]

(i) Failure to Turn over Fees

If the bankruptcy petition preparer fails to turn over disallowed fees within *30 days of service* of the court's order, the court will impose a *$500 fine* for each failure. [B.C. § 110(h)(5)]

(ii) Exempting Fees

An individual debtor may *exempt* any funds turned over. [B.C. § 110(h)(3)(C)]

(iii) The Motion

The court, on its own initiative, or the debtor, the trustee, a creditor, or the United States trustee or bankruptcy administrator may file a motion for disallowance and turnover of excessive fees. [B.C. § 110(h)(4)]

b. Fee Forfeiture

The bankruptcy court may order that the bankruptcy petition preparer *forfeit all fees in a case* in which the preparer fails to comply with § 110's rules governing bankruptcy petition preparers. [B.C. § 110(h)(3)(B)]

e.g. **Example:** Debtor hired Bankruptcy Petition Preparer ("BPP") to prepare various documents, including the petition, schedules, and statements, necessary to file for relief under Chapter 13. BPP failed to put his name or signature on any of the documents, as required by § 110(b)(1). None of the documents contained BPP's social security number, as required by § 110(c). Finally, BPP failed to file the declaration disclosing fees received from the debtor, as required by § 110(h)(2). The bankruptcy court concluded that these violations warranted forfeiture of all fees in the case. [*In re* **Warren**, 2012 WL 8145781 (Bankr. E.D. Cal. 2012)]

7. Damages and Fines

The Code provides for damages payable to the debtor and fines payable to the United States Trustee Fund for violations of the Code's rules governing bankruptcy petition preparers.

a. Damages

The debtor, trustee, or United States trustee or bankruptcy administrator may move for an award of *damages to the debtor* based on the conduct of a bankruptcy petition preparer. After notice and a hearing, the court must award damages to the debtor if a bankruptcy petition preparer violated any of the Code's rules governing bankruptcy petition preparers or the court determines that a bankruptcy petition preparer engaged in any *fraudulent, unfair, or deceptive act.* [B.C. § 110(i)(1)] The award of damages to the debtor shall include the following:

(i) the debtor's *actual damages* [B.C. § 110(i)(1)(A)];

(ii) the *greater* of either *$2,000* or *twice* the amount that the *debtor paid* for the bankruptcy petition preparer's services [B.C. § 110(i)(1)(B)]; *and*

(iii) reasonable *attorneys' fees and costs* in moving for damages [B.C. § 110(i)(1)(C)]

If the trustee or a creditor successfully moves for damages on the debtor's behalf, then the bankruptcy petition preparer must pay an *additional $1,000 to the trustee or creditor,* as well as reasonable attorneys' fees and costs. [B.C. § 110(i)(2)]

b. Fines

The debtor, trustee, creditor, United States trustee, or bankruptcy administrator may file a motion for an order imposing a fine on a bankruptcy petition preparer. [B.C. § 110(*l*)(3)] For *each failure* to comply with the Code's rules governing the conduct of bankruptcy petition preparers, the bankruptcy court may fine the bankruptcy petition preparer *$500.* [B.C. § 110(*l*)(1)] The bankruptcy court must *triple the fine* in any case in which the court finds that the bankruptcy petition preparer:

(i) *advised* the debtor to *exclude assets or income* that should have been disclosed on an applicable schedule [B.C. § 110(*l*)(2)(A)];

(ii) *advised* the debtor to use a *false social security number* [B.C. § 110(*l*)(2)(B)];

(iii) *failed* to tell the debtor that the debtor was filing for bankruptcy relief [B.C. § 110(*l*)(2)(C)]; or

(iv) prepared a document for filing that *failed to disclose the identity of the bankruptcy petition preparer* [B.C. § 110(*l*)(2)(D)]

In districts in which the United States trustee operates, any fine imposed must be paid to the United States trustee, who must deposit it in the **United States Trustee Fund.** [B.C. § 110(*l*)(4)(A)] In one of the six judicial districts in which bankruptcy administrators operate, the fine must be deposited into the special fund of the Treasury available to *offset funds appropriated for operation and maintenance of the courts* of the United States. [B.C. § 110(*l*)(4)(B); 28 U.S.C. § 1931]

Example: Bankruptcy Petition Preparer ("BPP") prepared seven documents for Debtor's Chapter 13 filing. None of the documents contained BPP's name or social security number, as required by the Code. [*See* B.C. § 110(b)(1), (c)] While the Code provides that the court may fine a BPP $500 for each failure to comply with the Code's rules, the bankruptcy court determined that $7,000 (7 documents x $500 for failure to provide name and 7 documents x $500 for failure to provide social security number) was excessive, given that court was not aware of any other case in which BPP had failed to comply with § 110's rules. Instead, court concluded that $1,400 was the appropriate fine under § 110(*l*)(1). However, BPP's failure to disclose his identity on the documents prepared for Debtor meant that the $1,400 fine was tripled, pursuant to § 110(*l*)(2)(D). [*In re* **Warren**, *supra*]

8. Injunctions

The bankruptcy court may enjoin a bankruptcy petition preparer from engaging in certain conduct or from acting as a bankruptcy petition preparer. A debtor, trustee, creditor, the United States trustee for the district in which the bankruptcy petition preparer resides or has conducted business, or the United States trustee for the district in which the debtor resides may bring a civil action for such an injunction. [B.C. § 110(j)(1)] The bankruptcy petitioner preparer must pay the *reasonable attorneys' fees and costs* to a debtor, trustee, or creditor that brings a successful action for injunctive relief. [B.C. § 110(j)(4)]

a. Injunction: Particular Acts

If the bankruptcy court determines that the bankruptcy petition preparer has (i) *violated* any of the *Code's rules governing bankruptcy petition preparers* or any other provision of the Bankruptcy Code; (ii) *misrepresented* her *experience or education* as a bankruptcy petition preparer; or (iii) engaged in any *fraudulent, unfair, or deceptive conduct,* then the court may enjoin the bankruptcy petition preparer from engaging in such conduct if injunctive relief is appropriate to prevent a recurrence of the conduct. [B.C. § 110(j)(2)(A)]

b. Injunction: Acting as Bankruptcy Petition Preparer

The bankruptcy court may enjoin a person from acting as a bankruptcy petition preparer if:

(i) she has *continually engaged* in any of the proscribed conduct described above and an *injunction is not sufficient* to prevent her interference with the proper administration of the Code;

(ii) she has *not paid a penalty* imposed; or

(iii) she has *failed to disgorge all fees* ordered by the court.

[B.C. § 110(j)(2)(B)]

c. Injunction: Contempt Power

As part of its contempt power, the bankruptcy court may enjoin a bankruptcy petition preparer who has failed to comply with a prior order of the court under § 110. The court may issue such an injunction on its own motion or on the motion of the trustee, United States trustee, or bankruptcy administrator. [B.C. § 110(j)(3); *see* **Fuller v. United States Trustee,** 2012 WL 4514174 (N.D. W.Va. 2012) (affirming bankruptcy court order under § 110(j)(3) permanently enjoining two bankruptcy petition preparers from acting as bankruptcy petition preparers in district, based on multiple violations of prior bankruptcy court order that defined and limited services preparers could provide, and requiring preparers to turn over excessive fees charged)]

Chapter Two
Jurisdiction and Procedure; Sovereign Immunity

Chapter Approach

This Chapter covers the structure and operation of the bankruptcy court system, and the limitations, constitutional and statutory, on the powers exercised by bankruptcy courts.

A bankruptcy court is an Article I court and constitutes a unit of the federal district court. The federal district court *refers cases and proceedings* to the bankruptcy judges in the district. The district court can withdraw the reference, and this Chapter covers the rules on *permissive* and *mandatory withdrawal of the reference.*

Because the bankruptcy court is an Article I court, there are certain types of proceedings in which the court cannot render a *final judgment or order.* Your professor may test your understanding of the types of proceedings in which the bankruptcy court may issue a final judgment or order. The following series of questions should guide your analysis.

1. Is the pending matter a *statutory core* or a *non-core* proceeding?

2. Even if the matter falls within one of the non-exclusive sixteen categories of statutory core proceedings under 28 U.S.C. § 157(b)(2), you still must ask whether it is a *Stern claim.*

3. If the matter is a *Stern* claim, have the parties *consented* to the bankruptcy court entering a final order or judgment?

4. If the parties have not consented, did the bankruptcy court follow the procedure for *non-core proceedings* set forth at 28 U.S.C. § 157(c)?

    Remember: Absent consent of the parties, it is the district court, *not the bankruptcy court,* which must enter final orders and judgments on *Stern* claims and non-core proceedings.

Your professor also may test your knowledge of abstention—*permissive and mandatory.* Make sure that you distinguish between abstaining from hearing a *single proceeding* that is but one component of the bankruptcy case versus abstaining, under § 305, from hearing the *entire bankruptcy case*.

You should know the *four statutory alternatives* to establish appropriate venue for filing a bankruptcy petition. What does the bankruptcy court consider when ruling on a request for change of venue?

Understand the *three paths* available for appealing a decision of the bankruptcy court. You should know when a *bankruptcy appellate panel* can hear an appeal, and the precedential value of the panel's decision. You also should know the requirements for a *direct appeal* to the circuit.

The Chapter wraps up with a short discussion of sovereign immunity and Code § 106.

A. Bankruptcy Courts: Structure and Operation

1. Unit of a District Court

The bankruptcy court in each federal judicial district constitutes a unit of the district court, which *refers* cases and proceedings to the bankruptcy judges for the district. [28 U.S.C. §§ 151, 157(a)] Bankruptcy judges serve as *judicial officers* of the United States district court established under Article III of the Constitution. [28 U.S.C. § 152(a)(1)] The bankruptcy court is an *Article I, not an Article III, court.*

2. Appointment of Bankruptcy Judges

Bankruptcy judges are appointed for a judicial district by the United States court of appeals for the circuit in which the district is located. For example, the Sixth Circuit Court of Appeals appoints the bankruptcy judges for the Eastern District of Michigan. The judge's *term is for 14 years.* [28 U.S.C. § 152(a)(1)] Only the judicial council for the circuit in which the bankruptcy judge's official duty station is located may remove the judge during the judge's term, but removal is only for incompetence, misconduct, neglect of duty, or physical or mental disability. [28 U.S.C. § 152(e)]

3. Chief Bankruptcy Judge

In each district court having more than one bankruptcy judge the district court must designate one judge to serve as *chief bankruptcy judge* of such bankruptcy court. The chief bankruptcy judge must ensure that the bankruptcy court and district court rules are observed and that the business of the bankruptcy court is handled effectively and expeditiously. [28 U.S.C. § 154(b)]

4. Staff of the Bankruptcy Court

Each bankruptcy judge may appoint a secretary and a law clerk, as well as any additional assistants deemed necessary by the Director of the Administrative Office of the United States Courts. [28 U.S.C. § 156(a)] If there is a sufficient number of bankruptcy cases and proceedings within a particular jurisdiction, the bankruptcy judges for that district may appoint a clerk of the court. [28 U.S.C. § 156(b)] The bankruptcy court clerk is the official custodian of all bankruptcy court records and dockets, and must pay into the United States Treasury all fees, costs, and other monies that she collects. [28 U.S.C. § 156(e), (f)]

5. Bankruptcy Court Records

With certain exceptions, any papers filed in a bankruptcy case and all dockets are *public records* and open to examination by any entity at reasonable times without charge.

a. Exceptions: Trade Secrets and Defamation

The bankruptcy court must, on request of a party in interest, or may, on its own motion, protect:

(i) an entity with regard to a *trade secret or confidential research, development, or commercial information* [B.C. § 107(b)(1)]; or

(ii) a person with regard to *scandalous or defamatory matter* contained in a paper filed in a bankruptcy case [B.C. § 107(b)(2)]

b. Exceptions: Identify Theft

In 2005, Congress added protections to the Code related to concerns about identify theft. The court also may protect an *individual* with regard to the following kinds of information to the extent that the court finds that *disclosure of such information* would create an *undue risk of identity theft* or other *unlawful injury* to the individual or the individual's property:

(i) Any *means of identification,* e.g., social security number, driver's license number, birth date, contained in a paper or to be filed in a bankruptcy case. [B.C. § 107(c)(1)(A); 18 U.S.C. § 1028(d)(7)]

(ii) Any *other information* contained in a paper containing a means of identification that is filed or is to be filed in a bankruptcy case. [B.C. § 107(c)(1)(B)]

Exception: Upon an *ex parte application demonstrating cause,* the court must provide access to the information described above to an entity acting pursuant to the *police or regulatory power* of a domestic governmental unit. [B.C. § 107(c)(2)]

c.   Access to Information

The United States trustee, bankruptcy administrator, trustee or any auditor serving under 28 U.S.C. § 586(f) (case audits) must have *full access to all information* contained in any paper filed or submitted in a bankruptcy case and *must not disclose* any information specifically protected under § 107 of the Code. [B.C. § 107(c)(3)]

B. Bankruptcy Courts: Powers

1. Power of Court

The bankruptcy judge may issue any *necessary or appropriate order, process, or judgment* to carry out the Code's provisions. [B.C. § 105(a); *see* **Marrama v. Citizens Bank,** 549 U.S. 365 (2007) (stating that "broad authority granted to bankruptcy judges" under § 105(a) was "surely adequate" to authorize the bankruptcy court, notwithstanding the language of § 706(a), to deny Chapter 7 debtor's motion to convert to Chapter 13, in order to address abusive litigation practices)] The bankruptcy court, however, may not exercise its power under § 105(a) in such a fashion as to "contravene specific statutory provisions." [**Law v. Siegel,** 571 U.S. 415 (2014) (in unanimous opinion, stating that § 105(a) does not authorize a bankruptcy court " 'to override explicit mandates of other [Code] sections' " and holding that bankruptcy court erred in surcharging all of debtor's homestead exemption to pay administrative expenses associated with debtor's misconduct, because the surcharge contravened the provisions of § 522 of the Code)] The bankruptcy court does not have the authority to appoint a receiver. [B.C. § 105(b)]

a.   Sua Sponte Action by Court

Nothing in the Bankruptcy Code precludes the bankruptcy court from, *sua sponte,* taking any necessary or appropriate action to enforce its orders or rules, or to prevent an abuse of process. [B.C. § 105(a); *see, e.g.,* **McInnis v. Santa Cruz County Tax Collector (***In re* **McInnis),** 2018 Bankr. LEXIS 3933 (B.A.P. 9th Cir. 2018) ("§ 105(a) allows a bankruptcy court to dismiss a case sua sponte for abuse of process")]

b.   Status Conferences

The court, on its own motion or on the request of a party in interest, must hold such status conferences as are necessary to further the *expeditious and economical resolution* of the bankruptcy case. Unless inconsistent with the Code or the Bankruptcy Rules, the court may issue orders at such conferences that it considers appropriate to ensure that the case is handled expeditiously and economically. [B.C. § 105(d)(2)] Such orders may:

(i)   set a deadline for the trustee to assume or reject an executory contract or unexpired lease [B.C. § 105(d)(2)(A)]; or

(ii) in a non-subchapter V Chapter 11 case,

    (1)   set a deadline for the debtor or trustee to file a disclosure statement and plan or to solicit acceptances of a plan [B.C. § 105(d)(2)(B)(i), (ii)];

(2) set a deadline for other parties in interest to file a plan or solicit acceptances of a plan [B.C. §§ 105(d)(2)(B)(iii), (iv)];

(3) fix the scope and format of the notice of the hearing on the disclosure statement [B.C. § 105(d)(2)(B)(v)]; or

(4) provide that the disclosure statement hearing be combined with the confirmation hearing. [B.C. § 105(d)(2)(B)(vi)]

(iii) Subchapter V

Section 105(d) **does not apply** in subchapter V. [B.C. § 1181(a); *see infra* Chapter Thirteen, § H.5.g on the subchapter V status conference]

c. Contempt

Most courts have held that the bankruptcy court has the authority, either inherently or under § 105, to impose sanctions for civil contempt. [**Price v. Lehtinen (*In re* Lehtinen),** 564 F.3d 1052 (9th Cir. 2009) (stating that bankruptcy courts "generally have the power to sanction attorneys pursuant to (1) their civil contempt authority under 11 U.S.C. § 105(a); and (2) their inherent sanction authority")] In **Taggart v. Lorenzen,** 139 S. Ct. 1795 (2019), the Supreme Court, in a unanimous decision, adopted the **fair ground of doubt** standard for determining whether a creditor's conduct violates a bankruptcy court's discharge order, thereby subjecting the creditor to sanctions for civil contempt. The Court held that §§ 524 and 105(a) "authorize a court to impose civil contempt sanctions when there is **no objectively reasonable basis** for concluding that the creditor's conduct" was lawful.

It is unclear whether a bankruptcy court may impose criminal contempt sanctions. The circuits are split on the issue. [*See* discussion of cases in *In re* **Hake,** 350 B.R. 628 (B.A.P. 6th Cir. 2006); *see also* **Kittywalk Systems v. Midnight Pass Inc. (*In re* Midnight Pass Inc.),** 2009 WL 3583957 (Bankr. D. Mass. 2009) (noting circuit split)]

d. Sanctions

The bankruptcy court may impose sanctions on attorneys, law firms, or parties who sign, file, or submit pleadings or other documents, or advocate for positions that (i) are **not well-grounded in fact or in law,** allowing for good faith arguments for change of existing law, or (ii) are filed for any **improper purpose.** [Bankruptcy Rule 9011(b), (c)] The court may impose sanctions only after notice and a reasonable opportunity to respond. [Bankruptcy Rule 9011(c)] This rule on sanctions does not apply to disclosures and discovery requests, responses, objections, and motions subject to bankruptcy rules governing adversary proceedings. [Bankruptcy Rules 9011(d), 7026–7037]

e. Substantive Consolidation

In appropriate circumstances, the court may order the substantive consolidation of debtors' estates, i.e., the pooling of their assets, debts, and causes of action. The power to substantively consolidate debtors' estates is derived from § 105(a). There is no single test that courts use in making the decision to substantively consolidate. Courts have developed "two distinct types of tests"—"a more traditional, factor based test and a balancing test." "Under the traditional test, courts look to several factors in determining whether substantive consolidation is appropriate" while the balancing test "focus[es] on the impact of consolidating the creditors and weighing it against the benefits of consolidation." [*In re* **Introgen Therapeutics,** 429 B.R. 570 (Bankr. W.D. Tex. 2010)]

(i) Distinguish—Procedural Consolidation

Substantive consolidation is rare. ***Procedural consolidation,*** also known as ***joint administration,*** is more common. A court may grant a motion for joint administration for administrative purposes for cases involving two or more related debtors, such as (i) a husband and wife, (ii) a partnership and a general partner, (iii) two or more general partners, or (iv) affiliated entities. [Bankruptcy Rule 1015(b); *see* B.C. § 101(2) (definition of affiliate)] Joint administration is a "procedural tool permitting use of a single docket for administrative matters, including the listing of filed claims, the combining of notices to creditors of the different estates, and the joint handling of other ministerial matters that may aid in expediting the cases." [**Reider v. FDIC (*In re* Reider),** 31 F.3d 1102 (11th Cir. 1994)]

C. Personal Jurisdiction

1. In General

The Bankruptcy Rules provide for ***nationwide service of process*** by first class prepaid mail, except for subpoenas, in adversary proceedings and contested matters. [Bankruptcy Rules 7004(b), (d), 9014(b)] Personal jurisdiction is established over a defendant in an adversary proceeding or respondent in a contested matter if service of process conforms with Rule 7004 and "the exercise of jurisdiction is consistent with the Constitution and laws of the United States." [Bankruptcy Rule 7004(f)] Courts typically do not use the "minimum contacts" test. Instead, many conclude that because bankruptcy issues are matters of federal question jurisdiction and the bankruptcy rules provide for nationwide service, a court has personal jurisdiction over any person with ***sufficient minimum contacts with the United States,*** not with the state in which the bankruptcy case is pending. Not all courts, however, use this ***"national contacts" test.*** Some courts have held that due process requires consideration of the ***Fifth Amendment's reasonableness and fairness*** requirements. [*See, e.g., **In re* Correra,** 589 B.R. 76 (Bankr. N.D. Tex. 2018) (discussing two approaches courts take to analysis of personal jurisdiction); **Gonzales v. Miller (*In re* Texas Reds, Inc.),** 2010 WL 1711112 (Bankr. D. N.M. 2010)]

2. Service of Process: Insured Depository Institutions

Service of process on an insured depository institution requires certified mail, rather than simply first class mail, to an officer of the institution, unless

a. the institution has appeared by its attorney, in which case the attorney must be served by first class mail [Bankruptcy Rule 7004(h)(1)];

b. the institution has waived in writing its entitlement to certified mail by designating an officer to receive service [Bankruptcy Rule 7004(h)(3)]; or

c. the court orders otherwise after service by certified mail of an application to permit service by first class mail is sent to an officer of the institution that the institution designates. [Bankruptcy Rule 7004(h)(2)]

The officer does not have to be correctly named, or even be named, if the envelope is addressed to the proper address and directed to the attention of the officer's position or title. [Bankruptcy Rule 7004(i)] Thus, service to an insured depository institution at its proper address and directed to the attention of the President, Chief Executive Officer, Officer for Receiving Service of Process, or similar titles suffices. [Bankruptcy Rule 7004(i), Committee Notes on 2022 Amendment]

D. Subject Matter Jurisdiction

1. District Courts

The United States district courts have *original and exclusive jurisdiction* over *all cases* under the Bankruptcy Code. [28 U.S.C. § 1334(a)] The district courts have *original but not exclusive* jurisdiction over *all civil proceedings* arising under, or arising in or related to the bankruptcy case. [28 U.S.C. § 1334(b)] Finally, the district courts have *exclusive jurisdiction* (i) of all of the *debtor's property*, wherever located, as of the commencement of the bankruptcy case; (ii) of *property of the estate;* and (iii) over *all claims or causes of action* involving construction of or rules relating to disclosure requirements under *§ 327* on employment of professional persons. [28 U.S.C. § 1334(e)]

2. Referral to Bankruptcy Courts

Each district has its own rule automatically referring all bankruptcy cases and proceedings to the bankruptcy judges in the district. [*See* 28 U.S.C. § 157(a); *see, e.g.,* W.D. Mich. LCivR 3.1(a) (Western District of Michigan); L.R. 81.1 (Northern District of New York)]

E. Core Versus Non-Core Proceedings

1. Introduction

There are three categories of proceedings in a bankruptcy case: proceedings that (i) *arise under* title 11; (ii) *arise in* a bankruptcy case; or (iii) *are related to* a bankruptcy case. [28 U.S.C. § 157(a)] Whether the bankruptcy court may enter *final judgments and orders* in a proceeding depends on whether the proceeding is a *statutory core or non-core proceeding* and, if the former, *whether it is a Stern claim.* The bankruptcy judge, either on her own motion or on the timely motion of a party, must determine whether a proceeding is core or non-core. The fact that State law may affect the resolution of the proceeding is not solely determinative of the core versus non-core nature of the proceeding. [28 U.S.C. § 157(b)(3)]

a. Core Proceedings

Core proceedings are those that *arise under title 11* or *arise in a bankruptcy case.* [28 U.S.C. § 157(b)(1); **Stern v. Marshall,** 564 U.S. 462 (2011) (stating that "core proceedings are those that arise in a bankruptcy case or under Title 11")] In a *core proceeding,* the bankruptcy court has the *statutory authority* to enter *final judgments and orders,* subject to regular appellate review. [28 U.S.C. §§ 157(b)(1), 158(a)] Congress apparently took the word "core" from Justice Brennan's plurality opinion in *Marathon.* [*See* **Northern Pipeline Construction Co. v. Marathon Pipe Line Company,** 458 U.S. 50 (1982) (noting that "the restructuring of debtor-creditor relations [ ] is at the core of the federal bankruptcy power")]

(i) Statutory Categories

After *Marathon,* Congress passed the Bankruptcy Amendments and Federal Judgeship Act of 1984, which, in part, created a *non-exclusive list* of *16 categories of core proceedings.* [Pub. L. No. 98–353 (1984) (15 categories in original legislation)] The statutory core proceedings include the following:

(1) matters involving *estate administration* [28 U.S.C. § 157(b)(2)(A)];

(2) the allowance or disallowance of *claims* against the estate or *exemptions* from estate property, and *estimation of claims and interests* for purposes of confirming a plan, *but not* the liquidation or estimation of contingent or unliquidated personal injury tort or wrongful death claims for purposes of distribution in a bankruptcy case [28 U.S.C. § 157(b)(2)(B)];

(3) *counterclaims* by the estate against persons filing claims [28 U.S.C. § 157(b)(2)(C)];

(4) orders to *obtain credit* [28 U.S.C. § 157(b)(2)(D)];

(5) *turnover* orders [28 U.S.C. § 157(b)(2)(E)];

(6) *preference* actions [28 U.S.C. § 157(b)(2)(F)];

(7) motions to terminate, annul, or modify *the automatic stay* [28 U.S.C. § 157(b)(2)(G)];

(8) *fraudulent conveyance* actions [28 U.S.C. § 157(b)(2)(H)];

(9) determinations of *dischargeability* [28 U.S.C. § 157(b)(2)(I)];

(10) *discharge objections* [28 U.S.C. § 157(b)(2)(J)];

(11) determinations of the *validity, extent, or priority of liens* [28 U.S.C. § 157(b)(2)(K)];

(12) *plan confirmations* [28 U.S.C. § 157(b)(2)(L)];

(13) orders approving the *use or lease of property,* including the use of cash collateral [28 U.S.C. § 157(b)(2)(M)];

(14) orders approving the *sale of property,* except property resulting from claims brought by the estate against persons who had not filed claims [28 U.S.C. § 157(b)(2)(N)];

(15) with the exception of personal injury tort or wrongful death claims, *other proceedings* affecting liquidation of estate assets or adjustment of the debtor-creditor or equity security holder relationship [28 U.S.C. § 157(b)(2)(O)]; and

(16) recognition of *foreign proceedings and other matters under Chapter 15* [28 U.S.C. § 157(b)(2)(P)].

(ii) The *Stern* Problem

(1) In ***Stern v. Marshall,*** the Supreme Court drew into question the framework that Congress had created post-*Marathon.* The Court held that while the bankruptcy court had *the statutory authority under § 157(b)(2)(C)* to enter a final judgment on the debtor's counterclaim for tortious interference, it *did not have the constitutional authority* to do so.

> **Example:** Debtor Vickie filed a state probate court action prior to bankruptcy against Pierce, her husband's son, claiming that Pierce had fraudulently induced Vickie's husband to sign a living trust that did not include her. After her husband died, Vickie filed for bankruptcy, and Pierce filed a complaint in the bankruptcy case claiming that Vickie had defamed him by having her lawyers tell members of the press that Pierce had engaged in fraud to gain control of his father's assets. Pierce filed a proof of claim for the defamation action and sought to have any debt declared non-dischargeable. Vickie filed a counterclaim for tortious interference with the gift that she had

expected from her deceased husband. The Supreme Court agreed that Vickie's counterclaim was a statutory core proceeding under § 157(b)(2)(C), but that Article III of the Constitution did not permit the bankruptcy court to enter a final judgment on Vickie's counterclaim. The Court explained that Vickie's counterclaim did not involve public rights, but instead was a claim "under state common law between two private parties." Moreover, the Court concluded that the fact that Pierce had filed a claim in Vickie's case was not relevant, because the issue was the nature of Vickie's counterclaim for tortious interference; it was the "very type of claim" that the Court had held in its earlier decisions in *Marathon* and **Granfinanciera v. Nordberg,** 492 U.S. 33 (1989) had to be decided by an Article III court. The Court also noted "there was never any reason to believe that the process of adjudicating Pierce's proof of claim would necessarily resolve Vickie's counterclaim." Finally, the Court rejected the idea that Pierce had consented to the bankruptcy court's resolution of Vickie's counterclaim, stating that Pierce "had nowhere else to go if he wished to recover from Vickie's estate." [**Stern,** *supra*]

(2) ***Remember:*** A *Stern* claim is one that falls within the list of core proceedings under § 157(b)(2), but on which the bankruptcy court cannot enter a final judgment or order, because doing so would violate Article III of the Constitution.

(iii) Dealing with *Stern* Claims

The Supreme Court handed down two decisions after *Stern* that explained how bankruptcy courts should handle *Stern* claims.

(1) *Executive Benefits*

In *Executive Benefits,* the Supreme Court, in a unanimous decision, held that the procedure governing non-core proceedings under *§ 157(c) applies to Stern claims.* The Court explained that when faced with a *Stern* claim, the bankruptcy court should enter proposed findings of fact and conclusions of law, which the district court reviews *de novo* before entering a final judgment in the proceeding. [**Executive Benefits Insurance Agency v. Arkison,** 573 U.S. 25 (2014)]

(2) *Wellness*

In *Wellness,* the Supreme Court held that if the parties to a *Stern* claim consent, then the bankruptcy court may enter a final order or judgment on the *Stern* claim. Consent must be ***knowing and voluntary,*** but ***need not be express.*** [**Wellness International Network, Ltd. v. Sharif,** 575 U.S. 665 (2015)]

b. Non-Core Proceedings

In a ***non-core*** proceeding that is otherwise related to the bankruptcy case, the bankruptcy court must submit ***proposed findings of fact and conclusions of law*** to the district court, which enters a final judgment or order, after conducting a ***de novo review*** on all matters on which a party has timely and specifically objected. [28 U.S.C. § 158(c)(1)] If all the parties ***consent,*** however, the bankruptcy court may enter final judgments and orders, subject to appellate review, in a ***non-core*** proceeding. [28 U.S.C. § 157(c)(2)]

(i) Personal Injury and Wrongful Death Claims

Proceedings to estimate or liquidate personal injury tort or wrongful death claims for purposes of distribution are not core and must be tried in the district court. [28 U.S.C. § 157(b)(2)(B), (b)(5)]

e.g. **Example:** Prior to bankruptcy, Debtor sold her home to the Deans. The Deans subsequently discovered that the basement of the home was contaminated with mold. The Deans filed suit against Debtor, and the case was submitted to binding arbitration. The arbitrator ruled in favor of the Deans on their property damage claim, and Debtor subsequently filed for relief under Chapter 13. The Deans filed an adversary proceeding in Debtor's Chapter 13 case, objecting to the discharge of a personal injury claim that the automatic stay prevented them from pursuing in state court. (Debtor had scheduled the claim as disputed, contingent, and unliquidated.) The bankruptcy court held that it lacked the "authority to liquidate or estimate the Deans' personal injury claim" and, thus, could not determine whether the claim was nondischargeable. As a result, the court granted the Debtor's motion to dismiss the Deans' adversary proceeding. [**Dean v. Lane (*In re* Lane)**, 2018 WL 1027339 (Bankr. W.D. Ky. 2018)]

c. Summary

(i) If the proceeding falls into one of the statutory categories of core proceedings and is not a *Stern* claim, then the bankruptcy court may enter a final judgment or order.

(ii) If the proceeding falls into one of the statutory categories of core proceedings and is a *Stern* claim, then the bankruptcy court may enter a final judgment or order only with the parties' consent.

(iii) If the proceeding falls into one of the statutory categories of core proceedings and is a *Stern* claim but the parties do not consent to the bankruptcy court entering a final order or judgment, then the bankruptcy court must submit proposed findings of fact and conclusions of law to the district court to review *de novo*.

(iv) If the proceeding is non-core, then the bankruptcy court may enter a final judgment or order with the parties' consent.

(v) If the proceeding is non-core but the parties do not consent to the bankruptcy court entering a final order or judgment, then the bankruptcy court must submit proposed findings of fact and conclusions of law to the district court to review *de novo*.

F. Jury Trials

1. Right to Jury Trial

The United States Supreme Court has held that the Seventh Amendment to the Constitution entitles a party that has ***not filed a claim*** against the bankruptcy estate to a jury trial of an action by the bankruptcy trustee against that party to recover an allegedly fraudulent conveyance. The Court set out the following framework for analyzing the right to a jury trial.

a. Would the cause of action have been brought ***at law*** in 18th Century England "prior to the merger of the courts of law and equity"?

b. Is the remedy requested ***legal*** in nature?

c. Does the action involve a ***private as opposed to a public right?***

[**Granfinanciera, S.A. v. Nordberg**, 492 U.S. 33 (1989)]

Example—No Claim Filed Against Estate: Debtor Corporation filed for relief under Chapter 11. The Chapter 11 trustee filed suit against two corporations (Granfinanciera and Medex), seeking $1.7 million in allegedly fraudulent transfers. Neither corporation had filed a claim against Debtor's estate; both requested a jury trial of the trustee's fraudulent conveyance action. The Supreme Court held that Granfinanciera and Medex were entitled under the Seventh Amendment to a jury trial. The Court first concluded that in 18th-century England the trustee would have had to bring his fraudulent conveyance action at law, because it involved a "determinate sum of money" and a "court of equity would not have adjudicated it." The Court next explained that the Chapter 11 trustee sought the payment of money, which is the traditional relief at law. Finally, the Court concluded that a fraudulent conveyance action under § 548(a)(2) is "more accurately characterized as a private rather than a public right as [the Court] used those terms in [its] Article III decisions." The fact that Congress had designated fraudulent conveyance actions as "core" did not alter the Court's conclusion. [**Granfinanciera,** *supra; see* **Schoenthal v. Irving Trust Co.,** 287 U.S. 92 (1932) (Bankruptcy Act case in which bankruptcy trustee sought to recover preferences from recipients who had not filed claims against the bankruptcy estate, holding that bankruptcy trustee had an adequate remedy at law and a suit in equity could not be maintained, and, thus, recipients of alleged preferences had a Seventh Amendment right to jury trial)]

Example—Claim Filed Against Estate: Debtors were uninsured, non-bank institutions that filed for relief under Chapter 11. Creditors held savings certificates issued by Debtors. In the 90 days prior to Debtors' bankruptcy filing, Creditors redeemed some, but not all, of those savings certificates. Creditors filed proofs of claim in Debtors' bankruptcy case. The Chapter 11 trustee filed adversary proceedings in the bankruptcy case to recover the preferential payments. In a per curiam opinion, the Supreme Court held that Creditors were not entitled to a jury trial in the trustee's preference action because they had filed claims in Debtors' bankruptcy case. The Court noted that in *Granfinanciera* it had explained that a creditor triggers the claims allowance process when the creditor files a claim. If the trustee then commences a preference action, that action "becomes part of the claims-allowance process which is triable only in equity." Thus, by filing claims, Creditors brought "themselves with the equitable jurisdiction of the Bankruptcy Court" and were not entitled to a jury trial. [**Langenkamp v. Culp,** 498 U.S. 42 (1990)]

2. Power of Bankruptcy Judges to Hold Jury Trials

In *Granfinanciera,* the Supreme Court did not decide whether bankruptcy courts could conduct jury trials. [**Granfinanciera,** *supra* (stating that it was not deciding whether 28 U.S.C. § 1411 allowed "bankruptcy courts to conduct jury trials in fraudulent conveyance actions")] In 1994, Congress amended title 28 of the United States Code to authorize bankruptcy judges to conduct jury trials, provided that the ***district court specially designates the exercise of this jurisdiction*** and ***all parties expressly consent.*** [28 U.S.C. § 157(e)] The reason for the 1994 amendment was to clarify the Supreme Court's *Granfinanciera* decision and resolve a circuit split. [H.R. Rep. No. 103–385, at 42 (1994) (explaining that "[T]he *Granfinanciera* court had no finding on whether bankruptcy judges could conduct civil trials, and the circuits have reached contrary opinions regarding this issue")] The requirement of express consent in § 157(e) resolves the constitutional question of whether a bankruptcy court—an Article I court—may hold a jury trial. [1 Collier ¶ 3.08(3); *see* **Wellness International v. Sharif,** 575 U.S. 665 (2015) (holding that Article III is not violated if the parties "knowingly and voluntarily consent to adjudication by a bankruptcy judge")]

3. Involuntary Cases

The district court may order that the issues arising in an involuntary bankruptcy case be tried without a jury. [28 U.S.C. § 1411(b)]

4. Personal Injury and Wrongful Death

Nothing in the Bankruptcy Code or in Chapter 87 (district courts) of Title 28 of the United States Code affects an individual's right to a jury trial under applicable nonbankruptcy law with regard to a *personal injury or wrongful death tort claim.* [28 U.S.C. § 1411(a)]

G. Withdrawal of the Reference

1. Permissive Withdrawal

The district court, either on its own motion or on the timely motion of a party, *for cause* may withdraw, in whole or in part, a case or proceeding that has been referred to the bankruptcy court. [28 U.S.C. § 157(d)] The district court judge must hear the motion to withdraw the reference. [Bankruptcy Rule 5011(a)] Courts have articulated various factors that they consider relevant to the permissive withdrawal analysis. [*See, e.g.,* **Shalom Torah Centers v. Philadelphia Indemnity Insurance Companies,** 2011 WL 1322295 (D. N.J. 2011) (stating that court first should determine whether the proceeding is core or non-core, and then evaluate whether withdrawal would promote uniformity, reduce forum shopping, further the economical use of debtor's and creditors' resources, and expedite the bankruptcy process)] It is important to remember that the statute uses the term "may" not "shall" in the first sentence; therefore, even if the court finds cause, it still may decline to withdraw the reference. [28 U.S.C. § 157(d)]

2. Mandatory Withdrawal

On a timely motion, the district court must withdraw a proceeding from the bankruptcy court if *its resolution* requires consideration of *both* the Bankruptcy Code *and* a *nonbankruptcy federal statute* "regulating organizations or activities affecting interstate commerce." [28 U.S.C. § 157(d)] While the statute says that withdrawal is mandated when resolution requires consideration of *both* the Code and a non-Code federal statute, the vast majority of courts have ignored the express statutory language. Instead, they have interpreted § 157(d) to mandate withdrawal if resolution of the dispute requires "*substantial and material*" consideration of the *non-Code federal statute* and that statute has *more than a de minimis impact* on interstate commerce. [1 Collier ¶ 3.04(2)] Withdrawal is not mandated if the dispute only involves a " 'simple application of well-settled law' "; withdrawal is mandated, however, to resolve " 'complicated, interpretive issues' ", in particular issues of first impression. [**Harrelson v. DSSC, Inc.,** 2015 WL 1043338 (M.D. Ala. 2015)] Mandatory withdrawal is not implicated if the dispute requires resolution of a state law, as opposed to a nonbankruptcy federal law. [**Mooring Capital Fund, LLC v. Sullivan,** 2016 WL 4628572 (N.D. W. Va. 2016)]

3. Appeals

A district court order either denying or granting a motion to withdraw the reference is not an appealable final order. [28 U.S.C. § 158(d)(1); *see* **Khan v. Mahia,** 567 Fed. Appx. 53 (2d Cir. 2014) (denial of motion to withdraw the reference of adversary proceeding is not a final order); **Springel v. Prosser (*In re* Prosser),** 2009 WL 798842 (D. V.I. 2009) (stating in footnote that " 'orders granting or denying motions for withdrawal of reference are not final' appealable orders")] As interlocutory orders, § 1292(b) provides the rule for appellate review. [28 U.S.C. § 1292(b)]

H. Abstention

1. Permissive Abstention

The district court may abstain from hearing a *particular* proceeding arising under the Code or arising in or related to a bankruptcy case when *justice, comity with state courts, or respect for state law* favors resolution of the matter in a state forum. [28 U.S.C. § 1334(c)(1)] Courts have used various multi-factor tests to decide whether to permissively abstain. [*See, e.g.,* **Watson v. Zigila,** 2010 WL 3582504 (E.D. Mich. 2010) (12-factor test); **McDaniel v. ABN Amro Mortgage Group,** 364 B.R. 644 (S.D. Ohio 2007) (13-factor test)]

e.g. **Example:** McKitrick represented Debtor Corporation in its Chapter 11 case. After the bankruptcy case closed, Debtor sued McKitrick in state court for malpractice. McKitrick removed the case to the federal district court, which referred the case to the bankruptcy court. The bankruptcy court abstained from hearing the malpractice case and remanded it to state court. On appeal, the bankruptcy appellate panel ("BAP") affirmed the bankruptcy court's decision. The BAP noted that the bankruptcy court had reached its conclusion after having found that 8 of the 12 factors that the court had examined weighed in favor of abstention. The court explained that the Debtor's creditors had been paid in full and, thus, any recovery in the malpractice action would not benefit bankruptcy creditors. The issue in the proceeding was governed by state law, i.e., malpractice, and abstention would return the claim to the court in which it originally was filed. In addition, allowing the malpractice claim to proceed in the bankruptcy court would mean that a state law claim, that otherwise could not be filed in federal court, would proceed in a forum not available to other alleged victims of malpractice. The BAP held that the bankruptcy court had not abused its discretion in abstaining from hearing the malpractice claim against McKitrick. [**Roberts Broadcasting Co. v. DeWoskin (*In re* Roberts Broadcasting Co.),** 568 B.R. 310 (B.A.P. 8th Cir. 2017)]

Remember: There are two statutory grounds for abstention: Code § 305 and 28 U.S.C. § 1334(c). The difference between the two provisions is that under § 305(a), "the court may dismiss a case or suspend *all* proceedings in a bankruptcy case" while § 1334(c) "provides for abstention from *particular* proceedings in a bankruptcy case." [**Efron v. Candelario (*In re* Efron),** 529 B.R. 396 (B.A.P. 1st Cir. 2015)]

2. Mandatory Abstention

On a *timely motion,* the district court must abstain from hearing *a particular proceeding* if all of the following requirements are satisfied:

a. the proceeding is *related to the bankruptcy case* (non-core), but not arising in the bankruptcy case or under the Code;

b. the proceeding is based on a *state law claim or cause of action;*

c. without § 1334(b), the proceeding could not have been brought in a federal court;

d. the proceeding already has been *filed in an appropriate state court;* and

e. the proceeding can be *timely adjudicated* in that forum.

[28 U.S.C. § 1334(c)(2)] The language of § 1334(c)(2) is more restrictive than that of (c)(1), which "applies to a broader range of civil proceedings. [1 Collier ¶ 3.05(1)]

a. Personal Injury Tort and Wrongful Death

Proceedings based on personal injury tort or wrongful death claims are not subject to mandatory abstention. [28 U.S.C. § 157(b)(2)(B), (b)(4); *see* **Massey Energy Co. v.**

West Virginia Consumers for Justice, 351 B.R. 348 (E.D. Va. 2006) ("mandatory abstention is not available for personal injury tort claims")]

3. Distinguish Proceeding from Case

It is important to differentiate between the court's abstaining from hearing a *single proceeding* that is only one component of the bankruptcy case and abstaining from hearing the *whole bankruptcy case.* The court is "limited to abstaining from a particular proceeding" under § 1334(c) while it "may either dismiss the case or, in the alternative, suspend all proceedings within the case" under § 305. [**Graham v. Yoder Machinery Sales (*In re* Weldon F. Stump & Co.),** 373 B.R. 823 (Bankr. N.D. Ohio 2007); *compare* 28 U.S.C. § 1334(c) *with* B.C. § 305(a)]

The bankruptcy court may, at any time, abstain from hearing *an entire case* by dismissing it or by suspending all proceedings if it finds that abstention would better serve the *interests of creditors and the debtor.* [B.C. § 305(a)(1)] Notice and a hearing are required.

e.g. **Example:** Debtor obtained a divorce in 2001, and the Commonwealth court in Puerto Rico ("CFI") ordered him to pay $50,000 per month to his former spouse until the marital assets were divided and liquidated. Debtor never voluntarily paid the $50,000 per month, and he and his ex-wife fought in the CFI for a decade before the CFI awarded the ex-wife approximately $3.3 million in past-due payments and interest. Several weeks later, Debtor filed for relief under Chapter 11. The bankruptcy court dismissed the case on two grounds, one of which was abstention under § 305(a)(1). The bankruptcy court found that Debtor's case served no bankruptcy purpose because it basically was a two-party dispute between Debtor and his ex-wife. The court explained that the CFI was the appropriate forum for resolving issues of local family and inheritance law, given that court's expertise in those areas of law. The bankruptcy court also noted that because Debtor had refused to pay the monthly sum owed to his ex-wife, which the court had determined was a domestic support obligation, Debtor could not confirm a Chapter 11 plan. The court also found that dismissal would not prejudice Debtor's other unsecured creditors, whom he proposed to pay in full. Finally, the bankruptcy court explained that dismissal would save the administrative costs associated with bankruptcy; money spent on estate professionals was money not used to pay Debtor's creditors. The BAP affirmed the bankruptcy court's decision. The BAP noted that courts examine a "wide variety" of factors in making an abstention decision pursuant to § 305(a). "A significant factor in favor of dismissing a case pursuant to § 305(a)(1) is the absence of a true bankruptcy purpose, particularly where the bankruptcy case constitutes a two-party dispute between the debtor and a single creditor." The BAP rejected Debtor's arguments that his bankruptcy case was not simply a two-party dispute, and concluded that "the bankruptcy court's findings amply support[ed] its decision that the interests of all creditors and the debtor [were] better served by dismissing the case pursuant to § 305(a)." [**Efron v. Candelario (*In re* Efron),** 529 B.R. 396 (B.A.P. 1st Cir. 2015)]

4. Appeals of Abstention Orders

With one exception, a bankruptcy court's order to abstain or not abstain, whether permissive or mandatory, from hearing a particular proceeding may be appealed to the district court or bankruptcy appellate panel. An abstention decision by the district court or bankruptcy appellate panel, however, may not be appealed to the court of appeals or the Supreme Court. [28 U.S.C. § 1334(d)] There is one *statutory exception*: a decision *not to abstain* under mandatory abstention may be appealed not only to the district court or bankruptcy appellate panel, but also the court of appeals and the Supreme Court. [28 U.S.C. § 1334(d)]

I. Removal

1. Claims Related to Bankruptcy Case

A party may remove any claim or cause of action in a civil proceeding from a nonbankruptcy court to the federal district court for the district where the civil action is pending, if there is proper jurisdiction under 28 U.S.C. § 1334. [28 U.S.C. § 1452(a)] Upon removal to the district court, the action then is automatically referred to the bankruptcy court based on the district's standing referral order. [28 U.S.C. § 157(a); *see* § D.2 of this Chapter]

a. Exceptions

Proceedings in the United States Tax Court or civil actions by governmental units to enforce their police or regulatory powers are not subject to removal. [28 U.S.C. § 1452(a)]

2. Remand

The court to which a claim or cause of action has been removed has the power, based on the equities, to remand the action to the forum where it was pending. [28 U.S.C. § 1452(b)]

a. Appeal

A bankruptcy court's order to remand or not to remand a removed proceeding is reviewable by the district court, but a remand decision by the district court is not reviewable by the court of appeals or the Supreme Court. [28 U.S.C. § 1452(b)]

J. Venue

1. Bankruptcy Case

The appropriate venue for the *filing of a bankruptcy petition* is in the federal district where the debtor has maintained her *residence, domicile, principal place of business* in the United States, or *principal assets* in the United States during, or for the longest portion of, the 180-day period immediately before commencement of the case. [28 U.S.C. § 1408(1)] The statute is written in the disjunctive; thus, a person or entity may file for relief under the Bankruptcy Code in any district that satisfies one of the four alternatives for venue: (i) the debtor's *domicile,* (ii) the debtor's *residence,* (iii) the location of the debtor's *principal place of business* in the United States, *or* (iv) the location of the debtor's *principal assets* in the United States. [*In re* **First Fruits Holdings, LLC,** 2018 WL 2759384 (Bankr. E.D. N.C. 2018)] Venue is also proper in a district where a bankruptcy case concerning a general partner, partnership, or affiliate of the debtor is pending. [28 U.S.C. § 1408(2); B.C. § 101(2) (definition of affiliate)]

Example: Debtor filed for bankruptcy in the Western District of Missouri. Debtor's residence and domicile were in Colorado, but Debtor's principal place of business—his law office—was located in the Western District of Missouri. Creditor filed a motion to dismiss the bankruptcy case for improper venue. The bankruptcy court granted the motion, concluding that Debtor was a resident of Colorado and that the majority of his assets were located in Colorado. On appeal, the court reversed and remanded. The Bankruptcy Appellate Panel explained that because § 1408 provides "four alternative bases for venue, the statute allows many possible locations where an entity or individual may file for bankruptcy protection." The Debtor did not contest that his residence, domicile, and the location of his principal assets were in Colorado. Debtor argued, however, that his principal place of business was in Missouri, thereby making venue proper. The BAP reversed the bankruptcy court's decision, concluding that the bankruptcy court had erred in finding that the residence and principal place of business of a sole proprietor necessarily must be the same. The BAP remanded for a determination by the bankruptcy court of the Debtor's principal place of business. [**Broady v. Harvey (*In re* Broady**), 247 B.R. 470 (B.A.P. 8th Cir. 2000)]

Remember: The state law exemptions applicable to debtor's case may *not* be the exemptions for the state in which debtor files for bankruptcy and in which venue is proper. [B.C. § 522(b)(3)]

2. Bankruptcy Proceedings

With certain exceptions, for a ***proceeding*** arising under the Code, or arising in or related to a bankruptcy case venue lies in the ***district in which the case is pending.*** [28 U.S.C. § 1409(a)]

Note: The venue rules under 28 U.S.C. § 1408 apply to filing of the bankruptcy case itself, i.e., where you file the bankruptcy petition. The venue rules under 28 U.S.C. § 1409 apply to ***proceedings*** arising under the Code, or arising in or related to the bankruptcy case.

a. Exception—Proceedings for Recovery of Small Debts

With the exception of certain post-petition claims, a bankruptcy trustee must file a proceeding ***arising in or related to*** the bankruptcy case in the district where the defendant resides if the proceeding is to recover:

(i) *a money judgment or property* worth less than *$1,525;*

(ii) *a consumer debt* of less than *$22,700;* or

(iii) *a non-consumer debt against a non-insider* of less than *$27,750.*

[28 U.S.C. § 1409(b)]

The reason for this "small debt" exception is to "prevent[ ] unfairness to distant debtors of the estate, when the cost of defending would be greater than the cost of paying the debt owed." [H.R. Rep. No. 95–595, at 446 (1977) (discussion of 28 U.S.C. § 1473(b), which has been superseded and replaced by § 1409(b); *see* 1 Collier ¶ 4.03(2))]

Note: The language of § 1409(a) and (b) differ. Section 1409(a) covers proceedings arising under the Bankruptcy Code, or arising in or related to a bankruptcy case. Section 1409(b) covers proceedings arising in or related to a bankruptcy case. [**Creditors' Trust v. Crown Packaging Corp. (*In re* Nukote International, Inc.**), 457 B.R. 668 (Bankr. M.D. Tenn. 2011) (noting that "there is no reference to proceedings 'arising under title 11' in § 1409(b)")] The legislative history does not explain the difference in wording. [*See* **Creditors' Trust,** *supra* (after exhaustive review of legislative history, concluding that "no discussion of the inclusion or exclusion of the phrase 'arising under title 11' in either subsection (a) or (b) ha[d] been discovered")]

(i) Exception to the Small Debt Exception—Certain Post-Petition Claims of Trustee

There is an ***exception*** to the ***small debt exception.*** The trustee may bring a proceeding ***arising under the Code, or arising in or related to*** a bankruptcy case based on a claim that arises ***post-petition from the operation of the debtor's business*** only in the district where the action could have been filed under applicable nonbankruptcy venue law. [28 U.S.C. § 1409(d)] This rule applies even if the trustee's claim is for a small amount that, otherwise, would qualify for the small debt exception contained in 28 U.S.C. § 1409(b).

b. Post-Petition Claims Against Representative of the Estate

A proceeding arising under the Code or arising in or related to a bankruptcy case based on a post-petition claim from *operation of the debtor's business* may be brought *against the representative of the estate* either in the district where the case is pending *or* in the district where the action could have been commenced under applicable nonbankruptcy venue law. [28 U.S.C. § 1409(e)] The trustee is the representative of the estate. [B.C. § 323(a)] But representative of the estate also includes the debtor in possession. [B.C. § 1107(a); *see* H.R. Rep. No. 95–595, at 326 (1977) (when debtor remains in possession in non-subchapter V Chapter 11 case, "the debtor in possession becomes the representative of the estate"); *see id.* at 447 (explaining that "representative of the estate" is used to make clear that the non-subchapter V Chapter 11 debtor in possession "is liable to suit in the venue prescribed" by § 1409(e)]

c. Alternative: Trustee as Statutory Successor

The trustee, as the statutory successor to the debtor or to creditors under Code §§ 541 or 544(b), has the *option* of commencing a proceeding arising in or related to the bankruptcy case in the district where the case is pending *or* in the district where it could have been brought by the debtor or such creditors under applicable nonbankruptcy venue law if the bankruptcy case had not been filed. [28 U.S.C. § 1409(c)] This provision is subject to the small debt exception. [28 U.S.C. § 1409(b)] But § 1409(c) is rarely used. After all, the trustee likely will prefer "bring[ing] suit in the home court." [1 Collier ¶ 4.03(3)(a)]

d. Personal Injury Tort and Wrongful Death Claims

The district court in which the bankruptcy case is pending determines whether a claim for personal injury tort or wrongful death is tried in the district court where the *bankruptcy case is pending or* in the district court in the district where the *claim arose*. [28 U.S.C. § 157(b)(5)]

3. Change of Venue

A district court may transfer a case or proceeding to another district court "in the *interest of justice or for the convenience of the parties.*" [28 U.S.C. § 1412; Bankruptcy Rule 1014(a)(1)] The bankruptcy court can order a transfer, because motions to change venue generally are treated as core proceedings. [*See, e.g.,* **Terry Manufacturing Co. v. Steel Law Firm, P.C. (*In re* Terry Manufacturing Co.),** 323 B.R. 507 (Bankr. M.D. Ala. 2005)]

a. When Venue of the Case Is Proper

The decision to transfer venue lies within the bankruptcy court's sound discretion, and the moving party bears the burden of proof. [**Gentry Steel Fabrication, Inc. v. Howard S. Wright Construction Co. (*In re* Gentry Steel Fabrication, Inc.),** 325 B.R. 311 (Bankr. M.D. Ala. 2005)] If the bankruptcy case was filed in a proper district, the court examines various factors in ruling on a request to change the venue to another district. The tests used by the courts vary. Some courts use different multi-factor tests, depending on whether the court is analyzing the transfer motion under the "interest of justice" or the "convenience of the parties" prong of § 1412. [*See, e.g.,* **Terry Manufacturing,** *supra* (using 7-factor test for evaluating the "interest of justice" and 5-factor test for evaluating "convenience of the parties"); **Gentry Steel,** *supra* (same)] Other courts employ a single, multi-factor test in ruling on a motion to transfer venue of a bankruptcy case. [*See, e.g.,* *In re* **Rehoboth Hospitality, LP,** 2011 WL 5024267 (Bankr. D. Del. 2011) (using 8-factor test] The factors used in these various tests, however, often are similar. Some common factors include (i) the economics of estate administration; (ii) the proximity of needed witnesses to the court; and (iii) the proximity of the debtor and creditors to the court.

b. When Venue of the Case Is Improper

If a case was filed in the wrong district, i.e., venue is improper, the bankruptcy court, upon motion of a party in interest or *sua sponte,* may transfer the case to another district if transfer is in *the interest of justice* or for the *convenience of the parties.* Notice and a hearing are required. [Bankruptcy Rule 1014(a)(2)]

(i) May the Bankruptcy Court Dismiss the Case?

What is unclear is whether the court may *dismiss the case.* While Bankruptcy Rule 1014 provides that the court "may dismiss the case or transfer" it, 28 U.S.C. § 1412 is silent on dismissal, stating only that the court "may transfer" the case. [28 U.S.C. § 1412; Bankruptcy Rule 1014(a)(2)] The difference in language has led to confusion, but a noted commentator concludes that dismissal should not be an option for the *bankruptcy court,* in part, due to the fact that 28 U.S.C. § 1406 provides that if venue is improper in the *district court,* the court may dismiss or transfer the case. [1 Collier ¶ 4.05(4)(a); *compare* 28 U.S.C. § 1406(a) *with* 28 U.S.C. § 1412]

(ii) Must Transfer Be to a Proper Venue?

Unlike § 1406, § 1412 does not provide that the transfer be to a district in which the case "could have been brought." [*Compare* 28 U.S.C. § 1406(a) *with* 28 U.S.C. § 1412] Bankruptcy Rule 1014 also does not require transfer to a proper venue. [Bankruptcy Rule 1014(a)(2); *see* 1 Collier ¶ 4.05]

(iii) Retain the Case

May the bankruptcy court simply *not* transfer the case and instead retain it? The answer to that question is not clear. [1 Collier ¶ 4.05(4)(a)]

K. Appeals

1. Appeal from Bankruptcy Court

An appeal may be taken from the bankruptcy court to the federal district court or to a bankruptcy appellate panel, if the jurisdiction has such a panel. [28 U.S.C. § 158] Under certain limited circumstances, a party may appeal directly to the court of appeals. [28 U.S.C. § 158(d)(2)]

a. District Court

The appellate jurisdiction of the district court and the bankruptcy appellate panel includes appeals from final orders, judgments, and decrees of the bankruptcy court, and from interlocutory orders extending or shortening the debtor's exclusivity period for filing a plan. [28 U.S.C. § 158(a); B.C. § 1121(d)] For other interlocutory orders, appellate jurisdiction is by leave of the district court or the bankruptcy appellate panel. [28 U.S.C. § 158(a)(3); Bankruptcy Rule 8004]

(i) Distinguish—Recommendations from Bankruptcy Court

Proposed *findings of fact and conclusions of law* submitted by the bankruptcy court to the district court in a *non-core matter* or a *Stern claim* are *not issues on appeal,* but merely recommendations to the district court for: (i) its consideration; (ii) *de novo* review of matters objected to; and (iii) entry of final order or judgment. [28 U.S.C. § 157(c)(1); *see* Bankruptcy Rule 9033]

b. Bankruptcy Appellate Panels: Overview

The judicial council of each circuit must establish a bankruptcy appellate panel, composed of bankruptcy judges from that circuit, to hear appeals *unless* (i) there are *insufficient judicial resources* available in the circuit or (ii) the procedure would cause *undue delay or increased cost* to parties in bankruptcy cases. [28 U.S.C. § 158(b)(1)] Each appeal is to be heard by three members of the bankruptcy appellate panel who are not from the district where the appeal arises. [28 U.S.C. § 158(b)(5), (c)(1)]

Unless the appellant elects at the time of the appeal or any other party elects, no later than *30 days* after service of the appeal notice, to have the district court hear the appeal, the bankruptcy appellate panel will hear the appeal. [28 U.S.C. § 158(c)(1); *see* Bankruptcy Rule 8005]

Note: Currently, the First, Sixth, Eighth, Ninth, and Tenth Circuits have established Bankruptcy Appellate Panels.

c. Bankruptcy Appellate Panel Decisions: Precedential Value

Decisions of the bankruptcy appellate panel bind the parties to the dispute before the court. Whether the panel's decisions are binding on bankruptcy courts within the circuit is unclear. Some courts hold that decisions of the bankruptcy appellate panel are binding on all bankruptcy courts within the circuit. Other courts conclude that the decisions are not binding on any bankruptcy court within the circuit. Still other courts hold that the decisions are binding only on the bankruptcy courts in the district from which the appeal arose. [*See* **Rhiel v. Ohio-Health Corp. (*In re* Hunter),** 380 B.R. 753 (Bankr. S.D. Ohio 2008) (discussing various approaches taken by the courts); *but see* H.R. Rep. No. 109–31, at 148 (2005) (noting that decisions by a bankruptcy appellate panel "lack stare decisis value")]

d. Direct Appeal to Circuit Court

In 2005, Congress added a new subsection to § 158(d) to provide, under certain circumstances, for a direct appeal to the circuit court. The legislative history shows that Congress added the subsection because it wanted to " 'establish[ ] a dependable body of case law' " and was concerned about "the paucity of settled bankruptcy-law precedent." [**Weber v. United States Trustee,** 484 F.3d 154 (2d Cir. 2007)]

(i) File Notice of Appeal

A direct appeal may be taken to the appropriate court of appeals from final orders, judgments, and decrees; interlocutory orders expanding or shortening the exclusivity period under § 1121; and, with leave of the court, other interlocutory orders and decrees. [28 U.S.C. § 158(a), (d)(2)(A)] The party seeking a direct appeal must file a *timely notice of appeal.* [Bankruptcy Rule 8006(a)(2) (stating certification is effective when, among other things, a "timely appeal has been taken" under Bankruptcy Rules 8003 or 8004)] The process for securing a direct appeal requires: (1) certification by the bankruptcy court, district court, or bankruptcy appellate panel; and (2) authorization by the circuit court of appeals. [28 U.S.C. § 158(d)(2)(A); *see* H.R. Rep. No. 109–31, at 148 (2005)]

(ii) Certification

Certification must be made either by (a) the ***bankruptcy court, district court, or bankruptcy appellate panel*** involved or (b) ***all the appellants and appellees,*** if any. The court may act on its own motion or on the request of a party in interest. [28 U.S.C. § 158(d)(2)(A)] The request for certification must be made ***no later than 60 days*** after entry of the judgment, order, or decree. [28 U.S.C. § 158(d)(2)(E)]

(1) Circumstances Justifying Direct Appeal

The statute provides three alternative sets of circumstances that justify a direct appeal. Thus, the certification must state that:

(a) the judgment, order or decree involves a legal question on which there is ***no controlling decision*** from the Supreme Court or the court of appeals for the circuit ***or*** that involves a matter of ***public importance*** [28 U.S.C. § 158(d)(2)(A)(i)];

(b) the judgment, order, or decree involves a legal question requiring ***resolution of conflicting decisions*** [28 U.S.C. § 158(d)(2)(A)(ii); *see **In re* MPF Holding US LLC,** 444 B.R. 719 (Bankr. S.D. Tex. 2011) (certifying direct appeal, because bankruptcy court's interpretation of Fifth Circuit precedent conflicted with interpretation of other bankruptcy courts, including two other judges in Northern District of Texas)]; *or*

(c) an immediate appeal from the judgment, order, or decree may ***materially advance the progress*** of the case or proceeding [28 U.S.C. § 158(d)(2)(A)(iii)].

Note: Section 158(d)(2) is drafted in the disjunctive, so only *one of the three conditions* must be satisfied.

(2) When the Court Must Certify

If the bankruptcy court, district court, or bankruptcy appellate panel, either on it its own motion or on request of a party in interest, determines that one of the three reasons outlined above for certification exists, then the court must make the certification. [28 U.S.C. § 158(d)(2)(B)(i)] The court also must make the certification if it receives a request from a ***majority of appellants and a majority of appellees,*** if any, to make the certification. [28 U.S.C. § 158(d)(2)(B)(ii)]

There is a drafting glitch in § 158(d)(2)(B)(ii); unlike § 158(d)(2)(B)(i), it fails to specifically state that one of the three circumstances must exist before the court must make the certification. Thus, it is unclear whether a certification by a majority of appellants and appellees, without more, suffices. [1 Collier ¶ 5.06(1)] As Collier explains, however, "[o]ne might [ ] anticipate a cold reception by a circuit court if one of the circumstances is not present." [1 Collier ¶ 5.06(1)]

(iii) Authorization by Court of Appeals

The Court of Appeals must authorize the direct appeal. [28 U.S.C. § 158(d)(2)(A), hanging sentence] Thus, even if there is a certification that complies with the statutory requirements, the Court of Appeals may decide not to accept the direct appeal. [**Weber v. United States Trustee,** 484 F.3d 154 (2d Cir. 2007) (denying motion for leave to take a direct appeal)]

e. "Clearly Erroneous" Standard

On appeal, the reviewing court must use the "clearly erroneous" standard with regard to the bankruptcy court's findings of fact. [**Anderson v. Cordell (*In re* Infinity Business Group, Inc.),** 628 B.R. 213 (D. S.C. 2021)] The bankruptcy court's conclusions of law, however, are subject to *de novo* review. [***In re* Swift Air,** 624 B.R. 694 (D. Ariz. 2020)]

f. Interlocutory Orders

The district court or bankruptcy appellate panel may grant leave to appeal an interlocutory order of the bankruptcy court. A party seeking leave to appeal must file a notice of appeal with the bankruptcy court clerk within *14 days* of the bankruptcy court's order. [28 U.S.C. § 158(a)(3); Bankruptcy Rules 8004(a), 8002(a)(1)] Neither the Code nor the Bankruptcy Rules provides a standard for determining whether to grant leave to appeal. Most courts, however, apply the "analogous standard for certifying an interlocutory appeal set forth in 28 U.S.C. § 1292(b)." [**Law Debenture Trust Co. v. Calpine Corp. (*In re* Calpine Corp.),** 356 B.R. 585 (S.D. N.Y. 2007); *see also* **Cadles of Grassy Meadows II, LLC v. St. Clair (*In re* St. Clair),** 2014 WL 279850 (E.D. N.Y. 2014) (stating that "majority of courts in [Second Circuit] and elsewhere" have held that the appropriate standard is set forth in § 1292(b))] Section 1292(b) provides for review of an interlocutory order if (i) there is a "controlling question of law as to which there is substantial ground for difference of opinion," and (ii) an immediate appeal "may materially advance the ultimate termination of the litigation." [28 U.S.C. § 1292(b)] In other words, leave to appeal an interlocutory order is justified only under *exceptional circumstances.* [**Law Debenture,** *supra*]

g. Time for Appeal

With certain limited exceptions, a party must file a notice of appeal *14 days* after entry of the bankruptcy judge's order, judgment, or decree being appealed. The notice of appeal must be filed with the clerk of the *bankruptcy court.* [28 U.S.C. § 158(c)(2); Bankruptcy Rules 8002(a)(1)] The district court or bankruptcy appellate panel lacks jurisdiction to hear a case in which a timely notice of appeal is not filed. [***In re* Dorsey,** 870 F.3d 359 (5th Cir. 2017) (stating that failure to timely file a notice of appeal is jurisdictional); *see* Bankruptcy Rule 8003(a)(1)]

2. Appeal from District Court or Bankruptcy Appellate Panel

An appeal may be taken to the circuit court from a *final decision, order, or judgment* of (i) the district court, in its *appellate capacity* or (ii) the bankruptcy appellate panel. [28 U.S.C. § 158(d)(1)]

a. Remands

What if the district court or appellate panel, in reviewing a bankruptcy court final order, remands the case to the bankruptcy court? Is the district court's or appellate panel's decision final or interlocutory? The majority of circuits hold that a district court or BAP order remanding a case to the bankruptcy court for "significant further proceedings" is not final and appealable. If the remand order is for a "purely ministerial function," then it is final and appealable under § 158(d)(1). [*See, e.g.,* **Gordon v. Bank of America (*In re* Gordon),** 743 F.3d 720 (10th Cir. 2014) (holding that district court order reversing bankruptcy court order confirming debtors' Chapter 13 plan and remanding to the bankruptcy court for entry of plan confirmation and related orders was not final and appealable order); ***In re* Swegan,** 555 F.3d 510 (6th Cir. 2009) (holding that bankruptcy appellate court order reversing bankruptcy court order granting summary judgment to debtor on his motion to discharge debt and remanding the adversary proceeding for trial was not final and appealable); **Settembre v. Fidelity & Guaranty Life Insurance Co.,** 552 F.3d 438 (6th Cir. 2009) (holding that district court order reversing bankruptcy court order granting summary judgment to creditor on its denial of discharge complaint and remanding case for trial was not final and appealable order)]

b. What Constitutes a Final Order?

Deciding whether a particular order is final is not an easy task, but it is an important one because § 158 provides that the courts of appeals have jurisdiction of *final* orders, judgments, and decrees. [28 U.S.C. § 158(d)(1)] The reason for the finality requirement is to promote judicial efficiency and prevent piecemeal review. [*See* **Eisen v. Carlisle & Jacquelin,** 417 U.S. 156 (1974) (discussing finality in appellate context in a non-bankruptcy case)]

Unlike ordinary civil litigation, bankruptcy cases involve an "aggregation of individual controversies." [1 Collier ¶ 5.08(1)(b)] As a result, in the bankruptcy context, courts have taken a pragmatic approach and apply what some courts call "flexible finality," which recognizes that the "breadth of bankruptcy cases necessitates an approach that allows for the efficient resolution of certain discrete disputes that may arise in a given bankruptcy." [*In re* **McKinney,** 610 F.3d 399 (7th Cir. 2010)] Courts have developed a liberal definition of finality in the context of bankruptcy by viewing *a proceeding* as the "relevant judicial unit for purposes of finality." Thus, an order that "conclusively determines a separable dispute over a creditor's claim or priority" is final. [*In re* **Saco Local Development Corp.,** 711 F.2d 441 (1st Cir. 1983)]

(e.g.) **Example—Final Order:** An order holding that Insurance Company's claim for Debtor's "employee group life, health, and disability insurance premiums" was entitled to priority status under § 507(a)(4) constituted a final appealable order, because it "effectively settle[d] the amount due the creditor." [*In re* **Saco Local Development Corp.,** *supra*]

(e.g.) **Example—Not Final:** Debtor filed for relief under Chapter 13. Debtor owned property on which Bank held the mortgage. Debtor proposed a Chapter 13 plan; Bank objected to its treatment under the plan. The bankruptcy court denied confirmation and ordered Debtor to propose a new plan within 30 days. In a unanimous decision, the Supreme Court held that an order denying confirmation of a plan is not a final order that a debtor can immediately appeal. The Court explained that the "relevant proceeding is the process of attempting to arrive at an approved plan that would allow the bankruptcy to move forward." The bankruptcy court's order denying confirmation did not terminate that proceeding because Debtor was free to propose another plan. [**Bullard v. Blue Hills Bank,** 575 U.S. 496 (2015)]

3. District Court as Trial Court

When the district court sits as a trial court rather than as an appellate court, e.g., in *non-core or Stern-claim* proceedings in which the parties do not consent or in proceedings in which the reference has been *withdrawn,* the normal standard for an appeal to the circuit court of the district court's final decision governs. [*See* 28 U.S.C. §§ 1291, 1292]

4. Orders Concerning Automatic Stay

In **Ritzen Group, Inc. v. Jackson Masonry, LLC,** 140 S. Ct. 582 (2020), the Supreme Court, in a unanimous opinion, held that a bankruptcy court's ruling on a motion for relief from the automatic stay "forms a discrete procedural unit" in the bankruptcy case and "[t]hat unit yields a final, appealable order when the bankruptcy court unreservedly grants or denies relief." [*See* 28 U.S.C. § 158 (appeals), Bankruptcy Rule 8002(a) (time for filing notice of appeal)]

L. Sovereign Immunity

1. Waiver

Bankruptcy Code § 106 waives the sovereign immunity of governmental units with respect to a number of bankruptcy issues. [*See* B.C. § 106(a)(1) (listing 59 sections for which sovereign immunity is abrogated)] This waiver applies to monetary recoveries, other than punitive damages awards, as well as to declaratory or injunctive relief. [B.C. § 106(a)(1), (3)]

a. Illustrations of Waiver

A governmental unit's sovereign immunity is waived with respect to the trustee's avoidance powers, because §§ 544–551 are included in the list in § 106(a)(1).

b. Distinguish § 541 Property Provision

Section 541 on property of the estate is excluded from the sections specified in § 106(a)(1). Thus, if property of the estate includes a debtor's cause of action against a governmental unit that is barred by sovereign immunity, the trustee cannot pursue the action.

e.g. **Example:** Debtor was a farmer who entered into a ten-year lease with Tribe for more than a million acres of farmland. The leased property was held in trust for the Tribe by the United States. The Bureau of Indian Affairs ("BIA") approved the lease. Several years into the lease, the BIA informed Debtor that a bridge connecting the north and south portions of the property was dangerous and would be removed. Debtor was unsuccessful in working out an arrangement with the BIA or a reduction in rent from the Tribe, and was unable to use the north end of the property as a result of the bridge's removal. Debtor defaulted on the lease and subsequently filed for relief under Chapter 11. Debtor filed an inverse condemnation action against the BIA in bankruptcy court and asked for $2 million in damages. Debtor's action could not proceed against the BIA in bankruptcy court. The cause of action belonged to the bankruptcy estate and any recovery became property of the estate, but § 106 of the Bankruptcy Code did not waive the government's sovereign immunity as to Debtor's takings clause cause of action. Instead, the Tucker Act waived the government's sovereign immunity, but only for suits filed in the United States Court of Federal Claims. Because the bankruptcy court lacked jurisdiction to hear Tucker Act claims, the cause of action was transferred to the Federal Court of Claims. [**McGuire v. United States,** 550 F.3d 903 (9th Cir. 2008)]

2. Offset Against Governmental Claims Permitted

If property of the estate includes a claim against a governmental unit that would be barred by sovereign immunity, the trustee can offset that claim against a claim that the governmental unit holds against the estate, e.g., an unrelated tax claim, but only up to the amount of the government's claim. [B.C. § 106(c)] "No affirmative recovery is permitted." [H.R. Rep. No. 95–595, at 317 (1977)] Section 106(c) applies *regardless of whether the governmental unit filed a proof of claim.* [*Compare* B.C. § 106(b) *with* B.C. § 106(c); *see* 2 Collier ¶ 106.06(2)(c)] The estate's claim and the claim of the governmental unit "may arise from the same or different transactions." [2 Collier ¶ 106.06(2)(a)]

3. Compulsory Counterclaims: Sovereign Immunity Waived

If a governmental unit has filed a proof of claim in the bankruptcy case, then it is deemed to have waived sovereign immunity with regard to a compulsory counterclaim to its claim that arose out of the same transaction or occurrence. [B.C. § 106(b)] The purpose of the rule is to prevent a "one-sided" result in which the governmental unit "receive[s] [a] distribution from the estate without subjecting itself to any liability it has to the estate within the confines of a compulsory counterclaim rule." [H.R. Rep. No. 95–595, at 317 (1977)]

4. State Sovereign Immunity and § 106

The Supreme Court has concluded that the States, by giving Congress the power to make uniform laws on bankruptcy, agreed "not to assert any sovereign immunity defense they might have had in proceedings" created by Congress under the Bankruptcy Clause. In a case involving a preference avoidance action brought by the liquidating supervisor in a Chapter 11 case against a State entity, the Court explained that the issue was not whether Congress had abrogated the State's sovereign immunity under § 106(a). Rather, the question was whether Congress' decision to make States amenable to preference actions fell within the scope of its powers under the Bankruptcy Clause. The Court concluded that it was "beyond peradventure" that Congress had such power, which "arises from the Bankruptcy Clause itself." [**Central Virginia Community College v. Katz,** 546 U.S. 356 (2006)]

The Supreme Court's opinion in a nonbankruptcy case decided prior to *Katz* raised serious questions about the validity of § 106's waiver of the states' Eleventh Amendment sovereign immunity. [*See* **Seminole Tribe of Florida v. Florida,** 517 U.S. 44 (1996)] In *Katz,* the majority acknowledged that statements made in *Seminole Tribe* "reflected an assumption that the holding in that case would apply to the Bankruptcy Clause." But, after "[c]areful study and reflection," the Court concluded "that that assumption was erroneous." [**Katz,** *supra*] Thus, the Court's decision in *Katz* appears to have settled the question of § 106(a)'s constitutionality. [2 Collier ¶ 106.02]

Chapter Three

Commencement and Administration of the Case

Chapter Approach

This topics in this Chapter largely, although not exclusively, involve issues that arise at the start of the bankruptcy case. The Chapter begins with the requirements *all debtors* must satisfy to be eligible for bankruptcy relief. It then sets out the specific requirements for relief under each chapter of the Code. It is important to know the *chapter-specific eligibility* requirements because your professor may ask you to evaluate whether a debtor is eligible for relief under Chapter 7 or Chapter 13, for example. A bankruptcy case normally is begun by the debtor's filing of a *voluntary petition.* *Involuntary cases* are rare, but this Chapter explains not only how creditors may begin such a case but also the specific sections of the Code that address issues arising in an involuntary case, e.g., *gap creditors.* At the start of the case, the debtor must file not only the petition but also numerous *schedules and statements*, some of which are chapter-specific. The Chapter provides a great deal of detail about these documents, which your professor may or may not wish you to master for the exam.

The first meeting of creditors—the *§ 341 meeting*—occurs within 21 to 50 days after the order for relief, depending on the chapter of the Code. This Chapter explains what happens at and the purposes of the § 341 meeting. The Chapter ends with a brief overview of *conversion* and *dismissal*. A case may be converted to another chapter of the Code or dismissed early in the case. For example, a Chapter 13 debtor may decide early on in her case that Chapter 7 would better serve her needs. But conversion and dismissal also may occur later in the debtor's case. The material in this Chapter merely introduces the concepts of conversion and dismissal. More detail on the chapter-specific rules for conversion and dismissal appear later in this study guide.

A. Eligibility Requirements: All Chapters

1. Only Persons May File

Only a *person* (individual, partnership, or corporation) that *resides* or has a *domicile, a place of business, or property in the United States* is eligible to be a debtor under the Bankruptcy Code. [B.C. § 109(a)]

a. Insolvency Not Required

A person need not be insolvent to file for relief under Chapters 7, 11, 12, or 13. [*See* B.C. § 109(b), (d)–(f)]

b. Corporation Is a Person

The bankruptcy definition of the term "corporation" is expansive and includes business trusts and most companies or associations with corporate attributes. [B.C. § 101(9)(A)] A limited partnership is not a corporation for purposes of the Bankruptcy Code. [B.C. § 101(9)(B)] Determining whether an entity qualifies as a corporation for purposes of the Bankruptcy Code is a federal question, so the fact that an entity is a corporation for state law purposes is not dispositive. Nonetheless, if an entity is a corporation under state law, then it "enjoys a presumption of being a corporation for purposes of § 101(9)" and the party claiming that the entity is not a corporation under § 101(9) bears the burden of proof on that issue. [*In re* **Charles St. African Methodist Episcopal Church,** 478 B.R. 73 (Bankr. D. Mass. 2012)]

Example—Labor Union: A labor union is eligible for relief under the Bankruptcy Code. The Code defines the term "corporation" to include an "unincorporated company or association." [B.C. § 101(9)(A)(iv)] The legislative history shows that the term "unincorporated association" was "intended specifically to include a labor union." [H.R. Rep. No. 95–595, at 309 (1977)]

Example—Business Trust: Debtor Catholic School Employees Pension Trust ("Pension Trust") filed for relief under Chapter 11. Numerous creditors filed motions to dismiss, claiming that the Pension Trust was not eligible to file a bankruptcy petition because it was not a business trust and, hence, not a corporation for purposes of the Bankruptcy Code. The bankruptcy court dismissed the petition. The court explained that the Pension Trust was established to preserve the trust *res,* not to generate income or profit. In addition, the Pension Trust did not engage in business activities other than activities incidental to protecting and preserving the trust corpus. Thus, the court held that Pension Trust was not a business trust and, thus, not eligible to file for relief under the Bankruptcy Code. [*In re* **Catholic School Employees Pension Trust,** 584 B.R. 82 (Bankr. D. P.R. 2018); B.C. § 101(9)(A)(v)]

2. When a Debtor May Not File for Bankruptcy Relief

In 2005, Congress added a pre-bankruptcy credit counseling requirement for *individual debtors.* With limited exceptions, an individual may not file for bankruptcy until she has satisfied this credit counseling requirement. The Code also prevents certain individual debtors from re-filing for bankruptcy after dismissal of their earlier bankruptcy case.

a. Individual Credit Counseling Requirement

An *individual debtor* may not file for relief under any chapter of the Bankruptcy Code for which she is otherwise eligible unless *prior to filing* she first obtained *credit counseling* from an *approved nonprofit budget and credit counseling agency* during the *180 days* before filing her bankruptcy petition. Credit counseling may be in the form of *individual or group briefings* conducted in person, over the *phone, or on the Internet.* [B.C. § 109(h)(1)]

b. Exceptions to Credit Counseling Requirement

In the following situations, an individual debtor need not satisfy the Code's credit counseling requirement before filing for bankruptcy.

(i) No Agencies in District

The credit-counseling requirement does not apply to a debtor who resides in a district for which the United States trustee or the bankruptcy administrator has determined that the credit counseling agencies in the district are not *reasonably able* to provide such services. [B.C. § 109(h)(2)]

(ii) Temporary Exigent Circumstances Certification

A debtor who, due to *exigent circumstances,* was unable to obtain credit-counseling services *during the 7 days* starting on the date on which she requested such services may obtain a *temporary waiver* of the requirement that she obtain credit counseling *prior* to filing for relief under the Bankruptcy Code. To obtain a waiver of the pre-filing credit-counseling requirement, the debtor must submit to the bankruptcy court a *certification* that

(1) describes the *exigent circumstances;*

(2) states the debtor's efforts to obtain counseling during the *7-day period;* and

(3) is *satisfactory to the court.* [B.C. § 109(h)(3)(A)]

Note: This exception is only a *temporary,* pre-filing waiver of the credit counseling requirement. The debtor who uses this exception must obtain credit counseling services *no later than 30 days after filing the petition,* unless the bankruptcy court, on a showing of *cause, extends* the 30 days an additional *15 days.* [B.C. § 109(h)(3)(B)]

(iii) Disabled, Incapacitated, or Active Military Duty

The credit counseling requirement does not apply to a debtor whom the court, *after notice and a hearing,* determines is unable to meet the requirement due to *incapacity, disability, or active military duty in a military combat zone.* The Code defines *"incapacity"* to mean the debtor is so "impaired by reason of mental illness or mental deficiency" as to be unable to make rational decisions about her financial responsibilities. *"Disability"* means that the debtor is so physically impaired that, even with reasonable effort, she cannot participate in any form of credit counseling—in person, on the phone, or on the Internet. [B.C. § 109(h)(4)]

c. Nonprofit Budget and Credit Counseling Agencies

The bankruptcy court clerk must maintain a *publicly available list* of nonprofit budget and credit counseling services that the United States trustee or bankruptcy administrator has approved. [B.C. § 111(a)(1)] To qualify, an agency must demonstrate that it will provide *qualified counselors,* maintain adequate provision for *safekeeping and payment* of *client funds,* provide *adequate counseling* for client credit problems, and deal responsibly and effectively with other matters related to the *quality, effectiveness, and financial security of its services.* [B.C. § 111(c)(1)] If the agency charges a fee, the *fee must be reasonable,* and services must be provided without regard to ability to pay. [B.C. § 111(c)(2)(B)] The agency *cannot pay commissions or bonuses* to its trained counselors that are based on the outcome of the agency's counseling services. [B.C. § 111(c)(2)(F)] No agency may provide to a *credit reporting agency* information about whether a debtor has received or sought instruction on personal financial management from the agency. [B.C. § 111(g)(1)]

(i) Damages

If a nonprofit budget and credit counseling agency *willfully or negligently* fails to comply with any Code requirement with respect to the debtor, it will be liable for *actual damages* that the debtor incurred as a result of the violation and any *court costs or reasonable attorneys' fees* incurred in an action to recover such damages. [B.C. § 111(g)(2)]

d. Multiple Petitions

An *individual* or a *family farmer* is not eligible to file a petition under any chapter of the Bankruptcy Code if she has been a debtor in a case that was *pending in the preceding 180 days* and *dismissed,* either because of the debtor's willful failure to obey court orders or "to appear before the court in proper prosecution of the case," *or* because she requested a voluntary dismissal of the case following a party's request for relief from the automatic stay. [B.C. § 109(g)] *Rationale:* This provision is intended to curtail abusive and repetitive filings, particularly in consumer bankruptcy cases. Another Code provision that addresses Congress' concern with abusive and repetitive filings is § 362(c), which Congress amended with the passage of BAPCPA in 2005.

Example—Failure to obey court orders or prosecute case: Husband and Wife filed for relief under Chapter 7. The bankruptcy court dismissed their petition for "cause," citing debtors' failure (i) to attend at least two § 341 meetings, (ii) to produce business records, and (iii) to truthfully and fully disclose their assets and business enterprises. Thirty-six days after dismissal, Husband filed again for relief under Chapter 7 and Creditor filed a motion to dismiss the petition pursuant to § 109(g). The bankruptcy court granted Creditor's motion to dismiss. First, the court held that Husband's failure to attend multiple § 341 meetings constituted willful failure to abide by court orders. The court noted that most courts have found that "attendance at section 341 meetings is mandated by court order, as that term is used in section 109(g)(1)." Second, the court held that Husband's petition merited dismissal under the second prong of § 109(g)(1)— willful failure to properly prosecute the bankruptcy case. The bankruptcy court explained that proper prosecution is not limited to physical appearance before the court; it applies to the debtor's compliance with his statutory duties. Because Husband had failed in his prior Chapter 7 case to attend § 341 meetings and accurately disclose assets and liabilities on both his schedules and to the Chapter 7 trustee, Husband had failed to perform his statutory duties. This conduct constituted willful failure to appear before the court in proper prosecution of the case. [*In re* **Wen Hua Xu,** 386 B.R. 451 (Bankr. S.D. N.Y. 2008)]

Example—Debtor's voluntary dismissal following creditor's request for relief from stay: Husband and Wife filed for relief under Chapter 13 in April of 2015. (Prior to April 2015, Wife had filed four petitions for relief under Chapter 13 dating back to September of 2011, and Husband had filed two petitions for Chapter 13 relief in 2013 and 2014.) In their joint April 2015 Chapter 13 case, Creditor moved for relief from the automatic stay as to debtors' homestead; later that same day, debtors sought voluntary dismissal of their case. The bankruptcy court granted the debtors' motion to dismiss at the end of July of 2015. About two and half months later, in October of 2015, Husband and Wife filed again for relief under the Bankruptcy Code, although this time they filed a Chapter 11 case. The bankruptcy court dismissed debtors' Chapter 11 case, because debtors were ineligible for bankruptcy relief under § 109(g)(2). [*In re* **Gibas,** 543 B.R. 570 (Bankr. E.D. Wis. 2016)]

B. Chapter-Specific Eligibility Requirements

1. Chapter 7: "Liquidation"

With certain exceptions, Chapter 7 relief is available to *any person* that resides or has a domicile, a place of business, or property in the United States. [B.C. §§ 109(a), (b), 101(41)] *Stockbrokers, commodity brokers, and clearing banks* may be debtors under special provisions of Chapter 7, which are beyond the scope of this summary. [B.C. §§ 741 *et seq.* (stockbrokers), 761 *et seq.* (commodity brokers), 781 *et seq.* (clearing banks)]

a. Exception: Individual Debtors Who Fail "Means" Test

Individual debtors with primarily consumer debts who fail the "means test" are not eligible to file for relief under Chapter 7. [B.C. § 707(b)]

b.   Exception: Railroads

Railroads are not eligible for Chapter 7 relief. [B.C. § 109(b)(1)]

c.   Exception: Domestic Savings Institutions and Insurance Companies

Domestic banks, insurance companies, credit unions, savings and loan associations, building and loan associations, homestead associations, cooperative banks, and other similar domestic institutions are not eligible for relief under Chapter 7. However, certain banking institutions may file for relief under Chapter 7 if a petition is filed at the direction of the Board of Governors of the Federal Reserve System. [B.C. § 109(b)(2)]

(i)   Rationale

The banking and insurance industries directly regulate these kinds of financial institutions, and "alternate provision is made for their liquidation under various regulatory laws." [H.R. Rep. No. 95–595, at 318 (1977)]

d.   Exception: Small Business Investment Companies

Small business investment companies licensed by the Small Business Administration under the Small Business Investment Act of 1958 are not eligible for Chapter 7 relief. [B.C. § 109(b)(2); 15 U.S.C. § 681] The reason for the exclusion is to protect the interests of the Small Business Administration from being subordinated to those of other creditors. [2 Collier ¶ 109.03(3)(a)]

e.   Exception: Foreign Savings Institutions and Insurance Companies

A foreign insurance company that is *engaged in such business in the United States* is not eligible for relief under Chapter 7. [B.C. § 109(b)(3)(A)] Foreign banks, savings and loan associations, and other similar financial institutions that have a *branch or agency in the United States* are not eligible for Chapter 7 relief. [B.C. § 109(b)(3)(B)]

2.   Chapter 11: "Reorganization"

Generally, only an individual, partnership, or corporation that is eligible for relief under Chapter 7 may be a debtor under Chapter 11. [B.C. § 109(d)] There are several differences, however, between eligibility under Chapter 7 and eligibility under Chapter 11.

a.   Difference #1: Individual Debtors with Primarily Consumer Debts

An individual debtor with primarily consumer debts who fails the "means test" may not file for relief under Chapter 7. Chapter 11 does not have a "means test." Chapter 11 is designed principally for business reorganizations, but the Supreme Court has held that a consumer debtor, i.e., an individual not engaged in business, also may qualify for relief under this chapter. [**Toibb v. Radloff,** 501 U.S. 157 (1991)] The vast majority of individual consumer debtors do *not* file for relief under Chapter 11. For example, in calendar year 2020, individuals with non-business liabilities filed only 288 of the 8,333 Chapter 11 cases filed, or approximately 3.5%. [BAPCPA Report—2020; Report F-5A]

b.   Difference #2: Stockbrokers and Commodity Brokers

Stockbrokers and commodity brokers *cannot* be debtors under Chapter 11. [B.C. § 109(d)]

c. Difference #3: Railroads

Railroads *are eligible* for relief under special provisions of Chapter 11. [*Compare* B.C. § 109(b)(1) *with* B.C. §§ 109(d), 1161 *et seq.*] This study guide does not cover railroad reorganization.

3. Chapter 12: "Family Farmer or Family Fisherman with Regular Annual Income"

A *family farmer or family fisherman* whose *yearly income* is sufficiently *stable and regular* to fund a Chapter 12 plan may file a petition under that chapter. [B.C. §§ 109(f), 101(19), 101(19B)] Individuals, individuals and their spouses, corporations, or partnerships may qualify as family farmers or family fishermen. [B.C. §§ 101(18), 101(19A)] In order to qualify for Chapter 12 relief, a *family farmer* cannot have aggregate debts in *excess of $11,097,350.* [B.C. § 101(18)] A *family fisherman* cannot have aggregate debts in *excess of* $2,268,550. [B.C. § 101(19A)]

A Chapter 12 case may be commenced only by the filing of a *voluntary* bankruptcy petition; it can never be commenced by an involuntary petition. [B.C. § 303(a)]

4. Chapter 13: "Adjustment of Debts of Individual with Regular Income"

Only *an individual with regular income* who, on the petition date, has noncontingent, liquidated *debts* less than *$2,750,000* is eligible for relief under Chapter 13. [B.C. § 109(e)]

Note: The $2.75 million aggregate debt limit is in effect until *June 21, 2024,* at which point, unless Congress acts, the separate secured and unsecured debt limits in effect on June 20, 2022, will apply to a debtor's eligibility for relief under Chapter 13. (BTATCA § 2(i)(1)(A), (2)).

a. "Individual with Regular Income"

An individual with regular income is an "individual whose income is sufficiently stable and regular to enable such individual to make payments under a plan under Chapter 13." [B.C. § 101(30)]

(i) Sources of Regular Income

Wages and salary are typical forms of regular income. But, any legitimate source of regular income qualifies, e.g., pension income, rental income, public assistance benefits. The key issue is whether it is sufficiently stable and capable of funding the debtor's repayment plan.

Note on Social Security Income: Courts are divided on whether Social Security benefits may be considered in determining a debtor's regular income for purposes of eligibility for relief under Chapter 13. [*See* **Santiago-Monteverde v. Pereira (*In re* Santiago-Monteverde),** 512 B.R. 432 (S.D. N.Y. 2014) (noting split in authority and holding that "Social Security income may not be considered in a Chapter 13 eligibility determination"); *but see* 2 Collier ¶ 109.06(1)(a)]

b. Voluntary Petition

A Chapter 13 case must be commenced by the debtor's voluntary petition. The Code does not authorize an involuntary Chapter 13 filing. [B.C. § 303(a)]

c. Joint Case

An individual with regular income and his spouse may file a joint petition under Chapter 13. The debt limit still applies, which means that the couples' *aggregate* indebtedness cannot equal or exceed *$2,750,000.* [B.C. §§ 302(a), 109(e)]

d. Exception: Stockbrokers and Commodity Brokers

Stockbrokers and commodity brokers do *not* qualify for relief under Chapter 13. [B.C. § 109(e)]

PERSONS *NOT* ELIGIBLE FOR RELIEF UNDER PARTICULAR CHAPTERS—A SUMMARY			GILBERT
CHAPTER 7	**CHAPTER 11**	**CHAPTER 12**	**CHAPTER 13**
Individual who has not satisfied credit counseling requirement or an exception to requirement § 109(h)	Individual who has not satisfied credit counseling requirement or an exception to requirement § 109(h)	Individual who has not satisfied credit counseling requirement or an exception to requirement § 109(h)	Individual who has not satisfied credit counseling requirement or an exception to requirement § 109(h)
Individual or family farmer with multiple petitions § 109(g)	Individual or family farmer with multiple petitions § 109(g)	Individual or family farmer with multiple petitions § 109(g)	Individual or family farmer with multiple petitions § 109(g)
Individual with primarily consumer debts who fails "means test" § 707(b)	Domestic banks, savings institutions, credit unions, insurance companies, and the like § 109(b), (d)	Persons who do not qualify as family farmers or family fishermen with regular annual income § 109(f)	Persons who are not individuals, such as corporations and partnerships § 109(e)
Railroads § 109(b)(1)	Small business investment companies § 109(b)(2)	Family farmers with aggregate debts > $11,097,350 § 101(18)	Individuals who do not have sufficiently stable and regular income to fund a plan § 109(e)
Domestic banks, savings institutions, credit unions, insurance companies, and the like § 109(b)(2)	Foreign insurance companies engaged in business in the United States § 109(b)(3)(A), (d)	Family fishermen with aggregate debts > $2,268,550 § 101(19A)	Individuals whose debts are ≥ $2,750,000 § 109(e)
Small business investment companies § 109(b)(2)	Foreign savings institutions and the like with branch or agency in United States § 109(b)(3)(B), (d)		Stock brokers § 109(e)
Foreign insurance companies engaged in business in the United States § 109(b)(3)(A)	Stock brokers § 109(d)		Commodity brokers § 109(e)
Foreign savings institutions and the like with branch or agency in United States § 109(b)(3)(B)	Commodity brokers § 109(d)		

C. Voluntary Case

1. Filing the Petition

A voluntary case is *commenced* when an eligible debtor files a petition under Chapter 7, 11, 12, or 13. At that time, the appropriate filing fee should be paid. [28 U.S.C. § 1930]. In an *individual* case, the debtor may file a signed application with the petition requesting to pay the filing fee in installments. [Bankruptcy Rule 1006; Official Form 103A (application)] The filing of a voluntary petition constitutes an *order for relief.* [B.C. § 301(b)]

a. Consumer Debtor

Before the start of the bankruptcy case, the clerk of the court must provide a debtor who is an *individual with primarily consumer debts* written notice that contains the following information:

(i) a brief description of chapters 7, 11, 12, and 13, and the *purposes, benefits, and costs of proceeding under each chapter* [B.C. § 342(b)(1)(A)];

(ii) available *services* from *credit counseling agencies* [B.C. § 342(b)(1)(B)];

(iii) a statement notifying the debtor that she may be *fined, imprisoned,* or both for knowingly and fraudulently *concealing assets or* making *false oaths or statements* under penalty of perjury [B.C. § 342(b)(2)(A)]; and

(iv) a statement that all information that the debtor provides in the case is *subject to examination by the Attorney General.* [B.C. § 342(b)(2)(B)]

Form 2010 contains the information required to be disclosed by § 342(b) of the Bankruptcy Code.

b. Notice

Notice of the order for relief must be sent to *all parties in interest,* including the debtor, all creditors, equity security holders in a Chapter 11 case, indenture trustees, and the United States trustee. [B.C. § 342(a); Bankruptcy Rule 2002(d), (f), (k)] State and federal taxing authorities and, if the debtor is subject to regulation, the regulatory agency with jurisdiction also will receive notice of the bankruptcy filing. [H.R. 95–595, at 331 (1977)] Holders of community claims should receive notice to avoid issues arising under § 524(a)(3). [3 Collier § 342.02(2)] A debt is not dischargeable if the creditor did not receive notice (or have actual knowledge) in time to file a proof of claim and, for certain debts, in time to request a nondischargeability determination. [B.C. § 523(a)(3)] The notice generally is included in the same document as the notice of the § 341 meeting of creditors. [*See* Official Forms 309A–I]

c. Joint Case of Husband and Wife

An individual debtor who wants to file a single petition with his spouse may commence a joint case. [B.C. § 302(a)] Debtors electing to file jointly pay only one filing fee. The filing of a joint petition operates automatically as an order for relief in the case. [B.C. § 302(a)]

(i) Legally Married

The debtors must be legally married; a joint petition may not be filed if they merely cohabitate. [*In re Lucero,* 408 B.R. 348 (Bankr. C.D. Cal. 2009)] After the Supreme Court's decision in *Obergefell v. Hodges,* same-sex couples may legally marry; thus, they are eligible to file a joint bankruptcy petition. [B.C. § 302; *see also* **Obergefell v. Hodges,** 576 U.S. 644 (2015)] Bankruptcy courts have reached different conclusions on whether same-sex individuals who are not married but are partners in a state-recognized civil union or domestic partnership qualify to file a joint petition under § 302 of the Bankruptcy Code. [*Compare In re* **Villaverde,** 540 B.R. 431 (Bankr. C.D. Cal. 2015) (holding that a same-sex couple registered in California as domestic partners is not eligible to file a joint Chapter 13 petition, because they are not spouses for bankruptcy purposes) *with In re* **Simmons, 584 B.R. 295** (Bankr. N.D. Ill. 2018) (same-sex individuals holding a certificate of civil union under Illinois law have a status that is "substantively identical" to that of a couple married under Illinois law and, therefore, are considered spouses for purposes of the Bankruptcy Code and may file a joint petition)]

(ii) Only in a Voluntary Case

The option to file a joint petition is available only in a voluntary case. [B.C. § 302(a)]

(iii) Consolidation

In a joint case, the court *may* consolidate the debtors' estates by pooling their assets and liabilities, especially if their property and debts are held jointly. [B.C. § 302(b)] Filing a joint petition does not automatically consolidate the joint debtors' respective estates. Consolidation "merges the debtors' estates, thereby subjecting all assets held by either debtor to the claim of all creditors," regardless of whether the claims were incurred by one or both debtors. [*In re* **Eichhorn,** 338 B.R. 793 (Bankr. S.D. Ill. 2006)]

(1) Distinguish Joint Administration

Substantive consolidation of the debtors' estates should be distinguished from *joint administration.* Under certain circumstances, e.g., when there is a joint petition, two or more separate petitions concerning a husband and wife in the same court, a petition by a debtor and an affiliate, the judge may expedite the cases by ordering joint administration regarding matters such as notices to creditors, listing of claims, other similar functions, and the appointment of a single trustee. [Bankruptcy Rule 1015(b)]

d. Corporation

State law determines who has authority to file a voluntary bankruptcy petition on behalf of a corporation or a limited liability company. [*See* **Price v. Gurney,** 324 U.S. 100 (1945) (holding under Chapter X of the Bankruptcy Act that the court must dismiss a petition filed by an entity without the authority to do so under local law); **DB Capital Holdings, LLC v. Aspen HH Ventures, LLC (***In re* **DB Capital Holdings, LLC),** 463 B.R. 142 (B.A.P. 10th Cir. 2010) (citing *Price* for proposition that state law determines who has authority to file a bankruptcy case on behalf of a limited liability company organized under state law)] If the person or entity filing the petition lacks authority to do so under state law, then the bankruptcy court must dismiss the petition. [**Franchise Services of North America v. United States Trustee (***In re* **Franchise Services of North America),** 891 F.3d 198 (5th Cir. 2018)]

e. Partnership

A petition filed by fewer than all the general partners in a partnership is treated as an involuntary petition. [B.C. § 303(b)(3)(A)]

2. Schedules, Statements, Documents and Debtor Duties in General

Congress created a number of new filing obligations and other duties for individual debtors with the passage of BAPCPA. A debtor's failure to file certain forms or paper work, or to perform certain statutory duties may result in dismissal of the case or lifting of the automatic stay.

a. Schedules, Statements and Documents with the Petition

In a voluntary case, the debtor must file the following schedules, statements, and documents *with the petition:*

(i) a *list of creditors* with addresses [B.C. § 521(a)(1)(A); Bankruptcy Rule 1007(a)(1)];

(ii) for *an individual debtor with primarily consumer debts,* a certificate by the debtor's attorney or if the debtor is not represented by an attorney a statement by the debtor that the attorney delivered or that the debtor read the notice required by *§ 342(b),* which explains the various chapters available to the debtor and the costs and benefits of each chapter [B.C. § 521(a)(1)(B)(iii)];

(iii) for *an individual debtor,* a statement showing compliance with the *credit counseling* requirement and a copy of any *debt repayment plan* [B.C. §§ 109(h), 521(b); Bankruptcy Rule 1007(b)(3) & (c)];

(iv) for *an individual debtor* who *rents* her residence and *wishes to stay in the rented residence after filing for bankruptcy* even though the *landlord has obtained an eviction judgment* against her, the *Initial Statement About an Eviction Judgment Against You* and deposit with the bankruptcy court clerk of the *amount of rent due during the 30 days after filing for bankruptcy* [Official Form 101A];

(v) for *an individual debtor,* a statement of the debtor's *social security number* [Bankruptcy Rule 1007(f)]; and

(vi) for a *corporate debtor,* other than a governmental unit, a *corporate ownership statement* that discloses any corporation owning 10% or more of the debtor's stock. [Bankruptcy Rule 1007(a)(1), 7007.1(a)]

b. Schedules, Statements and Documents Within 14 Days

All debtors, except a municipal debtor, must file the following schedules, statements, or documents either *with the petition* or *14 days* thereafter [Bankruptcy Rule 1007(c)]:

(i) a *schedule of assets and liabilities* along with a *summary table* of those assets and liabilities [B.C. § 521(a)(1)(B)(i); Bankruptcy Rule 1007(b)(1)(A)];

(ii) for *an individual debtor,* a schedule of *current income and expenditures* [B.C. § 521(a)(1)(B)(ii); Bankruptcy Rule 1007(b)(1)(B)];

(iii) a schedule of *executory contracts and unexpired leases* [Bankruptcy Rule 1007(b)(1)(C)];

(iv) a *statement of financial affairs* [B.C. § 521(a)(1)(B)(iii); Bankruptcy Rule 1007(b)(1)(D)];

(v) copies of all *pay stubs* that the debtor received from her employer within *60 days* of the bankruptcy filing [B.C. § 521(a)(1)(B)(iv); Bankruptcy Rule 1007(b)(1)(E)];

(vi) a record, if applicable, of any interest that the debtor has in an *education individual retirement account* [B.C. § 521(c); Bankruptcy Rule 1007(b)(1)(F)];

(vii) for *individual debtors* filing under Chapters 7, 11, or 13, *except an individual debtor under subchapter V,* an itemized statement of *current monthly income* [B.C. § 521(a)(1)(B)(v); Bankruptcy Rule 1007(b)(4)–(6), (c); Official Forms 122A-1, 122B, 122C-1]; and

(viii) a statement disclosing any reasonably anticipated *increase in income or expenditures* for the *12-month period* following the filing of the petition. [B.C. § 521(a)(1)(B)(vi); *see* **CFCU Federal Credit Union v. Frisbie,** 2009 WL 3153247 (W.D. N.Y. 2009) (holding that "the duty to disclose only exists if the debtor reasonably anticipates her income or expenses may increase")]

3. Chapter-Specific Schedules, Statements, Documents and Duties

In addition to the schedules, statements, documents and duties required of all debtors, the Code imposes additional filing requirements and obligations based on the nature of the debtor and filing chapter.

a. Chapter 7: Individual Debtor

An *individual* debtor filing for relief under *Chapter 7* must file the following additional paperwork and perform the following additional duties.

(i) Either *with the petition or no later than 14 days* thereafter, file the *Chapter 7 Means Test Calculation* form but only if the debtor has *primarily consumer debts* and her income *exceeds the median income* for her state and household size. [B.C. § 707(b)(2); Bankruptcy Rule 1007(b)(4); Official Form 122A-2]

(ii) Within the *earlier of 30 days from the petition* or the *§ 341 meeting,* with regard to property subject to a security interest *state her intention* to (1) *surrender* the property; (2) *redeem* the property; or (3) *reaffirm the debt* that the property secures. [B.C. § 521(a)(2)(A); Official Form 108]

(iii) *Within 30 days* of the first date set for the *§ 341 meeting, perform her intention* with regard to the property as to which she filed her statement of intention. [B.C. § 521(a)(2)(B)]

(iv) *No later than 7 days before the § 341 meeting,* provide a copy of the federal income tax return filed for the year immediately before the filing of the bankruptcy petition to the *trustee* and any *creditor* that makes *a timely request* for a copy. [B.C. § 521(e)(2)]

(v) No later than *60 days* from the date first set for the *§ 341 meeting,* file a statement that she has completed an *approved instructional course on personal financial management.* [B.C. § 727(a)(11); Bankruptcy Rule 1007(b)(7), (c)]

b. Chapter 11: Small Business Debtor

With the passage of BAPCPA in 2005, Congress amended the Bankruptcy Code to add a new § 308, which lists reporting duties for debtors in a *small business case.* A *subchapter V* case is *not* a small business case, but the Code provides that a subchapter V debtor must comply with the requirements of § 308. [B.C. §§ 101(51C), 1187(b)] Therefore, a debtor in a small business case or a subchapter V debtor must file *periodic financial and other reports* that contain information as to the following:

(i) the debtor's *profitability* [B.C. § 308(b)(1)];

(ii) *reasonable approximations* of debtor's *projected cash receipts and disbursements* over a reasonable time frame [B.C. § 308(b)(2)];

(iii) *comparisons* of *actual* cash receipts and disbursements with *earlier projections* [B.C. § 308(b)(3)];

(iv) debtor's *compliance* with *reporting requirements* under the Code and the Bankruptcy Rules [B.C. § 308(b)(4)(A)];

(v) debtor's *timely filing of tax returns* and other required *government filings,* and *payment of taxes* and *administrative expenses* when due [B.C. § 308(b)(4)(B)]; and

(vi) other matters that are in the *best interests of the debtor and creditors,* and in the public interest in *fair and efficient bankruptcy procedures.* [B.C. § 308(b)(6)]

If the debtor is not in compliance with its reporting obligations under the Code, is not filing tax returns or other government filings on time, or is not paying taxes and administrative expenses when due, then the debtor must explain what obligations it is not performing, the cost of such failures, and when the debtor intends to remedy such failures. [B.C. § 308(b)(5)]

In a *small business* or a *subchapter V case,* the debtor also must file with the petition a list of the names and addresses of the *creditors holding the 20 largest unsecured claims* (excluding insiders) and the amounts of their claims. [Bankruptcy Rule 1007(d)] If the debtor has equity security holders, it must file a detailed list of its equity security holders no later than *14 days* after filing its voluntary petition. [Bankruptcy Rule 1007(a)(3)]

c. **Chapter 11: Individual Debtor**

(i) The debtor must file with the petition a list of the names and addresses of the *creditors holding the 20 largest unsecured claims* (excluding insiders) and the amounts of their claims. [Bankruptcy Rule 1007(d); Official Form 104]

(ii) If the debtor claims a *state exemption* in *excess of $189,050* in a *burial plot,* property used by the debtor or a dependent as a *residence,* or property claimed by a debtor or dependent as a *homestead,* the debtor must file a statement as to whether a *proceeding is pending* in which the debtor may be found *guilty of certain felonies* or liable for certain debts. The debtor must file the statement *no earlier* than the *last plan payment* or the filing of a *motion for discharge.* [B.C. § 522(p), (q); Bankruptcy Rule 1007(b)(8), (c)]

(iii) *If* § 1141(d)(3) applies, then no later than the date of the *last plan payment* or filing of a motion for a *hardship discharge,* the individual Chapter 11 debtor must file a statement that she has completed an *approved instructional course on personal financial management.* [B.C. § 1141(d)(3); Bankruptcy Rule 1007(b)(7), (c)]

d. **Chapter 11: Other Debtors**

Other Chapter 11 debtors, e.g., corporations that are not small businesses, must file with the petition a list disclosing the names and addresses of the *creditors holding the 20 largest unsecured claims* (excluding insiders) and the amounts of their claims. [Bankruptcy Rule 1007(d)] The debtor also must file a detailed list of its equity security holders no later than *14 days* after filing its voluntary petition. [Bankruptcy Rule 1007(a)(3)]

e. **Chapter 12**

(i) A Chapter 12 debtor must file a *proposed plan* of repayment *with the petition* or *within 90 days* after the order for relief. [B.C. § 1221; Bankruptcy Rule 3015(a)]

(ii) If an *individual Chapter 12* debtor claims a *state exemption* in *excess of $189,050* in a *burial plot,* property used by the debtor or a dependent as a *residence,* or property claimed by a debtor or dependent as a *homestead,* the debtor must file a statement as to whether a *proceeding is pending* in which the debtor may be found *guilty of certain felonies.* The debtor must file the statement *no earlier* than the *last plan payment* or the filing of a *motion for discharge.* [B.C. § 522(p), (q); Bankruptcy Rule 1007(b)(8), (c)]

f. Chapter 13

A Chapter 13 debtor must file or provide the following additional statements and documents.

(i) The debtor must file a *proposed plan* of repayment *with the petition* or *within 14* days thereafter. [B.C. § 1321; Bankruptcy Rule 3015(b)]

(ii) No later than the date of the *last plan payment* or filing of a motion for a *hardship discharge*, the debtor must file a statement that she has completed an *approved instructional course on personal financial management.* [B.C. § 1328(g)(1); Bankruptcy Rule 1007(b)(7), (c)]

(iii) *No later than 7 days before the § 341 meeting,* the debtor must provide a copy of the federal income tax return filed for the year immediately before the filing of the bankruptcy petition to the *trustee* and any *creditor* that makes *a timely request* for a copy. [B.C. § 521(e)(2)]

(iv) If the debtor claims a *state exemption* in *excess of $189,050* in a *burial plot,* property used by the debtor or a dependent as a *residence,* or property claimed by a debtor or dependent as a *homestead,* the debtor must file a *statement* as to whether a *proceeding is pending* in which the debtor may be found *guilty of certain felonies.* The debtor must file the statement *no earlier* than the *last plan payment* or the filing of a *motion for discharge.* [B.C. § 522(p), (q); Bankruptcy Rule 1007(b)(8), (c)]

4. Automatic Stay

When a *bankruptcy petition is filed,* the automatic stay becomes effective against *all entities,* including a governmental unit, to protect the debtor, her property, and the property of the bankruptcy estate from creditors, while the debtor is granted a respite. [B.C. § 362(a)] The stay provides the debtor with a "breathing spell" and stops the rush to the courthouse. There are numerous exceptions to the stay. *See infra* Chapter Ten.

D. Involuntary Case

1. Eligibility

A creditor may file an involuntary petition only under *Chapter 7 or Chapter 11* against a person who otherwise qualifies as a debtor under those chapters. [B.C. § 303(a)] Involuntary petitions are exceedingly rare. In calendar years 2011 through 2015, they comprised less than one-tenth of one percent of all bankruptcy filings.

a. Exceptions

An involuntary petition under Chapter 7 or Chapter 11 cannot be filed against (i) a farmer, (ii) a family farmer, or (iii) a nonprofit or charitable corporation. [B.C. § 303(a)]

2. Filing the Petition

a. Petitioning Entities

Whether an involuntary petition can be filed depends on the number of creditors the debtor has and the aggregate amount of their claims. [B.C. § 303(b)]

(i) Debtor Has 12 or More Creditors

If the debtor has *at least 12 creditors holding unsecured, noncontingent, undisputed claims*, then *three or more of these creditors* whose claims aggregate *at least $18,600* may file an involuntary petition against the debtor. [B.C. § 303(b)(1)] BAPCPA added "as to liability or amount" to the language modifying "bona fide dispute" in § 303(b). As a result, a dispute about any part of a claim, even if the debtor does not dispute the entire dollar amount, means that the entire claim is subject to bona fide dispute and cannot count for purposes of § 303(b). [*In re* **Vicor Techs.,** 2013 WL 1397460 (Bankr. S.D. Fla. 2013)]

(ii) One or More Creditors

If there are *fewer than 12 creditors holding unsecured, noncontingent, undisputed claims,* excluding the debtor's insiders and employees, and transferees of voidable transfers, then *one or more of these creditors* whose claims aggregate *at least $18,600* may file an involuntary petition against the debtor. [B.C. § 303(b)(2)]

(iii) General Partner

An involuntary case against a partnership debtor may be filed by fewer than all of the general partners. [B.C. § 303(b)(3)(A)] If relief has been ordered concerning all of the general partners, an involuntary petition against the partnership may be filed by (i) a general partner, (ii) the trustee of a general partner, or (iii) a creditor holding a claim against the partnership. [B.C. § 303(b)(3)(B)]

b. Indemnity Bond

The bankruptcy court may order the petitioners to file a bond to indemnify the debtor for any damages that might be awarded if the involuntary petition subsequently is dismissed. Notice and a hearing are required, and *cause* must be shown for the filing of the bond. [B.C. § 303(e), (i)]

3. Answer

Only the debtor, or in the case of a partnership debtor a non-petitioning general partner, may file an answer to the involuntary petition. [B.C. § 303(d)] A failure to answer and controvert the petition's allegations will result in the entry of an order for relief. [B.C. § 303(h)]

4. Entry of an Order for Relief

The court will enter an order for relief against the debtor if:

a. **the debtor fails to timely controvert the allegations in the petition** [B.C. § 303(h); Bankruptcy Rules 1011(b), 1013(b)];

b. the court finds, after trial, that the debtor is *generally not paying her undisputed debts as they come due* [B.C. § 303(h)(1); *see In re* **Vicor Techs.,** 2013 WL 1397460 (Bankr. S.D. Fla. 2013) (court should consider " 'the number of unpaid claims, the amount of the claims, the materiality of nonpayment and the overall conduct of the debtor's financial affairs' ")]; or

c. the court finds, after trial, that within *120 days* before the petition was filed, a *custodian was appointed or took charge* of the debtor's property, other than for the purpose of enforcing a lien against less than substantially all of such property. [B.C. §§ 303(h)(2), 101(11)]

---

5. Gap Period

As mentioned above, the filing of an involuntary petition does not constitute an order for relief. In this *gap period* between filing of the petition and entry of the order for relief, the debtor continues to operate her business and continues to use, acquire, and dispose of property, unless the bankruptcy court orders otherwise. [B.C. § 303(f)]

a. Transfers During Gap Period

If the debtor makes a transfer during the gap period, the transfer is not subject to the trustee's avoiding powers *to the extent of post-petition value given* by the transferee, including services, *in exchange for the transfer.* The transferee is protected notwithstanding any notice or knowledge that she has of the bankruptcy case. To be free of the trustee's avoiding power, the purpose of the transfer must not be to satisfy or secure a pre-petition debt. [B.C. § 549(b)]

b. Priority for Gap Creditors

The Code provides *priority status* for the claims of gap creditors. [B.C. § 507(a)(3)] A gap creditor claim is one that arises in the ordinary course of the debtor's business or financial affairs before the *earlier of* the appointment of a trustee or entry of the order for relief. [B.C. § 502(f)]

c. Interim Trustee

During the gap period in a Chapter 7 case, on request by a party in interest and after notice to the debtor and a hearing, the court may direct the United States trustee to appoint an interim trustee if the court finds that such an appointment is needed to *preserve property of the estate* or to *avoid loss.* If an interim trustee is appointed, she takes possession of property of the estate and, if applicable, operates the debtor's business. [B.C. § 303(g)]

6. Dismissal of Involuntary Petition

a. Damages Possible

If the court dismisses an involuntary petition other than on the consent of all the petitioning entities *and the debtor,* and if the debtor has not waived her right to damages, then the court may award a judgment to the debtor and against the petitioners for costs and/or reasonable attorneys' fees. [B.C. § 303(i)(1)]

Note: Without such a provision, some creditors likely would file involuntary petitions as leverage against a debtor.

(i) Punitive Damages for Bad Faith

If the bankruptcy court dismisses the petition and finds that a petitioning entity filed the petition in *bad faith,* then the court may award the debtor damages proximately caused by the involuntary petition and/or punitive damages. [B.C. § 303(i)(2)] The debtor may recover for actual damages, costs and attorneys' fees, and punitive damages. [2 Collier ¶ 303.33(3) (stating that a "debtor can recover under both paragraphs (1) and (2) of section 303(i)")]

b. Protection for Individuals

BAPCPA added certain protections for an *individual debtor* whose involuntary bankruptcy petition is dismissed by the court.

(i) If the petition was *false* or contained *materially false, fictitious, or fraudulent statements,* the court, upon the debtor's motion, must *seal all court records* related to the petition and all references to such petition. [B.C. § 303(k)(1)]

(ii) If the court dismisses an involuntary petition against an *individual,* the court also may issue an order *preventing all consumer reporting agencies* from making a consumer report containing information about the petition or the involuntary bankruptcy case. [B.C. § 303(k)(2)]

(iii) The court may, upon motion of the debtor and for *good cause, expunge* any records related to an involuntary bankruptcy petition involving *bankruptcy crimes.* [B.C. § 303(k)(3); 18 U.S.C. §§ 152, 157] For example, filing a fraudulent involuntary petition is bankruptcy fraud punishable by five years' imprisonment, a fine, or both. [18 U.S.C. § 157(1)] The court, however, may not expunge the records related to such an involuntary petition until the relevant statute of limitations has expired. [B.C. § 303(k)(3)]

c. Notice and Hearing

The court may dismiss an involuntary petition on the motion of a petitioning creditor, on the consent of all petitioning creditors and the debtor, or for lack of prosecution only after *notice* and an opportunity for a *hearing* is given to *all creditors.* [B.C. § 303(j)]

7. Schedules to Be Filed

If the court enters an order for relief, then the debtor must file the lists, schedules, and statements required by the Code within the time limits fixed by Bankruptcy Rule 1007.

E. Section 341 Meeting of Creditors

1. Time and Place

In a *Chapter 7 or Chapter 11* case, within *21 to 40 days after* the order for relief, the United States trustee must convene a meeting of creditors. In a *Chapter 12 case*, the meeting is held within *21 to 35 days after* the order for relief. In a *Chapter 13 case*, the meeting is held within *21 to 50 days after* the order for relief. This meeting is called the *§ 341 meeting* of creditors. [B.C. § 341(a); Bankruptcy Rule 2003(a)]

a. Meeting of Equity Security Holders

The United States trustee also may convene a meeting of the debtor's equity security holders. [B.C. § 341(b)] The United States trustee sets the date for the meeting and presides at it. [Bankruptcy Rule 2003(b)(2)]

2. No § 341 Meeting

If the debtor has filed a plan on which it solicited acceptances prior to bankruptcy, then the bankruptcy court, on request of a party interest and for *cause,* may order the United States trustee not to convene a meeting of creditors or equity security holders. Notice and a hearing are required. [B.C. § 341(e)]

3. Notice

The clerk of the court provides by mail at least *21 days' notice* of the § 341 meeting to the debtor, the trustee, all creditors, and indenture trustees. If notice by mail is impracticable, the court may order that notice be given by publication. [Bankruptcy Rule 2002(a)(1), (*l*)] In a reorganization case under Chapter 11, equity security holders must be notified of any § 341 meeting of equity security holders. [Bankruptcy Rule 2002(d)] *See* Official Forms 309A–I for the notice of the § 341 meeting and other deadlines in the bankruptcy case.

4. Purpose of Section 341 Meeting

The § 341 meeting is not a judicial hearing. In fact, the bankruptcy judge may neither preside at nor attend the § 341 meeting. [B.C. § 341(c)] The *United States trustee presides* over the meeting. [B.C. § 341; Bankruptcy Rule 2003(b)] In the six judicial districts in Alabama and North Carolina, where the United States trustee program does not operate, the *bankruptcy administrator* presides. The primary purpose of the meeting is to afford creditors, any trustee or examiner in the case, any indenture trustee, and the United States trustee or bankruptcy administrator to examine *the debtor under oath.* [B.C. § 343] A creditor holding a *consumer debt* in a *Chapter 7 or Chapter 13* case may participate in the § 341 meeting, even if she is not represented by an attorney. [B.C. § 341(c)]

a. Trustee Exam in Chapter 7 Case

In a Chapter 7 case, the *trustee,* before the end of the meeting of creditors or of equity security holders, must *orally examine the debtor* to ensure that the debtor is aware of:

(i) the possible consequences of seeking a bankruptcy discharge, including the effect on the *debtor's credit history* [B.C. § 341(d)(1)];

(ii) the ability to file for relief under *another bankruptcy chapter* [B.C. § 341(d)(2)];

(iii) the effect of receiving a *bankruptcy discharge* [B.C. § 341(d)(3)]; and

(iv) the effect of *reaffirming a debt*, including what effect reaffirmation has on the *debtor's discharge*. [B.C. §§ 341(d)(4), 524(d)]

b. Election of Trustee or Committee in Chapter 7 Case

If creditors holding a sufficient percentage of unsecured claims make the request, unsecured creditors eligible to vote may vote to elect the Chapter 7 trustee at the § 341 meeting. [B.C. § 702(b)] Unsecured creditors eligible to vote on a Chapter 7 trustee under § 702 also may elect a committee of unsecured creditors that would consult with the trustee and United States trustee on administration of the debtor's Chapter 7 case. [B.C. § 705] Unsecured creditors' committees in Chapter 7 are rare.

c. Immunity

The Code provides that a person required to submit to examination, to testify, or to provide information in a bankruptcy case may be granted immunity pursuant to the conditions and procedures set forth at 18 U.S.C. §§ 6001–6005 [B.C. § 344]

5. Debtor Must Attend

The debtor must attend the § 341 meeting. [*See* B.C. § 343] The courts are divided about whether a bankruptcy court has the discretion under § 343 to waive the debtor's attendance at the § 341 meeting. [*In re* **Palmer,** 2015 WL 534503 (Bankr. W.D. La. 2015); B.C. § 343] A majority of courts, however, waive physical attendance at the § 341 meeting for good cause. [*In re* **Alleca,** 582 B.R. 530 (Bankr. M.D. Ala. 2018)]

e.g. **Example:** Debtor filed a petition for relief under Chapter 13. Debtor was 83 years old, had suffered a stroke, was bedridden, partially paralyzed, and unable to hold a conversation for more than five minutes because she was in a "confused state." Debtor appointed her granddaughter as power of attorney to appear on her behalf in the bankruptcy proceeding. The court concluded that "Congress did not intend to remove bankruptcy courts' discretion to waive debtor's appearance at § 341 meetings," in particular in cases in which the debtor's appearance was impossible. The court went on to explain that it would be the rare case, however, in which the debtor could not attend in person or telephonically; in those rare cases, a representative of the debtor with full knowledge of the debtor's financial affairs must appear. [*In re* **Palmer,** *supra*]

e.g. **Example:** Debtor, incarcerated in federal prison for his role in a Ponzi scheme, filed for relief under Chapter 7. Debtor moved the court to excuse his attendance at the § 341 meeting and instead have the trustee examine him through the use of interrogatories. The bankruptcy court denied Debtor's motion and found that Debtor had not met his burden of showing an alternative method existed that was equivalent to his attendance at a § 341 meeting. First, Debtor failed to comply with the local bankruptcy rule's requirement to provide copies of both his judgment and conviction. Second, the bankruptcy court found that the use of interrogatories, given the complexity of Debtor's bankruptcy case and the Ponzi scheme that led to his imprisonment, would create "insurmountable difficult[ies] [for the trustee] in fulfilling her duties." [*In re* **Alleca,** *supra*]

F. Conversion

1. Authorization

A debtor cannot convert her case to a chapter of the Bankruptcy Code for which she is ineligible. For example, a Chapter 7 debtor cannot convert her case to Chapter 13 if either her secured or unsecured debts exceed the statutory limits for Chapter 13 cases. A court may order conversion of a Chapter 7 or Chapter 11 case to Chapter 12 or Chapter 13 ***only upon the debtor's request.*** [B.C. §§ 706(c), 1112(d)] A Chapter 12 or Chapter 13 debtor may convert her case to Chapter 7 at any time. [B.C. §§ 1208(a), 1307(a)]

2. Effects of Conversion

The ***conversion*** of a case to another chapter constitutes an ***order for relief*** under that new chapter. With ***certain exceptions***, however, conversion does not alter the date of the filing of the bankruptcy petition, the commencement of the case, or the order for relief. [B.C. § 348(a)]

a. Exceptions

Section 348(b) lists a number of Code sections in which the phrase "the order for relief" means the conversion of the case to the new chapter.

> **Example:** Section 1221 of the Code requires the Chapter 12 debtor to file its plan no later than *90 days after the order for relief.* If a debtor converts its case from Chapter 11 to Chapter 12, the 90 days runs from the conversion of the case to Chapter 12, not from the initial filing of the Chapter 11 petition.

Section 348(c) provides that for §§ 342(a) and 365(d), the ***conversion order*** is treated as the ***order for relief.*** Section 342(a) requires notice of the order for relief. Section 365(d) sets time periods within which the trustee must assume or reject an executory contract or unexpired lease of the debtor.

> **Example:** On March 1, Darren filed for relief under Chapter 13. Darren rents his home. On May 3, Darren converted his case to Chapter 7. Section 365(d)(1) provides that an unexpired lease of residential real property is deemed rejected if the trustee has not assumed (or rejected) the lease within 60 days of the order for relief. If § 365(d)(1)'s time period ran from March 1—the date of the Chapter 13 petition—then the 60 days would have expired by the time of conversion. Section 348(c) provides that § 365(d) applies to the converted Chapter 7 case as if the conversion order were the order for relief. Therefore, the Chapter 7 trustee has 60 days from conversion, not the filing of the Chapter 13 petition, to assume or reject the lease.

3. Pre-Conversion Claims

Except for administrative expenses, any claims arising in a Chapter 11, 12, or 13 case after the order for relief but before conversion to another chapter are considered pre-petition claims for all purposes. [B.C. § 348(d)]

4. Trustee or Examiner Service Terminated

Conversion of a Chapter 7, 11, 12, or 13 case terminates the service of any trustee or examiner serving in the case prior to conversion. [B.C. § 348(e)]

5. Conversion from Chapter 13: Special Rules

a. Property of the Estate

If a case is converted from Chapter 13 to another chapter of the Code, property of the estate in the converted case consists of property of the estate *on the date of the Chapter 13 filing* that remains in the debtor's possession or control on the date of conversion. [B.C. § 348(f)(1)(A)] But, if the debtor converts her case in *bad faith,* property of the estate in the converted case consists of estate property *on the date of conversion,* which includes property acquired after the date of the Chapter 13 filing. [B.C. § 348(f)(2)]

> **Example:** Debtor filed for relief under Chapter 13. During her Chapter 13 case, Debtor made payments from her earnings to the Chapter 13 trustee. Debtor was unable to confirm a Chapter 13 plan and converted her case to Chapter 7. The Chapter 13 trustee distributed to the Chapter 7 trustee the payments made from Debtor's earnings. Debtor claimed that the funds should have been returned to her because they were not property of the Chapter 7 estate. The court agreed with Debtor. The payments were from wages that Debtor earned *after* filing her Chapter 13 case and, thus, were not property of the estate at the time that she filed her Chapter 13 case. Therefore, under § 348(f)(1)(A), they were not property of the estate in the converted Chapter 7 case. [**Stamm v. Morton (*In re* Stamm),** 222 F.3d 216 (5th Cir. 2000)]

Note: Had Debtor converted her case to Chapter 7 in bad faith, the wages she earned after filing for relief under Chapter 13 would have been property of the estate in the converted Chapter 7 case.

b. Secured Claims

Valuations of *property* and of *allowed secured claims* in the Chapter 13 case *only* apply in a case converted to Chapters 11 or 12. Any amounts paid on allowed secured claims in the Chapter 13 case *reduce* the amount of the secured claim in the converted Chapter 11 or 12 case. [B.C. § 348(f)(1)(B)]

With the enactment of BAPCPA, Congress added two new rules applicable to cases converted from Chapter 13. The first provides that unless a secured claim was paid in full as of the date of conversion from Chapter 13, the claim is still secured, notwithstanding any valuation or determination of the amount of the secured claim in the Chapter 13 case prior to conversion. [B.C. § 348(f)(1)(C)(i)] The second states that unless a *pre-bankruptcy default* has been cured under the plan as of the date of conversion, the default has the effect given under nonbankruptcy law. [B.C. § 348(f)(1)(C)(ii)]

G. Dismissal

1. Different Rules for Chapters 7, 11, 12, and 13

The Code provides different rules for dismissal depending on the chapter of the Code under which the debtor filed its petition. [*See* B.C. §§ 707, 1112, 1208, 1307] The chapter-specific dismissal rules are discussed later in this study guide.

2. Effect of Dismissal

Unless the bankruptcy court, for cause orders otherwise, the dismissal of a case is *without prejudice* to the debtor's right to file a subsequent petition, with the exception of the rule in § 109(g), and obtain a discharge of debts that could have been discharged in the case dismissed. [B.C. § 349(a)]

a. Section 109(g) Exception

Section 109(g) provides that *no individual or family farmer* is eligible to file for bankruptcy if she has been a debtor in a case *pending in the preceding 180 days* and (i) that case was dismissed due to the debtor's *willful failure* to abide by court orders or to *appear in proper prosecution* of the case; or (ii) the debtor sought and obtained voluntary dismissal of the case after the *filing of a motion to lift the stay*. [B.C. § 109(g)] If the court dismisses the case and makes either of the § 109(g) findings, then the dismissal is *with prejudice* as to the debtor's eligibility to refile for bankruptcy within 180 days.

3. Automatic Dismissal

If an *individual* in a *voluntary Chapter 7 or Chapter 13 case* fails to file all the information required by § 521(a)(1) *within 45 days* of filing her petition, then her case is *automatically dismissed* on Day 46. [B.C. § 521(i)(1)] While the Code provides for automatic dismissal, it is unclear how that happens, and it is possible, notwithstanding the "automatic dismissal" language that a court order is needed. [3 Collier ¶ 349.01(3)(h); § 521(i)(1), (2)] Any party in interest may request that the court enter an order dismissing the case. The bankruptcy court must enter such an order *no later than 7 days* after the request. [B.C. § 521(i)(2)] The debtor, within the 45-day period, may request and the bankruptcy court may allow additional time, *not to exceed 45 days,* to file the information required by § 521(a)(1) if the court finds justification for extending the time period. [B.C. § 521(i)(3)] The bankruptcy court may decline to dismiss the case, on motion of the trustee file within the 45-day period, if the court determines that the debtor *attempted in good faith* to file all the information required by § 521(a)(1)(B)(iv) (payment advices) and the *best interests of creditors* would be served by not dismissing the case. [B.C. § 521(i)(4)]

Chapter Four

Case Administration: Officers of the Estate

Chapter Approach

This chapter discusses the roles and duties of a bankruptcy trustee, an examiner, professional persons, and the United States trustee. The relevant provisions of the Bankruptcy Code are contained in §§ 321 through 333.

Make sure you distinguish between the trustee for an individual bankruptcy case and the United States trustee. In Chapters 7, 12, and 13, a trustee is appointed to handle the individual case. A trustee also is appointed in a *subchapter V Chapter 11* case. Appointment of a trustee in a non-subchapter V Chapter 11 case is rare.

In Chapter 7, the bankruptcy trustee collects and liquidates the assets of the estate and distributes the proceeds to creditors. In Chapters 12, 13, and subchapter V Chapter 11 cases, the *debtor remains in possession* of the property of the estate even though a trustee is appointed. Chapter 12 and Chapter 13 trustees are *standing trustees* for all cases in the jurisdiction. The United States trustee also may appoint a standing trustee for subchapter V cases in a jurisdiction.

In a non-subchapter V Chapter 11 case, the bankruptcy court may appoint an *examiner* to investigate the debtor's conduct and business operations, help determine the advisability of continuing the debtor's business, and report to the court. The debtor remains a debtor in possession notwithstanding the appointment of an examiner.

The *United States trustee* assumes many of the *administrative responsibilities* previously performed by the bankruptcy court, including the appointment and supervision of bankruptcy trustees, as well as the review of fee applications of attorneys and other professional persons, thereby helping to separate the administrative and judicial functions in bankruptcy cases. Remember that the United States trustee system does not operate in the six judicial districts in Alabama and North Carolina; instead, *bankruptcy administrators* perform many of the functions performed by the United States trustee.

It is important to remember that the bankruptcy court must approve the employment and compensation of a *professional person,* e.g., an attorney. The court may deny compensation to a professional person who fails to obtain court approval of her employment. Furthermore, make sure that a professional hired by a trustee or a debtor in possession is a *disinterested person* and that she does not have an interest adverse to the estate.

BAPCPA added two new types of officers: the *consumer privacy ombudsman* and the *patient care ombudsman.* The consumer privacy ombudsman's role is limited; she is appointed in a case in which there is a hearing on the trustee's proposal to sell or lease *personally identifiable information*. In a Chapter 7 or Chapter 11 case involving a *health care business*, the bankruptcy court must appoint a patient care ombudsman to represent the interests of patients of the health care business.

A. Trustee

1. Role and Capacity

The trustee is the official representative of the estate. The trustee's duties are set by statute. Besides various administrative powers, the trustee has authority to initiate and defend lawsuits. [B.C. § 323]

2. Eligibility

a. Chapter 7, 12, or 13 Case

An individual or corporation is eligible to serve as a trustee. The trustee does not have to be a lawyer. An individual must be competent to perform the required responsibilities, and a corporation must be authorized by its charter or bylaws to serve as a trustee. In a Chapter 7, 12, or 13 case, the trustee also must reside, or have an office, in the judicial district where the bankruptcy case is pending or in the adjacent district. [B.C. § 321(a)] The Code's general eligibility requirements to serve as a trustee do not include disinterestedness. [B.C. § 321] Nonetheless, courts have held that a trustee must be disinterested in order to avoid not only actual conflicts of interest but also the appearance of conflicts that may undermine the integrity of the bankruptcy system. [*In re* **Barkany**, 542 B.R. 699 (Bankr. E.D. N.Y. 2015)]

b. Subchapter V Chapter 11 Case

Section 321 of the Code, which elaborates on the eligibility requirements for a trustee, is limited to cases under Chapters 7, 12, and 13. [B.C. § 321] If § 321 does not provide the qualifications for a subchapter V trustee, then what are those qualifications? Section 1182 provides little help. [*See* 8 Collier ¶ 1183.02 (stating that "Subchapter V gives no guidance as to the qualifications for subchapter V trustees")] Section 1183 states that *an individual* appointed by the United States trustee may serve as a *standing trustee* if that individual posts the bond required by § 322. [28 U.S.C. § 586(b)] If no standing trustee is appointed, then the United States trustee must appoint a *disinterested person* to serve as trustee in the subchapter V case or the United States trustee may serve as the case trustee. [B.C. § 1183(a)]

c. "Disinterested Person"

The Code's definition of a disinterested person *excludes* the following entities:

(i) *creditors, equity security holders, and insiders* [B.C. § 101(14)(A)];

(ii) current *directors, officers, and employees* of the debtor, and those who have been directors, officers, of employees of the debtor within two years prior to the commencement of the case [B.C. § 101(14)(B)]; and

(iii) *any person with a materially adverse interest* to the estate or to any class of creditors or equity security holders. [B.C. § 101(14)(C)]

d. Examiner Precluded

Any person who has served as an examiner is prohibited from becoming a trustee in the same case. [B.C. § 321(b)] The Code's provisions on appointment and duties of an examiner *do not apply* to a subchapter V case. [B.C. § 1181(a)]

e. United States Trustee

If necessary, the United States trustee for the respective judicial district may serve as the trustee in a Chapter 7, 12, or 13 case. [B.C. § 321(c)] The United States trustee also may serve as the trustee in a subchapter V case but not in a non-subchapter V Chapter 11 case. [B.C. §§ 1104(d), 1183]

3. Qualification of Trustee—Bond

Within seven days after appointment or election, and before beginning service, a trustee must file with the court a *bond,* in favor of the United States, in the amount set by the United States trustee. [B.C. § 322(a)] The United States trustee determines the amount of the bond and must approve the sufficiency of the surety on such bond. [B.C. § 322(b)]

4. Selection of Trustee

The rules for determining when and how a trustee is selected vary depending on the chapter of the Code under which the bankruptcy case was filed.

a. Chapter 7 Case

All Chapter 7 cases require the services of a trustee. Each United States trustee establishes and maintains a panel of private trustees to serve in the Chapter 7 cases for the particular region. [28 U.S.C. § 586(a)(1)] There are 21 regions. [28 U.S.C. § 581(a)] In the six judicial districts in Alabama and North Carolina that are not part of the U.S. trustee system, the bankruptcy administrator maintains the panel of private trustees.

(i) Interim Trustee

Promptly after the entry of the order for relief in a Chapter 7 case, the United States trustee appoints a disinterested member of the private panel to serve as the interim trustee until the § 341 meeting. At the § 341 meeting, the interim trustee will become the permanent trustee unless another person is elected by creditors. In most cases, no election is held and the interim trustee serves as the permanent trustee in the case. [B.C. §§ 701(a), (b), 702(b), (d)]

(ii) Election of Trustee

If an election is requested by creditors who hold at least *20% in amount of the claims* entitled to vote for a trustee, an election is conducted at the § 341 meeting. [B.C. § 702(b)]

(1) Who May Vote

A creditor is eligible to vote for a trustee only if the creditor: (i) holds an allowable, *unsecured, nonpriority,* undisputed, fixed, and liquidated claim; (ii) does not have an interest that is materially adverse to other creditors holding such claims; and (iii) is not an insider. [B.C. § 702(a)] The courts are split on whether Bankruptcy Rule 2003(b)(3) further limits the creditors eligible to vote. Rule 2003(b)(3) provides that a creditor is entitled to vote if, at or before the § 341 meeting, the creditor has filed a *proof of claim* or a writing setting forth facts evidencing a right to vote *unless* an objection is made to the claim or the proof of claim is insufficient on its face. [Bankruptcy Rule 2003(b)(3)] Some courts limit eligible voters to those satisfying Rule 2003(b)(3). Other courts take a more "expansive view" and "note that section 702 does not specifically require that a proof of claim be filed in order for the creditor to be eligible to vote." [6 Collier ¶ 702.03(2)]

b. Votes Needed to Be Elected

Election of a candidate as the permanent trustee requires (i) that creditors holding at least *20% in amount* of the eligible voting claims *actually vote,* and (ii) that the candidate receive votes representing a majority *in amount* of the claims that have been voted. [B.C. § 702(c)]

c. **Non-Subchapter V Chapter 11 Case**

In a non-subchapter V Chapter 11 case, the debtor generally remains in possession of property of the estate and continues to manage the business, in an effort to reorganize, *without the necessity of a trustee's appointment.* The rationale is that the debtor's current management ordinarily is better acquainted with and more experienced in the particular business operations than an outside trustee. A party in interest or the United States trustee, however, may move at any time after the filing of the bankruptcy petition but before confirmation of a Chapter 11 plan for appointment of a Chapter 11 trustee. [B.C. § 1104(a)]

Reasons for appointment of a trustee are:

(i) *cause,* which includes *fraud, dishonesty, incompetence, or gross mismanagement* by current management either before or after the start of the bankruptcy case [B.C. § 1104(a)(1)];

(ii) appointment is in the *interests of creditors, any equity security holders,* and other interests of the estate [B.C. § 1104(a)(2)]; or

(iii) grounds exist to *convert or dismiss* the case, but the bankruptcy court determines that appointment of a trustee is in the *best interests of creditors and the estate.* [B.C. § 1112(b)(1)]

(i)   When the United States Trustee Must Act

BAPCPA added a new subsection (e) to § 1104 that requires the United States trustee to move for the appointment of a Chapter 11 trustee if *reasonable grounds* exist to suspect that current members of the debtor's governing body, debtor's chief executive or chief financial officer, or members of the governing body that selected the chief executive or chief financial officer participated in *actual fraud, dishonesty, or criminal conduct* in *managing the debtor* or the *debtor's public financial reporting.* [B.C. § 1104(e)]

d. **Appointment of Trustee**

If the bankruptcy court orders the appointment of a trustee, the United States trustee, after consulting with parties in interest, must appoint a disinterested person to serve as trustee, subject to the court's approval. [B.C. §§ 1104(d), 322] The United States trustee may not serve as the trustee in the case. [B.C. § 1104(d)]

e. **Election of Trustee**

The Code authorizes *election* of the trustee, *rather than appointment,* if a party in interest requests an election within *30 days* after the court orders appointment of a trustee. The United States trustee must convene a meeting of creditors for the purpose of electing a *disinterested person* to serve as trustee. [B.C. § 1104(b)(1)] The election is conducted in the same manner as the election of a trustee under Chapter 7. [*See* B.C. § 702(a)–(c)] If a Chapter 11 trustee is elected, then the United States trustee must file a report certifying the election. Upon filing of the report, the services of any trustee already appointed by the United States trustee under § 1104(a) are terminated. [B.C. § 1104(b)(2)]

f. **Subchapter V Chapter 11 Cases**

Chapter 11's provisions on appointment and election of a trustee *do not apply* in a *subchapter V case.* [B.C. § 1181(a)] Instead, as in Chapter 12 and Chapter 13, a trustee is appointed in a subchapter V case. The Code provides that if the number of cases in a region warrants it, the United States trustee will appoint a *standing trustee* for all *subchapter V Chapter 11 cases* in that region. [28 U.S.C. § 586(b); B.C. § 1183(a)] But, as of the writing of this study guide, the Executive Office of the United States Trustees has not appointed subchapter V standing trustees. [8 Collier ¶ 1183.02] Instead, a subchapter V trustee is appointed on a "case-by-case basis" from a panel or pools of subchapter V trustees created across the country. [Department of Justice, Private Trustee Information *available at https://www.justice.gov/ust/private-trustee-information*]

g. **Chapter 12 and Chapter 13 Cases**

If the number of cases in a region warrants it, the United States trustee will appoint *standing trustees* for all Chapter 12 and Chapter 13 cases in the region. [28 U.S.C. § 586(b); B.C. §§ 1202(a), 1302(a)] If a standing trustee is not appointed, then the United States trustee will appoint a *disinterested person* as the trustee for a particular case, or the United States trustee may serve as the trustee in the case. [B.C. §§ 1202(a), 1302(a)] Notwithstanding the appointment of a trustee, Chapter 12 and 13 debtors remain in possession of property of the estate. [B.C. §§ 1207(b), 1306(b)]

5. Duties of Trustee

The duties of a trustee vary according to the chapter under which the trustee is serving, although some of the basic functions overlap. [B.C. §§ 704, 1106(a), 1183(b), 1202(b), 1302(b)]

a. **Chapter 7 Case: Primary Responsibilities**

The primary responsibilities of a Chapter 7 trustee are to *collect and reduce to cash* property of the estate, to *make distributions* to claimants in the order prescribed by the Code, and to *close the estate* as expeditiously as is compatible with the best interests of parties in interest. [B.C. §§ 704(a)(1), 725, 726]

b. **Chapter 7 Case: Additional Responsibilities**

A Chapter 7 trustee has the following additional duties:

(i)   to *account* for all property received [B.C. § 704(a)(2)];

(ii)   to *ensure* an individual debtor's performance of her intentions regarding collateral securing debts [B.C. §§ 704(a)(3), 521(a)(2)(B)];

(iii)   to *investigate* the debtor's financial affairs [B.C. § 704(a)(4)];

(iv)   to *examine proofs of claims* and to object to the allowance of any improper claims [B.C. § 704(a)(5)];

(v)   to *object to the debtor's discharge,* if circumstances warrant [B.C. § 704(a)(6)];

(vi)   to *provide information* requested by parties in interest about the estate and the administration of the estate [B.C. § 704(a)(7)];

(vii)   to *file periodic financial reports,* including a statement of receipts and disbursements with the court, the United States trustee, and the appropriate taxing authorities, if the trustee is operating the debtor's business [B.C. § 704(a)(8)];

(viii) to *prepare and file* with the court and the United States trustee a *final report and account* concerning the case [B.C. § 704(a)(9)];

(ix)   to *continue to perform* the duties of an *administrator of an employee benefit plan,* if, at the commencement of the case, the debtor served as such an administrator [B.C. § 704(a)(11)];

(x) to *use reasonable and best efforts,* in a case involving a *health care business* that is closing, to *transfer patients* to a *facility* that is in the *vicinity* of the business that is closing, that maintains a *reasonable quality of care,* and that provides *services substantially similar* to the health care business that is closing [B.C. § 704(a)(12)];

(xi) to *file,* no later than *10 days after* the date of the first *§ 341 meeting,* a statement with the court as to whether the filing of an *individual* debtor's Chapter 7 bankruptcy case creates a presumption of abuse [B.C. §§ 704(b)(1)(A), 707(b)]; and

(xii) if there is a claim for a *domestic support obligation:*

    (1) to *provide written notice* to the holder of a *domestic support obligation claim* of the right to assistance from a state child support enforcement agency in collecting child support both during and after the case, and of the claim holder's right to payment in a Chapter 7 case [B.C. § 704(a)(10), (c)(1)(A)];

    (2) to *provide written notice* to the applicable state child support enforcement agency of the existence of a *domestic support obligation* [B.C. § 704(a)(10), (c)(1)(B)]; and

    (3) to *provide written notice* both to the holder of a *domestic support obligation claim* and the applicable state child support enforcement agency of the *granting of a discharge* to the debtor. [B.C. § 704(a)(10), (c)(1)(C)]

c. **Non-Subchapter V Chapter 11 Case**

A Chapter 11 trustee, appointed in a non-subchapter V case to replace a debtor in possession, ordinarily is authorized to *operate the debtor's business* [B.C. § 1108] and is charged with the following responsibilities:

(i) *to account* for all property received, to *examine proofs of claims* and object to improper ones, to *provide information* to parties in interest about the estate or its administration, to *file periodic financial reports* with the court, the United States trustee, and taxing authorities, to *prepare and file a final report and account,* to *continue,* in the appropriate case, to perform the duties of an *administrator of an employee benefit plan,* and to use *reasonable and best efforts* to transfer patients of a *health care business* that is closing to a facility with *substantially similar services.* [B.C. §§ 1106(a)(1), 704(a)(2), (5), (7), (8), (9), (11), (12)];

(ii) to file any documents required under section 521(a)(1), e.g., schedules, statements, pay stubs, that the debtor has not filed [B.C. §§ 1106(a)(2), 521(a)(1)];

(iii) to *investigate* the debtor's conduct, financial condition, and business operations, as well as the *advisability of continuing the debtor's business* [B.C. § 1106(a)(3)];

(iv) to *file a report of the investigation* relating any facts evidencing fraud, dishonesty, incompetence, misconduct, mismanagement, or irregularity in managing the debtor's affairs, or pertaining to a cause of action that the estate holds, and to send a copy of the findings to any creditors' committee, equity security holders' committee, indenture trustee, or any entity that the court designates [B.C. § 1106(a)(4)];

(v) to *file a Chapter 11 plan* as soon as feasible, or recommend conversion of the case to another chapter or dismissal [B.C. § 1106(a)(5)];

(vi) to *provide information,* if available, to the taxing authorities concerning any year for which the debtor failed to file a return [B.C. § 1106(a)(6)];

(vii) *after a plan has been confirmed,* to *file* any required reports [B.C. § 1106(a)(7)]; and

(viii) if there is a claim for a *domestic support obligation:*

    (1) to *provide written notice* to the holder of a *domestic support obligation claim* of the right to assistance from a state child support enforcement agency in collecting child support both during and after the case [B.C. § 1106(a)(8), (c)(1)(A)];

    (2) to *provide written notice* to the applicable state child support enforcement agency of the existence of a *domestic support obligation* [B.C. § 1106(a)(8), (c)(1)(B)]; and

    (3) to *provide written notice* both to the holder of a *domestic support obligation claim* and the applicable state child support enforcement agency of the *granting of a discharge* to the debtor. [B.C. § 1106(a)(8), (c)(1)(C)]

d. Subchapter V Case

A subchapter V trustee has the following duties:

(i) to *account* for all property received, to *examine proofs of claims* and to object to the allowance of any improper claims, to *object to the debtor's discharge,* if circumstances warrant, to *provide information* requested by parties in interest about the estate and the administration of the estate, and to *prepare and file* with the court and the United States trustee a *final report and account* concerning the case [B.C. §§ 1183(b)(1), 704(a)(2), (5), (6), (7), (9)];

(ii) to perform the *following duties* if the court, for *cause* and on request of a party in interest, the trustee, or the United States trustee, so orders:

    (1) *investigate* the debtor's conduct, financial condition, and business operations, as well as the *advisability of continuing the debtor's business* [B.C. §§ 1183(b)(2), 1106(a)(3)];

    (2) *file a report of the investigation* relating any facts evidencing fraud, dishonesty, incompetence, misconduct, mismanagement, or irregularity in managing the debtor's affairs, or pertaining to a cause of action that the estate holds, and to send a copy of the findings to any creditors' committee, equity security holders' committee, indenture trustee, or any entity that the court designates [B.C. §§ 1183(b)(2), 1106(a)(4)]; and

    (3) *after a plan has been confirmed, file* any required reports [B.C. §§ 1183(b)(2), 1106(a)(7)];

(iii) to *appear and be heard* at the subchapter V case *status conference* [B.C. § 1183(b)(3)];

(iv) to *appear and be heard* at any hearing on *plan confirmation*, post-confirmation *modification* of the plan, *sale* of property of the estate, or the *value of property* subject to a lien [B.C. § 1183(b)(3)];

(v) to ensure that the debtor begins making *timely plan payments* [B.C. § 1183(b)(4)];

(vi) if the debtor is *removed as debtor in possession*:

    (1) to *file periodic financial reports,* including a statement of receipts and disbursements with the court, the United States trustee, and the appropriate taxing authorities [B.C. §§ 1183(b)(5), 704(a)(8)];

(2) *to perform the duties* listed in (i) above, *continue,* in the appropriate case, to perform the duties of an *administrator of an employee benefit plan,* and use *reasonable and best efforts* to transfer patients of a *health care business* that is closing to a facility with *substantially similar services* [B.C. §§ 1183(b)(5), 1106(a)(1), 704(a)(2), (5), (7), (9), (11), (12)];

(3) to file any documents required under section 521(a)(1), e.g., schedules, statements, pay stubs, that the debtor has not filed [B.C. §§ 1183(b)(5), 1106(a)(2), 521(a)(1)];

(4) to *provide information,* if available, to the taxing authorities concerning any year for which the debtor failed to file a return [B.C. §§ 1183(b)(5), 1106(a)(6)];

(vii) if there is a claim for a *domestic support obligation:*

(1) to *provide written notice* to the holder of a *domestic support obligation claim* of the right to assistance from a state child support enforcement agency in collecting child support both during and after the case [B.C. §§ 1183(b)(6), 704(c)];

(2) to *provide written notice* to the applicable state child support enforcement agency of the existence of a *domestic support obligation* [B.C. §§ 1183(b)(6), 704(c)]; and

(3) to *provide written notice* both to the holder of a *domestic support obligation claim* and the applicable state child support enforcement agency of the *granting of a discharge* to the debtor. [B.C. §§ 1183(b)(6), 704(c)];

(viii) to *facilitate* development of a *consent plan* [B.C. § 1183(b)(7)]; and

(ix) to *distribute payments* pursuant to a confirmed plan [B.C. § 1194(a), (b)]

e. Chapter 13 Case

A Chapter 13 trustee has the following duties:

(i) *to account* for all property received, to *ensure* debtor performs her intentions regarding collateral securing debts, to *investigate* debtor's financial affairs, to *examine proofs of claims* and object to improper ones, to *object* to debtor's discharge, if circumstances warrant, to *provide information* to the parties in interest about the estate and its administration, and to *prepare and file a final report and account* of the estate's administration. [B.C. §§ 1302(b)(1), 704(a)(2), (3), (4), (5), (6), (7), (9)];

(ii) *to appear and be heard* at any hearing regarding (i) valuation of property on which there is a lien, (ii) confirmation of a Chapter 13 plan, or (iii) post-confirmation modification of a plan [B.C. § 1302(b)(2)];

(iii) *to advise the debtor,* other than on legal matters, and to assist the debtor in implementing the plan [B.C. § 1302(b)(4)];

(iv) *to ensure that the debtor begins making the payments* proposed by the plan no later than 30 days after the filing of the plan or the order for relief, whichever is earlier [B.C. §§ 1302(b)(5), 1326(a)(1)];

(v) if there a claim for a *domestic support obligation*:

(1) to *provide written notice* to the holder of a *domestic support obligation claim* of the right to assistance from a state child support enforcement agency in collecting child support both during and after the case [B.C. § 1302(b)(6), (d)(1)(A)];

    (2) to *provide written notice* to the applicable state child support enforcement agency of the existence of a *domestic support obligation* [B.C. § 1302(b)(6), (d)(1)(B)]; and

    (3) to *provide written notice* both to the holder of a *domestic support obligation claim* and the applicable state child support enforcement agency of the *granting of a discharge* to the debtor [B.C. § 1302(b)(6), (d)(1)(C)];

(vi) if the debtor is engaged in business, to *investigate* the debtor's conduct, financial condition, and business operations, as well as the *advisability of continuing the debtor's business* [B.C. §§ 1302(c), 1106(a)(3)];

(vii) if the debtor is engaged in business, to *file a report of the investigation* relating any facts evidencing *fraud, dishonesty, incompetence, misconduct, mismanagement,* or *irregularity* in managing the debtor's affairs, or pertaining to a cause of action that the estate holds, and to send a copy of the findings to any entity that the court designates [B.C. §§ 1302(c), 1106(a)(4)]; and

(viii) *to disburse the payments* to creditors under a confirmed plan. [B.C. § 1326(c)]

f. Chapter 12 Case

(i) Debtor Is Debtor in Possession

If the Chapter 12 debtor continues to be a debtor in possession, the duties of the Chapter 12 trustee are the same as those of a Chapter 13 trustee but for the following *three differences.*

    (1) The Code *does not require* the Chapter 12 trustee, unlike the Chapter 13 trustee, to *investigate* the debtor's financial affairs. [B.C. §§ 1202(b)(1), 1302(b)(1), 704(a)(4)]

    (2) The Chapter 12 trustee's obligation to *investigate and file a report* on the debtor's business operations, and *investigate the advisability of continuing the debtor's business* are triggered by a request for *cause* by a party in interest, the trustee, or the United States trustee. [B.C. § 1202(b)(2)] By comparison, the Chapter 13 trustee must carry out these duties if the debtor is engaged in business operations. [B.C. § 1302(c)]

    (3) The Chapter 12 trustee must *appear and be heard* at any hearing about value of property subject to a lien, plan confirmation, post-confirmation plan modifications, and the sale of property of the estate. [B.C. § 1202(b)(3)] The Code has no requirement that the Chapter 13 trustee appear and be heard on sale of estate property. [B.C. § 1302(b)(2)]

(ii) Debtor Removed as Debtor in Possession

If a Chapter 12 debtor is removed as debtor in possession, the trustee has the same duties as those of a Chapter 11 trustee, including operation of the debtor's farm or commercial fishing operation, except the obligation to investigate the debtor and report the results of that investigation. [B.C. §§ 1202(b)(5), (6), 1204]

CHAPTER	APPOINTMENT & ESTATE PROPERTY	PRIMARY DUTIES
CHAPTER 7	Promptly after entry of the order for relief, the United States trustee appoints an interim trustee, who usually becomes the permanent trustee unless, at the meeting of creditors, an election is requested by creditors holding at least 20% in amount of the claims entitled to vote for a trustee. Debtor must relinquish to the trustee all property of the estate. Any entity in possession of property that the trustee can use, sell, or lease *or* that the debtor can exempt must turn the property over to the trustee (with a few exceptions).	The trustee: • Collects and reduces to money property of the bankruptcy estate; • Makes distributions to creditors in the order prescribed by the Code; and • Closes the estate as expeditiously as is compatible with the best interests of parties in interest.
CHAPTER 11 (OTHER THAN SUBCH. V)	Generally, a trustee is **not** appointed, and the debtor remains in possession of the estate property and continues to operate the business. However, the court may order appointment of a trustee **for cause** (e.g., fraud, dishonesty, incompetence, or gross mismanagement by **current management**), if appointment is in the **interests of creditors,** or if grounds exist to **convert or dismiss** but the court decides that appointing a trustee is in the **best interests of creditors and the estate.** If the court orders appointment, then: • The United States trustee will appoint a trustee—after consulting with creditors, equity security holders, and any other parties in interest—who will serve, subject to court approval. The United States trustee may not serve as the trustee. • Alternatively, within 30 days after the court orders the appointment, a party in interest can request election of a trustee.	If a trustee is appointed, the trustee: • Replaces the debtor in possession; • Takes possession of the property; • Is authorized to operate debtor's business unless the court orders otherwise; • Investigates the debtor's conduct and financial condition, as well as the advisability of continuing the business, and files a report of the investigation; and • Files a Chapter 11 plan as soon as feasible (or recommends dismissal or conversion of the case to another chapter).
CHAPTER 11 (SUBCH. V)	**Appointment:** While the Code authorizes appointment of standing trustees, currently a subchapter V trustee is appointed on a case-by-case basis from panels or pools created across the country. **Estate Property:** The debtor remains in possession of all property of the estate, unless the debtor is removed as debtor in possession or unless the confirmed plan or the confirmation order provides otherwise.	The trustee has several of the same duties as a Chapter 7 trustee, e.g., accounting for property received and objecting to improper proofs of claim. The court, **for cause,** may require the trustee to assume additional duties performed by a non-subchapter V Chapter 11 trustee, such as investigating and reporting on the debtor's financial affairs. If the debtor is **removed as debtor in possession**, the trustee must operate the debtor's business and file periodic reports with the court, United States trustee, and any governmental taxing authority responsible for collecting taxes resulting from operation of the business.
CHAPTER 13	**Appointment:** In regions where there are many such cases, the United States trustee ordinarily appoints a standing trustee to serve in all such cases in the region. Otherwise, the United States trustee serves or appoints a trustee for each particular case.	The trustee is primarily a disbursing agent who: • Ensures that the debtor begins to make payments within the **earlier of** (i) **30 days** after the plan is filed or (ii) the order for relief;

	Estate Property: The debtor retains possession of all property of the estate, unless a confirmed plan or a plan order provides otherwise.	• Disburses payments to creditors under a confirmed plan; and • Testifies at hearings about confirmation (or post-confirmation modification) of a plan or valuation of property subject to a lien.
CHAPTER 12	**Appointment:** Same as Chapter 13. **Estate Property:** Same as Chapter 13.	The trustee's duties are very similar to those in Chapter 13 as long as the debtor continues to be a debtor in possession. If a Chapter 12 debtor is **removed from possession**, the trustee has the same duties as those of a Chapter 11 trustee, including operation of the debtor's farm or commercial fishing operation, except the obligation to investigate the debtor and report the results of that investigation.

6. Liability of Trustee

As a fiduciary of the estate, a trustee may be held *personally liable* for a "willful and deliberate" breach of her fiduciary duties. [**Mosser v. Darrow,** 341 U.S. 267 (1951)] The Supreme Court in *Mosser,* however, "did not address a trustee's personal liability with regard to negligent actions." [**Dodson v. Huff (***In re* **Smyth),** 207 F.3d 758 (5th Cir. 2000)] After *Mosser*, the Circuits split on the "question whether a bankruptcy trustee can be held personally liable for negligence (as opposed to deliberate misconduct)." [**LeBlanc v. Salem (***In re* **Mailman Steam Carpet Cleaning Corp.),** 196 F.3d 1 (1st Cir. 1999)] Some jurisdictions hold trustees personally liable for *either* intentional or negligent violations of their fiduciary duties. [*See, e.g.,* **LeBlanc,** *supra* (stating that after *Mosser* there was "no principled way . . . to avoid the conclusion that a bankruptcy trustee can be personally liable for negligent breach of fiduciary duty")] Other Circuits impose personal liability only for willful and deliberate violations of the trustee's fiduciary duties. [**Yadkin Valley Bank & Trust Co. v. McGee,** 819 F.2d 74 (4th Cir. 1987)] The Fifth Circuit has taken an intermediate position and has held that the "proper standard is gross negligence." [**Dodson v. Huff,** *supra*]

7. Powers of Trustee

The bankruptcy trustee, as the representative of the estate, is entrusted with a variety of administrative powers. Included among them are the powers to:

a. *file a proof of claim on behalf of a creditor* who has not timely filed his claim [B.C. § 501(c)];

b. *operate the debtor's business* (i) for a limited time in a *Chapter 7* case if in the estate's *best interests* and consistent with orderly liquidation of the estate; (ii) in a *non-subchapter V Chapter 11 case* in which the court ordered appointment of a trustee; or (iii) in a subchapter V Chapter 11 or a Chapter 12 case in which the court has removed the debtor in possession [B.C. §§ 721, 1108, 1183(b)(5), 1185, 1202(b)(5), 1203, 1204];

c. *deposit or invest money* of the estate [B.C. § 345];

d. *employ professional persons,* such as attorneys, accountants, auctioneers, or appraisers [B.C. § 327(a), (b)];

e. *avoid certain transfers and liens,* and thereby enlarge the estate for the benefit of creditors [B.C. §§ 544–551, 553];

f. *use, sell, or lease property* of the estate [B.C. § 363];

g. **obtain credit** [B.C. § 364];

h. **assume or reject executory contracts or unexpired leases** [B.C. § 365];

i. **demand utility services** for the estate [B.C. § 366];

j. **abandon property** of the estate [B.C. § 554]; and

k. **waive a debtor corporation's attorney-client privilege** concerning communications made by former officers and directors to the debtor's attorney before the bankruptcy petition was filed. [**Commodity Futures Trading Commission v. Weintraub,** 471 U.S. 343 (1985)]

 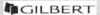
---

8. Removal of Trustee

A trustee, other than the United States trustee, or an examiner may be removed by the court *for cause.* The Bankruptcy Code does not define "cause," but most courts require actual fraud or injury for removal of a trustee. [3 Collier ¶ 324.02(2)] Notice and a hearing are required. [B.C. § 324(a)] If the court removes a trustee or examiner for cause in a particular case, the trustee or examiner is *removed in all other cases* in which the trustee or examiner is serving, unless the court orders otherwise. [B.C. § 324(b)]

B. Examiner

1. Role and Capacity

The Code's provisions on appointment and duties of an examiner *do not apply to subchapter V cases.* [B.C. § 1181(a)] In a non-subchapter V Chapter 11 case in which the court does not order the appointment of a trustee, a party in interest or the United States trustee may request, at any time prior to plan confirmation, the appointment of an examiner to conduct an investigation of the debtor, including an investigation of charges of *fraud, dishonesty, incompetence, mismanagement, or irregularity in managing the debtor's affairs,* on the part of the debtor's present or former management. [B.C. § 1104(c)(1)] The debtor in possession retains her property and continues to operate the business.

2. Eligibility

The United States trustee selects a *disinterested person* other than herself to act as examiner. [B.C. § 1104(d)]

3. Reasons for Appointment

When a party in interest or the United States trustee requests appointment of an examiner, the court, after notice and a hearing, *must order* that an examiner be appointed if the debtor's fixed, liquidated, unsecured debts *exceed $5 million, excluding* debts for goods, services, or taxes, or any debts owed to an insider. [B.C. § 1104(c)(2)] The court also must order the appointment of an examiner if such action is in the *best interests of creditors, equity security holders, and the estate.* [B.C. § 1104(c)(1)] The appointment is then made by the United

States trustee, after consulting with the parties in interest, and is subject to approval by the court. [B.C. § 1104(d)]

4. Duties of Examiner

An examiner's duties include the following:

a. *to investigate the debtor's conduct, financial condition, and business operations,* as well as the *advisability of continuing* the debtor's business [B.C. § 1106(b), (a)(3)];

b. *to file a report of the investigation,* including any facts evidencing *fraud, dishonesty, incompetence, misconduct, mismanagement,* or *irregularity in managing the debtor's affairs,* or a cause of action available to the estate [B.C. § 1106(b), (a)(4)(A)];

c. *to send a copy of the findings* of the investigation to any creditors' committee, equity security holders' committee, any indenture trustee or any other entity that the court designates [B.C. § 1106(b), (a)(4)(B)]; and

d. *any other responsibilities of a trustee* that the judge directs the debtor in possession not to perform. [B.C. § 1106(b)]

5. Examiner May Not Serve as Trustee or Professional Person

An examiner in a Chapter 11 case may not serve as the trustee, if one is appointed, or be employed as a professional person by the trustee *in the same case.* [B.C. §§ 321(b), 327(f)]

C. Professional Persons

1. Role and Capacity

A trustee, a debtor in possession, or creditors' or equity security holders' committees in a Chapter 11 case, with court approval, may hire professional persons, e.g., attorneys or accountants, to perform services with respect to the bankruptcy estate. [B.C. §§ 327(a), 1102, 1107(a), 1184, 1203]

2. Eligibility

Professional persons must be *disinterested persons* who *do not have an interest adverse* to the estate. [B.C. §§ 101(14), 327(a)] Court approval *must* be obtained *prior to performing services;* otherwise, the professional's application for compensation may be denied by the court.

a. Who Is a Professional Person?

The Bankruptcy Code includes *attorneys, accountants, auctioneers, and appraisers* as professional persons. [B.C. § 327(a)] The Bankruptcy Code defines attorney as an "attorney, professional law association, corporation, or partnership, authorized under applicable law to practice law." [B.C. § 101(4)] The Code defines "accountant" as an "accountant authorized under applicable law to practice public accounting, and includes [a] professional accounting association, corporation, or partnership, if so authorized." [B.C. § 101(1)] If a law firm or accounting partnership or corporation is approved for employment, then any partner, associate, or member of the firm may serve as an attorney or an accountant in the case without further order of the bankruptcy court. [Bankruptcy Rule 2014(b)]

The Code contains no definitions for auctioneers or appraisers, but no officer or employee of the judicial branch or of the Department of Justice may serve as an auctioneer or appraiser. [Bankruptcy Rule 6005] The courts have held a wide range of persons to be professional persons, including "personal property brokerage firms, management consultants, employment agencies, pension plan administrators, secretaries for the statutory creditors' committee, mediators, and a public relations firm." [3 Collier ¶ 327.02(6)(a)]

(i) Executives and Officers of the Debtor

Before evaluating whether a person is disinterested or has an interest adverse to the estate, make sure that the individual or firm is a ***professional person.*** The issue arises with regard to the debtor's executives and officers. If they are professional persons, then court approval is necessary for their continued employment and compensation. For many courts, the test for deciding whether an executive or officer is a professional person turns on whether the officer or executive plays a "central role in the administration" of the bankruptcy case. If not, and the debtor corporation needs the services of the officer or executive *regardless* of whether the corporation is in bankruptcy, then that officer or executive is not a professional person. If an officer or executive is *not* a professional person, then "disinterestedness is not an issue" and the debtor does not have to obtain prior court approval for the continued employment of that officer or executive. [*In re* **Dairy Dozen-Milnor, LLP,** 441 B.R. 918 (Bankr. D. N.D. 2010)]

b. Approval Before Hiring

Section 330 of the Code provides that the bankruptcy court may award compensation to a professional person employed pursuant to § 327. While the statute has no requirement of *prior* approval, many bankruptcy courts have interpreted the Code to mean that a professional person must obtain court approval *before* commencing services or risk not being compensated for those services, even if they benefit the estate. [*See, e.g.,* ***In re* Land,** 943 F.2d 1265 (10th Cir. 1991) (affirming bankruptcy court decision that ordered return of attorney's fees to debtor's brother, who had financed state court litigation that was primary asset in debtor's bankruptcy case, because attorney had not sought bankruptcy court approval prior to employment)] Bankruptcy courts, however, have issued *nunc pro tunc* retention orders in order to avoid the inequitable result of not compensating a professional person whose services did indeed provide a benefit to the bankruptcy estate. It is unclear whether the practice of issuing *nunc pro tunc* retention orders survives the Supreme Court's decision in **Roman Catholic Archdiocese of San Juan v. Acevedo Feliciano,** 140 S. Ct. 696 (2020).

(i) Various Standards for Granting Retroactive Relief Pre-*Acevedo Feliciano*

Prior to the Supreme Court's decision in *Acevedo Feliciano,* the courts had adopted several tests for determining when to grant retroactive relief. [***In re* Kearney,** 581 B.R. 644 (Bankr. D. N.M. 2018)] Most courts required ***extraordinary or exceptional circumstances.*** Courts differed, however, as to whether inattention or inadvertence precluded a finding of extraordinary or exceptional circumstances.

e.g. **Example:** Debtors filed for relief under Chapter 11. They hired SRR to appraise two pieces of real property for Debtors, but failed to obtain bankruptcy court approval prior to SRR's hiring. Ten months later, Debtors filed an application to employ SRR. No party disputed that SRR's work had provided some benefit to the bankruptcy court. Nonetheless, the bankruptcy court concluded that exceptional circumstances did not exist and denied the application. The court noted that SRR was a sophisticated party and the facts showed nothing more than inattention and inadvertence. The bankruptcy court concluded that if such behavior constituted "exceptional circumstances," then the exception would swallow the rule requiring approval prior to employment. [*In re* **Greektown Holding, LLC,** 2010 WL 7343848 (Bankr. E.D. Mich. 2010)]

e.g. **Example:** Debtor filed for relief under Chapter 7. Debtor owned two parcels of real property with his brother that the Chapter 7 trustee concluded had value for the estate. The trustee hired the law firm of Danning Gill to pursue the estate's interest in the properties. Danning Gill began its work for the trustee in late January, but did not file an employment application. Danning Gill and Debtor's attorney negotiated a settlement and sale of the properties to the Debtor. The bankruptcy court approved the settlement. Approximately 11 months after hiring Danning Gill, the Chapter 7 trustee filed an application to employ the firm. The bankruptcy court approved the application, and the Ninth Circuit's B.A.P. affirmed. The B.A.P. explained that to establish exceptional circumstances the applicant had to (i) provide a satisfactory explanation for not obtaining approval prior to employment and (ii) show that its services provided a significant benefit to the estate. There was no dispute that Danning Gill's work was of significant benefit to the estate. Even though Danning Gill acknowledged that its failure to file a timely application for employment resulted from "inadvertence or oversight," the B.A.P. affirmed the bankruptcy court's determination that Danning Gill had provided a satisfactory explanation for not timely filing an application for employment. [**Watson v. Gill (***In re* **Watson),** 2015 WL 3939781 (B.A.P. 9th Cir. 2015)]

Some courts adopted the ***excusable neglect*** standard. [*In re* **Singson,** 41 F.3d 316 (7th Cir. 1994) (rejecting the "extraordinary circumstances" test but also explaining that "excusable neglect" is a higher standard than "simple neglect"); **Blocksom v. Brown (***In re* **Brown),** 555 B.R. 854 (Bankr. S.D. Ga. 2016) (applying excusable neglect standard and explaining that "the mere presence of neglect is not fatal if it is excusable")] Yet other courts used ***multi-factor tests,*** the most common being the nine-factor test adopted in *Twinton Properties,* which requires that the applicant demonstrate each factor by clear and convincing evidence. [*In re* **Twinton Properties Partnership,** 27 B.R. 817 (Bankr. M.D. Tenn. 1983)]

(ii) Impact of *Acevedo Feliciano*

In *Acevedo Feliciano,* the Court explained that " 'nunc pro tunc orders are not some Orwellian vehicle for revisionist history—creating 'facts' that never occurred in fact. . . Put plainly, the court 'cannot make the record what it is not.' " *Acevedo Feliciano* did not involve a *nunc pro tunc* retention order. Some bankruptcy courts, however, have concluded that the common practice of issuing *nunc pro tunc* orders, "particularly with respect to employment under § 327 . . . must now stop." [*In re* **Miller,** 620 B.R. 637 (Bankr. E.D. Cal. 2020); *see also In re* **Benitez,** 2020 WL 1272258 (Bankr. E.D. N.Y. 2020) (interpreting *Acevedo Feliciano* to mean that the use of *"nunc pro tunc* orders to approve the retention of estate professionals retroactive to some date prior to the actual date of court approval is inappropriate")]

Eliminating the use of *nunc pro tunc* retention orders, however, does not mean that a bankruptcy court will not compensate a professional person who provided beneficial services without first obtaining the court's approval of her employment.

e.g. **Example:** Prior to bankruptcy, Debtor entered into a 40% contingency fee arrangement with Law Firm ("Special Counsel") to file suit for personal injuries arising from surgical implant of a medical device. Debtor subsequently filed for relief under Chapter 7 but his medical device claim was not scheduled and not administered in his no-asset case. When the claims administrator in the medical device litigation offered $165,000 to settle Debtor's claim, the Chapter 7 trustee reopened Debtor's Chapter 7 case to administer the asset. In the reopened case, the Chapter 7 trustee identified Special Counsel and the 40% contingency fee arrangement but failed to file an application under § 327 for court approval of Special Counsel's employment until almost a year after reopening the case. No one disputed the settlement terms or Special Counsel's role in settling the medical device claim. The bankruptcy court first noted that after the Supreme Court's decision in *Acevedo Feliciano* the common practice of issuing *nunc pro tunc* retention orders had to stop. Nonetheless, the court said that *Acevedo Feliciano* did not proscribe all retroactive relief. The bankruptcy court explained that "although an order authorizing employment under § 327 is a prerequisite to awarding compensation under § 330" the Code contains no "requirement that compensated services must have been performed only after the effective date of an employment order." The court, however, appeared to limit compensation to cases involving exceptional circumstances in which the pre-employment services benefitted the estate in some significant way. In addition, the court noted that the professional person requesting retroactive compensation has the burden of proof and must satisfy all of § 327's requirements, except that of pre-employment approval. Finally, the bankruptcy court concluded that the length of the delay between beginning services and applying for judicial approval of employment "affects the analysis of extraordinary circumstances—the longer the delay, the more difficult to explain." [*In re* **Miller,** *supra*]

Example: Married couple filed for relief under Chapter 13. Two months later, Husband and Daughter were involved in an auto accident. Husband retained Special Counsel to represent him and his daughter with regard to personal injuries they sustained in the car accident. Married couple's bankruptcy lawyer failed to apply for authorization under § 327 for Special Counsel because he mistakenly believed that only Daughter had sustained injuries in the car crash. When Debtors' counsel discovered his mistake he filed an application under § 327 for Special Counsel; the filing occurred about nine months after Husband hired Special Counsel. The bankruptcy court held that after the Supreme Court's decision in *Acevedo Feliciano,* "the use of *nunc pro tunc* orders to retroactively seek employment of professionals is an improper use of the mechanism and this court will no longer enter such orders." The court then explained that its decision to abandon *nunc pro tunc* retention orders did not mean that it would not order compensation for services rendered prior to entry of an order authorizing the professional person's employment. The bankruptcy court noted that nothing in the Code or the Bankruptcy Rules "require[s] employment to be authorized prior to performance of services." Thus, the court concluded that it would authorize, under certain circumstances, an award of compensation to a professional person using the factors it had "previously used to establish the basis for entry of tardy orders of employment." [*In re* **Roberts,** 618 B.R. 213 (Bankr. S.D. Ohio 2020)]

c. **"Disinterested"**

The Code provides that the following persons are *not* disinterested:

(i) a *creditor, insider, or equity security holder* [B.C. § 101(14)(A)];

(ii) a person who is or was an *officer, director or employee of the debtor* within *two years* prior to the bankruptcy filing [B.C. § 101(14)(B)]; or

(iii) a person with *an interest materially adverse* to the interest of the *estate* or any class of *creditors or equity security holders.* [B.C. § 101(14)(C)]

(i) Officers, Directors, and Employees

A professional person, such as an attorney or an accountant, who is or has been an officer, a director, or an employee of the debtor *within two years prior to bankruptcy* is not considered to be *disinterested* and, therefore, generally may not be employed as a professional person by the trustee or the debtor in possession. [B.C. §§ 101(14), 327(a)] Also, a finding that one member of a law firm is *not* disinterested may disqualify any other member of that firm under § 327.

Note: Make sure you distinguish between an executive or officer of the employee who does not play a central role in the administration of the bankruptcy case [*see supra* § 2.a(i)] and a current or former officer, director, or employee that the debtor seeks to employ to actively participate in the debtor's bankruptcy case.

e.g. **Example:** Related corporate Debtors filed for relief under Chapter 11 and filed an application to retain Law Firm as their counsel. Within two years prior to Debtors' bankruptcy filings, Partner of Law Firm had served as Secretary for several Debtors. The bankruptcy court first rejected Debtors' argument that Partner's role as Secretary was merely ministerial. The court concluded that it was not its job to "inquire into what role the officer may have played but need only determine whether the professional was an officer within the proscribed time." The bankruptcy court also rejected Debtors' § 1107(b) argument. Section 1107(b) provides that a professional person is not disqualified for employment under § 327 *solely* because of his prior employment by the debtor. Debtors claimed that the *only* basis for disqualifying Partner was his pre-bankruptcy employment by Debtors as Secretary. The court narrowly construed § 1107(b), holding that § 1107(b) did not "eliminate all the specific tests for disqualification enumerated in section 101(14)." Because Partner had served as an officer within two years of bankruptcy, he was not disinterested under § 101(14). Finally, the bankruptcy court held that Partner's disqualification also disqualified any member of Law Firm from representing Debtors. "We conclude that having one member's independence and disinterestedness impugned because he was an officer must equally affect the firm's independence and disinterestedness such that the firm must be disqualified under section 327(a) of the Code." *In re* **Essential Therapeutics, Inc.,** 295 B.R. 203 (Bankr. D. Del. 2003)]

d. Interest Adverse to the Estate

Unlike the term "disinterested person," the Code does not define what is an "interest adverse to the estate." But the fact that the Code defines a "disinterested person", in part, as a person without interests *materially adverse* to the estate demonstrates that there is some overlap between the two concepts. [3 Collier ¶ 327.04(2)(b)] What, then, is the difference between disinterestedness and adverse interest, in particular because the disinterested person definition requires that the person not have an interest materially adverse to the estate? In **Bank Brussels Lambert v. Coan (*In re* AroChem Corp.),** 176 F.3d 610 (2d Cir. 1999), the Second Circuit explained that under § 101(14)(C) (then § 101(14)(E)) the "professional personally must 'have' the prohibited interest." But § 327(a) provides that the professional person cannot *hold or represent* an interest adverse to the estate. Thus, a professional person who does not *personally have* a prohibited interest may be disinterested, but if she *represents* such a prohibited interest, then she is disqualified under the adverse interest portion of § 327. [*See* 3 Collier 327.04(2)(b)]

e. **Limited Exceptions to § 327(a)**

Be careful applying these exceptions. Note that all three exceptions contain the word "solely." The professional person still must be disinterested and neither hold nor represent an interest adverse to the estate. [*See, e.g.,* **Essential Therapeutics,** *supra* (stating that § 1107(b) does not "eliminate all the specific tests for disqualification enumerated in section 101(14)"]

(i) Creditor Representation

In a Chapter 7, 11, or 12 case, a professional person is not disqualified from *employment by a trustee solely* because of her employment by or representation of a creditor, unless another creditor or the United States trustee objects and the court finds an *actual conflict of interest.* [B.C. § 327(c)]

(ii) Non-Subchapter V Chapter 11 Case

In a non-subchapter V Chapter 11 case, a person is not disqualified for employment by a debtor in possession *solely* because that person was employed by or represented the debtor prior to the bankruptcy case. [B.C. § 1107(b)]

(iii) Subchapter V Chapter 11 Case

In a *subchapter V case,* a person is not disqualified from employment under § 327(a) *solely* because of holding a *pre-petition claim of less than $10,000.* [B.C. § 1195]

f. **Salaried Professionals of the Debtor**

A trustee who is authorized to operate the debtor's business may *retain or replace salaried professionals,* such as attorneys and accountants, who have been *regularly employed* by the debtor and are *necessary to operation* of the business. [B.C. § 327(b); *see* B.C. §§ 721, 1108, 1202]

g. **Special Purpose Attorney**

The court may authorize a trustee or a debtor in possession to employ a former attorney of the debtor for a *special purpose,* such as continuing legal expertise in an intricate proceeding, provided that the employment is in the *estate's best interest* and the lawyer does not represent or have an interest adverse to the debtor or to the estate concerning the specific subject matter of the employment. The purpose may *not* be to represent the trustee in administering the bankruptcy case. [B.C. § 327(e)]

h. **Trustee as a Professional Person**

The court may permit the trustee also to serve as an attorney or an accountant for the estate if that employment is in the *estate's best interest.* [B.C. § 327(d)]

3. Creditors' Committee May Hire Professional Persons

In a Chapter 11 case, a creditors' committee or an equity security holders' committee may employ attorneys, accountants, or other professionals to perform services for the committee. [B.C. § 1103(a)] While representing or in the employ of the committee, the professional person may not represent an entity having an *adverse interest.* Representation of a creditor of the same class as the committee represents, however, does not per se constitute representation of an adverse interest. [B.C. § 1103(b)]

Note: Typically, a creditors' committee is not appointed in a small business or subchapter V Chapter 11 case. [B.C. § 1102(a)(3)]

D. Ombudsmen

1. BAPCPA's Changes

BAPCPA added two new sections on the appointment of ombudsmen to Chapter 3 of the Bankruptcy Code. Section 332 provides for the appointment of a *consumer privacy ombudsman* while § 333 provides for the appointment of a *patient care ombudsman.*

a. Consumer Privacy Ombudsman

A bankruptcy court cannot approve a sale of *personally identifiable information* that is inconsistent with the debtor's privacy policy unless the court first orders the appointment of a *consumer privacy ombudsman* and subsequently holds a hearing, after notice, on the proposed sale. [B.C. § 363(b)(1)(B)] If the court orders the appointment of a consumer privacy ombudsman, then the United States trustee must appoint *one disinterested person,* other than the United States trustee, to serve as ombudsman *no later than 7 days* before the start of the sale hearing. [B.C. § 332(a)]

(i) Sale Hearing

The consumer privacy ombudsman may appear and be heard at the sale hearing and must provide information to the court to assist with the court's consideration of the facts, circumstances, and conditions of the proposed sale. The information may include the following:

(1) the *debtor's privacy policy;*

(2) the possible *losses or gains of privacy* to consumers if the court approves the sale;

(3) the potential *costs and benefits* to consumers if the court approves the sale; and

(4) any *alternatives* that would mitigate potential losses of privacy or potential costs to consumers. [B.C. § 332(b)]

(ii) Confidentiality

The consumer privacy ombudsman cannot disclose any personally identifiable information she obtains. [B.C. § 332(c)]

b. Patient Care Ombudsman

If a health care business files for relief under *Chapters 7, 9 or 11*, then the bankruptcy court must order the appointment, within *30 days* of the start of the case, of a *patient care ombudsman,* unless the court finds that appointment is not necessary for the protection of patients in a specific case. The job of the patient care ombudsman is to *monitor the quality of patient care* and to *represent the interests of patients* of the health care business. [B.C. § 333(a)(1)]

(i) Health Care Business

A *health care business* is any public or private entity, whether for profit or not for profit, that is primarily engaged in offering to the general public *facilities and services* for the *diagnosis or treatment of injury, deformity or disease* and *surgical, drug treatment, psychiatric, or obstetric care.* [B.C. § 101(27A)(A)] A health care business includes any general or specialized hospital, ancillary ambulatory, emergency, or surgical treatment center, hospice, home health agency, or any similar health care entity. [B.C. § 101(27A)(B)] The debtor must satisfy the following four elements, distilled from the Code's definition, in order to qualify as a health care business:

(1) debtor is a *public or private* entity;

(2) debtor is primarily engaged in offering facilities and services to the *general public;*

(3) the facilities and services are offered to the public for *diagnosis and treatment* of injury, deformity, or disease; and

(4) the facilities and services are offered to the public for *surgical care, drug treatment, psychiatric care, or obstetric care.*

[*See In re* **Smiley Dental Arlington PLCC,** 503 B.R. 680 (Bankr. N.D. Tex. 2013) (noting that a "plain reading of section 101(27A) requires the existence of four elements"); *In re* **Medical Associates of Pinellas, LLC,** 360 B.R. 356 (Bankr. M.D. Fla. 2007) (stating four elements)]

(ii) Long-Term Care Facility

A long-term care facility is a *health care business.* A long-term care facility includes a skilled nursing facility, intermediate care facility, assisted living facility, home for the aged, or domiciliary care facility. It also includes any health care institution related to one of the above facilities if that institution is primarily engaged in offering room, board, laundry, or personal assistance with activities of daily living. [B.C. § 101(27A)(B)(ii)(VI)]

(iii) Determining Nature of Debtor

If a debtor checks the "Health Care Business" box on the voluntary petition, then the case proceeds as one involving a health care business. [Bankruptcy Rule 1021(a); Official Form 201] The United States trustee or any party in interest may file a motion to determine whether the debtor is a health care business. [Bankruptcy Rule 1021(b)]

(iv) Appointment

If the bankruptcy court orders the appointment of an ombudsman, then the United States trustee appoints *one disinterested person,* other than the United States trustee, to serve as the patient care ombudsman for the health care business. [B.C. § 333(a)(2)(A)] If the debtor is a *long-term care facility,* the United States trustee may appoint the State Long-Term Care Ombudsman under the Older Americans Act of 1965 for the state in which the bankruptcy case is pending. [B.C. § 333(a)(2)(B)] If the United States trustee does not appoint the State Long-Term Care Ombudsman, then the court must provide notice to the State Long-Term Care Ombudsman of the name and address of the person appointed as the patient care ombudsman. [B.C. § 333(a)(2)(C)]

(v) Protection of Patients

A debtor may be a health care business, but the court still may decide not to appoint an ombudsman based on the specific facts of the debtor's case. In deciding whether appointment is necessary for the *protection of patients,* many courts examine a non-exclusive list of the following nine factors:

(1) the *cause of the bankruptcy;*

(2) whether there are *licensing or supervising authorities overseeing* the debtor;

(3) the debtor's *history* of patient care;

(4) patients' ability to *protect their rights;*

(5) the level of *dependency of patients* on the debtor's facility;

(6) the likelihood there will be *tension* between the *interests of patients and those of the debtor;*

(7) the *potential harm* to patients if the debtor drastically reduces its level of patient care;

(8) the presence and sufficiency of *internal safeguards* for appropriate care; and

(9) the effect that the *cost* of appointing an ombudsman will have on the likelihood that the debtor will *successfully reorganize.*

[*In re* **Alternate Family Care,** 377 B.R. 754 (Bankr. S.D. Fla. 2007) (declining to appoint a patient care ombudsman)]

(vi) Duties

The patient care ombudsman has the following statutory duties:

(1) to *monitor the quality of patient care,* to the extent necessary, including interviewing patients and doctors [B.C. § 333(b)(1)];

(2) to *report,* at a hearing or in writing, on the *quality of care* no later than *60 days after appointment* and at least every 60 days thereafter [B.C. § 333(b)(2)];

(3) to *file a motion or written report,* with notice to the parties in interest, if the ombudsman determines that the quality of care is *declining significantly* or is being *materially compromised* [B.C. § 333(b)(3)];

(4) to *maintain as confidential* any information related to patients, including patient records [B.C. § 333(c)(1)]; and

(5) to *obtain prior court approval* for any review of *confidential patient records* and to abide by any restrictions that the bankruptcy court imposes in order to protect confidentiality. [B.C. § 333(c)(1)]

E. Compensation of Officers

1. In General

Officers of the estate, including a trustee, an examiner, a Chapter 12 or 13 individual debtor's attorney, a consumer privacy ombudsman, a patient care ombudsman, and any professional person properly employed by a trustee, a debtor in possession, or a creditors' committee may be awarded by the court a *reasonable fee* for actual and necessary services, as well as *reimbursement* for *actual and necessary expenses.* [B.C. § 330(a)(1), (a)(4)(B)]

2. Debtor's Attorney

The right of the debtor's attorney to compensation from estate funds varies depending on the chapter of the Code under which the debtor files for relief.

a. Chapter 12 or 13

The Bankruptcy Code expressly provides that the court may award reasonable compensation to the attorney of an individual Chapter 12 or Chapter 13 debtor, based on the benefit and necessity of the services to the debtor and the statutory criteria listed below. [B.C. § 330(a)(4)(B)]

b. Chapter 7

The Supreme Court has held that § 330(a)(1) does not authorize payment of compensation to the Chapter 7 debtor's lawyer from the estate, unless the lawyer was employed pursuant to § 327. Section 327, however, speaks in terms of the *trustee's* employment of professional persons, including attorneys. Thus, a Chapter 7 attorney is only entitled to compensation under § 330(a)(1) if she is hired by the trustee and approved by the bankruptcy court. [**Lamie v. United States Trustee,** 540 U.S. 526 (2004)] Because the debtor hires the attorney to file her Chapter 7 case, the attorney representing a Chapter 7 debtor must obtain her fee upfront and not rely on compensation from estate funds under § 330(a)(1).

c. Chapter 11

A Chapter 11 debtor normally is a debtor in possession and, as such, has the rights, other than the right to compensation, of a trustee. Thus, the Chapter 11 debtor may hire an attorney and so long as the bankruptcy court approves the employment, the attorney is entitled to compensation according to the standards set forth in § 330. [B.C. §§ 1107(a), 1184, 327]

In a non-subchapter V case, however, once the bankruptcy court orders appointment of a Chapter 11 trustee, the debtor is no longer a debtor in possession and does not have the rights and powers of a trustee under § 1107(a). Therefore, after the appointment of a Chapter 11 trustee, the debtor's attorney must look to the debtor, not the estate, for compensation for services rendered. [*See* **Morrison v. United States Trustee,** 2010 WL 2653394 (E.D. N.Y. 2010) (noting that the language interpreted in *Lamie* "is not limited to Chapter 7, and there is no basis in law to presume that a different result would follow where a Chapter 11 trustee has been appointed"); *see also* **Millburn Partners, LLC v. Miles (*In re* Miles),** 2011 WL 1124183 (Bankr. N.D. Ga. 2011)]

3. Fee Application

An application for compensation for services or reimbursement of necessary expenses must include a ***detailed*** statement of (i) the services performed, (ii) the time spent, (iii) the expenses incurred, and (iv) the amounts requested. It also must include disclosures concerning (i) payments that have been made or promised to the applicant, (ii) the source of such payments, (iii) the sharing of, or any agreement to share, compensation previously received or to be received, and (iv) the details concerning any sharing of, or agreement to share, compensation, unless the sharing is with other members of the same firm of attorneys or accountants. A copy of the fee application must be sent to the United States trustee. [Bankruptcy Rule 2016(a)] The application must contain all information required by the ***procedural guidelines issued by the Executive Office for United States Trustees.*** [28 C.F.R. Part 58, Appendix A] Also, local bankruptcy rules may require additional information and always should be consulted.

a. Fees Incurred Defending Challenge to Fee Application

In **Baker Botts LLP v. ASARCO LLC,** 576 U.S. 121 (2015), the Supreme Court held that § 330(a)(1) does not authorize bankruptcy courts to award compensation to attorneys for work defending their fee applications. The Court concluded that "[b]ecause § 330(a)(1) does not explicitly override the American Rule with respect to fee-defense litigation, it does not permit bankruptcy courts to award compensation for such litigation."

4. Criteria for Determining Reasonable Compensation

In determining a reasonable fee, the court must consider the nature, extent, and value of the services, taking into account all relevant factors, including the following:

a. the *time* spent [B.C. § 330(a)(3)(A)];

b. the *rates* charged [B.C. § 330(a)(3)(B)];

c. whether the *services were necessary* to the administration of, or *beneficial* at the time services were rendered toward completion of, the case [B.C. § 330(a)(3)(C)];

d. whether the services were performed within a *reasonable time,* considering the nature, complexity, and importance of the work [B.C. § 330(a)(3)(D)];

e. whether the professional person is *board certified* or has otherwise shown *skill and experience* in the field of bankruptcy [B.C. § 330(a)(3)(E)]; and

f. whether the *compensation is reasonable* based on the *customary fees* charged by comparably skilled practitioners in nonbankruptcy cases. [B.C. § 330(a)(3)(F)]

The court cannot allow compensation for services that are (i) unnecessarily duplicative, (ii) not reasonably likely to benefit the estate, or (iii) not necessary to the administration of the case. [B.C. § 330(a)(4)(A)]

The bankruptcy court has wide discretion in awarding compensation. The court, on its own motion, or on the motion of the United States trustee, a trustee, or any party in interest may award compensation that is *less than* the requested compensation. [B.C. § 330(a)(2); *see, e.g.,* **Houlihan Lokey Howard & Zukin Capital v. Unsecured Creditor' Liquidating Trust (*In re* Commercial Financial Services), 427 F.3d 804 (10th Cir. 2005)** (affirming bankruptcy court order reducing fees from $1.9 million to $904,000 for a firm hired by committee of creditors holding asset-based securities)]

5. Limitations on Professionals' Compensation

An award of compensation to a professional person is subject to certain statutory limitations. [B.C. § 328]

a. Modification by Court

A trustee, a debtor in possession, or a creditors' or equity security holders' committee may hire a professional person on any reasonable basis, including on a retainer, on an hourly basis, or on a contingent fee basis. However, the compensation ultimately allowed by the court may vary from the agreed-upon terms if those terms prove to be *improvident in light of later developments* that could not have been anticipated at the time the fee arrangement was approved. [B.C. § 328(a)]

b. Denial of Compensation

If, at any time during employment, a professional person is *not disinterested* or *has an interest adverse to the estate* regarding the subject matter of her employment, the court may deny her compensation for services and reimbursement of expenses. [B.C. § 328(c)]

(i) Exceptions

This rule is subject to three exceptions for (i) a creditor's representative [B.C. § 327(c)], (ii) a "special purpose" attorney [B.C. § 327(e)], and (iii) a professional who was employed by the debtor or who represented the debtor before filing of the bankruptcy case [B.C. § 1107(b)]. A noted bankruptcy commentator explains that these three exceptions "permit the retention of a professional who might otherwise be unable to comply strictly" with § 327's requirements and "make clear that certain relationships do not, *per se*, create an appearance of impropriety on the professional's part." [3 Collier ¶ 328.05(1)]

c. Bifurcation of Trustee's Compensation

If a trustee also serves as an attorney or an accountant for the estate, her fee for professional employment may not include compensation for the performance of her duties as trustee. Compensation for services as trustee must be accounted for separately. [B.C. § 328(b)]

6. Trustee Compensation

A bankruptcy court, in determining *reasonable compensation to award a trustee*, must treat such compensation as a *commission,* based on § 326. [B.C. § 330(a)(7)] Section 326 provides limitations on compensation awarded to a trustee, and has different rules for Chapter 7 and non-subchapter V Chapter 11 cases versus subchapter V, Chapter 12, and Chapter 13 cases. [*See* B.C. § 326(a), (b)]

a. Chapter 7 and Non-Subchapter V Chapter 11 Trustees

In a Chapter 7 or non-subchapter V Chapter 11 case, a trustee's compensation may not exceed 25% of the first $5,000 disbursed by the trustee to parties in interest, 10% of the next $45,000, 5% of any amount disbursed in excess of $50,000 but not more than $1 million, and reasonable compensation not to exceed 3% of amounts disbursed in excess of $1 million. [B.C. § 326(a)]

(i) Exclusion of Disbursements to Debtor

Any disbursements by the trustee to the debtor, such as exempt property, are excluded from the computation. [B.C. § 326(a)]

(ii) Inclusion of Disbursements to Secured Creditors

The calculation of the trustee's total disbursements includes payments made to holders of secured claims. [B.C. § 326(a)] Courts, however, have held that a credit bid under § 363(k) is not included in the trustee's total disbursements for purposes of calculating the trustee's compensation. [*See, e.g.,* **Tamn v. United States Trustee (*In re* Hokulani Square, Inc.),** 776 F.3d 1083 (9th Cir. 2015) (holding that § 326(a) does not allow the trustee to collect fees on a credit bid transaction, because the statute says "moneys disbursed" and a credit bid involves the trustee turning property over to a secured creditor in exchange for a reduction in the amount that the estate owes to the secured creditor); *compare* **In re WM Six Forks, LLC,** 502 B.R. 88 (Bankr. E.D. N.C. 2013) (finding that the amount of a credit bid is included in calculating the quarterly fee due the United States trustee under § 1930(a)(6) and comparing the language of § 326—moneys disbursed—with that of § 1930(a)(6)—disbursements)]

(iii) Property Abandoned or Turned over

The maximum fee paid to the Chapter 7 or non-subchapter V Chapter 11 trustee is based on disbursements by the trustee. When the trustee abandons property or turns the property over to the secured creditor, however, no monies are disbursed. Thus, the value of the property abandoned or turned over is not included in total disbursements and does not increase the base on which the trustee's maximum fee is calculated. [H.R. Rep. No. 95–595, at 327 (1977)]

(iv) Minimum Fee for Chapter 7 Trustee

What if there is no property from which the Chapter 7 trustee may make disbursements to creditors? In a *no-asset case*, § 330 provides for a *fee of $60*: $45 under § 330(b)(1) and an additional $15 under § 330(b)(2). In the ***Bankruptcy Administration Improvement Act of 2020***, enacted January 12, 2021, Congress added a new subsection (e) to § 330. [Pub. L. No. 116–325 (2021)] It provides, for fiscal years 2021 through 2026, for the Chapter 7 trustee to receive the *lesser of $60* or a pro rata share of the net fees collected for each Chapter 7 case. [B.C. § 330(e)(4)] This payment is *in addition* to the amount provided for by § 330(b). [B.C. § 330(e)(5)] Therefore, in a no-asset case, the *largest minimum compensation* that the trustee will receive is $120: $60 under § 330(b) and an additional $60 under § 330(e)(4). [*See* H. Jason Gold & Marc E. Albert, *The History of the Chapter 7 Raise*, AM. BANKR. TRUSTEE J. 28 (2021)]

b. Subchapter V Chapter 11, Chapter 12, and Chapter 13 Trustees

(i) Standing Trustee

The bankruptcy court does not determine what constitutes reasonable compensation for a standing trustee in subchapter V Chapter 11, or Chapter 12 or 13 cases. [B.C. § 326(b)] Instead, the method for calculating compensation is provided by 28 U.S.C. § 586(e).

(ii) Non-Standing Trustee

The bankruptcy court may allow reasonable compensation under § 330 for a non-standing trustee appointed in a particular case under Chapter 12 or Chapter 13 not to exceed *5% of all payments made under the plan*. [B.C. § 326(b)] The problem is with non-standing *subchapter V Chapter 11 trustees.* The second clause of § 326(b) states that the bankruptcy court "may allow compensation under section 330 [ ] of a trustee appointed under section 1202(a) or 1302(a) [ ] for the trustee's services, . . . , not to exceed five percent upon all payments under the plan." The second clause does *not* include § 1183 on subchapter V trustees. The bankruptcy court in *In re Tri-State Roofing*, 2020 WL 7345741 (Bankr. D. Idaho 2020) concluded that the omission of the subchapter V non-standing trustee in the second clause of § 326(b) is subject to three interpretations: (1) subchapter V trustees are entitled to no compensation under § 330; (2) subchapter V trustees are entitled to reasonable compensation under § 330 subject to the 5% cap; or (3) subchapter V trustees are entitled to reasonable compensation with no 5% cap. The *Tri-State Roofing* court held that "§ 326(b) does not prevent an award of compensation to the Trustee under § 330(a)(1), nor does it place a cap on such compensation." [*But see* 3 Collier ¶ 326.02(2)(b) (stating that a non-standing trustee under subchapter V, Chapter 12, or Chapter 13 is "subject to the cap provided in section 326(b) of 5 percent of payments 'under the plan' ")]

7. Interim Compensation

A trustee, examiner, debtor's attorney, or other professional person may apply for interim compensation or reimbursement of expenses *once every 120 days* after the order for relief, or more frequently, if the court allows, instead of waiting until the conclusion of the bankruptcy case to be paid. [B.C. § 331] After notice and a hearing, the court may approve the application. Any award of interim compensation will cause a reduction, by that amount, in an award of compensation made under § 330. [B.C. § 330(a)(5)] Interim compensation is generally not an issue in Chapter 12 or 13 cases. Bankruptcy courts have standing orders for such cases that provide an allowed standard fee awarded without application or a hearing and paid as an administrative claim through the plan. [3 Collier ¶ 331.07]

8. Debtor's Transactions with Attorneys

Even if the debtor's attorney does not apply to the court for compensation, she still must file a statement of any fees paid or any fee agreement made within one year before bankruptcy for legal services related to the case. The statement also must indicate the source of payment. [B.C. § 329(a); Bankruptcy Rule 2016(b)] If the court determines that the compensation is unreasonable, it may cancel the fee agreement or order that any excessive portion be returned to the estate or to the entity that made the payment. [B.C. § 329(b); Bankruptcy Rule 2017] While the debtor's attorney must report any fees paid within the year prior to filing for bankruptcy, there is no limitations period for disgorgement of excessive fees. [B.C. § 329(b); Bankruptcy Rule 2017(a); **Arnes v. Bouhgton (*In re* Prudhomme)**, 43 F.3d 1000 (5th Cir. 1995) (ordering disgorgement of excessive fees paid more than one year before bankruptcy as a sanction for nondisclosure)]

9. Sharing of Fees Prohibited

A trustee, examiner, attorney, accountant, or other professional person employed in a bankruptcy case and who receives compensation or reimbursement as an administrative expense is prohibited from sharing such compensation or reimbursement with another person. [B.C. § 504(a); § 503(b)(2), (b)(4)] This rule is subject to two exceptions.

a. Exception—Members of Same Firm

Compensation or reimbursement may be shared with another member, partner, or associate of the same professional firm. [B.C. § 504(b)(1)]

b. Exception—Involuntary Case

An attorney representing a creditor who files an involuntary petition is permitted to share her fee with any other attorney who contributes to her services or expenses. [B.C. § 504(b)(2)]

F.   United States Trustee

1. Appointment and Term

For each of the 21 regions throughout the nation, the Attorney General appoints one United States trustee for a five-year term. If necessary, the Attorney General also may appoint one or more assistant United States trustees in any region when public interest so requires. [28 U.S.C. §§ 581, 582]

a. **Exceptions**

The judicial districts for Alabama and North Carolina are served by bankruptcy administrators appointed by the United States Courts of Appeals for the Fourth and Eleventh Circuits.

2. Administrative Duties

The United States trustee performs numerous administrative functions under the supervision of the Attorney General. Some of these duties are as follows:

a. *to establish and supervise a panel of private trustees* to serve in Chapter 7 cases [28 U.S.C. § 586(a)(1)];

b. *to appoint an interim trustee* from the private panel in a Chapter 7 case [B.C. § 701(a)(1)];

c. *to appoint a trustee or an examiner* in a non-subchapter V Chapter 11 case when the court orders such appointment to be made, or *to convene a meeting of creditors to elect a trustee* when the court orders a trustee's appointment and a party in interest timely requests an election, instead [B.C. § 1104(b), (d)];

d. *to appoint a standing trustee* for Chapter 12 or Chapter 13 cases, or, instead, *to appoint a trustee* for a particular case under Chapter 12 or Chapter 13 [28 U.S.C. § 586(b); B.C. §§ 1202(a), 1302(a)];

e. in a Chapter 11 case, *to appoint and monitor creditors' committees and equity security holders' committees* [B.C. § 1102(a); 28 U.S.C. § 586(a)(3)(E)];

f. *to convene and preside at the § 341 meeting* of creditors and, if appropriate, *to examine the debtor* at that meeting [B.C. §§ 341, 343];

g. *if necessary, to serve as the trustee* in a case under Chapter 7, 12, 13, or in a subchapter V, but not a non-subchapter V, Chapter 11 case [28 U.S.C. § 586(a)(2); B.C. §§ 701(a)(2), 1104(d), 1183(a), 1202(a), 1302(a)];

h. *to supervise the administration of bankruptcy cases and trustees* [28 U.S.C. § 586(a)(3)];

i. *to monitor applications for the employment of professional persons* and, if appropriate, file comments with the court regarding their approval [28 U.S.C. § 586(a)(3)(I)];

j. *to review fee applications* of trustees, examiners, attorneys, ombudsmen, and other professional persons, in accordance with procedural guidelines adopted by the Executive Office of the United States Trustee, file comments with the court concerning the applications, and, if appropriate, file objections [28 U.S.C. § 586(a)(3)(A); B.C. § 330];

k. *to monitor plans* filed in cases under Chapter 11, 12, and 13, and, if appropriate, to file with the court comments regarding such plans [28 U.S.C. §§ 586(a)(3)(B), (C)];

l. *to monitor Chapter 11 disclosure statements* and, if appropriate, file comments with the court [28 U.S.C. § 586(a)(3)(B)];

m. *to monitor the progress of bankruptcy cases* and take actions that are necessary to avoid undue delay [28 U.S.C. § 586(a)(3)(G)];

n. to take appropriate action *to ensure that the debtor timely files all necessary reports,* schedules, and fees [28 U.S.C. § 586(a)(3)(D)];

o. *to inform the United States Attorney about crimes* that may have been committed under federal law [28 U.S.C. § 586(a)(3)(F)];

p. *to deposit or invest under § 345 money* received as the trustee in bankruptcy cases [28 U.S.C. § 586(a)(4)];

q. *to make any reports* that the Attorney General directs, including the debtor audits required by BAPCPA [28 U.S.C. § 586(a)(6)];

r. *to perform an initial debtor interview in a small business case* as soon as possible after the order for relief but before the first § 341 meeting [28 U.S.C. § 586(a)(7)(A)];

s. if appropriate, *to visit the business premises of a small business debtor,* ascertain the state of the *books and records,* and *verify* that the small business debtor has *filed its tax returns* [28 U.S.C. § 586(a)(7)(B)];

t. *to review and monitor* the small business debtor's activities to determine whether the debtor will be unable to confirm a plan [28 U.S.C. § 586(a)(7)(C)]; and

u. *to promptly file a motion to convert or dismiss* a Chapter 11 case after finding *material grounds* for such relief [28 U.S.C. § 586(a)(8); B.C. § 1112]

3. Right to Raise Issues

The Bankruptcy Code grants the United States trustee the right to raise, appear and be heard with respect to any issue in a bankruptcy case. The United States trustee may not file a plan pursuant to § 1121(c). [B.C. § 307]

Chapter Five
The Bankruptcy Estate

Chapter Approach

The Code's definition of property of the estate is broad. Congress intended to bring into the bankruptcy estate "anything of value that the debtors have" at the time of filing for bankruptcy. [H.R. Rep. No. 95–595, at 176 (1977)] Thus, § 541(a)(1) of the Code provides that "all legal or equitable interests of the debtor in property as of the commencement of the case" constitute property of the estate.

The Chapter begins with numerous examples of property held to be estate property—bank accounts, liquor licenses, and even social media accounts. The estate also includes community property, certain post-petition acquisitions of property, and property recovered by the trustee using the Code's avoiding powers. *See* Chapter Six on the avoiding powers. Property of the estate is a central concept in bankruptcy. The definition is comprehensive, but there are a number of types of property excluded from property of the estate. This Chapter covers the ***ten categories of property that do not become estate property*** upon commencement of the bankruptcy estate. While the debtor may exempt property from the estate, exemptions are the subject of Chapter Eight.

The debtor may not have possession, custody, or control of all estate property at the start of the bankruptcy case. This Chapter covers the Code's ***turnover provisions***, which require both custodians and non-custodians to turn over estate property that is not in the debtor's hands to the trustee. The Chapter ends with the ***trustee's abandonment power***. Under § 554, the trustee may abandon—typically to the debtor—property that is of inconsequential value or burdensome to the estate. There are limits, however, on the exercise of the abandonment power. The Supreme Court created a "narrow exception" to the power, holding that the trustee cannot abandon estate property that is in violation of state or federal environmental laws that are "reasonably designed to protect the public health or safety from identified hazards." [**Midlantic National Bank v. New Jersey Department of Environmental Protection**, 474 U.S. 494 (1986)]

A. The Bankruptcy Estate

1. Property Included in Bankruptcy Estate

The filing of a petition creates the bankruptcy estate. [B.C. § 541(a)] The estate consists of "all interests, such as interests in real or personal property, tangible and intangible property, choses in action, causes of action, rights such as copyrights, trade-marks, patents, and processes, contingent interests and future interests, whether or not transferable by the debtor." [H.R. Rep. No. 95–595, at 175–76 (1977)] The Supreme Court has held that Congress generally has left to state law "the determination of property rights in the assets of a bankrupt's estate . . . [u]nless some federal interest requires a different result." [**Butner v. United States,** 440 U.S. 48 (1979) (decided under Bankruptcy Act); *see also* **Travelers Casualty & Surety Co. v. Pacific Gas and Electric Co.**, 549 U.S. 443 (2007) (citing *Butner* for proposition that " 'state law governs the substance of claims' " and holding that the Bankruptcy Code does not disallow a contract-based claim for attorney's fees simply because the fees were incurred litigating issues of bankruptcy law)]

a. All Legal and Equitable Interests of Debtor

The estate includes all of the debtor's legal and equitable interests in property ***at the time the petition is filed.*** [B.C. § 541(a)(1)] The estate also includes certain property acquired post-petition as well as property that the trustee, using her avoiding powers, brings back into the estate. [*See infra* subsection (c)] The Bankruptcy Code's definition of property of the estate is expansive, as evidenced by the following examples of legal and equitable interests in property that may be included in the estate:

(i) ***bank deposits*** [5 Collier ¶ 541.08 (stating that the "bank deposit is a chose in action evidencing the debt owed by the bank to the debtor")];

(ii) ***stocks and stock options*** [**Doucet v. Drydock Coal Com (*In re Oakley*)**, 421 B.R. 602 (B.A.P. 6th Cir. 2009) (debtor's shares in his family firm)];

(iii) ***insurance policies and payments under those policies*** [**Stinnett v. LaPlante (*In re Stinnett)*,** 465 F.3d 309 (7th Cir. 2006) (noting that "[a]s a general matter, insurance contracts in which the debtor has an interest" when bankruptcy is filed are estate property and concluding that disability payments under a disability insurance contract are proceeds of that policy); ***In re* Sunland,** 2014 WL 7011747 (Bankr. D. N.M. 2014) (citing cases, including those involving product liability insurance)];

(iv) ***compensation*** received post-petition (or right to compensation) for ***pre-petition*** employment services [***In re* Moulton,** 113 B.R. 732 (Bankr. M.D. Fla. 1990) (finding an implied contract for the reasonable value of services debtor provided pre-petition to wife's firm and concluding that value of those services constituted property of the estate)];

(v) ***executory contracts*** [*see* § 365; *see also infra* Chapter Eleven];

(vi) ***pre-petition personal injury claims*** by the debtor [**Cabral v. Shamban (*In re Cabral)*,** 285 B.R. 563 (B.A.P. 1st Cir. 2002) (stating that debtor's pre-petition personal injury claim was property of the estate and noting that such a claim is estate property regardless of "whether the claim is unliquidated or settled at the time of filing the bankruptcy petition")];

(vii) causes of action for ***damage to the debtor's property*** [4 Norton § 61:7];

(viii) ***other causes of action,*** including derivative suits against corporate officers and directors for breach of their fiduciary duties [**Torch Liquidating Trust v. Stockstill,** 561 F.3d 377 (5th Cir. 2009) (stating that suit by trustee of liquidating trust was not a derivative action but citing cases in which bankruptcy court permitted such suits); *see also* 4 Norton § 61:7];

(ix) ***income tax refunds*** based on ***pre-petition*** earnings or losses [**Kokoszka v. Belford,** 417 U.S. 642 (1974) (decided under Bankruptcy Act); **Garcia Matos v. Oliveras Rivera (*In re* Garcia Matos),** 478 B.R. 506 (B.A.P. 1st Cir. 2012) (citing cases)];

(x) ***net operating loss carryovers*** [**Official Committee of Unsecured Creditors v. PSS Steamship Lines, Inc. (*In re* Prudential Lines, Inc.),** 928 F.2d 565 (2d Cir. 1991)];

(xi) ***earned income credit,*** prorated to the date of the bankruptcy petition [**Wood v. Jones (*In re* Montgomery),** 224 F.3d 1193 (10th Cir. 2000); **Johnston v. Hazlett (*In re* Johnston),** 209 F.3d 611 (6th Cir. 2000) (citing cases)];

(xii) ***intellectual property***, such as patents, copyrights, and trademarks [**Hook v. United States (*In re* Hook),** 2008 WL 4424811 (D. Colo. 2008) (in a footnote, noting the broad scope of § 541(a)'s definition and stating a "debtor's intellectual property, such as interests in patents, trademarks and copyrights" is included in estate property)];

(xiii) *a remainder interest in real property* [*In re* **Saunders,** 2011 WL 671765 (Bankr. M.D. Ga. 2011) (stating that "[i]t is [ ] well-known that a vested remainder interest in real property is property of the estate")];

(xiv) *a liquor license* [**Abboud v. Ground Round, Inc. (*In re* Ground Round, Inc.),** 482 F.3d 15 (1st Cir. 2007)];

(xv) *business social media accounts* [*In re* **CTLI, LLC,** 528 B.R. 359 (Bankr. S.D. Tex. 2015)];

(xvi) a debtor's right to *redeem pawned property* under state law [**Schnitzel, Inc. v. Sorensen (*In re* Sorensen),** 586 B.R. 327 (B.A.P. 9th Cir. 2018)];

(xvii) *a debtor's right of redemption under state law arising at a post-petition foreclosure sale of real property* in which the estate had not abandoned its interest [**Schlarman v. Nageleisen (*In re* Nageleisen),** 527 B.R. 258 (Bankr. E.D. Ky. 2015)]; and

(xviii) right to *alimony payments* under a pre-petition divorce decree. [**Mehlhaff v. Allred (*In re* Mehlhaff),** 491 B.R. 898 (B.A.P. 8th Cir. 2013)]

b. **Limited by Debtor's Interest**

While the Code's definition of estate property is broad, there is an important limitation: the estate has no greater interest in property than the debtor had prior to filing for bankruptcy. [**Witko v. Menotte (*In re* Witko),** 374 F.3d 1040 (11th Cir. 2004) ("Congress expressly cautioned that the Bankruptcy Code 'is not intended to expand the debtor's rights against others more than they exist at the commencement of the case. . . .[The trustee] could take no greater rights than the debtor himself had' ") (quoting from legislative history)]

c. **Other Kinds of Estate Property**

Property of the estate also includes *community property,* property recovered by the trustee using her *avoiding powers,* and certain property acquired *post-petition.*

(i) **Community Property**

All of the debtor and debtor's spouse's community property, as defined under applicable state law, at the time of the filing of the bankruptcy petition becomes property of the estate if the property is under the debtor's sole or joint control or is liable for a claim against the debtor or for a joint claim against the debtor and debtor's spouse. [B.C. § 541(a)(2)]

(ii) **Property Recovered by Trustee**

Property of the estate includes any interests in property that the trustee recovers or preserves for the estate's benefit. For example, if the trustee avoids a preferential transfer and recovers the property transferred, that property is property of the estate. [B.C. § 541(a)(3), (4)]

(iii) **Certain Property Acquired Post-Petition**

The following types of property interests are property of the estate *if* the interest would have been estate property had the debtor had such *interest at the time of bankruptcy filing and* the debtor acquires or becomes entitled to acquire the property interest within *180 days after filing of the petition*:

(1) by bequest, devise, or inheritance [B.C. § 541(a)(5)(A)];

(2) as a result of a property settlement with the debtor's spouse or property included as part of a divorce decree [B.C. § 541(a)(5)(B)]; or

(3) as a beneficiary of a life insurance policy or death benefit plan. [B.C. § 541(a)(5)(C)]

Example: Debtor filed for relief under Chapter 7. Within 180 days after filing for bankruptcy, Debtor received a distribution from an inter vivos spendthrift trust after the trust's settlor, a distant relative of the Debtor's, passed away. The Chapter 7 trustee claimed that the distribution constituted property of the estate under § 541(a)(5), but the bankruptcy court disagreed. The court found that the Debtor had not acquired or become entitled to the distribution by "bequest, devise, or inheritance", under § 541(a)(5)(A) and, thus, the distribution was not estate property. (Neither § 541(a)(5)(B) nor (C) applied to the facts of the case.) The court explained that an inter vivos trust, unlike a testamentary trust, is not created by a will. Thus, Debtor did not receive the distribution by bequest or devise. The court noted that there was no evidence that the relative had died intestate and, thus, Debtor did not receive the distribution as an inheritance under the laws of intestacy. Therefore, the distribution was not estate property under § 541(a)(5)(A). [*In re* **Dayton,** 2018 WL 576748 (Bankr. W.D. Mo. 2018)]

(iv) Proceeds of Estate Property

With one important exception, proceeds, rents, profits, products, or offspring of or from estate property also are property of the estate. [B.C. § 541(a)(6)] Congress intended for the word "proceeds" to "not [be] used in a confining sense" but "to be a broad term to encompass all proceeds of property of the estate." [H.R. Rep. No. 95–595, at 368 (1977)]

Example: Debtor filed for relief under Chapter 13, but her case was dismissed. After dismissal, Bank obtained a default judgment against Debtor that ordered a sale of real property that the Debtor and her non-filing spouse owned. Before the property was sold, Debtor filed for relief under Chapter 7. After the bankruptcy court ordered a lift of stay "without abandonment," a foreclosure sale took place. The amount obtained at the foreclosure sale was so small that it triggered Debtor's right of redemption under applicable nonbankruptcy law. The bankruptcy court held that Debtor's right of redemption was estate property because under § 541(a)(6) it was a proceed of the foreclosure sale. [**Schlarman v. Nageleisen (***In re* **Nageleisen),** 527 B.R. 258 (Bankr. E.D. Ky. 2015)]

Example: Husband and Wife filed a joint petition for relief under Chapter 7. Prior to bankruptcy, Husband took a job with D&G, a holding company for a number of car dealerships. Husband also purchased a 33% interest in D&G. Husband's compensation with D&G included a base salary of $10,000 per month and a 5% monthly bonus based on the net profit of the D&G companies. If the companies did not make a profit in a particular month, then Husband did not earn a bonus that month. Husband and Wife argued that Husband's post-petition bonuses constituted earnings from service performed after the commencement of the case. The bankruptcy court rejected that argument and found that the bonuses were actually dividends from D&G's earnings. The court concluded that because the "bonuses" were "proceeds" or "profits" from Debtor's ownership interest in D&G, they constituted property of the estate under § 541(a)(6). [*In re* **Cook,** 454 B.R. 204 (Bankr. N.D. Fla. 2011)]

(1) Exception: Individual Chapter 7 Debtor's Post-Petition Earnings

In an *individual Chapter 7* case, the *debtor's earnings* for services rendered *after* the filing of the petition are *not* included in property of the estate. [B.C. § 541(a)(6)] In a Chapter 11 case in which the *individual debtor* elects to proceed under *subchapter V*, the *debtor's earnings* for services rendered *after* the filing of the petition but *before* the Chapter 11 case is closed, dismissed, or converted to Chapter 7, 12, or 13, whichever first occurs, are *not* included in property of the estate *unless* the debtor's plan is confirmed under § 1191(b) (cram down). [B.C. § 1186(a)(2); *see* § 1181(a)(1) (excluding § 1115)]. In Chapters 11 (with the exception stated above), 12, and 13, however, an individual debtor's earnings from services rendered after the filing of the petition but before the earlier of the closing, dismissal, or conversion of the case, whichever first occurs, are included in property of the estate. [B.C. §§ 1115(a)(2), 1207(a)(2), 1306(a)(2)]

Note: Section 1207(a), unlike § 1115, is not limited to individual debtors. The language of § 1306 also is not so limited, but only individual debtors are eligible to file for relief under Chapter 13.

(v) Property Acquired by Estate After Bankruptcy

Any property that the *estate* acquires *after the filing* of the petition is property of the estate. [B.C. § 541(a)(7)] Be careful to distinguish between property that the *debtor acquires* from property that the *estate acquires* after filing of the petition. This subsection of the Code applies only to property acquired by the *estate,* not by the *debtor. See infra* next subsection.

Example: In August of 2013, Debtor's spouse filed a divorce action in state court. The following summer, in July of 2014, Debtor filed for relief under Chapter 7. In March of 2015, Debtor's spouse filed a motion for relief of stay to allow the divorce proceeding to continue. The bankruptcy court granted the spouse's motion, and in June of 2015, the state court entered a consent judgment of divorce. That judgment awarded Debtor a 50% interest in certain inventory and required Debtor's spouse to pay Debtor $2,700 within 30 days of entry of the consent judgment. The Debtor claimed that the inventory and $2,700 were not property of the estate, because he acquired them pursuant to the consent judgment of divorce, which was entered more than 180 days after filing of his Chapter 7 case and, thus, § 541(a)(5)(B) did not apply. The bankruptcy court held that the inventory and $2,700 were estate property under §§ 541(a)(1) and (a)(7). The court explained that in Michigan the filing of an action for divorce creates a marital estate. When Debtor filed for bankruptcy, his interest in the marital estate became property of the estate under § 541(a)(1), even though Debtor's interest in the marital property was contingent at the time. Debtor's contingent interest vested, however, upon entry of the consent judgment of divorce; at that time, the Debtor's right to the inventory and $2,700 became estate property under § 541(a)(7). Therefore, the court concluded that it was "immaterial" that the state court had entered the consent judgment of divorce more than 180 days after Debtor had filed for bankruptcy. [*In re* **Kooi,** 547 B.R. 244 (Bankr. W.D. Mich. 2016)]

(vi) Property Acquired by the Debtor After Bankruptcy

In Chapters 12 and 13, and individual Chapter 11 cases (with an exception in subchapter V) *all property* of the kind described in § 541 that the *debtor acquires after bankruptcy* but before the closing, dismissal, or conversion of the case, whichever first occurs, is *property of the estate*. [B.C. §§ 1115(a)(1), 1207(a)(1), 1306(a)(1)] In a Chapter 11 case in which the debtor elects to proceed under *subchapter V*, all property acquired by the debtor *after* the filing of the petition but *before* the Chapter 11 case is closed, dismissed, or converted to Chapter 7, 12, or 13, whichever first occurs, is *not* included in property of the estate *unless* the debtor's plan is confirmed under § 1191(b) (cram down). [B.C. § 1186(a)(1); *see* § 1181(a)(1) (excluding § 1115)]

2. Invalid Clauses: Ipso Facto or "Bankruptcy" Clauses

Even if nonbankruptcy law or a clause in a contract or deed restricts or conditions the debtor's transfer of property, that property becomes property of the estate. [B.C. § 541(c)(1)(A)] A clause in the parties' agreement that provides for possible forfeiture, termination, or modification of the debtor's interest in the property due to (i) the debtor's insolvency, (ii) the debtor's financial condition, (iii) the debtor's filing of a bankruptcy case, or (iv) the appointment of a bankruptcy trustee or a pre-petition nonbankruptcy custodian are unenforceable under the Bankruptcy Code and do not prevent the property from being included in the bankruptcy estate. [B.C. § 541(c)(1); *see also* B.C. § 365(e)(1)]

a. Exception for Certain Trusts

A restriction on the transfer of the debtor's beneficial interest in a trust, if that restriction is enforceable under *applicable nonbankruptcy law,* is *enforceable* in bankruptcy. [B.C. § 541(c)(2)] Congress intended that spendthrift trusts be excluded from estate property to the extent that state law protects the trusts from creditors. [H.R. Rep. No. 95–595, at 176 (1977)] Courts consistently have applied this exception to traditional spendthrift trusts, and the Supreme Court has held that it also covers ERISA-qualified pension plans. [**Patterson v. Shumate,** 504 U.S. 753 (1992)] The exception operates to *exclude* the debtor's interest in the trust of the ERISA plan from property of her bankruptcy estate.

Note: BAPCPA added § 541(b)(7), which is a new exclusion from estate property for a variety of pension plans that might not qualify as ERISA-qualified. This new exclusion has eliminated in many cases the need to litigate the question of whether § 541(c)(2) excludes the debtor's pension benefits from her estate.

(i) Distinguish Payment of Trust Income to Debtor

It is important to distinguish *the income* from the *corpus* of the spendthrift trust for purposes of this exception. The income a debtor receives from a testamentary spendthrift trust within 180 days of the bankruptcy filing may be considered a bequest and, thus, become property of the estate *even though* the trust corpus is *not* estate property. [*See, e.g., In re* **Hecht,** 54 B.R. 379 (Bankr. S.D. N.Y. 1985) (holding that income received from the spendthrift trust within the 180 days after bankruptcy filing "constitute[d] bequests and [became] property of the estate under § 541(a)(5)(A)"]

3. Property Excluded from Estate

The Bankruptcy Code *excludes* ten types of interests from the bankruptcy estate. [B.C. § 541(b)(1)–(10)]

a. Certain Powers

A power that the debtor may exercise *solely for the benefit of an entity other than the debtor* is not part of the bankruptcy estate. [B.C. § 541(b)(1)]

e.g. **Example:** Debtor filed for relief under Chapter 13. Debtor used the Tennessee state exemptions and on Schedule C exempted the full fair market value of about $30,000 in child support arrearages. The Chapter 13 trustee objected to Debtor's plan, claiming, in part, that the plan was not proposed in good faith because Debtor had claimed inappropriate exemptions in the child support arrearages. The bankruptcy court overruled the trustee's objection. The court explained that under Tennessee law a custodial parent holds child support payments in a constructive trust for the minor child as beneficiary. The debtor holds these monies "for the benefit of an entity other than the debtor" and, therefore, they are excluded from the bankruptcy estate under § 541(b)(1). [*In re* **Turner,** 2014 Bankr. LEXIS 5417 (Bankr. W.D. Tenn. 2014)]

b. Expired Commercial Lease of Real Property

A debtor's interest *as a lessee* of *nonresidential real property* is excluded from property of the estate if the lease term expired before the filing of the petition. Property of the estate also ceases to include any interest of the debtor as a lessee if the lease's term expires *during* the bankruptcy case. [B.C. § 541(b)(2)]

c. Certain Property of Educational Institutions

The debtor's eligibility to participate in programs under the Higher Education Act of 1965 or the debtor's accreditation status or state licensure as an educational institution are excluded from estate property. [B.C. § 541(b)(3)]

d. Farmout Agreements and Production Payments

The debtor's interest in liquid or gaseous hydrocarbons that the debtor either transferred or promised to transfer pursuant to a farmout agreement is excluded from the estate. [B.C. §§ 541(b)(4)(A), 101(21A)] Also excluded are production payments from liquid or gaseous hydrocarbons if the debtor transferred her interest in the production payments pursuant to a written conveyance to an entity that does not participate in the property's operation. [B.C. §§ 541(b)(4)(B), 101(42A)] But, any consideration that the debtor retains, receives, or is entitled to receive for transferring an interest in liquid or gaseous hydrocarbons under a farmout agreement is not excluded from the estate. [Hanging sentence after B.C. § 541(b)(10)]

e. Education IRA

BAPCPA created an exclusion from estate property for certain funds placed into an education individual retirement account *no later than one year* before filing for bankruptcy. The exclusion applies *only if* all the following conditions are satisfied:

(i) the designated *beneficiary* is the debtor's *child, stepchild, grandchild, or stepgrandchild* for the taxable year in which the funds were placed in the account [B.C. § 541(b)(5)(A)];

(ii) the funds are not pledged or promised in connection with a credit extension [B.C. § 541(b)(5)(B)(i)]; and

(iii) the funds are *not excess contributions,* as defined by § 4973(e) of the Internal Revenue Code [B.C. § 541(b)(5)(B)(ii)].

There is a limitation, however, on the amount of funds excluded from the estate in the case of funds placed into such accounts between *720 and 365 days preceding bankruptcy.* In such a case, the debtor may exclude no more than a total of *$7,575* in all accounts for each designated beneficiary. [B.C. § 541(b)(5)(C)]

f. State Tuition Programs

BAPCPA added an exclusion from estate property for funds used to buy tuition credits or certificates, or contributed to an account that qualifies as a *State tuition program* pursuant to *§ 529(b)(1)* of the Internal Revenue Code *no later than one year prior* to the bankruptcy filing. [B.C. § 541(b)(6)] The funds are excluded from the bankruptcy estate only if all the following conditions are satisfied:

(i) the designated *beneficiary* is the debtor's *child, stepchild, grandchild, or stepgrandchild* for the taxable year in which the funds were paid or contributed [B.C. § 541(b)(6)(A)]; and

(ii) the *aggregate* amount paid or contributed for *each beneficiary* does not exceed total contributions allowed under *§ 529(b)(6)* of the Internal Revenue Code, as adjusted for inflation as of the date of the bankruptcy filing. [B.C. § 541(b)(6)(B)]

As with education IRAs, there is a limitation on the amount of funds excluded from the estate in the case of funds paid or contributed to such § 529 plans between *720 and 365 days preceding bankruptcy.* In such a case, the debtor may exclude no more than a total of *$7,575* in all accounts for each designated beneficiary. [B.C. § 541(b)(6)(C)]

g. Pension Plan, Deferred Compensation, and Tax-Deferred Annuity Monies

BAPCPA added an exclusion from estate property for funds withheld by an employer from employee wages or received by an employer from employees for payment as *contributions* to any of the following *four types of plans*:

(i) *employee benefit plans* under Title I of ERISA or a governmental employee benefit plans under § 414(d) of the Internal Revenue Code [B.C. § 541(b)(7)(A)(i)(I), (B)(i)(I)];

(ii) *deferred compensation plans* under § 457 of the Internal Revenue Code, which includes certain pension plans for state and local government employees, and charities [B.C. § 541(b)(7)(A)(i)(II), (B)(i)(II); 5 Collier ¶ 541.23(1)];

(iii) *tax deferred annuities* under § 403(b) of the Internal Revenue Code, which includes retirement plans for certain public school employees and ministers [B.C. § 541(b)(7)(A)(i)(III), (B)(i)(III); 5 Collier ¶ 541.23(1)]; and

(iv) *health insurance plans* regulated by State law [B.C. § 541(b)(7)(A)(ii), (B)(ii)].

Courts have held that *any* amounts in a retirement, deferred compensation plan, or health insurance plan are excluded from the bankruptcy estate, not simply monies that the employer holds at the commencement of the bankruptcy case.

Example: Husband and Wife filed for relief under Chapter 7. At the time of the bankruptcy filing, Wife had approximately $120,000 in a 403(b) retirement plan. Debtors exempted about one third of the monies using Vermont's exemptions, and argued that the remainder of the funds were not part of the bankruptcy estate under § 541(b)(7). The trustee argued that the exclusion under § 541(b)(7) only applied to the "gap period" between withholding and remittance of the monies to the plan. Thus, the trustee claimed that Debtors could not exclude the remaining $78,000 in Wife's 403(b) account. The bankruptcy court rejected the trustee's argument. The court noted that while there were no cases dealing specifically with 403(b) plans, the cases on 401(k) and ERISA-qualified savings plans spoke "with one voice in concluding that [such plans] are not property of the bankruptcy estate." The court noted that the same logic that applied to other type of plans under § 541(b)(7) applied to 403(b) plans. Thus, the court held that the $78,000 in Wife's 403(b) plan that Debtors had not exempted was not an issue, because those funds "were never part of the bankruptcy estate in the first instance." [***In re* Leahy,** 370 B.R. 620 (Bankr. D. Vt. 2007)]

h. Pawnbrokers

BAPCPA added an exclusion from estate property for ***personal property*** that the debtor has ***pledged or sold*** as collateral for a loan or advance from a ***person licensed*** to make such loans or advances. [B.C. § 541(b)(8)] For the exclusion to apply, all the following conditions must be met:

(i) the ***pledgee or transferee*** must be in ***possession*** of the personal property [B.C. § 541(b)(8)(A)];

(ii) the debtor is not required to repay the loan or advance or redeem the property or buy it back at a ***specific price*** [B.C. § 541(b)(8)(B)]; and

(iii) neither the debtor nor the trustee has exercised any right under the contract or State law to ***redeem*** the property in the time period provided by State law or § 108(b) of the Code. [B.C. § 541(b)(8)(C)]

Finally, § 541(b)(8) provides that it is subject to §§ 541 through 562 of the Code. As a result, the trustee may seek to avoid a pledge or sale of personal property that otherwise is covered by this subsection. [5 Collier ¶ 541.24]

Example: Debtor pledged jewelry to R&J, a licensed pawnbroker, as collateral for pawn loans. Before the loans' termination date, Debtor filed for relief under Chapter 13. R&J sent Debtor a notice of the loans' termination date, which provided for the ten-day right to redeem under California law. Debtor did not redeem the jewelry, and instead proposed a plan under which she would make monthly payments on the pawn loans. Debtor filed an adversary proceeding against R&J, asking the court to enjoin R&J from disposing of the jewelry. R&J responded that the jewelry was not property of the bankruptcy estate under § 541(a)(8), because Debtor had not redeemed the jewelry within the time frame provided by § 541(a)(8)(C). The Ninth Circuit's Bankruptcy Appellate Panel found that the time period for redemption had *not* lapsed. The court explained that the time period under state law applied, as it was later than the 60-day period provided by § 108(b)(2). The court then found that R&J's notice was void *ab initio* because R&J had sent the notice during the bankruptcy case without first moving to lift the automatic stay. As a result, the ten-day redemption period never began to run and Debtor's right to redeem was not extinguished. Thus, the jewelry was not removed from the bankruptcy estate under § 541(b)(8). The court distinguished its decision from those cases in which state law provides that pawned property *automatically* vests in the pawnbroker following the expiration of the redemption period. By comparison, California and a minority of other states require the pawnbroker to give notice before the pawned property vests in the pawnbroker. Because R&J did not move to lift the automatic stay, its notice was void and Debtor's redemption right did not terminate. [**Schnitzel, Inc. v. Sorensen (*In re* Sorensen),** 586 B.R. 327 (B.A.P. 9th Cir. 2018)]

i. Proceeds of Money Orders

If the debtor and money order issuer had an agreement prohibiting the debtor from commingling the proceeds of the money order sales with other debtor funds *and* the money order issuer took action to require the debtor's compliance with the prohibition before bankruptcy, then proceeds of any sales of money orders in the **14 days** prior to bankruptcy are excluded from the bankruptcy estate. [B.C. § 541(b)(9)]

j. ABLE Funds

As part of the Tax Increase Prevention Act of 2014, Congress added § 541(b)(10) to the Code, which excludes from estate property funds placed in a *qualified ABLE account,* as defined by § 529A(b) of the Internal Revenue Code, no later than *one year prior to the bankruptcy* filing. [B.C. § 541(b)(10); 5 Collier ¶ 541.25A] A State may create an ABLE program that allows contributions to ABLE accounts to cover certain disability expenses for *disabled* state residents. [5 Collier ¶ 541.25A] The exclusion applies if all the following conditions are satisfied:

(i) the designated *beneficiary* is the debtor's *child, stepchild, grandchild, or stepgrandchild* for the taxable year in which the funds were placed in the account [B.C. § 541(b)(10)(A)];

(ii) the funds are *not pledged or promised* in connection with a *credit extension* [B.C. § 541(b)(10)(B)(i)]; and

(iii) the funds are *not excess contributions,* as defined by § 4973(h) of the Internal Revenue Code [B.C. § 541(b)(10)(B)(ii)].

There is a limitation on the amount of funds excluded from the estate in the case of funds placed into such accounts between *720 and 365 days preceding bankruptcy.* In such a case, the debtor may exclude no more than a total of *$7,575* in all accounts for each designated beneficiary. [B.C. § 541(b)(10)(C)]

4. Distinguish Exemptions

Do not confuse *exclusions* from estate property with *exemptions.* If property is excluded from the estate under § 541(b), it means that the property never comes into the bankruptcy estate. Therefore, there is no need to exempt it. [*See* **Traina v. Sewell (*In re* Sewell),** 180 F.3d 707 (5th Cir. 1999) (stating that "[e]xemptions come into play only when property is included in the bankruptcy estate . . . ; by definition, *excluded* property never forms part of the bankruptcy estate and thus need not be tested for exempt status")] By comparison, exemptions apply to estate property. In doing an analysis, first ask whether the property is excluded from the bankruptcy estate. If it is, then do *not* look for exemptions. If the property comes into the bankruptcy estate, the debtor may exempt it, thereby removing the possibility, if the full value is exempted, of the trustee selling the property to distribute the proceeds to unsecured creditors. [B.C. § 522(b)]

B. Turnover of Property to Trustee

1. Turnover by Entity Other than Custodian

An *entity, other than a custodian,* in possession, custody, or control of property that the trustee may use, sell, or lease under § 363 or that the debtor may exempt under § 522 must deliver the property to the trustee and account for such property or the property's value. The turnover requirement does *not apply* to property of *inconsequential value or benefit to the estate.* [B.C. § 542(a)]

a. "Entity"

The Code defines the word "entity" more broadly than the term "person." Thus, even a governmental unit or a trust is subject to the turnover provisions. [B.C. § 101(15)]

b. Turnover of Property Repossessed Before Bankruptcy

A secured creditor that prior to bankruptcy repossessed collateral but has not yet sold the collateral to a bona fide purchaser must turn over the collateral to the trustee or the debtor in possession, because ownership is not transferred until a sale occurs. [**United States v. Whiting Pools, Inc.,** 462 U.S. 198 (1983)] However, the secured creditor is entitled to adequate protection of its interest. [B.C. §§ 363(e), 361; **United States v. Whiting Pools, Inc.,** *supra*]

(i) Note

In *Whiting Pools,* the Supreme Court made clear that it expressed no view on whether § 542(a) applied as broadly in Chapter 7 and 13, as it did in Chapter 11. Nonetheless, many courts have extended the reasoning of *Whiting Pools* to cases involving a pre-petition repossession by a secured creditor in a Chapter 13 case. [*See, e.g.,* **Weber v. SEFCU (*In re* Weber),** 719 F.3d 72 (2d Cir. 2013) (noting that debtor had equitable interest in property because repossession did not transfer ownership and that under *Whiting Pools* this equitable interest gave the estate a possessory interest in the secured property); **Transouth Financial Corp. v. Sharon (*In re* Sharon),** 234 B.R. 676 (B.A.P. 6th Cir. 1999) (applying *Whiting Pools* and concluding that possession of the vehicle "was part of the bundle of rights" that became estate property upon filing of the petition); *but see* **Bell-Tel Federal Credit Union v. Kalter (*In re* Kalter),** 292 F.3d 1350 (11th Cir. 2002) (not discussing *Whiting Pools* but holding that under Florida law, ownership of vehicles transferred upon pre-petition repossession and, therefore, were not property of the estate and not subject to turnover)] The *Whiting Pools* reasoning also has been extended to pledged property in the possession of a secured creditor in a Chapter 7 liquidation case. [*In re* **Gerwer,** 898 F.2d 730 (9th Cir. 1990)]

(ii) Automatic Stay

In **City of Chicago v. Fulton,** 141 S. Ct. 585 (2021), the Supreme Court resolved a split of authority as to whether a creditor that does not turn over property of the estate, but merely continues to hold it, violates the automatic stay provision found in § 362(a)(3), which stays not only "any act to obtain possession of property of the estate," but also an act *"to exercise control over property of the estate."* *Fulton* involved Chapter 13 debtors whose cars were impounded prior to bankruptcy by the City of Chicago for failure to pay fines for motor vehicle infractions. When the City refused to turn over the vehicles, the bankruptcy court in each case held that the City had violated the automatic stay. In a consolidated opinion, the Seventh Circuit affirmed the various bankruptcy courts' decisions. The Supreme Court vacated the judgment of the Court of Appeals and remanded for further proceedings. The Supreme Court held that "mere retention of estate property after the filing of a bankruptcy petition does not violate § 362(a)(3) of the Bankruptcy Code." The Court, however, declined to "decide how the turnover obligation in § 542 works." In her concurring opinion, Justice Sotomayor noted that turnover proceedings were notoriously slow—over 100 days for proceedings filed in the one-year period between July 2019 and June 2020. Justice Sotomayor called on the Advisory Committee on Rules of Bankruptcy Procedure to amend the Rules to ensure expedited review of turnover proceedings involving a debtor's vehicle. She also explained that Congress "could offer a statutory fix" by either ensuring expedited review for proceedings under § 542(a) or by "enacting entirely new statutory mechanisms that require creditors to return cars to debtors in a timely manner."

2. Payment of Debt That Is Estate Property

An entity that owes a debt that is *property of the estate* and that is matured, payable on demand, or payable on order must pay the trustee the amount of the debt in excess of any setoff permitted the entity under § 553. [B.C. § 542(b)] An example is a bank's obligation to pay to the trustee money in debtor's checking account.

a. Bank's Freeze of Debtor's Account

In **Citizens Bank of Maryland v. Strumpf,** 516 U.S. 16 (1995), the United States Supreme Court held that § 542(b)'s setoff exception coupled with the general rule on setoff in § 553(a) justify a bank's *temporary hold* on a debtor's checking account up to the amount allegedly subject to setoff. The administrative freeze provides the bank with time to seek relief from the automatic stay and a determination by the court of its right to a setoff. Without such a freeze, the debtor could spend the funds in the bank account, thereby rendering useless the bank's right to setoff.

3. Exceptions to Turnover

a. Property of Inconsequential Value

The turnover requirement does *not apply* to property of *inconsequential value or benefit to the estate.* [B.C. § 542(a)]

b. Transfer Without Actual Notice or Knowledge of Bankruptcy Case

Turnover is not required if an entity, such as a bank, *in good faith* and without either actual notice or knowledge of the bankruptcy petition transfers property of the estate or pays a debt owing to the debtor to an entity other than the trustee. [B.C. § 542(c)] Section 542(c) "codifies the result of *Bank of Marin v. England,* 385 U.S. 99 (1966)." [H.R. Rep. No. 95–595, at 369 (1977)]

Example: In late August and early September of 1963, Marin Seafoods drew and delivered several checks on its commercial account with Bank of Marin in favor of Eureka Fisheries. The checks totaled $2318.82. On September 26, 1963, Marin Seafoods filed for bankruptcy. On October 2, 1963, Eureka presented the checks to Bank or Marin for payment. At that time, Bank of Marin had neither notice nor knowledge of the Marin Seafoods bankruptcy filing. The Supreme Court, in a pre-Code case, held that Bank of Marin was not liable to the trustee for the amount of the checks paid when the Bank had no knowledge or notice of the bankruptcy proceeding. [**Bank of Marin v. England,** 385 U.S. 99 (1966)]

(i) Transferee Not Protected

Note that § 542(c) does *not* apply to the payee or transferee in such a transaction. The payee or transferee may be subject to the trustee's avoiding power under § 549 and to liability under § 550. [5 Collier ¶ 542.05; *see* **Bank of Marin,** *supra* (stating that the payee of the check is a creditor of the debtor and requiring him to "reimburse the trustee is only to deprive him of preferential treatment")]

(ii) Post-Petition Setoff Not Excepted

Even if a bank lacks actual notice or knowledge of the bankruptcy petition, it may not set off a pre-petition debt without first obtaining relief from the automatic stay. [B.C. §§ 542(c), 362(a)(7); *see* H.R. Rep. No. 95–595, at 369 (1977) (explaining that § 542(c) codifies the result in *Bank of Marin* "but does not go so far as to permit bank setoff in violation of the automatic stay")]

4. Turnover of Property by Custodian

A custodian with knowledge of the bankruptcy filing cannot disburse from or take any action to administer (i) any property of the debtor; (ii) any proceeds, rents, profits, products, or offspring of the debtor's property; or (iii) any property of the estate in her possession, custody, or control, except action needed to preserve such property. The custodian must turn over the property to the trustee and file an accounting. [B.C. § 543(a), (b)]

a. "Custodian" Defined

The Code defines a custodian as:

(i) a receiver or trustee of the debtor's property appointed in a nonbankruptcy action [B.C. § 101(11)(A)];

(ii) an assignee under a general assignment for the benefit of the debtor's creditors [B.C. § 101(11)(B)]; or

(iii) a trustee or receiver appointed or authorized to take control of the debtor's property to enforce a lien against such property or for the purpose of general administration of such property for the benefit of debtor's creditors. [B.C. § 101(11)(C)]

e.g. **Example:** Debtors, fifty-seven financially distressed cash currency exchanges, filed for relief under Chapter 11. Prior to bankruptcy, thirty-three of the exchanges were placed under state administrative receiverships pursuant to Illinois law. A receiver for the Director of Financial Institutions ("Director"), which regulates currency exchanges, was appointed. The receiver took title to all of Debtors' assets, and state liquidation proceedings were commenced against Debtors. The Seventh Circuit rejected the Director's argument that the term "custodian" included only court-appointed receivers and not administrative receivers. The court concluded that the state administrative receiver was a custodian under federal bankruptcy law, and affirmed the bankruptcy court's order directing the Director to turn over debtor's property to the bankruptcy trustee. [*In re* **Cash Currency Exchange, Inc.,** 762 F.2d 542 (7th Cir. 1985)]

b. Exceptions to Requirement of Turnover by Custodian

After notice and hearing, the bankruptcy court may *excuse* a custodian's duty to turn over property if the interests of creditors and, if the debtor is solvent, the interests of equity security holders are better served by allowing a custodian to remain in possession, custody, or control of the property. [B.C. § 543(d)(1)]

After notice and hearing, the bankruptcy court *must excuse* the custodian's obligation to turn over property if the custodian is an assignee for the benefit of creditors who was appointed or took possession of the debtor's property *more than 120 days* before the commencement of the bankruptcy case. If necessary to prevent fraud or injustice, however, the court is not required to excuse the custodian's compliance with the Code's turnover obligations [B.C. § 543(d)(2)]

c. Compensation or Surcharge

A bankruptcy court, after notice and a hearing, may award a custodian reasonable compensation for her services and actual expenses. [B.C. § 543(c)(2)] With the exception of an assignee for the benefit of creditors who was appointed or took possession more than 120 days before bankruptcy, a custodian may be liable for improper or excessive disbursements. [B.C. § 543(c)(3)]

5. Turnover of Books and Records

The bankruptcy court, after notice and a hearing, may order, subject to any valid privilege, an attorney, accountant, or other person to turn over to the trustee any books, documents, records, and papers concerning the debtor's finances or property. [B.C. § 542(e)]

a. Waiver of Corporate Attorney-Client Privilege

In the case of a *corporate debtor,* the trustee has the power to waive the corporation's attorney-client privilege concerning *pre-bankruptcy communications* made by former officers and directors to the debtor's attorney. The corporation's attorney may then be required to testify. [**Commodity Futures Trading Commission v. Weintraub,** 471 U.S. 343 (1985)]

(i) Rationale

In *Weintraub,* the Court concluded that in light of how the Code allocates responsibilities, "it is clear that the trustee plays the role most closely analogous to that of a solvent corporation's management." Thus, vesting the trustee with the power to waive the attorney-client privilege "most closely comports with the allocation of the waiver power to management outside of bankruptcy."

(ii) *Weintraub* and Individual Cases

The Supreme Court in *Weintraub* specifically noted that its holding had "no bearing on the problem of individual bankruptcy, which [it had] no reason to address." The lower courts since *Weintraub* have adopted several approaches to the issue with the most common being a case-specific analysis that weighs the harm to the individual against the duty of the trustee to maximize the estate. [*In re* **Tarkington,** 2010 WL 1416813 (Bankr. E.D. N.C. 2010)] Courts have held, however, that the attorney-client privilege does not apply to information that the debtor discloses in preparing her petition and schedules. [*See, e.g.,* **United States v. White,** 950 F.2d 426 (7th Cir. 1991); **Tarkington,** *supra; but see In re* **Stickle,** 2016 WL 417047 (Bankr. S.D. Fla. 2016) (disagreeing with those cases like *White* and *Tarkington* in which the court "applied a bright-line rule" that information disclosed in preparing schedules and the petition was not protected by the attorney-client privilege)]

b. No Accountant-Client Privilege

Where access to information relating to the debtor's financial condition is needed for complete and accurate disclosure, an accountant or an accounting firm must turn over documents and work papers in its possession. There is no accountant-client privilege under federal law. [*See* **Couch v. United States,** 409 U.S. 322 (1973) (noting in a criminal case that no such privilege existed under federal law)] Courts also have refused to recognize state evidentiary accountant-client privileges in proceedings involving traditional questions of federal bankruptcy law. [*In re* **International Horizons, Inc.,** 689 F.2d 996 (11th Cir. 1982)]

C. Abandonment of Estate Property

1. Inconsequential or Burdensome Property

After notice and a hearing, the trustee may abandon property that is ***burdensome or of inconsequential value and benefit*** to the estate. [B.C. § 554(a)] Normally, abandoned property returns to the debtor; it no longer is property of the estate. Abandonment, however, does not affect the validity of any lien on the property. Even though the abandoned property no longer is property of the estate, the automatic stay protects the debtor from actions by a secured creditor to collect on a pre-petition claim or judgment, or to enforce a lien on the debtor's property. [B.C. § 362(a)(1), (2), (5), (6); *see* 5 Collier ¶ 554.02(4)]

a. Exception: Violation of Environmental Laws

The trustee is prohibited from abandoning estate property that is in violation of state or federal environmental laws that are "reasonably designed to protect the public health or safety from identified hazards." [**Midlantic National Bank v. New Jersey Department of Environmental Protection,** 474 U.S. 494 (1986)] The Court in *Midlantic* explained that its exception to the abandonment power was a "narrow one" and that the abandonment power "is not to be fettered by laws or regulations not reasonably calculated to protect the public health or safety from imminent or identifiable harm."

Example: Debtor operates a waste oil processing facility. Debtor violates a state environmental law by accepting oil contaminated with certain prohibited toxic chemicals, which are extremely dangerous both to the natural environment and to the public. Debtor files a voluntary Chapter 11 petition and subsequently is ordered by the state environmental protection agency to clean up the site. There is no equity in the property, and the expected cost of cleanup is $2.5 million. The case is converted to Chapter 7, and the trustee seeks to abandon the property as burdensome to the estate. Abandonment is not permitted because it would violate the state environmental law and would constitute an imminent threat to the health and safety of the community. [**Midlantic National Bank v. New Jersey Department of Environmental Protection,** *supra*]

(i) Automatic Stay

The Code provides an exception to the automatic stay for the commencement or continuation of a proceeding by a governmental unit to enforce its "police and regulatory power, including the enforcement of a judgment other than a money judgment." [B.C. §§ 362(b)(4), 101(27) (definition of "governmental unit"] Thus, a cleanup order by a state or federal environmental regulatory agency does not violate the automatic stay.

2. Request to Abandon Burdensome Property

A party in interest may make a motion for abandonment, and the court, after notice and a hearing, may order the trustee to abandon property that is burdensome or of inconsequential value to the estate. [B.C. § 554(b)]

3. Close of the Case: Unadministered Property

At the close of the case, unless the bankruptcy court rules to the contrary, any property that the debtor scheduled that was not administered before case closing is abandoned to the debtor. [B.C. §§ 554(c), 521(a)(1)]

Chapter Six

The Bankruptcy Estate: The Trustee's Avoiding Powers

Chapter Approach

As mentioned in the introduction to Chapter Five of this study guide, the bankruptcy estate includes property that the trustee brings into the estate by exercising her *avoiding powers.* Your professor is likely to ask you about the trustee's avoiding powers on your final examination. There are two steps involved in the process: (1) *avoidance* of the transfer; and (2) *recovery* of the transferred property for the benefit of the estate.

This Chapter walks you through the *avoiding powers* in the order in which they appear in the Bankruptcy Code. The Chapter starts with § 544(a), which contains the Code's *strong arm clause.* At the start of the bankruptcy case, the trustee has the rights and powers of a *hypothetical* (i) judicial lien creditor, (ii) creditor with an unsatisfied execution, and (iii) bona fide purchaser who has perfected the transfer of real property from the debtor. Section 544(b) allows the trustee to step into the shoes of an *actual creditor* and use nonbankruptcy law, e.g., a state voidable transactions statute, to avoid a pre-petition transfer. The trustee also may avoid certain *statutory liens* under § 545. Section 547 authorizes the trustee to avoid pre-petition *preferential transfers*, thereby effectuating the important bankruptcy policy of *equality of distribution*. This portion of the Chapter contains a number of examples to illustrate what constitutes a preference and how the numerous creditor defenses to a preference action work. The next section of the Chapter discusses § 548 on *fraudulent transfers*—both transfers based on an *actual intent to hinder, delay, or defraud* creditors and transfers that are *constructively fraudulent.* Up to this point in the Chapter, the avoiding powers deal with pre-petition transactions. But § 549, with certain exceptions, authorizes the trustee to avoid *post-petition transfers*, as well. The Chapter then moves on to discuss the *statute of limitations* for the various avoidance actions, as well as certain *other limitations* on the trustee's avoiding powers, such as *retroactive perfection* or the creditor's right, under certain circumstances, to *reclaim goods.*

The second step in the process is *recovery* of the property that is the subject of the *avoided* transfer for the *benefit of the bankruptcy estate*. Section 551 provides that any avoided transfer or voided lien under § 506(d) is *preserved for the estate's benefit*. Section 550 describes the parties from whom the trustee may recover the transferred property or its value.

Remember: The *initial transferee* cannot defend against the trustee's recovery action by claiming good faith or lack of knowledge of the voidability of the transaction.

The Chapter closes out with an examination of §§ 552 and 553 of the Code. *Section 552* of the Bankruptcy Code technically is not an avoidance provision. Nonetheless, it operates in a similar fashion by *preventing a pre-petition lien from attaching* to property acquired post-petition and thereby partially avoiding that lien. *Section 553* recognizes that a creditor entitled to a *right of setoff* under state law may set off a debt he owes to the debtor against a claim he holds against the debtor, if *both the debt and the claim are mutual and arose prior to the filing of the bankruptcy case.* Section 553 is included in this Chapter, because it places limitations on the creditor's right to setoff during the *90 days prior* to bankruptcy while the debtor was *insolvent.* These exceptions to the creditor's right of setoff echo the Code's preference provisions.

A. Trustee's Avoiding Powers as Hypothetical Creditor or Purchaser, and as Successor to Certain Actual Creditors

1. Strong Arm Provision

The Bankruptcy Code grants to the trustee, at the commencement of the bankruptcy case, the hypothetical status and the rights and powers of (i) a *judicial lien creditor,* (ii) a creditor with an *unsatisfied execution,* and (iii) a *bona fide purchaser of real property.* Consequently, the trustee is able to avoid any transfer of the debtor's property that any of these entities—*regardless of whether one really exists*—could avoid, "without regard to any knowledge of the trustee or of any creditor." [B.C. § 544(a)]

a. Judicial Lien Creditor

The trustee is accorded the rights and powers of a *hypothetical* creditor who furnishes credit to the debtor at the time that the bankruptcy case is commenced, and who simultaneously acquires a *judicial lien* on as much of the debtor's property as is permitted under applicable state or other nonbankruptcy law. [B.C. § 544(a)(1)]

Example: On June 1, Debtor borrows $5,000 from Finance Company, granting a security interest in a famous painting recently inherited by Debtor. On December 1, Debtor files a voluntary bankruptcy petition. At this time, Finance Company has not perfected its security interest in the painting. Under the Uniform Commercial Code ("U.C.C.") § 9–317(a)(2), a judicial lien has priority over an unperfected security interest. As a hypothetical lien creditor as of the filing of the bankruptcy case, the trustee prevails over Finance Company's unperfected security interest in the painting. Hence, the trustee will be able to avoid the security interest and thereby increase the amount available for distribution to the unsecured creditors. [B.C. § 544(a)(1)] If Finance Company had filed a UCC financing statement (or UCC–1) prior to Debtor's bankruptcy filing on December 1, then the trustee could *not* have avoided Finance Company's security interest in the painting under § 544(a)(1).

(i) Exception: Purchase Money Security Interest

The rights and powers of the trustee under § 544 are subject to any retroactive perfection allowable under applicable nonbankruptcy law. [B.C. § 546(b)] The U.C.C. provides that if a person files a UCC–1 with regard to a purchase money security interest *within 20 days* of the debtor *receiving delivery* of the collateral, then that secured creditor has *priority* over the rights of a *lien creditor* that arise between the time of attachment and filing of the U.C.C. financing statement. [U.C.C. § 9–317(e)]

Example: On May 1, Equipment Co sells a $25,000 machine on credit to Atlas Corporation. On May 2, Atlas takes delivery of the machine. The parties sign a valid security agreement in which Atlas grants a security interest to Equipment Co in the machine. This is a *purchase money security interest*, because Atlas is using the funds extended through credit to buy the machine and the security interest granted is in the machine purchased on credit. [U.C.C. § 9–103(a), (b)] On May 15, Atlas files for bankruptcy. Equipment Co files a financing statement on the equipment on May 18. At the commencement of the case on May 15, the trustee became a hypothetical lien creditor. But, the trustee cannot avoid the grant of the security interest to Equipment Co. The trustee's powers under § 544 are subject to retroactive perfection allowable under applicable nonbankruptcy law. [B.C. § 546(b)] Section 9–317 is applicable nonbankruptcy law, and it provides that the creditor takes priority over a lien creditor whose rights arise between attachment and filing of a UCC–1 so long as the creditor files its financing statement within *20 days* of the *debtor taking delivery* of the collateral. The security interest attached on May 1, and Atlas took delivery on May 2. The trustee became a hypothetical lien creditor on May 15 when Atlas filed for bankruptcy. Equipment Co filed its financing statement on May 18, within 20 days of May 2. Therefore, while ordinarily the trustee would be able to avoid the Equipment Co security interest, it cannot do so here because it is a purchase money security interest, the trustee became a lien creditor between attachment and filing of the financing statement, and the creditor perfected by filing its financing statement within 20 days of the debtor taking delivery of the machine.

Note: Equipment Co's filing of a U.C.C. financing statement after the start of the bankruptcy case does not violate the automatic stay. Section 362(b)(3) of the Code provides an exception for acts to perfect an interest in property to the extent that the trustee's rights and powers are subject to such perfection under § 546(b). [B.C. §§ 362(b)(3), 546(b)]

 Example:

#1	#2	#3	Chapter 7 filing	#4
June 1	*July 5*	*August 29*	*September 2*	*September 6*

#1: On June 1, Creditor loaned Debtor $50,000, and took a security interest in Debtor's existing office equipment. Creditor filed a UCC–1 in the proper state office on August 5. The Chapter 7 trustee cannot avoid Creditor's security interest because Creditor perfected on August 5, about a month before the Chapter 7 trustee became a lien creditor by virtue of Debtor's Chapter 7 filing on September 2. [B.C. § 544(a)(1); U.C.C. § 9–317(a)(2)]

#2: On July 5, Creditor loaned Debtor $100,000. Creditor and Debtor signed a security agreement that granted Creditor a security interest in a valuable painting that Debtor owned. Creditor did not file a UCC–1. The Chapter 7 trustee can avoid Creditor's security interest, because the Chapter 7 trustee became a lien creditor *before* Creditor *either* (i) perfected its interest *or* (ii) satisfied the requirements of U.C.C. § 9–203(b)(3), e.g., signing a security agreement, *and* filed a UCC–1. While Creditor has a valid security agreement, it failed to file a UCC–1. Therefore, the Chapter 7 trustee prevails.

#3 & #4: On August 29, Debtor received office computers that it had purchased with a $75,000 loan that it had received from Creditor. The parties signed a security agreement that granted Creditor a security interest in Debtor's office computers. Creditor filed its UCC–1 on September 6. Section 9–317(e) of the UCC provides that a creditor with a purchase-money security interest will have priority over the rights of a lien creditor that arise between attachment and the UCC–1 filing if the creditor files a UCC–1 within 20 days of the debtor taking delivery of the collateral.

Creditor filed its UCC–1 on September 6, which is within 20 days of August 29, when Debtor received the collateral. In addition, Creditor's filing of a UCC–1 does not violate the automatic stay. [*See* B.C. §§ 362(b)(3), 546(b)]

b. Creditor with Unsatisfied Execution

The trustee also is granted the rights and powers of a *hypothetical* creditor who extends credit to the debtor at the time that the bankruptcy case is filed, and who acquires, at that time, an *unsatisfied execution* concerning the indebtedness. [B.C. § 544(a)(2)]

c. Bona Fide Purchaser of Real Property

The trustee is given the rights and powers of a *hypothetical bona fide purchaser who has perfected the transfer of real property* from the debtor at the time of bankruptcy. Thus, the trustee may avoid any transfer voidable by such a bona fide purchaser. The trustee's avoidance power does not extend to fixtures. [B.C. § 544(a)(3)]

(i) Exception: Constructive Notice

A trustee cannot avoid an unrecorded transfer of real property if, under state law, she is charged with constructive notice of the rights of another entity. The trustee's personal knowledge is not relevant. The issue is whether *constructive notice under nonbankruptcy law* suffices to defeat the priority of a bona fide purchaser. If so, then the bankruptcy trustee cannot avoid the transfer of the real property. [B.C. § 544(a)(3); *see, e.g.,* **Loyd v. Ball (*In re* Dailey),** 463 B.R. 142 (B.A.P. 10th Cir. 2009)]

e.g. **Example:** Creditor Bank held a recorded mortgage on debtors' home. While the mortgage correctly stated the street address and parcel identification number, it incorrectly stated the lot number of the property. Under Kansas law, however, recorded documents in the debtors' chain of title would have put a purchaser on constructive notice of the Bank's interest in the debtors' property or on constructive notice of facts requiring investigation that would have led to discovery of the Bank's mortgage. Therefore, the trustee could not avoid the mortgage. [**Hamilton v. Washington Mutual Bank (*In re* Colon),** 563 F.3d 1171 (10th Cir. 2009)]

2. Trustee's Avoiding Power Based on Actual Unsecured Creditors

If at the start of the bankruptcy case, an *actual creditor* exists that has an allowable unsecured claim and that has the right, under applicable nonbankruptcy law, to avoid a transfer of the debtor's property, then the trustee can avoid the whole transfer *for the benefit of the estate,* even if its value exceeds the amount of the creditor's claim. [B.C. § 544(b)(1)] Unlike § 544(a), § 544(b) requires the existence of an *actual creditor* at the time of the bankruptcy filing who could avoid the transaction in question.

The trustee's recovery is for the benefit of all creditors, even those that extended credit *after* the transaction sought to be avoided. [**Moore v. Bay,** 284 U.S. 4 (1931)] Nonbankruptcy law determines the extent of the trustee's right to avoid under § 544(b). The Uniform Fraudulent Transfer Act and the 2014 Voidable Transactions Act are the nonbankruptcy laws most commonly used by trustees under § 544(b). [5 Collier ¶ 544.06(2)]

e.g. **Example:** On March 1, 2015, Bank made a $10,000 unsecured loan to Debtor. On January 2, 2016, Debtor transferred real property, valued at $50,000, to Best Friend for no consideration and with the undisputed intention of defrauding Debtor's creditors. On

April 1, 2018, Debtor, who still owed $10,000 to Bank, filed a voluntary bankruptcy petition. All of the events took place in a state with a four-year "lookback" period under the state's Uniform Voidable Transactions Act ("UVTA"). The trustee cannot avoid Debtor's fraudulent transfer of the property under Bankruptcy Code § 548(a) because it occurred more than two years prior to bankruptcy. Bank is an *actual unsecured creditor* that (i) extended credit before January 2, 2016, (ii) may avoid the transfer under state law, and (iii) holds an allowable claim as of April 1, 2018. Thus, under Bankruptcy Code § 544(b)(1), the trustee may use the state UVTA to avoid the transfer and thereby bring the real property or its total value into the estate *for the benefit of all the unsecured creditors,* including Bank, which then will share *pro rata* with the other unsecured creditors.

a. Exception for Certain Charitable Contributions

The trustee cannot use § 544(b)(1) to avoid the transfer of a charitable contribution not deemed to be a fraudulent transfer under Code § 548(a)(2). The commencement of the bankruptcy case preempts any person's claim to recover such a transferred contribution under federal or state law. [B.C. § 544(b)(2)]

B. Trustee's Avoidance of Statutory Liens

1. In General

The trustee may avoid the fixing of a *statutory lien* on the debtor's property if the lien (a) arose due to the debtor's *financial condition*; (b) is not perfected against a *bona fide purchaser* of the property; or (c) is for *rent* or (d) is a lien of *distress for rent*. [B.C. § 545] A statutory lien "arises automatically, and is not based on an agreement to give a lien or on judicial action." Examples of statutory liens are mechanics' liens, warehousemen's liens, and tax liens. [H.R. Rep. No. 95–595, at 314 (1977); *compare* B.C. § 101(53) (statutory lien) *with* B.C. § 101(51) (security interest)]

2. Avoidable Statutory Liens

a. Liens Arising Due to Debtor's Financial Condition

Section 545(1) provides for avoidance of liens that arise *because* of the debtor's *bankruptcy, insolvency, or poor financial condition*. The purpose of the section is to prevent state or local laws from " 'impermissibl[y] . . . circumvent[ing] federal priorities for paying creditors' claims in bankruptcy.' " [*In re* **Swafford,** 160 B.R. 246 (Bankr. N.D. Ga. 1993)] The trustee may avoid a *statutory lien* that *first becomes effective* against the debtor upon the happening of one of the following events:

(i) *the filing of a bankruptcy petition* concerning the debtor [B.C. § 545(1)(A)];

(ii) *the filing of an insolvency proceeding* concerning the debtor *other than* one under the Code [B.C. § 545(1)(B)];

(iii) *the appointment of a custodian* or authorization of a custodian to *take possession of the debtor's property* [B.C. § 545(1)(C)];

(iv) *the debtor's insolvency* [B.C. § 545(1)(D)];

(v) the failure of the *debtor's financial condition* to meet a *certain standard* [B.C. § 545(1)(E)]; or

(vi) *an execution against the debtor's property* by an entity *other than the statutory lien holder.* [B.C. § 545(1)(F)]

b. Liens Not Perfected Against Bona Fide Purchaser

The trustee also may avoid a statutory lien that is not perfected or enforceable against a hypothetical bona fide purchaser at the time that the bankruptcy petition is filed, *unless* the purchaser is one described under § 6323 of the Internal Revenue Code or any similar provision in State or local law. [B.C. § 545(2)] To resolve a pre-BAPCPA split of authority as to the trustee's authority under § 545(2) to avoid filed federal tax liens, Congress added the language excepting certain purchasers from the trustee's avoiding power under § 545(2). For example, the Internal Revenue Code protects certain purchasers from the operation of the tax lien *even if* notice of the lien has been filed. [26 U.S.C. 6323] Thus, the purpose of the § 545(2) exception is to make clear that even a tax lien filed prior to bankruptcy is still valid "as against a trustee because the trustee is only afforded the status of a hypothetical bona fide purchaser, not a purchaser as defined in § 6323(h)." [5 Collier ¶ 545.03(4); *see* H.R. Rep. No. 109–31, at 102 (2005) (stating that the § 545(2) exception is "to prevent [§ 6323's] special protections from being used to avoid an otherwise valid lien")]

e.g. **Example:** Mainline Equipment did not pay personal property taxes assessed by Los Angeles County ("County"). The County then recorded certificates of tax liens that resulted in broad liens on all of Mainline's personal property located within the County. Mainline subsequently filed for relief under Chapter 11. As debtor in possession, Mainline had the same rights as a trustee in bankruptcy and, thus, sought to avoid, pursuant to § 545(2), the County's tax liens. Mainline argued that the liens were not perfected as against it, a bona fide purchaser. The Bankruptcy Appellate Panel for the Ninth Circuit agreed. California's revenue and tax code provided that tax liens were not valid against a subsequent purchaser in good faith for value. Mainline, as DIP, enjoyed the status of a bona fide purchaser and, thus, could avoid the tax liens. (The exception in § 545(2) apparently did not apply. California law made tax liens subject to the rights of a bona fide purchaser and, thus, was not a State law provision "similar" to § 6323 of the Internal Revenue Code.) [**Los Angeles County Treasurer & Tax Collector v. Mainline Equipment, Inc.,** 539 B.R. 165 (B.A.P. 9th Cir. 2015)]

(i) Retroactive Perfection

The trustee's avoiding power under § 545(2) is subject to any retroactive perfection permitted under state or other nonbankruptcy law. [B.C. § 546(b)]

c. Liens for Rent

The trustee also may avoid statutory liens for rent or a lien for distress of rent. [B.C. § 545(3), (4)]

C. Trustee's Power to Avoid Preferences

1. In General

The bankruptcy trustee may avoid pre-petition preferential transfers. [B.C. § 547] Section 547 accomplishes two main goals. First, by allowing the trustee to avoid transfers close in time to the debtor's bankruptcy filing, "creditors are discouraged from racing to the courthouse to dismember the debtor during his slide into bankruptcy." [H.R. Rep. No. 95–595, at 177 (1977)] Second, the preference provisions "facilitate the prime bankruptcy policy of equality of distribution . . . [because] [a]ny creditor that received a greater payment than others of his class is required to disgorge so that all may share equally." [H.R. Rep. No. 95–595, at 177–78 (1977)]

e.g. **Example:** Debtor owes $5,000 to Bank and $5,000 to Credit Union. Both creditors are unsecured, and neither is entitled to priority under the Code. On May 1, Debtor, who is insolvent, uses all of her remaining cash to repay Credit Union in full, while paying nothing to Bank. On June 1, Debtor files a voluntary Chapter 7 petition, and there are no assets available for distribution. The trustee may avoid the preferential transfer to Credit Union and recover the $5,000 payment for the benefit of the estate. After full payment of all priority claims in the case, including administrative expenses, Credit Union and Bank will share *pro rata* with any other general unsecured creditors. [B.C. § 547(b)]

2. Elements of Preference

To establish a preference, the trustee must prove a *transfer* of an *interest of the debtor in property:*

a. made *to or for the benefit of a creditor* [B.C. § 547(b)(1)];

b. for or on account of an *antecedent debt* [B.C. § 547(b)(2)];

c. made at a time *when the debtor was insolvent* [B.C. § 547(b)(3)];

d. *within 90 days* prior to filing of the bankruptcy petition or *one year* if the creditor was an *insider* [B.C. § 547(b)(4)]; and

e. that *results in the creditor receiving a larger share* than the creditor would have received if the estate had been *liquidated under Chapter 7* and the transfer had *not been made.* [B.C. § 547(b)(5)]

If *any* of the above elements is absent, the trustee may not set aside the transaction as a voidable preference. In addition, the SBRA amended the Code's preference section to require the trustee to exercise *"reasonable due diligence"* and to take into "account a party's known or reasonably knowable affirmative defenses" before seeking to avoid a possible preferential transfer. [B.C. § 547(b); *see* H.R. Rep. No. 116–171, at 8 (2019)]

a. Transfer of the Debtor's Interest in Property

(i) Transfer

The Code defines a transfer as:

(1) *creation of a lien* [B.C. § 101(54)(A)];

(2) *retention of title* as a security interest [B.C. § 101(54)(B)];

(3) foreclosure of the debtor's *equity of redemption* [B.C. § 101(54)(C)]; or

(4) any *voluntary or involuntary, direct or indirect, or absolute or conditional* disposition of property or an interest in property [B.C. § 101(54)(D)].

(ii) Debtor's Interest in Property

The subject matter of the transfer must be a *property interest of the debtor.* [B.C. § 547(b)] Examples include transfers of money, transfers of personal or real property, granting of a security interest in personal property, or granting of a mortgage on real property.

(1) The Earmarking Doctrine

The *earmarking doctrine* is a "judicially created exception to the statutory power of the bankruptcy trustee under § 547 to avoid or set aside an otherwise preferential transfer of assets." [**Campbell v. Hanover Ins. Co. (*In re* ESA Environmental Specialists),** 709 F.3d 388 (4th Cir. 2013)] The earmarking doctrine exception applies in cases in which there is no diminution in the value of the debtor's estate, because another entity's property is used to repay a creditor. A majority of courts place the burden of proof of the earmarking defense on the defendant in the preference action. [**Campbell,** *supra*]

> **Example:** Darien is in significant financial distress. He owes his unsecured creditors $50,000. One of those creditors is Carl, who is owed $5,000. Lulu, Darien's sister, pays Carl $5,000. A few days later, Darien files for relief under Chapter 7. There are insufficient funds to pay anything to Darien's general unsecured creditors. Carl received a preference because he obtained full payment pre-petition while Darien's other unsecured creditors received nothing in the Chapter 7 case. But, the payment to Carl did not affect Darien's bankruptcy estate; the estate's assets were no less than before Lulu's transfer to Carl. The transfer merely substituted Lulu for Carl with respect to the debt owed by Darien.

(2) Trust-Fund Taxes

In **Begier v. I.R.S.,** 496 U.S. 53 (1990), the Supreme Court held that a debtor's payments to the I.R.S. of trust-fund taxes, e.g., withheld federal income and Federal Insurance Contribution Act taxes, from its general accounts were not voidable preferences because they were not transfers of the debtor's property but rather were transfers of property held in trust for the federal government. [**Begier,** *supra*]

b. To or for the Benefit of a Creditor

The entity receiving or benefitting from the transfer must be the *debtor's creditor.* The fact that the creditor is a creditor of another entity closely connected to the debtor, e.g., a corporate debtor's president, is not sufficient to make a transfer preferential. [B.C. §§ 547(b)(1), 101(10); *see* **Howell v. US Foods, Inc. (*In re* Bilbo),** 2014 WL 689097 (Bankr. N.D. Ga. 2014)]

(i) Transfer *Benefits* a Creditor

The trustee may avoid a transfer *even if* another entity receives the property transferred. The key is whether the transfer *benefits the creditor.*

> **Example:** Archie is the sole owner of *Archie Comics Company* ("ACC"). On January 5, ACC borrows $5,000 from Richie Rich, who requires Archie to sign a personal guarantee for the funds loaned to ACC. On March 2, ACC repays the $5,000 loan to Richie Rich. On May 3, ACC files for relief under Chapter 7. The trustee may recover the $5,000 payment from Richie Rich *or* Archie. [B.C. § 550(a)(1)] The $5,000 was a transfer of the debtor's property *for the benefit* of creditor Archie within the 90 days prior to bankruptcy. At the time that ACC paid Rich, Archie was a creditor of ACC, because he held a contingent reimbursement claim against ACC. Archie's obligation to pay Rich was contingent on ACC's default on its promise to repay the $5,000. If ACC had defaulted, Archie would have had to pay Rich and, thus, would have had a right to reimbursement from ACC.

When ACC repaid the loan in full, Archie benefitted because the repayment eliminated his guarantee liability and improved Archie's position relative to what he would have received as a creditor in ACC's Chapter 7 case.

c. On Account of an Antecedent Debt

The transfer must concern a debt that was incurred by the debtor *before the transfer was made.* [B.C. § 547(b)(2)] In other words, the debt *precedes* the transfer in time. The Bankruptcy Code defines "debt" as "liability on a claim." [B.C. § 101(12)]

e.g. **Example:** Two months prior to filing for bankruptcy, Debtor purchased a used lawn mower from his neighbor for $200. Neighbor showed Debtor the lawn mower and they negotiated a $200 price; Debtor paid Neighbor $200 in cash on the spot and took the lawn mower to his house. Debtor subsequently filed for relief under Chapter 7. There is no preference, because there is no transfer on account of an antecedent debt. The debt and the transfer happened at the same time. Had Neighbor agreed to sell and transfer the mower to Debtor with Debtor coming back in a few days with the cash for the mower, then the $200 would be a transfer for an antecedent debt. In this second scenario, the debt arose when the parties made the contract for the mower. Payment (the transfer) followed several days later, so the debt was incurred before the transfer happened. Even if the $200 payment satisfied the elements of a preference, however, the *de minimis* exception at § 547(b)(8) would prevent the trustee from pursuing Neighbor for the $200.

d. Debtor's Insolvency

The transfer must have occurred when the debtor was insolvent, which means that her debts were greater than the value of her assets, excluding exempt property and property that was fraudulently transferred. [B.C. §§ 547(b)(3), 101(32)] There is a *rebuttable presumption* that the debtor is insolvent during the *90 days* immediately prior to the date on which the petition was filed. [B.C. § 547(f)] If the transferee or the beneficiary of a transfer presents evidence to rebut the presumption of the debtor's insolvency, then the trustee must prove insolvency to avoid the transfer.

e. Preference Period: Within Ninety Days Before Filing

The transfer must have been made *within 90 days prior to the filing of the bankruptcy petition.* If the creditor was an insider at the time of the transfer, then the preference period extends to one year before bankruptcy. [B.C. §§ 547(b)(4), 101(31)]

Note: The rules set forth in § 547(e) determine *when* a transfer is deemed to have been made for purposes of § 547.

(i) Presumption of Insolvency Is Limited to Ninety Days

Even when the preference period is one year before bankruptcy because the creditor was an insider, the *period during which the presumption of insolvency applies remains the same*—90 days. [**Lanik v. Smith (*In re* Cox Motor Express of Greensboro, Inc.),** 2016 WL 4259801 (Bankr. M.D. N.C. 2016) (insolvency presumption applies only for 90 days prior to filing of petition and "trustee must prove the debtor's insolvency during the remainder of the insider preference period")]

f. Creditor Improves Her Position

The trustee must show that the transfer enabled the creditor to obtain a larger distribution than the creditor would have received in a Chapter 7 case if the transfer had not occurred.

[B.C. § 547(b)(5)] This computation is based on a hypothetical liquidation of the estate as of the date of the filing of the bankruptcy petition. Therefore, unless unsecured creditors would recover 100% of their claims in a Chapter 7 case, any payment to a general unsecured creditor during the 90-day period may constitute a preference. [**Moser v. Bank of Tyler (*In re* Loggins**), 513 B.R. 682 (Bankr. E.D. Tex. 2014)]

Example: Dionysus filed for relief under the Bankruptcy Code. He owes his general unsecured creditors $50,000, and it is expected that such creditors would receive a 20% dividend in a Chapter 7 liquidation case. Frank is a friend of Dionysus, and loaned him $5,000 about a year ago. Dionysus paid Frank $1,000 on the eve of bankruptcy. Unless one of the exceptions under § 547(c) applies, the trustee may avoid the payment to Frank as a preference. Frank is a creditor who received a transfer of property from the debtor within 90 days of the bankruptcy filing when the debtor is presumed insolvent. Frank also received more than he would have received in a Chapter 7 case. With the pre-petition payment, Frank receives $1,000, which was paid on the eve of bankruptcy, plus $800, which is 20% of the remaining $4,000 debt. If there were no pre-petition payment, then Frank would receive $1,000, which is 20% of the $5,000 debt owed to him. Therefore, with the pre-petition payment, Frank's recovery is 36% ($1,800/$5,000) while without the pre-petition payment it is 20% ($1,000/$5,000). (*Note:* the numbers are approximate, because recovery of the preferential payment will increase the *pro rata* distribution to general unsecured creditors.)

(i) Secured Creditors

Payments made within 90 days of bankruptcy to a wholly secured creditor do not constitute a preference because the creditor does not receive a greater distribution than she would receive in a Chapter 7 case.

Example: Two years ago, Bank loaned Debtor $50,000 and took a security interest in a valuable painting that Debtor owned. Debtor made the regular monthly payments on the Bank loan, but in the 90 days prior to filing for bankruptcy Debtor paid an additional $5,000 to Bank towards the loan's principal. The $5,000 payment was not made in the ordinary course. When Debtor filed for relief under the Bankruptcy Code, the painting was valued at $75,000, and the loan balance was $40,000 ($45,000 − $5,000 paid in the 90-day period). The $5,000 payment to Bank is not a preference. In a Chapter 7 case, if the painting were sold to pay the Bank's loan, the Bank would recover $40,000 along with the $5,000 paid pre-petition on the loan. Had the $5,000 payment not been made pre-petition, the Bank would receive $45,000 from the sale of the painting. In other words, the Bank would receive $45,000 regardless of whether the payment had been made pre-petition.

Example: Two years ago, Bank loaned Debtor $50,000 and took a security interest in a valuable painting that Debtor owned. Debtor made the regular monthly payments on the Bank loan, but in the 90 days prior to filing for bankruptcy Debtor paid an additional $5,000 to Bank towards the loan's principal. The $5,000 payments were not made in the ordinary course. When Debtor filed for relief under the Bankruptcy Code, the painting was valued at $30,000, and the loan balance was $40,000 ($45,000 − $5,000 paid in the 90-day period). In this case, the $5,000 payment *is* a preference. Courts generally apply the pre-petition preferential payment first to the unsecured portion of the creditor's claim. Bank would receive $30,000 on its secured claim (the value of the painting). If the general unsecured creditors received a 10% dividend, then Bank would get $1,000 on its unsecured claim of $10,000 ($40,000 − $30,000 collateral value). With the $5,000 pre-petition payment, Bank would receive $36,000: $30,000 + $1,000 + $5,000. Without the

$5,000 pre-petition payment, however, Bank would receive only $31,500: $30,000 on its secured claim and $1,500 (10% of $15,000) on its unsecured claim. (*Note:* The numbers are approximate, because recovery of the preferential payment will increase the *pro rata* distribution to general unsecured creditors.)

3. Exceptions to Preference Rule

The trustee may not avoid any of the following transfers. [B.C. § 547(c), (h)] The *creditor* or party in interest against whom avoidance is sought has the *burden of proving* any of the *defenses under § 547(c).* [B.C. § 547(g)]

a. Substantially Contemporaneous Exchange for New Value

If a transfer is a substantially contemporaneous exchange for new value, the trustee may not avoid it. This exception applies *if:* (i) the debtor and the creditor *intended* the transfer to be a contemporaneous exchange *for new value* furnished to the debtor, and (ii) the transfer *actually was* a *substantially contemporaneous exchange*. [B.C. § 547(c)(1)]

(i) Parties' Intent

The debtor and creditor must intend that the transfer be a *contemporaneous exchange* for *new value.* [Hechinger Inv. Co. of Delaware v. Universal Forest Prods. (*In re* Hechninger Inv. Co. of Delaware), 489 F.3d 568 (3d Cir. 2007) ("Whether the parties intended a contemporaneous exchange is a question of fact to be decided in the first instance by the factfinder")]

Example: The Bison companies filed for relief under Chapter 11. In the 90 days prior to bankruptcy, Bison paid more than $63,000 to Tomball Forest, Ltd. for lumber products that Tomball Forest had delivered to Bison. The parties had agreed that Bison would send payment about a month after Tomball Forest invoiced Bison for delivery of the lumber products. The four payments totaling more than $63,000 all were sent within 30 to 45 days from the date of Tomball Forest's invoices. The Post-Confirmation Committee in the Bison Chapter 11 case sued Tomball Forest to recover the $63,000 as preferences under § 547. The bankruptcy court rejected Tomball Forest's argument that the contemporaneous exchange exception at § 547(c)(1) applied. The court noted that it did not have to determine whether the payments were "in fact substantially contemporaneous", as required by § 547(c)(1)(B), because Bison and Tomball Forest did not satisfy § 547(c)(1)(A)'s intent requirement. "The 'contemporaneous in fact' requirement is modified by the adverb 'substantially' . . . . The intent requirement contains no such modification." Because the parties had agreed that Bison would pay Tromball Forest at least one month after delivery of lumber products, the parties did not intend a contemporaneous exchange. **Post-Confirmation Committee v. Tomball Forest, Ltd. (*In re* Bison Building Holdings, Inc.)**, 473 B.R. 168 (Bankr. S.D. Tex. 2012)]

(1) "New Value" Defined

The Code defines new value as "money or money's worth in goods, services, or new credit, or release by a transferee of property previously transferred to such transferee in a transaction that is neither void nor voidable by the debtor or the trustee under any applicable law. . . ." New value does not include "an obligation substituted for an existing obligation." [B.C. § 547(a)(2); **Manchester v. First Bank & Trust Co. (*In re* Moses),** 256 B.R. 641 (B.A.P. 10th Cir. 2000) (paying on an existing bank loan is satisfaction of an antecedent debt and, hence, is not new value)]

(a) Proof

Some courts have held that proof of the *specific dollar amount* of new value given to the debtor (i.e., not merely "some" new value) is required to satisfy this exception. [*In re* **Spada**, 903 F.2d 971 (3d Cir. 1990) (finding that "a determination of how much 'new value' was involved in the exchange is mandated")]

(ii) In Fact Substantially Contemporaneous

The transfer also must *in fact* be substantially contemporaneous. [**Gold v. Myers Controlled Power, LLC (*In re* Truland Group, Inc.),** 2018 WL 333865 (Bankr. E.D. Va. 2018) (citing cases on time periods courts consider to be and not to be substantially contemporaneous, and concluding that "a gap of 44 days, and a gap of 23 days, are simply too long to be considered truly 'contemporaneous'' under Section 547(c)(1)")] Determining what constitutes a substantially contemporaneous exchange requires the court to look at the totality of the circumstances in each case. [**Gordon v. Novastar Mortgage, Inc. (*In re* Hedrick),** 524 F.3d 1175 (11th Cir. 2008) (joining the Eighth and Ninth Circuits in holding that "the 'substantially contemporaneous' rule of § 547(c)(1)(B) requires an examination of all the facts and circumstances"); *see also* **Burtch v. Connecticut Community Bank (*In re* J. Silver Clothing, Inc.),** 453 B.R. 518 (Bankr. D. Del. 2011); **Reynolds v. Quality Timber Products (*In re* Git-N-Go, Inc.),** 2007 WL 3232195 (Bankr. N.D. Okla. 2007)]

b. Transfer in Ordinary Course of Business

To satisfy the ordinary course of business exception, the creditor must demonstrate two things. First, the *debt was incurred* in the *ordinary course of business* or *financial affairs* of the debtor and the transferee. Second, the *transfer was made* either (i) in the *ordinary course of business* or *financial affairs* of the debtor and the transferee *or* (ii) according to *ordinary business terms.* [B.C. § 547(c)(2)]

(i) Ordinary Course Transfer

(1) Ordinary Course of Business or Financial Affairs

This is the subjective prong of the test, because it looks at whether the transfer is consistent with past business or financial practices of the debtor and creditor. In order to apply the test, courts first must determine the baseline period against which to compare the transfer. The baseline should be a period during which the debtor was financially healthy. Factors that courts consider " 'include the amount transferred, the timing of the payment, the historic course of dealings between the debtor and the transferee, and the circumstances under which the transfer was effected.' " [**Wiscovitch-Rentas v. Villa Blanca VB Plaza LLC (*In re* PMC Mktg. Corp.),** 543 B.R. 345 (B.A.P. 1st Cir. 2016)] A first-time transaction may qualify for the ordinary course exception, because the Bankruptcy Code directs the court to examine the ordinary course of business of the debtor and creditor/transferee, not the ordinary course of business *between* the debtor and creditor/transferee. [**Jubber v. SMC Elec. Prods. (*In re* CW Mining Co.),** 798 F.3d 983 (10th Cir. 2015)]

(2) Ordinary Business Terms

Determining whether the transfer was made *"according to ordinary business terms"* is an objective test. [**Wiscovitch-Rentas v. Villa Blanca VB Plaza LLC,** *supra*; **Stahl v. Whelan Elec., Inc. (*In re* Modtech Holdings, Inc.),** 503 B.R. 737 (Bankr. C.D. Cal. 2013)] The test requires the court to compare the challenged transfer with the norms in the relevant industry. A transfer made according to ordinary business terms is a transaction that is not so unusual or out of line with relevant industry practice that it is an aberration or a flagrant deviation from relevant industry norms. [**Sass v. Vector Consulting, Inc. (*In re* Am. Home Mortg. Holdings, Inc.),** 476 B.R. 124 (Bankr. D. Del. 2012) (summarizing tests from various Courts of Appeals)]

(ii) Late Payments

Late payments, by themselves, do not defeat a creditor's claim that transfers were made in the ordinary course of the creditor's and debtor's business. Instead, courts look to whether the debtor made late payments *outside* the 90-day preference period and, if so, compare the lateness of preference period payments against non-preference period payments. [**Wiscovitch-Rentas v. Villa Blanca VB Plaza LLC,** *supra*]

(iii) Long-Term Debt

The Supreme Court has held that payments on long-term debt, as well as payments on short-term debt, may qualify for the "ordinary course of business" exception. [**Union Bank v. Wolas,** 502 U.S. 151 (1991)]

c. Purchase-Money Security Interest Securing New Value

A *security interest* securing *new value* extended to the debtor for the purpose of acquiring certain property described in the security agreement and actually purchased by the debtor with the funds furnished by the creditor is protected from avoidance by the trustee. [B.C. § 547(c)(3)]

(i) Tracing Necessary

For this exception to apply, the debtor actually must use the new value received from the creditor to purchase the collateral. In other words, the creditor must prove that the security interest is a purchase-money security interest. [B.C. § 547(g)] If the creditor's funds are commingled with funds in a general debtor account, then it may prove difficult for the creditor to satisfy the exception's requirement that the debtor used *creditor funds* to purchase the collateral. If the creditor is unable to trace its funds, then it cannot prove it has a purchase-money security interest and § 547(c)(4)'s exception does not apply. [B.C. § 547(c)(3)(A)(iv); 5 Collier ¶ 547.04(3)]

(ii) Perfection Within Thirty Days After Possession

The secured party must perfect his purchase-money security interest no later than *30 days* after the debtor takes possession of the collateral; failure to perfect within that time renders the transfer voidable. [B.C. § 547(c)(3)(B)]

Example: On December 15, Diane Debtor purchased and took possession of a new car using funds from Creditor Financial Services to do so. Thirty-two days later, on January 16, Creditor Financial Services took the steps necessary under state law to perfect its security interest. State law provides creditors with 40 days to perfect their liens on motor vehicles. Federal, not state, law governs the relation-back or grace period for perfection. Thus, Creditor does not satisfy the requirements of § 547(c)(3) and the trustee may avoid Creditor Financial's security interest in the vehicle as a preference. [*See* **Fidelity Financial Services, Inc. v. Fink, 522 U.S. 211 (1998)** (holding 20-day rule, then in effect under § 547(c)(3)(B), controlling even though applicable state law provided for a longer grace period)]

Example: Same facts as in the above example, but the 30th day fell on a Saturday and, therefore, Creditor Financial Services perfected on the first business day after the 30th day, which was Monday, January 16 and 32 days after Debtor took possession of the vehicle. The bankruptcy court applied Bankruptcy Rule 9006(a), which provides that if the last day of the counting period is a "Saturday, Sunday, or legal holiday, the period continues to run until the end of the next day that is not a Saturday, Sunday, or legal holiday." [Bankruptcy Rule 9006(a)(1)(C)] Because Creditor Financial Services perfected its interest on Monday, January 16—the next day that was not a Saturday, Sunday, or legal holiday—the trustee could not avoid the security interest as a preferential transfer. [**Viegelahn v. Ruben's Auto Sales (*In re* Daniel)**, 619 B.R. 635 (Bankr. W.D. Tex. 2020)]

d. Subsequent Advance of New Value

A transfer is not avoidable to the extent that, ***subsequent to the transfer,*** the creditor extended ***new value*** that is "not secured by an otherwise unavoidable security interest" and "on account of which new value the debtor did not make an otherwise unavoidable transfer." [B.C. § 547(c)(4)] The purpose of the exception is to induce creditors to continue extending credit and doing business with debtors that are in financial trouble. [*See* **IRFM, Inc. v. Ever-Fresh Food Co.,** 52 F.3d 228 (9th Cir. 1995)] While the exception protects the creditor that has received a preferential payment, it is "not unfair" to the debtor's other creditors because the new value replenishes the estate. [*See* **Laker v. Vallette (*In re* Toyota of Jefferson),** 14 F.3d 1088 (5th Cir. 1994)]

There are several points to keep in mind in applying this exception.

(i) The exception only applies to new value extended *after* the preferential transfer.

(ii) The exception does *not* apply if the creditor extending the new value has a security interest that is "valid and enforceable at the time of the bankruptcy." [*See* **IRFM, Inc. v. Ever-Fresh Food Co.,** *supra*; **Intercontinental Polymers, Inc. v. Equistar Chems., LP (*In re* Intercontinental Polymers, Inc.),** 359 B.R. 868 (Bankr. E.D. Tenn. 2005)]

(iii) The ***majority rule*** is that the new value may be applied to offset any preferential transfer that precedes the new value and not simply the preferential transfer *immediately* preceding the provision of new value.

Example: *Epicerie,* the debtor, is a high-end grocery market that filed for bankruptcy on August 3. *Laitier* is one of *Epicerie's* suppliers of cheese and dairy products. While the parties' terms of payment required *Epicerie* to pay for goods upon delivery, *Epicerie* paid *Laitier* a week or more after delivery during the 90 days prior to the bankruptcy filing. *Epicerie's* payments also did not comport with industry standards. During the 90 days prior to *Epicerie's* bankruptcy filing, the following transactions occurred:

June 18: $20,000 payment to *Laitier*

June 30: $28,000 of goods shipped to *Epicerie*

July 10: $15,000 payment to *Laitier*

July 15: $10,000 of goods shipped to *Epicerie*

July 23: $20,000 payment to *Laitier*

The June 30 shipment of goods is new value, which means that the trustee may not recover the $20,000 payment made to *Laitier* on June 18. The trustee may recover $5,000 of the July 10 payment and the entire $20,000 payment made on July 23, however. The $8,000 by which the June 30 new value exceeds the June 18 preferential payment *may not* be used to protect the July 10 $15,000 payment to *Laitier.*

Remember: The new value exception requires that the creditor extend new value *after* the preferential transfer. The June 30 new value *precedes* the July 10 preferential payment of $15,000. The July 15 new value is only $10,000, so $5,000 of the July 10 payment to *Laitier* is avoidable by the trustee. In addition, there is no new value extended after the July 23 payment; hence the entire $20,000 payment is avoidable.

Note: None of the payments qualify for the ordinary business transaction exception because the facts state that the payments were not made according to either industry standards or the parties' typical payment terms.

 Example: Same facts as in the above example, except the payments and deliveries during the 90 days prior to bankruptcy were as follows:

June 18: $20,000 payment to *Laitier*

June 30: $15,000 of goods shipped to *Epicerie*

July 10: $15,000 payment to *Laitier*

July 15: $20,000 of goods shipped to *Epicerie*

The trustee cannot avoid the June 18 $20,000 payment or the July 10 $15,000 payment. The $15,000 new value on June 30 protects $15,000 of the June 18 preferential transfer. The July 15 new value of $20,000 protects both the July 10 $15,000 preferential payment *and* the remaining $5,000 of the June 18 preferential payment. The majority of courts do not require that the new value apply *only* to the immediately preceding preferential transfer.

(i) Comment

Some courts have held that a creditor that receives administrative priority payments pursuant to § 503(b)(9) for the new value provided to the debtor cannot also use the new value exception under § 547(c)(4) as a defense to a preference action. [5 Collier ¶ 547.04(4)(e)]

e. Security Interest in Inventory and Receivables

A transfer that creates a perfected security interest in the debtor's ***inventory, receivables, or proceeds of inventory or receivables*** is voidable only ***to the extent that the creditor's position has improved,*** to the prejudice of the estate, during the period ***beginning*** on the later of the 90th day before bankruptcy ***or*** the first date on which the creditor gave new value pursuant to the security agreement, and ***ending*** on the date that the petition was filed. [B.C. § 547(c)(5); B.C. § 547(a)(1) (definition of inventory) & (a)(3) (definition of receivable)] For a secured party that is an insider, the ***beginning*** time period is the later of one year before the filing of the petition or the first date on which the creditor gave new value.

(i) Why Is an Exception Needed?

Floating liens create a preference problem for secured creditors. The transfer of a security interest does not occur until the debtor has rights in the collateral. [B.C. § 547(e)(3)] If a secured creditor takes a security interest in a debtor's inventory, whether now owned or hereafter acquired, the security interest attaches to after-acquired inventory when the debtor acquires rights in the collateral, e.g., makes a contract for a delivery of inventory, not when the creditor originally perfected its security interest in the inventory. That means that the security interest attaching to the after-acquired inventory creates a transfer on account of an antecedent debt, which is one of the elements of a preference. [B.C. § 547(b)(2)] If the after-acquired inventory is purchased by the debtor during the 90-day window preceding the debtor's bankruptcy filing, then there is a transfer (security interest) to a creditor on account of an antecedent debt during the 90 days preceding bankruptcy when the debtor is presumed insolvent and the creditor is secured, as opposed to unsecured, in that inventory, which seems to improve the secured creditor's position. [B.C. § 547(b), (f)]

(ii) Improvement in Position Test

This exception protects a creditor with a "floating lien" so long as the creditor's position does not improve during the time period described in § 547(c)(5). [5 Collier ¶ 547.04(5)] The key is whether there is "prejudice [to] other creditors holding unsecured claims." [B.C. § 547(c)(5)] In other words, if the position of the creditor with the "floating lien" on the date of bankruptcy filing has not improved relative to its position 90 days prior to the bankruptcy filing, then there is no improvement in position and no preference to avoid. In determining how much, if any, a creditor has improved her position, the court examines the amount of any insufficiency, i.e., the difference between the outstanding balance of the debt owed and the value of the collateral, existing at *two specific times*:

- the 90th day before bankruptcy (or the first date on which new value was extended) and

- the date that the bankruptcy petition was filed.

Thus, regardless of any fluctuations during the preference period, the transfer will be voidable only to the extent that the insufficiency has been reduced between these two dates.

Example: Two years ago, Financier extended Acme a revolving line of credit to use for Acme's purchase of inventory. The parties signed a valid security agreement giving Financier a security interest in all Acme's inventory whether now owned or hereafter acquired. On October 2, Acme filed for relief under Chapter 11. Acme's inventory normally turns over completely every 30–40 days; therefore, all inventory on the date of bankruptcy filing was acquired within 90 days of the filing. On the date of bankruptcy, Acme owed Financier $1 million and Acme's inventory was valued at $1.1 million. (Acme made no payments to Financier between July 3 and October 2.) On July 3, 90 days prior to Acme's filing, Acme owed Financier $1 million, and Acme had inventory valued at $1 million. While the inventory increased from $1 million to $1.1 million during the 90-day period prior to filing for bankruptcy, Financier's position did not improve. Financier was fully secured on July 3 and fully secured on October 2. In other words, if the inventory were sold on July 3 Financier would receive $1 million. If the inventory were sold on October 2, Financier would receive $1 million. Therefore, there is nothing for the trustee to avoid.

Example: Two years ago, Financier extended Acme a revolving line of credit to use for Acme's purchase of inventory. The parties signed a valid security agreement giving Financier a security interest in all Acme's inventory whether now owned or hereafter acquired. On October 2, Acme filed for relief under Chapter 11. Acme's inventory normally turns over completely every 30–40 days; therefore, all inventory on the date of bankruptcy was acquired within 90 days of the bankruptcy filing. On the date of bankruptcy, Acme owed Financier $1 million and Acme's inventory was valued at $900,000. (Acme made no payments to Financier between July 3 and October 2.) On July 3, 90 days prior to Acme's filing, Acme owed Financier $1 million, and Acme had inventory valued at $800,000. The trustee may avoid $100,000 of Acme's security interest, because Acme's position improved by that amount from July 3 to October 2. On July 3, Acme was unsecured in the amount of $200,000 [$1 million loan − $800,000 in collateral]. On October 2, Acme was unsecured in the amount of only $100,000 [$1 million loan − $900,000 in collateral].

Note: The transfer is not voidable if the creditor's improvement in position did not harm the unsecured creditors, such as a case in which the insufficiency's reduction was caused *solely* by a seasonal appreciation in the value of collateral consisting of an inventory of swimwear held in storage in New York for 90 days from January until the filing of the petition in April. [*See* 5 Collier ¶ 547.04(5)]

(iii) "Receivable"

For purposes of a preference, the Code defines a receivable as a "right to payment, whether or not such right has been earned by performance." [B.C. § 547(a)(3)]

f. Statutory Lien

The trustee cannot avoid as a preference the fixing of a statutory lien *if the lien cannot be avoided under Bankruptcy Code § 545*. [B.C. § 547(c)(6); 5 Collier ¶ 547.04(6)]

Example: CTI performed construction work for Lionel Leisure ("LL") prior to LL's bankruptcy. LL failed to pay CTI almost $170,000 for work performed, and in June CTI filed notice of a mechanic's lien against LL. Also in June, LL filed for relief under Chapter 11. CTI's mechanic's lien was the fixing of a statutory lien that LL acknowledged could not be avoided under § 545. Therefore, CTI's mechanic's lien was not avoidable as a preference because it was the fixing of a statutory lien that could not be avoided under § 545. [*See* **Klein v. Civale & Tovato (***In re* **Lionel Corporation)**, 29 F.3d 88 (2d Cir. 1994).

g. Domestic Support Obligation

Bona fide payment of a *domestic support obligation* is not avoidable by the trustee. [B.C. §§ 547(c)(7), 101(14A)]

h. Consumer Payments Under $600

A transfer of property worth less than $600 in a case filed by an *individual debtor with primarily consumer debts* is not avoidable by the trustee. [B.C. § 547(c)(8)] The majority of courts *aggregate all transfers* made in the 90-day period to a single creditor rather than consider each transfer individually when determining whether the $600 exception applies. Most courts also allow the trustee to *avoid the entire amount* of money transferred and not simply the amount exceeding $599.

Example: Debtor filed for relief under Chapter 7. In the 90 days prior to the bankruptcy filing, $857 of Debtor's wages had been garnished pursuant to a state court judgment obtained by Creditor. None of the six garnishment payments exceeded $151. Creditor claimed that *each* garnishment payment was less than $600 and, thus, each payment was protected by § 547(c)(8). The bankruptcy court disagreed and concluded that the aggregated transfers totaling $857 were not protected from avoidance pursuant to § 547(c)(8). [**Rainsdon v. Action Collection Service, Inc. (*In re* Robles),** 2007 WL 1792320 (Bankr. D. Idaho 2007)]

Example: Debtor filed for relief under Chapter 7. In the 90 days prior to the bankruptcy filing, $1,108 of Debtor's wages had been garnished pursuant to a state court judgment obtained by Creditor. The largest of the individual garnishment payments was $116.10. Creditor claimed that *each* garnishment payment was less than $600 and, thus, each payment was protected by § 547(c)(8). The bankruptcy court disagreed and concluded that the aggregated transfers totaling $1,108 were not protected from avoidance pursuant to § 547(c)(8). Creditor also argued that only the amount over $599 was subject to avoidance. The bankruptcy court disagreed and held that the *entire* $1,108 was subject to avoidance. [**Maus v. Joint Twp. Dist. Mem. Hosp. (*In re* Maus),** 282 B.R. 836 (Bankr. N.D. Ohio 2002)]

i. Non-Consumer Payments Less than $7,575

A transfer of property worth less than $7,575 by a debtor whose debts are *not primarily consumer debts* is not avoidable by the trustee. [B.C. § 547(c)(9)] The issues of aggregation and the amount to avoid under § 547(c)(8) also are issues under § 547(c)(9). There is little case law on these issues under § 547(c)(9). The Ninth Circuit's B.A.P., however, turned to the case law under § 547(c)(8), noting the similarity of the language in subsections (c)(8) and (c)(9). [**Western States Glass Corp. v. Barris (*In re* Bay Area Glass),** 454 B.R. 86 (B.A.P. 9th Cir. 2011) ("Where Congress employs the same language in sequential subsections of a statute, we may infer that it intended the same meaning for the language in both subsections.")]

j. Alternative Repayment Schedules

The trustee may not avoid a transfer if the transfer was made as part of an *alternative repayment schedule* between the debtor and an approved nonprofit budget and counseling agency. [B.C. §§ 547(h), 111]

k. Rental and Supplier Arrearages

The CAA amended § 547 of the Code to provide that the trustee *cannot avoid as a preference* any covered payment for *rental arrearages or supplier arrearages.* [CAA § 1001(g) creating temporary § 547(j)] This *temporary* amendment, which sunsetted on *December 27, 2022,* sought to protect agreements made between business debtors and lessors or suppliers to defer payments that business debtors were unable to make due to COVID-19.

Important note: **The CAA's amendment to § 547 now *only* applies to bankruptcy cases commenced *before the sunset date of December 27, 2022.*** [CAA § 1001(g)(2)(B)]

(i) Covered Payment of Rental Arrearages

The CAA defines *covered payment of rental arrearages* as a payment made in connection with an agreement

(1) entered into between the debtor and a lessor of *nonresidential real property;*

(2) to defer or postpone the *payment of rent* and other periodic charges; and

(3) entered into *on or after March 13, 2020.*

[B.C. § 547(j)(1)(A)(i)] The CAA imposes *limitations* on what is included as a covered payment of rental arrearages. Any amount excluded as a covered payment of rental arrearages *does not qualify* for the CAA's exception to § 547's preference rules. In other words, the trustee may seek to recover these excluded amounts as preferences.

(1) The payment of arrearages cannot *exceed* the amount of rent and periodic charges agreed to under the lease *before March 13, 2020.* [B.C. § 547(j)(1)(A)(ii)]

(2) The payment of arrearages *does not include fees, penalties, or interest in an amount greater* than the fees, penalties, or interest provided by the lease. [B.C. § 547(j)(1)(A)(iii)(I)]

(3) The payment of arrearages *does not include* fees, penalties, or interest that the debtor would owe had the debtor made every lease payment due on time and in full *before March 13, 2020.* [B.C. § 547(j)(1)(A)(iii)(II)]

Example: Debtor Company owns a coffee and dessert shop, and rents its business premises from Lessor under a ten-year lease. Debtor had been a good tenant (Year 4 of the lease) and always had paid rent on time, but was unable to pay in the fall of 2020 due to the lockdowns and reduction of in-person dining from COVID. Debtor Company and Lessor entered into an agreement in September of 2020 in which Lessor agreed to accept 50% of rent due under the rental agreement for the months of September through December of 2020, with the remaining 50% due by the end of January of 2021. Debtor paid Lessor the arrearages, as promised, at the end of January. Debtor's business, however, did not recover and Debtor Company filed for relief under Chapter 11 at the end of March 2021. Lessor is an unsecured creditor and normally payment in full of an antecedent debt (past-due rent) within 90 days prior to bankruptcy filing would constitute a preference under § 547. The CAA's temporary amendments, however, mean that the trustee cannot recover, as a preference, the past-due rent paid to Lessor at the end of January, 2021.

(ii) Covered Payment of Supplier Arrearages

The CAA defines *covered payment of supplier arrearages* as a payment made in connection with an agreement

(1) entered into between the debtor and a supplier of goods or services under an *executory contract for goods or services;*

(2) to defer or postpone the *payment of amounts due* under an executory contract for goods or services; and

(3) entered into *on or after March 13, 2020.*

[B.C. § 547(j)(1)(B)(i)] The CAA imposes *limitations* on what is included as a covered payment of supplier arrearages. Any amount excluded as a covered payment of supplier arrearages *does not qualify* for the CAA's exception to § 547's preference rules. In other words, the trustee may seek to recover these excluded amounts as preferences.

(1) The payment of arrearages cannot *exceed* the amount due under the executory contract *before March 13, 2020.* [B.C. § 547(j)(1)(B)(ii)]

(2) The payment of arrearages **does not include fees, penalties, or interest in an amount greater** than the fees, penalties, or interest scheduled to be paid under the executory contract. [B.C. § 547(j)(1)(B)(iii)(I)]

(3) The payment of arrearages **does not include fees, penalties, or interest** that the debtor would owe had the debtor made every payment due under the executory contract on time and in full **before March 13, 2020.** [B.C. § 547(j)(1)(B)(iii)(II)]

CHECKLIST OF EXCEPTIONS TO THE PREFERENCE RULE

THE FOLLOWING TRANSFERS ARE EXCEPTED FROM THE VOIDABLE PREFERENCE RULE:

☑ Transfers that the debtor and creditor intended to be a **contemporaneous exchange** and that actually were **substantially contemporaneous exchanges** for new value

☑ Transfers made **in the ordinary course of business** of the debtor and creditor **or** according to **ordinary business terms,** for the purpose of repaying a **debt that was incurred** in the **debtor's and creditor's ordinary course of business**

☑ **Purchase-money security interests** securing new value given to the debtor to acquire certain property (actually purchased with the new value) if the creditor perfects within 30 days of the debtor's possession of the collateral

☑ An **extension of new value** made subsequent to the transfer

☑ Perfected **security interests in inventory or receivables** (or proceeds of either) to the extent that they did not improve the creditor's position to the prejudice of the estate during the pre-petition period stated in Code § 547(c)(5)

☑ The fixing of a **statutory lien** that **cannot be avoided under Bankruptcy Code § 545**

☑ A transfer that was a **bona fide** payment of a **domestic support obligation**

☑ Transfers to the same creditor in a case by an individual debtor with **primarily consumer debts** of **property whose aggregate value is less than $600**

☑ Transfers to the same creditor in a case by a debtor whose debts are **not primarily consumer debts** of **property whose aggregate value is less than $7,575**

☑ Transfers pursuant to an **alternative repayment schedule** with an approved nonprofit budget and counseling agency

☑ In any case **filed before December 27, 2022,** payments of certain **supplier or rental arrearages**.

---

4. Special Rules for Preferences

Section 547 specifies when certain transfers **are deemed to have been perfected** and when certain transfers are **considered to have been made.** [B.C. § 547(e)]

a. When Perfection Occurs

A transfer of **real property** is perfected when, under state law, i.e., recording statutes, a **bona fide purchaser** of the property cannot acquire an interest superior to that of the transferee. A transfer of **fixtures or personal property** is perfected when, under state law, i.e., U.C.C. Article 9, a creditor on a simple contract cannot acquire a **judicial lien** that is superior to the transferee's interest. [B.C. § 547(e)(1)]

b. When Transfer Is Made

It helps when working through these rules to consider them in the context of a debtor granting a consensual lien, e.g., a security interest, to a creditor in exchange for the creditor extending credit or loaning money to the debtor. The *transfer* is the grant of the consensual lien.

(i) Perfection Within Thirty Days

If the creditor perfects its interest within *30 days of the transfer*, then the transfer is made at the time that it takes effect between the debtor and creditor. [B.C. § 547(e)(2)(A)]

e.g. **Example:** Debtor needs funds to operate its business. On April 5, Bank and Debtor enter into a security agreement, which provides that Debtor grants Bank a security interest in Debtor's equipment in exchange for Bank's loan of $500,000 to Debtor. On April 25, Bank properly files a UCC–1 on the equipment. The transfer is the grant of the security interest. Bank perfected within 30 days of Debtor granting Bank a security interest, which means that for purposes of § 547, the transfer occurred on April 5—when it took effect—*not* April 25. Why is that important? Because if the Debtor became indebted to Bank on April 5—when Bank agreed to loan $500,000 to Debtor—and the transfer of the security interest occurred on April 5, then there is *no transfer on account of an antecedent debt.* Therefore, there is no preference and the trustee cannot avoid the security interest to Bank.

(ii) Perfection After Thirty Days

If the creditor perfects its interest *more than 30 days* after the transfer originally became effective, then the transfer is made on the date it is *perfected.* [B.C. § 547(e)(2)(B)]

e.g. **Example:** Same facts as prior example *except* Bank does not file its UCC–1 until May 10. The transfer is made on May 10, not April 5. Why is that important? Because now the transfer is on account of an antecedent debt—the Debtor incurred the debt on April 5. *If* Debtor files for bankruptcy on July 25, then the grant of the security interest to Bank is a preference. It was a transfer on account of an antecedent debt, made within 90 days of bankruptcy (May 10 to July 25), the debtor is presumed insolvent for those 90 days (§ 547(f)), and Bank is better off as a secured creditor than an unsecured creditor in a Chapter 7 case. Therefore, the trustee can avoid the security interest to Bank, unless one of the exceptions at § 547(c) applies.

e.g. **Example:** On December 5, 2017, Dylan purchased a new car from Cathay Luxury Motors ("CLM"). He signed a promissory note for the $48,000 purchase price and granted CLM a security interest in the vehicle. CLM, however, did not perfect the security interest until April 5, 2018. Dylan filed for relief under Chapter 7 on May 10, 2018. The trustee can avoid CLM's security interest in the vehicle. The granting of the security interest was a transfer to the creditor of the debtor's interest in property. [B.C. § 547(b)(1)] Because perfection did not occur within 30 days of December 5, the transfer of the security interest is deemed to have occurred on April 5, when CLM perfected. [B.C. § 547(e)(2)(B)] As a result, the transfer is on account of an antecedent debt, because the debt arose on December 5 and the transfer occurred four months later. [B.C. § 547(b)(2)] April 5 is within 90 days of the bankruptcy filing when the debtor is presumed to be insolvent. [B.C. §§ 547(b)(3) & (4), 547(f)] Finally, the transfer of the security interest makes CLM a secured creditor but had the transfer not occurred CLM would be a general unsecured creditor in the Chapter 7 case; therefore, the transfer allows CLM to receive more than it would had the transfer not taken place. [B.C. § 547(b)(5); *see* **Howell v. Brown (*In re* Pritchett),** 515 B.R. 656 (Bankr. N.D. Ga. 2014)]

(iii) If No Perfection Before Bankruptcy

A transfer is made immediately prior to bankruptcy if perfection has not occurred by the time the *petition is filed* or within *30 days after* the transfer became effective between the parties, *whichever is later*. [B.C. § 547(e)(2)(C)]

e.g. **Example:** In 2003, Bank loaned Debtor $196,000, and Debtor granted Bank a mortgage on his home. Bank failed to record the mortgage. Debtor subsequently filed for relief under Chapter 7. Bank's failure to record the mortgage means that the transfer of the mortgage occurred immediately prior to Debtor's filing for bankruptcy, which creates a preference problem for the Bank. [B.C. § 547(e)(2)(C); *see* **Wells Fargo Home Mortgage, Inc. v. Lundquist,** 592 F.3d 838 (8th Cir. 2010)]

(iv) Debtor's Rights in Property

Keep in mind that a debtor cannot grant a security interest in property unless it has rights to that property. [U.C.C. § 9–203(b)] Therefore, a transfer is not made until the debtor acquires rights in the property transferred. [B.C. § 547(e)(3)]

(1) Inventory and Receivables

Make sure to always check the improvement-in-position test for inventory and receivables at § 547(c)(5). [B.C. § 547(c)(5)]

In exchange for a line of credit from a bank to finance its purchases of inventory, a debtor often will grant the bank a security interest in debtor's inventory, whether "now owned or hereafter acquired." The reason for doing so is that inventory turns over quickly. If the security interest did not "float" to cover new purchases of inventory, the bank quickly could end up an unsecured creditor. Section 547(e)(3) provides that a transfer does not occur until the debtor has rights in the collateral. If a debtor buys inventory in the 90 days prior to filing for bankruptcy, there is a preference issue. The bank's security interest floats and attaches to the inventory, but not until the debtor acquires rights in the inventory. That means that the debtor has transferred an interest in property—the lien on the inventory—to a creditor, within 90 days of bankruptcy when the debtor is presumed insolvent, on account of an antecedent debt (line of credit), and the transfer of the security interest to the new inventory improves the bank's position. The Code's solution to this problem is the improvement-in-position test for inventory and receivables at § 547(c)(5). [*See* Collier ¶ 547.04(5) (stating that § 547(c)(5) "is indispensable to secured parties with floating liens because of the timing of transfer rules in section 547(e)")]

c. Rights in Garnished Wages

The vast majority of cases hold that, even if a garnishment lien has been executed more than 90 days before bankruptcy, the amounts of the debtor's wages garnished during the preference period are voidable transfers because the debtor does not acquire rights in wages until she has earned them. [**Morehead v. State Farm Mutual Auto Insurance Co. (*In re* Morehead),** 249 F.3d 445 (6th Cir. 2001); **Tower Credit, Inc. v. Schott,** 550 B.R. 299 (M.D. La. 2016)] If during the 90 days prior to bankruptcy, the aggregate value of the garnishments against an individual debtor with primarily consumer debts is less than $600, then the exception at § 547(c)(8) applies and the trustee may not avoid the transfer of the garnished wages.

d. When Transfer Occurs if Debtor Pays by Check

If the debtor pays a creditor by check, the *transfer* is deemed to have occurred, for purposes of the § 547(b) preference period, *at the time the bank honors the check.* [**Barnhill v. Johnson,** 503 U.S. 393 (1992)] In *Barnhill,* the Supreme Court noted that the Courts of Appeals that had considered the question had unanimously used the date of delivery for purposes of the preference exceptions under § 547(c). But the question of whether the date of delivery versus the date of honor applied to the preference *exceptions* was not before the Court; thus, it expressed no view on the issue. *Barnhill* is important in cases in which the debtor pays by check *more than 90 days* before bankruptcy but the bank honors the check *within the 90-day period.*

When deciding whether a *preference exception* under § 547(c) applies, most courts hold that the transfer occurs on the date that the *check is delivered, not honored.* [*See, e.g.,* **Littleton v. Hinton (***In re* **Triple H Auto & Truck Sales, Inc.),** 2009 WL 348858 (Bankr. S.D. Ala. 2009) (stating that for purposes of § 547(c)(1), the transfer occurs on the date that the check is delivered so long as the check is presented within a reasonable time and honored by the bank); **Rifken v. Entec Distribution, LLC (***In re* **Felt Mfg. Co.),** 2009 WL 3348300 (Bankr. D. N.H. 2009) (stating that "[c]ourts consistently hold that for new value purposes under § 547(c)(4), the transfer involving a payment by check occurs when the check is received by the creditor"); **Savage & Associates v. Mandl (***In re* **Teligent Inc.),** 380 B.R. 324 (Bankr. S.D. N.Y. 2008) (stating that for purposes of § 547(c)(2) the transfer happens when the check is delivered, so long as the check is honored within 30 days of delivery)]

5. Burden of Proof

The trustee has the burden of proving a preference exists. [*See* B.C. § 547(b)] The creditor has the burden of proving a defense under § 547(c). [B.C. § 547(g)]

D. Trustee's Power to Avoid Fraudulent Transfers

1. In General

The trustee may avoid a fraudulent transfer of the debtor's interest in property or the fraudulent incurring of an obligation if the transfer was made or the obligation was incurred by the debtor, voluntarily or involuntarily, *within two years* prior to bankruptcy. [B.C. § 548(a)] The trustee also may avoid certain transfers made by the debtor to a *self-settled trust within ten years* prior to bankruptcy. [B.C. § 548(e)]

2. "Transfer"

The Code defines a transfer as

a. *creation of a lien* [B.C. § 101(54)(A)];

b. *retention of title* as a security interest [B.C. § 101(54)(B)];

c. *foreclosure* of the debtor's equity of redemption [B.C. § 101(54)(C)]; or

d.   any direct or indirect, absolute or conditional, voluntary or involuntary *disposition of or parting with property or an interest in property.* [B.C. § 101(54)(D)].

a.   When Transfer Occurs

A transfer is made when it is sufficiently perfected that a bona fide purchaser cannot acquire an interest in the property superior to that of the transferee. If such perfection has not occurred prior to the filing of the petition, the transfer is deemed to be made immediately prior to bankruptcy. [B.C. § 548(d)(1)]

3.   "Fraudulent" Transfer

A trustee may avoid a transfer if there is *actual intent* to hinder, delay, or defraud a creditor. [B.C. § 548(a)(1)(A)] The trustee also may avoid a transfer that is *constructively fraudulent.* [B.C. § 548(a)(1)(B)]

a.   Actual Intent to Hinder, Delay, or Defraud

A transfer of the debtor's property is fraudulent if it was made with *actual intent* to hinder, delay, or defraud a creditor. [B.C. § 548(a)(1)(A)]

e.g.   **Example:** On March 1, Debtor, who was hopelessly in debt, transferred all of his assets into his wife's name for no consideration and for the express purpose of placing them out of the reach of his creditors. On March 3, Debtor filed a voluntary bankruptcy petition. The trustee may avoid the conveyance of Debtor's assets as a fraudulent transfer and may recover them for the benefit of the estate. [B.C. §§ 548(a)(1)(A), 550(a)]

(i)   Badges of Fraud

Because a debtor does not announce her intention to defraud creditors, the law has developed certain "badges of fraud" from which *actual intent may be inferred.* Both the Uniform Fraudulent Transfer Act and the Uniform Voidable Transactions Act provide the following non-exhaustive list of badges of fraud, which many courts use:

(1)   *inadequate or no consideration* is received for the transfer made or obligation incurred;

(2)   the *transferee is an insider,* **e.g., *a relative,*** of the debtor;

(3)   the *debtor keeps possession or control of the transferred property;*

(4)   the *transfer occurs or the obligation is incurred at a time after creditors have filed suit or threatened to file suit against the debtor;*

(5)   the debtor is *insolvent or becomes insolvent* shortly after the transfer was made or obligation incurred;

(6)   the transfer or obligation is *concealed;*

(7)   the transfer is of *substantially all the debtor's assets;*

(8)   the debtor *absconds;*

(9)   the transfer occurs shortly before or shortly after a *substantial debt* is incurred; and

(10) the debtor transferred her *essential business assets* to a lienor who then transfers the assets to an insider of the debtor.

[Uniform Fraudulent Transfer Act § 4(b); Uniform Voidable Transactions Act § 4(b)] It is not necessary to prove all the badges of fraud. The presence or absence of any particular badge of fraud is not dispositive. The inquiry is fact intensive, and courts look to all the circumstances surrounding the transfer made or obligation incurred. [**Osherow v. Texas Silica Logistics J.V. (*In re* FWLL, Inc.),** 2018 WL 1684308 (Bankr. W.D. Tex. 2018)]

(ii) Insolvency Not Required

If actual intent can be proved, the transfer is voidable regardless of whether the debtor was insolvent at the time of the transfer. [*See* B.C. § 548(a)(1)(A)]

(iii) Ten-Year Reach Back Period

BAPCPA added a provision to § 548 that extends the reach back period to *ten years* for certain cases of *actual fraud* involving transfers to *self-settled trusts.* [B.C. § 548(e)] The trustee may avoid the transfer if:

(1) the debtor made the transfer [B.C. § 548(e)(1)(B)];

(2) the transfer was to a *self-settled trust* [B.C. § 548(e)(1)(A)];

(3) the debtor is the *beneficiary* of that trust [B.C. § 548(e)(1)(C)]; and

(4) the debtor made the transfer with *actual intent to hinder, delay, or defraud* current creditors or entities that become creditors after the date of the transfer. [B.C. § 548(e)(1)(D)]

The Code defines a *transfer,* for purposes of § 548(e), to include a transfer the debtor made in anticipation of a money judgment, settlement, civil penalty, equitable order or criminal fine incurred or that the debtor believe would be incurred for (i) violations of *state or federal securities laws,* (ii) violations of *regulations or orders* issued under state or federal securities laws, or (iii) *fraud, deceit or manipulation in a fiduciary capacity* under §§ 12 or 15(d) of the Securities Exchange Act of 1934 or under § 6 of the Securities Act of 1933. [B.C. § 548(e)(2)]

b. Constructive Fraud

The Code provides that the trustee may prove *constructive fraud* by demonstrating that the debtor did not receive something of *reasonably equivalent value* in exchange for the transfer or obligation *and* the debtor (i) was *insolvent* or rendered insolvent by the transfer or obligation, (ii) was *undercapitalized* after the transfer or incurring of the obligation, (iii) intended to incur debts *beyond her ability to repay, or* (iv) made the transfer or incurred the obligation to or for the *benefit of an insider under an employment contract* and not in the ordinary course of business. [B.C. § 548(a)(1)(B)(i), (ii)(I)–(IV)]

(i) What Is Reasonably Equivalent Value?

The *first step* in determining reasonably equivalent value is determining whether the debtor received *any* value for the transfer. This part of the analysis is simple, because the Code defines value. For purposes of § 548, value includes not only property, but also the "satisfaction or securing of a present or antecedent debt of the debtor." [B.C. § 548(d)(2)(A)] If the debtor receives value, then the *second step* is deciding whether the value received is reasonably equivalent to the value transferred. This inquiry is fact intensive.

In **BFP v. Resolution Trust Corporation,** 511 U.S. 531 (1994), the Supreme Court held that the sale price received at a *non-collusive* foreclosure sale conclusively establishes reasonably equivalent value, if "all the requirements of the State's foreclosure law have been complied with." Any fraud, collusion, or other defect in the sale that would invalidate it under state law "will deprive[ ] the sale price of its conclusive force" and subject the sale to possible avoidance under § 548.

(ii) Receipt of Less than Reasonably Equivalent Value and Debtor's Insolvency

A transaction is considered to be fraudulent if the debtor received *less than reasonably equivalent value* for the transfer or obligation *and* was *insolvent* on the date the transfer or obligation occurred or *became insolvent* as a consequence of it. [B.C. § 548(a)(1)(B)(i), (ii)(I)]

Example: Debtor filed for relief under Chapter 7. For two years prior to filing for bankruptcy, Debtor paid about $5,500 to University to cover some of her son's tuition and educational expenses. The Chapter 7 trustee filed an adversary proceeding to avoid and recover the money paid to University under § 548(a)(1)(B)(i), (ii)(I). The Debtor was insolvent at the time she paid University or was rendered insolvent by virtue of the transfers made to University. Thus, the only issue before the court was whether Debtor received reasonably equivalent value in exchange for the tuition payments made to University. The bankruptcy court held that Debtor received no "legally cognizable value" and, thus, could not have received reasonably equivalent value for the transfers. The court explained that the Code's definition of value is "limited to economic benefits" and does not take account of "moral or familial obligations." [*See* **Boscarino v. Board of Trustees of Connecticut State Univ. System (*In re* Knight),** 2017 WL 4410455 (Bankr. D. Conn. 2017)]

Example: On May 1, 2001, Debtor's auction bid of $1 billion to purchase 14 radio spectrum licenses at their current market value was accepted by the F.C.C. as the high bid, and Debtor made a down payment of $100 million. On June 1, 2001, Debtor filed license application forms. On December 1, 2001, the F.C.C. approved the applications and granted Debtor the licenses, which had declined significantly in value to $200 million, rendering Debtor insolvent. Also on December 1, 2001, Debtor executed promissory notes totaling $900 million to the F.C.C. for the balance of the purchase price. On July 1, 2002, Debtor filed a Chapter 11 bankruptcy petition and also sought to avoid the transaction as a constructive fraudulent transfer under Code § 548(a)(1)(B)(i), (ii)(I). If the date of the transfer is deemed to be May 1—the date the auction closed—then Debtor loses because the value of the licenses was "by definition" the fair market value. [*See* **FCC v. NextWave Personal Communications, Inc. (*In re* NextWave Personal Communications, Inc.),** 200 F.3d 43 (2d Cir. 1999) (holding that Debtor's obligation to pay for spectrum licenses was not a fraudulent transfer, because the licenses' fair market value was equivalent to the bids that the F.C.C. had accepted at the close of the auction)] However, if the date of the transfer is deemed to be December 1—the date the licenses were approved and the promissory notes signed—then Debtor wins because Debtor did not receive reasonably equivalent value. [*See* **United States v. GWI PCS 1, Inc. (*In re* GWI PCS 1 Inc.),** 230 F.3d 788 (5th Cir. 2000) (holding that Debtor's obligation to pay for spectrum licenses was a fraudulent transfer, because that obligation did not arise at the close of the auction but only later after the F.C.C. had approved Debtor's application and Debtor had executed the notes for the balance of the purchase price)]

(iii) Receipt of Less than Reasonably Equivalent Value and Debtor's Undercapitalization

A transaction is constructively fraudulent if the debtor received *less than reasonably equivalent value* for the transfer or obligation and was left with *unreasonably small capital* for the operation of the debtor's business. [B.C. § 548(a)(1)(B)(i), (ii)(II)]

(1) Leveraged Buyout

In a *leveraged buyout,* the purchasing company uses the assets of the target corporation as collateral for a bank loan obtained to finance the purchase price. Suppose Acme, the acquiring company, borrows money to buy the stock of Theta, the target corporation. The shareholders of Theta are cashed out using the borrowed funds. Acme uses the assets of Theta as collateral for the loan. Theta increases its debt burden; the risk of default is borne by Theta's general unsecured creditors. Thus, Theta receives no *direct* benefit from the LBO. If the transaction results in Theta's undercapitalization or insolvency, the transfer might constitute a fraudulent conveyance if Theta subsequently files for bankruptcy, because Theta did not receive reasonably equivalent value in exchange for the grant of a security interest in *its own assets. Remember:* The funds from the bank (value) went to Acme, the *acquiring company, not* to Theta, *the target company.* [**United States v. Tabor Court Realty Corp.,** 803 F.2d 1288 (3d Cir. 1986) (case under Pennsylvania Uniform Fraudulent Conveyances Act holding that fraudulent conveyance law applied to LBOs, and upholding district court's determination that LBO transaction had rendered target insolvent and target did not receive fair consideration); *but see* **Mellon Bank, N.A. v. Metro Communications, Inc.,** 945 F.2d 635 (3d Cir. 1991) (court may take into account indirect benefits, e.g., debtor's ability to borrow money and creation of strong synergy by new affiliation, in deciding the question of reasonably equivalent value)]

(iv) Receipt of Less than Reasonably Equivalent Value and Debtor's Over-Extension

A transaction is constructively fraudulent if the debtor receives *less than reasonably equivalent value* for the transfer or obligation, and intends to incur or believes she will incur debts that she will be *unable to repay* as they mature. [B.C. § 548(a)(1)(B)(i), (ii)(III)]

(v) Receipt of Less than Reasonably Equivalent Value and Transfer to Insider

BAPCPA added a type of avoidable transaction that specifically involves insiders. This new subsection in § 548(a)(1)(B) applies if the debtor made a transfer or incurred an obligation (1) for *less than reasonably equivalent value*, (2) to or for the benefit of an *insider*, (3) under an *employment contract*, and (4*) not in the ordinary course* of business. [B.C. § 548(a)(1)(B)(i), (ii)(IV)]

c. Constructive Fraud: Exception for Certain Charitable Contributions

Certain charitable contributions are not treated as transfers for less than reasonably equivalent value under § 548(a)(1)(B). The trustee cannot avoid any transfer of cash or a financial instrument, e.g., stocks or bonds, by a *natural person* to a *qualified charitable or religious entity or organization*, as defined by the Internal Revenue Code, if the contribution:

(i) does not exceed 15% of the debtor's gross annual income for the year of the contribution *or*

(ii) if the contribution *does* exceed 15% of the debtor's gross annual income, it is consistent with the practices of the debtor in making charitable contributions.

[B.C. § 548(a)(2), (d)(3) (defines "charitable contribution"), (4) (defines "qualified religious or charitable entity or organization")]

d. Distinguish Third-Party Transactions with Indirect Benefit to Debtor

Courts generally find that there is no reasonably equivalent value if a transfer or obligation benefits a *third party and not the debtor*. Some courts, however, have recognized an exception, known as the *"indirect benefit rule,"* to this general principle. For example, if the transfer does not adversely affect the debtor's net worth, because there is an indirect benefit to the debtor, then a court may find reasonably equivalent value. Courts require that this indirect benefit be quantifiable. [5 Collier ¶ 548.05(2)(b); **Rubin v. Manufacturers Hanover Trust Co.,** 661 F.2d 979 (2d Cir. 1981)]

Example: Debtor was in the business of selling general merchandise to grocery stores. Debtor tried to obtain a $150,000 working capital loan from Bank, but Bank refused to make the loan due to Debtor's financial performance. Bank, however, agreed to loan the necessary capital to Debtor's three individual shareholders ("Shareholders"). While Shareholders were responsible for the loan, the loan proceeds were deposited directly into Debtor's corporate checking account. Debtor then granted Bank a security interest in its inventory, equipment, and accounts. Less than a year later, Debtor stopped doing business, and Debtor's creditors filed an involuntary petition under Chapter 7 against Debtor. The Chapter 7 trustee sought to avoid the security interest granted to Bank and claimed that the $150,000 loan that Shareholders contributed to Debtor was a capital contribution. Thus, the trustee argued that Debtor's grant of a security interest to Bank diminished the estate by $150,000. The bankruptcy court and the B.A.P. agreed with the trustee, but the Ninth Circuit reversed. The court explained that while Debtor was not a party to the $150,000 loan, it clearly benefited from that loan. In fact, Bank deposited the loan proceeds directly into Debtor's corporate account. Debtor benefited from the loan in the amount of $150,000, and Bank received a security interest in Debtor's collateral equivalent to Shareholders' $150,000 debt to Bank. The court concluded that there was no "net loss to Debtor's estate nor the funds available to the unsecured creditors." As a result, Debtor received reasonably equivalent value for the security interest granted to Bank. [**Frontier Bank v. Brown (*In re* Northern Merchandise, Inc.),** 371 F.3d 1056 (9th Cir. 2004)]

4. Good Faith Transferee

A *good faith transferee* or obligee for value is entitled to retain, or to receive a lien on, any property conveyed to her or to enforce an obligation incurred, *to the extent of any value given* by the transferee or obligee to the debtor. [B.C. § 548(c)] This provision applies to transfers voidable under § 548, unless the transfer also is subject to the trustee's avoiding power under §§ 544, 545, or 547.

a. Good Faith

In determining good faith, courts use an *objective, not a subjective, test.* They look to whether a transferee has information that puts it on inquiry notice about the fraudulent nature of the transaction or the debtor's insolvency. Failure to diligently inquire may result in a finding that the transferee is not a good faith transferee for purposes of § 548(c).

[**Christian Brothers High School Endowment v. Bayou No Leverage Fund, LLC (*In re* Bayou Group, LLC)**, 439 B.R. 284 (S.D. N.Y. 2010)]

b. Value

The Code defines value as "property, or satisfaction or securing of a present or antecedent debt of the debtor." An unperformed promise to provide the debtor or a relative of the debtor with support does not constitute value. [B.C. § 548(d)(2)(A)]

5. Partnership Debtor

The trustee may avoid any transfer by a partnership debtor *to a general partner* within *two years* prior to bankruptcy if the debtor was *insolvent* at the time of the transfer or the transfer caused the debtor to become insolvent. [B.C. § 548(b)]

EXAM TIP   GILBERT

Remember that the trustee has multiple avoiding powers. With the exception of self-settled trusts, if the transfer occurred more than two years prior to bankruptcy, it cannot be avoided under § 548. But, there may be a longer reach-back period if the trustee can find an *actual creditor* who, at the time of bankruptcy, has an allowable *unsecured claim* and has the right under *applicable nonbankruptcy law* to avoid a transfer of the debtor's property. [B.C. § 544(b)]

E. Post-Petition Transactions

1. General Rule

The trustee may avoid a transfer of estate property occurring after the filing of the bankruptcy petition, unless the transfer falls within one of the exceptions described below or is authorized under the Bankruptcy Code or approved by the court. [B.C. § 549(a)]

e.g. **Example:** Lewis, the chief financial officer for Cresta Corporation, issued a check to Castello, the attorney Cresta had hired to represent the firm in bankruptcy. Castello declined the check and asked for payment by cashier's check instead. Lewis delivered a cashier's check to Castello drawn on Lewis's personal bank account. The next day, Cresta issued a check to reimburse Lewis, and Cresta filed for relief under Chapter 7 that same day. Four days after Cresta filed for bankruptcy, its reimbursement check to Lewis cleared the bank. The transfer of the check to Lewis is a post-petition transfer that the Chapter 7 trustee may avoid. The transfer occurred post-petition on the date that the bank honored the check, and was not authorized by either the Code or the bankruptcy court. [**Lewis v. Kaelin (*In re* Cresta Technology Corp.),** 583 B.R. 224 (B.A.P. 9th Cir. 2018)]

cf. **Compare:** Debtor, a widget manufacturer, files a voluntary Chapter 11 petition. A trustee is not appointed, and Debtor continues to operate the business as a debtor in possession, making numerous sales of widgets in the ordinary course of business. Because the Bankruptcy Code permits these types of transactions without court approval, they are valid post-petition transfers and are not subject to avoidance. [B.C. § 363(c)(1)]

2. Entity Without Notice or Knowledge

An entity that has neither actual notice nor knowledge of the bankruptcy case is protected from liability concerning a good faith post-petition transfer. [B.C. §§ 549(a)(2)(A), 542(c); *see supra* Chapter Five, § B.3.b] For example, if a bank honors the debtor's check after the commencement of the case, the bank is not liable for honoring the check, if it had neither actual notice nor knowledge of the bankruptcy case. The transferee/payee on the check, however, may be subject to the trustee's avoiding power under § 549(a)(2)(A).

Example: Prior to filing for bankruptcy, Debtor took out a loan from Payday Loans ("PL"). Debtor gave PL a postdated check that covered the loan's principal and interest. About a week later, Debtor filed for relief under Chapter 13. After the commencement of Debtor's bankruptcy case, PL presented Debtor's check to Bank for payment. Bank, without notice or knowledge of the bankruptcy case, honored the check and paid PL. Section 542(c) authorized the transfer that took place when Bank honored Debtor's check. But, § 542(c) only protects the drawee bank, not the transferee PL. Thus, under § 549(a)(2), the trustee may avoid the post-petition transfer to PL of funds from Debtor's checking account. [B.C. § 549(a)(2)(A); *see* **Buckeye Check Cashing, Inc. v. Meadows (*In re* Meadows),** 396 B.R. 485 (B.A.P. 6th Cir. 2008)]

3. Exceptions to Trustee's Avoidance

The trustee cannot avoid a post-petition transfer (a) to a *gap transferee* that *gives value* post-petition in exchange for the transfer *or* (b) of *real property* to a *good faith purchaser* that gave *present fair equivalent value* and that had *no knowledge* of the bankruptcy case.

a. Gap Transferee in Involuntary Case

The debtor may continue to operate its business and dispose of property during the gap period—the time between the filing of an involuntary petition and the entry of an order for relief. [B.C. § 303(f)] The trustee, however, cannot avoid a transfer made during the gap period *to the extent that the transferee gave value, including services, after the start* of the *bankruptcy case* in exchange for the transfer. This exception does not apply to a transaction that involves the satisfaction or securing of a pre-petition debt. [B.C. § 549(a)(2)(A), (b)] The exception applies even if the gap transferee has notice or knowledge of the bankruptcy case. [B.C. § 549(b)]

Rationale: The purpose of this exception is to allow a business to continue its normal business operations during the gap period. If creditors feared having the trustee pursue them to recover post-petition transfers for goods or services rendered to the debtor, then filing of an involuntary petition could cause substantial harm to the debtor.

Example: Debtor Michael Mastro operated Mastro Properties, a sole proprietorship in the real estate and investment business. MKM is Debtor's son and the sole member of MKM LLC, which was formed to hold life insurance policies on Debtor. MKM LLC's transactions were run through Mastro's accounting system and MKM LLC had no independent financial existence until June when it opened a bank account with $900,000 in insurance proceeds provided by Mastro. On July 10, three of Debtor's secured creditors filed an involuntary Chapter 7 petition against Debtor. Between July 10 and August 21, when the court entered an order for relief, Mastro issued six checks totaling $362,000 to MKM and MKM LLC. The Chapter 7 trustee sought to avoid these transfers. MKM LLC claimed that the checks were compensation for services that MKM had provided to Debtor, and that the net effect of various transfers between Mastro and MKM LLC had benefited, not harmed, Debtor. The court rejected both claims. First, the court noted that MKM offered no evidence of the services provided to Debtor during the gap period. Second, the court explained that MKM LLC offered no evidence that the cash payments it had received were used to fund Mastro's operations during the gap period. The fact that MKM LLC never had been a supplier of cash to the Debtor, did not have cash of its own and relied on Debtor's assets for the cash in its bank account, and had no independent financial existence until shortly before the filing of the involuntary petition led the court to agree with the trustee that the gap period transfers to MKM LLC did not merit the exception at § 549(a)(2)(A). [**Mastro v. Rigby (*In re Mastro*), **2011 WL 3300370 (B.A.P. 9th Cir. 2011)]

b. Good Faith Purchaser of Real Property

The trustee cannot avoid a ***post-petition transfer of real property*** to a ***good faith purchaser*** that has ***no knowledge*** of the bankruptcy case and has paid ***present fair equivalent value*** if notice of the bankruptcy case has not been filed, prior to perfection of the transfer, in the office where real property transactions are recorded for the county in which the land is located. [B.C. § 549(c)] A party that buys property at a judicial or tax sale cannot take advantage of this exception to the trustee's avoiding power under § 549. The exception applies to a good faith *purchaser* and the Code defines *purchaser* as the "transferee of a voluntary transfer." [B.C. § 101(43); 5 Collier ¶ 549.06]

(i) Less than Present Fair Equivalent Value

If notice of the bankruptcy petition has not been filed in the proper office for recording before perfection of the transfer, and a good faith purchaser without knowledge of the case has given less than present fair equivalent value, she is entitled to a lien on the property, but only to the extent of the ***present value furnished.*** [B.C. § 549(c)]

F. Limitations on Trustee's Avoiding Powers

1. Statute of Limitations for Avoidance, *Except* Post-Petition Transfers

Most of the trustee's avoiding powers are subject to a statute of limitations requiring that the trustee *file an action* to avoid a transfer before the *earlier* of the following time periods:

a. the *later* of (i) *two years* after the entry of the order for relief *or* (ii) *one year* after the appointment or election of the first trustee, if the appointment or election occurs before the two-year period expires [B.C. § 546(a)(1)]; *or*

b. *the time* the case is *closed or dismissed*. [B.C. § 546(a)(2)]

a. Transfers Affected

This period of limitations applies to a trustee's action to avoid:

(1) a transfer avoidable under the strong arm clause [B.C. § 544(a)];

(2) a transfer avoidable by the trustee as successor to certain actual creditors [B.C. § 544(b)];

(3) a statutory lien [B.C. § 545];

(4) a preference [B.C. § 547];

(5) a fraudulent transfer [B.C. § 548]; or

(6) a setoff [B.C. § 553].

2. Statute of Limitations for Avoidance of Post-Petition Transactions

The trustee must file an action to avoid a post-petition transfer before the *earlier* of:

a. two years after the *transfer* was made [B.C. § 549(d)(1)]; *or*

b. the time the case is *closed or dismissed.* [B.C. § 549(d)(2)]

3. Equitable Tolling

Limitations periods may be equitably tolled because of fraud or misrepresentation that the trustee did not discover notwithstanding due diligence on her part, or extraordinary circumstances beyond the trustee's control that make it impossible for her to file an action on time. [5 Collier ¶ 546.02(3)] Courts use equitable tolling sparingly. [*See, e.g.,* **Montoya v. Sasso (*In re* Sasso)**, 550 B.R. 550 (Bankr. D. N.M. 2016) (stating that "[e]quitable tolling should be applied sparingly"); **Gugino v. Turner (*In re* Clark)**, 2015 WL 5545258 (Bankr. D. Idaho 2015) (stating that in the Ninth Circuit equitable tolling is " 'rarely applied and disfavored' " and "should be applied 'only sparingly' ")]

4. Statute of Limitations for *Recovery* of Avoided Transfer

If a transfer is *avoided*, the trustee must commence, an action to *recover* transferred property or, if the court orders, the value of such property *no later than the earlier of:*

a. *one year after avoidance* of the transfer [B.C. § 550(f)(1)]; *or*

b. the time that the case is *closed or dismissed.* [B.C. § 550(f)(2)]

5. Retroactive Perfection

The trustee's avoiding powers under Code §§ 544(a) (strong arm clause), 544(b) (successor to certain actual creditors), 545 (certain statutory liens), and 549 (post-petition transactions) are subject to any applicable nonbankruptcy law that permits retroactive perfection of a security interest. For example, U.C.C. § 9–317(e) provides that a creditor that perfects within *20 days* of the debtor taking delivery of the goods will have priority over the rights of an intervening lien creditor. Moreover, the Code provides an *exception to the automatic stay* for a post-petition act to perfect or to maintain or continue perfection provided that the action taken occurs within the time permitted under the applicable nonbankruptcy law. [B.C. §§ 362(b)(3), 546(b)(1)]

Example: On May 30, Debtor borrows $10,000 from Bank and grants Bank a purchase-money security interest in a new business computer that it had contracted to purchase from CompuWorld. Debtor receives delivery of the computer on April 1. On April 5, Debtor files a voluntary bankruptcy petition, and on April 6, Bank files a UCC–1 to perfect its security interest in the computer.

If this were not a purchase money security interest, the trustee would be able to avoid Bank's security interest, because the trustee became a hypothetical lien creditor on April 5 *before* Bank filed a UCC–1. [U.C.C. § 9–317(a)(2)]. But, the Uniform Commercial Code provides an exception for purchase money security interests. If the secured party files a UCC–1 within 20 days of the debtor taking delivery of the collateral, then the secured party has priority over a lien creditor that arose between attachment and the filing of the UCC–1. Attachment occurred on May 30. Trustee became a hypothetical lien creditor on April 5 when Debtor filed for bankruptcy. Bank filed its UCC–1 on April 6—within 20 days of Debtor taking delivery of the computer. Therefore, the trustee, having the rights of a hypothetical judicial lien creditor on the date of bankruptcy, is subject to Bank's retroactive perfection, and will be unable to avoid Bank's purchase-money security interest. [B.C. §§ 546(b), 544(a)(1); U.C.C. § 9–317(e)] Moreover, the Bank's post-petition filing of a UCC–1 does not violate the automatic stay. [B.C. § 362(b)(3)]

Keep in mind the possibility of retroactive perfection. If a creditor perfects a security interest after a bankruptcy petition is filed, the creditor might be able to trump the trustee's avoiding power if a **nonbankruptcy law** permits retroactive perfection of the creditor's security interest. The most common such law is U.C.C. § 9–317(e), under which post-petition perfection of a **purchase-money security interest** may relate back to a pre-petition date if the creditor files a financing statement within 20 days after the debtor receives delivery of the collateral.

a.   Note

Section 546(b)(1)(A) is not limited to statutes allowing retroactive perfection. [*See* **229 Main Street Ltd. Partnership v. Massachusetts EPA (*In re* 229 Main Street),** 262 F.3d 1 (1st Cir. 2001) (holding that "there is no requirement that the 'generally applicable law' referenced in section 546(b) contain an explicit relation-back mechanism")] Section 546(b)(1)(A) covers any law that "permits perfection of an interest in property to be effective against an entity that acquires rights in such property before the date of perfection." For example, in **229 Main Street,** the First Circuit held that the post-petition perfection of an environmental superlien which, under state law, "trumps all other encumbrances, no matter when filed," satisfied the "combined requirements of section 362(b)(3) and 546(b)(1)(A) and therefore [fell] within the exception carved out by these provisions." [**229 Main Street,** *supra*]

b.   Continuation Statements

The trustee's rights and avoiding powers under sections 544(a) (strong arm clause), 544(b) (successor to certain actual creditors), 545 (certain statutory liens), and 549 (post-petition transfers) also are subject to any applicable law permitting secured creditors to maintain or continue perfection of an interest in property, such as by filing a continuation statement under U.C.C. § 9–515(e). [B.C. § 546(b)(1)(B)] Taking any action allowed under § 546(b)(1)(B) to continue perfection, such as by filing a continuation statement, also does not violate the automatic stay. [B.C. §§ 362(a)(3), 546(b)(1)(B)]

6. Seller's Reclamation of Goods

The trustee's power to avoid (i) a transfer under the strong arm clause [B.C. § 544(a)], (ii) a statutory lien [B.C. § 545], (iii) a preference [B.C. § 547], or (iv) a post-petition transfer [B.C. § 549] is subject to the right of a seller, under certain circumstances, to **reclaim** goods that it sold to the debtor. [*See* B.C. § 546(c)]

a.   Elements Required for Reclamation

Congress substantially changed § 546(c) with the passage of BAPCPA in 2005. The following elements must be present for a **seller to reclaim goods** sold to the debtor. [B.C. § 546(c)]

(i)   Goods

The property sought to be reclaimed must be **goods.** Courts usually use the U.C.C.'s definition to determine what constitutes "goods." [U.C.C. § 2–105; 5 Collier ¶ 546.04(2)(b)(i)]

(ii) Sale in Ordinary Course of Seller's Business

For the seller to reclaim the goods, the seller must have sold the goods to the debtor in the ***ordinary course of the seller's business***. [B.C. § 546(c)]

(iii) Debtor Insolvent

The debtor must have ***received the goods while insolvent***. [B.C. § 546(c); *see* B.C. § 101(32) for definition of insolvency]

(1) "Receipt"

Courts usually use the U.C.C.'s definition of "receipt" to determine when the debtor received the goods subject to a seller's claim for reclamation. [U.C.C. § 2–103(1)(c); 5 Collier ¶ 546.04(2)(b)(v)] Therefore, the debtor is deemed to have received the goods when it has taken ***physical possession*** of them.

(iv) Received Within 45 Days

The seller's right to reclaim goods sold to the seller is limited to goods that the debtor ***received within 45 days*** of the start of debtor's bankruptcy case. [B.C. § 546(c)]

(v) Written Demand for Reclamation

The seller ***must make a written demand*** for reclamation ***no later than***:

(1) ***45 days*** after the debtor received the goods [B.C. § 546(c)(1)(A)]; *or*

(2) ***20 days*** after the start of the bankruptcy case, if the 45-day period expires after the commencement of the bankruptcy case. [B.C. § 546(c)(1)(B)]

(1) Computing the Time Period

The seller's right to reclamation only applies to goods received by the debtor within 45 days of the bankruptcy case. Thus, it appears that the language in § 546(c) referencing a 45-day period for making a written demand for reclamation is superfluous. Except in a case in which Day 45 lands on the date of bankruptcy filing, the 45-day period will *always* expire after the filing of the bankruptcy case. Therefore, the seller always will have 20 days after the bankruptcy case has begun to make a written demand for reclamation. [5 Collier ¶ 546.04(2)(b)(iv)]

> **Example:** Debtor receives goods from Seller on April 1. Debtor files for relief under Chapter 7 on May 15. The Federal Rules of Bankruptcy Procedure provide that in counting days, the day triggering the event is not included. [Bankruptcy Rule 9006(a)(1)] April 1—the day that Debtor received the goods—is not included when counting the 45 days; thus, Day 45 is May 16. Because the 45-day period expires after the start of the bankruptcy case, Seller has 20 days to make a written demand for reclamation. [5 Collier ¶ 546.04(2)(b)(iv)]

b. Subject to Secured Creditor Interest

The seller's right to reclaim goods is subject to the prior rights of a creditor with a security interest in the goods or the proceeds of those goods. [B.C. § 546(c)(1)]

c. Seller Fails to Give Notice

If the seller of goods fails to provide the debtor with the required notice for reclamation, the seller still may qualify for an administrative expense claim under § 503(b)(9). [B.C. §§ 546(c)(2), 503(b)(9)]

d. Grain Farmers and United States Fishermen

The trustee's power to avoid (i) a transfer under the strong arm clause [B.C. § 544(a)], (ii) a statutory lien [B.C. § 545], (iii) a preference [B.C. § 547], or (iv) a post-petition transfer [B.C. § 549] is subject to any *statutory or common law right* of a grain farmer or a United States fisherman to reclaim grain or fish sold, in the *ordinary course* of the seller's business, to a grain storage facility or a fish processing facility, respectively, that is owned or operated by the debtor, if the debtor *received such goods while insolvent.* [B.C. § 546(d)]

(i) Written Demand

The grain farmer or U.S. fisherman must make a written demand for reclamation no later than *10 days* after the debtor received the grain or fish. [B.C. § 546(d)(1)]

(ii) Grant of Lien

The bankruptcy court may deny reclamation to a grain farmer or U.S. fisherman that has made a proper demand for reclamation only if the court grants the seller a lien securing her claim. [B.C. § 546(d)(2)]

7. Securities Safe Harbor, Repo Agreements, Swap Agreements

a. Securities Safe Harbor

The securities safe harbor is an *exception* to the trustee's avoiding powers. [B.C. § 546(e)] It provides that the trustee *cannot avoid* a transfer that is a *margin payment* or a *settlement payment* made by or to or for the benefit of a *commodity broker, forward contract merchant, stockbroker, financial institution, financial participant, or securities clearing agency.* The trustee also *cannot avoid a transfer* made by or to or for the benefit of any of the above-mentioned entities in connection with a *securities contract, commodities contract, or forward contract.* The exception applies to *pre-petition, not post-petition,* transfers. [B.C. § 546(e); *see* §§ 101, 741, and 761 for definitions.

There is an *exception to this exception.* The safe harbor *does not apply* to transfers made with *actual intent to hinder, delay, or defraud.* [B.C. § 548(a)(1)(A)]

Example: Bedford Downs (Bedford) and Valley View entered into a pre-petition agreement pursuant to which Valley View agreed to buy all of Bedford's stock for $55 million. Valley View arranged with Credit Suisse to finance the purchase of Bedford and Credit Suisse wired the purchase money to Citizens Bank of Pennsylvania, which had agreed to act as the third-party escrow agent for the transaction. Bedford's shareholders, including Merit Management (MM), deposited their stock certificates into escrow and at closing Citizens Bank disbursed the funds to Bedford's shareholders. MM received $16.5 million from the sale of its Bedford stock to Valley View. Valley View subsequently filed for relief under Chapter 11 and appointed FTI Consulting to serve as trustee of debtor's litigation trust. FTI filed suit against MM seeking to avoid the $16.5 million transfer as constructively fraudulent under § 548(a)(1)(B). MM argued that the safe harbor at § 546(e) precluded FTI from avoiding the transfer from Valley View to

MM. MM argued that the safe harbor applied to the transaction because the transfer was a settlement payment made by or to or for the benefit of a financial institution—both Credit Suisse and Citizen's Bank. The Supreme Court ruled against MM, holding that the "relevant transfer for purposes of the § 546(e) safe-harbor inquiry is the overarching transfer that the trustee seeks to avoid under one of the substantive avoidance provisions." The Court explained that the status of the banks as financial institutions was irrelevant because the focus of the § 546(e) inquiry is on the "overarching transfer," not its "component parts." Because neither Valley View nor MM qualified as financial institutions or any other § 546(e) covered entity, the safe harbor did not protect the transfer from avoidance by FTI. [**Merit Management Group, LP v. FTI Consulting, Inc.,** 138 S. Ct. 883 (2018)]

b. Repurchase Agreements

The trustee *cannot avoid* a *pre-petition* transfer made by or to or for the benefit of a *repo participant or financial institution* in connection with a *repurchase agreement.* [B.C. § 546(f); for definitions, *see* §§ 101(22) (financial institution), 101(46) (repo participant), 101(47) (repurchase agreement)] This *exception does not apply* to transfers made with *actual intent to hinder, delay, or defraud.* [B.C. § 548(a)(1)(A)]

c. Swap Agreements

The trustee *cannot avoid* a *pre-petition* transfer made by or to or for the benefit of a *swap participant or financial participant* under or in connection with any *swap agreement.* [B.C. § 546(g); for definitions, *see* §§ 101(22A) (financial participant), 101(53B) (swap agreement), 101(53C) (swap participant)] This *exception does not apply* to transfers made with *actual intent to hinder, delay, or defraud.* [B.C. § 548(a)(1)(A)]

d. Master Netting Agreement

The trustee *cannot avoid* a *pre-petition* transfer made by or to or for the benefit of a *master netting agreement participant* under or in connection with any *master netting agreement* or individual contract covered thereby. [B.C. § 546(j); for definitions, *see* §§ 101(38A) (master netting agreement), 101(38B) (master netting agreement participant)] This *exception does not apply* to transfers made with *actual intent to hinder, delay, or defraud.* [B.C. § 548(a)(1)(A)] The exception also *does not apply* to an individual contract covered by the master netting agreement if the trustee could otherwise avoid a transfer made under that individual contract. [B.C. § 546(j)]

8. Return of Goods

The trustee's power to avoid (i) a transfer under the strong arm clause [B.C. § 544(a)], (ii) a statutory lien [B.C. § 545], (iii) a preference [B.C. § 547], (iv) a post-petition transfer [B.C. § 549], or (v) a setoff [B.C. § 553] is subject to the right of a Chapter 11 debtor, under certain circumstances, to *return* pre-petition goods. A Chapter 11 debtor, with the creditor's consent and subject to the prior rights of a creditor with a security interest in the goods or the proceeds of such goods, may return goods shipped by the creditor before bankruptcy, and the *creditor may offset* the purchase price against any pre-petition claim. This action requires a motion by the trustee within *120 days* after the order for relief, notice and a hearing, and a determination by the court that a *return is in the estate's best interests*. [B.C. § 546(h)]

9. Warehouseman's Lien

BAPCPA added protection for certain liens by warehousemen. The trustee may not avoid a warehouseman's lien for *storage, transportation, or costs incidental to the storage and handling of goods,* notwithstanding the Code's provisions on avoidance of statutory liens under § 545(2) and (3). [B.C. §§ 546(i)(1), 545(2), (3)] Courts are to apply the prohibition against avoidance in a manner consistent with U.C.C. § 7–209 or similar state laws. [B.C. § 546(i)(2)] The Code does not define what constitutes storage, transportation, or costs incidental to storage and handling of goods. U.C.C. § 7–209, however, provides that the warehouseman's lien covers such storage and transportation costs as "demurrage and terminal charges, insurance [and] labor," and the Official Comments provide that the "lien is limited to the usual charges arising out of a storage transaction." [U.C.C. § 7–209(a), Official Comment 1; *see also* 5 Collier ¶ 546.10]

G. Transferee's Liability to Estate for Avoided Transfer

1. Automatic Preservation for Benefit of Estate

Any transfer that has been avoided or any lien that is void under Bankruptcy Code § 506(d) is automatically preserved for the estate's benefit. [B.C. § 551]

2. What Trustee May Recover

By avoiding a transfer, the trustee may recover *either the property transferred* or, if ordered by the court, *its value.* [B.C. § 550(a)]

3. From Whom Trustee May Recover

The trustee may recover the transferred property or its value from (i) the initial transferee, (ii) the entity for whose benefit the transfer was made, or (iii) any subsequent transferee of the initial transferee. [B.C. § 550(a)] While the trustee may sue any of these entities for recovery, she is entitled to only a *single satisfaction*. [B.C. § 550(d)] In other words, if trustee recovers transferred property from a subsequent transferee, she may *not* also recover the value of that property from the initial transferee.

a. Initial Transferee

Unlike a secondary or other subsequent transferee, the initial person to whom the debtor makes a transfer cannot defend against the trustee's recovery action by claiming good faith or lack of knowledge of the voidability of the transaction. Thus, whether an entity is an initial transferee is important to determining the party from whom the trustee may recover the property transferred in the avoided transaction.

(i) Conduit Test

An entity that receives a transfer directly from the debtor is an *initial transferee.* Courts, however, have carved out an exception for initial transferees "who are 'mere conduits' with no real control" over the transferred funds. Under the *"control" or "conduit" test,* an entity is an initial transferee "only if [it] exercise[s] legal control over the assets received, such that [it] [has] the right to use the assets for [its] own purposes, and not if [it] merely served as a conduit for assets that were under the actual control of the debtor-transferor or the real initial transferee." [**Andreini & Co. v. Pony Express Delivery Services,** 440 F.3d 1296 (11th Cir. 2006); *see also* **Martinez v. Hutton (*In re* Harwell),** 628 F.3d 1312 (11th Cir. 2010) (in addition to showing transferee's lack of control over the assets received also requiring good faith on the part of that transferee in a fraudulent conveyance case)] For example, banks and insurance brokers are fiduciaries or agents for the debtor and, thus, may have limited control over the funds transferred to them. [*See* **Andreini & Co.,** *supra*]

Example: Insurance Broker ("Broker") arranged insurance coverage for its clients and billed those clients for the premiums due under the relevant insurance policies. Under state law, premium payments had to be deposited into a client trust account with Broker. When Broker received premiums, it sent those payments on to the insurance company. Debtor wrote a check to Broker's client trust account to cover premiums due for Debtor's workers' compensation insurance. Broker then transferred the premium payments to the insurance company, because those premiums either were overdue or shortly due. Unbeknownst to Broker, Debtor was in serious financial trouble, and its premium check bounced. About three weeks later, Debtor directly wired the amount due on the bounced check to Broker's client trust account. Two days later, Debtor filed for relief under Chapter 11. Both the bankruptcy and district courts concluded that Broker was an initial transferee from whom the trustee could recover the funds wired by Debtor into Broker's client trust account. The Eleventh Circuit, however, reversed after concluding that Broker was *not* an initial transferee. The court provided several reasons for its conclusion. First, Broker never intended to become a creditor of Debtor; instead, it was simply Broker's practice to immediately forward premium payments received in the client trust account. Second, Broker did not know of Debtor's financial problems and Debtor had never before sent Broker an insufficient funds check. Third, Debtor's check to make good on the earlier bounced check was transferred directly into Broker's client trust account. Under state law, Broker had limited control over the account. Broker was a fiduciary of the trust account monies, which could be used only to pay clients' insurance premiums. Debtor's transfer to Broker's client trust account was a preference and avoidable; however, the trustee could not recover the money from Broker as an initial transferee under § 550(a)(1). [**Andreini & Co.,** *supra*]

b. Exception for Good Faith Future Transferees

The trustee may not recover from a ***subsequent transferee*** who (i) did not know that the transfer was voidable, (ii) took the transfer in *good faith,* and (iii) *gave value* in exchange. A subsequent transferee is an entity in the chain of transfer from the initial transferee. A subsequent transferee who gives value, takes in good faith, and lacked knowledge of the voidability of the transfer *shelters* all subsequent *good faith transferees.* [B.C. § 550(b)]

(i) Value

For purposes of this exception, value includes the "satisfaction or securing of a present or antecedent debt." [B.C. § 550(b)(1)]

Example: Debtor transfers a painting to Allen, the initial transferee. Allen, in turn, sells the painting to Barbara, who pays value, in good faith, and without knowing that the transfer to Allen was voidable. Barbara, in turn, gives the painting to Carl as a gift. Carl takes the painting in good faith. Carl has not paid value, but because Barbara "shelters" Carl, the trustee may not recover the painting or its value from Carl.

c. Insiders and Non-Insiders

With the Bankruptcy Reform Act of 1994, Congress provided protection from trustee recovery actions to non-insiders in *preference cases* involving insiders. Thus, if a trustee avoids a preference made between 90 days and one year prior to bankruptcy for the benefit of a creditor that is an insider, the trustee *may not recover* the preferential transfer from a transferee that is not an insider. [B.C. §§ 547, 550(c)] With BAPCPA, Congress expanded the protection for non-insiders in preference actions involving insiders. The Code now provides that if the trustee avoids a preferential transfer made to a non-insider between 90 days and one year prior to bankruptcy for the benefit of a creditor that is an insider, the transfer is *avoided only as to the insider*, not the non-insider. [B.C. § 547(i)]

Example: On January 1, Debtor Corporation, while insolvent, paid $100,000 to Bank in full satisfaction of an unsecured antecedent loan, which Officer of Debtor Corporation had guaranteed. Still insolvent on June 1, Debtor Corporation filed a voluntary bankruptcy petition. The trustee can *avoid* the January 1 transfer as a preference. Even though the transfer occurred more than 90 days before bankruptcy, it benefitted Officer, an insider-guarantor, and was made within one year before the bankruptcy petition was filed. [B.C. § 547(b)(4)(B)] The transfer is considered avoided *only* as to Officer, not as to Bank, and the trustee cannot *recover* the $100,000 from Bank, a non-insider; any recovery must come from Officer, the insider-guarantor. [B.C. §§ 547(i), 550(c); *see* H.R. Rep. No. 109–31, at 144 (2005) (noting that the 1994 amendment to § 550 coupled with "the perfecting amendment to section 547 protect the noninsider from the avoiding powers of the trustee exercised with respect to transfers made during the 90-day to one year pre-filing period")]

4. Good Faith Transferee's Lien

If the trustee recovers from a good faith transferee under § 550(a), the transferee receives a *lien on the property recovered,* for the purpose of securing the cost of *the lesser* of:

a. the cost of any *improvements* she made after the transfer *minus* any profits she received from the property due to those improvements [B.C. § 550(e)(1)(A)]; or

b. the amount by which such improvements increased the property's value. [B.C. § 550(e)(1)(B)]

a. What Is an Improvement?

Improvements include any of the following:

(i) *physical additions* or changes to the property;

(ii) property *repairs;*

(iii) *payment of taxes* on the property;

(iv) *payment of any debt secured by a lien that is superior or equal* to the rights of the trustee; and

(v) *preservation of the property.* [B.C. § 550(e)(2)]

Example: Dan and Ben are long-time friends. A year ago, Ben loaned Dan, who was in financial trouble, $25,000. Dan recently filed for relief under Chapter 7. About two months prior to filing for bankruptcy, Dan gave Ben an old camper worth about $20,000 as repayment for the loan. Ben has spent about $5,000 refurbishing the camper and has had offers to buy it for $30,000. The trustee will be able to avoid the transfer of the camper to Ben as a preference under § 547(b). In addition, the trustee can recover the property from Ben, who is an initial transferee. So long as Ben is a good faith transferee, however, he will have a lien on the camper in the amount of $5,000, which is the lesser of the cost of improvements and the $10,000 increase in value of the camper due to Ben's improvements.

5. Statute of Limitations

The trustee must bring any action to recover transferred property or its value under § 550 *before the earlier* of (i) *one year* after the corresponding transfer was avoided, or (ii) the time the case *is closed or dismissed.* [B.C. § 550(f)]

H. Post-Petition Effect of Security Interest

1. General Rule for After-Acquired Property Clauses

Section 552 of the Bankruptcy Code is not really an avoidance provision. Nonetheless, it operates in a similar fashion by preventing a pre-petition lien from attaching to property acquired post-petition and thereby partially avoiding that lien. To understand how § 552 functions, you need to understand how an after-acquired property clause works. An *after-acquired property clause* is a clause in the parties' security agreement that creates a floating lien such that the security interest granted by the debtor to the creditor extends to collateral acquired by the debtor *after* signing the security agreement. [U.C.C. § 9–204] For example, if Acme signs a security agreement that grants a security interest to Bank Two in all of Acme's inventory, whether now owned or hereafter acquired, Bank Two's lien attaches to each new acquisition of inventory by Acme. With certain exceptions, however, § 552 of the Bankruptcy Code stops that lien from floating so that the creditor's security interest does not attach to *property acquired after* the filing of the bankruptcy case. [B.C. § 552(a)]

Note: Section 552 applies only to *consensual liens* and, thus, does not apply to federal tax liens, which are statutory. [B.C. § 101(50), (51); *In re* **Wampler,** 345 B.R. 730 (Bankr. D. Kan. 2006)]

2. Exception for Certain Post-Petition Proceeds

If the pre-petition security agreement provides that the security interest attaches not only to collateral that the debtor *acquired prior to bankruptcy* but also to the proceeds, profits, products, or offspring of such collateral, then the creditor's security interest attaches to any *traceable post-petition proceeds, products, offspring, or profits* of the collateral acquired pre-petition. [B.C. § 552(b)(1)]

Note: The exception does *not* apply to proceeds, products, offspring, or profits of collateral acquired post-petition.

Example: Debtor is a small business. Two years ago, Debtor obtained a working capital loan from Bank. Debtor granted Bank a security interest in Debtor's inventory and accounts receivable, whether "now owned or hereafter acquired." Bank properly perfected its interest. Debtor recently filed for relief under Chapter 11. After filing for bankruptcy, Debtor bought new inventory using cash from its corporate account. The cash is traceable to sales of inventory acquired pre-petition. Therefore, Bank's security interest attaches to the new inventory, because the post-petition inventory is proceeds of cash, which, in turn, were proceeds of pre-petition collateral on which the Bank has a valid security interest. [B.C. § 552(b)(1); U.C.C. § 9–315(d)(3)]

a. Note: Judicial Discretion Allowed

The court has authority not to apply this exception, depending on the equities of the case. Notice and a hearing are required. [B.C. § 552(b)(1)]

Example: Secured Creditor has a security interest in raw materials valued at $1 million. Debtor invests $100,000 and turns those raw materials into product that Debtor sells for $1.5 million. Secured Creditor claims that it has a security interest in those sale proceeds under § 552(b). The bankruptcy court, however, may decide that to add the sale proceeds to the secured creditor's collateral would be inequitable because "the general creditors were in effect responsible for much or all of the increase in the value of the proceeds over the original collateral." [*See* **J. Catton Farms v. First National Bank of Chicago,** 779 F.2d 1242 (7th Cir. 1985) (example is drawn from court's opinion)]

3. Exception for Certain Post-Petition Rents and Room Revenues

If a pre-petition security agreement extends to amounts paid as rent or for charges, fees, accounts, or other payments for hotel, motel, or similar lodgings, then the security interest extends to these post-petition rents, charges, fees, accounts or other payments. As with the exception for proceeds, products, offspring, and profits, the court, after notice and a hearing, may decide not to apply this exception based on the equities of the case. [B.C. § 552(b)(2)]

I.   Creditor's Right of Setoff

1. Right of Setoff

A creditor entitled to a right of setoff under state law may set off a debt he owes to the debtor against a claim he holds against the debtor, if *both the debt and the claim are mutual and arose prior to the filing of the bankruptcy case.* [B.C. § 553(a)] The Bankruptcy Code does not create a right of setoff; it merely preserves whatever right otherwise exists. [*See* **Citizens Bank v. Strumpf,** 516 U.S. 16 (1995)] The Bankruptcy Code does not define "mutual debt." The courts, however, apply a three-prong test for mutuality. The debts must be between the *same parties* who stand in the *same capacity,* and the debts must be in the *same right.* [*See, e.g.,* **Faasoa v. Army & Air Force Exchange Serv. (*In re* Faasoa),** 576 B.R. 631 (Bankr. S.D. Cal. 2017)]

a.   Same Parties

(i)   The same party requirement means that *triangular setoffs* generally are not allowed.

Example: Debtor Steel Corporation owes $100,000 to Outland, Inc. for steel that Steel had purchased from Outland prior to Steel's filing for relief under Chapter 11. Also prior to bankruptcy, Steel had sold $115,000 of finished product to Riley Company, a wholly owned subsidiary of Outland. Outland may not set off Riley's $115,000 debt to Steel against Outland's $100,000 claim against the debtor Steel. Outland and Riley are separate corporate entities. Thus, Steel's debt to Outland and Riley's debt to Steel are not mutual. [B.C. § 553(a); *see In re* **Berger Steel Co.,** 327 F.2d 401 (7th Cir. 1964) (decided under Bankruptcy Act of 1898)]

(ii)   The federal government is considered a *unitary creditor.* As a result, one federal agency may offset a debt that it owes to the debtor against a debt that the debtor owes to another federal agency. Some courts have applied this *unitary creditor* theory not only to the federal government but also to state governments. [*See, e.g.,* **Cottle v. Arizona Corp. Comm'n (*In re* Cottle),** 2016 WL 6081030 (B.A.P. 9th Cir. 2016) (holding that the bankruptcy court had not erred in treating Arizona Corporation Commission and State of Arizona as a unitary creditor for purposes of setoff under § 553)]

b. Same Capacity

The *same capacity* requirement often arises in the context of *fiduciary relationships.* Money received by a trustee in trust or by a person acting in a fiduciary capacity may not be used to set off an obligation owed by the debtor to the trustee or fiduciary in her *individual* capacity.

e.g. **Example:** David owes Fiona $500 in his individual capacity. Fiona, as trustee for a trust, owes David $100. Fiona may not setoff the $100 against the debt David owes to her. The debts are not mutual, because Fiona's obligation arises in her capacity as trustee, while David's obligation arises in his individual capacity. [5 Collier ¶ 553.03(3)(c)]

Note: While exceptions do exist, the general rule is that a bank and a person holding a general deposit account at the bank stand in the position of debtor and creditor. [**Libby v. Hopkins,** 104 U.S. 303 (1881)] Thus, the bank and depositor stand in the same capacity, and setoff is possible.

c. Same Right

Setoff is not allowed if the debt is not in the *same right.* The issue arises in cases involving joint debts.

e.g. **Example:** Amy and Ben are jointly liable on a $1,200 debt to Delilah, who has filed for relief under Chapter 7. Delilah owes an unrelated debt of $1,200 to Ben and his sister Clara. Ben may not setoff his debt to Delilah in her Chapter 7 case against his and his sister's joint claim against Delilah. The debts are not mutual. [*See, e.g.,* **Gray v. Rollo,** 85 U.S. 629 (1873)]

2. Automatic Stay

Once a bankruptcy petition has been filed, the automatic stay enjoins the post-petition setoff of a pre-petition debt owed to the debtor against a creditor's claim. [B.C. § 362(a)(7)] Therefore, a creditor must obtain *relief from the stay* before a setoff may be exercised.

a. Post-Petition Administrative Freeze of Debtor's Bank Account

The United States Supreme Court has held that a bank's *temporary hold* on a debtor's deposit account up to the amount allegedly subject to setoff, while the bank seeks relief from the automatic stay and the court's determination of its right to a setoff, does not violate the automatic stay. A temporary administrative freeze, pending a judicial determination of the bank's motion to lift the stay *does not constitute a setoff.* [**Citizens Bank v. Strumpf,** *supra*] It is a permissible response to the bank's dilemma of protecting its right of setoff, if one exists, from the debtor's dissipation of the cash in his deposit account.

Note: Based on the facts in *Strumpf,* it appears that the creditor should *promptly request relief from the automatic stay* and a determination of its right of setoff.

3. Secured Status of Claim Subject to Setoff

A creditor's allowed claim that is subject to setoff is a *secured claim* to the extent of the amount subject to setoff. [B.C. § 506(a)] Therefore, a creditor holding such a claim is entitled to *adequate protection,* unless the court lifts the automatic stay and permits the creditor to exercise her right of setoff. [B.C. § 362(d)(1)]

4. Exceptions to Right of Setoff

a. Disallowed Claim

There is no right of setoff to the extent that the court has disallowed the creditor's claim against the debtor. [B.C. § 553(a)(1)]

b. Claim Transferred by Non-Debtor Party

A creditor is not entitled to setoff if the claim on which the creditor bases its right to setoff was transferred to the creditor by *an entity other than the debtor after the filing* of the bankruptcy petition *or* within *90 days prior* to the bankruptcy petition at a time when the debtor was *insolvent.* [B.C. § 553(a)(2)]

Note: The debtor is presumed to be insolvent during the 90 days immediately preceding bankruptcy. [B.C. § 553(c)]

Example: Digby, Inc. recently filed for relief under Chapter 11. Digby operates a small business that has been in financial trouble for the past six months. At the time of bankruptcy filing, Local Bank held $30,000 of Digby's funds in a general account. Prior to bankruptcy, Tito Company sold goods worth $30,000 to Digby on unsecured credit. When Tito was unable to collect from Digby, Tito sold its $30,000 claim to Local Bank for $25,000 in the month prior to Digby's bankruptcy filing. Local Bank cannot setoff its $30,000 debt against the $25,000 claim against Digby, because Tito transferred the claim to Local Bank during the 90 days prior to the bankruptcy filing while Digby was presumed to be insolvent.

c. Exceptions to the Exception

With the enactment of BAPCPA, Congress carved out a number of exceptions to the rule that claims transferred by a non-debtor party within 90 days of the bankruptcy filing cannot serve as the basis for setoff. These exceptions involve sophisticated financial arrangements, such as swaps, master netting agreements, repo agreements, and commodities and forward contracts. [B.C. §§ 553(a)(2), 362(b)(6), 362(b)(7), 362(b)(17), 362(b)(27), 555, 556, 559, 560 & 561] A transaction falling into one of these enumerated exceptions *does not run afoul* of the prohibition against setoff for traded claims.

d. Debt Created for Purpose of Setoff

The creditor does not have a right of setoff if she incurred the debt owed to the debtor *within 90 days prior* to the bankruptcy petition, while the debtor was *insolvent*, for the *purpose* of creating a right of setoff. [B.C. § 553(a)(3)]

Note: Congress carved out the same exceptions under § 553(a)(3) that exist for traded claims under § 553(a)(2).

Example: Bank loaned Debtor, a small business, $200,000 on an unsecured basis. Debtor keeps its corporate account at Bank. Bank realizes that Debtor is in financial difficulty. One month before Debtor files for bankruptcy, Bank requires Debtor to keep at least 10% of its outstanding loan balance in its corporate account at the Bank. Debtor files for relief under Chapter 11, at which time Debtor has $50,000 in its corporate account. Bank may set off only $30,000 of the $50,000 in Debtor's account. Bank's requirement that Debtor maintain at least a $20,000 balance (10% of $200,000 loan) runs afoul of § 553(a)(3), because Bank required the balance within 90 days of bankruptcy while Debtor was insolvent for the purpose of creating a right of setoff.

e. Creditor's Improved Position Due to Pre-Bankruptcy Setoff

With certain exceptions, the trustee may avoid and recover for the estate a setoff made by a creditor within 90 days prior to the filing of the petition *to the extent that* the creditor (usually a bank) has improved its position. [B.C. § 553(b)(1)]

(i) Rationale

In the run-up to bankruptcy, debtors often are strapped for cash. The purpose of this exception is to prevent lenders, e.g., a bank, from making the debtor's financial situation worse by using funds that the debtor maintains at the bank to set off debts that the debtor owes to the lender.

(ii) Amount Recoverable

The amount that the trustee may recover is based on a *comparison* of the *insufficiency* on the date of setoff *with* the insufficiency on the *later of two dates: 90 days* before bankruptcy *or* the *first day during the 90 days* when there is an insufficiency. [B.C. § 553(b)(1)] If the insufficiency on the date of setoff *is less than* the insufficiency on the later of these two dates, then the trustee can recover the difference.

(1) "Insufficiency" Defined

The Code defines "insufficiency" as the amount by which the creditor's claim against the debtor *exceeds* the debtor's claim against the creditor. In other words, you end up with an insufficiency when the debtor owes more to the creditor than the creditor owes to the debtor. [B.C. § 553(b)(2)]

e.g. **Example:** Debtor owed Bank $100,000 on an unsecured loan. On the 90th day before the filing of Debtor's bankruptcy petition, Debtor's checking account with Bank had a balance of $100,000. At this point, there is no insufficiency—the Debtor owes Bank $100,000, and Bank owes Debtor $100,000. This balance remained unchanged until the 60th day before bankruptcy, when the account balance fell to $60,000. This was the first date on which an insufficiency existed. (The debtor owes the Bank $40,000 more than the Bank owes Debtor. Debtor owes $100,000 on the loan, but Bank owes Debtor only the $60,000 balance in Debtor's account.) On the 50th day before bankruptcy, the account balance was $50,000, but on the 40th day before bankruptcy it was $70,000, at which time Bank set off $70,000 against the unpaid loan. The amount recoverable by the trustee is $10,000. On the date of setoff, the insufficiency was $30,000; Debtor owed Bank $100,000 *minus* the $70,000 in the account that Bank owed Debtor. Day 60 prior to bankruptcy was the first date within the 90 days that there was an insufficiency; the amount of that insufficiency was $40,000. Thus, the trustee recovers $10,000—the difference between $40,000 (first insufficiency within 90 days) and $30,000 (date of setoff). Bottom line: Within the 90 days prior to bankruptcy, the bank improved its position by $10,000. [B.C. § 553(b)(1); *see* examples at 5 Collier ¶ 553.09(2)(b)]

(iii) Debtor May Be Solvent

Section 553(b)(1) applies even if the debtor is solvent.

(iv) Exceptions

The trustee's avoidance and recovery powers under § 553(b) *do not apply* to setoff rights arising from:

(1) certain *sophisticated financial transactions,* e.g., swaps, repo agreements [B.C. §§ 362(b)(6), (7), (17) & (27); 555, 556, 559, 560 & 561];

(2) the *rejection of unexpired leases of real property* in which the *debtor is the lessor* [B.C. § 365(h)];

(3) the *rejection* of a debtor's *executory contract* for the *sale of real property* or the sale of a *timeshare interest* [B.C. § 365(i)]; or

(4) the *return of goods* that a creditor had *shipped pre-petition* to the debtor in a Chapter 11 case. [B.C. § 546(h)]

f.   Creditor's Bad Faith Conduct

Setoffs are permissive, not mandatory, and lie within the court's equitable discretion. [**Faasoa v. Army & Air Force Exchange Service (*In re* Faasoa),** 576 B.R. 631 (Bankr. S.D. Cal. 2017)] Therefore, a court may deny setoff if the creditor's conduct is inequitable or in bad faith. [**Regal Financial Bank v. Heaton (*In re* Heaton),** 2011 WL 1980936 (Bankr. N.D. Cal. 2011) (disallowing Bank to set off attorney fees owed to debtors, resulting from loss in adversary proceeding, against debtors' pre-petition debt not only because of lack of mutuality but also because setoff would be inequitable)]

5. Distinguish Recoupment

It is important that you are able to distinguish setoff from the equitable doctrine of recoupment. It is not always easy and courts, at times, "use the terms 'setoff' and 'recoupment' interchangeably or indiscriminately." [5 Collier ¶ 553.10] The *setoff* of mutual debts between two parties involves independent obligations that usually are derived from *separate transactions. Recoupment*, on the other hand, is used by a creditor to reduce its liability to the debtor because of a right that the creditor has arising out of the *same transaction* or occurrence. Recoupment is basically a defense, e.g., overpayment, to the debtor's claim and not a mutual obligation. The distinction is important because neither the *automatic stay nor § 553's limitations* on setoffs *apply to recoupments*. [**Malinowski v. New York State DOL (*In re* Malinowski),** 156 F.3d 131 (2d Cir. 1998) (explaining that recoupment "comes into bankruptcy law through the common law, rather than statute . . . and is not subject to the limitations of section 553 or the automatic stay); *see also* **United States v. Johnson (*In re* Johnson),** 586 B.R. 449 (N.D. Ill. 2018) (noting that a "significant body of authority holds that recoupment does not violate the automatic stay")]

e.g. **Example:** Debtor, a nursing home, filed for relief under Chapter 11. Debtor participated in the Medicare program and was overpaid approximately $370,000 by Medicare. During the bankruptcy case, Debtor billed Medicare and Medicare adjusted its reimbursements to Debtor to account for the $370,000 overpayment. The court concluded that the contractual relationship between Debtor and Medicare constituted a single, ongoing transaction. Thus, Medicare's adjustment for the overpayments constituted recoupment, not setoff. Moreover, § 362(a)(7) did not apply, because Medicare's efforts to recover the overpayments constituted a recoupment, rather than a setoff. [**Slater Health Center, Inc. v. United States (*In re* Slater),** 398 F.3d 98 (1st Cir. 2005)]

Chapter Seven

Claims of Creditors

Chapter Approach

This Chapter covers claims. The Bankruptcy Code *broadly defines the term "claim"* to include a right to payment regardless of whether the creditor's claim is unliquidated, contingent, or subject to dispute. The Chapter begins with the rules on filing a *proof of claim* or *interest*—who may file, the time period for filing, and what happens if a proof of claim or interest is filed late. Creditors file proofs of claims while equity holders, for example, file proofs of interest.

In order for a creditor or interest holder to participate in any distribution made from the bankruptcy estate, however, the claim or interest must be *allowed.* The general rule is that absent objection, any proof of claim or interest that is filed is deemed allowed. There are *nine categories* of claims that the Code disallows or limits. For example, the Code limits the recovery by a lessor on a claim for termination of a lease of real property.

You must understand the different types of creditors, because they have different rights under the Code. In Chapter 7, for example, there is a payment hierarchy: secured creditors, unsecured priority creditors, and general unsecured creditors.

A *secured creditor* has a lien on some or all of the debtor's property. Some secured creditors are *oversecured.* An *oversecured creditor* is a creditor with a lien on property worth *more* than the debt owed to that creditor. It is important to distinguish between the *oversecured creditor* and the *secured creditor* whose debt *equals* the value of the property securing the debt. Oversecured creditors are entitled to interest—up to the value of the collateral—in the period between filing of the petition and confirmation of the plan. An *undersecured creditor,* on the other hand, holds a debt in *excess* of the value of the collateral securing that debt. That means, with a few exceptions described in this Chapter, that the creditor's claim is split between a secured claim (up to collateral value) and an unsecured claim. *Bifurcation* of the undersecured creditor's claim means that in a Chapter 11 case, for example, the undersecured creditor has two votes on the plan—for the secured creditor class to which it belongs and as part of the class of general unsecured creditors.

There are two types of *unsecured creditors—priority unsecured* and *general unsecured.* As the name suggests, *priority creditors* have priority of payment over the class of general unsecured creditors. There are *ten tiers* of priority creditors. Some priority classes, e.g., certain pre-petition wage claims, have monetary caps. Pay attention to these caps when answering an exam question. Any amount owed in *excess of the cap* is a general unsecured claim.

With a few exceptions, priority creditors *within a tier* share equally in any distribution from the bankruptcy estate. The Code, however, creates a *hierarchy* of priority creditors. *Administrative expense claims* and *tax claims,* both of which this Chapter discusses in some detail, have *second and eighth priority*, respectively. Why does that matter? In a *Chapter 7 case*, for example, if estate funds are exhausted after paying the administrative expense creditors, then no other priority creditor on the payment ladder below administrative expense claims will receive a distribution in the bankruptcy case. Not receiving a distribution in a Chapter 7 case, however, is not the end of the story for some priority creditors because under the Code there is some overlap between *priority status* and *nondischargeability.* For example, a tax claim that qualifies for *priority treatment* under § 507(a)(8) also is *nondischargeable* under § 523(a)(1). In *Chapters 11, 12, and 13*, the Code requires for confirmation that the plan provide particular treatment for the various types of priority creditors.

General unsecured creditors may receive no distribution in bankruptcy. Many Chapter 7 cases are *no asset,* which means that there is no dividend to pay to general unsecured creditors.

This Chapter wraps up with the Code's rules on *subrogation under § 509* and *subordination under § 510.* Remember that an entity must choose between a claim for reimbursement or contribution, on the one hand, and a claim for subrogation to the rights of the principal creditor, on the other. Finally, keep in mind that the bankruptcy court in cases involving inequitable conduct by a claimant may *equitably subordinate* all or part of an allowed claim or interest to another allowed claim or interest, or order that any lien securing the subordinated claim be transferred to the bankruptcy estate.

A. Filing Proofs of Claims

1. Claim

Congress intended the "broadest possible definition" of the word "claim" to include "all legal obligations of the debtor, no matter how remote or contingent" so as to provide "the broadest possible relief in the bankruptcy court." [H.R. Rep. No. 95–595, at 309 (1977)] Thus, the Code defines "claim," in part, as a *"right to payment,* whether or not such right is reduced to judgment, liquidated, unliquidated, fixed, contingent, matured, unmatured, disputed, undisputed, legal, equitable, secured, or unsecured." [B.C. § 101(5)(A)]

e.g. **Example:** Husband and Wife were in divorce proceedings when Husband filed for relief under Chapter 7. Wife timely filed a proof of claim for approximately $578,000 against Husband's estate based on an estimate of her expected share of the marital assets. Husband argued that Wife's interest in equitably dividing the marital property in Husband's bankruptcy estate was not a "claim," because the state court had not entered a final divorce decree and under state law a spouse's right to share in marital property through equitable distribution arises upon entry of the divorce judgment. The court found that even though there was no final divorce judgment when Husband filed for bankruptcy, Wife's interest, though "unliquidated and contingent on a final decree apportioning marital property, perhaps unmatured, and likely disputed" constituted a claim under § 101(5). Noting the "expansive definition" of "claim" in the Bankruptcy Code, the court distinguished between when a claim *accrues* and when a claim *exists.* While Wife's right to payment was contingent on entry of a final divorce decree, that right to payment *existed* at the time of bankruptcy filing; therefore, she had a claim in Husband's bankruptcy case. [*In re* **Ruitenberg,** 745 F.3d 647 (3d Cir. 2014)]

The second half of the Code's definition of the word "claim" is a *"right to an equitable remedy* for breach of performance if such breach gives rise to a right to payment, whether or not such right to an equitable remedy is reduced to judgment, fixed, contingent, matured, unmatured, disputed, undisputed, secured, or unsecured." [B.C. § 101(5)(B)]

e.g. **Example:** Prior to bankruptcy, Debtor Kovacs signed a stipulation and judgment entry settling a lawsuit by the State of Ohio against him and other companies, including Chem-Dyne, the firm for which he was CEO, for violation of state environmental laws related to an industrial and hazardous waste site that they operated ("Chem-Dyne site"). The stipulation enjoined Kovacs, Chem-Dyne, and other firms (the "defendants") from further polluting the air and public waters, forbade them from bringing more industrial waste onto the Chem-Dyne site, required them to remove certain wastes from the Chem-Dyne site, and ordered them to pay the State of Ohio $75,000 for injury to wildlife. When the defendants failed to abide by these obligations, the State had a receiver appointed to take possession of all the defendants' assets and to implement the judgment entry by cleaning up the Chem-Dyne site. Before the receiver completed his tasks, Kovacs filed for bankruptcy. The State of Ohio argued that the obligation to clean up the Chem-Dyne site was not a debt and, therefore, not discharged in Kovacs' bankruptcy case. The Supreme Court rejected this argument. The Court explained that the state court appointment of a receiver "dispossessed Kovacs, removed his authority over the site, and divested him of assets that might have been used by him to clean up the property." In other words, after the receiver's appointment, the "only performance sought from Kovacs was the payment of money." What the State of Ohio sought from Kovacs was *not* enforcement of the clean-up order but rather money to pay for the receiver undertaking that clean-up obligation Thus, the Supreme Court affirmed the decision of the Court of Appeals, which had concluded "that the cleanup order had been converted into an obligation to pay money, an obligation that was dischargeable in bankruptcy." The Court made clear, however, that its decision did *not* mean that the injunction against further pollution or bringing of hazardous waste onto the Chem-Dyne site was dischargeable in bankruptcy. [**Ohio v. Kovacs,** 469 U.S. 274 (1985)]

Note: "Courts have disagreed about whether injunctions requiring a debtor to clean up contaminated property constitute 'claims.' So long as a monetary payment is not being sought, or monetary payment is viewed as a 'suboptimal' remedy for the creditor, a growing number of courts will not classify a request for injunctive relief as a claim." [2 Collier ¶ 101.05(5)]

a. Covenant Not to Compete

While the courts are split on whether an equitable remedy for breach of a covenant not to compete constitutes a claim, the *majority of courts* have held that the right to equitable relief for breach of such covenants is *not a claim* for purposes of § 101(5). Some courts have relied on the Supreme Court's reasoning in *Kovacs* that complying with an injunction does not require the expenditure of money. Other courts have concluded that because injunctive relief is granted when the remedy at law is inadequate no alternative right to payment exists, as required by § 101(5)(B). [*In re* **Lafemina,** 2017 WL 4404254 (Bankr. E.D. N.Y. 2017) (discussing approaches)] If neither state law nor the parties' agreement provides for a right to payment as an alternative to injunctive relief, then a creditor's right to equitable relief for breach of a covenant not to compete does not constitute a claim and, therefore, is not dischargeable in bankruptcy. [*See In re* **Hurvitz,** 554 B.R. 35 (Bankr. D. Mass. 2016)]

b. Claims Against Property

The phrase "claim against the debtor" includes a claim against property of the debtor. [B.C. § 102(2)]

c. Broad Interpretation of "Claim"

As the Supreme Court has made clear in several decisions, "Congress intended . . . to adopt the broadest available definition of 'claim.' " [**Johnson v. Home State Bank,** 501 U.S. 78 (1991); *see* **Pennsylvania Dep't of Public Welfare v. Davenport,** 495 U.S. 552 (1990) ("Congress chose expansive language" when defining the term "claim"); **Ohio v. Kovacs,** 469 U.S. 274 (1985) ("Congress desired a broad definition of a 'claim' ")] Recognizing this intent to give "claim" an expansive definition in the bankruptcy context, a majority of courts have held that pre-petition claims may include causes of action arising from pre-bankruptcy conduct and pre-petition legal relationships, even if the cause of action under state or other applicable nonbankruptcy law did not accrue until after the petition was filed. [*In re* **Johns-Manville Corp.,** 57 B.R. 680 (Bankr. S.D. N.Y. 1986)]

(i) When a Claim Arises

The courts have devised *three tests* for when a *claim arises.* The minority position is the *accrued state law claim test,* also known as the *right to payment test.* Under this test, " 'a 'claim' does not arise in bankruptcy until a cause of action has accrued under nonbankruptcy law.' " [*In re* **Cleveland,** 349 B.R. 522 (Bankr. E.D. Tenn.

2006)] This test has been "widely criticized as inconsistent with the broad definition of 'claim' intended by Congress." [*In re* **Parks,** 281 B.R. 899 (Bankr. E.D. Mich. 2002)]

A claim arises under the ***debtor's conduct test*** when the conduct of the debtor occurs, even if the injury only manifests itself later. The following two examples are cases in which the court followed the debtor's conduct test.

Example: Victim was a user of an intrauterine device ("IUD") manufactured and sold by Debtor Corporation. The device caused serious bodily harm to Victim before Debtor Corporation filed a Chapter 11 petition, although Victim did not discover the cause of her injury until shortly after the bankruptcy case was filed. Victim has a pre-petition claim that arose "when the acts giving rise to the alleged liability were performed." [*In re* **A.H. Robins Co.,** 63 B.R. 986 (Bankr. E.D. Va. 1986), *aff'd,* 839 F.2d 198 (4th Cir. 1988)]

Example: Debtors, who operated a joint dental practice, filed for relief under Chapter 7. Patient received dental treatment from both Debtors prior to bankruptcy. After the bankruptcy filing, Patient experienced serious problems with the dental work and filed suit in state court against Debtors alleging negligent treatment. Debtors moved for sanctions for violation of the automatic stay, so Patient filed an adversary proceeding in the bankruptcy court seeking a declaration that her claim arose post-petition upon discovery of her injuries. The bankruptcy court held that Patient's claim arose at the time of Debtors' pre-petition conduct. Thus, the automatic stay prohibited her state court action against Debtors. [**Roach v. Edge (***In re* **Edge),** 60 B.R. 690 (Bankr. M.D. Tenn. 1986)]

The third approach is the ***fairly contemplated*** or ***pre-petition relationship test.*** This test "looks at whether there was a prepetition relationship between the debtor and the creditor such that a possible claim is within the fair contemplation of the creditor at the time the petition is filed." [*In re* **Parks,** *supra*]

Example: Married Couple entered into a contract with Vision Construction to renovate their home. Parks owned Vision. Married Couple obtained a loan from Bank, which purchased title insurance from Devon Title. The loan required that Vision provide Devon Title with lien waivers. Parks, on behalf of Vision, certified to Devon Title that no money was owed to subcontractors when there were subcontractors that had not been paid. These subcontractors placed liens on Married Couple's home. Parks subsequently filed for relief under Chapter 7 and received a discharge. After Parks received his discharge, Married Couple sued Devon Title, among others, and Devon Title filed a third-party complaint against various parties, including Parks. Parks claimed that the third-party complaint violated the discharge injunction. Devon Title argued that its complaint did not violate the discharge injunction because any claim it had did not arise until the post-discharge litigation by Married Couple. Devon Title contended its claim was not a pre-petition claim and, therefore, was not discharged in Parks' bankruptcy case. The bankruptcy court ruled against Devon Title. The court explained that it "was within the fair contemplation of Devon Title before [Parks'] bankruptcy was filed" that it might have a claim against Parks. Devon Title had a pre-petition relationship with Parks and "was in a position to ascertain whether the representations made by Parks were accurate." The court noted that Devon Title could have confirmed that there were no unpaid subcontractors by contacting the subcontractors. Thus, the court held that Devon Title's claim was a pre-petition claim and discharged in Parks' bankruptcy case. [*In re* **Parks,** *supra*]

d. Future Tort Claims

Courts have struggled with how to deal with future tort claimants in mass tort cases. The problem is the same regardless of the nature of the product involved—asbestos, silicone gel implants, or IUDs. The debtor files for relief under Chapter 11 and there are an unknown number of people who have used or been affected by the debtor's product, but have not yet manifested an injury. The problem is best illustrated by the asbestos tort claims of victims who have been exposed to asbestos but *whose injuries have not yet become apparent.* For example, mesothelioma, which results from exposure to asbestos, does not occur until decades after exposure. These circumstances possibly are covered by the broad definition of "claim." Significantly, courts have held that these potential tort claimants are parties in interest and are entitled to the appointment of a legal representative. [B.C. § 1109(b); *In re* **Johns-Manville Corp.,** 36 B.R. 743 (Bankr. S.D. N.Y. 1984), *aff'd,* 52 B.R. 940 (S.D. N.Y. 1985) (finding that future tort claimants "are parties in interest under Code Section 1109(b) in need of a legal representative to act independently and impartially where appropriate in the case")] The bankruptcy court in the *Johns-Manville* case confirmed a plan that provided for an Asbestos Health Trust to satisfy the claims of present and future asbestos victims. Funding for the trust included monies from settlements with the firm's insurers and a percentage of future firm profits. But all claimants, both present and future, were subject to an "injunction channeling all asbestos-related personal injury claims to the Trust," thereby precluding any suit against the reorganized company and limiting claimants to recovery from the Trust. [*See* **Kane v. Johns-Manville Corp.,** 843 F.2d 636 (2d Cir. 1988) (describing the Trust)] The Bankruptcy Code now provides for the type of trust/injunction used in the *Johns-Manville* case in Chapter 11 cases involving *asbestos-related liabilities.* [B.C. § 524(g)]

2. Claimants

a. Filing a Proof of Claim or Interest

With certain exceptions, a *creditor,* whether secured or unsecured, must file a proof of claim and an *equity security holder must* file a proof of interest for the claim or interest to be allowed. [Bankruptcy Rule 3002(a)]

(i) Creditor

The Bankruptcy Code defines a creditor to include an entity

(1) holding a *claim against the debtor* that arose or is deemed to have arisen *at or prior to the order for relief* [B.C. § 101(10)(A)];

(2) possessing a community claim [B.C. § 101(10)(C)]; or

(3) that has a claim *against the estate* for any of the following:

    (a) in an *involuntary case,* a claim arising in the *ordinary course* of debtor's business during *the gap period* between the start of the case and the order for relief [B.C. §§ 101(10)(B), 502(f)];

    (b) a claim arising from the *rejection* of an *executory contract or unexpired lease* [B.C. §§ 101(10)(B), 502(g)(1)];

    (c) a claim for *damages arising from the rejection* of a swap agreement, securities contract, forward contract, commodity contract, repurchase agreement, or master netting agreement [B.C. §§ 101(10)(B), 502(g)(2), 562];

(d) a claim arising from the *recovery of property* under §§ 522, 550, or 553 [B.C. §§ 101(10)(B), 502(h)];

(e) a claim that arises *post-petition* for a *tax entitled to priority* under § 507(a)(8) [B.C. §§ 101(10)(B), 502(i)]; or

(f) a claim that arises *post-petition but prior to conversion* in a case converted from chapter 11, 12 or 13, *except* a claim for administrative expenses. [B.C. §§ 101(10)(B), 348(d)]

(ii) Equity Security Holder

An equity security holder is the holder of:

(1) a share in a corporation [B.C. § 101(16A)];

(2) an interest of a limited partner in a limited partnership [B.C. § 101(16B)]; or

(3) a warrant or right (other than a right to convert) to buy, sell, or subscribe to a share, security, share in a corporation, or interest of a limited partner in a limited partnership [B.C. § 101(16C)]

b. Who Else May File a Proof of Claim or Interest?

(i) Debtor or Trustee

If a creditor does not timely file a proof of claim, the debtor or the trustee may file a proof of claim *in the creditor's name* within 30 days after the expiration of the time provided for filing claims. [B.C. § 501(c); Bankruptcy Rule 3004] The debtor may wish to file a proof of claim if the debt owed to the creditor is nondischargeable, because any distribution in the bankruptcy case would reduce the debtor's post-bankruptcy liability for a debt that is not discharged. [*See* B.C. § 501(c) Historical and Statutory Notes ("[t]he purpose of [§ 501(c)] is mainly to protect the debtor if the creditor's claim is nondischargeable"); Bankruptcy Rule 3004, 2005 Advisory Committee Notes (giving the debtor the chance "to file a claim ensures that the claim will participate in any distribution . . . [which] is particularly important for claims that are nondischargeable.")]

(ii) Co-Debtor, Surety, or Guarantor

If a creditor fails to timely file a proof of claim, a co-debtor, surety, or guarantor of the debtor may file a proof of claim *for the creditor* within 30 days after the expiration of the time provided for filing claims. [B.C. § 501(b); Bankruptcy Rule 3005(a)]

(iii) Indenture Trustee

In a Chapter 11 case, an indenture trustee may file a proof of claim "on behalf of all known or unknown holders of securities issued pursuant to the trust instrument under which it is trustee." [B.C. § 501(a); Bankruptcy Rule 3003(c)(5)] An indenture trustee is a trustee under a mortgage, deed of trust, or indenture relating to an outstanding security that constitutes a *claim* against the debtor, a *claim secured by a lien* against any of the debtor's property, or an *equity security* of the debtor. [B.C. § 101(28), (29)] For example, if the debtor issues $10 million of debentures, the indenture is the bond contract, and the indenture trustee is the representative of the bondholders.

3. Time to File

The time within which to file a proof of claim or interest depends on the chapter of the Bankruptcy Code governing the particular case.

a. Chapters 7, 12, and 13

Subject to the exceptions below, in a *voluntary case begun in Chapter 7, 12, or 13,* a proof of claim must be filed no later than *70 days* after the order for relief. In an *involuntary Chapter 7 case,* a proof of claim is timely filed if it is filed no later than *90 days* after the order for relief. [Bankruptcy Rule 3002(c)]

Note: A secured creditor's lien is not void simply because the creditor fails to file a proof of claim. [B.C. § 506(d)(2); Bankruptcy Rule 3002(a)]

b. Converted Cases

In a case *converted to Chapter 12 or 13,* a proof of claim is timely filed if it is filed no later than *70 days* after the order of conversion. [Bankruptcy Rule 3002(c); 2017 Advisory Committee Notes] In a case converted *from Chapter 11, 12, or 13 to Chapter 7,* all claims *actually filed before conversion* of the case are considered automatically filed in the Chapter 7 case. Thus, a second filing is not required. [Bankruptcy Rule 1019(3)] However, a claim must be filed if it was only deemed filed in a case converted from Chapter 11.

c. Chapter 11

In a Chapter 11 case, the court fixes and sends notice of a *bar date,* which operates as a deadline for the filing of proofs of claims or interests. [Bankruptcy Rules 3003(c)(3), 2002(a)(7)] Any claim or interest listed in the debtor's schedules is *deemed filed automatically* for the scheduled amount, unless the claim or interest is scheduled as contingent, unliquidated, or disputed. [B.C. § 1111(a); Bankruptcy Rule 3003(b)] Thus, if the debtor schedules a creditor's claim and does not indicate that the claim is contingent, unliquidated, or disputed, the creditor need not file a proof of claim.

d. Exceptions

The following are *exceptions to the general time periods* for filing proofs of claims.

(i) Governmental Unit Claims

With the exception of a claim resulting from a tax return filed under § 1308, a claim by a *governmental unit* in a Chapter 7, 12 or 13 case is timely if it is filed *no later than 180 days* after the order for relief. A claim by a governmental unit resulting from a *tax return filed under § 1308* is timely if it is filed *no later than 180 days* after the order for relief or *60 days* after the filing of the tax return. [Bankruptcy Rule 3002(c)(1)]

(ii) Infants or Incompetent Persons

In a Chapter 7, 11, 12 or 13 case, the court may extend the time period for filing a proof of claim by an *infant, incompetent person, or the representative* of the infant or incompetent person if extending the time period is in *the interest of justice* and will not *unduly delay administration of the case.* [Bankruptcy Rules 3002(c)(2), 3003(c)(3)]

(iii) Entry of Judgment

In a Chapter 7, 11, 12 or 13 case, an **unsecured claim** arising in favor of an entity or that becomes allowable as a result of the entry of a judgment may be filed **within 30 days after the judgment becomes final** if the judgment is for recovery of money or property from the entity, or denial or avoidance of the entity's interest in property. [Bankruptcy Rules 3002(c)(3), 3003(c)(3)]

(iv) Rejection of Executory Contract or Unexpired Lease

In a Chapter 7, 11, 12 or 13 case, the bankruptcy court may set a time for filing of claims arising from the rejection of executory contracts or unexpired leases. [Bankruptcy Rules 3002(c)(4), 3003(c)(3)]

(v) Chapter 7 "No Asset" Cases

If the Chapter 7 trustee notifies the court that unsecured creditors will receive a dividend in the Chapter 7 case, after creditors have received a notice indicating that no dividend would be paid, the bankruptcy clerk must give **at least 90 days' notice** by mail to creditors of the fact that a dividend will be paid and of the date by which creditors must file a proof of claim. [Bankruptcy Rules 3002(c)(5), 2002(e)]

(vi) Creditor Motion to Extend Time Period

In a Chapter 7, 11, 12, or 13 case, a creditor may file a motion to extend the time within which to file a proof of claim. The creditor may file such a motion either before or after the time period for filing proofs of claim has expired. The bankruptcy court may extend the time period if the court finds that notice was insufficient under the circumstances to give the creditor a reasonable time to file a proof of claim. The court may extend the time period **no more than 60 days** from the order granting the creditor's motion. [Bankruptcy Rules 3002(c)(6), 3003(c)(3)]

(vii) Secured Creditor on Debtor's Principal Residence

In a Chapter 7, 12 or 13 case, a proof of claim filed by the holder of a claim secured by the **debtor's principal residence** is timely filed if:

(1) the proof of claim and the documents required by Bankruptcy Rule 3001(c)(2)(C) are filed **no later than 70 days** after the order for relief [Bankruptcy Rules 3002(c)(7)(A), 3001(c)(2)(C); Official Form 410A]; and

(2) any attachments supporting creditor's interest in the property securing the claim, e.g., a copy of the mortgage, and evidence that the creditor's security interest is perfected, are filed as a supplement to the claim **no later than 120 days** after the order for relief. [Bankruptcy Rules 3002(c)(7)(B), 3001(c)(1), (d)]

e. Late Filing

(i) Filing by Debtor

In a Chapter 7, 11, 12 or 13 case, if a creditor fails to timely file a proof of claim, the debtor or trustee may file a proof of claim within **30 days after the claims filing period** provided by the relevant bankruptcy rule. [Bankruptcy Rules 3004, 3002(c), 3003(c)]

(ii) Excusable Neglect

In a Chapter 11 case, filing a proof of claim after the bar date is permitted based on excusable neglect. [Bankruptcy Rule 9006(b)(1)] Bankruptcy Rule 9006(b) provides that the bankruptcy court may enlarge the time for filing a proof of claim in a Chapter 7, 12 or 13 case only according to the terms provided in Bankruptcy Rule 3002(c); in other words, the excusable neglect standard of Rule 9006(b) does not apply in Chapters 7, 12, or 13. [Bankruptcy Rule 9006(b)(3); *see, e.g., In re* **Sunland, Inc.,** 536 B.R. 920 (Bankr. D. N.M. 2015) (explaining that Bankruptcy Rule 3002(c) governs claim filing deadlines in Chapter 7 and finding that "Rule 3002(c) has no 'excusable neglect' provision"); *In re* **Jackson,** 482 B.R. 659 (Bankr. S.D. Fla. 2012) (creditor failing to timely file a proof of claim may not rely on "excusable neglect" in Chapter 7, 12 or 13 cases); **Gold v. Gold (*In re* Gold),** 375 B.R. 316 (Bankr. N.D. Tex. 2007) (in Chapter 13, "Rule 9006(b)(3) does not permit extending the Rule 3002(c) deadline for 'excusable neglect' ")]

(1) Factors to Consider

In **Pioneer Investment Services Co. v. Brunswick Associates Limited Partnership,** 507 U.S. 380 (1993), the Supreme Court explained that the court's determination of what constitutes excusable neglect is "an equitable one, taking account of all relevant circumstances surrounding the party's omission." Those circumstances include:

(a) the danger of *prejudice to the debtor,*

(b) the *length of the delay* and its effect on judicial proceedings,

(c) the *reason for the delay* and whether it was within the reasonable control of the party and her attorney, and

(d) whether the party and counsel acted in *good faith.*

The Court ruled that the "proper focus" is on the *neglect of the party and her attorney* because clients will "be held accountable for the acts and omissions of their chosen counsel." The Court concluded that the neglect was excusable in *Pioneer* because of the unusual and inconspicuous placement of the bar date in the § 341 meeting notice, and the absence of any evidence of bad faith or prejudice to debtor or the administration of justice. The decision in *Pioneer,* according to the author of a leading treatise, created a "concept of excusable neglect governed, not by an easily ascertainable standard, but by one that leads to unpredictable results, dependent upon the equities of each case." [10 Collier ¶ 9006.06(3)]

f. Untimely Amendments to Timely Filed Claim

With the exception of certain late-filed claims in Chapter 7, an untimely filed claim is not allowed. [B.C. § 502(b)(9)] If a creditor files a timely claim, however, and later files an untimely amendment, is the amendment allowed? In making this determination, a bankruptcy court must determine whether the amendment relates back to the timely filed claim or is nothing more than a new claim disguised as an amendment. Generally, a bankruptcy court will allow an untimely amendment that: (i) cures a defect in the original claim, (ii) provides greater detail about a previously filed claim, or (iii) pleads a new theory of recovery on previously filed facts. [*In re* **Peak Web LLC,** 2017 WL 5197117 (Bankr. D. Ore. 2017)]

4. Filing on Certain Post-Petition Claims

A proof of claim may be filed on the following *post-petition claims* the same as if such claims had arisen *pre-petition* [B.C. § 501(d)]:

a. *a claim for reimbursement or contribution* that becomes fixed after the bankruptcy petition has been filed [B.C. § 502(e)(2)];

b. *a claim arising in the ordinary course of the debtor's business* or financial affairs during the *gap period* in an *involuntary case* [B.C. § 502(f)];

c. *a claim arising from the rejection of an executory contract or an unexpired lease* that the trustee or the debtor in possession has not assumed [B.C. § 502(g)(1)];

d. *a claim for damages* under § 562 for *rejection* of a swap agreement, securities contract, forward contract, commodity contract, repurchase agreement, or master netting agreement [B.C. § 502(g)(2)];

e. *a claim arising from the recovery of property* under §§ 522, 550, or 553 [B.C. § 502(h)]; and

f. *a claim* that does not arise until after the start of the bankruptcy case for a tax *entitled to eighth priority.* [B.C. §§ 502(i), 507(a)(8)]

5. Fuel Use Tax

In 2005, with the passage of BAPCPA, Congress added a provision to the Code permitting the filing of a single fuel use tax claim to cover fuel use taxes that the debtor owes to various state tax authorities. [4 Collier ¶ 501.06] This new subsection applies if the requirements of 49 U.S.C. § 31701 are met. [B.C. § 501(e)]

B.   Allowance of Claims

1.   General Rule: Allowance

Unless a party in interest objects, a claim or interest that has been filed will be allowed by the court and will serve as the basis for distribution. [B.C. § 502(a)] The Supreme Court has stated that the " 'basic federal rule' in bankruptcy is that state law governs the substance of claims" and that "claims enforceable under applicable state law will be allowed in bankruptcy unless they are expressly disallowed. *See* 11 U.S.C. § 502(b)." [**Travelers Casualty & Surety Co. v. Pacific Gas and Electric Co.,** 549 U.S. 443 (2007)]

a.   Partnership Debtor

If the debtor is a partnership in a Chapter 7 case, a creditor of any of the general partners of the partnership is considered a party in interest for the purpose of objecting to allowance of a claim. [B.C. § 502(a)]

b.   Objection

If a party in interest objects to a claim, the court, after notice and a hearing, determines the amount of the claim *as of the date of the filing of the bankruptcy petition,* and allows the claim unless it falls within one of the following recognized exceptions. [B.C. § 502(b)]

2. Exceptions to Allowance

a. Claim Unenforceable Due to Valid Defense

A claim that is unenforceable against the debtor and her property because the debtor has a *valid defense* under any applicable law or agreement, e.g., the statute of limitations or failure of consideration, is not allowable. Thus, the trustee may assert any defense that is available to the debtor with regard to a creditor's claim. [B.C. § 558] The fact that a claim is unenforceable under nonbankruptcy claim because it is contingent or unmatured *does not* render the claim unenforceable for purposes of § 502(b)(1). Congress intended that "[a]ll such contingent or unmatured claims [ ] be liquidated by the bankruptcy court in order to afford the debtor complete bankruptcy relief." [H.R. Rep. No. 95–595, at 352 (1977)]

Note: If state law does not extinguish a debt on which the statute of limitations has run, a creditor may file a claim for such a debt, because the debtor's liability for the debt still constitutes a claim under § 101(5)(A). [*See* **Midland Funding, LLC v. Johnson,** 581 U.S. 224 (2017) (specific issue arose under Fair Debt Collection Practices Act)] The trustee, of course, may object to the claim on the basis that the statute of limitations on the debt has expired, and the bankruptcy court may disallow the claim.

b. Claim for Post-Petition Interest

Unmatured interest on an *unsecured claim* is generally not allowable. Unmatured interest is interest that is not yet due and payable at the time of the bankruptcy filing. [B.C. § 502(b)(2); *see* **In re Energy Future Holdings Corp.,** 540 B.R. 109 (Bankr. D. Del. 2015) (sustaining debtor's objection to payment of post-petition interest and holding that creditor's allowed unsecured claim was limited to principal, accrued fees, and interest due as of the petition filing date)]

Note: In the rare case in which the bankruptcy estate is *solvent,* unsecured creditors are entitled to post-petition interest. [4 Collier ¶ 502.03(3)(c)] For example, in a Chapter 7 case, unsecured creditors will receive post-petition interest *if* all allowed (i) priority claims, (ii) timely filed unsecured claims, (iii) untimely filed unsecured claims, and (iv) claims for fines, penalties, or punitive damages that are not compensation for pecuniary loss are paid first and in full. [B.C. § 726(a)(5)]

c. Claim for Unsecured Property Tax in Excess of Debtor's Equity

An unsecured property tax claim in an amount owed *in excess* of the debtor's equity in the property is not allowed. The rationale for this limitation is to ensure that the estate is not depleted by paying taxes on property with no value to the estate that the trustee likely will abandon. [B.C. § 502(b)(3); 4 Collier ¶ 502.03(4)(a)]

Example: Debtor LLC, which owned a vacant hotel property, filed for relief under Chapter 11. At the time that Debtor filed for bankruptcy, it owed County $3,786,980, of which $1,916,782 was for taxes and $1,870,198 was for water and sewage charges. The hotel, however, was worth only $690,000. County filed a claim in Debtor's bankruptcy case for $3,786,980. The court held that § 502(b)(3) only applies to the tax portion of the County's claim, not to the charges for water and sewage. The tax portion of County's claim exceeded the value of the bankruptcy estate's interest in the hotel by $1,226,782 (tax portion of claim of $1,916,782 − $690,000 value of hotel); therefore, the court disallowed $1,226,782 of County's claim under § 502(b)(3). County had an allowed claim for $2,560,198: $690,000 (taxes) + $1,870,198 (water and sewage). [**In re Shefa, LLC,** 524 B.R. 717 (Bankr. E.D. Mich. 2015)]

Note: A tax claim disallowed under § 502(b)(3) is not entitled to priority under § 507(a)(8) and is not entitled to any distribution in the bankruptcy case. [*See In re* **Shefa,** *supra*]

d. Unreasonable Claim for Insider's or Attorney's Services

A claim for services by an insider or an attorney of the debtor will be disallowed for any amount *in excess of the reasonable value* of those services. [B.C. § 502(b)(4)]

e. Unmatured Claim for Domestic Support Obligation

A claim for a nondischargeable domestic support obligation that is unmatured as of the date of bankruptcy is not allowable. [B.C. §§ 502(b)(5), 523(a)(5)]

Example: Husband and Wife divorced prior to Husband's filing for relief under Chapter 11. Under the terms of the parties' divorce agreement, Husband was to pay Wife $33,333.34 each month for a period of ten years. At the time of his bankruptcy filing, Husband was current on these monthly payments. Wife filed a claim in Husband's bankruptcy case for $2.33 million in *future* spousal support payments. Wife asserted that the future spousal support payments were not "unmatured" because the divorce judgment no longer could be modified or reviewed and, therefore, the spousal support payments had vested. The bankruptcy court disagreed and held that the mere fact that Husband could not modify or seek review of the divorce agreement did not transform the future spousal support payments into a matured obligation. The court found that the payments were not yet due and owing and, thus, were unmatured and subject to the limitation provided by § 502(b)(4). The court disallowed Wife's claim for $2.33 million in spousal support payments due from Husband in the future. But, the court explained that while the Wife's domestic support obligation was not an allowed claim it still was nondischargeable. [*In re* **Meier,** 2014 WL 6686541 (Bankr. N.D. Ill. 2014)]

f. Excessive Claim for Damages for Terminated Lease of Real Property

The Bankruptcy Code caps a *lessor's damages* for termination of a *lease of real property.* [B.C. § 502(b)(6)] Congress designed this provision "to compensate the landlord for his loss while not permitting a claim so large (based on long-term lease) as to prevent other general unsecured creditors from recovering a dividend from the estate." [H.R. Rep. No. 95–595, at 353 (1977)]

The Code disallows any amount in *excess of* the *greater* of (i) the rent due under the lease, without acceleration, for one year *or* (ii) 15%, not to exceed three years, of the *remaining term* of the lease *after the earlier* of the date of bankruptcy *or* the date the property was repossessed or relinquished. [B.C. § 502(b)(6)(A)]. Section 502(b)(6)'s cap does *not* apply to unpaid rent due, without acceleration, on the earlier of these two dates. [B.C. § 502(b)(6)(B); 4 Collier ¶ 502.03(7)(e)]

Example #1: Debtor and Landlord sign a lease for ten years at a monthly rent of $10,000. Debtor repudiates the lease and immediately files for bankruptcy. Debtor is current on the rent at the time of bankruptcy filing, and at that time, there are seven years left on the lease. Landlord is quickly able to re-let the premises, but for only $7,500 per month, not $10,000 per month. Landlord files a claim in Debtor's bankruptcy case for $210,000 for the $2,500 difference in rent for the seven years (84 months) left on Debtor's lease. One year's rent is $120,000. Fifteen percent of the remaining term of the lease is 1.05 years (7 years x .15), which does not exceed three years, and amounts to $126,000 in rent (1.05 years x $120,000 yearly rent). Section 502(b)(6) provides for the *greater* of one year's rent ($120,000) or the rent for 15% of the remaining term, not to exceed three years ($126,000). Landlord's claim is not allowed for any amount in excess of $126,000. Therefore, Landlord may not recover for $84,000 ($210,000 – $126,000) in damages incurred by virtue of Debtor's breach of the lease.

Example #2: Same facts as in Example #1, except there are six years remaining on the lease at the time Debtor breaches and files for bankruptcy. Landlord's damages now are $180,000 (6 years at $30,000 [$2,500 per year difference x 12 months]). Landlord's claim, however, is allowable for only one year's rent of $120,000; the remaining $60,000 is disallowed under § 502(b)(6). The reason is that the remaining lease term now is less than 80 months. The calculation is as follows: 15% of the remaining six-year lease term is .9, which is less than three years, and translates into $108,000 (.9 x $120,000 yearly rent). Because one year's rent is greater than $108,000, Landlord's claim is disallowed for $60,000 ($180,000 damages – $120,000).

Shortcut: This section's language is complicated. A shortcut for determining which time period applies is as follows:

(i) **Remaining time on the lease is less than 80 months:** the time period is one year (*see* Example #2 above).

(ii) **Remaining time on the lease exceeds 240 months:** the time period is three years, because 240 months equals 20 years, and 15% of 20 years is three years, which is the maximum allowed under the statute.

(iii) **Remaining time on the lease is between 80 and 240 months:** the time period is 15% of the remaining term of the lease (*see* Example #1 above).

[4 Collier ¶ 502.03(7)(c)]

g. Excessive Claim for Employer's Termination of Contract

The Code also caps an employee's damages for termination of an employment contract. The Code disallows any amount in *excess* of *one year's compensation under the contract,* after the *earlier* of the date of the bankruptcy petition *or* the date the employee's performance was terminated. [B.C. § 502(b)(7)(A)] Section 502(b)(7)'s cap on the employee's claim does *not* apply to unpaid compensation due and owing on the earlier of these two dates. [B.C. § 502(b)(7)(B)]

h. Claim for Employment Tax Credit

A claim that results from a reduction, due to late payment, in the amount of an otherwise applicable federal tax credit available to the debtor in connection with a state employment tax on wages, salaries, or commissions earned from the debtor is not allowable. [B.C. § 502(b)(8); *see* H.R. Rep. No. 95–595, at 354 (1977)]

i. Tardy Claim

A tardily filed claim will be disallowed except to the extent permitted by the Federal Rules of Bankruptcy Procedure or one of the exceptions under § 726(a) applies. [B.C. § 502(b)(9); Bankruptcy Rule 3002(c)]

(i) The Chapter 7 Exceptions

(1) The bankruptcy court may allow a late-filed *priority* claim if the creditor filed the claim on or before the *earlier* of (i) 10 days after mailing of the trustee's final report; and (ii) the start of the trustee's distribution under § 726. [B.C. §§ 502(b)(9), 726(a)(1)]

Note: For late *administrative expense* claims, the bankruptcy court also must approve the tardy filing *for cause.* [B.C. § 503(a)]

(2) The bankruptcy court may allow a late-filed *nonpriority unsecured* claim if (i) the creditor did not have notice or actual knowledge of the bankruptcy case in time to file a timely claim or (ii) the claim was filed in time to permit payment of the claim. [B.C. §§ 502(b)(9), 726(a)(2)(C)]

(3) The bankruptcy court *may* allow any other late-filed *nonpriority unsecured* claim if money remains in the Chapter 7 estate after paying all timely filed priority and general unsecured claims *and* all untimely filed priority or general unsecured claims allowed under the two exceptions stated above. [B.C. § 726(a)(3)]

(ii) Certain Governmental Claims

Certain governmental claims are considered timely filed if they are filed within the time frames provided by § 502(b)(9). *Governmental claims, other than for taxes under § 1308*, are timely filed if filed up to *180 days* after the order for relief, unless the Federal Rules of Bankruptcy Procedure provide for a longer time. [B.C. § 502(b)(9); Bankruptcy Rule 3002(c)(1)] *Governmental claims for taxes under § 1308* are timely filed if filed no later than *180 days after the order for relief* or *60 days* after the date on which the return was filed. [B.C. §§ 502(b)(9), 1308; Bankruptcy Rule 3002(c)(1)]

j. Claim by Possessor of Estate Property or Transferee of Avoidable Transfer

Any claim of an entity from which property is recoverable under the Code's turnover, recovery of avoidable transfer, or setoff provisions or that is a transferee of an avoidable transfer is not allowable *unless* the entity has paid the amount, or turned over the property, for which it is liable. [B.C. § 502(d)]

k. Claim for Reimbursement or Contribution

The bankruptcy court will disallow any claim for reimbursement or contribution by an *entity that is liable with the debtor*, e.g., co-debtor, or an *entity that secured* the claim of a *creditor if:*

(i) the creditor's claim is disallowed [B.C. § 502(e)(1)(A)];

(ii) the reimbursement or contribution claim is *contingent* at the time of allowance or disallowance [B.C. § 502(e)(1)(B)]; or

(iii) the entity asserts a *right to subrogation* to the rights of the creditor under § 509 [§ 502(e)(1)(C)].

Note: If the co-debtor, surety, or guarantor pays the principal creditor after the petition has been filed, her claim for reimbursement or contribution then becomes fixed and will be allowed or disallowed as a *pre-petition claim.* [B.C. § 502(e)(2)]

■ GILBERT

CHECKLIST OF CLAIMS NOT ALLOWABLE

THE FOLLOWING CLAIMS ARE NOT ALLOWABLE IN A BANKRUPTCY CASE IF THERE IS AN OBJECTION:

☑ Claims that *are unenforceable due to a valid defense*

☑ *Unmatured interest on unsecured claims* unless the estate is solvent

☑ Claims for an *unsecured property tax* in excess of the debtor's equity in the property

- ☑ Claims *above a reasonable value for the services of an insider or attorney of the debtor*
- ☑ Claims for *nondischargeable domestic support obligations* that are unmatured as of the date of the bankruptcy
- ☑ Claims for *damages for a terminated lease of real property in excess of* the amount allowable under the formula in Code § 502(b)(6)
- ☑ Claims for *damages for an employer's termination of an employment contract in excess of* one year's compensation
- ☑ Claims for *disallowance of a federal employment tax credit* due to late payment of state unemployment insurance taxes
- ☑ Claims that are *filed tardily,* with certain exceptions
- ☑ Claims of entities from which *property is recoverable* and claims of *transferees of avoidable transfers,* unless the entity or transferee paid the amount, or turned over the property, for which it is liable
- ☑ Certain claims for *reimbursement or contribution*

3. Estimation of Claims

If the fixing or liquidation of a *contingent or unliquidated* claim would cause undue delay in the administration of the bankruptcy case, the bankruptcy court must estimate the claim. This estimate is *for the purpose of allowance* and, once allowed, the claim stands "on equal footing" with other allowed claims under § 502. [B.C. § 502(c)(1); 4 Collier ¶ 502.04(3)]

e.g. **Example:** Debtor Corporation, a manufacturer of asbestos-containing products that had seriously harmed the health of thousands of individuals, filed a Chapter 11 petition. Victim filed a motion to withdraw a proceeding to the district court for immediate trial of his personal injury claim in order to determine the amount of his damages and, thus, his claim against Debtor Corporation. The district court ruled against Victim and concluded that the motion to withdraw was premature. The court noted that Debtor Corporation had not yet developed a plan, and that the time and expense of thousands of individual trials to determine damages could "deplete the estate and leave other creditors with empty judgments." To avoid undue delay in the administration of the case, the bankruptcy judge could estimate the tort claim for the purpose of allowing the claim, and not for the purpose of distribution, since any trial of the latter issue had to occur in the district court. [*See In re* **Johns-Manville Corp.,** 45 B.R. 823 (S.D. N.Y. 1984)]

a. Equitable Remedy

The bankruptcy court also must estimate a claim for a *right to payment* arising from a *right to an equitable remedy* for breach of performance. [B.C. § 502(c)(2)]

4. Claims Deemed Pre-Petition

For the purpose of allowance or disallowance, the following *post-petition claims* are treated the same as if such claims had arisen *pre-petition:*

a. *a claim for reimbursement or contribution* that becomes fixed after the bankruptcy petition has been filed [B.C. § 502(e)(2)];

b. *a claim arising in the ordinary course of the debtor's business* or financial affairs during the *gap period* in an *involuntary case* [B.C. § 502(f)];

c. *a claim arising from the rejection of an executory contract or an unexpired lease* that the trustee or the debtor in possession has not assumed [B.C. § 502(g)(1)];

d.   *a claim for damages* under § 562 for *rejection* of a swap agreement, securities contract, forward contract, commodity contract, repurchase agreement, or master netting agreement [B.C. § 502(g)(2)];

e.   *a claim arising from the recovery of property* under §§ 522, 550, or 553 [B.C. § 502(h)];

f.   *a claim* that does not arise until after the start of the bankruptcy case for a tax *entitled to eighth priority* [B.C. §§ 502(i), 507(a)(8)]; and

g.   *a claim,* other than one for administrative expenses, *arising after the order for relief* but *before conversion* in a case converted from Chapter 11, 12, or 13. [B.C. §§ 348(d), 1112, 1208, 1307]

5. Reduction of Claim on Unsecured Consumer Debt

With the passage of BAPCPA, Congress added a provision to § 502 that allows a debtor to move to *reduce by no more than 20%* the amount of a *claim for an unsecured consumer* debt. The section only applies if the following requirements are satisfied:

a.   the claim is for a *consumer debt* that is *completely unsecured* [B.C. § 502(k)(1)];

b.   the creditor filing the claim *unreasonably refused to negotiate an alternative repayment schedule* that an approved nonprofit and credit counseling agency under § 111 proposed on the *debtor's behalf* [B.C. § 502(k)(1)(A)];

c.   the debtor's offer was made *at least 60 days* prior to filing of the petition [B.C. § 502(k)(1)(B)(i)];

d.   the debtor's offer provided for payment of *at least 60% of the debt* over a period not to exceed the loan's repayment period, or a reasonable extension of that period [B.C. § 502(k)(1)(B)(ii)]; and

e.   no portion of the debt under the alternative repayment schedule is *nondischargeable.* [B.C. § 502(k)(1)(C)]

The debtor must prove by *clear and convincing evidence* that (i) the creditor unreasonably refused to consider the debtor's proposal *and* (ii) the proposal was made before the expiration of the 60-day period referenced above. [B.C. § 502(k)(2)] At least one bankruptcy court has concluded that the standards that Congress created make the prospect of a debtor succeeding under § 502(k) "more illusory than practical and realistic." [*In re* **Hayes,** 385 B.R. 644 (Bankr. N.D. Ohio 2007)]

C.   Secured Claims

1. Definition

In bankruptcy, a secured claim is one that has been allowed and is either *secured by a lien* on property of the estate or is subject to *setoff.* [B.C. § 506(a)] The Bankruptcy Code treats a claim as secured *only to the extent of the value of the creditor's collateral* or up to the amount subject to setoff.

2. Undersecured Claims: Bifurcation

An *oversecured creditor* is a creditor with a lien on property worth *more* than the debt owed to that creditor. It is important to distinguish between the *oversecured creditor* and the *secured creditor* whose debt *equals* the value of the property securing the debt. Oversecured creditors are entitled to interest—up to the value of the collateral—in the period between filing of the petition and confirmation of a plan in one of the Code's reorganization chapters. [B.C. § 506(b)]

An **undersecured creditor,** on the other hand, holds a debt in **excess** of the value of the collateral securing that debt. With certain exceptions, if the amount of the creditor's claim exceeds the value of the collateral, the claim is undersecured and is divided into two separate claims: (i) a **secured claim** equal to the value of the collateral, and (ii) an **unsecured claim** equal to the amount by which the claim exceeds the value of the collateral. [B.C. § 506(a)]

 Example: Bank has an allowed claim against Debtor Company in the amount of $1,000,000 arising from a loan agreement secured by a security interest in Debtor Company's equipment and inventory. If the value of Debtor Company's equipment and inventory is $1,000,000, then Bank's claim is fully secured. If Debtor Company's equipment and inventory are valued at $800,000, then Bank is undersecured, and its $1,000,000 claim will be bifurcated into a secured claim for $800,000 and an unsecured claim for $200,000.

EXAM TIP   **GILBERT**

Bifurcation of undersecured claims is an extremely important concept in bankruptcy, and it is likely that you will be asked to apply it on an exam. Remember, if a creditor is **undersecured,** she is treated as if she has **two claims:** a secured claim equal to the value of the collateral and an unsecured claim for the rest of the debt.

---

3. Undersecured Claims and Bifurcation: Exceptions

The Bankruptcy Code contains certain notable exceptions to the general rule that an undersecured creditor's debt is divided into a secured and an unsecured claim.

a. Debtor's Principal Residence

In a case filed under Chapter 11 or 13, the plan may not modify the rights of a creditor holding a secured claim secured only by the debtor's principal residence. [B.C. §§ 1123(b)(5), 1322(b)(2)]

b. Hanging Paragraph

In a Chapter 13 case, the debtor may not bifurcate the claim of a creditor holding a **purchase-money security interest** (i) in a **motor vehicle** purchased within **910 days of bankruptcy** and acquired for the **debtor's personal use** or (ii) in **any other thing of value** if the debt was incurred within **one year of the bankruptcy filing.** [B.C. § 1325(a)(9) hanging paragraph]

c. Section 1111(b) Election

In a Chapter 11 case, if a creditor elects treatment under § 1111(b), the creditor's claim is treated as a secured claim to the extent that the claim is allowed. [B.C. § 1111(b)(2)]

4. Valuation of Collateral

The value of the collateral securing a creditor's claim is a question of fact. In determining the collateral's value, the bankruptcy court must take into account both the **purpose of the valuation** and the **intended disposition or use** of the collateral. [B.C. § 506(a)]

a. Purpose of the Valuation

During the bankruptcy case, the court must value the collateral securing a creditor's claim in order to effectuate the purposes of various provisions of the Bankruptcy Code. Some examples include:

(i) determining a creditor's entitlement to adequate protection [B.C. § 361];

(ii) deciding whether a creditor is entitled to *relief from the automatic stay* for a *lack of adequate protection* [B.C. § 362(d)];

(iii) determining a *debtor's equity in property* for purposes of a creditor's motion to lift the stay [B.C. § 362(d)(2)];

(iv) determining whether the amount of debtor's secured debts make her *ineligible for Chapter 13* [B.C. § 109(e)]; or

(v) deciding whether a debtor's plan under Chapter 11, 12, or 13 proposes to pay secured creditors the *present value* of their secured claims. [B.C. §§ 1129(b)(2)(A), 1225(a)(5), 1325(a)(5)]

[Examples from 4 Collier ¶ 506.03(4)(a)(iv)]

b. Proposed Use or Disposition

Collateral may have a different value depending on its use or disposition. For example, liquidation value may be appropriate if the secured party is permitted to foreclose on the collateral. While the Supreme Court and Congress have provided *some* guidance, many questions remain about both the appropriate valuation standard to use in some cases and the time for determining valuation.

(i) The Supreme Court's Decision in Rash

The Supreme Court has held that in a Chapter 13 case in which the debtor desires to keep and use a secured creditor's collateral over the creditor's objection ("cram down"), the collateral's value is its *replacement value,* which the Court described as the "cost the debtor would incur to obtain a like asset for the same 'proposed . . . use.' " The Court declined to elaborate on whether replacement value was retail or wholesale value, or some other value. It did explain, however, that replacement value does not include items, such as "warranties, inventory storage, and reconditioning", that the debtor does not receive when the debtor keeps a vehicle. [**Associates Commercial Corp. v. Rash,** 520 U.S. 953 (1997)]

(ii) BAPCPA Amendment to § 506(a)

Congress added subsection (2) to § 506(a) with the passage of BAPCPA in 2005. Section 506(a)(2) only applies to *personal property* and *individuals in Chapter 7 or 13.* The first sentence of § 506(a)(2) provides that in individual Chapter 7 or 13 cases, the value of *personal property* is its *replacement value,* without deduction for the costs of sale or marketing; the valuation time is the *time of the bankruptcy filing.* The second sentence of § 506(a)(2) then provides that *replacement value for personal property* in individual Chapter 7 or 13 cases is *retail value,* if the debtor acquired the collateral for *personal, family, or household purposes.* Retail value, however, is based on the *age and condition* of the personal property *at the time value is determined.* [B.C. § 506(a)(2)]

> **e.g.** **Example:** Debtor files for relief under Chapter 13, and plans to retain her car, which she purchased three years ago from Creditor. Debtor financed the purchase through Creditor; she acquired the vehicle for personal, family, or

household purposes. Debtor owes $10,000 on the car. Given its age and condition, the vehicle's retail value is $7,000. Creditor has a secured claim for $7,000 and an unsecured claim for $3,000 in Debtor's Chapter 13 case.

Note: The hanging paragraph of § 1325(a)(9) does *not* apply because Debtor purchased the vehicle more than 910 days prior to bankruptcy.

Remember: Section 506(a)(2) does not apply to Chapter 11 or 12 cases. It also does not apply to valuation of real property in Chapter 7 or 13 cases.

c. Time of Valuation

The first sentence of § 506(a)(2) provides that in an individual Chapter 7 or 13 case in which the collateral is personal property, valuation of the collateral is on the "date of the filing of the petition." The second sentence then provides that in an individual Chapter 7 or 13 case involving valuation of personal property acquired for *personal, family, or household use,* valuation is based on the "age and condition of the property at the time value is determined." In other words, § 506(a)(2) contains *two time periods* for determining the value of personal property in an individual Chapter 7 or 13 case. One reading of § 506(a)(2) is that the petition filing date (1st sentence) is the time used for valuing property that was *not* acquired for personal, family, or household purposes, e.g., for business purposes, while the "the time value is determined" (2d sentence) is used for property acquired for personal, family, or household purposes. [*See, e.g., In re* **Cook,** 415 B.R. 529 (Bankr. D. Kan. 2009) (holding that vehicle valuation is date of valuation hearing in Chapter 13 case)] For Chapter 11 and 12 cases, which are not governed by the language of § 506(a)(2), courts disagree as to the date to use for valuing collateral. [4 Collier ¶ 506.03(10)]

5. Oversecured Claims

If the value of a creditor's collateral exceeds the amount of the claim that it secures, including any surcharges under § 506(c), then the creditor is entitled to *post-petition interest,* regardless of whether the creditor's lien is consensual, e.g., a mortgage or a U.C.C. security interest, or nonconsensual, e.g., a tax lien. [**United States v. Ron Pair Enterprises, Inc.,** 489 U.S. 235 (1989) (holding that a nonconsensual, oversecured claim entitles the creditor holding that claim to post-petition interest under § 506(b)] To the extent that the claim is oversecured, the creditor also may recover any reasonable fees, e.g., attorneys' fees, costs, or other charges *specified in the agreement* or a *state statute under which the claim arose.* [B.C. § 506(b)]

Remember: Unsecured and undersecured creditors are not entitled to post-petition interest under § 506(b). [*See* **United Savings Association of Texas v. Timbers of Inwood Forest Associates,** 484 U.S. 365 (1988)]

a. Distinguish Time Periods

It is important to distinguish a secured creditor's entitlement to interest across three time periods in Chapter 11, 12, and 13 cases.

(i) Pre-Petition Interest

Any creditor, including an unsecured creditor, may add pre-petition interest to its claim if the creditor's agreement with the debtor provides for the payment of interest on tardily-paid pre-petition debts. Depending on the amount of interest and the value of any collateral, the interest claimed may end up as part of a creditor's unsecured claim.

Example: Creditor's and Debtor's agreement provides for the payment of interest at the contract rate of 10% on payments received more than 10 days after the payment due date. Creditor has a security interest in a piece of collateral owned by the Debtor. The collateral value is $10,000, while Debtor owes Creditor $11,000. At the time of bankruptcy filing, Debtor also owes Creditor $100 in interest for late payment. Creditor has a secured claim in Debtor's bankruptcy case for $10,000; Creditor's unsecured claim of $1,100 includes the pre-petition interest of $100.

(ii) Post-Petition, Pre-Confirmation Interest

Section 506(b) entitles oversecured creditors to the payment of interest up to the value of the creditor's oversecurity. Unsecured creditors or undersecured creditors are not entitled to post-petition, pre-confirmation interest on their claims.

Example: Debtor files for relief under Chapter 11. Creditor has a security interest in a piece of collateral owned by Debtor. The collateral is valued at $100,000; Creditor's claim is $98,000. Creditor is oversecured by $2,000, and is entitled to interest on its $98,000 claim during the period between filing of the petition and confirmation of the Chapter 11 plan. Creditor is limited, however, to $2,000 in interest. If post-petition, pre-confirmation interest is $3,000, Creditor is entitled to $2,000; a claim for the remaining $1,000 will be disallowed under § 502(b)(2).

(iii) Post-Petition, Post-Confirmation Interest

A plan under Chapters 11, 12, or 13 must pay interest on a creditor's secured claim in order to satisfy the requirement that secured creditors receive the ***present value*** of their secured claim. [B.C. §§ 1129(b)(2)(A)(i)(II) (cram down), 1225(a)(5)(B)(ii), 1325(a)(5)(B)(ii)] An undersecured creditor will receive post-confirmation interest on the secured portion of its claim, but is not entitled to post-petition, pre-confirmation interest under § 506(b) because it is not oversecured.

Note: Chapter 11, 12, and 13 each has a limited exception in which post-confirmation interest is paid on unsecured claims in order to achieve present value of the claim. But the exceptions are of limited utility because they each involve full payment over time of unsecured claims—a rare event. [*See* B.C. §§ 1129(b)(2)(B)(i) (cram down), 1225(b)(1)(A), 1325(b)(1)(A)]

Example: Creditor loaned Debtor $30,000, and perfected a security interest in a piece of collateral owned by Debtor. Debtor subsequently filed for relief under Chapter 13. The balance on the loan is $28,000, but the collateral is worth only $25,000. Creditor has a secured claim for $25,000 and an unsecured claim for $3,000. Creditor is not entitled to post-petition, pre-confirmation interest on its $28,000 claim, because Creditor is undersecured. Debtor's plan, however, must pay interest on Creditor's $25,000 secured claim in order to provide Creditor with the present value of its secured claim, which will be paid out over time under Debtor's Chapter 13 plan.

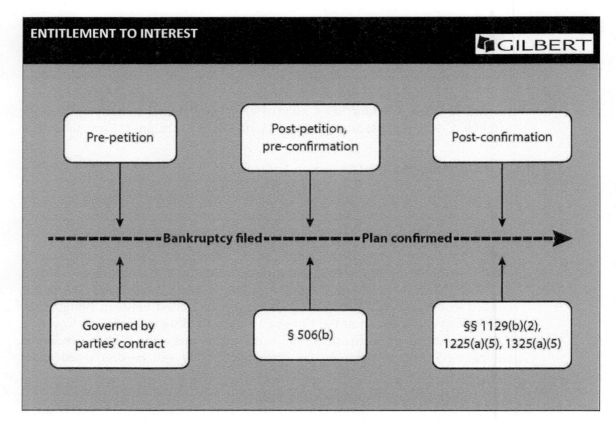

b. Payment of Interest and Fees

Any post-petition interest, and any fees, costs, or charges that are allowed to the holder of an oversecured claim, usually *accrue* unpaid until the claim is paid in full, e.g., when the property is sold, or as provided by the confirmed plan. [B.C. § 506(b); 4 Collier ¶ 506.04(4)]

c. Interest Rate

In the case of an oversecured consensual lien, most courts use the interest rate in the parties' contract. [*In re* **Smith,** 463 B.R. 756 (Bankr. E.D. Pa. 2012)] Whether a contractual post-default interest rate will be applied depends on the facts and equities of the particular case, with a rebuttable presumption in favor of the default rate. [**Prudential Insurance Co. v. City of Boston (*In re* SW Boston Hotel Venture, LLC),** 479 B.R. 210 (B.A.P. 1st Cir. 2012)]

6. Surcharge Against Collateral

To the extent that a secured creditor *benefits* from the *preservation or disposition* of the collateral, the trustee or the debtor in possession may be *reimbursed* from the collateral for the *necessary and reasonable costs* of preserving or disposing of the collateral. This surcharge is paid ahead of an award of post-petition interest or fees to an oversecured creditor. In 2005, Congress added the payment of "all ad valorem property taxes with respect to the property" to the expenses that may be charged against a secured creditor's recovery from the collateral. [B.C. § 506(c)]

a. Note

In **Hartford Underwriters Insurance Co. v. Union Planters Bank, N.A.,** 530 U.S. 1 (2000), the Supreme Court held that an administrative claimant does not have an independent right to recover its claim from a secured party's collateral under § 506(c). In *Hartford,* Debtor filed for relief under Chapter 11. Debtor owed Bank more than $4 million, and Bank held a security interest in essentially all of Debtor's real and personal property. After commencement of the case, the bankruptcy court approved a $300,000 post-petition loan by Bank to Debtor that authorized Debtor to use the loan proceeds to pay expenses, including workers' compensation expenses. During the Chapter 11 case, Insurer provided workers' compensation coverage to Debtor. Debtor, however, failed to pay the premiums and at the time that Debtor's case converted to Chapter 7, Debtor owed Insurer more than $50,000. Insurer had been unaware of the bankruptcy case until conversion, at which time it applied to the bankruptcy court for allowance of an administrative expense to be charged against the collateral securing Bank's claim under § 506(c). In a unanimous opinion, the Court held that the plain language of § 506(c) empowers only the *trustee* to recover costs from collateral securing an allowed secured claim. In a footnote, the Court expressly declined to address the question of whether third parties have a derivative right to act in the "trustee's stead" under § 506(c) if the trustee refuses to act. The issue remains unresolved.

7. Liens Deemed Void

a. Section 506(d)

A lien is *void* to the extent that it secures a claim that is *not an allowed secured claim unless*

(i) the claim is *disallowed only* under § 523(a)(5) as a *nondischargeable, unmatured domestic support obligation* [B.C. § 502(d)(1)];

(ii) the claim is for *reimbursement or contribution* and is *disallowed only under § 502(e)* [B.C. § 502(d)(1)]; or

(iii) the claim is not an allowed secured claim due *only to the failure of the creditor* to *file a proof of claim* under § 501. [B.C. § 502(d)(2)]

b. Real Property: *Dewsnup* and *Caulkett*

In a Chapter 7 case, if the collateral is real property worth less than the amount of the claim it secures, the debtor may not use Code § 506(d) to strip down the creditor's lien on the real property to the value of the collateral. [**Dewsnup v. Timm,** 502 U.S. 410 (1992)] In a later Chapter 7 case, the Supreme Court applied the rule from *Dewsnup* to preclude a debtor from stripping off a junior mortgage on real property when the debt owed on a senior mortgage exceeded the value of the real property. [**Bank of America v. Caulkett,** 575 U.S. 790 (2015)]

Example: Debtor owns a home subject to Bank's properly recorded mortgage of $80,000. When Debtor files a voluntary Chapter 7 petition, the present market value of the home is $50,000. Debtor seeks to avoid Bank's lien on his residence to the extent of $30,000. Debtor may not strip down Bank's lien to the value of the collateral.

Example: Debtor filed for relief under Chapter 7. Debtor's home is valued at $100,000. First Bank holds the senior mortgage on Debtor's home, and Debtor owes First Bank $105,000. Second Bank holds the junior mortgage on Debtor's home; Debtor owes Second Bank $50,000. Debtor moves to strip off Second Bank's mortgage, because Second Bank's lien is completely underwater; if Debtor sold his home today, Second Bank would receive nothing from the sale. Debtor may not void Second Bank's junior lien under § 506(d). The reasoning of *Dewsnup* also applies to a junior mortgage that is wholly underwater (due to the fact that the debt owed on the senior mortgage exceeds the value of the property).

8. Adequate Protection

A secured creditor has the right to receive adequate protection of her interest in the collateral. [B.C. § 361], and the failure to provide it constitutes cause to grant the creditor relief from the automatic stay. [B.C. § 362(d)(1)] The secured creditor may request adequate protection of her interest in collateral if her collateral is used, sold, or leased by the trustee or the debtor in possession. [B.C. § 363(e)] The Code also requires adequate protection of the interest of a secured creditor whose lien on the collateral is primed by a senior or equal lien authorized by the court for the purpose of enabling the trustee or the debtor in possession to obtain credit. [B.C. § 364(d)(1)(B)]

D. Administrative Expenses

1. Priority

Administration claims are **unsecured, priority** claims. Claims for administrative expenses have the second highest priority, after domestic support obligations, in the distribution of the assets of the estate. [B.C. §§ 503, 507(a)(1)]

2. Filing a Request

Generally, a request for administrative expenses must be **timely filed.** The court may approve, for cause, the late filing of such a claim. [B.C. § 503(a)] Not all creditors, however, must file a request in order to have their administrative expense claim paid. A creditor with a claim for **post-petition trade debt** incurred in the **ordinary course of the debtor's business** normally is paid without the creditor having to file a request for payment as an administrative expense. [4 Collier ¶ 503.02] In addition, in 2005, Congress added a subsection to § 503(b) that provides that a **governmental unit** is not required to file a request for payment of **certain taxes and related penalties and fines** that are allowable as administrative expenses. [B.C. § 503(b)(1)(B)–(D)]

3. Allowable Administrative Expenses

Section 503(b) lists **nine numbered categories** of expenses that qualify for administrative expense status. This list, however, is not exclusive because § 503(b) provides that "there shall be allowed administrative expenses . . . *including.*" [*See* B.C. § 102(3)] With certain important exceptions, any claim allowed as an administrative expense has **equal priority** with any other allowed administrative expense claim. [For the exceptions to this rule of equal priority, *see infra* § E.3]

a. Post-Petition Costs of Preserving Estate

The **actual and necessary post-petition costs of preserving the bankruptcy estate** are administrative expenses. The Code provides that post-petition **wages, salaries, and commissions** and certain **back pay awards** are actual, necessary costs and expenses of preserving the estate. [B.C. § 503(b)(1)(A)] But, § 503(b)(1)(A) uses the word "including," which means that a bankruptcy court may determine that costs and expenses not specifically described under § 503(b)(1)(A) are actual, necessary costs and expenses of preserving the estate and, thus, are entitled to administrative expense status.

(i) Wages, Salaries, and Commissions

Wages or salaries for employees operating the debtor's business in a reorganization case, for example, are allowable as administrative expense claims. [B.C. § 503(b)(1)(A)(i)] It is important to distinguish claims for post-petition wages and salaries, which may have administrative expense status and, thus, second priority of payment from pre-petition wages and salaries, which may qualify for fourth-priority of payment. [*Compare* B.C. § 507(a)(2) *with* § 507(a)(4)]

(ii) Back Pay Awards

Wages and benefits awarded in a judicial proceeding or a *National Labor Relations Board* proceeding as *back pay* for any post-petition period of time for the debtor's *violation of federal or state law* are allowable as administrative expenses if the bankruptcy court determines that paying such wages and benefits *will not substantially increase* the *probability of layoffs or termination* of current employees or the *nonpayment of domestic support obligations.* [B.C. § 503(b)(1)(A)(ii)] Congress added this new provision when it enacted BAPCPA. The back pay award must result from a violation of state or federal law, not a breach of a collective bargaining agreement. [*See In re* **Philadelphia Newspapers, LLC,** 433 B.R. 164 (Bankr. E.D. Penn. 2010)]

(iii) Examples of Other Administrative Expenses Under § 503(b)(1)

As mentioned above, § 503(b) uses the word "including." Therefore, a wide range of post-petition costs and expenses may qualify for administrative priority status.

(1) Environmental Clean-Up and Fines

Reasonable costs incurred by an environmental agency to clean up hazardous wastes that violate environmental laws, and civil fines and penalties imposed for post-petition violations of environmental laws are entitled to administrative expense priority. [B.C. § 503(b)(1)(A); *see* **Munce's Superior Petroleum Prods. v. New Hampshire Department of Environmental Services (*In re* Munce's Superior Petroleum Prods.),** 736 F.3d 567 (1st Cir. 2013) (holding that post-petition fine for contempt for debtor's failure to comply with earlier post-petition state court order requiring debtor to bring facilities into compliance with state environmental law was entitled to administrative expense priority)]

(2) Obtaining Unsecured Credit

A trustee authorized to run the debtor's business may obtain unsecured credit or incur unsecured debt in the *ordinary course of the debtor's business* that is allowable as an administrative expense. [B.C. §§ 364(a), 503(b)(1)] After notice and a hearing, the bankruptcy court may authorize the trustee to obtain unsecured credit or incur unsecured debt *other than in the ordinary course of the debtor's business* that is allowable as an administrative expense. [B.C. §§ 364(b), 503(b)(1)]

(3) Pre-Confirmation Retiree Benefits

In a Chapter 11 case, retiree benefit payments that must be made prior to the effective date of a confirmed plan are allowable as administrative expenses. [B.C. § 1114(e)(2)]

b. Post-Petition Taxes and Penalties

Post-petition taxes incurred by the estate, whether secured or unsecured, and including property taxes, are administrative expenses. [B.C. § 503(b)(1)(B)(i)] In addition, any tax attributable to an excessive allowance of a *tentative carryback adjustment* that the estate received, whether for a pre- or post-petition taxable year, is allowable as an administrative expense. [B.C. § 503(b)(1)(B)(ii)] A *fine, penalty,* or *reduction in credit* relating to such post-petition taxes of the estate also is allowable as an administrative expense. [B.C. § 503(b)(1)(C)]

Note: Make sure that you distinguish post-petition taxes accorded second priority status as administrative expenses from taxes accorded eighty priority status. [*Compare* § 507(a)(2) *with* § 507(a)(8)] Section 503(b) specifically excepts from administrative expense priority "a tax of a kind specified in section 507(a)(8)." [B.C. § 503(b)(1)(B)(i)]

c. Compensation and Reimbursement

Compensation and reimbursement awarded to a trustee, an examiner, a consumer privacy ombudsman, a patient care ombudsman, or a professional person employed under § 327 of the Code or by a Chapter 11 committee, are administrative expenses. [B.C. §§ 503(b)(2), 330(a), 332, 333]

d. Expenses of Filing an Involuntary Petition

The actual and necessary expenses of a creditor who files an involuntary petition against the debtor are administrative expenses. [B.C. § 503(b)(3)(A)] Administrative expenses include *reasonable compensation* for professional services, as well as *reimbursement* of actual and necessary expenses, of an *attorney or an accountant* of a creditor who files an involuntary petition. [B.C. § 503(b)(4)]

Note: In an *involuntary* case, post-petition claims that arise "in the ordinary course of the debtor's business or financial affairs . . . before the earlier of the appointment of a trustee [or] the order for relief" are *not* treated as administrative expense claims, but rather are given *third priority* in the order of distribution. [B.C. §§ 503(b), 507(a)(3), 502(f); *see infra* § E.2.c]

Keep in mind: Make sure you distinguish between the creditor filing the involuntary petition and the creditor that provides goods and services in the gap period. The former has an administrative expense claim, while the latter does not. The gap creditor's claim does have third priority, however.

e. Expenses of Recovery of Concealed or Transferred Property

The actual and necessary expenses of a creditor who, with court approval, *recovers* for the *benefit of the estate* any *property* that the *debtor has either concealed or transferred* are administrative expenses. [B.C. § 503(b)(3)(B)] Administrative expenses include *reasonable compensation* for professional services, as well as *reimbursement* of actual and necessary expenses, of *an attorney or an accountant* of such a creditor. [B.C. § 503(b)(4)]

f. Expenses of Criminal Prosecution

The actual and necessary expenses incurred by a creditor in connection with *prosecution of a criminal offense* related to the bankruptcy case, the debtor's property, or the debtor's business are administrative expenses. [B.C. § 503(b)(3)(C)] Administrative expenses include *reasonable compensation* for professional services, as well as *reimbursement* of actual and necessary expenses, of an *attorney or an accountant* of such a creditor. [B.C. § 503(b)(4)]

g. Expenses of Substantial Contributor

In a Chapter 11 case, the actual and necessary expenses of a creditor, an indenture trustee, an equity security holder, or an *unofficial* creditors' or equity security holders' committee, i.e., one not appointed by the United States trustee under § 1102, that makes a ***substantial contribution*** to the case are administrative expenses. [B.C. § 503(b)(3)(D)] Administrative expenses include ***reasonable compensation*** for professional services, as well as ***reimbursement*** of actual and necessary expenses, of an ***attorney or an accountant*** of such creditor, indenture trustee, equity security holder, or unofficial creditors' or equity security holders' committee. [B.C. § 503(b)(4)] Reasonable compensation for services rendered by an indenture trustee in making a substantial contribution to the Chapter 11 case also are administrative expenses. [B.C. § 503(b)(5)]

h. Expenses and Compensation of Pre-Petition Custodian

The actual and necessary expenses, as well as compensation, for the services of a pre-petition custodian who has been superseded under Bankruptcy Code § 543 are administrative expenses. [B.C. § 503(b)(3)(E)] Administrative expenses include ***reasonable compensation*** for professional services, as well as ***reimbursement*** of actual and necessary expenses, of an ***attorney or an accountant*** of the custodian. [B.C. § 503(b)(4)]

i. Expenses of Official Chapter 11 Creditors' Committee

The actual and necessary expenses incurred by the members of an official Chapter 11 creditors' or equity security holders' committee—one appointed under § 1102—in performing the duties of the committee are treated as administrative expenses. [B.C. § 503(b)(3)(F)] Such expenses include travel and lodging, for example, but not compensation for services rendered.

j. Witness Fees

Witness fees and mileage expenses are administrative expenses. [B.C. § 503(b)(6); 28 U.S.C. § 1821]

k. Nonresidential Real Property Leases

A landlord may have an allowable administrative expense claim for monies due under a ***nonresidential real property lease*** that was ***first assumed*** under § 365 and then ***later rejected.*** [B.C. § 503(b)(7)] The landlord's claim is for ***all monetary obligations*** due for the ***two-year period*** following the ***later*** of the rejection date or the date that the trustee turned the premises over to the landlord. Monetary obligations ***do not*** include ***penalty provisions*** under the lease or damages resulting from the ***trustee's failure to operate the premises.*** The landlord's claim is subject to setoff or reduction ***only*** for monies received from an entity other than the debtor. The rest of the landlord's claim is an unsecured claim subject to any relevant limitation placed on damages under § 502(b)(6). This is a new provision that Congress enacted as part of BAPCPA.

l. Closing Health Care Business

The actual, necessary costs and expenses that a trustee or a federal or state department or agency incurs in ***closing a health care business*** are allowable administrative expenses. [B.C. § 503(b)(8)] Such costs and expenses include ***disposing of patient records*** and ***transferring patients*** from the health care facility that is closing to another health care business. [B.C. §§ 503(b)(8)(A), (B), 351] This is a new provision that Congress enacted as part of BAPCPA.

m. Certain Pre-Petition Sales of Goods

A creditor that sold *goods* in the *ordinary course of the debtor's business* has an allowable administrative expense claim for the value of goods received by the debtor *within 20 days* of the start of the bankruptcy case. [B.C. § 503(b)(9)] This is a new provision that Congress enacted as part of BAPCPA. The Bankruptcy Code does not define "goods," but a number of courts have turned for guidance to the Uniform Commercial Code's definition at § 2–105. [*In re* **Pilgrim's Pride Corp.,** 421 B.R. 231 (Bankr. N.D. Tex. 2009)]

Note: A pre-petition seller of goods to the debtor also may have a right to reclaim goods sold within 45 days of the start of the debtor's bankruptcy case. [B.C. § 546(c)]

n. Small Business Act Loans: Temporary Amendment

The CAA added a *temporary* § 503(b)(10) granting administrative expense status to debts incurred under § 364(g)(1). [CAA § 320(a), (b); *see infra* Chapter Eleven, § C.9 on § 364(g)(1)] Section 364(g)(1) is itself a *temporary amendment* to the Code that provides that the bankruptcy court, after notice and a hearing, may authorize a trustee or debtor in possession in a Chapter 11 subchapter V case, or a Chapter 12 or 13 case to obtain a *loan under the Small Business Act,* and accords that debt *super-super priority* status if it is not forgiven pursuant to the provisions of the Small Business Act. [CAA § 320(a); B.C. §§ 1183, 1184, 1203, 1204, 1304; 15 U.S.C. § 636(a)] While the changes to both §§ 503(b) and 364 sunsetted on *December 27, 2022,* they apply to any case begun *before December 27, 2022.* [CAA § 320(f)(2)]

4. Exempt Property

As a general rule, administrative expenses are not payable out of property that the debtor exempts. [B.C. § 522(k)] However, the debtor's exempt property is liable for the share of administrative expenses related to the trustee's avoidance of a transfer of property or recovery of such property. The share of costs is computed based on the value of the *portion of the property exempted* in relation to the *value of the property recovered.* [B.C. § 522(g), (k)(1)] If the debtor avoids the fixing of a lien under § 522(f) or avoids a transfer of property that the trustee did not attempt to avoid, and then recovers such property for the estate, the exempt property is liable for any costs or expenses associated with the avoidance and recovery actions. [B.C. § 522(f), (h), (i)(1), (k)(2)]

5. Limitations on KERPS

In BAPCPA, Congress added language to the Code that limits a debtor's ability to claim administrative expense priority for *certain post-petition payments made to insiders.* The purpose of this new provision is to place restrictions on Key Employee Retention Plans ("KERPS"). The Code now provides that a payment made or obligation incurred for the *benefit of an insider* to induce the insider to remain with the debtor's business shall not be allowed or paid unless the court makes the following findings based on evidence in the record:

a. the transfer or obligation is essential to retain the insider because she has a *bona fide offer* from another business at the *same or greater compensation.* [B.C. §§ 503(c)(1)(A), 101(31)]; *and*

b. the insider's services are *essential to the business's survival* [B.C. §§ 503(c)(1)(B), 101(31)]; *and*

c. the court finds *either of the following:*

(i) the transfer or payment does not exceed an amount equal to *10 times the average* transfer or payment of a similar kind made to *non-management employees* during the calendar year in which the insider transfer or obligation was made [B.C. §§ 503(c)(1)(C)(i), 101(31)]; *or*

(ii) if the debtor made no transfers to non-management employees during the relevant calendar year, then the transfer or obligation for the insider's benefit does not exceed an amount that is *25% of the amount of any similar transfer or obligation* made to *the insider* in the *calendar year prior* to the calendar year in which the contested transfer or obligation takes place. [B.C. §§ 503(c)(1)(C)(ii), 101(31)]

A *severance payment* made to an insider also "shall neither be allowed nor paid" unless the payment is part of a *program applicable to all full-time employees* and the severance payment amount does not *exceed 10 times the average severance* paid to *non-management employees* during the same calendar year. [B.C. §§ 503(c)(2), 101(31)] Finally, any transfers made or obligations incurred *outside the ordinary course of business,* including those for the benefit of officers, managers, or consultants hired after filing of the bankruptcy petition, "shall neither be allowed nor paid" unless *justified* by the *facts and circumstances of the case.* [B.C. § 503(c)(3)]

E. Priority Claims

1. In General

Priority claims are *unsecured claims* but as the name suggests have priority of payment in bankruptcy. There are ten tiers of priority claims which, in a Chapter 7 case, are entitled to payment in the order of their priority ranking. [B.C. § 507(a)] Thus, all of the claims in a priority level must be paid in full before moving down to the next priority level. In a Chapter 7 case, then, the general (nonpriority) unsecured creditors receive payment only after all priority unsecured creditors are paid. [B.C. § 726(a)(1)]

Example: Debtor files for relief under Chapter 7. Debtor has $12,000 in unencumbered, non-exempt assets. Administrative expenses are $2,000, and Debtor has $20,000 in priority tax claims. Unsecured claims total $60,000. The administrative expenses will be paid in full, because they are second priority. The remaining $10,000 does not cover the $20,000 in priority tax claims; the tax claimants share *pro rata,* which means that each claimant receives 50% ($10,000 available/$20,000 claims) of its claim. The unsecured creditors receive nothing.

2. Order of Priority

BAPCPA made several changes to the Code's priority scheme. Among those changes was the addition of a tenth priority for personal injury claims resulting from debtor's operation of a vehicle or vessel while intoxicated. Congress also moved alimony and child support obligations—now termed domestic support obligations—from seventh to first priority.

Priority claims that have been *allowed* are paid in the following order. [B.C. § 507(a)]

a. First Priority: Domestic Support Obligations

The first priority under § 507(a) is for *domestic support obligations,* but within that priority scheme is a payment hierarchy. [*See, e.g., In re* **Yelverton,** 556 B.R. 1 (Bankr. D. D.C. 2016) (describing the payment hierarchy within § 507(a)(1)] First paid are certain *administrative expenses of a trustee* elected or appointed in Chapter 7, 11, 12, or 13, to the extent that the trustee *administers assets* that are *used to pay the domestic support* *obligation.* [B.C. § 507(a)(1)(C)] The Code allows first payment *only* for the trustee's expenses for the actual, necessary costs of preserving the estate, the trustee's compensation, and fees and mileage. [B.C. §§ 503(b)(1)(A), (2), (6), 330] Second paid are allowed unsecured claims for domestic support obligations *owed to or recoverable by* a spouse, former spouse, or child of the debtor, or the child's parent, legal guardian, or legal representative. The claim may be filed by the person owed the obligation or a governmental unit on behalf of such person. [B.C. §§ 507(a)(1)(A), 101(14A)] Third paid are domestic support obligations that a spouse, former spouse, or child of the debtor, or that child's parent, legal guardian, or legal representative have *assigned to a governmental unit.* (A voluntary assignment of a domestic support obligation to a governmental unit for purposes of collecting the obligation, however, falls within the category of second-paid, not third-paid, claims under § 507(a)(1).) Also included in this third category under § 507(a)(1) are domestic support obligations that *are owed directly to or recoverable by a governmental unit* under applicable nonbankruptcy law. [B.C. § 507(a)(1)(B)]

Example: Debtor files for relief under Chapter 7; at the time he files for bankruptcy, Debtor owes his former spouse ("Spouse") $10,000 in alimony and child support payments. Debtor has $20,000 in non-exempt assets. The Chapter 7 trustee incurs $4,000 in administrative expenses, of which $1,000 was spent administering assets to pay Spouse's domestic support obligation. The Chapter 7 trustee is paid $1,000 first; Spouse then is paid $10,000. The trustee's other $3,000 in administrative expenses are accorded second priority status under § 507(a)(2). The $6,000 remaining of the $20,000 in non-exempt assets is paid to other priority claimants, in the order provided by the Code, and then to timely filed general unsecured claims.

b. Second Priority: Administrative Expenses

The second priority includes allowed administrative expenses. [B.C. § 507(a)(2); *see supra* § D of this Chapter]

c. Third Priority: Involuntary Case Gap Claims

The third priority includes those allowed unsecured claims in an involuntary case that arise in the *ordinary course* of the debtor's business or financial affairs in the *gap period,* which is the time between *filing of the involuntary petition* and the *earlier* of the *order for relief* and the *appointment of a trustee.* [B.C. §§ 507(a)(3), 502(f)]

Distinguish: Third priority allowed claims of a creditor that provides goods or services to the debtor during the gap period from the second priority administrative expenses of a creditor that files the involuntary petition against the debtor. [*Compare* B.C. §§ 507(a)(3) *with* § 503(b)(3)(A), (b)(4); *see supra* § D.3.d of this Chapter]

d. Fourth Priority: Wages and Commissions

The fourth priority includes wages, salaries, or commissions earned by an *individual* within *180 days* before either bankruptcy or "the cessation of the debtor's business," whichever occurs first. This provision applies regardless of the individual's position of employment and includes vacation pay, severance pay, and sick leave pay. [B.C. § 507(a)(4)(A)] The fourth priority also includes commissions earned by an *individual or a corporation with only one employee,* acting as an *independent contractor* in the sale of goods or services for the debtor in the *ordinary course* of the debtor's business; the *180-day time limit* applies to these commissions, as well. In order to qualify for fourth-priority status, at least *75%* of the individual's or corporation's *earnings* from acting as an independent contractor during the *12 months prior to bankruptcy* must have been earned from the debtor. [B.C. § 507(a)(4)(B)]

(i) Limitation

Each fourth priority claim is *limited to $15,150*. [B.C. § 507(a)(4)]

Example: Patty Parker is the president of Debtor Corporation. Debtor Corporation filed for relief under Chapter 7 on June 1 and stopped doing business on the same day. From February 1 until June 1, Parker earned, in the employ of Debtor Corporation, $20,000 in salary, which remained unpaid as of June 1. Because any individual employee is entitled to a priority for wages or salaries earned within the 180-day period before either bankruptcy or cessation of debtor's business, whichever is earlier, Parker will receive fourth priority treatment of $15,150 of the $20,000 she is owed in past-due salary. Parker will have a general unsecured claim for the remaining $4,850. If funds remain after all priority creditors are paid, then Parker will share *pro rata* with other unsecured creditors in those funds. [B.C. § 507(a)(4)(A)]

e. "Cessation of Business"

The courts have construed the language "cessation of the debtor's business" to mean the date on which the debtor stops doing business altogether. There is no cessation of the debtor's business simply because the debtor closes some stores, outlets, or divisions, but continues to operate—albeit on a reduced scale. [B.C. § 507(a)(4)]

Example: Debtor Corporation owns and operates several seafood restaurants. In 2007, it closed one restaurant but continued to operate several others. Employees sued and, in 2008, ultimately settled with Debtor for $400,000. Debtor Corporation paid on the settlement until it filed for relief under Chapter 11 in 2010. Employees filed a claim for the remainder of the settlement and argued that the claim was entitled to fourth-priority status. The bankruptcy court held that Employees did not have a fourth priority claim. Employees' earnings were for a period in 2007, which was more than 180 days prior to Debtor's 2010 Chapter 11 filing. The court rejected Employees' argument that the closing of the restaurant at which they had worked constituted a "cessation of the debtor's business." The court noted that Debtor operated several other restaurants and that the closing of one of those restaurants did not constitute a cessation of Debtor's business. [*In re* **McGrath's Publick Fish House, Inc.,** 2011 WL 66026 (Bankr. D. Ore. 2011)]

f. Fifth Priority: Employee Benefit Plans

The fifth priority is for contributions to an employee benefit plan for services rendered within *180 days* before either bankruptcy or "the cessation of the debtor's business," whichever occurs first. [B.C. § 507(a)(5)]

(i) Limitation

This priority is limited to the *number of employees* covered by the plan *multiplied by $15,150 minus:* (i) the total amount paid to such employees as fourth priority wage claims and (ii) the total amount paid by the bankruptcy estate to any other benefit plan for such employees. [B.C. § 507(a)(5)(B)] As the Supreme Court noted in **Howard Delivery Service v. Zurich American Insurance Co.,** 547 U.S. 651 (2006), "§ 507(a)(5) covers fringe benefits that complete a pay package—typically pension plans, life insurance plans and group health, life, and disability insurance." But, the Court in *Howard Delivery,* held that unpaid premiums on a workers' compensation policy purchased by debtor for its employees do not enjoy fifth-priority status under the Bankruptcy Code.

Distinguish: The $15,150 limit for wages, salaries, and commissions under § 507(a)(4) is per employee. Note the language "for each individual" in § 507(a)(4). No such language appears in the provision on employee benefit plans. Thus, § 507(a)(5) "provides an aggregate limit on recovery" under that provision; not an individualized recovery per employee." [**Consolidated Freightways Corp. v. Aetna, Inc. (*In re* Consolidated Freightways Corp.),** 564 F.3d 1161 (9th Cir. 2009)]

g. Sixth Priority: Grain Farmers and United States Fishermen

The sixth priority is for allowed unsecured claims of grain producers or United States fishermen against a debtor who operates or owns a grain storage facility or against a debtor who operates a fish produce storage or processing facility, respectively. [B.C. § 507(a)(6)]

(i) Limitation

Each farmer or fisherman is limited to $7,475 for a sixth priority claim. [B.C. § 507(a)(6); § 557(b) (definitions of grain, grain storage facility, and producer)]

h. Seventh Priority: Consumer Claims

The seventh priority, which also is known as the "layaway" priority, is for allowed *unsecured claims of individuals* arising from the pre-petition deposit of money with the debtor for the purchase, lease, or rental of property *or* the purchase of services that were not delivered or provided. The property or services must have been for the individual's *personal, family, or household* use. [B.C. § 507(a)(7)]

(i) Limitation

Each individual is limited to $3,350 for a seventh priority claim. [B.C. § 507(a)(7)]

i. Eighth Priority: Taxes

Eighth priority claims include claims for unpaid income taxes, property taxes, trust fund taxes and various other unsecured pre-petition tax claims of governmental units. [B.C. § 507(a)(8)]

(i) Income Tax or Gross Receipts Tax

A tax on or measured by income or gross receipts for a *taxable year ending on or before the filing of the bankruptcy petition* are eighth priority claims.

(1) Return Last Due

An income tax or gross receipts tax for which a *return was last due,* including extensions, *within three years* prior to the date of the bankruptcy petition is an eighth priority claim. [B.C. § 507(a)(8)(A)(i)] Priority depends on when the return was last due, not when the return was filed.

Note: In a unanimous opinion, the Supreme Court held that the "three-year lookback period" of Code § 507(a)(8)(A)(i) is tolled during the pendency of a prior bankruptcy case. Thus, the time during which a debtor's prior bankruptcy case is pending does not count toward the three-year lookback period. [**Young v. United States,** 535 U.S. 43 (2002) (married debtors' taxes were nondischargeable because "the IRS was disabled from protecting its claim during the pendency of the [debtors' prior] Chapter 13 petition, and this period of disability tolled the three-year lookback period when the [debtors] filed their Chapter 7 petition")]

Example: Debtor filed for relief under Chapter 7 on March 5, 2018. Debtor has not paid his income taxes for 2014 or 2015. The income taxes for both years are entitled to priority under § 507(a)(8)(A). March 5, 2015 is three years prior to Debtor's filing of the Chapter 7 petition. Debtor's 2015 income taxes were last due on April 15, 2015, and his 2015 taxes were last due on April 15, 2016. Both dates fall *after* March 5, 2015; thus, both years' taxes are entitled to priority.

(2) Assessed Within 240 Days

An income tax or gross receipts tax that has been *assessed within 240 days* before the date of the petition is an eighth priority claim. [B.C. § 507(a)(8)(A)(ii)] There are two situations in which the Code extends the 240-day period. First, the time period during which an *offer in compromise* was pending or in effect *plus 30 days* is not counted in calculating the 240-day period. [B.C. § 507(a)(8)(A)(ii)(I)] Second, the period during which the *automatic stay* was in effect in a *prior bankruptcy case plus 90 days* is not counted in calculating the 240-day period. BAPCPA added this second time extension. [B.C. § 507(a)(8)(A)(ii)(II)]

Example: Tax Authority assessed taxes against Debtor on February 1. Debtor consulted with Attorney regarding the assessment and on September 1, Attorney, on Debtor's behalf, made an offer in compromise to Tax Authority. The offer was pending for two months. On December 15, Debtor filed for bankruptcy. The February 1 tax is entitled to eighth priority. The offer in compromise was pending for two months or 60 days. The Code adds another 30 days to that time period, which means a tax assessed within 330 days (240 days + 60 days for offer + 30 extra days) of filing for bankruptcy is entitled to priority. February 1 is less than 330 days before December 15. As the author of a leading treatise explains, the reason for extending the 240-day period is to allow the debtor and taxing authority to negotiate over the offer in compromise without the taxing authority worrying about losing rights in a subsequent bankruptcy case due to the negotiations. [4 Collier on Bankruptcy ¶ 507.11(2)(b)(ii)]

(3) Assessable Post-Petition

Eighth priority claims include an income tax or gross receipts tax that was not assessed pre-petition but which is *assessable post-petition* but *does not include* a tax that is nondischargeable because (a) a return was not filed, (b) a return was filed late and within two years prior to bankruptcy, or (c) the debtor filed a fraudulent return or intentionally tried to evade the tax. [B.C. §§ 507(a)(8)(A)(iii); 523(a)(1)(B), (C)]

Example: Debtor filed for relief under Chapter 11 in March 2017. At the time of his bankruptcy filing, the IRS was auditing his liability for federal income taxes for the years 2010, 2011, and 2012. In November 2017, the IRS issued a notice of deficiency to Debtor for tax years 2010 through 2012. The taxes are entitled to eighth priority under § 507(a)(8)(A)(iii), because they were not assessed pre-petition but were assessable post-petition.

Note: The taxes are outside the three-year reach back period under § 507(a)(8)(A)(i). [*See, e.g.,* **Fein v. United States (***In re* **Fein),** 22 F.3d 631 (5th Cir. 1994) (noting that § 507(a)(8)(A)(iii) provides priority treatment for "pre-petition federal income tax liabilities not yet assessed but still assessable, such as federal income tax liabilities still under audit")]

(ii) Property Tax

A property tax incurred prior to bankruptcy that was last payable without a penalty *within one year* before the date of the petition is an eighth priority claim. [B.C. § 507(a)(8)(B)]

Distinguish: Post-petition property taxes, which are allowable as an administrative expense claim and, thus, have second priority *from* pre-petition property taxes, which are eighth priority.

(iii) Trust Fund Tax

Any trust fund tax that the debtor was *obligated to collect or withhold* from a third party and for which the debtor is liable in any capacity is an eighth priority claim. [B.C. § 507(a)(8)(C)] For example, an employer must withhold income taxes and employees' share of Social Security taxes from employees' paychecks. If the employer files for bankruptcy but has not transmitted these withheld taxes to the government, the government has an eighth priority claim for those amounts withheld but not transmitted. Unlike income and property tax priority claims, there is no time limit in the Code for trust fund taxes. Such a tax enjoys priority regardless of its age. [*See* 4 Collier ¶ 507.11(4)(a)]

e.g. **Example—Sales Taxes:** Michael Calabrese owned a bagel store and under New Jersey law was required to collect sales tax from his customers. Calabrese filed a Chapter 11 case for the bagel store, but the case was converted to Chapter 7. Calabrese also filed a Chapter 13 case himself. New Jersey filed proofs of claim for more than $63,000 in Calabrese's individual bankruptcy case. Calabrese argued that the taxes were excise taxes and that more than $56,000 of that amount was not entitled to priority because they were for a period greater than the three-year reach back for excise taxes under § 507(a)(8)(E). The Third Circuit disagreed and held that the sales taxes were trust fund taxes and entitled to priority because the Code has no time limit for trust fund taxes. The court explained that the sales taxes collected by Calabrese were not owed by him or his business. Instead, customers owed those taxes and Calabrese collected them to transmit them to the taxing authority. Thus, the "third-party sales taxes resemble[d] trust fund taxes more than other sales taxes." [*See In re* **Calabrese,** 689 F.3d 312 (3d Cir. 2012)]

(iv) Employment Tax

An employment tax on wages, salaries, or commissions earned from the debtor before bankruptcy and for which a return was last due *within three years* before the date of the petition is an eighth priority claim. [B.C. § 507(a)(8)(D)] For example, the employer must withhold 7.65% of an employee's gross wages for Social Security and Medicare taxes. The employer also must pay its portion of Social Security and Medicare taxes on those wages, which is 7.65% of each employee's gross wages. The employer's 7.65% is a priority tax employment claim under § 507(a)(8)(D); the amount that an employer withholds from its employees' wages is a trust fund tax under § 507(a)(8)(C).

(v) Excise Tax

An excise tax concerning a transaction that occurred *or* for which a return was last due *within three years* before bankruptcy is an eighth priority claim. [B.C. § 507(a)(8)(E)]

(vi) Customs Duties

Customs duties relating to the *importation of merchandise* are entitled to eighth priority in any one of the following three situations.

(1) The imported merchandise entered for *consumption within one year* of the bankruptcy filing. [B.C. § 507(a)(8)(F)(i)]

(2) The merchandise is covered by an entry *liquidated or reliquidated within one year* before the bankruptcy filing. [B.C. § 507(a)(8)(F)(ii)]

(3) The merchandise entered for *consumption within four years* of the bankruptcy filing but the *customs tax was unliquidated* on that date and the *Secretary of the Treasury certifies* that the failure to liquidate was due *either* to a pending investigation into assessment of antidumping or countervailing duties or fraud *or* the information needed to appraise or classify the merchandise was not available to the customs officer before such date. [B.C. § 507(a)(8)(F)(iii)]

(vii) Penalty on Eighth Priority Tax Claim

A penalty attributable to an eighth priority tax claim is also an eighth priority claim, but only if the penalty constitutes *compensation for actual pecuniary loss.* [B.C. § 507(a)(8)(G)]

(viii) Additional Issues Related to Priority Tax Claims

(1) *Pro Rata* Distribution

In a Chapter 7 case, if there are insufficient funds to pay all eighth priority tax claims, those tax claims share on a *pro rata* basis any monies remaining for distribution. There is no payment hierarchy among the eighth priority tax claims, unlike the payment hierarchy that exists for first priority domestic support obligations. [*Compare* B.C. § 507(a)(8) *with* B.C. § 507(a)(1)]

e.g. **Example:** Debtor files for relief under Chapter 7. After paying all administrative expenses, the trustee has $10,000 left to distribute. Debtor owes $15,000 in federal income taxes, $5,000 in state income taxes, and $5,000 in property taxes. All taxes are entitled to eighth priority status. Each tax creditor receives 40% of its claim ($10,000 assets/$25,000 tax claims). Thus, the IRS receives $6,000, and the state and property taxing authorities each receive $2,000.

(2) Suspension of Time Periods

BAPCPA added language in a hanging paragraph at the end of § 507(a)(8). The new language provides that any applicable time limit under § 507(a)(8), e.g., one year for property taxes, *does not run for the period during* which:

(a) *applicable nonbankruptcy law prevented* a governmental unit from collecting a tax because the debtor had requested a hearing and an appeal of collection action taken or proposed against the debtor, *plus 90 days;* or

(b) the *automatic stay* was in effect in a prior bankruptcy case or collection was precluded because of one or more confirmed plans, *plus 90 days.*

(3) Erroneous Refund

The claim of a governmental unit for an *erroneous refund or credit* of a tax is entitled to the *same priority* as the tax to which it pertains. [B.C. § 507(c)]

(4) Pre-Petition Interest

Most courts view pre-petition interest as part of the tax claim and, therefore, the pre-petition accrued interest has eighth priority status. [*In re* **Colonial BancGroup, Inc.,** 2012 Bankr. LEXIS 3004 (Bankr. M.D. Ala. 2012) (stating that "[i]t is well established that interest has the same priority as the underlying tax provided that the interest accrued pre-petition")]

j. Ninth Priority: Failure to Maintain Capital Requirements of an Insured Depository Institution

The ninth priority is for allowed unsecured claims of a federal depository institutions regulatory agency, such as the Federal Deposit Insurance Corporation, for the amount of any deficiency under the debtor's agreement to maintain the capital of an insured depository institution. [B.C. §§ 507(a)(9), 101(21B), 101(35)]

k. Tenth Priority: Operation of a Vehicle or Vessel While Intoxicated

BAPCPA added a tenth priority to § 507(a). This priority applies to allowed claims for *death or personal injury* resulting from the operation of a *vessel or motor vehicle* if such operation was unlawful because the debtor was *intoxicated* from using alcohol, drugs, or other substances. [B.C. § 507(a)(10)]

PAYMENT OF CLAIMS　　　　　　　　　　　　　　　　　　　　　**GILBERT**

IN A CHAPTER 7 CASE, CLAIMS GENERALLY ARE SATISFIED IN THE FOLLOWING ORDER:

☑ **Secured claims,** out of the collateral securing them (cash or the collateral itself)

☑ **Unsecured priority claims:** All claims in each category are paid before any claims in a lower category are paid

　　First　　**Domestic support obligations and administrative expenses** of trustee to the extent the trustee administers assets to pay the domestic support obligation claim *but see* payment hierarchy described at § E.2.a *supra*

　　Second　　**Administrative expenses,** such as the actual and necessary costs of preserving the estate (e.g., normal operating expenses of a Chapter 11 business), post-petition taxes incurred by the estate, trustee and examiner fees, and the fees of professional persons, such as attorneys and accountants. A secured creditor may have a super-priority claim for adequate protection deficiencies. With court approval, a creditor that extends post-petition credit or debt to the debtor will have a super super-priority administrative expense that has priority over all other administrative expenses, including those with super-priority

Third	**Involuntary case gap claims** that arise in the ordinary course of the debtor's business or financial affairs between the time an involuntary petition is filed and the earlier of the appointment of a trustee or the order for relief
Fourth	**Claims for wages or commissions** earned up to 180 days before the earlier of the filing of the bankruptcy petition or the cessation of the debtor's business; limited to $15,150 per claim
Fifth	**Employee benefit plan contributions** for services rendered within 180 days before the earlier of the filing of the bankruptcy petition or the cessation of the debtor's business; limited to the number of employees covered by the plan times $15,150, minus (a) the total amount paid to such employees under the fourth priority plus (b) the total amount paid by the estate to any other benefit plan for such employees
Sixth	**Claims of grain farmers and U.S. fishermen** against debtors who run grain or fish processing or storage facilities; limited to $7,475 per claim
Seventh	**Claims of individuals for return of pre-petition deposits on consumer goods or services** that were not delivered or performed; limited to $3,350 per claim
Eighth	**Certain tax claims,** such as an income tax for which a return was due within three years before the bankruptcy petition was filed
Ninth	**Claims of a federal depository institutions regulatory agency** for the amount of any deficiency under the debtor's agreement to maintain the capital of an insured depository institution
Tenth	**Death or personal injury claims** arising from debtor's operation of a motor vehicle or vessel while intoxicated

☑ **General unsecured claims**

> IN A CASE UNDER CHAPTER 11, 12, OR 13, PAYMENT MUST COMPLY WITH THE
> REQUIREMENTS FOR CONFIRMATION UNDER THE RESPECTIVE CHAPTER,
> AND PAYMENT MAY BE ALTERED PURSUANT TO A PLAN.

3. Exceptions to Equal Treatment of Priority Creditors in a Class

The general rule is that priority creditors *within a class* share equally in any distribution. Thus, within a priority class, there is no payment hierarchy. There are several exceptions, however, to this general rule.

a. Domestic Support Obligations

There is a hierarchy of payment among first priority domestic support obligation claims. The trustee, if she administers assets to pay a domestic support obligation, is paid first, then a spouse, former spouse, or child of the debtor with a domestic support obligation claim, and finally, a governmental unit with a domestic support obligation assigned to it by a spouse, former spouse, or child of the debtor. [B.C. § 507(a)(1)(A)–(C); *see supra* §E.2.a of this Chapter]

b. Conversion to Chapter 7

If a case is converted from Chapter 11, 12, or 13 to a case under Chapter 7, the administrative expense claims in the Chapter 7 case *after conversion* have priority over the administrative expenses incurred prior to conversion. [B.C. § 726(b)] The reason for prioritizing payment of Chapter 7 post-conversion administrative expenses is to "provide an incentive to encourage capable trustees and professionals to act" in the converted case. [*In re* **Rittenhouse,** 76 B.R. 610 (Bankr. S.D. Ohio 1987)]

c. Super-Priority: Inadequately Protected Secured Creditor

If the trustee, under §§ 362, 363, or 364, provides adequate protection to a creditor whose claim is secured by a lien on the debtor's property, but the adequate protection ultimately proves to be deficient, the creditor will receive an administrative expense claim with *priority over all other administrative expenses* allowed against the debtor's estate. [B.C. § 507(b)]

e.g. **Example:** Debtor filed for relief under Chapter 11. Debtor owed Creditor $2.7 million, which was secured by a properly perfected security interest in Debtor's accounts receivable. Debtor sought an order to use cash collateral, and at the cash collateral hearing the accounts receivable were valued at $836,616. The bankruptcy court entered an order authorizing Debtor to use cash collateral and granting adequate protection to Creditor in the form of a replacement lien on Debtor's post-petition accounts receivable and inventory, up to $836,616. Debtor's reorganization effort failed, and there was a shortfall of more than $427,000 in Creditor's adequate protection. As a result, the bankruptcy court held that Creditor had a super-priority claim under § 507(b) for $427,766, which was the amount that Creditor was not adequately protected. There were not enough assets in the estate, however, to pay Creditor's claim. Because the Code provides that a super-priority administrative claim must be paid prior to any other administrative claim, the bankruptcy court ordered the disgorgement of interim fees paid to other professionals in the case—Debtor's attorneys and the lawyer for the unsecured creditors' committee. [*In re* **Wilson-Seafresh, Inc.,** 263 B.R. 624 (Bankr. N.D. Fla. 2001)]

d. Super Super-Priority: Post-Petition Credit

If the trustee or the debtor in possession is unable to obtain unsecured post-petition credit by means of an administrative expense priority, the court may approve new credit or the incurring of debt that has *priority over all other administrative expense* claims, *including any super-priority claims* arising from the failure of adequate protection. [B.C. § 364(c)(1)]

4. Subrogation

A third party, such as a co-debtor or a surety, who becomes subrogated to the rights of a holder of a claim entitled to a first priority or fourth through ninth priority does *not* become subrogated to the holder's right to priority. Therefore, the subrogated claim is treated as a nonpriority claim. [B.C. § 507(d)]

a. Distinguish Assignment

It is important to distinguish subrogation from assignment. Section 507(d) does not apply to assignments and, thus, an assignee of a priority claim should have the same right to priority as the assignor. A subrogee acquires a claim because it paid a debt on which it was legally or contractually obligated. With an assignment, however, the assignee pays a claim even though it has no legal or contractual obligation to pay. [4 Collier ¶ 507.16; *see* **Nova Information Systems v. Premier Operations, Ltd. (***In re* **Premier Operations),** 294 B.R. 213 (S.D. N.Y. 2003) (holding that creditor was not entitled to a priority claim under § 507(a)(7) [(a)(6) at time of the case] because it was a subrogee, not an assignee, of customers' claims, and noting the distinction between a creditor that voluntarily pays on claims in a negotiated transaction with consideration and a creditor that pays on a claim "unwillingly by operation of other contractual or legal obligations")]

b. Administrative Expense Claims, Gap Claims, and Personal Injury Claims

Keep in mind that § 507(d) applies *only* to first priority and fourth through ninth priority claims. Thus, an entity subrogated to the rights of (i) a holder of an administrative expense claim (second priority), (ii) a holder of a gap claim in an involuntary case (third priority), or (iii) a holder of a personal injury claim (tenth priority) become subrogated to the respective priorities of such claims. [4 Collier ¶ 507.16; § 507(d), 507(a)(2), (3), (10)]

F. Tax Claims

1. Determination of Tax Liability

The bankruptcy court has jurisdiction to determine the amount or legality of any tax, fine, penalty, or addition to tax that has ***not*** been contested in and adjudicated by an appropriate judicial or administrative court ***prior to bankruptcy.*** The court may exercise its power to determine tax liability regardless of whether the tax has been assessed or paid. [B.C. §§ 505(a)(1), (2)(A)] In BAPCPA, Congress created a limitation on the bankruptcy court's powers with regard to ad valorem taxes. Thus, the bankruptcy court ***may not*** determine the amount or legality of any amount arising in connection with an ***ad valorem tax*** on the estate's real or personal property if the applicable period for contesting or re-determining that amount under applicable nonbankruptcy law has expired. [B.C. § 505(a)(2)(C)]

Example: Debtor filed for relief under Chapter 11. Tax Collector filed a proof of claim in Debtor's bankruptcy case for unpaid ad valorem taxes, based on the appraised value of 20 investment properties that Debtor owned. Prior to bankruptcy, Appraiser had certified the tax rolls to Tax Collector for collection of taxes. Under state law, Debtor had 60 days from certification to file suit to challenge Appraiser's valuation for tax purposes. Debtor did not do so. Instead, after the 60-day period had expired, Debtor objected to Tax Collector's proof of claim and argued that the assessed value of the 20 properties exceeded their actual value. The bankruptcy court held that Debtor's objection was timely under § 108 of the Code, even though the time to contest the Appraiser's value had run under state law. The district court affirmed the bankruptcy court's decision. The Court of Appeals, however, reversed the district court's decision and held that Congress intended with § 505(a)(2)(C) "to create an exception to the general time limits for contesting a tax assessment set forth in § 108(a)." The court noted that § 505(a)(2)(C) speaks in terms of the expiration of a time period under applicable *nonbankruptcy* law and that § 108 is a bankruptcy law, not a nonbankruptcy law. Thus, the court found that because the time period for contesting the appraisal had run under state law, Debtor's objection to Tax Collector's claim was untimely. [**Dubov v. Read (*In re* Read),** 692 F.3d 1185 (11th Cir. 2012)]

2. Tax Refund

The bankruptcy court cannot determine the ***estate's*** right to a tax refund ***before the earlier of 120 days*** after the trustee properly requests a refund from the appropriate governmental unit, ***or*** a determination by that governmental unit of the trustee's request. [B.C. § 505(a)(2)(B)]

3. Tax Liability of Estate

Section 505(b) of the Bankruptcy Code provides a process by which the trustee "can obtain an expedited determination" of the estate's post-petition tax liability. [4 Collier ¶ 505.01] A trustee may request that the appropriate taxing authority determine any ***unpaid tax liability of*** *the estate* incurred during the administration of the case by submitting to the governmental unit a tax return accompanied by a request for a determination of the tax to the address provided by the governmental unit for making such requests. [B.C. § 505(b)(2); *see infra* § F.7 on Address for § 505 Requests]

a. Discharge upon Payment

Unless the return submitted is *fraudulent* or contains *material misrepresentations,* the estate, the trustee, and the debtor or a successor to the debtor are discharged from any liability for the tax in any of the following circumstances.

(i) The tax *indicated on the return is paid* and the taxing authority *either* (1) fails to notify the trustee *within 60 days* that the return has been *chosen for examination*, or (2) fails to complete an examination and notify the trustee of any tax owing *within 180 days* (or such additional time allowed by the court for cause) after the trustee's request for determination. [B.C. § 505(b)(2)(A)]

(ii) The *court, after notice and hearing, determines the amount* owed upon completion of the taxing authority's examination and that amount of *tax is paid.* [B.C. § 505(b)(2)(B)]

(iii) The amount of tax that the *taxing authority determines is due is paid*. [B.C. § 505(b)(2)(C)]

4. Assessment

After the court determines a tax under § 505, the taxing authority may assess the amount of the tax against the estate, the debtor, or a successor to the debtor, notwithstanding the automatic stay. [B.C. §§ 505(c), 362]

5. Interest on Tax Claims

BAPCPA added a new section to the Code that spells out the rate at which interest is to be paid on tax claims. If the Code requires the payment of interest on a *tax claim* or an *administrative expense tax* claim, or the payment of interest to enable a *tax creditor* to receive the *present value* of its claim, then the interest rate is the applicable *rate under nonbankruptcy law.* [B.C. § 511(a)] In the case of taxes paid pursuant to a *confirmed plan under Chapter 11, 12, or 13,* the date for determining the interest rate is the calendar month in which the plan is confirmed. [B.C. § 511(b)]

6. Proof

The Supreme Court, in a unanimous decision, held that "in the absence of modification in the Bankruptcy Code the burden of proof on a tax claim in bankruptcy remains where the substantive tax law puts it." [**Raleigh v. Illinois Department of Revenue,** 530 U.S. 15 (2000)]

7. Address for § 505 Requests

The bankruptcy clerk must maintain a list under which federal, state, and local taxing authorities may *designate an address for service of requests under § 505* and describe where to obtain more information for filing such requests. [B.C. § 505(b)(1)(A)] If the taxing authority does not provide the bankruptcy clerk with an address for service of § 505 requests, then these requests may be served at the address for filing of a tax return or protest with the relevant taxing authority. [B.C. § 505(b)(1)(B)] Congress added this subsection in BAPCPA.

G. Subrogation Claims

1. Subrogee

A subrogee is an entity that **has paid** a creditor's claim against the debtor because the entity either had secured the claim or was liable with the debtor on the claim as a co-debtor, co-maker, surety, or guarantor. [B.C. § 509(a)] "When the doctrine of subrogation applies, the party paying the loss or claim (the subrogee) steps into the shoes of the person who suffered the loss (the subrogor), thereby allowing the subrogee to succeed to the legal rights and claims of the subrogor with respect to the loss or claim." [**Milgard Tempering, Inc. v. DaRosa (*In re* DaRosa),** 318 B.R. 871 (B.A.P. 9th Cir. 2004)]

2. Subrogee Receives Creditor's Rights

With certain exceptions, a subrogee succeeds to the rights of the creditor whose claim it paid to the extent of the amount paid. [B.C. § 509(a)]

Remember: The subrogee of a first or fourth through ninth priority claim does not become subrogated to the holder's right to priority. [B.C. § 507(d); *see supra* § E.4 of this Chapter]

3. Exceptions

Subrogation to the rights of a creditor is not allowed in the following situations. [B.C. § 509(b)]

a. Reimbursement or Contribution Claim

The first **three exceptions** to the right of subrogation all relate to an entity's claim for **reimbursement or contribution** based the entity's payment of the creditor's claim. First, subrogation is not allowed to the extent that the entity's claim for reimbursement or contribution is **allowed** under § 502. [B.C. § 509(b)(1)(A)] Section 502(e) provides that an entity's claim for reimbursement or contribution is not allowable if the entity asserts a right of subrogation under § 509. [B.C. § 502(e)(1)(C)] Thus, the entity must choose: a right to subrogation under § 509 or filing a claim for reimbursement or contribution.

Second, subrogation is not allowed to the extent that the claim for reimbursement or contribution has been **disallowed,** for example for one of the reasons specified in § 502(b). This provision does **not** apply if the claim was disallowed on the basis of § 502(e). [B.C. § 509(b)(1)(B)]

Finally, subrogation is not allowed to the extent that the claim for reimbursement or contribution has been **subordinated under § 510.** [B.C. § 509(b)(1)(C); *see infra* § H of this Chapter on subordination]

b. Co-Debtor Received Consideration

To the extent that the co-debtor, rather than the debtor, received the consideration for the claim held by the principal creditor, subrogation is not allowed. [B.C. § 509(b)(2)] This provision of the Code ties back to the rationale underlying § 509. The co-debtor must be **secondarily, not primarily, liable** on the debt. Receiving consideration in exchange for agreeing to pay the debt suggests primary, not secondary, liability. As the author of a well-respected treatise explains: "courts refuse to extend section 509 to a party who is itself primarily liable on the creditor's claim or has otherwise received the consideration for the claim of the creditor." [4 Collier ¶ 509.02(2)]

4. Subordination to Principal Creditor's Claim

The bankruptcy court must subordinate a co-debtor's claim for subrogation or for reimbursement or contribution to the principal creditor's claim until the principal creditor's claim is paid in full, either through distribution under the Bankruptcy Code or by other means. [B.C. § 509(c)]

e.g. **Example:** Anderson Excavating Company subcontracted work to M&S Grading on a public construction project. State law required Anderson to post a bond to ensure payment of all labor and materials on the project. M&S had various collective bargaining agreements under which it owed monies to pension and health plans. During the construction project, M&S failed to make approximately $197,000 of contributions to these employee plans (the Plans). Because M&S was unable to make these contributions, Anderson paid more than $134,000 of the $197,000 owing in order to settle the Plans' claim against Anderson's bond. In the M&S bankruptcy, the Plans claimed that Anderson was not subrogated to the Plan's claim for the unpaid contributions. The bankruptcy court agreed with the Plans, explaining that "§ 509(c) requires that a subrogated claim is nevertheless subordinated to the primary creditor's claim until the primary creditor is paid in full." Therefore, Anderson would receive nothing until the Plans' claim was paid in full. [*In re* **M&S Grading, Inc.,** 2009 WL 1872600 (Bankr. D. Neb. 2009)]

H. Subordination of Claims

1. Subordination Agreement

A subordination agreement is an agreement in which one party (the subordinating party) agrees that its interest in property will have a lower priority than the interest to which it is subordinate. In bankruptcy, a subordination agreement is enforceable to the same extent it is enforceable under applicable nonbankruptcy law. [B.C. § 510(a)]

2. Subordination of Claims for Purchase or Sale of a Security

A claim for damages, rescission, or contribution or reimbursement arising from the purchase or sale of a security of the debtor or its affiliate *must be subordinated* to all claims or interests *senior or equal* to that which the security represents. [B.C. § 510(b)] One reason for the subordination rule is that Congress determined that the "risk of illegality in securities issuance should be borne by those investing in securities and not by general creditors." [H.R. Rep. No. 95–595, at 195 (1977)] Another is that creditors rely on the equity cushion that shareholder investment provides. [*In re* **Lehman Bros., Inc.,** 519 B.R. 434 (S.D. N.Y. 2014)]

a. Exception: Common Stock

If the security is common stock, then the claim will be subordinated to the *same priority as common stock,* not to a lower priority. [B.C. § 510(b)]

e.g. **Example:** Debtor Corporation files a voluntary Chapter 7 petition, and Security Holder files a claim for rescission of certain purchases of *preferred stock,* based on alleged violations by Debtor Corporation of § 10(b) of the Securities Exchange Act of 1934. [15 U.S.C. § 78j(b)] A claim for rescission means that Security Holder wants to *undo* the transaction. She no longer wants to hold an equity position in Debtor Corporation; she wants damages from Debtor Corporation based on a theory of restitution. Under § 510, however, a claim for rescission results in the Security Holder being subordinated to the interest (preferred shareholder) that she held prior to rescission. Thus, Security Holder does not share in any distribution as part of the class of general unsecured creditors based on undoing the sale of preferred stock to her. Nor does she share in any distribution made to the preferred shareholders. Instead, Security Holder's claim for rescission is be paid *after* preferred shareholders are paid. In other words, her claim for rescission is subordinated to a position *below* the interests of the preferred shareholders but *above* the interests of the common shareholders.

3. Equitable Subordination

The court, after notice and a hearing, also has the equitable power (i) to subordinate all or part of an allowed secured or unsecured claim to another allowed claim, (ii) to subordinate all or part of an allowed interest to another allowed interest, or (iii) to order that any lien securing such a subordinated claim be transferred to the estate. [B.C. § 510(c)]

a. Test

The Fifth Circuit in the pre-Code case of *In re Mobile Steel* established what has become the standard test for equitable subordination. [**United States v. Noland,** 517 U.S. 535 (1996) (noting that district courts and courts of appeals had "generally followed the *Mobile Steel* formulation"); **Sender v. Bronze Group, Ltd. (*In re* Hedged-Investment Assocs.),** 380 F.3d 1292 (10th Cir. 2004) (stating that *Mobile Steel* has become "the standard formulation of the common law of equitable subordination")] The *Mobile Steel* test requires proof of the following elements:

(i)   *inequitable conduct* on the part of the claimant to be subordinated;

(ii) *injury to the creditors* of the debtor, or an *unfair advantage* to the claimant, due to the misconduct; and

(iii) equitable subordination of the claim is *not inconsistent with the provisions of the Bankruptcy Code.*

[**Benjamin v. Diamond (*In re* Mobile Steel Co.),** 563 F.2d 692 (5th Cir. 1977)]

b. Inequitable Conduct

An essential element in the equitable subordination of a claim or interest is showing inequitable conduct on the claimant's part. Such misconduct falls into one of the following three categories: (i) fraud, illegality, or breach of fiduciary duties; (ii) undercapitalization; or (iii) the claimant's use of the debtor as a mere instrumentality or alter ego. [**Official Committee of Unsecured Creditors of HH Liquidation, LLC v. Comvest Group Holdings, LLC (*In re* HH Liquidation, LLC),** 590 B.R. 211 (Bankr. D. Del. 2018)] While citing favorably to the *Mobile Steel* test, the Supreme Court left open the question of whether "a bankruptcy court must always find creditor misconduct before a claim may be equitably subordinated." [**Noland,** *supra*]

c. Causation

A claim or interest is equitably subordinated *only* to the extent necessary to offset the harm caused to the debtor and his creditors by the claimant's conduct.

d. Insiders and Fiduciaries

Courts usually rigorously examine the dealings of insiders and fiduciaries for *good faith and fairness.* [**Pepper v. Litton,** 308 U.S. 295 (1939)] In a case involving an insider, the trustee has the burden of presenting material evidence of the insider's unfair conduct. The insider then must rebut that evidence by demonstrating that her transactions with the debtor were fair. If the case involves a non-insider, however, there must be evidence of more egregious behavior, such as " 'fraud, spoliation or overreaching.' " [**Schubert v.**

Lucent Technologies, Inc. (*In re* Winstar Communications, Inc.), 554 F.3d 382 (3d Cir. 2009)] The burden-shifting framework used in equitable subordination cases involving insiders does not apply to cases involving non-insiders. The "proponent of subordination" always has the burden of proof. [*In re* NJ Affordable Homes Corp., 2013 WL 6048836 (Bankr. D. N.J. 2013)]

I. Distribution Outside of Bankruptcy Code

1. Creditors of Partnership

A creditor of a partnership debtor who receives payment on an allowed claim against the partnership from a general partner who is not a debtor in a Chapter 7 case and who has not secured the creditor's claim with a lien on the general partner's own property is prohibited from receiving any payment on the claim until all of the creditors with whom she would have shared equally have received payment equal to the consideration she received from the general partner. [B.C. § 508]

Chapter Eight

Debtor's Exemptions

Chapter Approach

This is the first of two Chapters covering the areas of bankruptcy law that give the debtor a "fresh start." This Chapter covers *exemptions and redemption*; both topics deal with the debtor's ability to exit bankruptcy with property sufficient to embark on a fresh financial start. Chapter Nine covers discharge and the Code's provisions protecting debtors against discrimination post-bankruptcy.

An individual debtor is entitled to *exempt* certain *property* from the bankruptcy estate. By allowing the debtor to exempt property, the Code ensures that bankruptcy does not leave the debtor destitute and without the basic necessities of life. The debtor may elect either the exemptions provided for by the Bankruptcy Code, if the debtor's domiciliary state has *not opted out*, or those permitted under applicable state exemption law. Exemption law after BAPCPA is complicated. BAPCPA created *domiciliary rules* that raise questions about the extraterritorial effect of state exemption laws, for example. After BAPCPA, the Code now contains certain *federal limitations* on exemptions even for debtors using the exemptions provided by state law. Congress enacted these limitations to curtail debtors from forum shopping in an effort to obtain the benefit of more favorable exemptions.

Your professor may test you on the debtor's ability to avoid certain liens and security interests in order to take full advantage of available exemptions. You need to understand how to apply the Code's rules that allow a debtor to avoid judicial liens and certain nonpossessory nonpurchase-money security interests to the extent that they *impair an exemption* of the debtor.

Finally, an individual debtor may choose to *redeem* tangible personal property from a lien by paying the secured party the market value of the collateral. Redemption, however, is available only in a Chapter 7 case and only for dischargeable consumer debts.

A. Exemptions

1. Fresh Start: Exempt Property

As discussed earlier in Chapter Five, filing of the petition creates the bankruptcy estate which comprises all of the legal and equitable interests of the debtor. An individual debtor, however, does not emerge destitute from bankruptcy, because she is entitled to certain exemptions from property of the estate, either under the Bankruptcy Code or pursuant to applicable state law and nonbankruptcy federal law. These exemptions apply only to individual debtors—not to partnerships or corporations—in cases under Chapters 7, 11, 12, and 13. A waiver by the debtor of an exemption (or exemptions) in favor of an unsecured creditor is unenforceable in bankruptcy. [B.C. § 522(e)]

a. States Opting out

A majority of states have opted out of the federal bankruptcy exemption scheme, thereby restricting debtors domiciled there to the exemptions allowed under their state law and federal nonbankruptcy law. Section 522(b)(2) authorizes the states to opt out.

b. States Not Opting out

In states that have not opted out, the debtor may choose *either* the federal bankruptcy exemptions or those permitted under applicable state and federal nonbankruptcy law. [B.C. § 522(b)(1), (2)]

(i) Joint Case

If spouses file a joint petition for bankruptcy or if their individually filed cases are jointly administered, then both spouses must elect the same exemptions, either state or federal. [B.C. §§ 301–303, 522(b); Bankruptcy Rule 1015(b) (joint administration)] If the debtors are not able to agree, they will be deemed to have chosen the federal bankruptcy exemptions. [B.C. § 522(b)]

2. Federal Bankruptcy Exemptions

In states that have not opted out, the debtor may elect the federal exemptions. The maximum amount of the exemptions increases every three years. [B.C. § 104(a)] Currently, the maximum exemptions of a debtor's interests in property permitted under the Code are as follows. [B.C. § 522(d)]

a. Homestead

The debtor may exempt up to $27,900 in *real or personal property* used by the debtor or a dependent as a *residence,* in a *cooperative that owns property* that the debtor or a dependent uses as a *residence,* or in a *burial plot* for the debtor or a dependent. [B.C. § 522(d)(1)]

b. Motor Vehicle

The debtor may exempt up to $4,450 in *one motor vehicle.* [B.C. § 522(d)(2)]

c. Household Goods, Clothing, Books, Crops, Animals

The debtor may exempt up to *$14,875 in aggregate value* in household furnishings, household goods, clothing, appliances, books, musical instruments, crops, or animals that are held primarily for the *personal, family, or household use* of the debtor or a dependent.

But note: The debtor may not exempt more than *$700 in any single item* from the list above. [B.C. § 522(d)(3)]

 Example: Daria files for relief under Chapter 7. The total value of her household furnishings and goods, books, and clothing (with the exception of a fur coat) is $11,000. When she died several years ago, Daria's grandmother left her a fur coat worth about $2,000. Daria cannot use the household goods exemption to exempt the full $2,000 value of the fur coat. While her household belongings and clothing total $13,000, with the fur coat's value included, the Code caps out the exemption for any single item at $700. Therefore, Daria may exempt $700 of the coat's value using § 522(d)(3). She will have to use another exemption, e.g., the wildcard, to exempt the remaining value.

d. Jewelry

The debtor may exempt up to $1,875 in jewelry held primarily for the *personal, family, or household* use of the debtor or a dependent. [B.C. § 522(d)(4)]

e. Wildcard Exemption

The debtor may exempt up to $1,475, plus up to $13,950 of any unused portion of the homestead exemption, *in any property.* [B.C. § 522(d)(1), (5)] This exemption, with a current total ceiling of $15,425, is designed primarily for the benefit of non-homeowner debtors.

 Example: Doris rents an apartment. Several years ago, her grandmother passed away and left her a necklace and earring set valued at approximately $17,300.

Doris may use the jewelry exemption to exempt $1,875 of the set's value, and because she rents she may apply the entire wild card exemption of $15,425 to the remaining value of the necklace and earring set.

Example: Doris has $27,900 in equity in her home. Several years ago, her grandmother passed away and left her a necklace and earring set valued at approximately $14,000. Doris uses the homestead exemption to exempt $27,900 of the equity in her home. That leaves her only $1,475 of the wild card exemption to apply to the jewelry set. While Doris also may use the jewelry exemption, the combined wild card and jewelry exemptions permit Doris to exempt only $3,350 of the jewelry set's $14,000 value.

f. Tools of the Trade

The debtor may exempt up to $2,800 in her professional books or tools of the trade or those of a dependent. [B.C. § 522(d)(6)]

g. Life Insurance

The debtor may exempt any *unmatured* life insurance contract that she owns, except a credit life insurance contract. [B.C. § 522(d)(7)] This provision "refers to the life insurance contract itself [and] does not encompass any other rights under the contract, such as the right to borrow out the loan value." [H.R. Rep. No. 95–595, at 361 (1977)]

h. Loan Value or Accrued Interest of Life Insurance

The debtor may exempt up to $14,875 in the loan value or in accrued interest or dividends of any unmatured life insurance contract that the debtor owns. [B.C. § 522(d)(8)] The $14,875 exemption is reduced by the amount of any premium payment automatically transferred post-petition pursuant to the terms of the pre-petition insurance contract. [B.C. §§ 522(d)(8), 542(d)]

(i) Insured

For purposes of this exemption, *the insured* must be either the debtor or an individual of whom the debtor is a dependent. [B.C. § 522(d)(8)] For purposes of § 522, a dependent includes, but is not limited to, a spouse, regardless of whether the spouse is, in fact, dependent. [B.C. § 522(a)(1)]

i. Health Aids

The debtor may exempt health aids prescribed by a professional for the debtor or a dependent. [B.C. § 522(d)(9)] There is no monetary cap for this exemption.

j. Government Benefits

The debtor may exempt from the estate her right to receive social security benefits, veterans' benefits, local public assistance, unemployment benefits or compensation, or disability or illness benefits. [B.C. § 522(d)(10)(A)–(C)]

k. Alimony, Support, or Maintenance

The debtor may exempt payments received for alimony, support, or maintenance, to the extent that it is reasonably necessary to support the debtor and any dependent. [B.C. § 522(d)(10)(D)]

l. Pension Plan

The debtor may exempt payments under a stock bonus, pension, profit sharing, annuity, or similar plan that are based on length of service, age, illness, disability, or death, to the extent that such payment is reasonably necessary to support the debtor and any dependent. [B.C. § 522(d)(10)(E)]

Remember: The Supreme Court in **Patterson v. Shumate**, 504 U.S. 753 (1992) held that the debtor's rights in an ERISA-qualified pension plan are not property of the estate. [B.C. § 541(c)(2); *see supra* Chapter Five, § A.2.a] The debtor does not exempt property that is *excluded* from the bankruptcy estate.

(i) Exception

This exemption does not apply (1) to payments under a plan or contract that was established by or under the auspices of an insider that employed the debtor at the time that the debtor's rights arose; (2) such payments are on account of age or length of service; *and* (3) the plan or contract does not qualify under § 401(a), 403(a), 403(b), or 408 of the Internal Revenue Code. [B.C. § 522(d)(10)(E)(i)–(iii)]

m. Crime Victim Award

The debtor may exempt property or payments received pursuant to an award under a crime victim's reparation law. [B.C. § 522(d)(11)(A)]

n. Wrongful Death Award

The debtor may exempt her right to receive payment arising from the wrongful death of an individual of whom the debtor was a dependent, to the extent that the payment is reasonably necessary to support the debtor and any of her dependents. [B.C. § 522(d)(11)(B)]

o. Life Insurance Proceeds

The debtor may exempt a payment under a life insurance contract that insured the life of an individual if debtor was a dependent of that individual on the date of the individual's death. The debtor may exempt the payment only to the extent that the payment is reasonably necessary to support the debtor and any of her dependents. [B.C. § 522(d)(11)(C)]

p. Personal Injury Award

The debtor may exempt payments, up to a maximum of $27,900, arising from personal bodily injury of the debtor or an individual of whom the debtor is a dependent. This exemption does not include compensation for pain and suffering or compensation for actual pecuniary loss, such as medical expenses. [B.C. § 522(d)(11)(D)]

q. Loss of Future Earnings

The debtor may exempt compensation for the loss of future earnings of either the debtor or an individual of whom the debtor was or is a dependent, to the extent that the payment is reasonably necessary to support the debtor and any of her dependents. [B.C. § 522(d)(11)(E)]

r. Retirement Funds

Congress added an exemption in BAPCPA for the debtor's retirements funds, so long as the monies are in a fund or account that is exempt from taxation under certain provisions of the Internal Revenue Code. [B.C. § 522(d)(12); 26 U.S.C. §§ 401, 403, 408, 408A, 414, 457, 501(a)] At the same time, Congress created a limit on the aggregate value of assets in certain IRAs that an individual debtor may exempt. [B.C. § 522(n); 26 U.S.C. §§ 408, 408A] The *limitation* now stands at *$1,512,350.* The limitation does not apply to certain simplified employee pensions or simple retirement accounts. [B.C. § 522(n); 26 U.S.C. §§ 408(k), (p)] The aggregate value limitation also does not apply to certain rollover contributions and earnings on those contributions. [B.C. § 522(n); 26 U.S.C. §§ 402(c), (e)(6); 403(a)(4), (5); 403(b)(8)] Finally, a court may increase the monetary cap in the interests of justice. [B.C. § 522(n)]

3. State Exemption Law, Federal Limits, and Nonbankruptcy Federal Exemptions

a. Introduction

The exemptions available to the debtor are those allowable under applicable state law and nonbankruptcy federal law, subject to the Bankruptcy Code's domiciliary requirement and to new Code restrictions on state homestead exemptions. [B.C. § 522(b)(3), (o), (p), (q)]

b. *Which* State's Exemption Law?

BAPCPA made the determination of which state's exemption law applies to the debtor more difficult. Subject to the Code's domiciliary requirement and to federal restrictions on state homestead exemptions, the exemptions allowable under state law are those in effect: (i) as of the date the bankruptcy petition was filed and (ii) in the state where the debtor has been domiciled for the *730 days or two years* prior to filing the bankruptcy petition. If the debtor has not been domiciled in a single state for those 730 days, then the exemption law of the place where debtor has been domiciled for the *180 days immediately preceding the 730-day period* applies. If the debtor has not been domiciled in a single state for the *180-day period,* then the exemption law of the place where debtor has been domiciled for the *longest portion of the 180-day period* applies. State law exemptions vary widely from state to state. [B.C. § 522(b)(3)(A)]

Example: Darren files for relief under Chapter 7 on March 5, 2018, in the Western District of Michigan. Darren grew up in Chicago, Illinois, but changed his domicile to Grand Rapids, Michigan on July 5, 2017. As a result, Darren has lived in Michigan for only eight months, which is less than the 730 days required by the Bankruptcy Code. Two years or 730 days prior to March 5, 2018 is March 5, 2016. For the six months prior to March 5, 2016, Darren was domiciled in Chicago, Illinois. Therefore, the Illinois exemptions apply to Darren's case, even though he lives in Michigan at the time of his bankruptcy filing. Can Darren argue that Michigan is not an opt-out state and, thus, he can choose the federal exemptions? The problem is that Illinois exemption law governs, and Illinois is an opt-out state. But is the Illinois opt-out statute limited to Illinois residents? If so, then Darren can claim the federal exemptions and argue that Illinois opt-out law does not apply to him because he is not a resident of Illinois. [*See, e.g.,* **Camp v. Ingalls (*In re* Camp),** 631 F.3d 757 (11th Cir. 2011) (holding that Chapter 7 debtor who filed in Texas but whose domicile under § 522(b)(3)(A) was Florida could use federal exemptions because Florida's opt-out statute did not apply to non-residents); *In re* **Battle,** 366 B.R. 635 (Bankr. W.D. Tex. 2006) (same in Chapter 13 case)]

c. Problems with the Domiciliary Requirement

(i) The "Hanging Paragraph"

If the 730-day/180-day domiciliary requirement results in the debtor being ineligible for any exemption, then the debtor may elect the federal exemptions. This new "hanging paragraph" applies regardless of whether debtor's domicile is in an opt-out state. [B.C. § 522(b)(3)]

Example: On April 19, 2006, Debtor filed for relief under Chapter 7 in the bankruptcy court for the Middle District of Florida. At the time that he filed for bankruptcy, Debtor had lived in Florida for less than a year. Prior to the Florida move, Debtor's domicile was Indiana. In his bankruptcy case, Debtor claimed the federal exemptions, even though Florida is an opt-out state. The trustee objected, claiming that Debtor was limited to Indiana's exemptions. Indiana, however, limited its exemptions to debtors domiciled in the state on the date of the bankruptcy filing. The bankruptcy court held that Debtor could claim the federal exemptions based on the "hanging paragraph" at the end of § 522(b)(3). The court explained that Debtor could not claim the Florida exemptions, because he had not been domiciled in Florida for 730 days at the time of bankruptcy, and also could not claim the Indiana exemptions, which were limited to debtors domiciled in Indiana at the time of bankruptcy filing. Because the operation of the domiciliary requirement rendered Debtor ineligible for any exemption, the court concluded that Debtor could claim the federal exemptions. [*In re* **West,** 352 B.R. 905 (Bankr. M.D. Fla. 2006)]

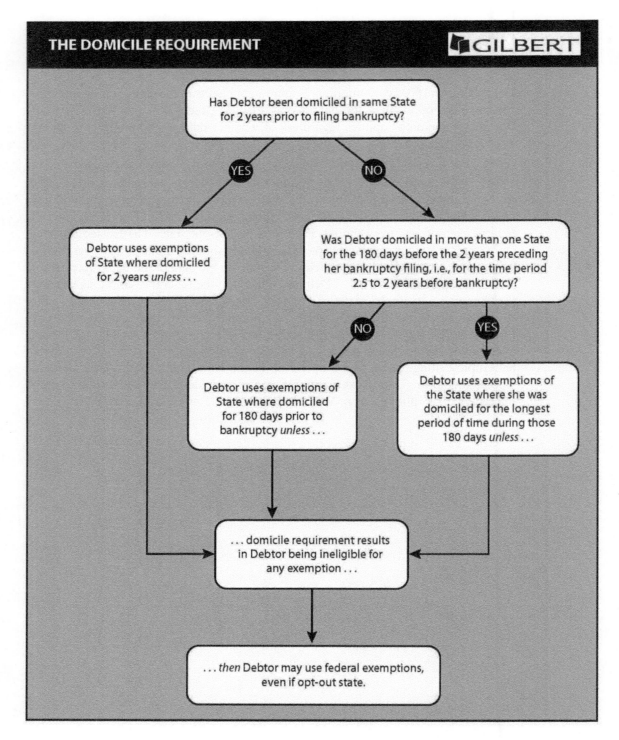

(ii) Application of a State's Exemptions to Property Located Outside the State

Another issue under the Code's new domiciliary requirement is whether a state's exemption laws apply to property located outside the state of bankruptcy filing when state exemption law is silent on that question. The *majority rule* is the *state-specific interpretation,* which provides that if a state does not limit the application of its exemption laws to property located inside the state then the bankruptcy court may apply a state's exemption laws to the debtor's property wherever it may be located.

Example: Married Debtors filed for relief under Chapter 7 in the Northern District of West Virginia approximately four months after moving from Louisiana. Debtors exempted real and personal property located in Louisiana using the Louisiana exemptions, but also exempted personal property located in West Virginia using the Louisiana exemptions. The Chapter 7 trustee objected to the Debtors' use of Louisiana exemptions to property not located in the State of Louisiana. The bankruptcy court held that Debtors could exempt their personal property in West Virginia using Louisiana's exemptions. On appeal, the district court affirmed the bankruptcy court's decision and adopted the state-specific interpretation. The district court held that the state-specific interpretation was the "plainest meaning of the statute" and the "most liberal interpretation that feasibly" could be applied to § 522(b)(3)(A) of the Bankruptcy Code. The Fourth Circuit affirmed the district court's decision and explained that "the state-specific approach 'best embodies congressional intent,' in that it treats § 522(b)(3)(A) as a 'straightforward . . . choice-of-law provision.'" [**Sheehan v. Ash,** 889 F.3d 171 (4th Cir. 2018)]

d. Federal Limitations on Homestead Exemptions

The Bankruptcy Code now contains three limitations on a debtor's right to fully exempt her homestead under state exemption laws. The limitations apply to *real or personal property* that the debtor or a dependent *uses as a residence* or *claims as a homestead,* a *cooperative* that owns property used by the debtor or a dependent as a *residence,* or a *burial plot* for the debtor or a dependent ("the Property").

(i) The Fraud Limitation

The fraud limitation reduces the amount of the debtor's state exemption to the extent that the debtor, *with intent to hinder, delay or defraud creditors,* disposed of *non-exempt property* in the *10-year period* preceding bankruptcy in order to increase the amount of the state-law exemption taken in the Property described above. Courts apply the same standard for *intent to hinder, delay or defraud creditors* under § 522(o) that they use under § 548. [B.C. §§ 522(o), 548(a)(1)(A)] If the debtor files for relief under Chapter 7, the trustee also may object to the debtor's discharge under § 727(a)(2).

Example: Debtor files for relief under Chapter 7. He owns a home valued, at the time of bankruptcy, at $400,000. A month prior to bankruptcy, Debtor had $100,000 in equity in his home. Debtor withdrew large sums of non-exempt cash from several accounts and applied these sums to pay down the mortgage on his home. At the time of bankruptcy, Debtor owned the home free and clear. Debtor lives in a state with a generous homestead exemption, so he exempts all $400,000 of his home's value. The Chapter 7 trustee objects to the exemption. If the trustee can show that Debtor acted with intent to hinder, delay, or defraud creditors, then Debtor may only exempt $100,000 of his home's value.

(ii) The 1215-Day Limitation

The Bankruptcy Code places a cap of *$189,050* on any interest that the debtor acquires in the Property described above during the *1215-day period* preceding the filing of bankruptcy. [B.C. § 522(p)(1)] This restriction does not apply to the *principal residence of a family farmer.* [B.C. § 522(p)(2)(A)] It also does not apply if the debtor uses the money received from sale of a residence acquired before the 1215-day period to acquire a new residence in the *same state* during the 1215-day period. [B.C. § 522(p)(2)(B)]

(iii) The "Bad Conduct" Limitation

The Bankruptcy Code caps the debtor's exemptible interest at *$189,050* on the Property described above in cases involving certain types of bad conduct by the debtor. The cap does not apply to the extent that the amount of the debtor's interest in the property is ***reasonably necessary for the support*** of the debtor and any dependents of the debtor. [B.C. § 522(q)(1), (2)] The cap applies to the debtor who:

(1) the bankruptcy court, after notice and a hearing, determines has been convicted of a *felony,* which under the circumstances demonstrates that filing for bankruptcy was an *abuse* of the Bankruptcy Code [B.C. § 522(q)(1)(A)];

(2) owes a debt arising from ***violations of federal or state securities laws,*** or regulations or orders issued pursuant to federal or state securities laws [B.C. § 522(q)(1)(B)(i)];

(3) owes a debt arising from ***fraud, deceit, or manipulation in a fiduciary capacity*** or in connection with the ***purchase or sale of securities registered under the federal securities laws*** [B.C. § 522(q)(1)(B)(ii)];

(4) owes a debt arising from any ***civil remedy under 18 U.S.C. § 1964*** [B.C. § 522(q)(1)(B)(iii)]; or

(5) owes a debt arising from any ***criminal act, intentional tort, or willful or reckless misconduct*** that caused ***serious physical injury or death*** to another person in the ***five years*** prior to the debtor filing for bankruptcy. [B.C. § 522(q)(1)(B)(iv)]

(iv) "Electing" State Exemptions

The Bankruptcy Code provides that the restrictions on exemptions in §§ 552(p) and (q) apply "as a result of [the debtor's] electing" the state law exemptions. Courts have grappled with whether Congress intended this language to apply only to debtors in states that have not opted out of the federal exemptions. In opt-out states, debtors must select the state exemptions and, therefore, do not elect them. The issue is limited to §§ 522(p) and (q), because § 522(o) does not contain the "as a result of electing" language. The *majority rule* is that *§§ 522(p) and (q) apply in both opt-out and non-opt-out states,* because Congress intended, when drafting those sections, to close the so-called mansion loophole.

> **Example:** Debtors filed for relief under Chapter 7. They listed a home worth $318,000 and noted that the home was subject to a mortgage of $158,000. The debtors used Nevada's exemptions to exempt the remaining $160,000 in equity in their home. (At the time, § 522(p)'s cap was $125,000.) The Chapter 7 trustee objected to the debtors' exemption, claiming that the debtors had not owned their home for at least 1215 days before the bankruptcy filing. The debtors argued that § 522(p) did not apply to them, because they filed for bankruptcy in an opt-out state and, thus, had not elected the state law exemptions. The bankruptcy court rejected the debtors' argument and concluded that the "electing" language in § 522(p) was a scrivener's error. The bankruptcy court held that "Congress intended to close the mansion loophole in opt-in states as well as opt-out states." [*In re* **Kane,** 336 B.R. 477 (Bankr. D. Nev. 2006)]

e. Nonbankruptcy Federal Law

Federal statutes other than the Bankruptcy Code sometimes provide exemptions that may be claimed under § 522(b)(3)(A), such as Social Security payments [42 U.S.C. § 407], veterans' benefits [38 U.S.C. § 5301], civil service retirement benefits [5 U.S.C. § 8346(a)], or military pension benefits. [38 U.S.C. § 5301] For a list of other benefits that the debtor may exempt, *see* 4 Collier ¶ 522.02(3).

f. Tenancy by the Entirety and Joint Tenancy

A debtor who uses the state exemptions also may exempt any interest in property she held, immediately prior to bankruptcy, as a tenant by the entirety or as a joint tenant, to the extent that applicable nonbankruptcy law exempts such interest from process. [B.C. § 522(b)(3)(B)] It is important to recognize that the treatment of property held by the entirety or in a joint tenancy depends on how state law treats such property.

(i) Which State Law Governs?

The location of the property determines the applicable state law. The 730-day/180-day domiciliary timelines are located in § 522(b)(3)(A), while the entireties property and joint tenancy provision is located in § 522(b)(3)(B). Therefore, the phrase "applicable nonbankruptcy law" in § 522(b)(3)(B) is the law of the state where such property is located. [4 Collier ¶ 522.06]

(ii) Tenancy by the Entirety

If only one of the tenants is a debtor in the case, her entitlement to exempt property under section 522(b)(3)(B) may depend not only on any protection from process afforded by applicable nonbankruptcy law, but also on the absence of any joint creditors. When a bankruptcy petition is filed by one spouse holding property as a tenant by the entirety with her non-filing husband, the property is exempt in most jurisdictions if there are *no joint* creditors. However, the First, Third, Fourth, Sixth and Eighth Circuits, interpreting various state exemption laws, have ruled that property held by the entirety is not exempt to the extent of any claims in the case by creditors to whom the debtor and her spouse are *indebted jointly.* [**Edmonston v. Murphy (*In re* Edmonston),** 107 F.3d 74 (1st Cir. 1997) (holding that debtor was not entitled to exemption for his residence, which was entireties property, because Massachusetts law allowed joint creditors to reach entireties property); ***In re* Garner,** 952 F.2d 232 (8th Cir. 1991) (holding that under Missouri law joint creditors may reach entireties property); **Sumy v. Schlossberg,** 777 F.2d 921 (4th Cir. 1985) ("reaffirming the guiding principle of all of [the Circuit's] relevant cases that joint creditors are entitled . . . to reach entireties property to satisfy their claims"); ***In re* Grosslight,** 757 F.2d 773 (6th Cir. 1985) (joint creditor may reach a "spouse's individual undivided interest in entireties property"); and **Napotnik v. Equibank & Parkvale Sav. Assoc.,** 679 F.2d 316 (3d Cir. 1982) (debtor could not avoid joint creditor's judicial lien on entireties property and could exempt only the equity in excess of that joint creditor's lien)]

The Seventh Circuit reached a different conclusion when interpreting Indiana's exemption laws. The court concluded that Indiana law "create[d] a blanket exemption for entirety property in the bankruptcy context." Thus, a debtor who owns entireties property with her non-debtor spouse and who takes Indiana's exemptions may exempt the entireties property in her bankruptcy case and protect it from the claims of joint creditors. [***In re* Paeplow,** 972 F.2d 730 (7th Cir. 1992)]

(iii) Joint Tenancy

When a joint tenant files for relief under the Bankruptcy Code, her proportionate interest in the joint tenancy becomes property of the estate. If the debtor owns property as a joint tenant with two other non-debtors, the debtor's one-third interest in the property becomes estate property. The issue, then, is the extent of the debtor's exemption in the property. The Bankruptcy Appellate Panel for the Eighth Circuit held that under Missouri law the debtor, one of three joint tenants, could take the entire state law homestead exemption, because there was no evidence that her non-debtor co-tenants had claimed an exemption in the property. [**Abernathy v. LaBarge (*In re* Abernathy),** 259 B.R. 330 (B.A.P. 8th Cir. 2001)]

The courts are split as to whether filing for bankruptcy severs the joint tenancy, thereby destroying the right of survivorship. The issue arises when one joint tenant dies during the pendency of the bankruptcy case. Does the trustee become a tenant in common with the surviving prior joint tenants?

Example: Debtor and her father were joint tenants of three certificates of deposit ("CDs"). Debtor filed for bankruptcy but died during the pendency of the bankruptcy case. The trustee claimed that one-half of the CD funds belonged to the bankruptcy estate, because filing for bankruptcy had severed the joint tenancy with the non-debtor father and, thus, destroyed the father's right of survivorship to the CDs. The trustee claimed that he and Debtor's father held the CDs as tenants in common. The bankruptcy court rejected the trustee's argument. The court held that § 522(b)(3)(B) "treats tenants by the entireties and joint tenants identically" and, thus, if filing for bankruptcy "does not sever the estate of [a] tenant by the entirety, then such filing does not sever joint tenants." The bankruptcy court also found that bankruptcy filing did not sever a joint tenancy under West Virginia law. Thus, the CD funds passed to Debtor's father by his right of survivorship. [*In re* **DeMarco,** 114 B.R. 121 (Bankr. W.D. W.Va. 1990)]

Compare: A married couple filed a joint petition for relief under the Bankruptcy Code. During the pendency of the case, the husband died. The couple owned real property as joint tenants. The bankruptcy court held that the bankruptcy filing severed the joint tenancy, thereby terminating the wife's right to survivorship and making her and the trustee tenants in common. The court ruled that the deceased husband's bankruptcy estate held a one-half interest in the real property. [*In re* **Tyson,** 48 B.R. 412 (Bankr. C.D. Ill. 1985)]

(iv) Sale of Property

The trustee may *sell* both the *estate's interest* and the *interest of any co-owner* in property in which the debtor, as of the commencement of the case, had an undivided interest as a *tenant in common, joint tenant, or tenant by the entirety*. The trustee must satisfy the conditions set forth in Bankruptcy Code § 363(h). [*See infra* Chapter Eleven, § B.8]

g. Retirement Funds

(i) Introduction

With BAPCPA, Congress expanded the right of debtors to exempt retirement funds. It added a new subsection to § 522(d) allowing debtors who elect the federal exemptions to exempt certain retirement funds. [B.C. § 522(d)(12); 26 U.S.C. §§ 401, 403, 408, 408A, 414, 457, 501(a)] At the same time, Congress gave debtors claiming state exemptions the same right to exempt retirement funds as provided to debtors claiming the federal exemptions. [B.C. § 522(b)(3)(C)]

(ii) Monetary Cap

The Bankruptcy Code places a cap of *$1,512,350* on the amount of retirement assets that a debtor may exempt in an *individual retirement account* under *§ 408 or § 408A (Roth IRA)* of the Internal Revenue Code. A *simplified employee pension plan* under *§ 408(k)* and a *simple retirement account* under *§ 408(p)* of the Internal Revenue Code are *not included* under the rule. The dollar limitation *does not apply* to amounts in the individual retirement account that are attributable to *rollover contributions* under §§ 402(c), 402(e)(6), 403(a)(4), 403(a)(5), and 403(b)(8) of the Internal Revenue Code or to *earnings on such rollover contributions.* [B.C. § 522(n)]

(iii) Type of Funds Covered

The debtor may exempt retirement funds, using either § 522(d)(12) (federal exemptions) or § 522(b)(3)(C) (state exemptions), in the following situations:

(1) the *retirement fund* has received a *favorable determination* under the relevant section of the Internal Revenue Code of 1986 and that determination is *in effect on the petition filing date* [B.C. § 522(b)(4)(A); 26 U.S.C. § 7805];

(2) the *retirement fund* has *not* received a *favorable determination* under the relevant section of the Internal Revenue Code of 1986 *but the debtor demonstrates* that:

 (a) there is no *prior determination to the contrary* by a court or the IRS; and

 (b) the retirement fund *substantially complies* with applicable requirements of the Internal Revenue Code *or* the *debtor is not materially responsible* for the fund's failure to *substantially comply* [B.C. § 522(b)(4)(B)];

(3) a *direct transfer from a tax-exempt fund* [B.C. § 522(b)(4)(C); 26 U.S.C. §§ 401, 401(a)(31), 403, 408, 408A, 414, 457, 501(a)];

(4) an eligible *rollover distribution* under the Internal Revenue Code [B.C. § 522(b)(4)(D)(i); 26 U.S.C. § 402(c)]; or

(5) a *distribution from a tax-exempt fund or account* that, to the extent allowed by law, is *deposited into a tax-exempt fund or account* no later than *60 days* after the distribution. [B.C. § 522(b)(4)(D)(ii); 26 U.S.C. §§ 401, 403, 408, 408A, 414, 457, 501(a)]

(iv) Inherited IRA

An inherited IRA is a traditional or a Roth IRA that is inherited after the death of the IRA's owner. The Supreme Court, in a unanimous opinion, held that monies in an inherited IRA do not qualify for exemption under § 522(b)(3)(C) because the monies do not constitute retirement funds. The Court explained that several characteristics of an inherited IRA, including the Tax Code's requirement that the heir withdraw all the funds within five years of the owner's death or take minimum annual distributions, differentiated it from traditional and Roth IRAs used for retirement planning. If a surviving spouse inherits the IRA, she may treat it as an inherited IRA *or* roll it over into her own IRA. If she rolls it over, then she can exempt it under § 522(b)(3)(C). The Internal Revenue Code, however, provides the roll over option only to a surviving spouse. [**Clark v. Rameker,** 573 U.S. 122 (2014); *see* **Lerbakken v. Sieloff and Associates (*In re* Lerbakken),** 590 B.R. 895 (B.A.P. 8th Cir. 2018) (holding that debtor could not exempt retirement monies that he received in divorce settlement, because the Supreme Court in *Clark v. Rameker* had "clearly suggest[ed] that the exemption is limited to individuals who create and contribute funds into the retirement account [and that] [r]etirement funds obtained or received by any other means do not meet this definition")]

4. Joint Case

In a joint case, *each debtor* is entitled to a separate claim of any allowable exemptions. [B.C. § 522(m)]

a. Federal Exemptions

The law is clear that joint debtors who elect the federal exemptions may stack their exemptions. Thus, a married couple may exempt up to $55,800 in their homestead and up to $29,750 in certain items intended for the personal, family, or household use of the debtors. [B.C. § 522(m)]

Note: Married debtors cannot double the $700 per item limit for household goods, however. The purpose of § 522(m) is not to give married couples the right to exempt better, i.e., more expensive, items of household goods than their single debtor counterparts.

(i) But Recall

In a joint case, *both debtors* must choose either the federal exemptions or the state exemptions, because the Code prohibits the stacking of federal and state exemptions. Thus, one spouse may not elect the federal exemptions while the other spouse elects the state exemptions. [B.C. § 522(b)(1)]

b. State Exemptions

In opt-out states, where debtors cannot elect the federal exemptions, the question has arisen as to whether married debtors may use § 522(m) to double the value of their states' exemption value. The majority of courts have held that state law controls whether debtors in opt-out states may stack state law exemption values. Thus, § 522(m) creates no "right to exemption doubling under state law where it does not otherwise exist." [*In re* **Pace,** 521 B.R. 124 (Bankr. N.D. Miss. 2014)]

Example: Husband and Wife filed a joint petition for relief under Chapter 7 in the bankruptcy court for the Northern District of Mississippi. Mississippi law, at the time, provided for a $75,000 homestead. Debtors doubled the homestead exemption value and exempted the full $130,000 value of their home. The Chapter 7 trustee objected to the exemption, and the bankruptcy court ruled in favor of the trustee. The court held that the Mississippi "statute [did] not provide for more than one homestead exemption to be applied to a single residence, regardless of how many individuals reside[d] therein." As a result, debtors only could exempt $75,000 of the $130,000 equity in their home. [*In re* **Pace,** *supra*]

Note: The analysis differs, however, in cases involving § 522(p). Section 522(m) provides that "*this* section shall apply separately with respect to each debtor in a joint case." [B.C. § 522(m)] Section 522(p) is a subsection of § 522 and, thus, included within § 522(m)'s "this section" language. As a result, some courts have held that married debtors may double the homestead value limitation in § 522(p). [*In re* **Rasmussen,** 349 B.R. 747 (Bankr. M.D. Fla. 2006)]

Example: Husband and Wife filed a joint petition for relief under Chapter 7 in the Middle District of Florida. The couple exempted equity worth $175,000 in their home. Because the debtors had not owned their home for at least 1215 days prior to filing for bankruptcy, the Chapter 7 trustee objected to the exemption under § 522(p). The bankruptcy court allowed the debtors to exempt the full $175,000 in equity by stacking, pursuant to § 522(m), the then-$125,000 exemption limitation for a homestead acquired within 1215 days of bankruptcy filing. [***In re* Rasmussen**, *supra*]

5. List of Exemptions

The debtor must file a list of the property that she claims as exempt. If the debtor fails to file a list of exemptions (Schedule C), a dependent of the debtor may file the list. [B.C. § 522(*l*); Bankruptcy Rule 4003(a); Official Form 106C]

a. Amendments

The debtor may amend her list of exemptions as a matter of course at any time before the close of the case. [Bankruptcy Rule 1009(a)] A bankruptcy court, however, has the discretion to deny an amendment if the debtor proposes the amendment in bad faith or the amendment would prejudice creditors. [**Grueneich v. Doeling (*In re* Grueneich),** 400 B.R. 680 (B.A.P. 8th Cir. 2009)]

b. Objections

(i) In General

Any party in interest may object to the debtor's claim of exemptions. With limited exceptions, the objection must be filed within *30 days after the later* of: (i) the conclusion of the § 341 meeting or (ii) the filing of an amendment to the list or supplemental schedules, unless *for cause* the court grants an extension. A request for an extension must be filed within the 30-day period to object. [Bankruptcy Rule 4003(b)(1)] Objections must be served on the trustee, the debtor and the debtor's attorney, and any person who filed the list and that person's attorney. [Bankruptcy Rule 4003(b)(4)]

(ii) By Trustee for Fraud

The *trustee* may file an objection to the debtor's claimed exemptions at any time *before one year after the closing* of the case if the debtor *fraudulently asserted* the claimed exemptions. The trustee must deliver or mail its objection to the debtor, the debtor's attorney, and to any person filing the list of exempt property as well as that person's attorney. [Bankruptcy Rule 4003(b)(2)]

(iii) Homestead Exemption Limitation

Any party in interest may object to the debtor's claim of exemption under § 522(q). The objection must be filed *before the case closes.* If the debtor first claims the exemption in a reopened case, then the objection must be filed before the reopened case closes. [Bankruptcy Rule 4003(b)(3); B.C. § 522(q)]

(iv) Failure to Object

If no objection is filed by a party in interest, the property described on the debtor's list of exemptions is deemed as exempt. [B.C. § 522(*l*)] In two cases, the Supreme Court has weighed in on the consequences of a failure to object within the 30-day time frame established by Bankruptcy Rule 4003(b)(1).

e.g. **Example:** Debtor exempted a potential award from a pending employment discrimination lawsuit and listed the value of the exemption as "unknown." The trustee did not object. After the period for objection had expired, the lawsuit settled for $110,000, and the trustee sought the proceeds, claiming that the debtor could legitimately exempt only a small portion of the $110,000 award. The Supreme Court held that a late objection will not be allowed even if the debtor has no colorable basis for claiming the exemption. [**Taylor v. Freeland & Kronz,** 503 U.S. 638 (1992)]

Example: Debtor listed $10,718 worth of business equipment and using the federal exemptions then in effect exempted the full value of that equipment. An appraisal of the equipment showed a value in excess of the $10,718 assigned by the debtor and the trustee moved to auction the equipment in order to capture the excess value for the benefit of the estate's creditors. The debtor objected, claiming that by equating the exemption amount with the value provided for the equipment she intended to exempt the full value of that equipment, regardless of whether it exceeded the value exempted or allowed under the exemption. The Supreme Court held that the trustee was not obligated to object within the time frame established by the Bankruptcy Rules in order to preserve the estate's right to value in excess of the debtor's claimed exemption. The Court distinguished *Taylor,* resting its decision on notice to the trustee and other possible objecting parties. If the trustee or objecting party knows or cannot determine that the exemption amount claimed, e.g., debtor puts "unknown" on Schedule C, exceeds the exemption's monetary limit, then the exemption stands if there is no timely objection. Where the exemption amount claimed, however, does not exceed the exemption's monetary limit, then there is no duty to object. [**Schwab v. Reilly,** 560 U.S. 770 (2010)]

Note: The current version of Schedule C (exemptions) now contains a box for the debtor to check that says "100% of fair market value, up to any applicable statutory limit." [Official Form 106C] Bankruptcy Rule 4003(b) also was amended to allow the trustee additional time to object in cases of alleged fraud.

6. Effect of Exemptions: Not Liable for Debts

The general rule is that, unless the case is dismissed, property exempted by the debtor is not liable *during or after the case* for any pre-petition debt or any debt deemed under § 502 to have arisen before bankruptcy. [B.C. § 522(c)]

a. Exceptions

Exempt property is liable for the following kinds of debts:

(i) *nondischargeable taxes* [B.C. §§ 522(c)(1), 523(a)(1)];

(ii) *domestic support obligations* [B.C. §§ 522(c)(1), 523(a)(5)];

(iii) *a debt secured by a lien* that is not void under § 506(d) *and* that has not been avoided under § 522(f) or (g), or §§ 544, 545, 547, 548, 549, or 724(a) of the Code [B.C. § 522(c)(2)(A)];

(iv) *a debt secured by a tax lien* if notice of the lien was filed properly [B.C. § 522(c)(2)(B)];

(v) *a debt for fraud or defalcation while acting in a fiduciary capacity, embezzlement, or larceny* owed by *an institution-affiliated party of an insured depository institution* to a federal depository institutions regulatory agency acting as the conservator, receiver, or liquidating agent for such institution [B.C. §§ 522(c)(3), 523(a)(4)];

(vi) *a debt for willful and malicious injury to another entity or its property* owed by *an institution-affiliated party of an insured depository institution* to a federal depository institutions regulatory agency acting as the conservator, receiver, or liquidating agent for such institution [B.C. §§ 522(c)(3), 523(a)(6)]; and

(vii) *a debt in connection with fraud* in obtaining or providing *any financial assistance* for purposes of *financing an education* at an institution of higher learning. [B.C. § 522(c)(4); 20 U.S.C. § 1001]

7. Avoidance of Liens That Impair Exemption

The debtor may avoid most judicial liens and certain nonpossessory, nonpurchase-money security interests if they *impair an exemption* that the debtor could otherwise claim. [B.C. § 522(f)(1)] To avoid such a lien, the debtor must have an interest in the property *before* the lien attaches, because under § 522(f) it is the *fixing of the lien* that is avoided. [**Farrey v. Sanderfoot,** 500 U.S. 291 (1991)] To commence a proceeding to avoid a lien under § 522(f), the debtor files a motion in the manner provided by the rules on contested matters or serves a Chapter 12 or Chapter 13 plan on the affected creditors. [Bankruptcy Rules 4003(d), 9014]

a. "Impair an Exemption"

The phrase "impair an exemption" is defined in terms of the following statutorily prescribed mathematical computation. [B.C. § 522(f)(2)(A)]

	Judicial lien or nonpossessory non-purchase-money security interest
+	All other liens
+	Amount of the exemption available in the absence of any lien

Sum X

−	The value of the debtor's interest in the property *without* any liens

Amount that lien impairs the exemption

If the value of the property is less than the total of the liens and the exemption, then the exemption is impaired to the extent of the difference. If the property is subject to more than one lien, the calculation should not include a lien that has been avoided. [B.C. § 522(f)(2)(B)] Note, however, that this formula does not apply to a mortgage foreclosure judgment. [B.C. § 522(f)(2)(C)]

Example: Debtor owns property worth $50,000. There is a judicial lien on the property of $20,000. The state homestead exemption is $30,000. The lien does not impair the debtor's exemption, because the difference between the value of the property and the judicial lien is $30,000; thus, Debtor has $30,000 in equity, all of which she may exempt using the state's $30,000 homestead exemption. The formula produces the same result. $20,000 (judicial lien) + $0 (all other liens) + $30,000 (amount of exemption if no liens) = $50,000 (Sum X in formula above). Conclusion: $50,000 (Sum X) − $50,000 (value of property without any liens) = $0, which means that the exemption is not impaired and the lien cannot be avoided at all.

Example: Same facts as in the prior example except the judicial lien is in the amount of $40,000. Sum X from the statutory calculation above is now $70,000: $40,000 (judicial lien) + $0 (all other liens) + $30,000 (exemption *if* no liens at all). Subtracting $50,000, which is the value of the property without any liens, from $70,000 leaves $20,000 or the extent of the impairment. Thus, the lien can be avoided in the amount of $20,000.

b. Judicial Lien

A judicial lien is avoidable to the extent that it impairs an exemption of the debtor. [B.C. § 522(f)(1)(A)] Under the Code, a judicial lien is a "lien obtained by judgment, levy, sequestration, or other legal or equitable process or proceeding." [B.C. § 101(36)] While a mortgage is a lien, it is a consensual, not a judicial, lien. [*Compare* B.C. § 101(36) *with* § 101(37)] Thus, a debtor may not invoke § 522(f) to avoid a mortgage on her home.

e.g. **Example:** Several years ago, Debtor took out a mortgage with Bank Three to purchase her home. Debtor recently filed for relief under Chapter 7. Her home is valued at $100,000, and the mortgage balance is $90,000. The state's homestead exemption is $30,000. Debtor may exempt the $10,000 in equity that she has in the home, but the mortgage is not a judicial lien. Therefore, the Debtor may not avoid it in order to take the full $30,000 state homestead exemption.

e.g. **Example:** Creditor obtains and records a judgment. Under state law, the judgment constitutes a lien on the debtor's home. Such a lien is called a judicial lien, and it can be avoided to the extent that it impairs an exemption.

(i) Exception: Domestic Support Obligations

A judicial lien securing a debt for a domestic support obligation is ***not avoidable.*** [B.C. § 522(f)(1)(A)]

c. Security Interest

The debtor may avoid a ***nonpossessory, nonpurchase-money*** security interest in any of the following items, to the extent that it "impairs an exemption to which the debtor would have been entitled:" [B.C. § 522(f)(1)(B)]

- ***household goods*** or furnishings, clothing, jewelry, appliances, books, musical instruments, crops, or animals that are held primarily for the debtor's (or a dependent's) ***personal, family, or household use*** [B.C. § 522(f)(1)(B)(i)];

- ***implements, professional books, or tools, of the trade*** of the debtor or a dependent [B.C. § 522(f)(1)(B)(ii)]; or

- ***health aids,*** e.g., a wheelchair, prescribed by a professional for the debtor or a dependent [B.C. § 522(f)(1)(B)(iii)].

(i) What Is a Nonpossessory, Nonpurchase-Money Security Interest?

(1) Nonpossessory

Nonpossessory means that the *creditor* does not possess the collateral. Recall from secured transactions that possession is one way for a creditor to perfect its security interest.

(2) Nonpurchase-Money

A purchase-money security interest arises if a creditor loans the debtor money or extends credit to the debtor and the debtor grants the creditor a security interest in the collateral that debtor purchased with the loan proceeds or credit extension. [*See* U.C.C. § 9–103]

e.g. **Example:** Debtor buys a car from Auto Dealer. Dealer extends credit to Debtor to buy the car, and the parties sign a note in which Debtor promises to make monthly payments over the course of sixty months. Debtor grants Auto Dealer a security interest in the automobile to secure his promise to repay the loan. Auto Dealer has a purchase money security interest.

Example: In need of cash, Debtor goes to Small Bank for a $5,000 loan. Debtor signs a note promising to make monthly payments on the loan over the next two years. Small Bank, however, wants more than the debtor's promise to repay so it asked Debtor for collateral. Debtor grants Small Bank a security interest in a valuable painting, valued at $6,500, which Debtor had inherited from her parents. Small Bank has a security interest in the painting, but it is *not* a purchase money security interest because Debtor did not use Small Bank's loan to purchase the collateral in which she granted a security interest.

(a) Refinancing

There is a split of authority concerning whether the refinancing of a debt secured by a purchase-money security interest extinguishes the purchase-money quality of the security interest. There are two basic rules—the transformation rule and the dual status rule—that courts apply not only to cases involving lien avoidance under § 522(f) but also to cases involving the hanging paragraph under § 1325(a)(9). Under the *transformation rule,* refinancing destroys the purchase-money status of the original loan, because the money provided through refinancing is not used to buy the collateral. [*See In re* **Huddle,** 2007 WL 2332390 (Bankr. E.D. Va. 2007) (hanging paragraph case); *see also* **United States v. Juan Madriz Haro,** 2009 U.S. Dist. LEXIS 73253 (C.D. Cal. 2009) (explaining rule but in context of real property mortgage)] Under the *dual status rule,* a security interest may be both purchase-money and non-purchase-money; it is purchase-money to the extent that the debtor used loan proceeds to purchase the collateral securing the interest and non-purchase-money with regard to any obligations unrelated to the purchase of the collateral. [*See In re* **McCauley,** 398 B.R. 41 (Bankr. D. Colo. 2008) (hanging paragraph case); *see also* U.C.C. § 9–103 Official Comment 7]

(b) U.C.C. Article 9

Article 9 leaves to the courts the choice of rule in consumer goods transactions. [U.C.C. § 9–103(h)] For nonconsumer goods transactions, it adopts the dual status rule, but this rule is not binding on the bankruptcy courts. [U.C.C. § 9–103(f), Official Comments 7 & 8]

(ii) What Are Household Goods?

With BAPCPA, Congress codified the definition of "household goods," using a modified version of the Federal Trade Commission's definition. The term "household goods" means:

(1) *clothing, furniture, appliances, linens, china, crockery, and kitchenware* [B.C. § 522(f)(4)(A)(i)–(iii), (vii)–(x)];

(2) one *radio,* one *television,* and one *VCR* [B.C. § 522(f)(4)(A)(iv)–(vi)];

(3) one *personal computer* and related equipment [B.C. § 522(f)(4)(A)(xv)];

(4) *educational materials and equipment* for primary use by the debtor's minor dependent children [B.C. § 522(f)(4)(A)(xi)];

(5) *medical equipment and supplies* [B.C. § 522(f)(4)(A)(xii)];

(6) *furniture* used *exclusively* for *minor children* or *elderly or disabled* dependents of the debtor [B.C. § 522(f)(4)(A)(xiii)]; and

(7) *personal effects* of the debtor and her dependents, including *wedding rings* and *toys and hobby equipment* of minor dependent children [B.C. § 522(f)(4)(A)(xiv)].

(iii) Not Household Goods

The term "household goods" does not include:

(1) *works of art,* unless the works of art were done by the debtor or a relative, or are of the debtor or a relative [B.C. § 522(f)(4)(B)(i)];

(2) *electronic equipment* (excluding one television, radio, and VCR) with a fair market value *in excess of $800* [B.C. § 522(f)(4)(B)(ii)];

(3) *antiques* with fair market value *in excess of $800* [B.C. § 522(f)(4)(B)(iii)];

(4) *jewelry* (excluding wedding rings) with fair market value *in excess of $800* [B.C. § 522(f)(4)(B)(iv)]; and

(5) *a computer* (excluding the personal computer described above), *motor vehicles,* including a tractor or lawn mower, *boats, or motorized recreational devices,* including *watercraft* and *aircraft.* [B.C. § 522(f)(4)(B)(v)]

(iv) What Are Tools of the Trade?

Courts differ about what constitutes tools or implements of the trade, in part, because the language of states' tools of the trade exemptions varies. [*See, e.g.,* **Larson v. Sharp (*In re* Sharp),** 508 B.R. 457 (B.A.P. 10th Cir. 2014) (requiring the court to interpret what constitutes "gainful occupation" under Colorado's tools of the trade exemption)] The ability to avoid a lien using § 522(f)(1)(B)(ii)'s tools of the trade provision also depends on whether the debtor uses the federal § 522(d)(6) tools of the trade exemption or a state law tools of the trade exemption. [*In re* **Nickeas,** 503 B.R. 453 (Bankr. W.D. Wis. 2013)] Thus, the Seventh Circuit held that debtors could use § 522(f)(1)(B)(ii) to avoid a lien on farm equipment because debtors had used Wisconsin's tools of the trade exemption. [*In re* **Thompson,** 867 F.2d 416 (7th Cir. 1989)] But, the Seventh Circuit also has held that because the federal exemptions were much narrower a debtor using the § 522(d)(6) tools of the trade exemption could not avoid a lien under § 522(f)(1)(B)(ii) on farm equipment similar to that in *Thompson.* [*In re* **Patterson,** 825 F.2d 1140 (7th Cir. 1987); *see In re* **Nickeas,** *supra* for an explanation of the difference between the two Seventh Circuit cases] The tools for which the debtor claims the exemption must not be for a hobby or pastime. [**Larson v. Sharp,** *supra*]

(1) Vehicles

While a car may qualify as a tool of the trade, the vehicle must be used for more than mere transportation to and from work. A car used only for commuting to and from work does not qualify as a tool of the trade. [*In re* **King,** 451 B.R. 884 (Bankr. N.D. Iowa 2011)] Thus, a debtor who worked as a law clerk and tutor could not avoid a lien on her car using § 522(f)(1)(B)(ii), because traveling was "merely incidental" to her work. [**Mitchell v. First Franklin Corp. (*In re* Mitchell),** 2018 WL 1442256 (Bankr. N.D. Ga. 2018)]

(2) Cap on Amount Avoided

A debtor *may not* avoid a *nonpossessory, non-purchase-money security interest* on *implements, professional books, or tools of the trade* to the extent that the property's value *exceeds $7,575.* [B.C. § 522(f)(3)]

The monetary limitation on lien avoidance, however, *only applies* if the following conditions are satisfied:

(a) a *state has opted out* of the federal exemptions or the *debtor has waived* the right to claim the federal exemptions [B.C. § 522(f)(3)(A)]; *and*

(b) applicable state law either (a) allows the *debtor unlimited exemptions except* to the extent that the property is subject to a *consensual lien,* or (b) *prohibits the avoidance of a consensual lien* on property that otherwise would be *exempt.* [B.C. § 522(f)(3)(B)]

(a) Problems with Interpreting § 522(f)(3)

The language of both § 522(f)(3)(A) and (B) is problematic. First, § 522(e) of the Code makes exemption waivers unenforceable.

Second, it is unclear how often § 522(f)(3)'s cap would apply to debtors seeking to avoid a lien on tools of the trade. The problem is that in most states neither of § 522(f)(3)(B)'s alternatives apply. Section 522(f)(3)(B) is satisfied if state law allows the debtor to claim unlimited exemptions. The provision does *not* say that state law permits an unlimited exemption for tools of the trade. Yet no state provides debtors with unlimited exemptions for *all* categories of collateral. [4 Collier ¶ 522.11(6)(c)] A second way to satisfy § 522(f)(3)(B) is if state law prohibits the avoidance of consensual liens. [4 Collier ¶ 522.11(6)(c)] Not many states do so, however. Does that mean that there is no monetary cap on lien avoidance for tools of the trade if neither of the two alternatives at § 522(f)(3)(B) applies?

e.g. **Example:** Married debtors filed for relief under Chapter 7, and moved to avoid liens on farm equipment and machinery in the amount of $26,000, pursuant to § 522(f)(1)(B)(ii). Minnesota allowed a $13,000 exemption for farm equipment and machinery, and each debtor claimed the full exemption. Lienholders objected, in part, on the ground of § 522(f)(3)'s monetary limitation, which then stood at $5,000. The bankruptcy court concluded that Minnesota did not have unlimited exemptions and that Minnesota law did not "speak to lien avoidance." Therefore, the court held that § 522(f)(3)'s then-$5,000 cap did not apply and debtors could avoid the liens in the amount of $26,000. [*In re* **Zimmel,** 185 B.R. 786 (Bankr. D. Minn. 1995)]

(3) Federal Wildcard Exemption

Remember that a nonpossessory, nonpurchase-money security interest in tools of the trade is avoidable only to the extent that it impairs an exemption to which the debtor would have been entitled. Although the maximum federal exemption for tools of the trade is $2,800, the exemption may be supplemented by an amount equal to $1,475 plus up to $13,950 of any unused part of the debtor's homestead exemption, or, in a joint case, $2,950 plus up to $27,900 of any unused part of the homestead exemptions. [B.C. §§ 522(d)(5), (6)]

8. Property Recovered by Trustee

The debtor may *exempt* property that the *trustee has recovered* and brought into the estate so long as the debtor, absent the transfer, could have exempted the property under applicable federal or state law, and only if:

a. the debtor *did not voluntarily* transfer the property *and* did *not conceal it* [B.C. § 522(g)(1)]; or

b. the debtor *could have avoided* the transfer under § 522(f)(1)(B). [B.C. § 522(g)(2)]

Example: Husband and Wife ("Debtors") filed for relief under Chapter 7. Prior to bankruptcy, Husband's brother loaned Debtors $80,000 and took a security interest in Debtors' Corvette. When Debtors realized that Brother had failed to properly perfect his security interest, they listed the Corvette as exempt. The Chapter 7 trustee moved to compel turnover of the Corvette to the bankruptcy estate, and Debtors responded that the Corvette was exempt. The 9th Circuit B.A.P. affirmed the bankruptcy court's determination that Debtors could not exempt the Corvette under § 522(g)(1)(A), because Debtors had voluntarily transferred a security interest in the Corvette to Brother. [**Wharton v. Schwartzer (*In re Wharton*),** 563 B.R. 289 (B.A.P. 9th Cir. 2017)]

Example: Husband and Wife filed for relief under Chapter 7. Prior to bankruptcy, Judgment Creditor obtained a $10,000 judgment in state court against Husband. Judgment Creditor later obtained an order authorizing a sheriff or court officer to seize personal property of the Husband to satisfy the state court judgment. Court Officer showed up at Husband's home about two weeks later to seize property in satisfaction of the judgment. Court Officer informed Husband that he would accept $4,000 in cash instead of seizing property in the Debtors' garage. Husband's father then wrote a check payable to Husband; Husband and Court Officer went to the bank where Husband cashed the check and gave Court Officer $4,000 in cash. After deducting statutory fees and expenses, Judgment Creditor received $3548.80 in partial satisfaction of the state court judgment. After Debtors filed their Chapter 7 petition, Judgment Creditor remitted $3548.80 to the Chapter 7 trustee in response to the trustee's demand for return of the funds as a preferential transfer. Husband then amended his schedules to exempt the recovered funds pursuant to the federal wild card exemption. The Chapter 7 trustee argued that Husband had voluntarily transferred the money pre-petition and, thus, § 522(g)(1)(A) precluded him from exempting the funds. The bankruptcy court held that because the transfer of funds "occurred by operation of law . . .[it] was [ ] involuntary for purposes of 522(g)." Thus, Husband was entitled to exempt the funds using § 522(d)(5). [*In re* **Hill,** 566 B.R. 891 (Bankr. W.D. Mich. 2017)]

a. Limitation

The debtor may exempt recovered property only to the extent that she has not already claimed the maximum amount allowable for the relevant category of exemption. [B.C. § 522(j)]

9. Avoidance by Debtor

If the trustee can avoid a transfer of property or recover a setoff but does not attempt to pursue it, the debtor may *avoid* the transfer or may *recover* the setoff to the extent that she could have exempted the property under § 522(g)(1) if the trustee had used his avoiding powers. [B.C. § 522(h)] Section 522(h) protects the debtor's exemption rights. The trustee may have little incentive to pursue an avoidance action in cases in which the recovery is not distributed to estate creditors but rather is claimed by the debtor as exempt.

Example: Debtor inherited her mother's home upon her mother's death in 2007. In 2014, the City of Milwaukee ("City") foreclosed on the property because real estate taxes had not been paid. Only after the foreclosure did Debtor take the steps necessary to record her interest in the property. Approximately a month after the foreclosure, Debtor filed for relief under Chapter 13. Debtor initiated an adversary proceeding against the City to set aside as a fraudulent conveyance the transfer of Debtor's home pursuant to the tax foreclosure judgment. The City moved to dismiss the adversary complaint and argued that Debtor had no standing to bring the proceeding under §§ 522(h) and 548(a)(1)(B)(i), (ii)(I), because she was not the record owner and, thus, there was no transfer of the debtor's interest in property. The bankruptcy court disagreed. The court held that under Wisconsin law Debtor acquired her interest in the home when her mother died and, thus, Debtor had an interest in the property at the time of the tax foreclosure sale. Because the Chapter 13 trustee had not sought to avoid the transfer, Debtor could use § 522(h) to do so. The transfer pursuant to the tax foreclosure sale was involuntary, the Debtor had not concealed the property, and if Debtor were successful in avoiding the transfer under § 548, then she would be able to exempt the full value of the home under Wisconsin law, thereby satisfying the requirements of § 522(g) and (h). [**Martin v. City of Milwaukee (*In re* Martin),** 2014 WL 7011042 (Bankr. E.D. Wis. 2014)]

10. Debtor's Recovery and Exemption

A debtor who avoids a transfer of property or recovers a setoff pursuant to §§ 522(f) or 522(h) may *recover* the property or the setoff in accordance with § 550 and may *exempt* it to the extent permitted under the applicable exemption scheme. [B.C. § 522(i)]

a. Limitation

Section 522(i) may be used to exempt property only to the extent that the debtor already has not claimed the maximum amount allowable for the relevant category of exemption. [B.C. § 522(j)]

11. Administrative Expenses

Subject to certain exceptions, exempt property usually is not liable for the payment of administrative expenses. [B.C. § 522(k); *see supra* Chapter Seven, § D.4 for discussion of exceptions]

B. Redemption: Chapter 7 Cases Only

1. Tangible Personal Property

In a Chapter 7 case, an *individual debtor* has the right to redeem *tangible personal property* from a lien that secures a dischargeable consumer debt if the property is held mainly for *personal, family, or household use,* and it either has been *exempted* by the debtor or has been *abandoned* by the trustee. The debtor may retain such collateral by paying the secured party the *amount of the allowed secured claim,* which is determined by the collateral's market value. [B.C. §§ 722, 506(a)]

Example: Debtor, an individual, files a Chapter 7 petition and lists among her assets the family car, which currently is valued at $7,000, is subject to a purchase-money security interest in favor of Bank, and is used solely for personal driving. The outstanding balance on the car loan is $10,000. Debtor may redeem the automobile by paying a lump sum of $7,000 to Bank.

a.   Lump Sum

To redeem collateral, the debtor must make payment in a lump sum and not by installment payments. In 2005, Congress added "in full at the time of redemption" to the end of § 722 to make clear the requirement of lump sum, not installment, payment.

2. Changed Intention

A debtor who has filed a statement of intention to reaffirm a secured consumer debt is not bound irrevocably by the decision and still may redeem the collateral, notwithstanding her original statement of intention. [*See* savings clause following B.C. § 521(a)(2)(B)] Keep in mind that BAPCPA has created a more complex set of rules regarding the debtor's statement of intention. [*See infra* Chapter Ten, § A.4]

3. No Waiver

A debtor may exercise her right to redeem collateral even if she has waived the right to redeem. [B.C. § 722]

Chapter Nine

Discharge of Indebtedness

Chapter Approach

This Chapter is the second of two Chapters addressing the areas of bankruptcy law that give the debtor a "fresh start." The Chapter covers the effects of the debtor's discharge, the ever-growing list of nondischargeable debts, and the Code's provisions protecting the debtor from discrimination post-bankruptcy.

The main source of the debtor's fresh start is the *discharge* of indebtedness. Remember that a discharge *relieves the debtor of personal liability* on all discharged debts and *permanently enjoins* creditors from attempting to collect or recover such claims from the debtor personally. There are two important points to bear in mind about the discharge. First, Congress continues to add to the list of *nondischargeable debts.* For example, a Chapter 7 discharge granted to an individual debtor does not include *nineteen categories* of *nondischargeable debts* described in Bankruptcy Code § 523(a). While the standard Chapter 13 discharge is more generous than the Chapter 7 discharge, Congress, in BAPCPA, expanded the list of nondischargeable debts in Chapter 13. The second important point to keep in mind is that the discharge does not wipe out *liens.* It eliminates the debtor's *personal* liability for discharged debts.

Notwithstanding the right to a discharge, a debtor may want to enter into a *reaffirmation agreement* if the debt is secured by a nonavoidable lien on collateral that the debtor wishes to retain. A reaffirmation agreement is enforceable only if it complies with the Code's requirements. BAPCPA added detailed disclosure rules that must be satisfied for any reaffirmation agreement.

Prior to BAPCPA's enactment, some courts allowed the debtor to continue paying on secured debt for her automobile, for example, and "ride through" bankruptcy without entering into a reaffirmation agreement. With BAPCPA, Congress enacted a number of changes to the Code, including to the automatic stay, in order to close off the "ride through" as an option in bankruptcy. These changes, however, did not eliminate the ability of debtors to "ride through" in all cases. You will find more discussion of the ride-through in Chapter Ten of this study guide.

Finally, remember that the law *prohibits discrimination* by a governmental unit, by a private employer, or by a lender engaged in a guaranteed student loan program against a person who was or is a debtor in bankruptcy, who was insolvent prior to or during the bankruptcy case, or who failed to pay a discharged debt.

A. Nondischargeable Debts

1. Exceptions to Discharge

Certain debts of an *individual debtor* are not dischargeable and, therefore, survive the bankruptcy of an individual who has received a discharge under Chapter 7, 11, 12, or 13. Some courts have held that *Chapter 12's discharge provision* applies not only to individual debtors but also to debtors that are artificial entities. [B.C. § 1228] Subchapter V of Chapter 11 contains a discharge provision for cram down cases that is similar to Chapter 12's rule. [B.C. § 1192] Subchapter V is new. Therefore, whether certain debts of a *non-individual subchapter V debtor* whose plan was confirmed by cram down are nondischargeable is an open question. To sum up: in any bankruptcy case, certain debts of *individual debtors* are nondischargeable. Whether certain debts of *artificial entities* are nondischargeable is less clear in Chapter 12 and in a subchapter V Chapter 11 case with a plan confirmed by cram down. [B.C. §§ 523(a), 1141(d)(2), 1192, 1228(a), 1328(a); *see infra* Chapters Twelve, § F, Chapter Thirteen, § H, Chapter Fourteen, § E, and Chapter Fifteen, § G for additional, specific discharge rules and exceptions, including exceptions to discharge for ***non-individual*** cases, that apply to bankruptcy filings under Chapter 7, 11, 12 and 13]

a. Effect of Nondischargeability

A creditor that obtains a judicial determination that a particular debt is nondischargeable is free to pursue the debtor and to attempt to recover that debt subsequent to the debtor's discharge. [*Compare* B.C. § 524(a)(2) *with* § 523(a)]

b. Distinguish: Denial of Debtor's Discharge

A determination of nondischargeability under § 523(a) excepts ***a specific debt*** from the debtor's discharge. On the other hand, the complete denial of a debtor's discharge allows ***all of the debtor's debts*** to survive bankruptcy, and thereafter all claimants may compete for satisfaction of their claims. The court may deny an individual Chapter 7 debtor a discharge based on certain misconduct. [*See, e.g.,* B.C. § 727(a)(1)–(7), (12)] The Code also provides for denial of discharge in a Chapter 7 or Chapter 13 case if a debtor files for bankruptcy too closely on the heels of a prior bankruptcy case in which she received a discharge, regardless of whether the prior case was filed under Chapter 7, 11, 12, or 13. [*See, e.g.,* B.C. §§ 727(a)(8), (a)(9), 1328(f)] The permissible time between filings depends on the chapter(s) under which the successive cases were filed.

2. Nondischargeable Debts Under § 523(a)

The debts listed at § 523(a) are not dischargeable in an ***individual Chapter 7 or Chapter 11*** case, or pursuant to a ***hardship discharge in Chapter 13.*** [B.C. §§ 523(a), 1141(d)(2), 1328(c)] In a ***Chapter 13 non-hardship or standard discharge*** case, some, but not all, of the debts listed in § 523(a) are not discharged. [B.C. § 1328(a)(2)] With a limited exception for unsecured debts for certain taxes, the debts listed at § 523(a) are not dischargeable in an individual ***Chapter 12*** case. [B.C. § 1228(a)] In Chapters 12 and 13, and subchapter V Chapter 11 cram down cases, the Code also excepts from discharge certain other debts.

Note the "Exception" section for each category of debt for distinctions among the various filing chapters.

a. Taxes

(i) Gap Period Taxes

Third priority claims are those that arise during the ***gap period*** in an involuntary case in the ordinary course of the debtor's business. [B.C. §§ 507(a)(3), 502(f)] The Code provides that in an individual case a tax claim that is a third priority claim, i.e., it arises during the gap period, is not dischargeable. [B.C. § 523(a)(1)(A)]

(ii) Income, Property, and Other Taxes

Eighth priority taxes include various unsecured pre-petition tax claims, e.g., an income tax for which a return was due within three years prior to bankruptcy. [B.C. § 523(a)(1)(A)]

Exception in Chapter 12: Debts for unsecured taxes that arise pre-petition and debts for unsecured taxes that arise post-petition but prior to discharge are ***dischargeable in a Chapter 12*** case if those taxes result from the sale, transfer, exchange or other disposition of property used in the ***debtor's farming operation.*** [B.C. § 1232(a)(4)] These taxes are treated as pre-petition claims that are not entitled to priority under § 507 and are ***not*** considered nondischargeable claims under

§ 523(a)(1)(A) or (B). [B.C. § 1232(a)(1), (2), (c)] The debtor must provide for them in the Chapter 12 plan. [B.C. § 1232(a)(3)]

Exception in Chapter 13: With the *exception of trust fund taxes* under § 507(a)(8)(C), eighth priority tax claims are dischargeable in a Chapter 13 case in which the debtor obtains a standard discharge. [B.C. § 1328(a)(2); *see In re* **Ladona,** 2017 WL 2437233 (Bankr. D. N.H. 2017) (stating that "based on their exclusion from 11 U.S.C. § 1328(a)(2), priority tax debts under 11 U.S.C. § 523(a)(1)(A) are dischargeable in Chapter 13 cases")]

(iii) Return Not Filed

Taxes for which a *return or equivalent report or notice either has not been filed or given,* or was filed or given *late and within two years* of bankruptcy are not dischargeable. [B.C. § 523(a)(1)(B)]

(iv) Fraudulent Return

Taxes for which the *debtor filed a fraudulent return or "willfully attempted in any manner to evade or defeat"* the tax are not dischargeable. [B.C. § 523(a)(1)(C)]

Note: This portion of the summary covers exceptions to discharge for *individual debtors.* In BAPCPA, however, Congress added a discharge exception for *corporate debtors* that tracks the language of § 523(a)(1)(C) without specifically referencing that subsection. Thus, confirmation of a plan does not discharge a corporate debtor from any debt for a *tax or customs duty* for which the debtor "made a fraudulent return" or "willfully attempted in any manner to evade or to defeat such tax or customs duty." [B.C. § 1141(d)(6)(B)]

(1) Definition of Return

BAPCPA added a hanging paragraph to the end of § 523(a) to define the word "return." [*See* **Wogoman v. IRS (*In re* Wogoman),** 475 B.R. 239 (B.A.P. 10th Cir. 2012)] The Code now defines "return" to mean a *return* that satisfies the *requirements of applicable nonbankruptcy law.* It includes a return prepared pursuant to § 6020(a) of the Internal Revenue Code or a similar State or local law, or a written stipulation to a judgment or final order entered by a nonbankruptcy tribunal. A return does *not* include a return made pursuant to § 6020(b) of the Internal Revenue Code or similar State or local law. [B.C. § 523(a)(19) hanging paragraph]

(v) Post-Petition Interest on Nondischargeable Tax Debt

In a case under the Bankruptcy Act, the Supreme Court, in a unanimous opinion, held that post-petition interest on a nondischargeable tax debt also is not dischargeable. [**Bruning v. United States,** 376 U.S. 358 (1964)] The vast majority of courts have held that *Bruning* applies to cases under the Code. [*See In re* **Tuttle,** 291 F.3d 1238 (10th Cir. 2002) (noting "the great weight of authority")] Thus, *post-petition interest* on a nondischargeable tax is also nondischargeable. Courts also have consistently held that *pre-petition interest* on a nondischargeable tax is nondischargeable. [3 Norton 3d § 57:8]

b. Fraud

(i) False Pretenses or Representation, or Actual Fraud

Debts for money, property, services, or an extension, renewal, or refinancing of credit obtained by *false pretenses or representation, or actual fraud,* other than a statement about the financial condition of the debtor or an insider, are not dischargeable if the creditor *justifiably* relies on the fraudulent representation. [B.C. § 523(a)(2)(A); **Field v. Mans,** 516 U.S. 59 (1995) (holding that "§ 523(a)(2)(A) requires justifiable, but not reasonable, reliance")] The Supreme Court has held that the words "actual fraud" in § 523(a)(2)(A) include "forms of fraud, like fraudulent conveyance schemes, that can be effected without a false representation."[**Husky International Electronics, Inc. v. Ritz,** 578 U.S. 355 (2016)]

Note: This portion of the summary covers exceptions to discharge for *individual debtors.* In 2005, however, Congress added an exception to § 1141 of the Code that provides that confirmation of a Chapter 11 plan does *not discharge a corporate debtor* from a debt owed to a *domestic governmental unit* that was obtained by *false pretenses, false representation, or actual fraud.* [B.C. §§ 1141(d)(6)(A), 523(a)(2)(A); *see* **United States v. Fusion Connect, Inc. (***In re* **Fusion Connect),** 634 B.R. 22 (S.D. N.Y. 2021) (holding that civil penalty owed to United States was not dischargeable under § 1141(d)(6)(A) because it arose from the fraud even though the United States was not a victim of that fraud)]

Example: In **Bartenwerfer v. Buckley,** 143 S. Ct. 665 (2023), the Supreme Court addressed the question whether a debtor found jointly liable for fraud in a state court judgment may discharge the debt for such fraud, notwithstanding § 523(a)(2)(A), because she "lacked the requisite knowledge" of the other party's fraud. The Bartenwerfers purchased a house in San Francisco and "[a]cting as business partners" decided to renovate the house and then sell it for a profit. While David Bartenwerfer took charge of the renovation project, Kate Bartenwerfer was "largely uninvolved." The Bartenwerfers sold the house to Buckley, who later obtained a state court judgment against them for more than $200,000, based, in part, on nondisclosure of material facts about the home's condition. When the Bartenwerfers filed for relief under Chapter 7, Buckley filed an adversary proceeding alleging that the state court judgment was not dischargeable under § 523(a)(2)(A). In a unanimous decision, the Supreme Court held that "[w]ritten in the passive voice, § 523(a)(2)(A) turns on how the money was obtained, not who committed fraud to obtain it." The Court concluded that an innocent person sometimes may be liable "for fraud they did not personally commit, and, if they declare bankruptcy, § 523(a)(2)(A) bars discharge of that debt." In a brief concurring opinion, Justice Sotomayor, joined by Justice Jackson, noted that the issue before the Court was not one "involving fraud by a person bearing no agency or partnership relationship to the debtor." Justice Sotomayor explained that because Kate Bartenwerfer had not "dispute[d] that she and her husband acted as partners, the debt [was] not dischargeable under the statute."

(1) Credit Cards: Implied Representation Theory

An issue with applying § 523(a)(2)(A) to credit cards is that the retailer taking the card receives payment from the credit card company. When the consumer/debtor presents her credit card to the retailer, the retailer does not expect payment from the debtor. It waits for approval from the credit card company, which makes payment to the retailer. In other words, there is no false representation by the consumer/debtor to the retailer. But without a false representation, where is the fraud? To deal with this problem, a number of courts have held that *each time* the debtor uses a credit card, she *impliedly represents* to the card issuer that she *intends to repay the debt.* [*See, e.g.,* **Citibank v. Spradley (*In re* Johnson),** 313 B.R. 119 (Bankr. E.D. N.Y. 2004) (citing cases)]

(2) Did Debtor Know?

The creditor must demonstrate that at the time that the debt was incurred the debtor *knew that the representation* of her intent to repay was *false.* Courts use various factors to determine whether the debtor *subjectively* knew her representation was false:

(a) the *time* between debtor using the card and filing for bankruptcy;

(b) whether *debtor consulted with an attorney* about filing for bankruptcy before using her card;

(c) the *number of charges;*

(d) the *amount* of the charges;

(e) the debtor's *financial condition* when she used her card;

(f) whether the charges *exceeded the card's limit;*

(g) whether debtor made *multiple charges* on the same day;

(h) whether the debtor was *employed;*

(i) debtor's *financial sophistication;*

(j) whether Debtor's *buying habits* changed suddenly; and

(k) whether the charges at issue were for *luxuries or for necessities.*

[**Citibank v. Spradley,** *supra*]

(3) Statutory Presumptions

Consumer debts totaling more than *$800* for *luxury goods or services* owed to a single creditor and incurred by an individual debtor within *90 days* before bankruptcy are presumed to be nondischargeable. Similarly, *cash advances* totaling more than *$1,100* that are extensions of consumer credit under an open-end credit plan received by an individual debtor within *70 days* before bankruptcy are presumed to be nondischargeable. [B.C. § 523(a)(2)(C)(i)]

(a) "Consumer"

The definition of the terms "consumer", "credit," and "open end credit plan" are the same as those in § 103 of the Truth in Lending Act. [B.C. § 523(a)(2)(C)(ii)(I)]

(b) "Luxury Goods or Services"

Luxury goods or services *does not* include goods or services reasonably necessary for the maintenance or support of the debtor or a dependent of the debtor. [B.C. § 523(a)(2)(C)(ii)(II)]

(4) Punitive Damages

In **Cohen v. De La Cruz,** 523 U.S. 213 (1998), the Supreme Court, in a unanimous opinion, held that § 523(a)(2)(A) makes nondischargeable "all liability arising from fraud, and that an award of treble damages therefore falls within the scope of the exception" to discharge.

(ii) False Financial Statements

A debt for money, property, services, or an extension, renewal, or refinancing of credit obtained by the use of a *statement in writing* is nondischargeable *only* if the following elements are present:

(1) the statement was *materially* false [B.C. § 523(a)(2)(B)(i)];

(2) the statement related to the *financial condition* of the *debtor or an insider* [B.C. § 523(a)(2)(B)(ii)];

(3) the creditor owed the debt *reasonably relied upon* the written statement [B.C. § 523(a)(2)(B)(iii)]; *and*

(4) the debtor made the statement with the *intent to deceive.* [B.C. § 523(a)(2)(B)(iv)]

e.g. **Example:** Appling hired the law firm of Lamar, Archer & Cofrin ("Lamar") to represent him in business litigation. By March of 2005, Appling owed the firm $60,000 in legal fees. Lamar told Appling that unless the past-due amount was paid, the firm would withdraw from the representation and put a lien on its work product. In March, Appling told his attorneys that he expected a $100,000 tax refund, which would have covered his outstanding legal fees. In reliance on Appling's statement, Lamar continued to represent Appling and did not start collection activities for the past-due bills. In October of 2005, Appling and his wife received a refund of only $59,851, which they put into their business. The next month, Appling met with his lawyers and told them that he had not yet received his tax refund. In reliance on that statement, Lamar completed the pending litigation on Appling's behalf and delayed collection activities on the past-due bills. Appling never paid his attorneys, so Lamar sued and obtained a judgment for more than $100,000 in outstanding legal fees. Appling and his wife then filed for relief under Chapter 7. The Supreme Court, in a unanimous opinion, held that "a statement about a single asset, [i.e., income tax refund], can be a 'statement respecting the debtor's financial condition' under § 523(a)(2) of the Bankruptcy Code." The Court explained that a "statement is 'respecting' a debtor's financial condition if it has a direct relation to or impact on the debtor's overall financial status. A single asset has a direct relation to and impact on aggregate financial condition." Statements about a single asset convey information about the debtor's solvency and ability to repay a debt. Appling's statements about his income tax refund were statements respecting his financial condition, because they indicated that he could pay his past-due attorney fees. Those statements, however, were oral, not written, as required by § 523(a)(2)(B). Therefore, the debt to his attorneys was dischargeable. [**Lamar, Archer & Cofrin, LLP v. Appling,** 138 S. Ct. 1752 (2018)]

Note: This portion of the summary covers exceptions to discharge for *individual debtors.* In 2005, however, Congress added an exception to § 1141 of the Code that provides that confirmation of a Chapter 11 plan does *not discharge a corporate debtor* from a debt owed to a *domestic governmental unit* that was obtained by use of a *false statement in writing* respecting the debtor's *financial condition.* [B.C. §§ 1141(d)(6)(A), 523(a)(2)(B)]

(iii) Costs and Attorneys' Fees

A creditor who unsuccessfully brings a proceeding to have a *consumer debt* declared nondischargeable under § 523(a)(2) is liable to the debtor for costs and reasonable attorneys' fees if the court finds that the creditor's complaint was *not substantially justified.* [B.C. § 523(d)] The court will not impose costs and attorneys' fees on the creditor if an award would be *unjust* due to special circumstances. [B.C. § 523(d)]

c. Failure to Schedule Debts in Current Case

Whether a debt that the debtor fails to list or schedule in her current case is nondischargeable depends on the nature of the debt.

(i) Sections 523(a)(2), (a)(4), or (a)(6) Debts

For debts involving fraud, misrepresentation, or use of a false written financial statement [§ 523(a)(2)], larceny, embezzlement, or fraud or defalcation while acting in a fiduciary capacity [§ 523(a)(4)], or willful and malicious injury [B.C. § 523(a)(6)], the debt is not dischargeable if the failure to list or schedule the debt precludes a *creditor without notice or actual knowledge of the bankruptcy case* from timely filing a proof of claim *and* a complaint to determine the dischargeability of the debt. [B.C. § 523(a)(3)(B), (c)]

(ii) Other Debts

For any debt other than those described in §§ 523(a)(2), (a)(4), or (a)(6), the debt is not dischargeable if the failure to list or schedule it precludes a creditor who has *no notice or actual knowledge of the bankruptcy case* from timely filing a proof of claim. [B.C. § 523(a)(3)(A)]

d. Fiduciary Fraud or Defalcation, and Embezzlement or Larceny

Debts for fraud or defalcation *while acting in a fiduciary capacity* are nondischargeable. Debts arising from *embezzlement or larceny* also are nondischargeable, but there is no requirement that the wrongdoing occur in a fiduciary context. [B.C. § 523(a)(4)]

(i) Fraud in a Fiduciary Capacity

Courts consistently have held that fraud, for purposes of § 523(a)(4), requires intentional deceit or wrongdoing. Implied or constructive fraud does not suffice. [**Bannon v. Tyson (*In re* Tyson),** 450 B.R. 514 (Bankr. E.D. Pa. 2011); **Marshall v. Youngblood (*In re* Youngblood),** 2009 WL 1232103 (Bankr. S.D. Tex. 2009); **Wood v. Borland (*In re* Borland),** 2009 WL 9084773 (Bankr. E.D. Cal. 2009)]

Note: For purposes of § 523(a)(4), any institution-affiliated party of an insured depository institution is deemed to be acting in a fiduciary capacity. [B.C. §§ 523(e), 101(33), (35)]

(ii) Defalcation in a Fiduciary Capacity

In **Bullock v. BankChampaign,** 569 U.S. 267 (2013), the Supreme Court, in a unanimous opinion, held that the term "defalcation" under § 523(a)(4) "includes a culpable state of mind requirement ... involving knowledge of, or gross recklessness in respect to, the improper nature of the relevant fiduciary behavior." Defalcation requires intentional wrongdoing when the conduct does not involve "bad faith, moral turpitude, or other immoral conduct." The Court explained that the requisite intentional wrongdoing includes "not only conduct that the fiduciary knows is improper but also reckless conduct of the kind that the criminal law often treats as equivalent." Thus, in a case in which there is no *actual knowledge* of wrongdoing, there may be defalcation if the "fiduciary 'consciously disregards' (or is willfully blind to) 'a substantial and justifiable risk' that his conduct will turn out to violate a fiduciary duty."

e. Domestic Support Obligations

Debts owed for *domestic support obligations* are nondischargeable. [B.C. §§ 523(a)(5), 101(14A)]

f. Property Settlements and Other Obligations Arising from Separation Agreements or Divorce Decrees

Debts that *do not qualify as domestic support obligations* but that are owed to a *spouse, former spouse, or child of the debtor* and that were incurred in the course of a *divorce or separation* or in connection with a separation agreement, divorce decree, other court order, or a governmental unit's determination based on state or territorial law, are nondischargeable. [B.C. § 523(a)(15)]

Exception—Chapter 13: Such debts are dischargeable for the debtor who receives a standard Chapter 13 discharge, but not the Chapter 13 debtor who receives a hardship discharge. [B.C. §§ 1328(a)(2), 1328(b), (c)(2), 523(a)(15)]

g. Willful/Malicious Injury

The Code has different tests for nondischargeability of debts for willful/malicious injury, depending on whether the case is filed under Chapter 7, 11, or 12 as opposed to under Chapter 13.

(i) Willful *and* Malicious Injury

Debts for *willful and malicious injury* caused by the debtor to *another entity or its property* are nondischargeable in a *Chapter 7, 11, or 12* case, or in a *Chapter 13* case in which the debtor receives a *hardship discharge.* [B.C. §§ 523(a)(6), 1141(d)(2), 1228(a)(2), 1328(b), (c)(2)]

e.g. **Example:** Debtor is a physician who treated Patient/Creditor for a foot injury. Debtor admitted Patient/Creditor to the hospital for treatment and prescribed oral penicillin, rather than intravenous penicillin, which would have been more effective. Debtor did so because he believed that Patient/Creditor was concerned with the cost of treatment. When Debtor left on a business trip, other doctors took over Patient's/Creditor's care and decided to transfer her case to an infectious disease specialist. When Debtor returned, he canceled the transfer and stopped all antibiotics, because he thought the infection had subsided. Instead, Patient/Creditor had to have her leg amputated below the knee. Debtor had no malpractice insurance. Patient/Creditor sued and obtained a $350,000 judgment against Debtor, who filed for relief under Chapter 7. The bankruptcy court found that the $350,000 judgment was nondischargeable under § 523(a)(6). But, in a unanimous decision, the Supreme Court held that the judgment did not qualify as a nondischargeable debt under § 523(a)(6). The Court explained that § 523(a)(6) required a "deliberate or intentional *injury,* not merely a deliberate or intentional *act* that [led] to injury." The Court explained that injuries caused by reckless or negligent conduct do not satisfy the requirements of § 523(a)(6). [**Kawaauhau v. Geiger,** 523 U.S. 57 (1998)]

(1) "Willful"

The Supreme Court held that because the word "willful" modifies the word "injury", "nondischargeability [under § 523(a)(6)] takes a deliberate or intentional *injury,* not merely a deliberate or intentional *act* that leads to injury." [**Kawaauhau v. Geiger,** *supra*] The issue left unanswered by the Supreme Court in *Geiger* was the state of mind needed to satisfy § 523(a)(6)'s requirement of a willful injury. Of the courts addressing the issue, most have adopted a *subjective* standard such that the willful injury requirement is satisfied "only when the debtor has a subjective motive to inflict injury or when the debtor believes that injury is substantially certain to result from his own conduct." [**Carillo v. Su (*In re* Su),** 290 F.3d 1140 (9th Cir. 2002); 4 Collier ¶ 523.12 (2)]

(2) "Malicious"

The predominant view is that the debtor's malice may be inferred from her deliberate conduct under the circumstances. [**Viener v. Jacobs (*In re* Jacobs),** 381 B.R. 128 (Bankr. E.D. Penn. 2008)] There are variations on the courts' basic formulation of the malice standard, but generally, malice means that the debtor intentionally engaged in a wrongful act or consciously disregarded a duty without just cause or excuse. [*See, e.g.,* **FNA Group, Inc. v. Arvanitis (*In re* Arvanitis),** 523 B.R. 633 (Bankr. N.D. Ill. 2015) ("Maliciousness requires proof of conscious disregard of a duty without just cause or excuse"); **Associated Receivables Funding, Inc. v. O'Donnell (*In re* O'Donnell),** 523 B.R. 308 (Bankr. D. Mass. 2014) (proof of malice requires an injury that was "objectively wrongful or lacking in just cause or excuse" and the debtor "inflicted the injury in 'conscious disregard' of her duties"); **Gross v. Osborne (*In re* Osborne),** 520 B.R. 861 (Bankr. D. N.M. 2014) ("The 'malicious' element requires proof of 'an intentional, wrongful act, done without justification or excuse' "] Personal animus or ill will are not required. [**Larson v. Bayer (*In re* Bayer),** 521 B.R. 491 (Bankr. N.D. Penn. 2014)]

e.g. **Example:** Husband and Wife ("Debtors") operated a small dairy farm. In order to keep the farm operating when dairy prices fell precipitously, Debtors took out three loans from the U.S. Farm Service Agency ("FSA"). As collateral for the loans, Debtors executed two mortgages on real property in FSA's favor and granted FSA a security interest in Debtors' farm equipment, machinery, crops, and cattle. FSA properly perfected its security interest. The loan documents contained very specific language requiring Debtors to obtain FSA's consent before disposing of any of the collateral securing the loans. Without obtaining FSA's consent, Husband sold, both under his own name and another person's name, more than one hundred head of cattle. The sales netted more than $84,000 in proceeds, of which FSA received nothing. When FSA discovered the sales, it demanded compensation for or replacement of the collateral. Debtors filed for relief under Chapter 7, and FSA filed an adversary proceeding to have the debt declared nondischargeable as a conversion that was willful and malicious under § 523(a)(6). The bankruptcy court found that Husband's conduct was willful and malicious, and held that his debt to FSA was not discharged. On the question of malice, the court first noted that it could infer, given the specific language in the loan documents, that Husband's "injurious acts were done in 'knowing disregard' of FSA's rights." Second, the court explained that while Husband did not use the sale proceeds for personal gain, he elevated the rights of certain creditors over those of FSA. Because there was no testimony from Husband, the court could not find just cause or excuse for Husband's conduct, e.g., Husband acted to keep the farm afloat or in the reasonable belief, based on past dealings, that he was allowed to dispose of FSA's collateral. [**United States v. Shelmidine (*In re* Shelmidine),** 519 B.R. 385 (Bankr. N.D. N.Y. 2014)]

(ii) Willful *or* Malicious

The standard Chapter 13 discharge excepts from discharge debts for restitution or damages awarded in a ***civil action*** against the debtor for ***willful or malicious injury*** resulting in ***personal injury or death*** of an ***individual.*** [B.C. § 1328(a)(4)] The Chapter 13 exception from discharge differs from § 523(a)(6)'s exception from discharge in the following ways:

(1) A creditor need only prove ***willful or malicious injury*** under § 1328(a)(4). By comparison, § 523(a)(6) requires proof of both ***willfulness and maliciousness.***

(2) Section 1328(a)(4) applies to harm by the debtor *only* to individuals. Section 523(a)(6) applies to harm against "entities," which includes individuals and corporations. [B.C. § 101(15), (41)]

(3) Section 1328(a)(4) only excepts from discharge willful or malicious injury that results in ***personal injury or death.*** Section 523(a)(6) includes not only personal injury or death, but ***also harm to property.***

(4) Section 1328(a)(4) says "awarded in a civil action." Section 523(a)(6) contains no such language. There is little case law on the issue, but there is a question as to whether the phrase "awarded in a civil action" requires the creditor to have obtained a judgment pre-petition against the debtor in order to have the debt declared nondischargeable. [*See* **Waag v. Perman (*In re* Waag),** 418 B.R. 373 (B.A.P. 9th Cir. 2009) (affirming bankruptcy court decision that § 1328(a)(4) did not require a pre-petition judgment for nondischargeability); **Morrison v. Harrsch (*In re* Harrsch),** 432 B.R. 169 (Bankr. E.D. Pa. 2010) (concerned about the "vagaries of timing" and holding that the "award" for damages could be entered after the start of debtor's bankruptcy case); *but see* **Parsons v. Byrd (*In re* Byrd),** 388 B.R. 875 (Bankr. C.D. Ill. 2007) (in the first published case on the issue post-BAPCPA, bankruptcy court held that the word "awarded" was past tense, which meant that a pre-petition award was a "prerequisite to a finding of nondischargeability under § 1328(a)(4)")]

h. Fines, Penalties, and Restitution

(i) Fines, Penalties, or Forfeitures

With the exception of certain tax penalties, in a case under Chapters 7, 11, or 12, or a hardship discharge case under Chapter 13, a ***fine, penalty, or forfeiture*** payable ***to and for the benefit*** of a ***governmental unit*** is nondischargeable to the extent that it is ***not compensation for actual pecuniary loss.*** [B.C. §§ 523(a)(7), 1328(b)] Section 523(a)(7) applies to both ***criminal and civil penalties, fines and forfeitures.*** [**Disciplinary Bd. v. Feingold (*In re* Feingold),** 730 F.3d 1268 (11th Cir. 2013)]

e.g. **Example:** The Commonwealth of Pennsylvania disbarred Debtor from the practice of law. The Disciplinary Board subsequently filed a complaint in state court to enjoin Debtor from the practice of law and to appoint a conservator to protect Debtor's clients and take possession of Debtor's client files. The state court, at the conclusion of its proceedings, assessed approximately $45,000 in costs and expenses associated with the conservatorship and disciplinary proceedings against the Debtor. Debtor then filed for relief under Chapter 7. The Eleventh Circuit held that the $45,000 debt was not dischargeable. The court held that the costs assessed in the attorney disciplinary proceedings were punitive and not compensatory in nature. Noting that the attorney disciplinary system served the dual functions of deterrence and protection of the public, the court concluded that the costs assessed against Debtor constituted a " 'fine, penalty, or forfeiture' within the meaning of § 523(a)(7)." The court also explained that the costs assessed were not for actual pecuniary loss, because the Disciplinary Board had to "perform its public function whether it could recoup the costs associated with it or not." [**Disciplinary Bd. v. Feingold (*In re* Feingold)**, *supra*]

cf. **Compare:** Client hired Debtor as his attorney to assist with modification of his home mortgage loan. Client paid Debtor $5,500 in advance of any modification; taking fees in advance of a residential home modification violated California law. Client fired Debtor and sought refund of the $5,500 under California's mandatory attorney fee arbitration program. The arbitrator ruled against Debtor and found that she owed Client a full refund of the $5,500. Debtor made a few payments on the arbitration award, but then claimed that she had insufficient funds to continue to pay. The arbitrator then filed an action in the state bar court, which found that Debtor could afford to pay and suspended Debtor's license to practice law until she refunded the remainder of the $5,500 to Client. Debtor then filed for relief under Chapter 7. The court held that the debt was dischargeable, because it was the amount that Debtor owed to Client; thus, it was compensation for actual pecuniary loss and not a fine or penalty. [**Scheer v. State Bar (*In re* Scheer),** 819 F.3d 1206 (9th Cir. 2016)]

(1) Tax Penalties

Section 523(a)(7) carves out *two exceptions* to nondischargeability for tax penalties. If a tax penalty fits within either exception, it is *dischargeable.*

(a) Dischargeable Tax: A tax penalty that relates to a tax that does *not* qualify as nondischargeable under § 523(a)(1) is dischargeable. [B.C. § 523(a)(7)(A)]

(b) More than Three Years Before Bankruptcy: A tax penalty that relates to a tax imposed with regard to a transaction or event that occurred *more than three years* prior to the bankruptcy filing is dischargeable. [B.C. § 523(a)(7)(B)]

(ii) State Criminal Restitution

Court-ordered state criminal restitution payments imposed as part of a defendant's sentence and as a condition for probation are penal in nature and, thus, nondischargeable. [B.C. § 523(a)(7); **Kelly v. Robinson,** 479 U.S. 36 (1986)] The Supreme Court in *Kelly* stated: "Because criminal proceedings focus on the State's interest in rehabilitation and punishment, rather than the victim's desire for compensation, we conclude that restitution orders imposed in such proceedings operate 'for the benefit of' the State . . . [and] are not assessed 'for . . . compensation' of the victim."

(iii) Civil Restitution

Courts are split on the question whether § 523(a)(7) excepts from discharge civil restitution awards. [*In re* **Styer,** 477 B.R. 584 (Bankr. E.D. Pa. 2012)]

Example: HUD obtained a judgment against Debtors making them jointly and severally liable for $8.65 million related to Debtors' violations of the Interstate Land Sales Full Disclosure Act, including sales of lots at over three times their assessed value. The Fourth Circuit held that the judgment was not dischargeable under § 523(a)(7). The court acknowledged that HUD intended to use all or some of the funds to reimburse the victims of Debtors' misconduct, but also noted that HUD had no obligation to remit funds to anyone. The court narrowly interpreted the phrase "not compensation for actual pecuniary loss" and focused on the nature of the government's interest. "So long as the government's interest in enforcing a debt is *penal,* it makes no difference that injured persons may thereby receive compensation for pecuniary loss. In other words, the 'not compensation for actual pecuniary loss' phrase in § 523(a)(7) refers to *the government's* pecuniary loss." [**Department of Housing & Urban Development v. Cost Control Marketing & Sales Management of Virginia, Inc.,** 64 F.3d 920 (4th Cir. 1995)]

Compare: The State of Illinois sued Debtor for violating the Illinois Consumer Fraud and Deceptive Business Practices Act. The state court found that Debtor had defrauded his customers and, among other things, ordered him to pay restitution in the amount of $210,000. The order provided for payment of restitution to the Illinois Attorney General, but for the victims of Debtor's fraudulent conduct. The Seventh Circuit held that the $210,000 civil restitution award was dischargeable because it was not paid "for the benefit of a government unit." While the money was paid *to* the State of Illinois, the funds were to be distributed to the victims of Debtor's fraudulent activity. Thus, the requirements of § 523(a)(7) were not satisfied. The civil restitution award was for the benefit of the victims, not for the benefit of the governmental unit—the State of Illinois. [*In re* **Towers,** 162 F.3d 952 (7th Cir. 1998)]

(iv) Restitution or Fines in Criminal Sentence in Chapter 13

Debts for *restitution or a criminal fine* that are included in the debtor's sentence for *conviction of a crime* are excepted from the standard Chapter 13 discharge. [B.C. § 1328(a)(3)] Section 1328(a)(3) differs from § 523(a)(7) in the following ways.

(1) Section 523(a)(7) applies to all fines owed to a governmental unit, while § 1328(a)(3) only excepts criminal fines from discharge if they are *included in the sentence for conviction* of a crime.

(2) Section 523(a)(7) specifically states that the fine or penalty must not be compensation for actual pecuniary loss. Section 1328(a)(3) contains no such limitation.

(v) Restitution for Federal Crimes

The payment of an order of *restitution* under title 18 of the United States Code, for most *federal* crimes, is nondischargeable in a Chapter 7, 11, or 12 case, or a Chapter 13 hardship discharge case. [B.C. § 523(a)(13)] *Fines* ordered in connection with certain *federal* crimes are nondischargeable under *all chapters* of the Code, and liens securing them filed in favor of the United States are *not avoidable* in bankruptcy. [18 U.S.C. § 3613(e)]

Note: Section 1328(a)(3) governs the dischargeability of debts for restitution in a Chapter 13 case. Section 1328(a)(3) is broader than § 523(a)(13), which is limited to restitution orders issued in federal criminal cases.

e.g. **Example:** Lagos owned Dry Van Logistics. Lagos created false invoices for services that Dry Van had not performed and used those false invoices as collateral to borrow money from General Electric Capital Corporation (GECC). Lagos pleaded guilty to wire fraud and Dry Van filed for bankruptcy. The district court ordered Lagos to pay restitution to GECC under the Mandatory Victims Restitution Act of 1996. Lagos challenged the portion of the restitution award— about $5 million—requiring him to reimburse GECC for monies that GECC spent on forensic experts, consultants, and lawyers in investigating Lagos's fraud and participating in Dry Van's bankruptcy. In a unanimous opinion, the Supreme Court interpreted the statutory phrase *incurred during participation in the investigation or prosecution of the offense or attendance at proceedings related to the offense* as limited to "government investigations and criminal proceedings." Therefore, the Court held that Lagos was not required to pay GECC that portion of the restitution award that included fees that GECC had incurred in its own private investigation of Lagos's fraud or fees incurred for its participation in Dry Van's bankruptcy proceedings. [**Lagos v. United States,** 138 S. Ct. 1684 (2018)]

i. Student Loans

Pre-BAPCPA, only educational loans funded by a governmental unit or nonprofit institution were nondischargeable. BAPCPA expanded the categories of educational loans subject to the Code's nondischargeability provision. Thus, absent an ***undue hardship*** on the debtor and her dependents, an educational loan made, insured, or guaranteed by a governmental unit, or extended under a program funded by a governmental unit or a nonprofit institution, or any other educational loan that is a qualified education loan under the Internal Revenue Code is nondischargeable. [B.C. § 523(a)(8)] The exception to discharge for student loans applies to Chapters 7, 11, 12, and all Chapter 13 cases, regardless of whether the debtor obtains a standard or hardship discharge. [B.C. §§ 523(a), 1141(d)(2), 1228(a)(2), 1328(a)(2)]

(i) Undue Hardship

A debtor will receive a discharge of her student loans if she can prove "undue hardship." Most courts use the *Brunner* test for undue hardship, which requires proof of the following elements:

(1) *the debtor and her dependents cannot maintain a "minimal standard of living,"* based on current income and expenses, if repayment is required;

(2) *the debtor's current situation,* e.g., finances, ability to get a job, medical condition, is likely to *persist for a significant portion of the repayment period;* and

(3) *the debtor has made good faith efforts to repay the student loan.*

[*In re* **Brunner,** 46 B.R. 752 (S.D.N.Y. 1985), *aff'd,* 831 F.2d 395 (2d Cir. 1987); B.C. § 523(a)(8)]

(ii) HEAL Loans

A Health Education Assistance Loan ("HEAL") is a loan extended for educational purposes to a health professional, e.g., a medical student, by a private lender, such as a bank. The United States Department of Health and Human Services guarantees the loan. A HEAL loan is not dischargeable unless three statutory conditions are satisfied, one of which is a finding by the court that the *failure to discharge* the debt would be *unconscionable.* [42 U.S.C. § 292f(g)]; **Woody v. DOJ (*In re* Woody),** 494 F.3d 939 (10th Cir. 2007)]

(1) Unconscionability

The unconscionability standard under 42 U.S.C. § 292f(g) is far more difficult to satisfy than the "undue hardship" test of § 523(a)(8). The bankruptcy court must determine whether "nondischarge would be shockingly unfair, harsh, or unjust, or otherwise unconscionable." The test is fact-intensive, and requires courts to examine the totality of the debtor's circumstances, including her income and earning ability, her health, the debtor's standard of living and expenses, the ability of dependents to provide financial support, the debtor's good faith attempts to pay her HEAL loans, the amount of debt owed and the interest rate on the loans, and whether the debtor has tried to maximize her income. These factors are not exclusive, and bankruptcy courts must consider any additional factors that bear on the unconscionability analysis. [**Woody v. DOJ (*In re* Woody),** *supra*]

(2) Other Elements

In addition to unconscionability, the discharge of a HEAL loan requires proof (i) that *seven years* have expired from the date that repayment was required to begin, not counting any period during which the obligation to repay was suspended, and (ii) that with regard to a HEAL borrower who is carrying on her profession but has not repaid her HEAL loans, the Secretary of Health and Human Services *has not waived statutory rights to reduce payments* owed to the HEAL borrower for health services provided under federal law up to an amount equal to the balance due on her HEAL loans. [42 U.S.C. § 292f(g), (f)]

j. Operating a Motor Vehicle, Vessel, or Aircraft While Intoxicated

Any debt for *death or personal injury* resulting from the debtor's use of a motor vehicle, vessel, or aircraft if such operation was unlawful because debtor was *intoxicated* from using alcohol, drugs, or another substance is nondischargeable. [B.C. § 523(a)(9)]

k. Prior Bankruptcy

A debt that was or could have been listed in a *prior case* in which the debtor *waived discharge* or in which the debtor was *denied discharge* under § 727(a)(2)–(7) is nondischargeable. [B.C. § 523(a)(10)] The denial-of-discharge language is tied to § 727, and only to specific subsections of § 727.

Exception: Such debts are dischargeable as part of a standard Chapter 13 discharge. [*See* B.C. § 1328(a)]

Distinguish: It is important to distinguish § 523(a)(10), which excepts *particular debts,* from a *complete denial of discharge* in a bankruptcy case filed within certain time periods after the debtor received a discharge in a prior bankruptcy case. [*Compare* B.C. § 523(a)(10) *with* B.C. §§ 727(a)(8) & (9), 1328(f)]

e.g. **Example:** In May of 2014, Debtor filed for relief under Chapter 7 but was denied a discharge under § 727(a)(2), because she had made a fraudulent conveyance of her property within a year of her Chapter 7 filing. Debtor subsequently files for relief under Chapter 13. Debtor will not be denied a discharge of the debts from her prior Chapter 7 case, because Chapter 13 does not except from discharge debts under

§ 523(a)(10). But, the date of Debtor's subsequent Chapter 13 filing affects her right to a standard discharge in the later Chapter 13 case. If Debtor filed her later Chapter 13 case in August of 2018, she will receive a standard discharge upon completing her plan payments. But, if Debtor filed her later Chapter 13 case in February of 2018, she will not receive a discharge, even if she completes her plan payments, because she filed her later Chapter 13 case *less than 4 years* after having filed for relief under Chapter 7. [B.C. § 1328(f)(1)]

Example: Debtor filed for relief under Chapter 7 in February of 2010. Debtor was denied a discharge in that case under § 727(a)(11), because she failed to complete the instructional course on personal financial management that is required by Bankruptcy Code § 111. Debtor files for relief under Chapter 7 in August of 2018. Section 523(a)(10) only applies to a denial of discharge under §§ 727(a)(2) through (7). As a result, the prior denial of discharge pursuant to § 727(a)(11) does not affect Debtor's ability to receive a discharge in her current Chapter 7 case. Moreover, § 727(a)(8) does not apply, because Debtor's August 2018 Chapter 7 case was filed more than eight years after the filing of her February 2010 Chapter 7 case.

l. **Fiduciary Fraud or Defalcation of Officers and Directors of Financial Institutions**

Any debt arising from a final judgment or order, or consent order or decree (i) entered by any federal or state court, (ii) issued by a federal depository institutions regulatory agency, or (iii) contained in a settlement agreement with the debtor, resulting from the debtor's *fraud or defalcation* while acting in a *fiduciary capacity* with respect to any *insured depository institution or insured credit union* is nondischargeable. [B.C. §§ 523(a)(11), 101(21B), (34), (35)]

Exception—Chapter 13: Such debts are dischargeable as part of a standard Chapter 13 discharge. [B.C. § 1328(a)]

Note: For purposes of § 523(a)(11), any institution-affiliated party of an insured depository institution is deemed to be acting in a fiduciary capacity. [B.C. §§ 523(e), 101(33), (35)]

m. **Failure to Maintain Capital of Insured Depository Institutions**

Any debt for *malicious or reckless* failure to maintain the capital of an insured depository institution in breach of a commitment to a federal depository institutions regulatory agency is nondischargeable. [B.C. § 523(a)(12)]

Exception—Chapter 13: Such debts are dischargeable as part of a standard Chapter 13 discharge. [B.C. § 1328(a)]

n. **Debts Incurred to Pay Taxes**

Debts incurred to pay taxes that would be nondischargeable under § 523(a)(1), or fines or penalties imposed under federal election law are nondischargeable. [B.C. § 523(a)(14), (14A), (14B)] Prior to BAPCPA's passage, § 523(a)(14) only applied to federal taxes that would be nondischargeable under § 523(a)(1). It now applies to *all* taxes that would be nondischargeable under § 523(a)(1), as well as to fines or penalties for federal election law violations.

Exception—Chapter 13: Such debts are dischargeable as part of a standard Chapter 13 discharge. [B.C. § 1328(a)]

o. Condominium Fees

Fees or assessments for a condominium, a share in a cooperative housing corporation, or a lot in a homeowners' association that become due and payable *after the order for relief* are nondischargeable for as long as the debtor or the trustee has a legal, equitable, or possessory ownership interest in the condominium, cooperative housing corporation, or lot. [B.C. § 523(a)(16)]

Exception—Chapter 13: Such debts are dischargeable as part of a standard Chapter 13 discharge. [B.C. § 1328(a)]

p. Court Costs

Fees imposed on a prisoner for filing a case, appeal, complaint, or motion, as well as any other costs assessed in connection with the filing are nondischargeable even if the debtor files *in forma pauperis* or has the status of a prisoner under 28 U.S.C. § 1915(h) or similar non-federal law. [B.C. § 523(a)(17)]

Exception—Chapter 13: Such debts are dischargeable as part of a standard Chapter 13 discharge. [B.C. § 1328(a)]

q. Pension Loans

A debt owed to a *pension, profit-sharing, stock bonus or other plan* established under the Internal Revenue Code for certain loans permitted by ERISA (29 U.S.C. § 1108(b)(1)), or subject to the Internal Revenue Code's rules on loans as distributions (26 U.S.C. § 72(p)), or loans from a thrift savings plan permitted under the federal employees retirement system (5 U.S.C. § 8433(g) are not dischargeable. [B.C. § 523(a)(18)] BAPCPA added this exception to discharge.

Exception—Chapter 13: Such debts are dischargeable as part of a standard Chapter 13 discharge. [B.C. § 1328(a)]

r. Securities Law Violations

A debt owed for violation of *state or federal securities laws,* or for *common law fraud, deceit or misrepresentation* in connection with the *purchase or sale of a security* is nondischargeable if it results from any (i) judgment, order, consent order, or decree entered in any federal or state court, or any administrative proceeding, (ii) settlement agreement entered into by the debtor, or (iii) any court or administrative order for damages, fines, penalties, citations, restitutionary payments, disgorgement payments, attorney fees, costs or any other payment owed by the debtor. The debt is nondischargeable regardless of when the liability determination is made: before, on, or after the petition filing date. [B.C. § 523(a)(19)] Congress added § 523(a)(19) to the Bankruptcy Code in 2002 as part of the Corporate and Criminal Fraud Accountability Act, which is Title VIII of the Sarbanes-Oxley Act of 2002. [**McKinny v. Allison,** 2013 U.S. Dist. LEXIS 155245 (E.D. N.C. 2013); *see* 107 Pub. L. No. 204 (2002)] In 2005, Congress closed a loophole that allowed debtors to argue that the exception applied only to judgments entered prior to the bankruptcy filing. [4 Collier ¶ 523.27]

Exception—Chapter 13: Such debts are dischargeable as part of a standard Chapter 13 discharge. [B.C. § 1328(a)]

3. Certain Long-Term Debts

A debtor may have certain long-term debts, e.g., mortgage, in which the last payment on the debt is due *after* the last payment is due under the debtor's three- or five-year plan. [B.C. §§ 1222(c), 1322(d)] These long-term debts are *not* part of the *Chapter 12 or Chapter 13 discharge*, regardless of whether it is a standard or hardship discharge. [B.C. §§ 1228(a)(1), 1228(b), (c)(1), 1222(b)(5), (9); §§ 1328(a)(1), 1328(b), (c)(1), 1322(b)(5)] In a **subchapter V Chapter 11** case in which the plan is **crammed down**, any debt on which the last payment is due after the plan's first three years, or such other time not to exceed five years, is not discharged. [B.C. § 1192(1)]

A "Y" IN THE CHAPTER COLUMN INDICATES THAT THE DEBT IN COLUMN A IS *NOT DISCHARGEABLE*. AN "N" MEANS THAT THE DEBT IS DISCHARGED. VARIATIONS ON THE NONDISCHARGEABILITY OF A DEBT ARE INDICATED IN COLUMNS B THROUGH F. WITH THE EXCEPTION OF COLUMN D, THE TABLE PROVIDES THE DEBTS THAT ARE *NOT DISCHARGEABLE* IN AN *INDIVIDUAL* CASE.

(A) CATEGORY OF DEBT	(B) CH. 7	(C) CH. 11 INCLUDES SUBCHAPTER V	(D) CH. 11 CORPORATE	(E) CH. 12	(F) CH. 13— STANDARD	(G) CH. 13— HARDSHIP
THIRD AND EIGHTH PRIORITY TAXES § 523(a)(1)(A)	Y	Y	N	Y, *except* taxes on disposition of property used in debtor's farming operation (§ 1232)	N Only trust fund taxes under § 507(a)(8)(C) are not dischargeable	Y
NO RETURN OR LATE RETURN § 523(a)(1)(B)	Y	Y	N	Y	Y	Y
FRAUDULENT RETURN § 523(a)(1)(C)	Y	Y	Y § 1141(d)(6)(B)	Y	Y	Y
FRAUD, FALSE PRETENSES, FALSE FINANCIAL STATEMENTS § 523(a)(2)	Y	Y	Y § 523(a)(2)(A), (B) § 1141(d)(6)(A)	Y	Y	Y
FAILURE TO SCHEDULE DEBT IN CURRENT CASE § 523(a)(3)	Y	Y	N	Y	Y	Y
FRAUD OR DEFALCATION IN FIDUCIARY CAPACITY, AND EMBEZZLEMENT OR LARCENY § 523(a)(4)	Y	Y	N	Y	Y	Y
DOMESTIC SUPPORT OBLIGATIONS (DSO) § 523(a)(5)	Y	Y	N	Y	Y	Y
SETTLEMENTS & OBLIGATIONS FROM SEPARATION OR DIVORCE—NOT DSO § 523(a)(15)	Y	Y	N	Y	N	Y
WILLFUL AND MALICIOUS INJURY TO PERSON OR PROPERTY § 523(a)(6)	Y	Y	N	Y	§ 1328(a)(4) requires willful *or* malicious injury and limited to harm to persons	Y

FINES, PENALTIES, FORFEITURES, RESTITUTION PAYABLE TO GOVERNMENTAL UNIT, EXCEPT CERTAIN TAX PENALTIES § 523(a)(7)	Y	Y	N	Y	§ 1328(a)(3) excepts from discharge debts for restitution or criminal fines included in debtor's sentence—state or federal	Y
RESTITUTION: SOME FEDERAL CRIMES § 523(a)(13)	Y	Y	N	Y	§ 523(a)(13) not apply, *but see* § 1328(a)(3)	Y
FINES: CERTAIN FEDERAL CRIMES; LIENS NOT AVOIDABLE 18 U.S.C. § 3613(e)	Y	Y	Y	Y	Y	Y
STUDENT LOANS UNLESS "UNDUE HARDSHIP" § 523(a)(8)	Y	Y	N	Y	Y	Y
HEAL LOANS 42 U.S.C. § 292f(g)	Y	Y	N	Y	Y	Y
DEATH, PERSONAL INJURY FROM OPERATING MOTOR VEHICLE, VESSEL OR AIRCRAFT WHILE INTOXICATED § 523(a)(9)	Y	Y	N	Y	Y	Y
WAIVER OF DISCHARGE OR DENIAL OF DISCHARGE IN PRIOR CASE § 523(a)(10)	Y	Y	N	Y	N	Y
FIDUCIARY FRAUD, DEFALCATION FINANCIAL INSTITUTIONS § 523(a)(11)	Y	Y	N	Y	N	Y
FAILURE TO MAINTAIN CAPITAL INSURED DEPOSITORY INSTITUTION § 523(a)(12)	Y	Y	N	Y	N	Y
DEBTS INCURRED TO PAY NONDISCHARGEABLE TAXES, ELECTION LAW FINES/PENALTIES § 523(a)(14), (14A), (14B)	Y	Y	N	Y	N	Y
CONDOMINIUM FEES § 523(a)(16)	Y	Y	N	Y	N	Y
COURT COSTS: PRISONERS § 523(a)(17)	Y	Y	N	Y	N	Y
PENSION LOANS § 523(a)(18)	Y	Y	N	Y	N	Y
SECURITIES LAW VIOLATIONS § 523(a)(19)	Y	Y	N	Y	N	Y
CERTAIN LONG-TERM DEBTS	N	N, except subchapter V cram down § 1192(1)	N	Y §§ 1228(a)(1), 1222(b)(5), (9)	Y §§ 1328(a)(1), 1322(b)(5)	Y §§ 1328(c)(1), 1322(b)(5)

CERTAIN POST-PETITION CONSUMER DEBTS	N	N	N	N	Y §§ 1328(d), 1305(a)(2)	Y §§ 1328(d), 1305(a)(2)

4. Proof

In a unanimous decision, the Supreme Court held that the ***preponderance-of-the-evidence*** standard of proof applies to the exceptions to discharge contained in § 523(a). [**Grogan v. Garner,** 498 U.S. 279 (1991)]

5. Prior State Court Judgments

In a Bankruptcy Act case, the Supreme Court, in a unanimous opinion, held that ***res judicata*** did not preclude the bankruptcy court's consideration of evidence of fraud in deciding whether a debt previously reduced to a state court judgment, pursuant to the parties' stipulation, was nondischargeable. [**Brown v. Felsen,** 442 U.S. 127 (1979)]

Example: Debtor owned a car dealership, and Creditor guaranteed Bank's loan that financed the purchase of vehicles for the dealership. When Bank sued to collect on the loan, Creditor alleged that Debtor had fraudulently induced Creditor to sign the guarantee for the loan. The parties entered into a stipulation that provided that Bank could recover against both Creditor and Debtor, but that Creditor had a right to judgment against Debtor. Both the stipulation and resulting judgment were silent on the basis for Debtor's liability to Creditor. Debtor subsequently filed for relief under the Bankruptcy Act. Creditor argued that the debt owed to him was nondischargeable, under § 17 of the Bankruptcy Act, because of Debtor's fraud. Debtor claimed that the prior state court action had not resulted in a finding of fraud and, thus, res judicata prevented Creditor from re-litigating the nature of the debt before the bankruptcy court. The bankruptcy court ruled in favor of Debtor and concluded that nothing in the state court record provided a basis for a finding of fraud. The district court and the Court of Appeals affirmed. The Supreme Court reversed. The Court held that "neither the interests served by res judicata . . . nor the policies of the Bankruptcy Act would be well served by foreclosing [Creditor] from submitting additional evidence to prove his case." The Court explained that when the issues related to nondischargeability of a debt for fraud are not the same as those underlying a state court collection proceeding, the parties do not have an incentive to litigate the discharge question in state court. A contrary rule, according to the Court, would force a creditor to litigate a fraud/nondischargeability issue simply to protect himself against the possibility of a future bankruptcy proceeding. The Supreme Court also noted that in 1970 Congress had amended the Bankruptcy Act to give exclusive jurisdiction over certain nondischargeability claims, including the fraud claim at issue, to the bankruptcy courts. The Court explained that "it would be inconsistent with the philosophy of the 1970 amendments to adopt a policy of res judicata which takes these § 17 questions away from bankruptcy courts and forces them back into state courts." [**Brown v. Felsen,** *supra*]

Example: Creditors purchased Company from Debtors for $610,000. Several months later, Creditors sued Debtors for fraud in connection with the sale of Company. The parties settled the lawsuit; the settlement agreement provided that Debtors would pay Creditors $300,000 and that Creditors would execute releases of all claims arising from the litigation. Debtors failed to pay $100,000 of the monies owed under the settlement agreement, and Creditors filed suit to collect in state court. Debtors then filed for relief under Chapter 7. Creditors argued that the $100,000 debt owed to them was nondischargeable based on fraud. The bankruptcy court ruled against Creditors, and both the district court and Court of Appeals affirmed. The Supreme Court reversed and held that the decision in *Brown v. Felsen* governed the outcome. The Court explained that the fact that the "relevant debt here is embodied in a settlement, not in a stipulation and consent judgment," as in *Brown,* was not dispositive. The

Court concluded that, as in *Brown,* what had not been established was that the parties had intended to resolve the question of fraud for purposes of a nondischargeability action in bankruptcy. Thus, the settlement agreement did not bar Creditors from showing that the debt owed to them arose from fraud and, therefore, was not dischargeable under § 523(a)(2)(A). [**Archer v. Warner,** 538 U.S. 314 (2003)]

a. Collateral Estoppel

In **Grogan v. Garner,** *supra,* the Supreme Court ruled that if the elements of the fraud discharge exception in bankruptcy and the fraud judgment obtained by a creditor are the same, and the standard of proof is the same, then the doctrine of collateral estoppel *applies* in discharge exception proceedings under § 523(a) to preclude the retrial of issues of fact that have been "actually litigated and determined" in an earlier action in a nonbankruptcy court.

The bankruptcy court applies "federal principles of collateral estoppel" to determine the "preclusive effect of a prior judgment rendered by a federal court." [**FTC v. Abeyta (*In re* Abeyta),** 387 B.R. 846 (Bankr. D. N.M. 2008); *see also* **Walker v. Walker (*In re* Walker),** 477 B.R. 111 (Bankr. E.D. Mo. 2012)] If a state court rendered the prior judgment, then the "collateral estoppel law of that state must be applied to determine the judgment's preclusive effect." [**St. Laurent v. Ambrose (*In re* St. Laurent),** 991 F.2d 672 (11th Cir. 1993); *see, e.g.,* **Rally Hill Products v. Bursack (*In re* Bursack),** 65 F.3d 51 (6th Cir. 1995) (in deciding whether to apply collateral estoppel, a court "first must determine if a state-court judgment would receive preclusive effect in the state where it was rendered"); **P.B. Surf, Ltd. v. Savage (*In re* Savage),** 2015 WL 4498910 (Bankr. N.D. Ala. 2015) ("a bankruptcy court should use the state's collateral estoppel principles"); **In re Stalnaker v. Stalnaker,** 408 B.R. 440 (Bankr. M.D. Ga. 2009) (the bankruptcy court "must apply the collateral estoppel law of the state where the judgment was rendered")]

(i) Consent Judgment

If the parties settled the prior state court action by a consent judgment, collateral estoppel may not apply because the *actually litigated* requirement may not be satisfied. [*See, e.g.,* **Giannetti Construction Corp. v. Fodale (*In re* Fodale),** 2012 WL 718904 (Bankr. E.D. Mich. 2012) (noting that under Michigan law "consent judgments are not generally given collateral estoppel effect" because the actual litigation element of collateral estoppel is missing)] The bankruptcy court must find that the parties understood that the agreement would conclusively determine the issue of dischargeability in the event of bankruptcy. [*See, e.g.,* **McKinny v. Allison,** 2013 U.S. Dist. LEXIS 155245 (E.D. N.C. 2013) (finding that bankruptcy court would need to conduct further proceedings to determine that the parties intended to foreclose litigation of the issue of liability under § 523(a)(19) when settlement agreement contained express statement that parties admitted no liability)] The consent judgment should include specific findings of fact supporting liability and nondischargeability. [*See, e.g.,* **P.B. Surf, Ltd. v. Savage (*In re* Savage),** *supra* (holding that consent judgment contained no findings of fact to support an admission by debtors that the elements of §§ 523(a)(2)(A), (4) or (6) had been established, even though debtors had stipulated that debt would not be dischargeable in bankruptcy]

6. Special Rules

a. Debts Under Bankruptcy Code § 523(a)(1), (a)(3), and (a)(8)

Debts for *taxes, unscheduled liabilities,* or *educational loans* that were held to be nondischargeable in a prior bankruptcy case concerning the debtor are dischargeable in a subsequent bankruptcy case, unless these debts are *independently* nondischargeable by the terms of § 523(a). [B.C. § 523(b)]

b. Debts Under Bankruptcy Code § 523(a)(2), (a)(4), and (a)(6)

For the following *three types of debts*, the creditor must file a complaint seeking a determination by the bankruptcy court that its debt is not dischargeable [B.C. § 523(c)(1)]:

(i) *debts for fraudulently obtaining money, property, services, or credit* [B.C. § 523(a)(2)];

(ii) *debts for fraud or defalcation by a fiduciary,* for embezzlement, or for larceny [B.C. § 523(a)(4)]; and

(iii) *debts for willful and malicious injury to persons or property.* [B.C. § 523(a)(6)]

With two exceptions, any of these three types of debts will be *discharged* if the creditor holding that debt fails to request that the bankruptcy court except that debt from discharge. [B.C. § 523(c)(1)]

In individual Chapter 7, 11, and 12 cases, and in a Chapter 13 case with a hardship discharge, debts under § 523(a)(2), (4), and (6) are excepted from discharge. In a Chapter 7, 11 or 12 case, a *complaint* requesting determination of the dischargeability of debts under § 523(a)(2), (a)(4), (a)(6) *must be filed by the creditor within 60 days after the first date set* for the § 341 meeting, unless the deadline is extended by the court for cause. [Bankruptcy Rule 4007(c)] Because debts under § 523(a)(6) are excepted from the *hardship discharge* under Chapter 13, when a Chapter 13 debtor moves for such a discharge, the bankruptcy court must enter an order fixing the time within which to file a complaint to determine dischargeability of a debt under § 523(a)(6). [Bankruptcy Rule 4007(d)]

Recall that the standard discharge in Chapter 13 excepts from discharge debts under § 523(a)(2) and (a)(4), but not § 523(a)(6). Instead, in Chapter 13, the exception for debts for certain *willful or malicious injuries* is found at § 1328(a)(4). Thus, in a Chapter 13 standard discharge case, a *complaint* requesting determination of the dischargeability of debts under § 523(a)(2) or (a)(4) *must be filed by the creditor within 60 days after the first date set* for the § 341 meeting, unless the deadline is extended by the court for cause. [Bankruptcy Rule 4007(c)]

(i) Exception to § 523(c)(1) for Creditor Without Notice

A creditor that fails to file a request with the bankruptcy court for a nondischargeability determination of a claim under § 523(a)(2), (4), or (6) does *not have its claim discharged* if the creditor's claim was not listed or scheduled and the creditor had neither notice nor knowledge of the bankruptcy case in time to file a proof of claim and request a nondischargeability determination from the bankruptcy court. [B.C. § 523(a)(3)(B), 523(c)(1)]

(ii) Exception to § 523(c)(1) for Federal Depository Institution Regulatory Agency

The requirement under § 523(c)(1) that a creditor request a nondischargeability determination from the bankruptcy court for certain debts does *not* apply to a federal depository institution regulatory agency, in its capacity as a conservator, receiver, or liquidating agent for an insured depository institution, to recover a debt under § 523(a)(2), (4), (6), or (11) owed to the institution by an institution-affiliated party. [B.C. § 523(c)(2); § 101(33), (35)] But, if the conservator, receiver, or liquidating agent was appointed in time to reasonably comply with the requirement to file a proof of claim and a nondischargeability complaint as a creditor of the institution-affiliated party, then the exception does not apply and § 523(c)(1) must be satisfied. [B.C. § 523(b)(3)(B), (c)(2)]

Note: An institution-affiliated party of an insured depository institution is considered to be acting in a fiduciary capacity for purposes of § 523(a)(4) and (11). [B.C. § 523(e)]

c. Other Dischargeability Proceedings

A complaint requesting a determination of the dischargeability of a debt, *other than* one under § 523(a)(2), (a)(4), or (a)(6) may be filed at any time, even if it requires reopening the case. [Bankruptcy Rule 4007(b)]

B. Effects of Discharge

1. Relief from Personal Liability

A debtor is relieved of *personal* liability for all debts that are discharged. [B.C. § 524(a)(1), (2)] Thus, while a valid lien that has not been avoided in the bankruptcy case generally survives *in rem* and ultimately may be enforced against the property securing the debt, no action is permitted against the debtor personally for a deficiency if the debt has been discharged.

EXAM TIP 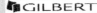 **GILBERT**

The main goal of bankruptcy is to give the honest debtor a fresh start. This is accomplished by relieving the debtor from *personal liability* for all debts that are discharged.

---

a. "Debt" Defined

The Bankruptcy Code defines "debt" as "liability on a claim." [B.C. § 101(12)]

b. Judgments

A discharge automatically *voids any judgment* against the debtor for *personal liability* on a debt that is included in the discharge. [B.C. § 524(a)(1)]

c. Injunction

A discharge also operates as an injunction prohibiting creditors from taking any action, or filing or continuing a law suit, designed to recover or collect any discharged debt as a *personal liability* of the debtor. [B.C. § 524(a)(2)]

e.g. **Example:** Debtor breached her lease with Landlord. Landlord filed state court actions for damages resulting from the nonpayment of rent and for possession of the premises. The state court granted judgment in favor of Landlord, but before Landlord could evict Debtor, she filed for relief under Chapter 7. The Chapter 7 trustee did not assume Debtor's lease and, thus, it was deemed rejected. Debtor received a discharge in her Chapter 7 case. Subsequently, Landlord filed a complaint in state court against Debtor for breach of the lease. The commencement of the post-bankruptcy state court action is a violation of the discharge injunction because it is an effort to collect on a pre-petition claim. [**Baxter v. Summerfield Investment Group, LLC (*In re* Baxter),** 2015 WL 6122158 (Bankr. D. Md. 2015)]

e.g. **Example:** Debtor enrolled in a master's program at University. Debtor stopped paying tuition, but University allowed her to sit for exams and to sign up for classes. Debtor completed her program and received her master's degree. When Debtor asked for a transcript, University refused to provide one to her until she paid her back tuition, which amounted to more than $6,000. Debtor then filed for bankruptcy and received a discharge. Debtor, once again, requested a transcript from University and agreed to pay the transcript fee. University, once again, refused to provide a transcript because Debtor had failed to pay the tuition she owed University. Debtor has a state law right to a certified copy of her transcript. Thus, University's failure to provide Debtor with a transcript violates the discharge injunction because it is an effort to collect on a pre-petition debt. (Debtor's past-due tuition was not a nondischargeable student loan.) [*In re* **Kuehn,** 563 F.3d 289 (7th Cir. 2009)]

d. Community Property

With two exceptions, in community property states, a discharge also enjoins any act by a creditor to collect or recover an allowable community claim from community property acquired by the debtor *after* the filing of the bankruptcy case. [B.C. § 524(a)(3)]

e.g. **Example:** Husband files for relief under Chapter 7, and has *no* nondischargeable debts. Wife does not file for bankruptcy but had she done so on the same day as Husband, she also would have had *no* nondischargeable debts. Creditors of Husband or Wife that hold community claims on the date of Husband's bankruptcy filing may not bring claims against community property that Husband and Wife acquire after Husband's bankruptcy. [*See* 4 Collier ¶ 524.02(3)(a)]

There are *two exceptions* to this rule.

(i) Nondischargeable Debts

If the community claim is *nondischargeable* under § 523(a), or under §§ 1192, 1228(a)(1) or 1328(a)(1) in the debtor's case *or would be nondischargeable* in the case of debtor's spouse had debtor's spouse filed a petition on the same day as debtor filed her petition, then the discharge injunction does not prohibit a creditor with an allowable community claim from taking action to recover on that claim from community property acquired after the filing of the bankruptcy petition. [B.C. § 524(a)(3)]

(ii) Discharge Denial

If the *debtor's spouse was denied a discharge* in a case filed within six years of the debtor's petition or *would be denied a discharge in a Chapter 7 case* had she filed bankruptcy on the date of the debtor's petition, then the discharge injunction does not prohibit a creditor with an allowable community claim from taking action to recover on that claim from community property acquired after the filing of the bankruptcy petition. [B.C. § 524(b)(1), (2); *see* 4 Collier ¶ 524.02(3)(b) ("Sections 524(b)(1)(A) and (B) apply if *both* spouses are debtors, and sections 524(b)(2)(A) and (B) apply if only one spouse is a debtor.")]

2. Co-Debtor or Surety—No Discharge

With limited exceptions, the discharge of a debt of the debtor does *not* affect the liability of any other entity, e.g., a co-debtor, surety, or guarantor, or the property of any other entity for that debt. [B.C. § 524(e)]

Exception: Under certain circumstances, the creditor of a non-debtor spouse may not collect against community property acquired post-petition. [B.C. § 524(a)(3)]

Exception: The Code allows a *channeling injunction* issued in a Chapter 11 asbestos case to bar actions against non-debtor third parties so long as certain statutory requirements are satisfied. [B.C. § 524(g)(4)(A)]

Exception: The courts are split as to whether the bankruptcy court may confirm a reorganization plan that includes a provision releasing certain non-debtors of liability or permanently enjoining suits against them. [4 Collier ¶ 524.05]

3. Voluntary Repayment

The Code expressly permits the debtor to voluntarily repay any debt. [B.C. § 524(f)] However, in the absence of an enforceable reaffirmation agreement with a creditor, the debtor has no personal *legal* obligation to repay a debt that has been discharged.

C. Reaffirmation Agreements

1. Definition

A reaffirmation agreement is a voluntary contract between the debtor and the holder of a dischargeable claim whereby the debtor promises to repay all or part of the debt after bankruptcy. [B.C. § 524(c)] The debtor may not unilaterally reaffirm a debt. [*In re* **Turner,** 156 F.3d 713 (7th Cir. 1998)]

2. Requirements for Enforceability

A reaffirmation agreement is enforceable only if all of the following conditions are satisfied. [B.C. § 524(c)]

a. Enforceable Contract

The reaffirmation agreement must be enforceable under nonbankruptcy law. [B.C. § 524(c)]

b. Made Before Discharge

The agreement must have been made prior to the granting of the debtor's discharge. [B.C. § 524(c)(1)]

c. Disclosures

At or before the time that the debtor signs the reaffirmation agreement, the debtor must receive a set of detailed *disclosures* that Congress added to the Code in 2005 with the passage of BAPCPA. [B.C. § 524(c)(2), (k)] If the disclosures are provided in *good faith,* then this requirement for an enforceable reaffirmation agreement is satisfied. [B.C. § 524(*l*)(3)]

The debtor must receive a *disclosure statement* that includes, among other things, the amount of the debt reaffirmed, the amount of any costs and fees, the annual percentage rate on the reaffirmed debt, a repayment schedule, and statements explaining the debtor's rights and obligations with regard to a reaffirmed debt. [B.C. § 524(k)(3)] The debtor also must receive the following:

(i) the ***reaffirmation agreement*** itself, the basic form of which is provided for in the Code [B.C. § 524(k)(1), (4)];

(ii) the ***declaration,*** which is a ***certification by the debtor's attorney, if any,*** that the attorney informed the debtor of the ***legal effect and consequences*** of entering into the reaffirmation agreement, that debtor made a ***voluntary and informed choice*** in making the agreement, and that the agreement does ***not impose an undue hardship*** on the debtor [B.C. § 524(k)(1), (5)];

(iii) the ***debtor's signed statement in support of the reaffirmation agreement,*** the language of which is provided in the Code [B.C. § 524(k)(1), (6)];

(iv) the ***motion for court approval*** of the reaffirmation agreement in cases in which the debtor is ***not represented*** by counsel or a ***presumption of undue hardship*** exists [B.C. § 524(k)(1), (7), (m)(1)]; and

(v) the form of ***court order*** approving the reaffirmation agreement in cases in which court approval is needed. [B.C. § 524(k)(1), (8)]

d. Filing with Court and Attorney's Declaration

The agreement, accompanied by a cover sheet prepared as prescribed by Official Form 427, must be filed with the court ***no later than 60 days*** after the first date set for the § 341 meeting. [B.C. § 524(c)(3); Bankruptcy Rule 4008(a); Official Form 427] If the debtor was ***represented by counsel,*** the declaration by the debtor's attorney also must be filed. [B.C. § 524(c)(3)] If an individual debtor was ***not represented by counsel*** when she negotiated a reaffirmation agreement and the debtor wants to reaffirm a ***consumer debt not secured by the debtor's real property,*** the bankruptcy court must find that the agreement is in the ***debtor's best interest*** and that it does ***not impose an undue hardship*** on the debtor or a dependent. [B.C. § 524(d)(2), (c)(6)(A)]

e. No Rescission

The debtor has not rescinded the reaffirmation agreement at any time before the ***later*** of the ***discharge*** or ***60 days after*** the reaffirmation agreement was ***filed*** with the court. [B.C. § 524(c)(4)]

f. Discharge Hearing

The requirements concerning a discharge hearing must have been fulfilled. [B.C. § 524(c)(5), (d)] A discharge hearing is a judicial hearing at which the court informs an ***individual debtor*** whether her discharge has been granted or denied under Chapter 7, 11, 12, or 13. [B.C. § 524(d)]

(i) Permissive

If the debtor either does not reaffirm any debts, or does reaffirm and was ***represented by an attorney*** when the agreement was negotiated, a discharge hearing is discretionary with the court. However, if the judge schedules a hearing, the debtor must attend. [B.C. §§ 524(d), 521(a)(5)]

(ii) Mandatory: Unrepresented Debtor

If an individual debtor who receives a discharge desires to enter into one or more reaffirmation agreements negotiated ***without attorney representation,*** the court must hold a discharge hearing and the debtor must attend in person. [B.C. §§ 524(d),

521(a)(5)] At that time, the court must advise the debtor that a *reaffirmation agreement* is completely voluntary and is *not required* either by the Bankruptcy Code or by state law. The judge also must inform the debtor that the legal effect of the agreement is to bind the debtor contractually to repay a debt that could have been discharged and, thus, expose the debtor to personal liability should the debtor default on the agreement in the future. [B.C. § 524(d)(1)] Finally, an agreement reaffirming a debt, other than a *consumer debt secured by the debtor's real property*, is enforceable *only if* the court finds that the agreement is in the *debtor's best interest* and that it does *not impose an undue hardship* on the debtor or a dependent. [B.C. § 524(d)(2), (c)(6)(A)]

Example: Married Debtors filed for relief under Chapter 7. Debtors' attorney negotiated several reaffirmation agreements between Debtors and Bank for debts secured by real property that Debtors operated as residential rental properties. Debtors' attorney declined to sign the declaration in support of the reaffirmation agreements. (The debt was not consumer debt.) Because Debtors' attorney did not file the required certification, the bankruptcy court treated Debtors' case as if they had not been represented by counsel during the negotiation of the reaffirmation agreements. Thus, the court had to make the "best interests" and "undue hardship" determinations required by the Code for unrepresented debtors. [*In re* **Martin**, 2011 WL 10818345 (Bankr. S.D. Ohio 2011); *see* § 524(a)(6)(A)]

(1) Best Interests of the Debtor

The Bankruptcy Code does not define what constitutes "best interests of the debtor." A bankruptcy court must determine whether the reaffirmation agreement benefits the debtor financially or economically. Courts examine a variety of factors in making a "best interests" finding. Those factors include the following:

- whether debtor's decision to reaffirm was *voluntary and informed*;

- the *nature of the debt*—secured or unsecured;

- the *amount of equity* debtor has in the collateral;

- the *likelihood* that the *creditor will repossess* the collateral if there is no reaffirmation agreement;

- the extent to which the *debtor needs the collateral*, e.g., car for work;

- the debtor's *payment history*; and

- the *alternatives to reaffirmation* that are available to the debtor.

[*In re* **Martin**, *supra*; *see* **BankBoston v. Claflin (*In re* Claflin),** 249 B.R. 840 (B.A.P. 1st Cir. 2000) (listing similar factors to determine "best interests" and "undue hardship" in a case decided prior to BAPCPA's creation of undue hardship presumption)]

Example: Debtor filed for relief under Chapter 7. Prior to bankruptcy, Debtor had purchased a vehicle and financed the purchase through Bank. Debtor entered into a reaffirmation agreement with Bank, in which Debtor agreed to pay Bank a total of $23,400 on the vehicle valued at $22,500. Debtor did not have the assistance of counsel when negotiating her agreement with Bank. Debtor entered into the reaffirmation agreement out of concern that post-bankruptcy Bank would repossess her vehicle based on an *ipso facto* clause in her contract with Bank. (The parties' contract provided that a default occurs if the Debtor files for bankruptcy.) State law, however, provided that a default was enforceable only to the extent that payment was not made as required by the parties' contract. State law did not allow Bank to repossess Debtor's vehicle post-bankruptcy so long as Debtor remained current on her car payments. Thus, reaffirmation did not make sense as a way to avoid the threat of repossession. Debtor avoided repossession by making her monthly car payments on time, not by signing a reaffirmation agreement. In addition, reaffirmation excluded the unsecured portion of Bank's debt from discharge. Therefore, the reaffirmation agreement was not in Debtor's best interest, because all reaffirmation did was increase the amount that Debtor had to pay to Bank if she defaulted by not paying on the vehicle after her discharge in bankruptcy. [*See In re* **Henderson,** 492 B.R. 537 (Bankr. D. Nev. 2013)]

g. Presumption of Undue Hardship

BAPCPA added a section to the Code that creates a *presumption of undue hardship* if the scheduled payments on the reaffirmed debt *exceed* the debtor's monthly *income minus expenses.* The presumption applies regardless of whether debtor was represented or not represented by counsel during negotiations for the reaffirmation agreement. [B.C. § 524(m)(1)] The presumption does not apply to reaffirmation agreements in which the creditor is a credit union. [B.C. § 524(m)(2)] The bankruptcy court must review the presumption, which is in effect for *60 days after* the reaffirmation agreement is filed with the court. The *debtor may rebut the presumption* with a written statement identifying other sources of funds for paying the reaffirmed debt. If the presumption is not rebutted, the bankruptcy court *may disapprove* the reaffirmation agreement. The Code does *not require* the court to disapprove the agreement; it only requires "review" of the presumption. The bankruptcy court, however, may not disapprove an agreement without first conducting *a hearing, upon notice, prior to the entry of debtor's discharge.* [B.C. § 524(m)(1)]

Note: While the Code does not require the court to disapprove a reaffirmation agreement if the presumption of undue hardship is not rebutted, keep in mind that the bankruptcy court must make a finding of no undue hardship before approving a reaffirmation agreement if the Debtor did not have counsel during negotiation of that agreement. [B.C. § 524(c)(6)(A)(i)] Therefore, in cases in which the Debtor did not have legal representation during negotiation of the reaffirmation agreement, the court should not approve that agreement if the presumption of undue hardship is not rebutted.

3. Creditor Pressure Forbidden

Most courts agree that a creditor does not violate the automatic stay by merely sending the debtor a letter proposing a reaffirmation agreement. [*See, e.g., In re* **Estrada,** 439 B.R. 227 (Bankr. S.D. Fla. 2010)] The creditor, however, may not threaten or coerce the debtor to reaffirm any pre-petition indebtedness; such conduct does violate the automatic stay. [B.C. § 362(a)(6)]

4. Permissible Creditor Actions

Notwithstanding the Code's requirements for reaffirmation agreements, a creditor may accept payments from the debtor before and after the filing of a reaffirmation agreement. [B.C. § 524(*l*)(1)] A creditor also may accept payments from the debtor under a reaffirmation agreement if the creditor *believes in good faith* that the agreement is effective. [B.C. § 524(*l*)(2)] Finally, the requirement to make certain disclosures to the debtor is satisfied if the required *disclosures are given in good faith.* [B.C. § 524(*l*)(3)] BAPCPA added these provisions to the Code's reaffirmation rules.

5. The "Ride Through"

Prior to BAPCPA's passage, several circuits permitted a debtor to "ride through" bankruptcy and retain collateral securing a debt so long as she continued to make regular loan payments to the secured creditor. For example, in a circuit that allowed the "ride through," a debtor who owned a car and was current on her car payments pre-bankruptcy could simply continue to pay the bank or secured lender that held the security interest in her vehicle; the debtor did not have to reaffirm the debt (or redeem the car) in order to keep the car. Congress, however, made a number of changes to the Code that affect the "ride through." Those changes are discussed more fully in Chapter Ten, because under some circumstances the debtor's failure to file or perform her intention, as required by § 521, triggers termination of the automatic stay.

CHECKLIST OF REQUIREMENTS FOR ENFORCEABILITY OF A REAFFIRMATION AGREEMENT　　　　　　　　　　　**GILBERT**

ALL OF THE FOLLOWING ELEMENTS ARE REQUIRED FOR A REAFFIRMATION AGREEMENT TO BE ENFORCEABLE:

- ☑ The agreement is *enforceable under nonbankruptcy law.*

- ☑ The agreement must be *made before the debtor's discharge is granted.*

- ☑ The debtor must receive the *disclosures set forth at § 524(k).*

- ☑ The agreement must be *filed with the court.*

- ☑ If the debtor is *represented by an attorney* during negotiation of the reaffirmation agreement, the attorney must file an *affidavit or declaration* stating that: (i) the debtor was *fully informed* and entered into the agreement voluntarily, (ii) the agreement will *not impose undue hardship* on the debtor or the debtor's dependents, and (iii) the attorney has fully advised the debtor of the *legal effect and consequences* of the reaffirmation and any subsequent default.

- ☑ If the debtor is an individual *not represented by an attorney* during the negotiation of the reaffirmation agreement, the court must hold a *discharge hearing and the debtor must attend.* The court must explain that the debtor is *not required to reaffirm* the debt, and the *legal effect and consequences* of the reaffirmation agreement and of default under such agreement. If the debt is a *consumer debt not secured by real property* of the debtor, the court must approve the agreement based on a finding that it is in the debtor's *best interest* and does not cause an *undue hardship* for the debtor or a dependent.

- ☑ The debtor must *not rescind* the reaffirmation agreement at any time before the *later* of the *discharge* or *60 days after* the reaffirmation agreement is *filed* with the court.

- ☑ If a *presumption of undue hardship* arises because the scheduled payments on the reaffirmed debt *exceed* the debtor's monthly *income minus expenses,* the bankruptcy court must review the presumption, which is in effect for *60 days after* the reaffirmation agreement is filed with the court. If the presumption is not rebutted, the bankruptcy court *may disapprove* the reaffirmation agreement. The bankruptcy court, however, may not disapprove an agreement without first conducting a hearing, upon notice, prior to the entry of debtor's discharge.

D. Protection Against Discrimination

1. Introduction

In addition to relieving the debtor of personal liability for any debts discharged, the law enhances her fresh start by providing express prohibitions against discriminatory treatment by employers or governmental units. [B.C. § 525]

2. Governmental Discrimination

A governmental unit may not discriminate against a ***person solely*** because that person (i) is or was a debtor in a bankruptcy case, (ii) was insolvent before or during such a case, or (iii) has not paid a debt that was discharged or is dischargeable in the case. The government also may not discriminate against any person with whom the debtor has been associated. This prohibition prevents a governmental unit from (i) terminating an employee; (ii) denying employment; (iii) discriminating with respect to employment; or (iv) denying, revoking, suspending, or declining to renew a license, permit, charter, franchise, or similar privilege for any of these reasons. [B.C. § 525(a); **FCC v. NextWave Personal Communications, Inc.,** 537 U.S. 293 (2003); **Perez v. Campbell,** 402 U.S. 637 (1971) (decided under Bankruptcy Act)]

a. Distinguish—Post-Bankruptcy Credit

Section 525 prohibits "discrimination or other action based *solely*" on the debtor's bankruptcy, insolvency, or failure to pay a discharged debt. "It does not prohibit consideration of other factors, such as future financial responsibility or ability . . . if applied nondiscriminatorily." [H.R. Rep. No. 95–595, at 367 (1977)]

3. Private Employer

A private employer may not discriminate with respect to employment against an ***individual*** or terminate the individual's employment, ***solely*** because (i) she is or was a debtor in bankruptcy; (ii) she was insolvent before or during her bankruptcy case; or (iii) she has not paid a dischargeable debt. A private employer also may not discriminate against any person with whom the debtor has been associated. [B.C. § 525(b)]

Example: Debtor filed for relief under Chapter 13 in 2006. The next year, she applied for a job with Employer who made her an offer of employment contingent on passing a drug test and a background check. When the background check revealed Debtor's Chapter 13 filing, Employer rescinded its offer. Debtor claimed that Employer had violated the anti-discrimination prohibition contained at § 525(b). The bankruptcy court and district court ruled against Debtor. The Fifth Circuit affirmed. The court compared the language of § 525(b) on private employers with that of § 525(a) on governmental units. Section 525(a) prohibits a governmental unit from *denying,* terminating, or discriminating with respect to employment of a debtor. By comparison, § 525(b) only prohibits terminating or discriminating with respect to debtor's employment. Thus, the court held that this difference in statutory language meant that "Congress did not prohibit employers from denying employment to persons based on their bankruptcy status." [**Burnett v. Stewart Title, Inc. (*In re* Burnett),** 635 F.3d 169 (5th Cir. 2011); *see also* **Myers v. TooJay's Management Corp.,** 640 F.3d 1278 (11th Cir. 2011)]

4. Student Loans

Any *governmental unit* operating a student grant or loan program or *lender* engaged in the business of *making loans guaranteed under a student loan program* is prohibited from discriminating against a student loan or grant applicant because the applicant (i) is or was a debtor in a bankruptcy case, (ii) was insolvent before or during such a case, or (iii) failed to pay a discharged debt. [B.C. § 525(c)(1)] The governmental unit or lender also may not discriminate against any person with whom the debtor has been associated. A student loan program means any program under Title IV of the Higher Education Act of 1965 or a similar program operated under State or local law. [B.C. § 525(c)(2)]

Chapter Ten

Administrative Powers: The Automatic Stay

Chapter Approach

Chapter 3 of the Bankruptcy Code includes a subchapter on various administrative powers. This Chapter of the study guide covers the automatic stay and is the first of two Chapters in this guide on those administrative powers. Chapter Eleven of the study guide covers the remaining powers— (1) adequate protection, (2) the use, sale, or lease of property, (3) obtaining credit, (4) executory contracts and unexpired leases, and (5) utility service.

Your bankruptcy exam likely will include questions requiring you to know the actions to which the stay applies, as well as the ever-growing number of exceptions that Congress has created to operation of the automatic stay.

The automatic stay *takes effect* when a debtor files for bankruptcy. The starting point for any analysis is determining whether the automatic stay *prohibits* the described conduct. Remember that the scope of the stay is broad. It covers actions against *the debtor, the debtor's property, and property of the estate.* But there now are *twenty nine exceptions to the stay.* Some are quite specific, e.g., the newly added § 362(b)(29) on certification of an amateur sports organization, and, thus, unlikely to be tested in a survey course on bankruptcy. But others, such as the exception for various family law proceedings or the exception for a governmental unit to exercise its police or regulatory powers, are likely to arise in a fair number of bankruptcy cases. In addition, although not included among § 362(b)'s exceptions to the stay, § 362(n) provides that the automatic stay *does not apply* in certain *small business cases.* Thus, determining whether a creditor's action violates the stay requires you to know which actions are prohibited by, which are not covered by, and which are excepted from the automatic stay.

While the automatic stay may initially apply in a case, ask yourself whether the debtor's bankruptcy case is one in which the automatic stay *terminates* based on the happening of certain events? With BAPCPA, Congress added new subsections to the Code, i.e., § 362(c)(3), (h), that *terminate the automatic stay* in cases involving *serial filers* and *individual Chapter 7 debtors* who fail to timely satisfy the requirements of § 521(a)(2). Pay attention to these provisions, which contain detailed and complicated rules. Understanding how the Code's various sections and subsections relate to each other is critical to your ability to correctly analyze exam questions and problems.

Finally, your professor may ask under what circumstances a creditor may obtain a *lift of the automatic stay.* The Code provides the following *four grounds* for lifting the stay.

1.   Is there *cause* to lift the stay, including the lack of *adequate protection*? [*See* Chapter Eleven of this study guide on adequate protection.]

2.   If the creditor requests a lift of the stay against property, does the debtor have *equity in the property* or is the property *necessary for an effective reorganization*? If the answer is "yes" to either question, then the court will not grant the lift-stay motion.

3.   If the motion involves *single asset real estate,* there are tight deadlines the debtor must satisfy to avoid the bankruptcy court lifting the stay.

4.   BAPCPA added the fourth ground for relief from the stay to address the problem of "abusive filings," e.g., a debtor who repeatedly files for bankruptcy in order to obtain protection of the stay with regard to real property to stop a foreclosure action. This final basis for stay relief requires the court to find that the debtor's filing for bankruptcy is part of a *scheme to delay, hinder, or defraud creditors.*

A. Automatic Stay

1. Introduction

The automatic stay is "one of the fundamental debtor protections provided by the bankruptcy laws." [H.R. Rep. No. 95–989, at 340 (1977)] The stay takes effect **when a bankruptcy petition is filed** and protects the debtor, the property of the estate, and the property of the debtor from certain actions by creditors. Thus, it provides the debtor with a "breathing spell" from collection efforts by her creditors. The stay, however, also benefits creditors because it prevents a rush to the courthouse, thereby ensuring an orderly administration of the bankruptcy case. The stay applies to **all entities.** [B.C. §§ 362, 101(15)]

EXAM TIP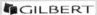

You need to remember that the automatic stay starts when the **bankruptcy petition** is filed. This rule applies in both voluntary and involuntary cases. Do not confuse it with the entry of an order for relief, which in an involuntary case, happens later.

---

2. Acts Stayed

The automatic stay operates to prohibit a broad range of actions against the **debtor, property of the estate,** or **property of the debtor.** Subsections (a)(1), (2), (6), (7), and (8) of § 362 stay actions against the **debtor.** Subsections (a)(2)–(4) of § 362 operate to stay actions against **property of the estate.** Finally, § 362(a)(5)'s prohibition applies to **property of the debtor.**

a. Proceedings Against Debtor

The commencement or continuation, including the issuance or service of process, of a **judicial, administrative, or other action or proceeding** against the **debtor** is stayed if the action is intended to recover a **pre-petition claim** against the debtor, or if the action was commenced or could have been commenced before the bankruptcy petition was filed. [B.C. § 362(a)(1)]

(i) Claim

Congress intended that the courts give an expansive definition to the word "claim" in the Code. [*See* **Johnson v. Home State Bank,** 501 U.S. 78 (1991) ("Congress intended . . . to adopt the broadest available definition of 'claim' "); **Pennsylvania Dep't of Public Welfare v. Davenport,** 495 U.S. 552 (1990) ("Congress chose expansive language" when defining the term "claim"); **Ohio v. Kovacs,** 469 U.S. 274 (1985) ("Congress desired a broad definition of a 'claim' ")] Recognizing this intent to give "claim" an expansive definition in the bankruptcy context, a majority of courts have held that pre-petition claims may include causes of action arising from pre-bankruptcy conduct and pre-petition legal relationships, even if the cause of action under state or other applicable nonbankruptcy law did not accrue until after the petition was filed. [*See supra* Chapter Seven, § A.1.c]

b. Pre-Petition Judgments

The enforcement against the **debtor** or against **property of the estate** of a pre-petition judgment is stayed. [B.C. § 362(a)(2)]

c. Acts Against Property of the Estate

Any act to obtain possession of *property of the estate* or property from the estate, or to exercise control over property of the estate is prohibited, regardless of whether the underlying claim arose before or after the filing of the bankruptcy petition. [B.C. § 362(a)(3)]

e.g. **Example:** City impounded Debtor's vehicle for failing to pay parking fines. Debtor subsequently filed for relief under Chapter 13. Debtor requested that City return his vehicle but City refused. City's mere retention of the vehicle after Debtor's bankruptcy filing is not an act "to exercise control over property of the estate" and, therefore, does not violate the automatic stay. **City of Chicago v. Fulton,** 141 S. Ct. 585 (2021)

e.g. **Example:** Insurance Company issued a "prepaid excess officers and directors liability" policy to Debtor, which shortly thereafter filed a voluntary Chapter 11 bankruptcy petition. Insurance Company then canceled the policy and sent notice to Debtor. Cancellation of the policy violated the automatic stay because the insurance policy constituted property of the estate. [B.C. § 362(a)(3); *In re* **Minoco Group of Companies, Ltd.,** 799 F.2d 517 (9th Cir. 1986)]

d. Liens Against Property of the Estate

Any act to create, perfect, or enforce a lien against *property of the estate* is stayed. [B.C. § 362(a)(4)]

e.g. **Example:** Debtor LLC owned property on which it had not paid property taxes for more than five years. As a result, County scheduled the property for sale at an internet auction. After Debtor's right of redemption expired and the internet auction started but before it concluded, Debtor filed for relief under Chapter 7. The auction continued, notwithstanding the bankruptcy filing, and the property sold the next day. Debtor's right of redemption expired the evening before the internet auction was to take place. The bankruptcy court held that sale of the property was "an action [by County] to enforce its tax lien post-petition to collect its pre-petition claim against the Debtor." Thus, the court concluded that County had violated § 362(a)(4) (as well as §§ 362(a)(3) and (a)(6)). [*In re* **RW Meridian LLC,** 553 B.R. 807 (Bankr. S.D. Cal. 2016)]

e.g. **Example:** Bank extended a loan to Debtor Corporation, and Debtor granted Bank a security interest in its equipment. (The loan was not used to purchase equipment.) Six months later, Debtor filed for relief under Chapter 11. Bank then filed a financing statement, under Article 9 of the Uniform Commercial Code, in an effort to perfect its security interest in the equipment. Bank has violated the automatic stay, because the equipment is property of the estate and Bank tried post-petition to perfect its lien against estate property. [B.C. § 362(a)(4)]

(i) Limited Exception

There is a limited exception to the stay that authorizes post-petition perfection in certain circumstances. [B.C. § 362(b)(3); *see, e.g., supra* Chapter Six, § A.1.a(i)]

e. Liens Against Debtor's Property

Any act intended to create, perfect, or enforce a lien against *property of the debtor* is prohibited *to the extent that the lien secures a pre-petition claim.* [B.C. § 362(a)(5)] Property that the trustee has *abandoned* under § 554 reverts to the debtor and is protected by the automatic stay from enforcement of any lien securing a pre-bankruptcy claim. The stay also shields the debtor's *exempt property* and property *acquired post-petition* from a lien securing a pre-petition claim. [B.C. § 362(a)(5)] The purpose of this provision is to avoid "certain creditors [receiving] preferential treatment . . . [and] circumvent[ion] [of] the debtors' discharge." [H.R. Rep. No. 95–595, at 341 (1977)]

EXAM TIP   ▐GILBERT

If your exam question involves property that the trustee has abandoned, remember that a creditor whose claim is secured by that property must obtain the *court's relief from the automatic stay* before proceeding against the property under nonbankruptcy law. Even if the debtor agrees to relinquish the collateral to the creditor, it is essential to first obtain a court order granting relief from the stay.

---

f. Collection Efforts

Any act to collect, recover, or assess a claim against the *debtor* that arose prior to the bankruptcy petition is forbidden. Thus, creditors may not bother or intimidate the debtor about repayment of pre-petition obligations. [B.C. § 362(a)(6)]

e.g. **Example:** On March 1, Debtor, owing $2,000 to Credit Union, filed a Chapter 7 petition, and notice of the case was sent to Credit Union. Between March 2 and April 1, Credit Union's agent telephoned Debtor on 10 different occasions, demanding repayment of its claim. These acts violate the automatic stay and may subject Credit Union to actual damages, including costs and attorneys' fees, and potentially punitive damages, as well. [B.C. § 362(a)(6), (k)(1)]

e.g. **Example:** Debtor enrolled in a master degree program. Debtor stopped paying tuition during her first year, but University allowed her to take exams and sign up for new classes. She completed her course work and received a degree. At graduation, Debtor owed more than $6,000 to University. Debtor filed for relief under Chapter 7 and during her bankruptcy case requested a transcript from University. While Debtor offered to pay the transcript fee, University refused to provide a transcript. The University's refusal to give Debtor a copy of her transcript was "an act to collect a debt and thereby violated the automatic stay." [*In re* **Kuehn,** 563 F.3d 289 (7th Cir. 2009)]

g. Setoffs

The automatic stay also stays the post-petition setoff of mutual debts. Thus, the setoff of a pre-petition debt owing to the debtor against a claim asserted against the debtor is prohibited unless the court grants relief from the stay. [B.C. §§ 362(a)(7), 553]

(i) Distinguish—Bank's Administrative Freeze

The United States Supreme Court, in a unanimous opinion, held that a bank's *temporary hold* on a debtor's deposit account, up to the amount allegedly subject to setoff, while the bank promptly seeks relief from the automatic stay, is not a setoff and, thus, does not violate the automatic stay. [**Citizens Bank of Maryland v. Strumpf,** 516 U.S. 16 (1995)]

h. Tax Court Proceedings

The Code stays the commencement or continuation of a case in the United States Tax Court concerning the tax liability of (i) a *corporate debtor* for a taxable period that the bankruptcy court may determine or (ii) an *individual debtor* for a taxable period ending before the order for relief. [B.C. §§ 362(a)(8), 505]

CHECKLIST OF ACTS ENJOINED BY THE AUTOMATIC STAY

AFTER THE BANKRUPTCY PETITION HAS BEEN FILED, THE FOLLOWING ACTS ARE ENJOINED BY THE AUTOMATIC STAY:

☑ The commencement or continuation of an action against the *debtor to recover a pre-petition claim*

☑ The enforcement against the *debtor* or against *property of the estate* of a *pre-petition judgment*

☑ Any act to *obtain possession of property of the estate or property from the estate,* or to exercise *control over property of the estate*

☑ Any act to create, perfect, or enforce a *lien against property of the estate*

☑ Any act to create, perfect, or enforce a *lien against property of the debtor to the extent the lien secures a pre-petition claim*

☑ Any act to *collect, recover, or assess a pre-petition claim* against the *debtor*

☑ The *setoff of a pre-petition debt owing to the debtor* against a claim against the debtor

☑ The commencement or continuation of a *case in the United States Tax Court concerning the tax liability of (i) a corporate debtor* for a taxable period that the bankruptcy court may determine *or (ii) an individual debtor* for a taxable period prior to the order for relief

3. Exceptions to the Automatic Stay

There is an ever-expanding list of exceptions to the automatic stay. [*See* B.C. § 362(b)(1)–(29)] Congress added a number of new exceptions to the stay in 2005. The filing of a bankruptcy petition does not operate as a stay of the following actions. [B.C. § 362(b)]

a. Criminal Proceedings

The commencement or continuation of a criminal action against the debtor is not stayed. [B.C. § 362(b)(1)] One issue on which there is a split of authority is whether the exception at § 362(b)(1) excepts from the automatic stay commencement or continuation of a criminal prosecution against a debtor who passed a bad check. [*See In re* **Bibbs,** 282 B.R. 876 (Bankr. E.D. Ark. 2002) (discussing split of authority)] Some courts have examined whether the real reason for prosecuting the debtor for passing bad checks is to exert pressure on the debtor to pay a dischargeable debt. [3 Collier ¶ 362.05(2)(a)] A majority of courts, however, have held that the plain language of § 362(b)(1) creates no "distinction based on a prosecutor's motive" and, thus, the automatic stay does not apply to the prosecution of a debtor on a bad check charge. [*See, e.g.,* **Hutchison-Corbin v. Burton,** 2009 WL 2407698 (W.D. Ky. 2009); *In re* **Caravona,** 347 B.R. 259 (Bankr. N.D. Ohio 2006)]

b. Family Law Matters

BAPCPA significantly expanded the Code's exception for actions taken regarding a number of family law matters, including the collection of domestic support obligations, child custody orders, and the establishment of paternity.

(i) Domestic Support Obligations

The automatic stay now does not apply to any of the following actions related to enforcement or collection of domestic support obligations:

(1) the commencement or continuation of a civil action or proceeding to *establish or modify* a domestic support obligation order [B.C. §§ 362(b)(2)(A)(ii), 101(14A)];

(2) the *collection* of a domestic support obligation from *assets that are not property of the estate,* such as property that is exempt or is acquired post-petition by the debtor [B.C. §§ 362(b)(2)(B), 101(14A); *see* B.C. § 522(c)(1)];

(3) the *withholding of income* that is property of the estate or debtor property to pay a domestic support obligation pursuant to judicial or administrative order or statute [B.C. §§ 362(b)(2)(C), 101(14A)];

(4) the *withholding, suspension, or restriction* of a *driver's license,* a *professional or occupational license,* of a *recreational license,* under state law, because of past-due support or failure to comply with warrants or subpoenas in child support proceedings, as provided for in the Social Security Act [B.C. §§ 362(b)(2)(D), 101(14A); 42 U.S.C. § 666(a)(16)];

(5) the *reporting to a consumer reporting agency* of overdue support owed by a parent [B.C. §§ 362(b)(2)(E), 101(14A); 42 U.S.C. § 666(a)(7)];

(6) the *interception of a tax refund* to apply to a past-due domestic support obligation as provided for under 42 U.S.C. §§ 664 and 666(a)(3), or similar state law [B.C. §§ 362(b)(2)(F), 101(14A)]; or

(7) the *enforcement of a medical obligation,* as specified in the Social Security Act. [B.C. §§ 362(b)(2)(G), 101(14A); 42 U.S.C. §§ 601 *et seq.*]

(ii) Paternity and Child Custody and Visitation

The filing of a bankruptcy petition does not stay the commencement or continuation of a civil action or proceeding to *establish paternity* or concerning *child custody or visitation.* [B.C. § 362(b)(2)(A)(i), (iii)]

(iii) Domestic Violence

The automatic stay does not apply to the commencement or continuation of any civil action or proceeding regarding domestic violence. [B.C. § 362(b)(2)(A)(v)]

(iv) Dissolution of Marriage

The commencement or continuation of a civil action or proceeding to *dissolve a marriage* is not a violation of the automatic stay. This exception to the stay *does not apply,* however, to the extent that the proceeding seeks to determine a *division of property that is property of the estate.* [B.C. § 362(b)(2)(A)(iv); *see In re* **Kallabat,** 482 B.R. 563 (Bankr. E.D. Mich. 2012) (holding that while the Code did not stay debtor's divorce proceeding, it was a violation of the automatic stay for attorney of debtor's former spouse to ask the state court judge to "adjudicate property rights in the marital home")]

c. Certain Acts of Perfection

The automatic stay does not prohibit the perfection of an interest in property to the extent that perfection occurs within the 30-day grace period allowed by § 547(e)(2)(A), or to the extent that the trustee's rights and powers are subject to such perfection under § 546(b), such as in the case of retroactive perfection of a purchase-money security interest within the 20-day grace period allowed under U.C.C. § 9–317(e). [*See supra* Chapter Six, § A.1.a(i)] The filing of a *continuation statement* also is excepted from the automatic stay to the same extent. [B.C. § 362(b)(3); U.C.C. § 9–515]

d. Police or Regulatory Powers: General Principles

The commencement or continuation of a proceeding by a governmental unit to enforce its police or regulatory power is not stayed. This exception to the stay is *limited to subsections (a)(1)–(3) and (a)(6)* of § 362. [B.C. § 362(b)(4); **Board of Governors of the Federal Reserve System v. MCorp Financial, Inc.,** 502 U.S. 32 (1991) (administrative proceedings against bank holding company by the Board of Governors of the Federal Reserve system were not stayed because Board's action fell "squarely within § 362(b)(4)")]

The courts use two tests to determine whether the police or regulatory exception to the stay applies to government action. If the government satisfies *either* test, then the automatic stay does *not* apply to the government's action. [3 Collier ¶ 362.05(5)(a)]

The two tests are the *"pecuniary purpose"* test and the *"public policy"* test. The "pecuniary purpose" test requires the court to determine whether the government's action primarily concerns *public safety and welfare or the government's pecuniary interest.* The stay applies *if* the government's primary concern is protection of its "pecuniary interest in the debtor's property." The public policy test requires the court to " 'distinguish[ ] between government actions that effectuate public policy and those that adjudicate private rights.' " Thus, if the government's conduct *furthers public policy by protecting public safety and welfare,* then the exception at § 362(b)(4) applies. [**United States v. Federal Resources Corp.,** 525 B.R. 759 (D. Idaho 2015); *see also* 3 Collier ¶ 362.05(5)(a)]

> **e.g.** **Example:** The Commonwealth of Pennsylvania issued an order to show cause to Debtor Corporation and its nondebtor principal regarding alleged violations of the Pennsylvania Prevailing Wage Act ("PPWA"). Thirty minutes before the show cause hearing, Debtor filed for relief under Chapter 7. The hearing took place, and Debtor filed an adversary complaint alleging violation of the automatic stay. The bankruptcy court "outright" rejected any argument that the Commonwealth was not acting pursuant to its police and regulatory powers. The court also rejected Debtor's argument that the hearing was an invalid exercise of the Commonwealth's police and regulatory powers, because Debtor had permanently ceased operations and, thus, there was no risk of future harm. The court first noted that the bankruptcy court was not the proper forum for determining the risk of future harm. The court also explained that the police and regulatory powers exception to the stay " 'includes actions to fix the amount of damages for past conduct, whether or not that conduct is continuing' because the Code distinguishes 'between entry and enforcement of a money judgment, *allowing entry but not enforcement.*' " Thus, the Commonwealth's conduct in holding the hearing fell within the stay exception at § 362(b)(4). [**Travacomm Communications, Inc. v. Pennsylvania (*In re* Travacomm Communications, Inc.),** 300 B.R. 635 (Bankr. W.D. Penn. 2003)]

> **e.g.** **Example:** The United States filed suit against various defendants under the Comprehensive Environmental Response, Compensation, and Liability Act ("CERCLA") for monies spent on cleaning up hazardous waste at two mines in Idaho. The federal district court granted summary judgment to the United States as to liability and damages on its CERCLA claim. It also ruled in favor of the government on its veil-piercing and Federal Debt Collection Procedures Act ("FDCPA") claims. Before the district court could enter final judgment, however, two defendants filed for bankruptcy. The district court held that it could enter final judgment, without violating the automatic stay, on all three claims: FDCPA, veil piercing, and CERCLA. First, the court relied on Ninth Circuit precedent to conclude that FDCPA claims fell squarely within the government's police and regulatory powers under § 362(b)(4). Second, the court

concluded that it could enter final judgment on the veil-piercing claim. The court explained that the purpose of its decision was to prevent fraud, which the Ninth Circuit previously had held fell within the scope of § 362(b)(4)'s exception to the automatic stay. Finally, the court held that the government's action to recover costs under CERCLA satisfied both the "pecuniary purpose" and the "public policy" tests and, thus, fell within the scope of § 362(b)(4). While the court held that it could enter final judgment, it stayed *execution* of that judgment against the two parties that had filed for relief under the Bankruptcy Code. [**United States v. Federal Resources Corp.,** *supra*]

(i) Police or Regulatory Powers: Enforcement of Judgments

The enforcement of a judgment obtained by a governmental unit in implementing its police or regulatory power is subject to the automatic stay if the judgment is *a money judgment.* [B.C. § 362(b)(4)]

e.g. **Example:** Debtor was the chief executive and stockholder of Corporation. Corporation and other business entities operated an industrial and hazardous waste site in State. State sued Debtor, Corporation, and the other companies in state court for violations of various state environmental laws. Debtor subsequently signed a stipulation in his individual capacity and on behalf of Corporation that settled the State's lawsuit. The stipulation, in part, enjoined Debtor and the other businesses from further polluting the air or public waters, prohibited them from bringing more waste onto the site, and required them to remove certain waste products from the site. In addition, the stipulation ordered the payment of $75,000 as compensation to the State for injuries to wildlife. Debtor and the other firms did not comply with the obligations set forth in the stipulation, which resulted in the appointment of a receiver; the state court ordered the receiver to take possession of the assets of the Debtor and the other business entities, and to clean up the site. The receiver took possession of the site, but Debtor filed for relief under Chapter 11 before site cleanup was complete. State argued that the clean-up obligation was not a debt under the Bankruptcy Code. The Supreme Court disagreed. The Court explained that the state court order had "dispossessed" Debtor and eliminated his authority over the site. Thus, the State only sought the payment of money from Debtor. [B.C. § 362(b)(4); *see* **Ohio v. Kovacs,** 469 U.S. 274 (1985) (decision in context of whether clean-up obligation was a debt and, thus, dischargeable under the Code)]

e. Setoffs and Other Contractual Rights: Commodities and Securities Brokers, Repo, Swap, and Master Netting Agreement Participants

Four exceptions to the automatic stay, including one added by BAPCPA, are Congressional reactions to concern for the stability of markets. If the stay applied in cases covered by these exceptions, it would prevent " 'prompt liquidation of an insolvent's positions [and] because [of] market fluctuations in the securities market [could] create an inordinate risk that the insolvency of one party could trigger a chain reaction of insolvencies of the others.' " [**Petersen v. Cargill, Inc. (***In re* **G&R Feed & Grain Co.),** 2013 WL 8351982 (Bankr. S.D. Iowa 2013)] Moreover, no court or administrative agency in any bankruptcy proceeding can stay the exercise of rights not subject to the stay pursuant to § 362(b)(6), (7), (17), or (27). [B.C. § 362(o); *see In re* **Weinraub,** 361 B.R. 586 (Bankr. S.D. Fla. 2007) ("The only reading of § 362 that gives effect to § 362(o) is to acknowledge that the Court has the power to stay any of the parts of § 362(b) that are not specifically listed in § 362(o)")] Congress added § 362(o) to the Code in 2005 with the passage of BAPCPA.

(i) Commodity Brokers, Stockbrokers

The automatic stay does not apply to the exercise by a *commodity broker, forward contract merchant, stockbroker, financial institution, financial participant, or securities clearing agency* of any contractual right, defined in Code §§ 555 or 556, under any security agreement or arrangement or other credit enhancement related to a commodity contract, forward contract or securities contract. [B.C. § 362(b)(6); § 101(6), (22), (22A), (25), (48), (50), (53A)] The contractual rights under §§ 555 and 556 are the rights to *liquidate, terminate, or accelerate a securities contract, a commodities contract, or a forward contract.* [B.C. §§ 555, 556] Also excepted from the automatic stay is the exercise of any contractual right by a *commodity broker, forward contract merchant, stockbroker, financial institution, financial participant, or securities clearing agency* to *set off or net out* any termination value, payment amount or other transfer obligation arising under a commodity contract, forward contract, or securities contract, including any master agreement for such contracts. [B.C. § 362(b)(6); § 101(6), (22), (22A), (25), (48), (50), (53A)]

(ii) Repurchase Agreements

The automatic stay does not apply to the exercise by a *repo participant or financial participant* of any contractual right, defined in Code § 559, under any security agreement or arrangement or other credit enhancement related to any *repurchase agreement.* [B.C. §§ 362(b)(7), 559; § 101(22A), (46), (47), (48), (50)] The contractual rights under § 559 are the rights to *liquidate, terminate, or accelerate* a *repurchase agreement.* [B.C. § 559] Also excepted from the automatic stay is the exercise of any contractual right by a *repo participant or financial participant to set off or net out* any termination value, payment amount or other transfer obligation arising under one or more repurchase agreements, including a master agreement. [B.C. § 362(b)(7); § 101(22A), (46), (47), (48), (50)]

(iii) Swap Agreements

The automatic stay does not apply to the exercise by a *swap participant or financial participant* of any contractual right, defined in Code § 560, under any security agreement or arrangement or other credit enhancement related to any *swap agreement.* [B.C. §§ 362(b)(17), 560; § 101(22A), (50), (53B), (53C)] The contractual rights under § 560 are the rights to *liquidate, terminate, or accelerate* a *swap agreement.* [B.C. § 560] Also excepted from the automatic stay is the exercise of any contractual right by a *swap participant or financial participant to set off or net out* any termination value, payment amount or other transfer obligation arising under one or more swap agreements, including a master agreement. [B.C. § 362(b)(17); § 101(22A), (50), (53B), (53C)]

(iv) Master Netting Agreements

Also excepted from the automatic stay is the exercise by a *master netting agreement participant* of any contractual right, defined in Code §§ 555, 556, 559, or 560, under any security agreement or arrangement or other credit enhancement related to any *master netting agreement.* [B.C. §§ 362(b)(27), 555, 556, 559, 560; § 101(38A), (38B), (50)] The contractual rights under §§ 555, 556, 559, and 560 are the rights to *liquidate, terminate, or accelerate* a *securities contract, a commodities contract, a forward contract, a repurchase agreement, or a swap agreement.* [B.C. §§ 555, 556, 559, 560; § 101(25), (47), (53B)] Also excepted from the automatic stay is the exercise of any contractual right by a *master netting agreement participant to set off or net out* any termination value, payment amount or other transfer obligation arising under one or more master netting agreements. This exception to that automatic stay applies *to the extent* that the *master netting agreement participant* is *eligible to exercise these rights* under § 362(b)(6), (7), or (17) for each individual contract under the master netting agreement in issue. [B.C. § 362(b)(27), (6), (7), (17)] Congress added this exception to the stay in 2005 with the passage of BAPCPA.

f. HUD Mortgage Foreclosures

The *commencement* of certain mortgage or deed of trust foreclosure actions by the Secretary of Housing and Urban Development is excepted from the automatic stay. [B.C. § 362(b)(8)]

g. Tax Audits and Assessments

A tax audit, an issuance of a notice of tax deficiency, a demand for tax returns, and an assessment of any tax and issuance of a notice and demand for payment of the assessed tax are excepted from the automatic stay. [B.C. § 362(b)(9)]

(i) Tax Lien

Any tax lien that otherwise would attach to property of the estate as a result of the assessment will *not be effective,* unless the tax debt is nondischargeable and the property or its proceeds are transferred out of the estate to the debtor or otherwise revest in the debtor. [B.C. § 362(b)(9)(D)]

h. Recovery of Property by Certain Lessors

The automatic stay also does not prohibit any act by a debtor's lessor to obtain possession of nonresidential real property if the lease has *terminated by the expiration of its stated term* prior to the filing of the bankruptcy petition or during the case. [B.C. § 362(b)(10)] This exception only applies if the termination occurs because the stated term of the lease expires. Thus, the stay prohibits a landlord of nonresidential real property from taking action to obtain possession based on lease termination due to a post-petition *default.* [3 Collier ¶ 362.05(10)]

(i) Relationship to Property of the Property

If a lease of nonresidential real property terminates prior to bankruptcy, then any interest the debtor had as lessee is not included in property of the estate. Any interest of the debtor as lessee also ceases to be property of the estate if the lease for nonresidential real property terminates during the bankruptcy case. [B.C. § 541(b)(2)]

i. Certain Actions Relating to Negotiable Instruments

The automatic stay does not stay the presentment of a negotiable instrument, sending notice of dishonor, or protesting dishonor of such instrument. [B.C. § 362(b)(11)]

j. Certain Actions Against Educational Institutions

The automatic stay does not apply to any action by an accrediting agency regarding the accreditation status or by a state licensing body concerning the licensure of the debtor as an educational institution. [B.C. § 362(b)(14), (15)] The stay also does not apply to any action by a guaranty agency or the Secretary of Education concerning the debtor's eligibility to participate in programs under the Higher Education Act of 1965. [B.C. § 362(b)(16); 20 U.S.C. § 1085(j)]

(i) Relationship to Estate Property

A debtor's eligibility to participate in programs authorized under the Higher Education Act of 1964, the debtor's accreditation status, and the State licensure of the debtor as an educational institution are not property of the estate. [B.C. § 541(b)(3)]

k. Repossession of Aircrafts and Vessels

The automatic stay does not apply in a *Chapter 11 case* to certain actions by the Secretary of Transportation or the Secretary of Commerce if the action is commenced, continued, or concluded *more than 90 days* after filing of the petition. [B.C. § 362(b)(12), (13)] Actions that fall within this exception to the stay are:

(i) foreclosure of a *preferred ship or fleet mortgage;*

(ii) foreclosure of a security interest in or relating to a *vessel or vessel under construction,* held by the Secretary of Transportation under chapter 537 of title 46, 49 U.S.C. § 109(h), or applicable state law; or

(iii) foreclosure of a mortgage, deed of trust, or other security interest in a *fishing facility* held by the Secretary of Commerce under chapter 537 of title 46.

Congress added these two exceptions to the stay in the Omnibus Budget Reconciliation Act of 1986, which provided that the exceptions applied to cases filed after August 1, 1986 and before December 31, 1989. [Pub. L. No. 99–509 § 5001(a), (b), (c) (1986); *see* 3 Collier ¶ 362.05(12) "[n]o action has been taken to extend the applicability of these sections")]

l. Ad Valorem Property Tax Liens and Special Assessments on Real Property

Section 362(b)(18) exempts from the automatic stay the creation or perfection of a statutory lien for *ad valorem property taxes,* imposed by a governmental unit, that *become due post-petition.* In 2005, Congress expanded this exception. Thus, § 362(b)(18) now also excepts from the stay *special taxes or special assessments* on real property, regardless of whether ad valorem, imposed by a governmental unit and that *become due post-petition.* [B.C. § 362(b)(18)]

m. Withholding of Income for Pensions

The automatic stay does not apply to the *withholding of income* from a debtor's wages and collection of those amounts withheld pursuant to the debtor's agreement authorizing withholding and collection for the benefit of a *pension, profit-sharing, stock bonus or other plan* established under certain sections of the Internal Revenue Code and sponsored by the debtor's employer, or an affiliate, successor, or predecessor of such employer to the extent that the monies withheld and collected are only used to repay certain loans. [B.C. § 362(b)(19); 26 U.S.C. §§ 401, 403, 408, 408A, 414, 457, 501(c)] The exception applies to loans from: (1) a plan under § 408(b)(1) of the Employee Retirement Security Act of 1974 ("ERISA"); (2) a plan subject to § 72(p) of the Internal Revenue Code; or (3) a thrift savings plan in the Federal Employee's Retirement System that meets the requirements of 5 U.S.C. § 8433(g). [B.C. § 362(b)(19)(A), (B); 29 U.S.C. § 1108(b)(1); 26 U.S.C. § 72(p); 5 U.S.C. § 8433(g); *see also* 3 Collier ¶ 362.05(18)] The exception makes clear that no loan under a government plan pursuant to § 414(d), or a contract or account under § 403(b), of the Internal Revenue Code constitutes a claim or debt under the Bankruptcy Code. [B.C. § 362(b)(19); 26 U.S.C. §§ 403(b), 414(d)] Congress added § 362(b)(19) to the Code in 2005 as part of several related changes "to expand the protection of tax-favored retirement plans or arrangements." [H.R. Rep. No. 109–31, at 63–64 (2005)] Thus, disposable income in Chapter 13 does *not* include amounts required to repay the loans described in § 362(b)(19). [B.C. § 1322(f)]

n. Prior Bankruptcy Cases

In 2005, Congress added two new exceptions to the stay for actions against *real property* based on what took place in a *prior bankruptcy* filing by the debtor.

Note: The exceptions *only* apply to debtors filing more than one bankruptcy case within the times specified.

(i) Scheme to Delay, Hinder, or Defraud

There are *two steps* necessary for this exception to the automatic stay to work. The *first step* requires action by the bankruptcy court under § 362(d)(4) in the debtor's *prior bankruptcy case.* In the prior case, the bankruptcy court had to grant relief from the automatic stay to a creditor whose claim is secured by *real property,* after having found that the debtor's filing for bankruptcy was part of a *scheme to delay, hinder, or defraud* creditors that involved either (1) *the transfer* of part or all of the real property *without the secured creditor's consent* or (2) *multiple bankruptcy filings* affecting such real property. [B.C. § 362(d)(4)] The court's stay relief order remains in effect in any *subsequent bankruptcy case* affecting such real property that is filed within *two years* after entry of the order, if the order is recorded in compliance with applicable state laws for recording real property liens or notices of interest in real property. [B.C. § 362(d)(4)]

The *second step* involves § 362(b)(20), which provides an exception to the automatic stay for any act to *enforce any lien against or security interest in* the *real property* following entry of an order pursuant to *§ 362(d)(4).* [B.C. § 362(b)(20)] In the *later bankruptcy* case, the debtor may move for relief from such order based on *changed circumstances* or for other *good cause.* The court may grant debtor relief from the order after notice and a hearing. [B.C. § 362(b)(20), (d)(4)]

(ii) Ineligible Debtor Based on Prior Bankruptcy Case

The automatic stay does not apply to any act to enforce a lien against or security interest in real property if the debtor is not eligible under § 109(g) to be a debtor or if the debtor filed the bankruptcy case in violation of an order in a prior case prohibiting the debtor from being a debtor in another bankruptcy case. [B.C. §§ 362(b)(21), 109(g)] Congress created this new exception to curb abusive filings. [H.R. Rep. No. 109–31, at 70 (2005)]

e.g. **Example:** Debtor filed for relief under Chapter 13. Creditor held the note and deed of trust on Debtor's home, and moved to lift the stay based on Debtor's default on the note. The bankruptcy court granted Creditor's motion, and Creditor noticed a trustee's sale (under state law) of the property. On the day scheduled for the trustee's sale of Debtor's property, Debtor filed a request to dismiss her Chapter 13 case and immediately filed a second bankruptcy case. The trustee's sale occurred after the filing of Debtor's second bankruptcy case, but before Creditor's attorney received notice of that case. The court held that the filing of Debtor's second bankruptcy petition did not stay the trustee's sale of her property. Debtor filed her second bankruptcy case within 180 days of requesting a voluntary dismissal of her prior Chapter 13 case after Creditor had filed a motion for and obtained relief from the stay. As a result, Debtor was not eligible under § 109(g)(2) to be a debtor in her second bankruptcy case. "The specific exception to the automatic stay under § 362(b)(21)(A) was directly applicable," and the trustee's sale of the property did not violate the stay. [*See* **Leafty v. Aussie Sonoran Capital, LLC (*In re* Leafty),** 479 B.R. 545 (B.A.P. 9th Cir. 2012)]

o. Eviction: Residential Real Property

In 2005, Congress added two new exceptions to the stay that affect the ability of a lessor to move forward with eviction proceedings, in certain circumstances, without obtaining relief from the automatic stay. Both subsections are exceptions to § 362(a)(3), which stays any act to obtain possession of or exercise control over estate property. [B.C. § 362(a)(3), (a)(22), (a)(23)]

(i) Pre-Petition Judgment for Possession

In 2005, Congress created an exception to the stay for the continuation of any *eviction, unlawful detainer, or similar proceeding* by a lessor of residential real property against a debtor/tenant if the lessor has obtained a *judgment for possession pre-petition.* [B.C. § 362(b)(22)] The exception, however, is subject to § 362(*l*), which keeps the automatic stay in place if the debtor/tenant satisfies certain conditions.

(1) Applicability of the Exception During the First 30 Days

The stay will go into effect (exception will not apply) for *30 days after the filing of the petition* if the debtor (1) files with the petition a *certification,* under penalty of perjury, that she has the right under nonbankruptcy law to *cure the entire monetary default* that gave rise to the judgment for possession; (2) *serves* such certification on the *lessor;* and (3) deposits with the court clerk any *rent that would come due during the 30-day period.* [B.C. § 362(*l*)(1); *see* Official Form 101A]

(2) Applicability of the Exception from Day 31 Forward

If the debtor takes the steps outlined above under (1) and within that 30-day period files with the court and serves on the lessor a *further certification,* under penalty of perjury, that debtor has *cured,* under nonbankruptcy law, the entire monetary default that gave rise to the judgment for possession, then the exception under § 362(b)(22) does not apply. In other words, the automatic stay applies and prevents the lessor from proceeding against the debtor. [B.C. § 362(*l*)(2)]

(ii) Objection by Lessor

If the lessor objects to either the debtor's initial certification or her further certification of cure and serves that objection on the debtor, then the court must hold a *hearing within 10 days* after filing and service of the objection to determine whether the debtor's certification is true. [B.C. § 362(*l*)(3)(A)] If the court upholds the lessor's objection, then the exception to the stay at § 362(b)(22) applies immediately; therefore, the lessor need not apply for relief from the stay in order to complete the process of recovering full possession of the property. [B.C. § 362(*l*)(3)(B)(i)] The court clerk must immediately serve upon the debtor and lessor a certified copy of the court's order upholding the lessor's objection. [B.C. § 362(*l*)(3)(B)(ii)]

(iii) Debtor's Failure to File Certification

The debtor must indicate on the petition whether there is a judgment for possession of the rental property where she resides, and must provide the lessor's name and address. [B.C. § 362(*l*)(5)] If the debtor indicates on the petition that there is a judgment for possession of her rental premises but fails to file either the initial certification or further certification described above, then the exception at § 362(b)(22) shall apply immediately upon failure to file the certification. The lessor is not required to file a motion to lift the automatic stay in order to complete the process of recovering full possession of the leased property. [B.C. § 362(*l*)(4)(A)] The clerk of the court also must immediately serve on the lessor and the debtor a certified copy of the docket indicating the absence of a filed certification and the applicability of § 362(b)(22). [B.C. § 362(*l*)(4)(B)]

(iv) Summary

The lessor may complete the process to recover possession of leased residential premises without moving to lift the automatic stay under § 362(a)(3) if there is a *pre-petition judgment for possession* and:

(1) the debtor/tenant *fails to file the initial certification* under § 362(*l*)(1)(A);

(2) the debtor/tenant *fails to deposit rent* that would become due during the 30-day period after filing of the petition [B.C. § 362(*l*)(1)(B)];

(3) the debtor/tenant, during the 30-day period after filing for bankruptcy, *fails to file the further certification of cure* under § 362(*l*)(2);

(4) the debtor/tenant files the *initial certification* under § 362(*l*)(1)(A), the *lessor objects to such certification,* and the *court upholds* the lessor's objection; *or*

(5) the debtor/tenant files the *further certification of cure* under § 362(*l*)(2), the *lessor objects to such certification,* and the *court upholds* the lessor's objection.

p. Property Endangerment or Controlled Substance Use

Congress added this exception to the automatic stay in 2005, and the structure of the exception is similar to that involving a pre-petition judgment for possession under § 362(b)(22). Section 362(b)(23), however, allows the lessor, under certain conditions, to *begin or continue an eviction action* without moving to lift the stay.

A lessor of residential real property may commence or continue an eviction action based on *endangerment of the property* or *illegal use of controlled substances on the property.* In order to take advantage of this exception, the lessor must file with the court and serve on the debtor a *certification,* under penalty of perjury, that such an *eviction action has been filed* or that the debtor, during the *30 days prior to filing of the certification,* has *endangered* the property or illegally used or allowed the use of a *controlled substance on the property.* [B.C. § 362(b)(23)] The exception, however, is subject to § 362(m), which keeps the automatic stay in place if the debtor/tenant satisfies certain conditions.

(i) When Exception Applies

The exception at § 362(b)(23), allowing the lessor to move forward with the eviction, applies on the date that is *15 days* after the lessor files and serves the certification. [B.C. § 362(m)(1)] The 15-day period does not apply, however, if the debtor takes certain action in response to the certification. [B.C. § 362(m)(2)]

(ii) Debtor Objection

If the debtor files with the court an *objection* to the *truth or legal sufficiency* of the lessor's *certification* and serves that objection on the lessor, then the exception to the stay at § 362(b)(23) does not apply, unless the court orders otherwise. [B.C. § 362(m)(2)(A)] The court must hold a *hearing within 10 days* after the filing and service of debtor's objection in order to determine if the situation giving rise to the lessor's certification existed or has been remedied. [B.C. § 362(m)(2)(B)]

(iii) Hearing Determination

If the debtor can *demonstrate,* to the court's satisfaction, that the situation giving rise to lessor's certification either *did not exist or has been remedied,* then the *automatic stay remains in effect* as otherwise provided by § 362. [B.C. § 362(a)(3), (m)(2)(C)] If the debtor fails to make such demonstration to the court's satisfaction, then the lessor does not need to move for relief from the stay under § 362(a)(3) in order to proceed with the eviction. [B.C. § 362(m)(2)(D)(i)] The court clerk, then, immediately must serve on the lessor and the debtor a certified copy of the court's order upholding the lessor's certification. [B.C. § 362(m)(2)(D)(ii)]

(iv) No Debtor Objection

If the debtor does not object to the lessor's certification within 15 days, then *§ 362(b)(23) immediately applies* and lessor does not have to move for relief from the stay under § 362(a)(3) in order to complete the process of recovering full possession of the leased property. [B.C. § 362(m)(3)(A)] The court clerk then shall immediately serve on the lessor and the debtor a certified copy of the docket indicating debtor's failure to file an objection. [B.C. § 362(m)(3)(B)]

(v) Summary

The lessor may complete the process to recover possession of leased residential premises without moving to lift the automatic stay under § 362(a)(3) if the lessor files with the court and serves on the debtor a *certification,* under penalty of perjury, that it has filed an eviction action based on *endangerment of the property* or *illegal use of controlled substances on the property* or that the debtor, during the *30 days prior to filing of the certification,* has *endangered* the property or illegally used or allowed the use of a *controlled substance on the property* and

(1) the debtor *fails to object* to lessor's certification within 15 days after lessor filed and served on debtor the certification; or

(2) the debtor filed an objection but failed to demonstrate to the court's satisfaction that the situation giving rise to lessor's certification either did not exist or had been remedied.

q. Non-Avoidable Transfers

This exception, added to the Code in 2005, provides that the automatic stay does not apply to any transfer that is not avoidable under § 544 and that is not avoidable under § 549. [B.C. § 362(b)(24)] Thus, if the trustee cannot avoid the debtor's post-petition transfer of estate property under § 549, the trustee cannot void that transfer by claiming it violates the automatic stay. The trustee must challenge the transfer under § 549, rather than "side step the limitations found in § 549 by asserting that an unauthorized transfer is also void in violation of the automatic stay." [**Slone v. Anderson (*In re* Anderson),** 511 B.R. 481 (Bankr. S.D. Ohio 2013) (also noting that § 362(b)(24) is " 'one of the oddest and perhaps the most poorly drafted of the BAPCPA provisions dealing with the automatic stay' ")]

r. Securities Self-Regulatory Organizations

In 2005, Congress added another exception to the automatic stay for certain conduct by securities self-regulatory organizations, which it defined as a securities association or a national securities exchange registered with the Securities Exchange Commission. [B.C. §§ 362(b)(25), 101(48A)] The exception covers the following actions:

(i) the commencement or continuation of an *investigation or action* by a securities self-regulatory organization to enforce the organization's regulatory power [B.C. § 362(b)(25)(A)];

(ii) the *enforcement* of an *order or a decision*, other than for monetary sanctions, obtained by a securities self-regulatory organization to enforce the organization's regulatory power [B.C. § 362(b)(25)(B)]; or

(iii) any action taken by a securities self-regulatory organization to *delist, delete,* or *refuse to permit quotation of stock* that fails to meet applicable regulatory standards. [B.C. § 362(b)(25)(C)]

s. Setoff Income Tax Refund

In 2005, Congress added an exception to the stay to permit a governmental unit to setoff, if allowed under nonbankruptcy law, an *income tax refund for a pre-petition taxable period against a pre-petition tax liability.* The income tax refund and the tax liability must be for a pre-petition taxable period. If applicable nonbankruptcy law does not allow the setoff because there is a pending action to determine the amount or legality of a tax liability, then the governmental unit may hold the refund until the pending action is resolved. The trustee, however, may move for turnover of the refund. The court, after notice and a hearing, may order turnover, but only if the court grants the government adequate protection, within the meaning of § 361, for any secured claim that the government unit has under § 506(a) by virtue of its right to setoff. [B.C. § 362(b)(26)]

e.g. **Example:** Debtor filed for relief under Chapter 13 in 2008. The IRS filed a proof of claim in her case for more than $44,000 owed in pre-petition income taxes. The IRS set off Debtor's pre-petition tax liability against $1,500 that Debtor had overpaid on her 2007 pre-petition taxes. Debtor argued that the setoff violated the automatic stay. The bankruptcy court held that there was no stay violation. The court explained that the IRS has the right to set off tax liabilities against tax refunds under nonbankruptcy law, specifically 26 U.S.C. § 6402(a). Because both the tax liability and the tax refund were for pre-petition taxable periods, the IRS's setoff fell "squarely within the exception of § 362(b)(26) and [did] not violate the automatic stay." [**Ewing v. United States (*In re Ewing*),** 400 B.R. 913 (Bankr. N.D. Ga. 2008)]

t. Federal Health Care Programs

It is not a violation of the automatic stay for the Secretary of Health and Human Services to exclude the debtor from participating in the Medicare program or any other federal health care program, as defined in the Social Security Act. [B.C. § 362(b)(28); 42 U.S.C. §§ 1320a–7b(f), 1301 *et seq.*, 1395 *et seq.*] Congress added this exception in 2005.

u. Amateur Sports

In 2020, Congress enacted the Empowering Olympic, Paralympic, and Amateur Athletes Act of 2020 ("Empowering Act"), whose purpose, in part, was to "protect amateur athletes from emotional, physical, and sexual abuse. [Pub. L. No. 116–189 (2020)]. The Empowering Act added § 362(b)(29) to the Code, which excepts from the automatic stay under § 362(a)(1) any action by an *amateur sports organization* to replace a governing body or any action by the *United States Olympic and Paralympic Committee* to revoke the certification of a national governing body. [B.C. § 362(b)(29)(A); 36 U.S.C. §§ 220501(b), 220521, 220528]

v. Small Business Debtor

In 2005, Congress added an exception to the stay to address what it perceived as a problem with serial filing by small business debtors. The stay exception only applies to a *small business case,* which is a term of art defined in the Code. [B.C. §§ 362(n), 101(51C)] This exception to the stay *only applies* if the debtor files a bankruptcy case and

(i) *is a debtor in a small business case pending* at the time debtor files its subsequent bankruptcy case [B.C. § 362(n)(1)(A)];

(ii) *was a debtor in a small business case* that was *dismissed for any reason* by an order that became final in the *two-year period* before the date of the order for relief in the subsequent bankruptcy case [B.C. § 362(n)(1)(B)];

(iii) *was a debtor in a small business case* in which a *plan was confirmed* in the *two-year period* before the date of the order for relief in the subsequent bankruptcy case [B.C. § 362(n)(1)(C)]; *or*

(iv) is an *entity that acquired substantially all of the assets or business of a small business debtor described above in (i)–(iii),* unless such entity establishes by a preponderance of the evidence that it acquired the assets or business in *good faith and not to evade the restrictions of § 362(n).* [B.C. § 362(n)(1)(D)]

(i) Inapplicability of the Small Business Exception

The Code provides that in certain circumstances, the *exception* to the automatic stay for small business cases *does not apply,* which means that the automatic stay *does* apply. The automatic stay applies

(a) to an *involuntary case,* so long as there is no collusion between the debtor and creditors [B.C. § 362(n)(2)(A)]; or

(b) to the filing of a petition if the debtor proves by a preponderance of the evidence that the filing resulted from *circumstances beyond the debtor's control not foreseeable at the time the case then pending was filed,* and it is more likely than not that the court will *confirm a feasible reorganization, not liquidating, plan within a reasonable time period.* [B.C. § 362(n)(2)(B)]

Example: Debtor owned and operated a boat marina business. She filed for relief under Chapter 11, and filed a reorganization plan and disclosure statement. Debtor was a small business debtor and her Chapter 11 case was a small business case. On April 1, 2010, the bankruptcy court dismissed Debtor's Chapter 11 case, because she failed to comply with the 45-day confirmation requirement at § 1129(e) for small business debtors. On April 9, 2010, Debtor filed a second small business Chapter 11 case. Debtor argued that the exception to the stay at § 362(n) did not apply to her second bankruptcy case, because she satisfied the requirements of § 362(n)(2)(B)(i)—her second bankruptcy filing resulted from circumstances not foreseeable at the time that she filed her first Chapter 11 case. Debtor posited that her first Chapter 11 case was "the case then pending." The court rejected Debtor's argument. It held that the "plain language" of § 362(n)(2)(B)(i) "refers to a separate case that *is* pending at the time that second petition is filed" and because there was no *pending* case at the time that Debtor filed her second bankruptcy case (her first case had been dismissed), § 362(n)(2)(B)(i) simply did not apply. Therefore, the court concluded that § 362(n)(1)(B) applied to Debtor's second bankruptcy filing on April 9, 2010, thereby "rendering the automatic stay inapplicable." [**Palmer v. Bank of the West,** 438 B.R. 167 (E.D. Wis. 2010)]

🔲 GILBERT

CHECKLIST OF EXCEPTIONS TO OR CASES IN WHICH THE AUTOMATIC STAY DOES NOT APPLY

THE AUTOMATIC STAY DOES NOT APPLY TO:

- ☑ The commencement or continuation of a *criminal action against the debtor*

- ☑ Various actions related to the collection of *domestic support obligations*

- ☑ The commencement or continuation of a civil suit to establish *paternity* or concerning *child custody or visitation*

- ☑ The commencement or continuation of any civil action regarding *domestic violence*

- ☑ The commencement or continuation of a civil action to *dissolve a marriage*

- ☑ Certain *acts of perfection or filings of continuation statements* to the extent that they occur within the applicable grace period, or to the extent that the trustee's rights and powers are subject to such perfection

- ☑ Governmental proceedings to *enforce police or regulatory powers* and enforcement of *nonmonetary judgments* resulting from such proceedings

- ☑ The exercise of certain contractual rights to *liquidate, terminate, or accelerate securities, commodities, or forward contracts; repurchase or swap agreements; or master netting agreements*

- ☑ Certain setoffs related to *securities, commodities, or forward contracts; repurchase or swap agreements; or master netting agreements*

- ☑ Certain *HUD mortgage foreclosures*

- ☑ *Tax audits and assessments*

- ☑ Actions to recover nonresidential real property under a lease that has *terminated by expiration of the lease's stated term* before or during the case

- ☑ *Presentment* of a negotiable instrument, sending a *notice of dishonor,* or *protesting dishonor*

- ☑ Certain actions against *educational institutions* relating to accreditation, licensure, or eligibility to participate in federal programs

- ☑ Actions by the Secretary of Transportation or the Secretary of Commerce in a *Chapter 11 case* to *foreclose a preferred ship or fleet mortgage,* to *foreclose on a security interest* relating to a *vessel or vessel construction* under applicable state or federal law, or *to foreclose a mortgage, deed of trust, or other security interest in a fishing facility* held by the Secretary of Commerce under federal law

- ☑ The creation or perfection of a *statutory lien for ad valorem property taxes that become due post-petition*

- ☑ *Special taxes or special assessments on real property,* regardless of whether ad valorem, imposed by a governmental unit, that *become due post-petition*

- ☑ **Withholding of income** from a debtor's wages and **collection of the withheld** amounts pursuant to an agreement with debtor authorizing such withholding and collection for the benefit of a **pension, profit-sharing, stock bonus or other plan** established pursuant to provisions of the Internal Revenue Code **to the extent** such monies are withheld and collected only to repay certain loans

- ☑ Any act to **enforce any lien against or security interest in real property** based on an order lifting the stay in the debtor's **prior bankruptcy case** because debtor engaged in a **scheme to delay, hinder, or defraud creditors** that involved either the transfer of real property without the secured creditor's consent or multiple bankruptcy filings affecting such real property

- ☑ Any act to **enforce a lien or security interest in real property** if the debtor is **ineligible under § 109(g)** to be a debtor or if the debtor's bankruptcy filing violates an **order entered in a prior bankruptcy case** prohibiting the debtor from filing another bankruptcy case

- ☑ Under certain circumstances, the **continuation of any eviction, unlawful detainer, or similar proceeding** by a lessor of **residential real property** if the lessor has obtained a **pre-petition judgment for possession** of the leased premises

- ☑ Under certain circumstances, the **commencement or continuation of an eviction action** based on the debtor's **endangerment of the leased property or illegal use of a controlled substance on the leased property**

- ☑ Any transfer that is **not avoidable under § 544 and not avoidable under § 549**

- ☑ A **securities self-regulatory organization's commencement or continuation** of an **investigation or action, enforcement** of an **order or decision** (other than for monetary sanctions), or action to **delist, delete or refuse to permit quotation of a stock** that fails to meet applicable regulatory standards

- ☑ If allowed under applicable nonbankruptcy law, the **setoff** by a governmental unit, of an **income tax refund for a pre-petition taxable period against a pre-petition tax liability**

- ☑ The **exclusion by the Secretary of Health and Human Services of the debtor** from participating in the Medicare program or any other federal health care program, as defined in the Social Security Act

- ☑ Any action by an **amateur sports organization** to replace a governing body or any action by the **United States Olympic and Paralympic Committee** to revoke the certification of a national governing body

- ☑ The debtor's filing of a bankruptcy case if the debtor is a debtor in a **pending small business case** at the time of the subsequent bankruptcy filing

- ☑ The debtor's filing of a bankruptcy case if the debtor was a debtor in a **small business case** that was **dismissed for any reason** by an order that became final in the **two years** prior to the date of the order for relief in debtor's subsequent bankruptcy filing

- ☑ The debtor's filing of a bankruptcy case if the debtor was a debtor in a **small business case in which a plan was confirmed** in the **two years** prior to the date of the order for relief in debtor's subsequent bankruptcy filing

- ☑ A case in which the debtor is an entity that **acquired substantially all of the assets or business of a small business debtor** described in the three scenarios immediately above, unless the debtor establishes by a preponderance of the evidence that it obtained the assets or business in **good faith** and **not to circumvent the Code's provisions on serial filing**

4. Expiration of Stay

Prior to BAPCPA's enactment, the Code's rules on when the stay expired were relatively simple. In 2005, however, Congress added new rules on stay termination for *personal property* in cases involving *individual Chapter 7 debtors.* [B.C. § 362(h)] Congress also significantly expanded § 362(c) by creating detailed rules about the operation of the stay in cases involving *serial filing by individual debtors.* [B.C. § 362(c)]

a. Individual Chapter 7 Debtors and Personal Property

Section 521(a)(2) of the Code requires an individual Chapter 7 debtor to file a statement of intention and perform that intention within certain time periods with regard to debts secured by property of the estate. [B.C. § 521(a)(2)] In 2005, Congress added § 362(h) to the Code and tied termination of the automatic stay to the debtor's performance of her obligations under § 521 with regard to *personal property of the estate or of the debtor* that secures a claim or that is subject to an unexpired lease. [B.C. § 362(h)(1)]

(i) Stay Termination

In an *individual Chapter 7* case, the automatic stay terminates with respect to *personal property of the estate or of the debtor* that secures a claim or that is subject to a lease and such property is no longer property of the estate if the debtor fails (i) to *timely file a statement of intention* or to indicate on such statement that it will *surrender or redeem, the property, reaffirm the debt secured by the property, or assume such unexpired lease* pursuant to § 365(p); or (ii) *timely take the action* specified in the statement. [B.C. § 362(h)(1)(A), (B)] The stay does not terminate if the debtor specifies an intention to reaffirm the debt on the original contract terms and the creditor refuses to agree to reaffirmation on those terms. [B.C. § 362(h)(1)(B); *In re* **Craker,** 337 B.R. 549 (Bankr. M.D. N.C. 2006)]

Note: The language of § 362(h) is not limited to Chapter 7 cases, but § 521(a)(2), to which § 362(h) specifically refers, *is* so limited. Thus, a noted commentator contends that "it is clear that an early stay termination under section 362(h) can occur only in a Chapter 7 case in which the debtor is an individual." [3 Collier ¶ 362.11; *see also In re* **Schlitzer,** 332 B.R. 856 (Bankr. W.D. N.Y. 2005) (holding that § 362(h) does not apply in a Chapter 13 case)]

(ii) Exception

The trustee may file a motion *before § 521(a)(2)'s time limits expire* asking the court to stop the operation of § 362(h). The *stay does not terminate* if the court, after notice and a hearing, determines that the *property is of consequential value or benefit* to the estate, orders *adequate protection* of the creditor's interest, and orders the debtor to *deliver to the trustee any collateral in the debtor's possession.* [B.C. § 362(h)(2)] If the court rules against the trustee's motion, however, the stay terminates at the conclusion of the hearing on the motion.

(iii) Comfort Order

Section 362(j) provides that a party in interest may request the court to issue an order that the automatic stay has terminated under § 362(c). Section 362(j) specifically mentions § 362(c), but not § 362(h). Thus, there is disagreement as to whether a court may issue a comfort order that the automatic stay has terminated under § 362(h).

cf. Compare: *In re* **Grossi,** 365 B.R. 608 (Bankr. E.D. Va. 2007) ("[e]ntry of a comfort order under 11 U.S.C. § 362(j) is not appropriate when the stay allegedly has been terminated under 11 U.S.C. § 362(h)") *with In re* **Espey,** 347 B.R. 785 (Bankr. M.D. Fla. 2006) (stating that because § 362(c)(1) provides that the stay continues only so long as property is estate property, once property no longer is estate property, e.g., when the stay terminates under § 362(h), "a party in interest may move the Court for an order confirming that the stay is terminated under § 362(j)").

(iv) Compare: Stay Termination § 521(a)(6)

Section 521(a)(6) also contains a stay termination provision, but with regard to *personal property securing a purchase-money security interest.* This provision applies *only* to an *individual Chapter 7 debtor.* If a Chapter 7 debtor fails to reaffirm the debt or redeem the property securing the creditor's purchase-money interest within *45 days* after the first meeting of creditors, then the *automatic stay terminates* and the property *no longer is estate property.* [B.C. § 521(a)(6)] Section 521(a)(6) is limited to *purchase-money security interests in personal property,* while § 362(h) "applies to all debts secured by personal property, not just purchase-money debts." [*In re* **Lopez,** 440 B.R. 447 (Bankr. E.D. Va. 2010)]

(v) The Ride-Through

Some jurisdictions, prior to the passage of BAPCPA, recognized what came to be known as the "ride-through." A debtor could continue to make payments on a current debt and keep the collateral securing the debt without redeeming the property or reaffirming the debt. BAPCPA's changes to the Code, e.g., the stay termination provisions at §§ 362(h) and 521(a)(6), limited, but did not eliminate, the ride-through. For example, the stay termination provisions at §§ 362(h) and 521(a)(6) apply to *personal,* not *real,* property. Thus, some courts have held that BAPCPA did not "eliminate the ride-through for debts secured by real property." [**Lopez,** *supra*]

Suppose a debtor who is current on her car payments decides neither to redeem the vehicle nor to reaffirm the debt secured by the car. When the stay lifts, can the creditor repossess the vehicle based on an *ipso facto* clause in the parties' contract? The answer to this question depends on whether a creditor can repossess under state law based on a contractual *ipso facto* clause when the debtor is current on her vehicle payments. [*In re* **Donald,** 343 B.R. 524 (E.C. N.C. 2006) (stating that when the debtor does not act, as required by § 521(a)(6) or § 362(h), § 521(d) merely eliminates the Code's prior limitations "on the operation of ipso facto clauses . . . [and] [c]reditors still must ensure that the contract, and their efforts to enforce the terms in it, do not run afoul of any applicable state laws"); *see, e.g.,* **Hall v. Ford Motor Credit, LLC,** 292 Kan. 176 (Kan. 2011) (affirming lower court holding that even though debtor was current on car payments creditor did not violate the Kansas Uniform Consumer Credit Code by repossessing debtor's vehicle post-bankruptcy based on ipso facto clause in parties' contract and debtor's failure to reaffirm the debt in bankruptcy on collateral worth substantially less than the debt itself)]

b. Section 362(c): General Rules

Unless the court grants relief from the automatic stay, it remains operative from the time that the bankruptcy petition is filed until it terminates as follows.

(i) The stay of an *act against property of the estate* is effective until the property no longer is property of the estate. [B.C. § 362(c)(1)]

(ii) The stay of *any other act* enjoined under § 362(a) continues until the case is dismissed, the case is closed, or a discharge in an individual Chapter 7 case or a case under Chapter 11, 12, or 13 is granted or denied, whichever occurs first. [B.C. § 362(c)(2)]

e.g. **Example:** Trustee, in compliance with § 363, sells an asset of the estate to Third Party. The automatic stay is terminated with respect to the asset at the time that it ceases to be property of the estate. [B.C. § 362(c)(1)]

e.g. **Example:** Trustee abandons an over-encumbered asset of the estate. Debtor has not been granted or denied a discharge, and the case has neither been closed nor dismissed. Although the asset is no longer property of the estate, it becomes Debtor's property and continues to be protected by the automatic stay. [B.C. § 362(a)(5), (c)(2)]

e.g. **Example:** Trustee abandons an over-encumbered asset of the estate. The bankruptcy court subsequently grants Debtor a discharge, which terminates the automatic stay. The secured creditor can proceed to foreclose her lien on the property. [B.C. § 362(c)(2)(C)]

(i) Chapter 11

Except as otherwise provided in the plan or the plan confirmation order, confirmation of a Chapter 11 plan vests all of the property of the estate in the debtor. [B.C. § 1141(b)] With certain exceptions, plan confirmation also discharges the debtor from pre-confirmation debts. [B.C. § 1141(d)(1)(A)] Thus, in such cases, plan confirmation terminates the automatic stay. [B.C. § 362(c)(1), (2)(C)]

(1) Individual Non-Subchapter V Case

For an individual non-subchapter V case, a distinction must be drawn between the *stay of an act against property* and the *stay of any other act*. Plan confirmation vests all estate property in the debtor; thus, the automatic stay as to that property terminates upon plan confirmation because the property no longer is estate property. [B.C. §§ 362(c)(1), 1141(b)]

But in an individual non-subchapter V Chapter 11 case, the debtor does not receive a discharge until she completes all plan payments. [B.C. § 1141(d)(5)(A); *see* § 1181(a) (§ 1141(d)(5) not applicable)] Therefore, after confirmation but before closing (or dismissal) of an individual non-subchapter V Chapter 11 case, the stay of any *other* act continues. [B.C. § 362(c)(2)]

But, what if the debtor moves for a final decree in order to close her case, even though she has not yet received a discharge, in order to avoid paying quarterly fees to the United States trustee? In **Rael v. Wells Fargo (*In re* Rael),** 527 B.R. 799 (B.A.P. 10th Circuit 2015), the Tenth Circuit's BAP held that closing of the case, even for mere administrative convenience to save on payment of fees, terminates the automatic stay as to any other act. The court noted that the Code "does not distinguish amongst motives for case closure."

(ii) Exempt Property

Property that the debtor exempts is no longer property of the estate. But, unless the debtor's case is dismissed, exempt property is not liable during or after the case for a debtor's pre-petition debts. [B.C. § 522(c)] There are exceptions, however, to this general rule. For example, exempt property is liable for nondischargeable tax and domestic support obligations. [B.C. §§ 522(c)(1), 523(a)(1), (a)(5)]

c. Section 362(c): Serial Filers and BAPCPA's Changes

The Code's provisions on serial filers apply only to *individual debtors,* and only if the debtor's prior case was *dismissed.* [*See* B.C. § 362(c)(3), (4)] The serial filer provisions do not apply, however, if the debtor filed her later case because her prior case was filed under Chapter 7 and dismissed pursuant to § 707(b). [B.C. § 362(c)(3), (c)(4)(A)(i)]

(i) Prior Pending Case: 30-Day Rule

If an *individual debtor* files for relief under Chapter 7, 11, or 13 and if the debtor had a case *pending in the prior year* that was *dismissed,* § 362(c)(3) provides that the stay in debtor's current bankruptcy case expires after *30 days.* The stay expires, however, only as to a debt, property securing that debt, or a lease *with respect to the debtor.* Therefore, the majority of courts have held that after 30 days, while the automatic stay expires as to *the debtor and property of the debtor,* it remains in place with regard to *estate property.* [**Rose v. Select Portfolio Servicing, Inc.,** 945 F.3d 226 (5th Cir. 2019); **Holcomb v. Hardeman (*In re* Holcomb),** 380 B.R. 813 (B.A.P. 10th Cir. 2008)] This stay-expiration rule does *not* apply to cases under Chapter 12. [B.C. § 362(c)(3)]

(1) What Does *Pending* Mean?

The stay-termination provision at § 362(c)(3) applies to a subsequent bankruptcy filing by an individual debtor if a prior Chapter 7, 11, or 13 case was *pending* during the prior year. The Bankruptcy Code does not define what "pending" means. For example, if the bankruptcy court dismisses the debtor's Chapter 13 case on March 1, 2017, but the clerk of court does not close the case until September 1, 2017, does debtor's filing another Chapter 13 case on June 1, 2018 run afoul of § 362(c)(3)? There is limited case law on the issue, but most courts run the time frame from the order of dismissal, not the administrative case closing. [*See, e.g., In re* **Linares,** 2010 WL 2788248 (Bankr. S.D. Fla. 2010) (holding that dismissal, not administrative closing, is relevant date from which to run the time period in § 362(c)(3)); *In re* **Easthope,** 2006 WL 851829 (Bankr. D. Utah 2006) (noting that it would be unfair to debtors to run the time period in § 362(c)(3) from the date of case closing because debtors cannot control when the clerk's office closes a case and, thus, holding that "[t]he plain meaning of the word 'pending' as well as policy considerations demonstrate that a case is no longer pending once it has been dismissed"); *In re* **Moore,** 337 B.R. 79 (Bankr. E.D. N.C. 2005) (stating that debtor's prior bankruptcy case was "no longer 'pending' for purposes of § 362(c)(3) as of the date of dismissal, regardless of when the case was closed")]

(2) Request for Stay Continuation: Procedure

A party in interest may file a motion to continue the automatic stay as to any or all creditors. To obtain relief, the party in interest must demonstrate that the filing of the subsequent case was in *good faith* as to the creditors to be stayed. The Code requires notice and a hearing, and that the *hearing be completed within the 30-day period* before the stay expires. [B.C. § 362(c)(3)(B)]

(3) Statutory Presumption: All Creditors

For purposes of a request to extend the stay under § 362(c)(3)(B), the filing of the subsequent case is *presumed not to be in good faith* as to *all creditors* if:

(a) **more than one prior case** filed by or against the debtor under Chapter 7, 11, or 13 was **pending** within the preceding one-year period [B.C. § 362(c)(3)(C)(i)(I)];

(b) a prior case filed by or against the debtor under Chapter 7, 11, or 13 was **dismissed** within the preceding one-year period because the debtor failed to (i) **without having a substantial excuse,** file or amend the petition or other required documents; (ii) **provide adequate protection,** as required by the court; or (iii) **perform the terms of a confirmed plan** [B.C. § 362(c)(3)(C)(i)(II)]; **or**

Note: Mere inadvertence or negligence does not constitute substantial excuse, unless the negligence of debtor's attorney resulted in the prior case's dismissal. [B.C. § 362(c)(3)(C)(i)(II)(aa)]

(c) there has been *no substantial change* in the *debtor's financial or personal affairs since the dismissal* of the next most prior case nor any other reason to conclude that the subsequent case will result in a discharge, if filed under Chapter 7, or a fully performed confirmed plan, if filed under Chapter 11 or 13. [B.C. § 362(c)(3)(C)(i)(III)]

(4) Statutory Presumption: Creditor Moved to Lift Stay

For purposes of a request to extend the stay under § 362(c)(3)(B), the filing of the subsequent case is *presumed not to be in good faith* as to any creditor that sought relief from the stay in the debtor's prior case and that *motion was pending at the time of dismissal* of the prior case *or* was *resolved by terminating, conditioning, or limiting the stay* as to such creditor's actions. [B.C. § 362(c)(3)(C)(ii)]

(5) Presumption Not Applicable

The presumption does not apply to a subsequent bankruptcy filing if the debtor's prior Chapter 7, 11 or 13 case was dismissed due to the creation of a *debt repayment plan.* [B.C. § 362(i)] The Code does not require that the debtor have completed this debt repayment plan in order for the presumption under § 362(c)(3) not to apply.

(6) Rebutting the Presumption

The debtor may rebut the presumption that her subsequent bankruptcy case was not filed in good faith. The debtor must rebut the presumption by *clear and convincing evidence.* [B.C. § 362(c)(3)(C)]

e.g. **Example:** Debtor filed for relief under Chapter 13 on October 23, 2012. That case was dismissed on November 14, 2013, because Debtor failed to make timely payments under his Chapter 13 plan. On August 26, 2014, less than one year from the dismissal of his earlier Chapter 13 case, Debtor filed his second Chapter 13 case. The next day, Debtor filed a motion to continue the automatic stay beyond the 30-day period. The court examined a number of factors, including the debtor's motive and reasons for dismissal of his first bankruptcy case. The court noted that Debtor's first bankruptcy case was dismissed because he could not make the Chapter 13 payments, not because of any improper conduct. At the hearing, Debtor testified that he could not make the Chapter 13 plan payments in his prior case because the business had lost its liquor license. The business, however, had regained the license and while Debtor testified that he had been seriously ill, he had since recovered. The court also concluded that based on the Debtor's credible testimony, Debtor had narrowly met his burden of establishing by clear and convincing evidence that he could fund and perform a plan in his second Chapter 13 case. The bankruptcy court, applying a totality-of-the-circumstances test, concluded that Debtor had established by clear and convincing evidence that his second Chapter 13 case was filed in good faith. Therefore, the court granted the Debtor's motion to extend the automatic stay beyond the 30-day period. [*In re* **Riedy,** 517 B.R. 88 (Bankr. W.D. Mich. 2014)]

(ii) Two or More Prior Pending Cases

If an individual debtor files for bankruptcy and there were *two or more bankruptcy cases pending in the prior year* that were *dismissed,* § 362(c)(4) provides that the automatic stay in debtor's current bankruptcy case does not go into effect. Section 362(c)(4) does *not* apply if the debtor files for bankruptcy, other than under Chapter 7, after her prior Chapter 7 case was dismissed under § 707(b). [B.C. § 362(c)(4)(A)(i)] Unlike § 362(c)(3), § 362(c)(4)(A) does not limit its operation to Chapter 7, 11, or 13; thus, it appears to apply to all prior bankruptcy filings, including those under Chapter 12. [*Compare* B.C. § 362(c)(3) *with* B.C. § 362(c)(4)(A)(i); *see In re* **Benefield,** 438 B.R. 706 (Bankr. D. N.M. 2010) (holding that automatic stay did not come into effect in debtors' Chapter 11 case because debtors' two prior Chapter 12 cases had been pending but dismissed during the preceding year)] On request of a party in interest, the court must promptly enter an order confirming that no stay is in effect in debtor's bankruptcy case. [B.C. § 362(c)(4)(A)(ii)]

(1) Request for Stay to Take Effect

Within *30 days of the filing of the debtor's subsequent bankruptcy case,* a party in interest may request that the court order the stay to take effect as to any or all creditors, subject to any conditions imposed by the court. The court may so order, after notice and a hearing, only if the party in interest demonstrates that the filing of the subsequent case was in *good faith as to the creditors to be stayed.* [B.C. § 362(c)(4)(B)] Unlike the hearing under § 362(c)(3), the hearing under § 362(c)(4) does not have to conclude within 30 days after the filing of the petition. [*Compare* § 362(c)(3)(B) *with* § 362(c)(4)(B)] If the court grants the request, the stay is effective on the date of the court's order allowing the stay to go into effect. [B.C. § 362(c)(4)(C)]

(2) Statutory Presumption: All Creditors

For purposes of a request under § 362(c)(4)(B), the filing of the subsequent case is *presumed not to be in good faith* as to *all creditors* if:

(a) *two or more prior cases* filed by or against the debtor were *pending* within the preceding one-year period [B.C. § 362(c)(4)(D)(i)(I)];

(b) a prior case filed by or against the debtor was *dismissed* within the preceding one-year period because the debtor (i) *without having a substantial excuse* failed to file or amend the petition or other required documents; (ii) failed to *provide adequate protection,* as required by the court; or (iii) failed to *perform the terms of a confirmed plan* [B.C. § 362(c)(4)(D)(i)(II)]; *or*

Note: Mere inadvertence or negligence do not constitute substantial excuse, unless the negligence of debtor's attorney resulted in the prior case's dismissal. [B.C. § 362(c)(4)(D)(i)(II)]

(c) there has been *no substantial change* in the *debtor's financial or personal affairs since the dismissal* of the next most prior case nor any other reason to conclude that the subsequent case will result in a discharge, if filed under Chapter 7, or a fully performed confirmed plan, if filed under Chapter 11 or 13. [B.C. § 362(c)(4)(D)(i)(III)]

(3) Statutory Presumption: Creditor Moved for Relief of Stay

For purposes of a request under § 362(c)(4)(B), the filing of the subsequent case is *presumed not to be in good faith* as to any creditor that sought relief from the stay in a prior case and that *motion was pending at the time of dismissal* of the prior case *or* was *resolved by terminating, conditioning, or limiting the stay* as to such creditor's actions. [B.C. § 362(c)(4)(D)(ii)]

(4) Rebutting the Presumption

The debtor may rebut the presumption that her subsequent bankruptcy case was not filed in good faith. The debtor must rebut the presumption by *clear and convincing evidence.* [B.C. § 362(c)(4)(D)]

(iii) Comfort Orders

Upon the request of a party in interest, the court shall issue an order under § 362(c) that the automatic stay has been terminated. [B.C. § 362(j)]

5. Relief from Stay

Upon request of a party in interest, and after notice and a hearing, the court may grant relief from the automatic stay by *terminating, modifying, annulling, or conditioning* the stay. [B.C. § 362(d)]

Example: Debtor owned a residential real estate development project and defaulted on a construction loan obtained from Bank. Bank foreclosed on the property but before the sheriff's sale Debtor's counsel filed for relief under Chapter 7. Debtor's counsel had intended to file for relief under Chapter 11, and when he learned that he could not withdraw the Chapter 7 petition he filed a Chapter 11 petition less than an hour after filing the Chapter 7 petition. The Chapter 11 case moved forward, and Bank filed a motion to lift the automatic stay. Construction Company, which had recorded a mechanic's lien against the property pre-petition based on its work on the property, had notice of both bankruptcy filings and did not object to Bank's motion. The bankruptcy court granted Bank's motion and the Chapter 11 case was subsequently dismissed. Several days after dismissal of the Chapter 11 case, the Debtor filed a motion to dismiss the Chapter 7 case. Construction Company received notice of the motion to dismiss. Before dismissal of the Chapter 7 case, there was a sheriff's sale of the property, at which Bank bid. Bank then sold the property to a third party. After dismissal of Debtor's Chapter 7 case, Construction Company filed a motion to vacate the foreclosure sale, arguing that at the time of the sale Debtor's Chapter 7 case was still open and, thus, the automatic stay was still in effect. Bank then moved for the bankruptcy court to retroactively annul the Chapter 7 automatic stay and the bankruptcy court granted Bank's motion. The district court affirmed. The court explained that Bank had not willfully violated the stay; no action had taken place in the Chapter 7 case, which had been filed in error. Once the Bank realized that the sale had taken place while the Chapter 7 case was still open, Bank filed its motion to retroactively annul the stay. The court also noted that Construction Company had received all relevant notices, and that vacating the foreclosure sale would prejudice the rights of an alleged bona fide purchaser. The district court affirmed the bankruptcy court's order, which retroactively annulled the automatic stay effective on the date that the court had lifted the stay in Debtor's Chapter 11 case. [**Arrow Road Construction Company v. Bridgeview Bank Group (*In re* Brittwood Creek, LLC),** 450 B.R. 769 (N.D. Ill. 2011)]

a. Grounds for Relief

The Bankruptcy Code spells out several grounds for moving for relief from the automatic stay. Commonly, these motions are filed by a secured creditor for the purpose of foreclosing on or taking other action with regard to the property securing its claim.

(i) "Cause"

After notice and a hearing, the bankruptcy court must grant relief from the automatic stay to a party in interest if *cause* exists to lift the stay. [B.C. § 362(d)(1)] The Code does not define the term "cause." Thus, the determination of whether cause exists to lift the stay is fact-intensive, and "there is no set formula courts can use to make the determination." [*In re* **Vista International Development,** 2008 Bankr. LEXIS 5139 (Bankr. W.D. Tenn. 2008)]

(1) Lack of Adequate Protection

The debtor's failure to provide adequate protection of an entity's interest in property is sufficient cause for the court to order relief from the stay. [B.C. § 362(d)(1)] Other than a case filed under Chapter 12, adequate protection may constitute cash payments, granting of an additional or replacement lien, or realization of the indubitable equivalent of the entity interest in the property. [B.C. § 361] Adequate protection of an entity's interest in property in a *Chapter 12 case* may require cash payments, granting of an additional or replacement lien, payment of a reasonable rent for use of farmland, or such other relief as will adequately protect the value of property securing the claim. [B.C. § 1205] Granting an administrative expense, however, does not constitute adequate protection under any chapter of the Bankruptcy Code. [B.C. §§ 361(3), 1205(b)(4)] Failing to insure collateral also may constitute a failure of adequate protection and, thus, cause to lift the automatic stay. [*In re* **Melincavage,** 2018 WL 3725746 (Bankr. D. N.J. 2018) (holding, in part, that cause existed to lift the stay because "[a]dequate protection includes providing proof of enforceable insurance on collateral")]

e.g. **Example:** Debtor owned real property on which her mother operated a car wash. Debtor failed to pay the real estate taxes, and the property was sold for nonpayment of taxes. Buyer then assigned its certificate of purchase to Waters, who filed a petition for a tax deed under state law. At the time of Debtor's bankruptcy filing, the time period under state law to redeem had not yet expired and Waters' petition for a tax deed was still pending. Debtor filed her Chapter 13 plan, which provided for payment of past-due taxes on the property. Waters moved for lift of the stay to proceed in state court with the tax deed proceeding. Post-petition, Debtor missed a tax payment on the property and failed to demonstrate that her mother could make the tax payments from the revenue from the car wash business. The bankruptcy court explained that the property could be sold again at another tax sale because of missed tax payments. In order to obtain a tax deed, Waters then would have to redeem from that property tax sale. The bankruptcy court concluded that because of the "great risk that another tax buyer [might] intercede, Waters's interest in

[Debtor's] property [was] not therefore adequately protected." Therefore, the court granted his motion to lift the stay. [*In re* **Scott,** 449 B.R. 535 (Bankr. N.D. Ill. 2011)]

(2) Lack of Good Faith

The debtor's lack of good faith in filing the bankruptcy petition can constitute cause for granting relief from the automatic stay. [B.C. § 362(d)(1); *see, e.g.,* **Alta Vista, LLC v. Juarez (***In re* **Juarez),** 533 B.R. 818 (Bankr. D. Colo. 2015) (Chapter 13); *In re* **Sterling Bluff Investors, LLC,** 515 B.R. 902 (Bankr. S.D. Ga. 2014) (Chapter 11)] Courts have used different tests and factors in their determination of whether a debtor's bankruptcy filing is in bad faith and, thus, constitutes cause to lift the automatic stay. [*See, e.g., In re* **Loucheschi, LLC,** 2011 WL 3319891 (Bankr. D. Mass. 2011) (discussing various tests and approaches taken by courts); *In re* **Reyes Ramos,** 2006 WL 3898377 (Bankr. D. P.R. 2006) (same)]; *see also In re* **Boates,** 2006 WL 166569 (E.D. Penn. 2006) (examining seven factors, including debtor's motives, effect on creditors, debtor's pre- and post-petition treatment of creditors, in bad-faith filing analysis)]

Note: A court's order to lift the stay due to bad faith filing of a petition differs from an order entered in a prior case pursuant to § 362(d)(4) based on a scheme to defraud or the debtor's multiple bankruptcy filings. [B.C. § 362(d)(4)]

(3) Judicial Economy and Other Tribunals

The lack of adequate protection is not the only cause for lifting the stay. "[A] desire to permit an action to proceed to completion in another tribunal may provide another cause." [H.R. Rep. No. 95–595, at 343 (1977)] In making the decision whether to lift the stay to allow pending litigation to go forward, courts examine several factors:

(a) whether the litigation involves *only state law issues,* such that it is not necessary to draw upon the expertise of the bankruptcy court;

(b) whether lifting the stay would *promote judicial economy;* and

(c) whether the *estate can be protected* by requiring creditors to seek enforcement of any judgment through the bankruptcy court.

[*See, e.g., In re* **Bayou Haven Bed & Breakfast, LLC,** 2018 WL 3956933 (Bankr. E.D. La. 2018)]

(ii) Acts Against Property

The bankruptcy court will grant relief from the stay of an act against property if (i) the debtor has *no equity* in the property and (ii) the property is *not necessary for an effective reorganization.* [B.C. § 362(d)(2)]

(1) No Equity

Most courts view equity as the difference between the total of all liens on the property and the property's value. [B.C. § 362(d)(2)(A); *see, e.g., In re* **Madco Products,** 2009 Bankr. LEXIS 5724 (Bankr. W.D. Tenn. 2009)]

e.g. **Example:** Debtor filed for relief under Chapter 13. Citizens Bank held the mortgage on Debtor's home, which was appraised at $168,000. The balance on the loan extended by Citizens to Debtor to purchase the home was

$216,000. Thus, Debtor had no equity in his home. [*In re* **Brown,** 606 B.R. 348 (Bankr. E.D. Ark. 2019)]

(2) Not Necessary for an Effective Reorganization

The property at issue also must not be necessary to an effective reorganization. [B.C. § 362(d)(2)(B); *see In re* **Heritage Oracle, LLC,** 2010 WL 4259772 (Bankr. D. Ariz. 2010) (finding that debtor's brokerage and property management business was a service business that could operate in any location and, thus, debtor did not need the particular commercial real property from which it was currently operating and for which creditor sought relief from stay)] While a Chapter 13 debtor does not reorganize, as does a Chapter 11 entity, the clear weight of authority is that § 362(d)(2) applies to a Chapter 13 case. [*In re* **Donahue,** 231 B.R. 865 (Bankr. D. Vt. 1998)]

The debtor's prospects for reorganization are relevant to the "necessary to an effective reorganization" prong of the lift-of-stay analysis. Property will be deemed not necessary for an effective reorganization upon a finding that the debtor does not have a reasonable possibility of successfully reorganizing within a reasonable time. [B.C. § 362(d)(2)(B); *see, e.g., In re* **Brown,** *supra* (noting that "[i]n addition to finding the property necessary, courts also evaluate whether the debtor can propose a confirmable plan")]

Example: Debtor LLC owned ten acres of land on which it was developing a retail shopping center and hotel complex. Secured Creditor filed a complaint in state court seeking judicial foreclosure and appointment of a receiver. The state court granted Creditor's request for relief, but before the receiver took possession of the property Debtor filed for relief under Chapter 11. Secured Creditor filed a motion to lift the stay. Relief from the automatic stay was appropriate under § 362(d)(2). The property was appraised at almost $26 million, but the Secured Creditor's claim alone was approximately $35 million. Therefore, Debtor had no equity in the property. The Debtor also failed to provide evidence that it could reorganize within a reasonable period of time. Debtor would be unable to obtain consent from creditors with impaired claims without making full or near full payment to those impaired claimants, but Debtor had not secured the monies necessary to fund such a full-payment plan. [**F&F, LLC v. U.S. Hung Wui Investments, Inc. (*In re* F&F, LLC),** 2010 WL 6452907 (B.A.P. 9th Cir. 2010)]

(iii) Single Asset Real Estate

The Code also contains special rules for stay relief on property that satisfies the definition of "single asset real estate." If a creditor's claim is secured by an interest in single asset real estate, the court must grant relief from the automatic stay if the debtor fails to do either of the following within certain prescribed time frames:

(1) *file a plan of reorganization* that has a *reasonable possibility of being confirmed* within a *reasonable time* [B.C. § 362(d)(3)(A)] or

(2) *start to make monthly payments* in an amount equal to the current nondefault contract rate of interest to each creditor with a claim secured by the real estate, other than creditors with a judgment lien or an unmatured statutory lien. [B.C. § 362(d)(3)(B)]

Note: In 2005, Congress added language to § 362(d)(3)(B) that now gives the debtor the discretion to make the monthly payments from *rents or other income generated*

before, on, or after the start of the bankruptcy case *from the single asset real estate.* [B.C. § 362(d)(3)(B)(i)]

(1) Action Required

The debtor must take one of these two actions by the *later of:*

- *90 days after the order for relief; or*

- *30 days after the court determines debtor is subject to § 362(d)(3).*

For cause, the court may extend the 90-day period by an order entered within the 90 days. [B.C. § 362(d)(3)]

(2) Single Asset Real Estate Defined

The Code defines "single asset real estate" as "real property constituting a *single property or project,* other than residential real property with fewer than four residential units, which generates *substantially all of the gross income* of a debtor who is not a family farmer and on which no substantial business is being conducted by a debtor other than the business of operating the real property and activities incidental thereto." [B.C. § 101(51B)] In 2005, Congress deleted the $4 million secured debt cap previously in the definition and excluded family farmers from the scope of the definition.

(iv) Abuse by Debtor: Real Property

In 2005, Congress added a new subsection to § 362(d) to address a perceived problem with abusive filings. Section 362(d)(4) does two things. First, it states that the court must provide relief from the stay of any *act against real property* to a creditor with an interest secured by that property if the court finds that filing of the petition was part of a *scheme to delay, hinder, or defraud creditors* that involved either of the following:

(1) the *transfer* of all or a part of the *real property* without the secured creditor's consent or court approval [B.C. § 362(d)(4)(A)]; or

(2) *multiple bankruptcy filings* affecting the real property. [B.C. § 362(d)(4)(B)]

Second, if the secured creditor takes certain action, the stay relief entered in the current bankruptcy case may extend for *two years* after entry of that stay relief order. If the stay relief order is *recorded* in such a way as to satisfy applicable state laws on notices of interests or liens on real property, then the order is *binding in any other bankruptcy case* purporting to affect the real property *filed within two years* of the entry of the order. The debtor in the subsequent bankruptcy case, however, may move for relief from the order based on *changed circumstances* or other *good cause* shown, after notice and a hearing. Any governmental unit that accepts notices of interests or liens on real property must accept a certified copy of such a stay relief order for indexing and recording. [B.C. § 362(d)(4)]

b. Lessors of Personal Property

If a *lessor of personal property* requests adequate protection of its interest in the property leased to the debtor, such relief is "to the exclusion of such property being subject to an order to grant relief from the stay." [B.C. § 363(e)] Thus, the lessor can request and receive adequate protection of its interest in the leased property but cannot obtain relief from the automatic stay in order to repossess that property. [*See* H.R. Rep. No. 103–835, at 50 (1994) (stating that § 363(e) was amended to "clarify that the lessor's interest is subject to 'adequate protection' [but] [s]uch remedy is to the exclusion of the lessor's being able to seek to lift the automatic stay")]

c. Procedure for Requesting Relief

To initiate stay litigation, a party in interest files a motion for relief from the stay. [Bankruptcy Rule 4001(a)(1)]

(i) Acts Against Estate Property: Hearing

When the relief sought is from the stay of an act against *property of the estate,* the stay terminates, by operation of law with respect to the party in interest making the request for stay relief, *30 days* after the motion is filed unless, after notice and a hearing, the court orders that the stay remain operative until a final hearing is concluded. The bankruptcy court will order that the stay continue in effect until conclusion of the final hearing "if there is a reasonable likelihood that the party opposing relief from the stay will prevail" at such final hearing. [B.C. § 362(e)]

(1) Preliminary Hearing

When the court directs that the stay will remain in effect until a final hearing has been concluded, the initial hearing is called a preliminary hearing. The final hearing must *conclude within 30 days* after the conclusion of the preliminary hearing, unless the 30-day period is extended by consent of the parties or by the court, for a specific time, due to compelling circumstances. The parties may agree, or the court may direct, that the preliminary and final hearings be consolidated. [B.C. § 362(e)]

(ii) Individual Chapter 7, 11, or 13 Case

In 2005, Congress added a subsection to § 362(e) to provide special rules that apply to a request for stay relief involving an individual debtor's Chapter 7, 11, or 13 case. In such a case, the automatic stay terminates, by operation of law, *60 days* after a request for relief is made by a party in interest, *unless*

(1) the court renders a *final decision during the 60-day period* starting on the date of the request for stay relief [B.C. § 362(e)(2)(A)]; or

(2) the 60-day period is extended by the *agreement of all parties in interest or* by the court for the time that the court finds is required for good cause. [B.C. § 362(e)(2)(B)]

(iii) Burden of Proof

In any hearing for relief from the stay under § 362(a), the *party seeking relief has* the burden of proof *regarding the debtor's equity* in property. The *party opposing relief* has the burden of proof *on all other issues.* [B.C. § 362(g)]

(iv) Ex Parte Relief

The bankruptcy court may grant *ex parte* relief from the stay as is necessary to prevent *irreparable harm* to an entity's interest in property that will occur before there is time for notice and a hearing. [B.C. § 362(f); Bankruptcy Rule 4001(a)(2)] But, § 362(f) is rarely used and "Bankruptcy Rule 4001(a)(2) sharply limits the availability of *ex parte* relief under section 362(f) to situations of extreme emergency." [3 Collier ¶ 362.09]

(v) Appeal

A decision to grant or deny relief from the stay is a final order, which may be appealed. In **Ritzen Group, Inc. v. Jackson Masonry, LLC,** 140 S. Ct. 582 (2020), the Supreme Court, in a unanimous opinion, held that a bankruptcy court's ruling on a motion for relief from the automatic stay "forms a discrete procedural unit" in the bankruptcy case and "[t]hat unit yields a final, appealable order when the bankruptcy court unreservedly grants or denies relief." [*See* 28 U.S.C. § 158 (appeals), Bankruptcy Rule 8002(a) (time for filing notice of appeal)] Unless the bankruptcy court orders otherwise, the order granting relief from the stay is stayed for *14 days* from entry. [Bankruptcy Rule 4001(a)(3)]

6. Willful Violation of Stay

An individual who is injured by a *willful* violation of the automatic stay may recover actual damages, costs, attorneys' fees, and, when warranted, punitive damages. [B.C. § 362(k)(1)] Several Circuits have held that actual damages under § 362(k) may include emotional distress damages in appropriate cases. [*See* **Lodge v. Kondaur Capital Corp.,** 750 F.3d 1263 (11th Cir. 2014) (stating that the court "join[ed] other circuits in concluding that emotional distress damages fall within the broad term of 'actual damages' in § 362(k)")] Section 362(k)(1) provides for damages to *individuals,* not to entities. Thus, damages for willful violations of the stay should not be available under § 362(k)(1) to corporations or other entities. [*See, e.g.,* **TLB Equipment, LLC v. Quality Car & Truck Leasing, Inc. (*In re* TLB Equipment, LLC),** 479 B.R. 464 (Bankr. S.D. Ohio 2012); **5th Avenue Real Estate Development, Inc. v. Countrywide Home Loans, Inc. (*In re* 5th Avenue Real Estate Development, Inc.),** 2008 WL 4371336 (Bankr. S.D. Fla. 2008)] Congress could have used the word "entity," as it did in § 362(k)(2), in order to make relief for stay violations more broadly available under § 362(k)(1). Nonetheless, a bankruptcy court may "under § 105 of the Bankruptcy Code and under its inherent equitable powers, enforce the automatic stay, even when the debtor is a corporation, even though § 362(k)(1) provides a remedy for a stay violation only to 'individuals.' " [*In re* **Mirabilis Ventures, Inc.,** 2011 WL 1167880 (Bankr. M.D. Fla. 2011)] Courts are split on whether "a bankruptcy trustee, acting as representative of a bankruptcy estate, is an 'individual' within the meaning of § 362(k)(1)" because the "bankruptcy estate is an entity but not a natural person." [*In re* **Sayeh,** 445 B.R. 19 (Bankr. D. Mass 2011)]

In 2005, Congress added a new subsection that provides that if the stay violation is based on an entity's *good faith belief* that the stay has terminated pursuant to § 362(h), then recovery is limited to *actual damages.* [B.C. § 362(k)(2), (h)] This limitation on damages makes sense if § 362(j) does not apply to § 362(h), and an entity is unable to obtain a comfort order that the stay has terminated.

Chapter Eleven

Administrative Powers: §§ 363–366 of the Code

Chapter Approach

This Chapter is the second of two that examine the various administrative powers set forth in Chapter 3 of the Bankruptcy Code. Chapter Ten covers the automatic stay, while this Chapter covers (1) adequate protection, (2) the use, sale, or lease of property, (3) obtaining credit, (4) executory contracts and unexpired leases, and (5) utility service. Your bankruptcy exam likely will include questions on some or all of these topics.

As you already learned in Chapter Ten, the bankruptcy court will *lift the automatic stay for cause*, including a *lack of adequate protection* of the creditor's interest in the property. But adequate protection also is required if the trustee or debtor in possession proposes to *use, sell, or lease* property in which the creditor holds an interest. In addition, if the trustee or debtor in possession incurs debt or obtains credit secured by a lien on property that is *equal to or senior* to a creditor's lien, the creditor's interest in the property must be adequately protected. A creditor's interest in property may be protected in various ways, including *cash or periodic payments* or even an *equity cushion* sufficient to protect against the collateral's depreciation.

Remember: Chapter 12 has its own adequate protection provision.

The *use, sale or lease* of property of the estate, whether in or out of the ordinary course of the debtor's business, is critical to the bankruptcy process. If the debtor in possession could not use estate property, how could it operate the business? Ask whether the use, sale, or lease of estate property is *in or out* of the *ordinary course of business.* How does the court make this determination, and why does it matter? What is required for the trustee or debtor in possession to use, sell, or lease *cash collateral?* Can the trustee or debtor in possession sell property of the estate, either in or out of the ordinary course, *free and clear* of any interest in the property held by an entity other than the estate? If so, under what circumstances?

A debtor needs money to operate its business and § 364 of the Code provides the rules for the trustee or debtor in possession to *incur debt or obtain credit post-petition*. When will the bankruptcy court authorize the incurring of debt or extension of credit with *super-super priority*? Will the court authorize a *priming lien*? If so, under what circumstances?

If the debtor has defaulted on an *executory contract or unexpired lease*, what must it do in order to *assume* that contract or lease? Which types of agreements are *not assumable or assignable*? What is the effect of the trustee's or debtor in possession's *rejection* of an executory contract or unexpired lease? What are the *time periods for assumption or rejection* of an executory contract or an unexpired lease in Chapter 7? Chapters 11, 12, or 13? How do the rules differ if the unexpired lease is for *nonresidential real property*? What is an *ipso facto* clause? What are the rights of a lessee of real property when the *debtor is the lessor* and rejects the unexpired lease? What are the licensee's rights when the *debtor is the licensor* of a *right to intellectual property* and the executory contract under which the license was granted is rejected in bankruptcy?

Finally, has a *utility discriminated* against the debtor in the provision of utility service *solely* because of the debtor's bankruptcy filing? Has the trustee or debtor provided the utility with *adequate assurance of payment* for post-petition services?

A. Adequate Protection

1. Interest in Property

The Bankruptcy Code mandates that in certain circumstances a party's interest in property be adequately protected. [B.C. § 361]

a. Property Subject to Automatic Stay

If an entity's interest in property is subject to the automatic stay and the entity moves to lift the automatic stay because of a lack of adequate protection, the court must grant relief from the stay or require that the entity's interest in the property be adequately protected. [B.C. § 362(d)(1)]

b. Property Used, Sold, or Leased

Upon the request of an entity with an interest in property that the trustee or debtor in possession proposes to use, sell, or lease, the bankruptcy court may condition such use, sale, or lease on the provision of adequate protection of the interest. [B.C. § 363(e)]

c. Equal or Senior Lien on Property

If the court authorizes the trustee or the debtor in possession to incur debt or to obtain credit secured by a lien on property of the estate that is equal or senior to a lien held by an entity on the same property, adequate protection of that entity's interest is required. [B.C. § 364(d)(1)(B)]

2. Methods of Providing Adequate Protection

An entity's interest in property may be adequately protected in a variety of ways; the Bankruptcy Code sets forth three *nonexclusive* methods. [B.C. § 361]

a. Cash Payments

The trustee or debtor in possession may provide adequate protection by making *cash or periodic cash payments* to the extent that an entity's interest in the property has decreased in value (i) due to the automatic stay; (ii) as a result of the use, sale, or lease of the property; or (iii) because of the grant of a lien of equal or higher priority on the property. [B.C. § 361(1)]

Example: Creditor has a $100,000 claim against Debtor; the claim is secured by collateral worth $75,000. The collateral is depreciating at a rate of approximately $500 per month. Thus, without adequate protection, Creditor's secured claim shrinks by $500 each month and its unsecured claim grows by $500 per month. One way to provide adequate protection of Creditor's interest in the collateral is to require the trustee or debtor in possession to make monthly cash payments of $500 during the pendency of the bankruptcy case. The adequate protection payments ensure that the value to pay Creditor's secured claim remains constant and that the unsecured claim does not increase by virtue of the Creditor's inability to enforce its rights to the collateral during the bankruptcy case. [Example from 3 Collier ¶ 361.03(2)]

b. Additional or Replacement Lien

The trustee or debtor in possession may provide adequate protection by furnishing an *additional or replacement lien* to the extent of any decrease in value of the entity's interest in the property caused by (i) the automatic stay; (ii) the use, sale, or lease of the property; or (iii) the grant of a senior or equal lien on the property. [B.C. § 361(2)]

c. Indubitable Equivalent

The third method described in § 361 for providing adequate protection is for the bankruptcy court to grant relief constituting the *indubitable equivalent* of the entity's interest in the property. Giving an entity an allowable administrative expense does not constitute the indubitable equivalent of the entity's interest in the property. [B.C. § 361(3)] The term "indubitable equivalent" comes from the phrase "the most indubitable equivalence" in a Bankruptcy Act case authored by Learned Hand. [*In re* **Murel Holding Corp.,** 75 F.2d 941 (2d Cir. 1935)] Bankruptcy courts have not required adequate protection to be of the *most* indubitable equivalent; they do, however, require adequate protection to be completely compensatory. [**Desert Fire Protection v. Fontainebleau Las Vegas Holdings, LLC (***In re* **Fontainebleau Las Vegas Holdings, LLC),** 434 B.R. 716 (S.D. Fla. 2010)]

d. Equity Cushion

An *oversecured* creditor often is adequately protected by an equity cushion, which is the amount by which the value of the collateral exceeds the debt owed to the creditor. A substantial equity cushion may adequately protect a secured creditor's interest from depreciation of the collateral that might occur while the property is being used, sold, or leased by the trustee or the debtor in possession, or while the automatic stay precludes the secured party from taking possession.

Example: Debtor, the owner of certain land valued at $100,000, files a Chapter 11 petition. First Mortgagee is owed $50,000, secured by a mortgage on the realty. Second Mortgagee holds a junior lien on the same property in the amount of $80,000. First Mortgagee files a motion to lift the automatic stay, under § 362(d)(1), on the ground of lack of adequate protection. Unless the land is expected to depreciate rapidly, the equity cushion of $50,000 appears to be sufficient to adequately protect First Mortgagee's interest. Therefore, First Mortgagee's motion for relief from the stay probably will be denied.

(i) Method of Determination

In determining whether the *equity cushion* adequately protects First Mortgagee's interest in the property in the example above, the court compares the value of the property to the amount of the secured claim plus all *senior* secured claims. [*See, e.g.,* **GVM, Inc. v. PeoplesBank (***In re* **GVM, Inc.),** 605 B.R. 315 (Bankr. M.D. Pa. 2019) ("when assessing the risk to a secured creditor's interest in collateral, most courts engage in an analysis of the property's equity cushion, which is the value of the property after deducting the claim of the creditor and all senior claims")] Therefore, the court does not take into consideration Second Mortgagee's *junior* lien of $80,000.

Example: Debtor LLC ("Debtor") filed for relief under Chapter 11 in early September 2017. Creditor Canyon was Debtor's pre-petition lender. Debtor filed a motion for bankruptcy court approval to borrow $22 million post-petition from Ardent Financial. In its motion, Debtor asked the court for a priming lien for Ardent pursuant to § 364(d)(1). The issue was whether there was adequate protection of Canyon's interest if the court granted a priming lien to Ardent. Debtor's expert testified to an "as is" value of approximately $77 million. The value of Canyon's liens ($59.6 million) and the amount of the proposed priming lien ($22 million) totaled $81 million, which *exceeded* the value of the property. Thus, there was no equity cushion under Debtor's "as is" valuation. The court evaluated other valuations provided by Debtor's expert and concluded that Debtor had failed to prove "adequate protection in the form of any equity cushion, let alone an adequate equity cushion, to protect the lien interests of the existing lien holders, including Canyon, if the proposed DIP loan and priming lien are approved." [*In re* **Packard Square LLC,** 574 B.R. 107 (Bankr. E.D. Mich. 2017)]

(1) Post-Petition Interest Oversecured Creditors

While an oversecured creditor is entitled to the *accrual* of post-petition interest, this allowance does not entitle the oversecured creditor to *present payments* of post-petition interest. [B.C. § 506(b)] Adequate protection protects the secured creditor against a decrease in the collateral securing the creditor's loan. The accrual of post-petition interest increases Creditor's claim, which, in turn, shrinks any existing equity cushion. The shrinkage of the equity cushion, however, is not due to a decrease in the collateral value and should not trigger adequate protection. Thus, a bankruptcy court should not provide adequate protection to a creditor in a case in which post-petition interest payments erode the equity cushion. [3 Collier ¶ 361.03(1); *see* **United Savings Association of Texas v. Timbers of Inwood Forest Associates,** 484 U.S. 365 (1988)]

e. Undersecured Creditors

The United States Supreme Court, in a unanimous opinion, held that the requirement of adequate protection does *not* entitle an undersecured creditor to receive compensation, i.e., interest, for the delay caused by the automatic stay in foreclosing on the creditor's collateral and reinvesting the proceeds. [**Timbers,** *supra*] The Court concluded that "the 'interest in property' protected by § 362(d)(1) does not include a secured party's right to immediate foreclosure." Moreover, the Court determined that the "phrase 'value of such creditor's interest' in § 506(a) means 'the value of the collateral' and "the phrase 'value of such entity's interest in § 361(1) and (2)' " has the same meaning. [**Timbers,** *supra*] The Code provides secured creditors with other remedies to safeguard against unreasonable delay. These other remedies include seeking relief from the automatic stay for the purpose of foreclosure if the debtor has no equity in the collateral and there is no reasonable possibility of a successful reorganization [B.C. § 362(d)(2)], requesting conversion or dismissal of the case [B.C. § 1112(b)], or proposing a Chapter 11 plan of reorganization or liquidation after the debtor's period of exclusivity has expired [B.C. § 1121(c)]. [*In re* **Timbers of Inwood Forest Associates, Ltd.,** 808 F.2d 363 (5th Cir. 1987), *aff'd,* 484 U.S. 365 (1988)]

3. Valuation of Collateral

To determine what constitutes adequate protection in any particular case, it is necessary to ascertain the value of the collateral as accurately as possible. But Congress did not specify how to determine value, instead leaving the determination to development by the courts. Congress did not anticipate development of a "hard and fast rule" to apply in all cases but rather recognized the importance of flexibility to allow courts to "adapt to varying circumstances and changing modes of financing." Congress also did not expect the courts to "construe the term value to mean, in every case, forced sale liquidation or full going concern value", and noted the "wide latitude between those two extremes." [H.R. Rep. No. 95–595, at 339 (1977)] Therefore, there is no single valuation standard. Congress anticipated a flexible approach with courts taking account of factors such as the *purpose of the valuation* and the *intended use or disposition of the collateral.* [B.C. § 506(a)]

4. Failure of Adequate Protection

If adequate protection is provided to a creditor whose claim is secured by a lien on property of the debtor, but the "adequate protection" eventually is shown to have been deficient, the secured creditor will receive an administrative expense claim with super-priority, which means priority over all other administrative expenses allowed in the case. [B.C. § 507(b); *see supra* Chapter Seven, § E.3.c]

Note: The bankruptcy court may authorize the post-petition obtaining of unsecured credit or incurring of unsecured debt with **super super-priority.** The post-petition lender in such a case has priority over creditors with super-priority claims based on a deficiency in the adequate protection provided to them. [B.C. § 364(c)(1)]

5. Chapter 12 Cases

The adequate protection provisions of § 361 do not apply to a case under Chapter 12 concerning a family farmer or family fisherman. [B.C. § 1205(a)] Instead, the trustee may provide adequate protection to a creditor by (a) making **cash or periodic cash payments,** (b) providing an **additional or replacement lien,** (c) paying **reasonable rent** customary in the community **for use of farmland,** or (d) such other relief, other than granting an allowable administrative expense, that will adequately protect the value of the property. [B.C. § 1205(b)]

EXAM TIP   **GILBERT**

Adequate protection is a very important concept in bankruptcy. If you encounter an exam question involving adequate protection, remember that it is **within the court's discretion** to approve or disapprove it. Consider **all possible methods** that could protect against depreciation in the value of the creditor's collateral under the particular circumstances.

B. Use, Sale, or Lease of Property

1. In General

The use, sale, or lease of estate property, both in and out of the ordinary course of the debtor's business, is an integral part of the bankruptcy process, such as when the trustee liquidates a Chapter 7 debtor's estate, or when a debtor in possession or trustee is authorized to operate the debtor's business, farm or commercial fishing operation in a case under Chapter 11 or Chapter 12. [B.C. § 363]

a. Debtor in Possession

Other than the right to compensation, a non-subchapter V Chapter 11 or Chapter 12 debtor in possession has nearly all of the rights, powers, functions, and duties of a Chapter 11 trustee, including the right to use, sell, and lease property of the estate. [B.C. §§ 1107(a), 1203] While a trustee is appointed in subchapter V, the subchapter V debtor is a debtor in possession, unless removed for cause or for failing to perform the plan's obligations. [B.C. §§ 1183–1185] The subchapter V debtor in possession has all the rights, other than the right to compensation, and nearly all the duties of a Chapter 11 trustee, including operating the business. [B.C. § 1184]

b. **Chapter 13**

There are also special provisions authorizing a debtor or a debtor engaged in business in a Chapter 13 case to use, sell, or lease property. [B.C. §§ 1303, 1304]

2. Out of Ordinary Course of Business

After *notice and a hearing,* a trustee or a debtor in possession may use, sell, or lease property of the estate out of the ordinary course of the debtor's business, unless the sale or lease involves *personally identifiable information,* in which case special rules apply. [B.C. § 363(b)(1)] Whether any individual sale, use, or lease of property is deemed to be outside the ordinary course of business is a question of fact.

a. **Personally Identifiable Information**

Customer lists and other customer information have value and, thus, a debtor may wish to sell such information during its bankruptcy case. In 2005, however, Congress created special rules for the *sale or lease* of personally identifiable information. The rules do not apply to the trustee's or debtor in possession's *use* of such personally identifiable information.

(i) **Definition of Personally Identifiable Information**

If an individual obtains a product or service from the debtor primarily for *personal, family, or household purposes,* then any of the following information constitutes *personally identifiable information* if provided in connection with obtaining that product or service:

(1) the individual's first name or initial, and last name [B.C. § 101(41A)(A)(i)];

(2) the address of the individual's residence [B.C. § 101(41A)(A)(ii)];

(3) the individual's electronic address, including an e-mail address [B.C. § 101(41A)(A)(iii)];

(4) a phone number dedicated to contacting the individual at her residence [B.C. § 101(41A)(A)(iv)];

(5) the individual's social security number [B.C. § 101(41A)(A)(v)];

(6) an account number of a credit card issued to the individual [B.C. § 101(41A)(A)(vi)];

(7) a birth date, number of a birth or adoption certificate, or a place of birth, if identified in connection with one or more of the items specified above in 1–6 [B.C. § 101(41A)(B)(i)]; or

(8) any other information about an identified individual that, if disclosed, will result in contacting or identifying such individual physically or electronically. [B.C. § 101(41A)(B)(ii)]

(ii) **Requirements for Approving Sale or Lease of Personally Identifiable Information**

If the debtor, in connection with offering a product or service, discloses to an individual a *policy prohibiting the transfer of personally identifiable information* to persons not affiliated with the debtor and if that *policy is in effect on the date debtor files for bankruptcy,* then the trustee or debtor in possession *cannot sell or lease personally identifiable information* to any person *unless*

(1) the sale or lease is *consistent with the policy* [B.C. § 363(b)(1)(A)]; or

(2) after appointment of a ***consumer privacy ombudsman,*** pursuant to § 332, and after notice and a hearing, the ***court approves the sale or lease*** giving due consideration to the facts, circumstances and conditions of the sale or lease ***and*** finds that there was no showing that the sale or lease would violate applicable nonbankruptcy law. [B.C. § 363(b)(1)(B)]

b. "Notice and a Hearing"

The Code authorizes the doing of an act ***without a hearing*** if appropriate notice is provided and no party in interest timely requests a hearing. [B.C. § 102(1)(B)(i); *see* H.R. Rep. No. 95–595, at 315 (1977) (stating that "[i]f there is no objection to the proposed action, the action may go ahead without court action" and noting that "[t]his is a significant change from present law, which requires the affirmative approval of the bankruptcy judge for almost every action")] The Bankruptcy Rules relax the notice requirement for small estates. [If the estate's non-exempt property has an aggregate gross value ***less than $2,500,*** then a ***general notice of intent to sell*** the property other than in the ordinary course suffices. [Bankruptcy Rule 6004(d); *see* B.C. § 102(1)(A) ("notice as is appropriate in the particular circumstances")]

c. Business Judgment Test

Courts apply a ***business judgment test*** to decide whether to approve a use, sale, or lease of estate property outside the ordinary course of business. Under the business judgment test, the court defers to the debtor's decision so long as the decision was a fair and reasonable exercise of the debtor's business judgment. [*See In re* **Alpha Natural Resources, Inc.,** 546 B.R. 348 (Bankr. E.D. Va. 2016); *see also In re* **Nine W. Holdings, Inc.,** 588 B.R. 678 (Bankr. S.D. N.Y. 2018) (court is not to "second guess" board's business judgment so long as board acted on an informed basis, in good faith, and in the honest belief the decision was in the firm's best interests)] The business judgment test applied by courts under § 363(b) is not the same as the business judgment rule applied outside bankruptcy to corporate law decisions. [3 Collier ¶ 363.02(4)]

d. Chapter 11 Case: Sales of Substantially All Assets

A sale of substantially all of the assets of a Chapter 11 estate raises questions of whether the sale is an effort to circumvent the protections afforded creditors under a Chapter 11 plan, e.g., disclosure, voting, confirmation. The concern is with the sale being the equivalent of a *sub rosa* plan. Such sales, while closely scrutinized by bankruptcy courts, are allowed. [*See* **Florida Department of Revenue v. Piccadilly Cafeterias, Inc.,** 554 U.S. 33 (2008) (stating in a footnote that while a Chapter 11 case normally ends with a confirmed reorganization plan, in some cases the debtor sells substantially all its assets prior to confirmation of a plan of liquidation)] The two most controversial cases of such sales were those in the GM and Chrysler bankruptcies during the height of the Great Recession. [*See* **Indiana State Police Pension Trust v. Chrysler LLC (*In re* Chrysler LLC),** 576 F.3d 108 (2d Cir. 2009) (affirming bankruptcy court order approving sale, under § 363, of substantially all of Chrysler's assets and rejecting argument that sale transaction constituted a *sub rosa* plan), *cert. dismissed,* 557 U.S. 961 (2009); ***In re* GMC,** 407 B.R. 463 (Bankr. S.D. N.Y. 2009) (approving GM's motion for an order under § 363 to sell, pursuant to a master purchase and sale agreement, substantially all its assets, free and clear, to a buyer sponsored by the U.S. Treasury)] When there is no "need for speed," the assets are not perishable and value will not be lost waiting for plan confirmation, the plan proponent must demonstrate why "there is a need to sell prior to the plan confirmation hearing." [***In re* Gulf Coast Oil, Corp.,** 404 B.R. 407 (Bankr. S.D. Tex. 2009) (declining to approve sale of substantially all assets under § 363, noting that proponents of transaction sought to avoid the Congressional scheme that required bargaining, voting, and satisfaction of the requirements of § 1129)] Even though a court may approve a sale of substantially all of a debtor's assets, it will scrutinize the proposed transaction and may decline to approve certain portions of the transaction that it considers a *sub rosa* plan of reorganization. [*In re* **On-Site Sourcing, Inc.,** 412 B.R. 817 (Bankr. E.D. Va. 2009) (approving motion for sale of substantially all assets because it was the best and only deal available, but excising certain provisions that "all furthered a *sub rosa* plan of reorganization")]

e. Secured Creditor's Right to Bid

A secured creditor whose lien secures an allowed claim on property sold *outside the ordinary course of business* may "credit bid" at the sale of such property. By doing so, the secured creditor offsets her claim against the purchase price of the property. [B.C. § 363(k)]

3. In Ordinary Course of Business

A trustee or a debtor in possession who is authorized to operate the debtor's business may use, sell, or lease property of the estate in the ordinary course of business *without notice or a hearing,* unless the court orders otherwise. [B.C. § 363(c)(1)]

a. Determining Ordinary Course of Business

There are two tests that courts use to determine whether a particular transaction is in or out of the *ordinary course of business*: (i) the *vertical dimension test,* also known as the *reasonable expectations or creditor's expectation test,* and (ii) the *horizontal dimension test.* [**Aalfs v. Wirum (***In re* **Straightline Investments),** 525 F.3d 870 (9th Cir. 2008) (applying both tests)]

(i) Vertical Dimension Test

The *vertical dimension test* examines the debtor's normal business practices to determine whether the transaction subjects creditors to risks of a different character than the risks present when credit was extended. [**Crawforth v. Wheeler (***In re* **Wheeler),** 444 B.R. 598 (Bankr. D. Idaho 2011)]

(ii) Horizontal Dimension Test

The *horizontal dimension test* compares the debtor's business to similar businesses and asks whether a similar business would enter into a transaction like the one proposed by the debtor's business. [**Aalfs v. Wirum,** *supra* (concluding that sale of debtor's accounts did not satisfy the horizontal dimension test because purchaser of accounts "failed to show that the sale of accounts receivable by a custom milling business was the type of transaction 'that other similar businesses would engage in as ordinary business' ")]

b. Exception—Cash Collateral

The trustee or the debtor in possession may use, sell, or lease *cash collateral* in the *ordinary course of business only* if she obtains either *court authorization,* after notice and a hearing, or the *consent* of all entities having an interest in the cash collateral. [B.C. § 363(c)(2)]

(i) Definition

The Code defines "cash collateral" as cash, negotiable instruments, documents of title, securities, deposit accounts, and other cash equivalents in which both the debtor's estate and a third party have an interest. Cash collateral includes proceeds, rents, profits, products, or offspring of property in which an entity has an interest. It also includes fees, charges, accounts or other payments for hotel or motel rooms, or other lodging properties. [B.C. §§ 363(a); 552(b)] The Code's definition of cash collateral is expansive and covers situations that may not involve a security interest. For example, a bank having a right to set off its claim against the debtor's deposit account has a secured claim, by virtue of § 506(a); thus, that deposit account constitutes cash collateral. [3 Collier ¶ 363.03(3)]

(ii) Hearing

When a request is made for authorization to use cash collateral, usually time is of the essence. Thus, the court must act promptly to schedule a hearing *based on the needs of the debtor.* [B.C. § 363(c)(3)] The hearing may be a preliminary hearing or may be consolidated with a hearing on adequate protection under § 363(e). If it is a preliminary hearing, the court may authorize the use, sale, or lease of cash collateral only if there is a *reasonable likelihood* that the trustee or the debtor in possession will prevail at the final hearing on adequate protection. [B.C. § 363(c)(3), (e); *see* Bankruptcy Rule 4001(b)]

(iii) Duty to Segregate

The trustee or the debtor in possession must *segregate and account for any cash collateral* in her possession, custody, or control, except to the extent that the cash collateral has been used, sold, or leased pursuant to court authorization or consent of all entities with an interest in the cash collateral. [B.C. § 363(c)(4)]

EXAM TIP   GILBERT

Suppose an exam question asks whether the debtor in possession may use cash collateral to pay its employees in the ordinary course of business. Your answer should explain that *either court authorization* or the secured party's *consent* is required. The hearing on this issue will be very important, because a Chapter 11 case may fail if the employees quit because the debtor cannot pay wages.

---

4. Automatic Stay

The trustee or debtor in possession may use, sell, or lease property in the ordinary or non-ordinary course only to the extent not inconsistent with any relief granted from the automatic stay. [B.C. §§ 363(d)(2), 362(c)–(f)] A noted bankruptcy commentator explains that § 363(d) ties together §§ 362 and 363, such that use of property in the ordinary course of business "is limited by any adequate protection" provided under § 362 and the use, sale, or lease of property outside the ordinary course "is limited by any stay relief" already provided. [3 Collier ¶ 363.04]

5. Nonprofit Corporations and Trusts

Section 363(d) also provides that the trustee or debtor in possession may use, sell, or lease property in the ordinary or non-ordinary course of business of a *corporation or trust* that is *not* a *moneyed business, commercial corporation, or trust only in accordance with nonbankruptcy law* that governs transfer of property by such a debtor. [B.C. § 363(d)(1)] A corporation or trust that is not a moneyed business, commercial corporation, or trust means a nonprofit corporation or trust. [H.R. Rep. No. 109–31, at 145 (2005) (stating that amendment of § 363(d) is to "restrict the authority of a trustee to use, sell, or lease property by a nonprofit corporation or trust")] The purpose of the restriction is to ensure that a nonprofit does not "escape supervision by its State's Attorney General, who is given standing to appear and be heard on this issue." [3 Collier ¶ 363.04]

6. Adequate Protection

Upon the motion of an entity having an interest in property that is, or is proposed to be, used, sold, or leased by the trustee or the debtor in possession, the court must *prohibit or condition* the use, sale, or lease in a manner that provides adequate protection of the entity's interest. [B.C. § 363(e); *see* Bankruptcy Rule 4001(a); *see supra* § A of this Chapter.] The trustee or debtor in possession has the burden of proof on the issue of adequate protection. [B.C. § 363(p)(1)]

a. Insurance

Frequently, the use, sale, or lease of property may be *conditioned* on the procurement of insurance as one of the elements of adequate protection. [B.C. § 363(e)]

b. Unexpired Leases of Personal Property

While the Code requires adequate protection of a lessor's interest in personal property that is subject to an unexpired lease, this remedy is to the exclusion of relief from the automatic stay under § 362(d). [B.C. § 363(e); *see supra* Chapter Ten, § A.5.b]

7. Ipso Facto or "Bankruptcy" Clauses

Subject to the requirements of § 365, the trustee or debtor in possession may use, sell, or lease property in or out of the ordinary course of business, or the terms of a Chapter 11, 12, or 13 plan may provide for such use, sale, or lease, notwithstanding provisions in a contract, lease, or nonbankruptcy law that otherwise would cause a forfeiture, modification, or termination of the debtor's interest in the property as a result of:

a. *the insolvency or financial condition* of the debtor;

b. *the commencement of a bankruptcy case* concerning the debtor;

c. *the appointment of a bankruptcy trustee or a nonbankruptcy custodian;* or

d. *the taking possession of property* by a bankruptcy trustee or a nonbankruptcy custodian.

[B.C. § 363(*l*)]

The trustee's or debtor in possession's sale, use, or lease of the property, however, is still subject to other restrictions on transfer or use that are unrelated to the debtor's filing for bankruptcy or its financial situation. [3 Collier ¶ 363.10(2); *see* **Board of Trade v. Johnson,** 264 U.S. 1 (1924) (Bankruptcy Act case in which the Court held that the bankruptcy trustee could sell a seat on the Chicago Board of Trade owned by debtor only if the trustee satisfied the Board's rule that a seat owner could not sell his seat until he had paid debts owed to fellow Board of Trade seat owners)]

8. Sale Free and Clear

The trustee or the debtor in possession may sell property of the estate, either in or out of the ordinary course of business, *free and clear* of any interest in the property held by an entity other than the estate. The sale may proceed *only if one of the following* statutory requirements is satisfied:

a.   *applicable state or other nonbankruptcy law allows* a free-and-clear sale of the property [B.C. § 363(f)(1)];

b.   the entity holding the interest *consents to the sale* [B.C. § 363(f)(2)];

c.   *if the interest is a lien*, the *sale price for the property is greater than the total value of all liens* on the property [B.C. § 363(f)(3)];

   Note: Courts disagree about the meaning of "aggregate value of all liens." Some courts hold that the phrase means the *economic value* of all liens under § 506(a). Thus, the face amount of a lien held by an out-of-the-money junior lienholder (insufficient collateral value to cover junior lienholder's claim) would not count in determining the "aggregate value of all liens." [*See, e.g., In re* **Collins**, 180 B.R. 447 (Bankr. E.D. Va. 1995)] Other courts hold that "aggregate value of all liens" means the *face value* of all liens. [*See, e.g.,* **Clear Channel Outdoor, Inc. v. Knupfer (*In re* PW, LLC),** 391 B.R. 25 (B.A.P. 9th Cir. 2008)]

d.   *there is a bona fide dispute* concerning the entity's interest in the property [B.C. § 363(f)(4)]; *or*

e.   *the entity holding the interest could be required to accept a money satisfaction* in a legal or equitable action. [B.C. § 363(f)(5)]

9. Sale Free and Clear Affecting Dower, Curtesy, or Co-Ownership Interests

a. Dower or Curtesy

Notwithstanding the conditions above for a *free and clear sale,* the trustee or the debtor in possession may sell property free and clear of an entity's *vested or contingent right of dower or curtesy.* [B.C. § 363(g)]

b. Co-Owner's Interest

If property of the estate is co-owned by the debtor and another entity, the trustee or the debtor in possession may *sell the interests of both* the estate *and* a tenant in common, a joint tenant, or a tenant by the entirety *only if all* of the following conditions are satisfied:

(i)   *it is impracticable to partition* the property between the estate and the co-owner [B.C. § 363(h)(1)];

(ii) *the amount realized* from the sale of the *estate's undivided interest* in the property is *substantially less* than from the sale of the property *free of the co-owner's interest* [B.C. § 363(h)(2)];

(iii) *the benefit to the estate* from a sale free of the co-owner's interest *outweighs the detriment to the co-owner* [B.C. § 363(h)(3)]; *and*

(iv) *the property is not used to produce, transmit, or distribute for sale electric energy or natural or synthetic gas* for heat, light, or power. [B.C. § 363(h)(4)]

c. Right of First Refusal

Before consummation of a sale of (i) property free and clear of dower or curtesy rights, (ii) a co-owner's interest in property, or (iii) community property, the debtor's spouse or a co-owner of the property may buy the property at the same price for which it is to be sold. [B.C. § 363(i), (g), (h)]

d. Distribution of Proceeds

After a sale of property free and clear of dower or curtesy rights, or a sale of a co-owner's interest in property, the trustee or the debtor in possession must pay the appropriate portion of the proceeds to the debtor's spouse or the co-owner, less costs and expenses of the sale. The trustee's compensation is not considered a cost or expense of the sale. [B.C. § 363(j)]

10. Not Free and Clear: Consumer Credit Transactions

In 2005, Congress added a new provision to § 363 that addresses the sale of an interest in a consumer credit transaction or consumer credit contract. The sale of any interest in a consumer credit transaction subject to the Truth in Lending Act or any interest in a consumer credit contract, as defined at 16 C.F.R. § 433.1, is *not free and clear* of any claim or defense related to such consumer credit transaction or consumer credit contract. [B.C. § 363(o)] All claims and defenses that a consumer could raise to the sale outside bankruptcy apply to the buyer in a sale under the Bankruptcy Code.

11. Burden of Proof

In any hearing concerning the use, sale, or lease of property, the trustee or debtor in possession has the burden of proof regarding the question of adequate protection, while the entity claiming an interest in property bears the burden of showing the validity, priority, or extent of that interest. [B.C. § 363(p)]

12. Appeal: Mootness

Section 363(m) provides *protection*, under certain circumstances, to the buyers or lessees of property *against the reversal or modification on appeal* of a sale or lease order. The provision is similar to that at § 364(e).

Absent a stay pending appeal, the validity of an authorization to sell or lease property, in or outside the ordinary course of business, is not affected by a reversal or modification on appeal if the purchaser or lessee acted in *good faith*, regardless of the purchaser's or lessee's knowledge of the appeal. [B.C. § 363(m)] Thus, in order to protect its rights, a party seeking to appeal a sale order must obtain a stay of that order pending appeal. A majority of circuits have held that § 363(m) creates "a *per se* rule automatically mooting appeals for failure to obtain a stay of the sale at issue." [*See* **Parker v. Goodman (*In re* Parker),** 499 F.3d 616 (6th Cir. 2007) (noting majority rule but declining to adopt it or minority approach)] Several Circuits, however, require that the party alleging mootness prove that the court cannot " 'grant effective relief without impacting the validity of the sale.' " [**Brown v. Ellman (*In re* Brown),** 851 F.3d 619 (6th Cir. 2017) (holding that trustee had failed to carry "his burden to demonstrate mootness under § 363(m)" because the court could "order relief without disturbing the earlier conveyance")]

Courts have adopted *no single definition* of "good faith." A buyer who shows a lack of integrity during the course of sale proceedings, who engages in fraud or collusion, or who tries to take grossly unfair advantage of other bidders does not act in good faith. [*In re* **GMC,** 407 B.R. 463 (Bankr. S.D. N.Y. 2009)]

a. Exceptions to Mootness Doctrine

The Ninth Circuit recognizes the following two limited exceptions to the mootness rule in § 363(m): (i) "where real property is sold subject to a statutory right of redemption", or (ii) the transaction otherwise could be set aside under state law. [*In re* **Ewell,** 958 F.2d

276 (9th Cir. 1992); *In re* **Mann,** 907 F.2d 923 (9th Cir. 1990); *see* **Fuentes v. Goodrich (*In re* Fuentes),** 2018 WL 2460283 (C.D. Cal. 2018) (noting two exceptions in footnote)]

13. Collusive Sale

If the sale price of the estate property is controlled by an agreement among bidders, the trustee or debtor in possession may avoid the sale, or may recover damages from any of the conspirators equal to the value of the property minus the price paid, plus any costs, attorneys' fees, or expenses of obtaining relief. Moreover, in a case in which a party entered into such an agreement in willful disregard of this Code provision on collusive sales, recovery also may include punitive damages. [B.C. § 363(n)]

14. Sales and Use Taxes Permitted

The United States Supreme Court has held that a bankruptcy liquidation sale is not immune from a nondiscriminatory state sales or use tax. [**California State Board of Equalization v. Sierra Summit, Inc.,** 490 U.S. 844 (1989)]

C. Obtaining Credit

1. In General

A debtor needs money to operate its business. Section 364 of the Code provides the rules for the trustee or debtor in possession under Chapter 11 (including subchapter V) or Chapter 12 to ***obtain credit***—unsecured or secured—or to ***incur debt***. [*See supra* § B.1.a of this Chapter on Chapter 11 debtor in possession status] A Chapter 13 debtor engaged in business may operate her business and, subject to any conditions or limitations imposed by the court, has the right to obtain credit or incur debt under § 364. [B.C. § 1304(a), (b)]

2. In Ordinary Course of Business

Unless the court orders otherwise, a trustee or debtor in possession authorized to operate the debtor's business may procure ***unsecured credit,*** e.g., trade credit, and incur ***unsecured debt*** in the ordinary course of business without notice or a hearing. Such credit or debt is allowable as an ***administrative expense.*** [B.C. §§ 364(a), 503(b)(1)] Administrative expense claims, if not timely paid, are entitled to second level priority under § 507(a)(2).

3. Out of Ordinary Course of Business

After ***notice and a hearing,*** the court may approve the request of a trustee or debtor in possession to obtain unsecured credit or to incur unsecured debt ***out of the ordinary course of business*** as an ***allowable administrative expense.*** [B.C. § 364(b)] What happens, however, if a creditor fails to obtain court approval before lending money or extending credit to the debtor out of the ordinary course of the debtor's business? The courts have reached different conclusions. Some courts allow for retroactive approval of the creditor's claim as an administrative expense, but normally only under extraordinary circumstances. [*See **In re Ockerlund Construction Co.,*** 308 B.R. 325 (Bankr. N.D. Ill. 2004) (citing cases); *see also **In re* Ohio Valley Amusement Co.,** 2008 WL 5062464 (Bankr. N.D. W.Va. 2008) (holding that creditor's loans to debtor were outside the ordinary course of business and denying *nunc pro tunc* approval of two loans made without prior court approval)]

Other courts deny the creditor an administrative expense claim priority but treat the creditor's claim as a general unsecured claim. Some courts, however, have gone so far as to find that a creditor that fails to obtain court approval for a post-petition loan or extension of credit has no bankruptcy claim at all and, thus, is not entitled to participate in any distribution during the bankruptcy case. [*See In re* **Ockerlund Construction Co.,** *supra* (holding that the "holder of a post-petition 'claim" that is not entitled to administrative-expense priority cannot be a creditor, cannot file a proof of claim, and, even if he could file one, cannot by definition have an 'allowed' claim as of the petition date"); *see also* 3 Collier ¶ 364.03(2)]

Important: Recently, the Supreme Court, in a per curiam opinion in **Roman Catholic Archdiocese of San Juan v. Acevado Feliciano,** 140 S. Ct. 696 (2020), noted that " '[n]unc pro tunc orders are not some Orwellian vehicle for revisionist history—creating facts that never occurred in fact.' " The bankruptcy court in **Zvoch v. Winnecour (*In re* Zvoch),** 618 B.R. 734 (Bankr. W.D. Pa. 2020) questioned whether "this kind of retroactive relief is still cognizable after the United States Supreme Court's ruling in *Roman Catholic Archdiocese of San Juan, Puerto Rico v. Acevedo Feliciano.*"

4. Priority or Security

Prospective post-petition lenders may not be satisfied with an administrative expense priority even though it is the second category of unsecured claims to be paid. [B.C. §§ 503(b)(1), 507(a)(2)] Thus, if the trustee or debtor in possession is *unable* to obtain unsecured credit allowable as an administrative expense, then the court, after notice and a hearing, may authorize the obtaining of credit or incurring of debt:

a. with *super super-priority status* entitling the creditor to payment ahead of not only all administrative expense claims but also any super-priority administrative expense claims resulting from the failure of adequate protection [B.C. §§ 364(c)(1), 361, 507(b)];

b. secured by a *lien on unencumbered estate property* [B.C. § 364(c)(2)]; *or*

c. secured by a *junior lien on encumbered estate property.* [B.C. § 364(c)(3)]

The trustee or debtor in possession may ask the court for any combination of the alternatives provided under § 364(c). The trustee or debtor in possession must show "that it has reasonably attempted, but failed, to obtain unsecured credit under sections 364(a) or (b)." [*In re* **Ames Department Stores, Inc.,** 115 B.R. 34 (Bankr. S.D.N.Y. 1990)] Some courts have adopted a three-part test to determine whether to authorize a post-petition loan or extension of credit under § 364(c): (1) Was the debtor unable to obtain unsecured credit with an administrative expense priority? (2) Is the transaction necessary to preserve estate assets? and (3) Are the transaction's terms fair, reasonable, and adequate, given the debtor's circumstances and the proposed lender? [*In re* **L.A. Dodgers LLC,** 457 B.R. 308 (Bankr. D. Del. 2011); *see also In re* **Republic Airways Holdings, Inc.,** 2016 WL 2616717 (Bankr. S.D. N.Y. 2016)] In the motion seeking relief pursuant to § 364(c), the trustee or debtor in possession must "describe the nature and extent" of any provision in the credit or loan agreement that grants priority or a lien on estate property and also identify the location of such a provision in the proposed agreement and order. [Bankruptcy Rule 4001(c)(1)(B)(i)]

5. Priming Lien

What happens if the debtor has no unencumbered property and the lender will not extend credit or loan money in exchange for administrative expense status or super-super-priority over all other administrative expenses? The bankruptcy court, after notice and a hearing, may approve new credit or incurring of debt secured by a *senior or equal* lien on property of the estate. [B.C. § 364(d)(1)] The trustee or debtor in possession must show that "less burdensome financing is unavailable," but it is not necessary to demonstrate that credit was sought "from every possible lender." [*In re* **Vegt,** 499 B.R. 631 (Bankr. N.D. Iowa 2013) (finding that requirement that credit is unavailable elsewhere was satisfied because financing had been sought unsuccessfully from between 15 to 20 other lenders); *see* § 364(d)(1)(A) ("trustee is unable to obtain such credit otherwise")] Adequate protection must be provided to the original lienholder, and the trustee or debtor in possession has the burden of proof on the issue of adequate protection. [B.C. § 364(d)(2)]

If you have an exam question concerning (i) a trustee, (ii) a Chapter 11 or Chapter 12 debtor in possession, or (iii) a Chapter 13 debtor engaged in business who needs to obtain credit or incur debt, you will need to remember the following rules.

(a) Generally, the trustee or debtor in possession may obtain *unsecured credit or incur unsecured debt in the ordinary course of business* without notice or a hearing, and it is allowable as an administrative expense.

(b) Obtaining *unsecured credit or incurring unsecured debt that is out of the ordinary course of business* requires prior court approval after notice and the opportunity for a hearing. Otherwise, the creditor's claim may be denied administrative expense status.

(c) In circumstances in which the trustee or debtor in possession can prove that it made a reasonable attempt but was unable to obtain unsecured credit or debt on an administrative expense basis, the court, after notice and opportunity for a hearing, may authorize credit or debt:

   (i) with a super super-priority that is *ahead of all other administrative expenses*, including a super-priority claim for the failure of adequate protection;

   (ii) *secured* by a lien on estate property that is unencumbered; or

   (iii) *secured* by a junior lien on estate property that is encumbered.

(d) If the trustee or debtor in possession cannot obtain credit or incur debt on any basis other than by granting to the creditor a lien that is senior or equal to an existing lien on estate property, the court, after notice and opportunity for a hearing, may authorize a *priming lien*, but only if the original lienholder is given *adequate protection*.

---

6. Certain Other Provisions in Post-Petition Lending Agreements

Post-petition financing agreements may contain controversial provisions that require the court to scrutinize the terms for fairness to the bankruptcy estate. The Bankruptcy Rules provide that a motion to authorize the obtaining of post-petition credit must describe the nature and extent of any of these controversial provisions and identify their specific location in the proposed agreement and order. [Bankruptcy Rule 4001(c)(1)(B)]

a. Cross-Collateralization

Cross-collateralization occurs when a pre-petition lender agrees to lend to the debtor post-petition but wants a security interest in unencumbered estate property to secure not only the post-petition loan but also existing pre-petition unsecured claims against the debtor. The Eleventh Circuit has held that cross-collateralization is an "impermissible means of obtaining post-petition financing" because it is "contrary to the basic priority structure of the Code." [**Shapiro v. Saybrook Manufacturing Co. (*In re* Saybrook Manufacturing Co.),** 963 F.2d 1490 (11th Cir. 1992)] Other courts have found the use of cross-collateralization permissible under certain circumstances. [*See **In re* Ellingsen MacLean Oil Co.,** 834 F.2d 599 (6th Cir. 1987) (noting that while controversial, cross-collateralization "is often used, and even the courts that discourage it have approved its use")] A motion for post-petition financing that includes a cross-collateralization provision must specifically identify the location of such provision in the proposed agreement and order, and describe the nature and extent of the provision. [Bankruptcy Rule 4001(c)(1)(B)(ii)]

b. Roll-Ups

In a roll-up, there is a pre-petition lender with pre-petition debt that agrees to lend to the debtor post-petition. Prior to the post-petition loan, that lender has pre-petition debt and pre-petition collateral securing that debt. The lender agrees to extend credit post-petition secured by post-petition collateral, but "as opposed to segregating the pre-petition collateral and applying it to pre-petition debt and applying post-petition collateral to the post-petition debt, *all* of the cash collateral generated by the debtor is applied first to reduce the pre-petition debt." [*See In re* **Cranberry Growers Cooperative,** 592 B.R. 325 (Bankr. W.D. Wis. 2018), *rev'd on other grounds,* 930 F.3d 844 (7th Cir. 2019)] As a result, the lender's pre-petition debt is "rolled up" into the lender's post-petition debt; the total post-petition debt is the sum of the pre-petition debt and any post-petition extensions of credit made by the lender. [*See In re* **Cranberry Growers,** *supra*] A motion for post-petition financing that includes a "roll up" must specifically identify the location of such provision in the proposed agreement and order, and describe the nature and extent of the provision. [Bankruptcy Rule 4001(c)(1)(B)(ii)]

7. Notice and Hearing

A motion for authority to obtain credit must be accompanied by a copy of the credit agreement and a proposed order. [Bankruptcy Rule 4001(c)(1)(A)] The court *cannot commence a final hearing* on the motion *earlier than 14 days* after service of the motion. The movant may request that the court conduct a hearing before that 14-day period expires, but the court may authorize the obtaining of credit only to avoid *immediate and irreparable harm to the estate pending a final hearing.* [Bankruptcy Rule 4001(c)(2)]

8. Appeal

Absent a stay pending appeal, the validity of the court's order authorizing the debtor to obtain credit or to incur debt, or the validity of any lien or priority granted by the court under § 364, is not affected by a reversal or modification on appeal, so long as the lender acted in *good faith.* This rule applies even if the lender knew of the appeal. [B.C. § 364(e)]

9. Temporary Change to § 364

The CAA added a *temporary* subsection (g) to § 364. It provides that the bankruptcy court, after notice and a hearing, may authorize a trustee or debtor in possession in a Chapter 11 subchapter V case, or a Chapter 12 or 13 case to obtain a *loan under the Small Business Act.* [CAA § 320(a); B.C. §§ 1183, 1184, 1203, 1204, 1304; 15 U.S.C. § 636(a)] If the loan is not forgiven pursuant to the provisions of the Small Business Act, then the loan is treated as a debt with *super-super priority.* [CAA § 320(a); B.C. § 364(c)(1)] While the CAA's amendment to § 364 sunsetted on *December 27, 2022,* it still applies to any case begun *before December 27, 2022.* [CAA § 320(f)(2)(B)]

D. Executory Contracts and Unexpired Leases

1. Definitions

The Bankruptcy Code does not define the terms "executory contract" or "unexpired lease." Thus, the courts have attempted to construe these terms in the bankruptcy context when applying § 365's provisions on assumption or rejection.

a. Executory Contract

In determining whether a contract is executory, many courts look to see whether the contractual obligations of **the debtor and the nondebtor party** are " 'so far unperformed that the failure of either to complete performance would constitute a material breach excusing performance of the other.' " [**Lewis Bros. Bakeries Inc. v. Interstate Brands Corp. (*In re* Interstate Bakeries Corp.),** 751 F.3d 955 (8th Cir. 2014); *In re* **Calpine Corp.,** 2008 WL 3154763 (Bankr. S.D. N.Y. 2008)] Professor Vern Countryman of Harvard Law School developed this "material breach" test. The contract is not executory under the Countryman test if the payment of money is the only remaining obligation. [*See* **Holzer v. Barnard,** 2016 WL 4046767 (E.D. N.Y. 2016)] Some courts, however, use the *functional approach* to determine whether a contract is executory. [**Holzer,** *supra* (stating that courts in the Second Circuit had "adopted two different standards as to executory contracts"—the Countryman test and the functional approach)] Under the functional approach, a court may deem a contract executory, even if *only one* party has outstanding material obligations under the contract, if "assumption[ ] [or] rejection would ultimately benefit the estate and its creditors.' " [**Thompkins v. Lil' Joe Records, Inc.,** 476 F.3d 1294 (11th Cir. 2007)] The Eleventh Circuit has used the functional test in some cases. [3 Collier ¶ 365.02(2)(a); *see* **Lil' Joe Records,** *supra* (noting that bankruptcy court had used the functional approach, which the Eleventh Circuit had "tacitly approved in [its] precedent")]

(i) Options

Most courts have held that a paid-for but unexercised option is an executory contract. Those courts that have held that such options are not executory contracts have rested their decisions on the fact that the optionor owes no performance unless and until the option is exercised. [*See* **COR Route 5 Co., LLC v. Penn Traffic Co. (*In re* Penn Traffic Co.),** 524 F.3d 373 (2d Cir. 2008) (listing cases)]

b. Unexpired Lease

Under § 365, an unexpired lease must be a true lease, rather than one intended as a secured transaction. The bankruptcy court should use applicable state law in making this determination. [*In re* **Montgomery Ward, LLC,** 469 B.R. 522 (Bankr. D. Del. 2012)] Courts look to the economic realities of the transaction, not to the labels that the parties assign to it. [*See* S. Rep. No. 95–989, at 64 (1978) (stating, in the context of real property, that "[t]he distinction between a true lease and a financing transaction is based upon the economic substance of the transaction and not, for example, upon the locus of title, the form of the transaction or the fact that the transaction is denominated a 'lease' ")]

To distinguish between a true lease and a security agreement, courts often consider the provisions of § 1–203(b) of the Uniform Commercial Code.

(i)   If the *lessee can terminate* the transaction, then the transaction is more likely a lease than a secured sale. [**Hitchin Post Steak Co. v. GE Capital Corp. (*In re* HP Distribution, LLP),** 436 B.R. 679 (Bankr. D. Kan. 2010)]

(ii) If the *lessee cannot terminate* the transaction *and* can **renew the lease** for the *remaining economic life* of the goods for *no additional or nominal additional consideration or* has an **option to purchase** for *no additional or nominal additional consideration,* then the transaction is a secured sale, not a lease. [U.C.C. §§ 1–203(b)(3), (4)]

(iii) If the lessee *cannot terminate* the transaction *and* the lease term is equal to or greater than the *remaining economic life of the goods,* then the transaction is a secured sale, not a lease. [U.C.C. § 1–203(b)(1)]

e.g. **Example:** Prior to filing for bankruptcy, Debtor signed an agreement called a "lease" with Creditor for a vehicle priced at $30,000. The vehicle has an economic life of 15 years, and the lease is for a five-year term. Debtor can terminate the agreement, but if she decides not to do so she has the option to buy the vehicle at the end of five years for a price that is equal to the reasonably predicted market value at that time. The transaction is a lease; it is structured so that Creditor/Lessor retains a valuable reversionary interest in the vehicle. [*See* U.C.C. § 1–203(c)(6)]

e.g. **Example:** Prior to filing for bankruptcy, Debtor signed an agreement called a "lease" with Creditor for a vehicle priced at $30,000. The vehicle has an economic life of 15 years. The lease term is five years, and Debtor cannot terminate the agreement. The reasonably predicted market value of the vehicle in five years is $8,000. The agreement gives Debtor the option to buy the vehicle for $10. The transaction is a disguised sale, not a lease. The lease cannot be terminated and Debtor can purchase the car for nominal additional consideration. [*See* U.C.C. § 1–203(b)(4)] The transaction is structured so as to give Debtor an enormous incentive to purchase the vehicle in five years; thus, Creditor/Lessor did not expect to receive the vehicle back from Debtor at the time that the parties signed the "lease."

2. Assumption or Rejection: General Principles

The debtor in possession or trustee, with the court's approval, may assume or reject an executory contract or an unexpired lease of the debtor. [B.C. § 365(a)] A motion is required, as are reasonable notice and an opportunity for a hearing. [Bankruptcy Rules 6006, 9014] In a case under Chapters 11, 12, or 13, assumption or rejection also may occur by a provision in a confirmed plan. [B.C. §§ 1123(b)(2), 1222(b)(6), 1322(b)(7)]

a. Court Approval Mandatory

The Code requires judicial authorization to assume or reject, except when rejection occurs automatically upon the expiration of certain statutory time limits placed on the power to assume or reject. [B.C. § 365(a); *In re* **Robb & Stucky, Ltd., LLLP,** 2011 WL 3948805 (Bankr. M.D. Fla. 2011)]

e.g. **Example:** Debtor, operating its business as a debtor in possession, made post-petition premium payments to Insurance Agent, pursuant to certain insurance policies. The payments represented both post-petition and pre-petition insurance coverage; no court approval was obtained to assume the agreements. Several months later, Debtor decided to reject the contracts, but Insurance Agent asserted that they had already been assumed by Debtor's post-petition conduct. The court ruled against Insurance Agent and noted that it was the rare case in which a debtor in possession's conduct constitutes assumption of an agreement under § 365. "The more generally followed rule is that acceptance of benefits (i.e. 'conduct') under an executory contract does not in and of itself work an assumption." Therefore, Insurance Agent had to repay the amounts received in payment of the pre-petition portion of the indebtedness. [*In re* **A. H. Robins Co.,** 68 B.R. 705 (Bankr. E.D. Va. 1986)]

b. Business Judgment Test

A majority of courts apply the *business judgment* test to the debtor in possession's or trustee's decision to assume or reject an executory contract or an unexpired lease. The test requires the court to put " 'itself in the position of the trustee or debtor in possession and determin[e] whether assuming the contract would be a good business decision or a bad one.' " The test "presupposes that the estate will assume a contract only where doing so will be to its economic advantage and will reject contracts whose performance would benefit the counterparty at the expense of the estate." [**Cor Route 5 Co., LLC v. Penn Traffic Co. (***In re* **Penn Traffic Co.),** 524 F.3d 373 (2d Cir. 2008)] While the *business judgment* test is not identical to the *business judgment rule* that courts use to review corporate decisions, it does have "similar factors" to the business judgment rule. [*In re* **The Great Atlantic & Pacific Tea Company, Inc.,** 544 B.R. 43 (Bankr. S.D. N.Y. 2016)]

Example: Debtor has a contract with Creditor to deliver 1,000 widgets for $10,000. Debtor files for bankruptcy and at that time the parties have not performed the contract. If performing the contract will cost $5,000, then the debtor in possession or trustee will assume the contract in order to obtain the benefit for the estate. If, however, it will cost $15,000 to supply the widgets, then there is no benefit to the estate and the debtor in possession or trustee will reject the contract. [*See In re* **Giordano,** 446 B.R.744 (Bankr. E.D. Va. 2010)]

(i) Exception: Collective Bargaining Agreements

Section 1113, not the business judgment test, governs the rejection of a collective bargaining agreement in Chapter 11.

c. Assume or Reject in Entirety

The trustee or debtor in possession may not assume the benefits and reject the burdens of an executory contract or an unexpired lease. The contract or lease must be either assumed or rejected in its entirety. [*In re* **Hagood Reserve, LLC,** 2010 WL 5067444 (Bankr. W.D. N.C. 2010); *In re* **Abitibibowater Inc.,** 418 B.R. 815 (Bankr. D. Del. 2009)]

d. Pre-Bankruptcy Termination

The trustee or debtor in possession cannot assume a contract or a lease that has legally terminated prior to the commencement of the bankruptcy case, with no right to cure. [*See, e.g., In re* **DBSI, Inc.,** 407 B.R. 159 (Bankr. D. Del. 2009)]

3. Assumption of Contracts and Leases in Default

If the debtor is not in default of the obligations under an executory contract or an unexpired lease, then the debtor in possession or trustee may assume and, perhaps, assign the contract or lease. In a case in which the debtor is in default, whether the default occurred pre- or post-petition, the trustee or debtor in possession may assume an executory contract or an unexpired lease *only* if the following three requirements are met at the time of assumption. [B.C. § 365(b)(1)]

a.   Cure

With certain exceptions, the trustee or debtor in possession must *cure* the default or provide *adequate assurance* that the default will be *cured promptly.* [B.C. § 365(b)(1)(A)] The Code does not define what constitutes a prompt cure. Thus, the issue is whether a debtor may cure over the entire length of the debtor's plan or whether prompt cure requires payment over some shorter period of time. The facts and circumstances of each case shape the court's determination of whether cure is prompt. [*In re* **M. Fine Lumber Co., Inc.,** 383 B.R. 565 (Bankr. E.D. N.Y. 2008)]

Example: Married Debtors filed for relief under Chapter 13. At the time of their bankruptcy filing, they owed approximately $1,400 in pre-petition arrearages on a car lease. Debtors proposed curing the arrearages by making payments over the 51 months of their Chapter 13 plan. Lessor objected and argued that Debtors had to complete their cure prior to the expiration of the vehicle lease. The bankruptcy court agreed with Lessor. The court explained that some courts had held that in a consumer case cure could not extend beyond six months while other courts had held that defaults had to be cured prior to the end of the lease term. The bankruptcy court concluded that it did not have to decide the appropriate time frame, because Lessor had asked that Debtors be required to cure by the lease termination date. The court held that Lessor's request was reasonable and that Debtors had to cure the pre-petition arrearages by the end of the lease's term rather than allowing Debtors to cure over the plan's 51-month period. [*In re* **Coffman,** 393 B.R. 829 (Bankr. S.D. Ohio 2008)]

(i)   Exceptions to Requirement of Cure

There are a number of exceptions to the requirement that the debtor in possession or trustee cure any default prior to assumption. The exceptions apply to the breach of any of the following provisions that the parties' contract defines as a default:

(1)   the debtor's *financial condition or insolvency* at any time before the bankruptcy case closes [B.C. § 365(b)(2)(A)];

(2)   the debtor's *filing for bankruptcy* [B.C. § 365(b)(2)(B)];

(3)   the appointment of a *bankruptcy trustee* or a *custodian prior to bankruptcy* [B.C. § 365(b)(2)(C)];

(4)   the *taking possession of property* by a bankruptcy trustee or a custodian prior to bankruptcy [B.C. § 365(b)(2)(C)];

(5)   failure to satisfy a *penalty rate or a penalty provision* arising from the debtor's failure to perform *nonmonetary obligations* under the lease or executory contract [B.C. § 365(b)(2)(D)]; or

(6)   except for a penalty rate or penalty provision, the failure to perform *nonmonetary obligations* under an unexpired *lease of real property,* if it is impossible to perform such obligations at or after the time of assumption [B.C. § 365(b)(1)(A)]. *Note: See infra* § (3)(b)2. on unexpired leases of nonresidential real property.

(ii)   Amendments to the Code's Cure Provisions

(1)   1994 Amendments and Cure

In 1994, Congress created an exception to the cure requirement such that the debtor in possession or trustee prior to assumption did not have to satisfy "any penalty rate or provision relating to a default arising from any failure by the debtor to perform nonmonetary obligations under the executory contract or unexpired lease." [Pub. L. No. 103–394 § 219(a)(3) (1994)] This provision is codified at § 365(b)(2)(D), and with the 2005 amendments now reads "penalty rate or penalty provision."

(2) BAPCPA and Cure

Prior to BAPCPA's passage, § 365(b)(2)(D) excepted from the requirement of cure "any penalty rate or provision relating to a default arising from any failure by the debtor to perform nonmonetary obligations under the executory contract or unexpired lease." [B.C. § 365(b)(2)(D) *pre-BAPCPA*] There was a split of authority as to the meaning of this provision. Some courts interpreted the language to mean that the debtor did not have to cure a penalty rate *or any other provision* relating to a default stemming from the breach of a nonmonetary obligation. Other courts read the word "penalty" as modifying *both* rate and provision, thereby limiting the exception to *penalty rates and penalty provisions* arising from nonmonetary defaults. In 2005, Congress amended § 365(b)(2)(D) by adding the word "penalty" before provision, thereby changing the language from "penalty rate or provision" to "penalty rate or penalty provision." [*See **In re** **Empire Equities Capital Corp.**,* 405 B.R. 687 (Bankr. S.D. N.Y. 2009)]

In 2005, Congress also amended § 365(b)(1)(A) to provide an exception to the Code's cure requirement for an **unexpired lease of real property** if the debtor's **default** relates to a **nonmonetary obligation** that **cannot be cured** at or after the time that the trustee assumes the lease. The exception to the cure requirement in such a case, however, does *not* apply to a penalty rate or penalty provision, which means that the debtor in possession or trustee must cure a breach of a penalty rate or penalty provision prior to assuming an unexpired lease of real property. [3 Collier ¶ 365.06(3)(c)] At the same time, Congress provided that for a nonmonetary default arising from failure to abide by the terms of a **commercial real property lease** the debtor in possession or trustee must cure by performing according to the lease terms after assumption and by providing compensation for pecuniary losses. [B.C. § 365(b)(1)(A)]

(3) What Does It All Mean?

The amendments to § 365(b), both in 1994 and in 2005, are not models of clarity. There are a few points on which most courts are in agreement, but a number of issues on which there is a split of authority or remaining questions of interpretation. It is important to recognize that some of these rules vary depending on whether the cure relates to an **unexpired lease of real property** versus an **executory contract or unexpired lease of personal property**.

(a) Courts in Agreement

1. The debtor in possession or trustee may assume an **unexpired lease of real property** without curing a default as to a nonmonetary obligation that is impossible to cure at the time of assumption. One example is "the prepetition breach of a continuous operation clause in a real property lease" because it is impossible for the trustee to "go back in time and cause the debtor to operate in the past during that the time that it did not operate." [3 Collier ¶ 365.06(3)(c)]

2. The debtor in possession or trustee cannot assume an *executory contract or an unexpired lease of personal property* if, at the time of assumption, it is impossible to cure the debtor's default of a nonmonetary obligation under the lease or executory contract.

Example: Debtor purchased an option from Capital to buy several loans secured by real property. The option expired on April 30, 2009 at 12 p.m. Debtor filed for relief under Chapter 11 39 minutes prior to expiration of the option, and argued that § 365 provided it with the time necessary to raise the money to purchase the loans and assume the contract. The court held that debtor's default—its failure to exercise the option within the time provided—was material and incurable. The court noted that the case involved a *non-lease executory contract* and that BAPCPA's amendments "establish[ed] that a debtor must cure most defaults arising from an executory contract that is not a real property lease." Because debtor's failure to timely exercise the option was not curable, the contract could not be assumed under § 365. (*Note:* The court did hold, however, that § 108(b) extended the option period for 60 days from the bankruptcy filing.) [*In re* **Empire Equities Capital Corp.,** 405 B.R. 687 (Bankr. S.D. N.Y. 2009); *see also* **Quantum Diversified Holdings, Inc. v. Wienheimer (*In re* Escarent Entities, L.P.),** 423 Fed. Appx. 462 (5th Cir. 2011) (holding that debtor could not assume contract because it could not cure non-monetary, material default in executory contract)]

(b) Questions of Interpretation

The amendments in 1994 and 2005 created some interpretation questions that remain unresolved.

1. It is unclear whether the Code's language "relating to a default arising from any failure by the debtor to perform nonmonetary obligations" applies to *both* "penalty rate" *and* "penalty provision" or only to "penalty provision." [B.C. § 365(b)(2)(D)] In other words, does § 365(b)(1) *not apply* to *any* penalty rate because the words "nonmonetary obligation" in § 365(b)(2)(D) modify *only* "penalty provision," not "penalty rate?" If the language applies only to "penalty provision," then the debtor need not cure any penalty rate, regardless of whether it arises from a failure by the debtor of a *monetary or nonmonetary* obligation. [*See, e.g., In re* **Zamani,** 390 B.R. 680 (Bankr. N.D. Cal. 2008) (holding that § 365(b)(2)(D)'s cure exception, incorporated into § 1124(2), relieved the debtor of satisfying any penalty interest rate related to a monetary or nonmonetary default)]

2. The 2005 amendments to § 365(b)(1)(A) provide that if "such default" arises from the failure of the debtor to abide by the terms of a *non-residential real property lease*, then the trustee must cure by performing according to the lease terms after assumption and providing compensation for pecuniary losses. The problem is that it is unclear what prior default Congress intended to reference when it used "such default": the default that § 365(b) requires be cured as a condition of assumption *or* the default of a nonmonetary obligation that is impossible to cure. Collier concludes that the words "such

default" refer back to nonmonetary obligation as a "substitute for cure of an incurable obligation." [3 Collier ¶ 365.06(3)(c); *see In re Patriot Place, Ltd.*, 486 B.R. 773 (Bankr. W.D. Tex. 2013) (holding that in the case of a nonmonetary default of a "nonresidential (commercial) real property lease, as long as [debtor] is not currently committing a nonmonetary default at the time of assumption, then it is performing under the lease and § 365(b)(1)(A) will excuse any previous uncurable nonmonetary defaults")]

b. Compensation

The trustee or debtor in possession must *compensate* or provide adequate assurance of prompt compensation to the non-debtor party for any *monetary loss* caused by the default. [B.C. § 365(b)(1)(B)]

c. Adequate Assurance of Future Performance

The trustee or debtor in possession must furnish *adequate assurance of future performance* of the executory contract or the unexpired lease. [B.C. § 365(b)(1)(C)]

(i) Criteria

In deciding whether the trustee has provided adequate assurance of future performance, the courts consider a number of factors, including the following: (i) the debtor's payment history; (ii) the debtor's profitability, if in business; (iii) the existence of a guarantee or other monies on deposit or dedicated to payment on the lease or executory contract; and (iv) the overall economic prognosis for the debtor's industry. [*See, e.g., In re* **M. Fine Lumber Co., Inc.**, 383 B.R. 565 (Bankr. E.D. N.Y. 2008)]

(ii) Shopping Center Leases

The Code provides more guidance about what constitutes adequate assurance of future performance of a shopping center lease. [B.C. § 365(b)(3)]

(1) "Shopping Center"

The Code does not define the term "shopping center." The decision as to whether the lease is in a shopping center is made on a case-by-case basis and courts normally consider a number of factors, including "combination of leases, whether all leases are held by [a] single landlord, [the] presence of common parking area, [the] existence of [a] master lease, and [the] contiguity of stores." [**Androse Associates of Allaire, LLC v. A&P (***In re* **A&P)**, 472 B.R. 666 (S.D. N.Y. 2012)] The most important factors likely are " 'a combination of leases held by a single landlord, leased to commercial retail distributors of goods, with the presence of a common parking area.' " [*In re* **Ames Department Stores, Inc.**, 348 B.R. 91 (Bankr. S.D. N.Y. 2006) (quoting Collier)]

(2) "Adequate Assurance"

Adequate assurance of future performance of a shopping center lease *includes* adequate assurance:

(a) of the *source of the rent* due under the lease [B.C. § 365(b)(3)(A)];

(b) if the lease is assumed and assigned, that the *financial condition and operating performance* of the proposed assignee and any guarantors is similar to the financial condition and operating performance of the debtor and any guarantors as of the time that the debtor became the lessee under the lease [B.C. § 365(b)(3)(A)];

(c) that any *percentage rent* due under the lease will not decline *substantially* [B.C. § 365(b)(3)(B)];

(d) that *assumption or assignment* of the lease is *subject to all lease terms,* including provisions concerning location, use, radius, or exclusivity [B.C. § 365(b)(3)(C)]; and

(e) that *assumption or assignment* will *not disrupt any tenant mix or balance* in the shopping center. [B.C. § 365(b)(3)(D)]

d. Incidental Services and Supplies

Prior to the assumption of an unexpired lease in default, other than a default under § 365(b)(2), the lessor is not obligated to provide incidental services or supplies, unless the trustee or debtor in possession pays, according to the terms of the lease, for any services or supplies furnished before assumption. [B.C. § 365(b)(4)]

4. Assignment

The trustee or debtor in possession may assign an executory contract or an unexpired lease only after assuming the contract or lease and providing adequate assurance of the assignee's future performance, regardless of whether there has been a default. [B.C. § 365(f)(2)] Unless assumption and assignment are provided for under the terms of the debtor's plan, the trustee or debtor in possession must file a motion to assume and assign an executory contract or unexpired lease. Reasonable notice and an opportunity for a hearing must be afforded to the party against whom relief is sought. [Bankruptcy Rules 6006(a), 9014(a)]

a. Ineffectiveness of Restrictions on Assignment

With the exception of contracts that cannot be assigned, an assignment that complies with the requirements of § 365(f)(2) is valid, notwithstanding any provision in the contract or lease or in applicable nonbankruptcy law that prohibits, restricts, or conditions the assignment, or that terminates or modifies the contract or lease because of the assignment. [B.C. §§ 365(f)(1), (3); *see infra* § 5]

b. Liability of Trustee

The assignment of an executory contract or an unexpired lease has the effect of relieving the trustee and the estate from any liability resulting from a breach occurring after the assignment. [B.C. § 365(k)]

c. Landlord's Deposit

The assignment of an unexpired lease under which the debtor is the lessee entitles the lessor to demand substantially the same deposit or other security that she would have required under the original lease from a comparable tenant. [B.C. § 365(*l*)]

5. Agreements Not Assumable or Assignable

The trustee may not assume or assign certain kinds of executory contracts and unexpired leases. [B.C. § 365(c)]

a.   Applicable Law Excuses Performance

If *applicable nonbankruptcy law* excuses the nondebtor party from accepting performance from, or furnishing performance to, an entity other than the debtor or the debtor in possession, the trustee may not assume or assign the contract or lease, unless the nondebtor party consents. [B.C. § 365(c)(1)] The prohibition only applies if "applicable law excuses the other party from performance"; thus, the contract or lease itself does not have to contain a prohibition or restriction on assignment. [H.R. Rep. No. 95–595, at 348 (1977)] As you learned in first-year Contracts, certain personal services contracts cannot be assigned. The Code's prohibition against assumption and assignment, however, is not limited to personal service contracts. [*See, e.g.,* **In re XMH Corp.,** 647 F.3d 690 (7th Cir. 2011) (trademark license not assignable without consent of trademark owner); **In re West Electronics, Inc.,** 852 F.2d 79 (3d Cir. 1988) (holding that debtor could not assume and assign a contract with the United States government for production of military equipment); **In re Virgin Offshore USA, Inc.,** 2013 WL 4854312 (E.D. La. 2013) (nonexclusive intellectual property licenses cannot be assigned without the licensor's consent)]

(i)   Hypothetical Versus Actual Performance Test

Can a Chapter 11 debtor in possession *assume and perform* a contract or lease that it could **not** *assume and assign* because of the prohibition at § 365(c)(1)? A majority of the Courts of Appeal to address the issue have adopted the "hypothetical test." Under the hypothetical test, "if the debtor in possession lacks hypothetical authority to assign a contract, then it may not assume it—even if the debtor in possession has no *actual* intention of assigning the contract to another." [**N.C.P. Marketing Group v. B.G. Star Products,** 556 U.S. 1145 (2009) (definition of test in statement of Justice Kennedy, joined by Justice Breyer, regarding denial of petition for certiorari)] The problem with the hypothetical test, of course, is that the third party originally contracted with the debtor (now the debtor in possession in Chapter 11); thus, the concerns underlying § 365(c)(1) of the Code, e.g., forcing a third party to accept performance of a non-delegable duty, simply do not apply if it is the original contracting party assuming performance of its original contractual obligations.

The First Circuit and most bankruptcy courts faced with the issue have adopted the "actual performance test." Under the "actual performance test," the bankruptcy court must determine whether the debtor in possession intends to assign the contract or lease after assumption. [**Institut Pasteur v. Cambridge Biotech Corp.,** 104 F.3d 489 (1st Cir. 1997)] If not, then the debtor in possession may assume the executory contract or unexpired lease.

b.   Contracts to Loan Money or to Issue Securities

The trustee or debtor in possession may not assume or assign an executory contract (i) to make a loan or to extend other debt financing or financial accommodations to or for the benefit of the debtor, or (ii) to issue a security of the debtor. [B.C. § 365(c)(2)] For example, "contracts such as loan commitment and letters of credit are nonassignable, and may not be assumed by the trustee." [H.R. Rep. No. 95–595, at 348 (1977)] This prohibition, however, does not apply to "an ordinary contract to provide goods or services that has incidental financial accommodations or extensions of credit." [3 Collier ¶ 365.07(2)] A credit card merchant agreement between the credit-card processor bank and the debtor merchant does not constitute a financial accommodations contract and, thus, the trustee or debtor in possession may assume such agreement in bankruptcy. [*See, e.g.,* **In re United Airlines, Inc.,** 368 F.3d 720 (7th Cir. 2004)]

c. Nonresidential Leases Terminated Before Bankruptcy

The trustee or debtor in possession may not assume or assign a lease of nonresidential real property that has terminated under nonbankruptcy law prior to the order for relief. [B.C. § 365(c)(3)] Some courts engage in a two-step analysis to determine whether § 365(c)(3) precludes assumption of a lease of nonresidential real property. The first step is to determine whether the lease was terminated under applicable nonbankruptcy law before the bankruptcy filing. If the lease was terminated, then the court must decide whether the termination was reversible under state anti-forfeiture law or other applicable state law. [*In re* **Waterkist Corp.**, 775 F.2d 1089 (9th Cir. 1985); *see In re* **Sterling Mining Co.**, 2009 WL 1377471 (D. Idaho 2009) (citing *Waterkist* test), *aff'd,* **Sunshine Precious Metals, Inc. v. Sterling Mining Co. (*In re* Sterling Mining Co.)**, 2010 WL 1816176 (D. Idaho 2010)]

6. Rejection Constitutes Breach

A rejection by the trustee or debtor in possession operates as a breach of the executory contract or the unexpired lease. Section 365(g) provides the rules for determining the time that the breach is deemed to have occurred, which, in turn, determines the nature of the non-breacher's claim.

a. No Assumption

If the trustee or debtor in possession has not assumed the contract or the lease under the terms of a confirmed plan or pursuant to the provisions of § 365, then the failure to assume constitutes a rejection and a breach. [B.C. § 365(g)(1)] The breach is deemed to occur *pre-petition,* immediately before the filing of the bankruptcy petition. [B.C. § 502(g)(1)] As a result, the non-breacher's claim is subject to any limitations that normally apply to the kind of pre-petition claim she holds. For example, the claim of a lessor that results from the rejection of a real property lease is limited to the amount fixed by § 502(b)(6), and an employee's claim for damages caused by the rejection of an employment contract is limited to the amount allowable under § 502(b)(7). [*See, e.g.,* **Rubloff Development Group, Inc. v. Kmart Corp. (*In re* Kmart Corp.)**, 389 B.R. 555 (N.D. Ill. 2008) (stating that damages arising from the breach of a lease, by virtue of rejection, are "only entitled to general nonpriority status and, in some circumstances, capped" under § 502(b)(6)]

(i) Distinguish Post-Petition Use

If the trustee or debtor in possession uses the leased premises post-petition but prior to rejection, then the benefit to the estate of that use is treated as an administrative expense. [B.C. § 503(b)(1)(A)] The administrative expense is determined based on the "fair and reasonable value of the lease", which is not necessarily the same as the rent charged under the lease. The contract rent, however, is "presumptive evidence of fair and reasonable value." [*In re* **Thompson**, 788 F.2d 560 (9th Cir. 1986)] Section 502(b)(6) does *not* limit the amount of the administrative expense. [*See* S. Rep. No. 95–989, at 63 (1978) (Section 502(b)(6) "does not apply to limit administrative expense claims for use of the leased premises to which the landlord is otherwise entitled")]

b. Assumption

If a trustee or debtor in possession *first assumes* and then *rejects* an executory contract or unexpired lease, the date that the breach is deemed to occur depends on whether the case was converted *from* Chapter 11, 12, or 13 *to* Chapter 7 before rejection, and if converted to Chapter 7, whether the assumption occurred *before or after* conversion to Chapter 7.

(i) No Conversion Prior to Rejection

If the case was not converted to Chapter 7 *before rejection,* then the breach is deemed to occur *at the time of rejection.* [B.C. § 365(g)(2)(A)]

(ii) Conversion to Chapter 7 Prior to Rejection

If the trustee or debtor in possession rejects after conversion a contract or unexpired lease it had previously assumed, the date of breach depends on whether the *assumption occurred pre- or post-conversion.* The breach is deemed to occur immediately *before conversion* if the lease or contract was *assumed before conversion.* [B.C. § 365(g)(2)(B)(i)] The breach is deemed to occur at the *time of rejection* if the lease was *assumed after conversion.* [B.C. § 365(g)(2)(B)(ii)]

(iii) Why Does It Matter?

When the trustee or debtor in possession first assumes and then rejects a contract or unexpired lease, "courts have granted administrative expense status to claims for damages arising from the breach." [*In re* **Juvennelliano,** 464 B.R. 651 (Bankr. D. Del. 2011)] If a case has been converted to Chapter 7 from Chapter 11, 12, or 13, the administrative expenses of the Chapter 7 case have priority over the administrative expenses of the prior Chapter 11, 12, or 13 case. [B.C. § 726(b)] If the breach is deemed to occur immediately before conversion, then administrative expenses incurred post-conversion to Chapter 7 have priority over the administrative expense claim for damages from rejection of the contract or unexpired lease.

> **e.g.** **Example:** On May 1, Debtor/Lessee filed for relief under Chapter 11 and, on June 1, obtained court approval to assume an unexpired lease of certain real property. On July 1, Debtor rejected the lease and, on August 1, converted the case to Chapter 7. The rejection of the lease constituted a breach deemed to have occurred on July 1, and for which Lessor is entitled to an administrative expense. [B.C. § 365(g)(2)(A)] Any administrative expenses arising *after conversion* in the Chapter 7 case have priority over Lessor's administrative expense claim, which was incurred prior to conversion. [B.C. § 726(b); *In re* **Multech Corp.,** 47 B.R. 747 (Bankr. D. Iowa 1985)]

c. Personal Property Leases and the Stay

Congress added subsection (p) to § 365 with the passage of BAPCPA. Section 365(p) provides rules related to *termination of the automatic stay* upon *rejection or deemed rejection* of a *personal property lease.* [B.C. § 365(p)(1), (3)] It also provides a process by which an individual Chapter 7 debtor may assume a lease that has been rejected or deemed rejected. [B.C. § 365(p)(2)]

(i) Not Estate Property

If a personal property lease is *rejected or deemed rejected* because it was not timely assumed under § 365(d), then the leased property *no longer is estate property* and the *automatic stay is automatically terminated.* [B.C. § 365(p)(1)]

(ii) Individual Chapter 7 Debtors

In an individual Chapter 7 case, if the trustee has rejected a personal property lease or the lease has been deemed rejected, the debtor may *notify the creditor in writing* that the debtor *wants to assume* the lease. The lessor, upon receiving such notice, may inform the debtor that it is willing to have the lease assumed and may condition assumption on the cure of any default according to the terms of the parties' contract. The lessor need not agree to assumption. [B.C. § 365(p)(2)(A)] If the debtor, no later than *30 days* after notice is provided, notifies the lessor in writing that the lease is assumed then the *debtor, not the estate, has assumed liability* for the lease. [B.C. § 365(p)(2)(B)] The Code does not specify *which* notice—that of the debtor or the lessor—starts the 30-day clock. The lessor's response to the debtor's notice that she wants to assume the lease violates neither the automatic stay nor the discharge injunction. [B.C. §§ 365(p)(2)(C), 362, 524(a)(2)] There is a split of authority as to whether a lease assumption under § 365(p) is enforceable after discharge if the debtor did not reaffirm the debt under the lease pursuant to § 524(c). [3 Collier ¶ 365.10(6); *see In re* **Bailly,** 522 B.R. 711 (Bankr. M.D. Fla. 2014) (discussing split of authority on issue and holding that debtor could assume his car lease "without separately reaffirming the debt and, indeed, without seeking any approval from the Court")]

(iii) Chapter 13 and Individual Chapter 11 Cases

In a Chapter 13 case or an individual Chapter 11 case in which the debtor is the lessee under a *personal property lease,* the lease is deemed rejected as of the conclusion of the confirmation hearing if the lease is not assumed in the confirmed plan. [B.C. § 365(p)(3)] Upon rejection, the automatic stay and the co-debtor stay are automatically terminated as to the property subject to the lease. [B.C. §§ 365(p)(3), 1301]

Note: This subsection does not terminate the stay with regard to the debtor or other property of the estate.

7. Time Limitations for Assumption or Rejection

The period within which the trustee or debtor in possession may assume or reject an executory contract or an unexpired lease depends on the chapter under which the case is filed and the nature of the property that is the subject matter of the contract or lease. [B.C. § 365(d)]

a. Chapter 7 Cases: Executory Contracts and Certain Leases

The trustee, in a case under Chapter 7, has *60 days* after the order for relief within which to assume or reject an *executory contract* or an unexpired lease of *personal property or residential real property.* Otherwise, the contract or the lease is deemed rejected. The court, during the 60-day period, may extend the period for cause. [B.C. § 365(d)(1)]

b. Chapter 11, 12, and 13 Cases

Assumption or rejection of an *executory contract* or unexpired lease of *personal property or residential real property* may occur at any time prior to the confirmation of a plan under Chapter 11, 12, or 13. [B.C. § 365(d)(2)]

(i) Expedited Decision

On request of the nondebtor party to an executory contract or unexpired lease, the court may order the trustee or debtor in possession to assume or reject the contract or lease within a fixed period of time. [B.C. § 365(d)(2)]

c. Time for Assumption of a Lease of Nonresidential Real Property

If the debtor is a lessee of nonresidential real property, then the trustee or the debtor in possession has until the *earlier of* the date of the entry of a *plan confirmation order or 120 days after the order for relief* within which to assume or reject the unexpired lease, or else the lease is deemed rejected and the property must be immediately surrendered to the lessor. [B.C. § 365(d)(4)(A)] During the 120-day period, the trustee or the lessor may move for an extension of this time period, and the bankruptcy court, for cause, may *extend* the period for *90 days.* [B.C. § 365(d)(4)(B)(i)] If the bankruptcy court grants such an extension, it may grant a subsequent additional extension of time *only* if the lessor consents in writing. [B.C. § 365(d)(4)(B)(ii)]

Note: For a subchapter V case commenced before *December 27, 2022,* the time period to assume the lease or to seek an extension to assume is *210, not 120, days.* [CAA § 1001(f)(1), (f)(2)(B)]

8. Trustee Obligations Prior to Assumption or Rejection

a. Lease of Nonresidential Real Property

The trustee or debtor in possession must timely perform all duties arising under an unexpired lease of nonresidential real property after the order for relief and until assumption or rejection. The only duties excluded are those described in § 365(b)(2). [B.C. § 365(d)(3)] Therefore, all rents due under such a lease during this period must be *timely paid at the rate specified in the lease.* [B.C. § 365(d)(3); *see, e.g., In re* **Shoot the Moon, LLC,** 2016 WL 1452671 (Bankr. D. Mont. 2016) (stating that § 365(d)(3) "requires immediate payment under the lease" based on the " 'contractual rate of rent, rather than any measure of the value of the trustee's actual use of the property' ")]

(i) Extending Time for Performance

The bankruptcy court, *for cause,* may extend the time for the trustee or debtor in possession to perform any lease obligations, including payment of rent, that arise within *60 days after* the order for relief. The court, however, may *not* extend the time for performance beyond such 60-day period. [B.C. § 365(d)(3)]

(1) Subchapter V

The CAA amended § 365(d)(3)'s time periods for subchapter V cases commenced before *December 27, 2022.* [CAA § 1001(f)(2)(B)] If the debtor is "experiencing or has experienced a material financial hardship" due to COVID-19, the bankruptcy court may extend the time for the debtor to perform its lease obligations until the *earlier of* (i) *60 days after* the order for relief, which may be extended an *additional 60 days* if the debtor continues to experience material financial hardship due to COVID-19 *or* (ii) the date on which the lease is *assumed or rejected.* [CAA § 1001(f)(1), creating temporary subsection (B) to § 365(d)(3)] The bankruptcy court may extend this initial 60-day period by *an additional 60 days* if the court finds that the debtor continues to experience, either directly or indirectly, *a material financial hardship* due to COVID-19. [CAA § 1001(f)(1)]

(ii) Failure to Perform

What happens if the trustee or debtor in possession fails to perform its lease obligations, e.g., does not pay post-petition rent, prior to assumption or rejection of that lease? The Bankruptcy Code does not answer the question.

A *majority of courts* treat the unpaid post-petition rent as an *administrative expense* arising under § 365(d)(3), not § 503(b)(1). In other words, administrative expense status is automatic and § 503(b)(1)(A)'s requirements, such as demonstrating a benefit to the estate, do not apply. [*See, e.g.,* **Towers v. Chickering & Gregory (*In re* Pacific-Atlantic Trading Co.),** 27 F.3d 401 (9th Cir. 1994) (holding that "[b]y providing for timely performance of *all* lease obligations, 'notwithstanding section 503(b)(1),' the statute has already granted priority payment status to the full amount of rent due under nonresidential leases"); *see also* 3 Collier ¶ 365.04(1)(b)] A *minority of courts* require the lessor to assert an administrative expense claim under § 503(b)(1). Notice and a hearing are required, and the lessor must demonstrate the benefit to the estate. These courts conclude that because Congress failed to provide a specific remedy for the debtor's or trustee's failure to perform, Congress left the remedy determination to the sound discretion of the bankruptcy court. [*See In re* **Simbaki, Ltd.,** 2015 WL 1593888 (Bankr. S.D. Tex. 2015) (discussing courts' approaches to issue)]

(1) Subchapter V

If the court extends the time period for the trustee to perform an obligation of the debtor's under a lease of nonresidential real property, then that obligation must be treated as an *administrative expense under § 507(a)(2)* for purposes of § 1191(e)'s special rule for payment of administrative and gap claims in a subchapter V case. [CAA § 1001(f)(1), creating temporary subsection (C) to § 365(d)(3), which applies to a subchapter V case commenced *before December 27, 2022.* (CAA § 1001(f)(2)(B)); *see infra* Chapter Thirteen, § H on subchapter V]

b. Lease of Commercial Personal Property in Chapter 11

In a *Chapter 11 case*, the trustee or debtor in possession must timely perform all obligations, except those specified under § 365(b)(2), in a lease of *non-consumer personal property* first arising *from or after 60 days after the order for relief* until the lease is assumed or rejected. After notice and a hearing, the bankruptcy court, based on the *equities of the case,* may order otherwise with regard to the lease obligations or their timely performance. [B.C. § 365(d)(5)]

This obligation to perform, unlike that in § 365(d)(3), does not apply until *60 days after the order for relief.* Thus, during the first 60 days, the estate pays for use of commercial personal property based on general concepts of benefit to the estate; if the estate does not use the property, then the lessor likely receives no payment for those first 60 days. After 60 days, however, the trustee or debtor in possession must pay at the lease rate for the noncommercial personal property. The most common type of unexpired commercial lease is an *equipment lease.*

c. Executory Contracts and All Other Leases

The Bankruptcy Code does not contain specific rules about the trustee's or debtor in possession's obligations to perform prior to assumption or rejection of executory contracts, or leases of residential property or consumer personal property. But the estate must pay for the benefit it receives from post-petition performance of such contracts or leases. That benefit is compensated as a priority administrative expense and only to the extent of any *actual benefit to the estate.* [*See* B.C. § 503(b)(1)]

9. Ipso Facto Provisions

With certain exceptions, an executory contract or unexpired lease may not be terminated or modified *after* the filing of a bankruptcy petition solely on account of an *ipso facto* or other bankruptcy termination clause in the contract or lease. Thus, the Code invalidates any contractual provision that terminates or modifies the parties' contract or lease based on:

a. the insolvency or financial state of the debtor [B.C. § 365(e)(1)(A)];

b. the commencement by the debtor of a bankruptcy case [B.C. § 365(e)(1)(B)];

c. the appointment of a bankruptcy trustee or a nonbankruptcy custodian [B.C. § 365(e)(1)(C)]; *or*

d. the taking possession of property by a bankruptcy trustee or a nonbankruptcy custodian [B.C. § 365(e)(1)(C)].

e.g. **Example:** The post-petition cancellation of Debtor's insurance policy under an "at will" clause of the contract, solely because of the filing of an involuntary petition against Debtor, is ineffective; thus, the policy continues in force. [B.C. § 365(e)(1)(B); *In re B. Siegel Co.,* 51 B.R. 159 (Bankr. E.D. Mich. 1985)]

Exceptions: The Code provides exceptions to the basic rule that *ipso facto* and other bankruptcy termination clauses are not effective post-petition. Such clauses are effective to terminate or modify the parties' agreement, if the non-debtor party invokes the clause, in either of the following two situations:

a. applicable law excuses the non-debtor party from accepting performance from or rendering performance to the trustee or an assignee, e.g., a personal services contract [B.C. § 365(e)(2)(A)]; *or*

b. the contract is one to make a loan or extend other debt or financial accommodations to or for the benefit of the debtor, or to issue a security of the debtor. [B.C. § 365(e)(2)(B)]

e.g. **Example:** Debtor Jonesboro Tractor Sales filed for relief under Chapter 11. Debtor and Kubota Tractor Corporation were parties to a Dealership Agreement that contained an *ipso facto* termination clause. Kubota argued that it could enforce the termination provision because the Dealership Agreement was a contract to extend financial accommodations to the debtor. The bankruptcy court disagreed. The court explained that under the Dealership Agreement, Kubota was not obligated to extend financing to Debtor. Under the terms of the Dealership Agreement, Kubota could have insisted on payment in cash on delivery for its products. Therefore, the Dealership Agreement was not a contract to extend financial accommodations, which meant that "the exception in Section 365(e)(2)(B) [did] not apply, and the Dealership Agreement [could] not be terminated solely because of the Debtor's bankruptcy filing." [*In re* **Jonesboro Tractor Sales, Inc.,** 619 B.R. 223 (Bankr. E.D. Ark. 2020)]

10. Debtor as Lessor of Real Property

If the trustee rejects an unexpired lease of real property under which the *debtor is the lessor,* then the lessee either may consider the lease terminated or, *if the term of the lease has commenced,* retain rights under the lease for the balance of the current term and for any period of renewal or extension enforceable under nonbankruptcy law. [B.C. § 365(h)(1)(A)] Similarly, if the trustee rejects a timeshare interest under a timeshare plan under which the *debtor is the seller* of the interest, then the purchaser of that interest either may treat the timeshare interest as terminated *or* if the term of the *timeshare interest has commenced,* retain its rights in the timeshare interest for the balance of the term and for any period of renewal or extension enforceable under nonbankruptcy law. [B.C. §§ 365(h)(2)(A), 101(53D)]

a. Continued Possession

If the lessee or timeshare interest purchaser elects to retain her rights, she may offset against her post-rejection rent or monies due for the timeshare interest any damages occurring after the date of rejection that flow from the failure of the trustee or debtor in possession to perform its obligations under the lease or the timeshare plan. The right of offset is the exclusive remedy against the estate or the debtor for post-rejection damages. [B.C. § 365(h)(1)(B), (2)(B)] The rejection of a lease of real property in a shopping center in which the lessee elects to retain its rights does not affect the enforceability of any lease provision related to radius, location, use, exclusivity, or tenant mix or balance. [B.C. § 365(h)(1)(C)]

11. Debtor as Seller of Real Property

If the trustee rejects an executory contract to sell real property or a timeshare interest under which the *debtor is the seller,* the buyer, *if in possession,* may treat the contract as terminated or may stay in possession of the real property or timeshare interest. [B.C. § 365(i)(1)]

a. Continued Possession

If the purchaser chooses to remain in possession, she must make all payments required by the contract. However, she may offset against these payments any damages occurring after the date of rejection that result from nonperformance of the debtor's obligations under the contract. The right of offset is the buyer's exclusive remedy against the estate for post-rejection damages. [B.C. § 365(i)(2)(A)]

(i) Title

The trustee or debtor in possession must deliver the title to the buyer as provided for in the contract, but is not obligated to perform any other duties under the contract. [B.C. § 365(i)(2)(B)]

b. Termination of Contract

A buyer that treats a rejected executory contract to sell real property as terminated *or* that is not in possession of the property has a *lien* on the property to the extent of any payments made toward the purchase price. [B.C. § 365(j)]

12. Intellectual Property

If the debtor is the licensor of a right to intellectual property, and the trustee or debtor in possession rejects an executory contract under which the license has been granted, the licensee may consider the contract terminated or may retain its contractual rights to the intellectual property, including any right to exclusivity, but excluding any other right to specific performance of the contract, and use the property for the remaining period of the contract and any rightful extension. [B.C. § 365(n)] Congress added § 365(n) to the Code in response to **Lubrizol Enterprises, Inc. v. Richmond Metal Finishers, Inc.,** 756 F.2d 1043 (4th Cir. 1985), which held that rejection of an intellectual property license terminated the licensee's right to use licensed copyrights, trademarks, and patents.

a. Retention of Rights

If the licensee elects to retain its contractual rights to the property, it must make all royalty payments due under the contract and any extension of the contract's term. The licensee waives any right of setoff concerning the contract and any claim for administrative expenses resulting from performance of the contract. [B.C. § 365(n)(2)(C)] Upon the licensee's written request, the trustee or debtor in possession must do the following:

(i) provide the licensee, to the extent required by the parties' contract or any supplementary agreement, the intellectual property, including such embodiment, that the trustee or debtor in possession holds [B.C. § 365(n)(3)(A)]; and

(ii) not interfere with the licensee's rights, as provided in the parties' contract or supplementary agreement, to the intellectual property, including such embodiment (non-interference includes the licensee's right to obtain the intellectual property or such embodiment from a third party). [B.C. § 365(n)(3)(B)]

b. "Intellectual Property" Defined

The Bankruptcy Code defines intellectual property as any of the following, to the extent protected by nonbankruptcy law:

(i) trade secrets [B.C. § 101(35A)(A)];

(ii) inventions, processes, designs, or plants protected under United States Code title 35 [B.C. § 101(35A)(B)];

(iii) patent applications [B.C. § 101(35A)(C)];

(iv) plant varieties [B.C. § 101(35A)(D)];

(v) works of authorship protected under title 17 of the United States Code [B.C. § 101(35A)(E)]; and

(vi) mask works (relating to semiconductor chip products) protected under chapter 9 of title 17 of the United States Code. [B.C. § 101(35A)(F)]

The Code's definition of intellectual property does not include trademarks, trade names, or service marks; thus, § 365(n) does not apply to them. But in **Mission Product Holdings v. Tempnology, LLC,** 139 S. Ct. 1652 (2019), the Supreme Court held that a debtor-licensor's rejection of a trademark licensing agreement was a breach of that contract, not a rescission of it. Because rejection does not rescind rights previously granted to the licensee, the debtor-licensor's rejection does not "deprive[ ] the licensee of its rights to use the trademark." The Court explained that its decision rested on § 365(g) and that Congress had done "nothing in adding Section 365(n) to alter the natural reading of Section 365(g)—that rejection and breach have the same results." Thus, the "debtor-licensor's rejection [did not] revoke the trademark license."

13. Capital Commitment of a Financial Institution

In a Chapter 11 case, the trustee or debtor in possession is deemed to have assumed and must immediately cure any deficiency under any commitment by the debtor to a federal depository institutions regulatory agency to maintain the capital of an insured depository institution. [B.C. §§ 365(o), 101(21B), (35)] Any subsequent breach of this obligation results in a priority claim under § 507(a)(9). [B.C. §§ 365(o), 507(a)(9)]

E. Utility Service

1. Protection for Debtor

A utility may not discontinue, alter, or refuse service to, or discriminate against, the trustee or debtor solely because of the filing of a bankruptcy case or because the debtor failed to timely pay a debt owed for utility services furnished prior to the order for relief. [B.C. § 366(a)]

 Example: Married Debtors filed for relief under Chapter 13 on October 26. At the time of their bankruptcy filing, Debtors owed Gas Utility more than $1,200. While

Gas Utility could have discontinued Debtors' gas service as of November 16 if Debtors failed to provide adequate assurance of payment, it instead gave Debtors until December 22 to pay a $217 deposit as adequate assurance of payment. Debtors paid the $217, but then accumulated more than $1,100 in unpaid, post-petition gas bills. After providing proper notice under state law, Gas Utility terminated Debtors' gas service for failure to pay their post-petition gas bills. Debtors sued for violation of the automatic stay. The bankruptcy court ruled against Debtors, and the district court affirmed. The district court held that "[i]t is well-established that § 366 permits a utility to terminate service to a debtor or trustee who has posted adequate assurance but fails to make post-petition payments on the utility service, and may do so without seeking relief from the automatic stay as long as the utility follows its state law termination procedures." [**Weisel v. Dominion Peoples Gas Co. (*In re* Weisel),** 428 B.R. 185 (W.D. Penn. 2010)]

2. Exception: Insufficient Security

Except in a Chapter 11 case, a utility may discontinue, alter, or refuse service if, within *20 days* after the order for relief, neither the debtor nor the trustee provides *adequate assurance of payment* for post-petition services, such as a deposit or other security. [B.C. § 366(b); *In re* **Hanratty,** 907 F.2d 1418 (3d Cir. 1990) (rejecting debtors' contention that a utility's request for a deposit from Chapter 13 debtors constituted discrimination against those debtors because the utility did not request such a deposit from new residential utility customers)]

a. Adequate Assurance of Payment

In BAPCPA, Congress defined what does and does not constitute assurance of payment. An administrative expense priority does *not* constitute assurance of payment. [B.C. § 366(c)(1)(B)] Assurance of payment means any of the following:

(i) a cash deposit [B.C. § 366(c)(1)(A)(i)];

(ii) a letter of credit [B.C. § 366(c)(1)(A)(ii)];

(iii) a certificate of deposit [B.C. § 366(c)(1)(A)(iii)];

(iv) a surety bond [B.C. § 366(c)(1)(A)(iv)];

(v) a prepayment of utility consumption [B.C. § 366(c)(1)(A)(v)]; *or*

(vi) another form of security on which the utility and debtor or trustee agree. [B.C. § 366(c)(1)(A)(vi)]

b. Modification of Payment

The bankruptcy court, upon the request of a party in interest and after notice and a hearing, may order reasonable modification of the amount of any deposit or security intended as adequate assurance of payment. [B.C. § 366(b)]

3. Exception: Chapter 11

In a *Chapter 11 case*, a utility may alter, refuse, or discontinue service if during the *30-day period* starting with the filing of the petition the debtor or trustee does not provide *adequate assurance of payment* that is *satisfactory to the utility.* [B.C. § 366(c)(2)] Congress added this provision to the Code in 2005.

a. Modification of Payment

In a Chapter 11 case, the bankruptcy court, upon request of a party in interest and after notice and a hearing, may order reasonable modification of the amount of any deposit or security intended as adequate assurance of payment. [B.C. § 366(c)(3)(A)]

b. Irrelevant Factors

In making its determination on the adequacy of an assurance of payment in the Chapter 11 context, the bankruptcy court *may not consider* any of the following factors:

(i) the absence of pre-petition security [B.C. § 366(c)(3)(B)(i)];

(ii) the debtor's timely payment of pre-petition charges [B.C. § 366(c)(3)(B)(ii)]; or

(iii) the availability of an administrative expense priority claim. [B.C. § 366(c)(3)(B)(i)]

Congress added this language to the Code in 2005.

4. Pre-Petition Deposit

A utility, without notice or order of the court, may set off or recover a pre-petition deposit provided to the utility by the debtor. [B.C. § 366(c)(4)] Congress added this provision to the Code in 2005.

Chapter Twelve

Bankruptcy Code Chapter 7: Liquidation

Chapter Approach

In a Chapter 7 case, the trustee collects the property of the estate, reduces it to cash, and pays claimants in a prescribed order.

Your professor is likely to ask you to decide whether a debtor may file for relief under Chapter 7. In 2005, Congress enacted BAPCPA, which established *new eligibility requirements for individual consumer debtors* filing for Chapter 7. The new financial eligibility test determines whether a debtor's filing for relief under Chapter 7 creates a *presumption of abuse*. If the debtor fails to rebut the presumption, then the debtor's Chapter 7 case will be dismissed. The following are some key things for you to keep in mind when answering this type of question.

1. The new eligibility requirements to file for relief under Chapter 7 *only apply to individual debtors with primarily consumer debts.*

2. If a debtor's *annual income is less than the state's median income,* then the Chapter 7 "means test" does not apply.

3. An *above-median income debtor* must "pass" the means test to file for or remain in Chapter 7.

4. The court may still dismiss the Chapter 7 case of a below-median income debtor or of an above-median income debtor who passes the means test if the court determines that the debtor filed the case *in bad faith* or that under the *totality of the circumstances* the filing of the case demonstrates *abuse.*

Your professor may ask you to determine the amount of any distribution made to creditors in the Chapter 7 case. Consider the following when answering a question of this type.

1. Ordinarily, *secured* creditors are paid out of their collateral.

2. *Unsecured priority creditors* are paid ahead of the general unsecured creditors, and are paid in the order that they appear in § 507(a) of the Code. Thus, if there is not enough money to pay all tax creditors (eighth priority), then the tax claimants share *pro rata* in the distributed funds.

3. If there are assets sufficient to pay a dividend to unsecured creditors, then unsecured creditors share *pro rata* in that distribution, including creditors with nondischargeable debts. Do *not* confuse nondischargeability of a debt with the right of the claimant to participate in any distribution from the bankruptcy estate.

4. The trustee can *avoid* liens for certain kinds of penalties, and *tax liens* are subject to subordination.

5. If your question concerns a *partnership* debtor, remember that special rules apply if there are insufficient assets to pay all the claims against the partnership.

Your professor also may ask you to determine whether the debtor should receive a *discharge* under Chapter 7. The Code currently contains *twelve numbered exceptions* to the Chapter 7 discharge. If any exception is satisfied, e.g., the debtor transferred property with the intent to hinder, delay, or defraud a creditor, then *none* of the Chapter 7 debtor's pre-petition debts is discharged. Remember to distinguish between a *global denial* of discharge and the *debt-specific* discharge exceptions in § 523 of the Bankruptcy Code. If the facts do not show any of the grounds for denial, then a discharge *must* be granted, although under appropriate circumstances, a discharge may be *revoked.*

Finally, keep in mind that the debtor may *convert* a Chapter 7 case to Chapter 11, 12, or 13, if the case has not been converted earlier and the debtor is eligible under the other chapter. The court also may *dismiss* a case for cause or if a consumer debtor has filed but does not qualify for relief under Chapter 7.

Note: This outline does not cover stockbroker, commodity broker, or clearing bank liquidation cases. [*See* B.C. §§ 741–53, 761–67, 781–84 (subchapters III, IV, and V of Chapter 7)]

A. Introduction

1. Eligibility for Relief

With the following exceptions, a person, e.g., an individual, partnership, or corporation that resides or has a domicile, a place of business, or property in the United States may be a debtor under Chapter 7. [B.C. § 109(a), (b)]

a. Exceptions for Certain Entities

The following persons are *not eligible* to be debtors under Chapter 7:

(i) *railroads* [B.C. § 109(b)(1)];

(ii) *domestic insurance companies,* banks, credit unions, savings and loan associations, building and loan associations, homestead associations, cooperative banks, industrial banks, small business investment companies licensed by the Small Business Administration, New Markets Venture Capital companies, and other similar institutions [B.C. § 109(b)(2)];

(iii) *foreign insurance companies* that are *engaged in such business in the United States* [B.C. § 109(b)(3)(A)]; and

(iv) *foreign banks, savings banks, savings and loan associations, credit unions* and other similar financial institutions with a *branch or agency in the United States.* [B.C. § 109(b)(3)(B)]

b. Exceptions: Financial Situation or Pre-Bankruptcy Conduct

The exceptions above are based on *entity type,* e.g., railroads. The Code also provides that certain debtors are not eligible for relief under Chapter 7 based on their *current financial situation* or *pre-bankruptcy conduct.* For this group of debtors, changing the time of the bankruptcy filing may remove the bar to eligibility. The following debtors also are not eligible for relief under Chapter 7:

(i) *an individual or a family farmer* who was a debtor in a case that was *pending in the preceding 180 days* and *dismissed* because of the debtor's willful failure to obey court orders or to appear before the court in proper prosecution of the case [B.C. § 109(g)(1)];

(ii) *an individual or a family farmer* who was a debtor in a case that was *pending in the preceding 180 days* and the debtor requested and obtained a voluntary dismissal of the case following a party's request for relief from the automatic stay [B.C. § 109(g)(2)];

Note: The disqualification *supra* (i) and (ii) [B.C. § 109(g)(2)] applies to individuals filing for relief not only under Chapter 7 but also under Chapters 11, 12, and 13.

(iii) *above-median income individual debtors with primarily consumer debts* who fail the "means test" [B.C. § 707(b)]; and

(iv) with certain limited exceptions, an *individual debtor* who has not obtained *credit counseling* during the *180 days* prior to seeking relief under the Bankruptcy Code. [B.C. § 109(h)]

Note: This disqualification applies not only to individuals filing for relief not only under Chapter 7 but also under Chapters 11, 12, and 13.

2. Chapter 7 Trustee

Promptly after the order for relief, the United States trustee must appoint a disinterested member of the panel of private trustees to serve as the interim trustee in a Chapter 7 case. [B.C. § 701(a)(1); 28 U.S.C. § 586(a)(1)] Then, either a trustee is elected at the § 341 meeting of creditors or, as usually occurs, the interim trustee automatically becomes the permanent trustee in the case. [B.C. § 702]

a. Duties of Trustee

In a Chapter 7 case, the trustee's primary responsibilities are to locate and collect property of the estate, convert the property to cash, make distributions to claimants in the order established by the Bankruptcy Code, and close the estate expeditiously. [B.C. §§ 704(a), 726] BAPCPA added a number of new responsibilities for the Chapter 7 trustee, including verifying that individual debtors are eligible for relief under Chapter 7 and providing various notices related to claims for domestic support obligations. [*See* B.C. §§ 704(a)(10), (b), (c)] Bankruptcy Code § 704 provides a full list of the administrative duties of the Chapter 7 trustee. [*See also* Chapter 4, § A.5]

3. Authority to Operate Debtor's Business

Occasionally, the trustee may receive authorization from the court to operate the debtor's business temporarily, under circumstances in which continuing the business for a limited time is in the *best interest of the estate* and consistent with its *orderly liquidation.* [B.C. § 721] "An example is the operation of a watch company to convert watch movements and cases into completed watches which will bring much higher prices than the component parts would have brought." [H.R. Rep. No. 95–595, at 380 (1977)]

4. Meeting of Creditors

No earlier than 21 and no later than 40 days after the order for relief, the United States trustee must convene and preside at the § 341 meeting. [B.C. § 341; Bankruptcy Rule 2003(a)]

a. Business Conducted

The business conducted at the § 341 meeting includes the following matters:

(i) *examination of the debtor,* under oath, by creditors, the trustee or an examiner in the case, an indenture trustee, or the United States trustee [B.C. § 343; Bankruptcy Rule 2003(b)(1)];

(ii) *the election of a trustee,* if requested by a sufficient number of unsecured creditors [B.C. § 702]; and

(iii) *election of a creditors' committee,* if desired, consisting of between 3 and 11 unsecured creditors, to act in an advisory role in consultation with the Chapter 7 trustee or the United States trustee. [B.C. § 705; Bankruptcy Rule 2003(b)(1)]

b. Conclusion of § 341 Meeting

Before concluding the § 341 meeting, the *trustee must orally examine the debtor* to make certain that the debtor is aware of the following matters:

(i) the possible consequences, including the impact on credit history, of obtaining a *bankruptcy discharge* [B.C. § 341(d)(1)];

(ii) the availability of relief under *other chapters* of the Bankruptcy Code [B.C. § 341(d)(2)];

(iii) the *effect of a discharge* of debts [B.C. § 341(d)(3)]; and

(iv) the *effect of reaffirming a debt*, including the debtor's knowledge of the impact of reaffirmation on discharge. [B.C. §§ 341(d)(1), 524(d)]

B. The Means Test

1. Introduction

BAPCPA created a financial eligibility test for *individual Chapter 7 debtors with primarily consumer debts.* The goal of this financial eligibility test is to force a debtor to file for relief under Chapter 13 (or Chapter 11) instead of Chapter 7 if the debtor has the financial means to pay some threshold amount of money to the debtor's unsecured creditors. BAPCPA provides that filing for relief under Chapter 7 for these "can pay" debtors creates a *presumption of abuse.*

The *first step* of this new financial eligibility test is determining whether the individual debtor's income is *above or below the median income* for the debtor's household size in the state in which the debtor resides. The *means test,* which is the second step, only applies to *above-median income debtors.*

2. The Below-Median Income Debtor

a.   The Bankruptcy Code provides that there is no *presumption of abuse* for a *below-median income debtor.* Therefore, no one may file a motion to dismiss the debtor's case on the *sole* ground that the filing for relief under Chapter 7 is presumed to be an abuse of the bankruptcy system. [B.C. § 707(b)(7)]

b.   The below median-income debtor's Chapter 7 case may be dismissed, however, if the court determines that the *petition was filed in bad faith* or *the totality of the debtor's financial situation demonstrates abuse.* [B.C. § 707(b)(3); *see also infra* § H.2.b of this Chapter]

c.   Only the *judge, United States trustee, or Bankruptcy Administrator* may move to dismiss the case of a below-median income debtor for *bad faith* or under the *totality-of-the-circumstances* test. [B.C. § 707(b)(6)]

3. The Above-Median Income Debtor

a.   An above-median income debtor must do the *means test* in order to determine whether the debtor's filing for relief under Chapter 7 creates a *presumption of abuse.* If there is no presumption of abuse, then the debtor's case still may be dismissed if it was *filed in bad faith* or if the *totality of the debtor's financial situation demonstrates abuse.* [B.C. § 707(b)(2), (3); *see also infra* § H.2.b of this Chapter]

b.   If there is a presumption of abuse, then the debtor may *rebut the presumption* by showing *special circumstances* that justify additional expenses or adjustments to current monthly income for which there is *no reasonable alternative.* Special circumstances may include *"a serious medical condition or a call or order to active duty in the Armed Forces."* [B.C. § 707(b)(2)(B)]

4. Current Monthly Income

a. All *individual* debtors must determine their *current monthly income,* because this figure determines the debtor's income status as above or below median.

Note: An *individual debtor whose debts are primarily business in nature* must submit a statement that she is *exempt* from the *presumption of abuse.* [Official Form 122A-1 Supp] The debtor still must complete and submit the statement of current monthly income form. [Official Form 122A-1]

b. *Current monthly income* is the debtor's *average monthly income from all sources* that the debtor receives during the *six-month period* prior to filing for bankruptcy. The six-month period *ends on the last day of the calendar month immediately preceding* the filing of the bankruptcy case. [B.C. § 101(10A)(A)]

> **e.g.** **Example:** Dale files for relief under Chapter 7 on October 20, 2021. Dale's current monthly income is computed by averaging his income for the months of April through September of 2021. Dale's income from October is not included, because the six-month period ends on the last day of the month prior to his filing for bankruptcy.

> **e.g.** **Example:** Dale's income varies by month, because commissions are a large part of his compensation. Dale files for relief under Chapter 7 on October 20, 2021. His gross wages in April and May of 2021 were $2,000; in June and July, his wages increased to $3,000; in August and September, his gross wages were $2,200. Dale's current monthly income is the average over the past 6 months or $2,400 ($14,400/6 months).

a. What Is Included in Current Monthly Income?

Current monthly income *includes* (1) non-taxable income or (2) amounts paid by any entity other than the debtor *on a regular basis* for the *household expenses* of the debtor or the debtor's dependents. [B.C. § 101(10A)] Current monthly income *does not include*

(i) *Social Security benefits*;

(ii) payments to *victims of war crimes or crimes against humanity* based on their status as victims of these crimes;

(iii) payments to *victims of domestic or international terrorism* based on their status as victims of terrorism; and

(iv) benefits paid in connection with a *disability, combat-related injury or disability, or death of a member of the uniformed services.*

[B.C. § 101(10A)]

Congress added the *fourth exclusion* above for certain benefits for members of the military in the Honoring American Veterans in Extreme Need Act of 2019 (HAVEN Act). [Pub. L. No. 116–52 (2019); *see* 2 Collier ¶ 101.10A]

> **e.g.** **Example:** Debbie is a retired school teacher. She has a modest pension and also collects Social Security benefits, which do not cover all of her household expenses. Debbie's son pays her utility bills each month. Debbie's current monthly income includes her pension payments as well as the amount her son contributes each month toward her utility payments. It does not include her Social Security benefits.

5. Above or Below Median?

a. Once the debtor determines her current monthly income, she *multiplies that number by 12* and compares it with the median income for her household size in the state in which she resides. If her income exceeds the state median, then she is an above-median income debtor and must complete the "means test." If her income is equal to or less than the state median, then she is a ***below-median*** income debtor and there is ***no presumption of abuse.***

> **Example:** Dilbert is single and his current monthly income is $2,000, for an annual income of $24,000. The median income for a single person in the state where Dilbert resides is $32,000. Dilbert is a below-median income debtor; therefore, Dilbert's filing of relief under Chapter 7 does not create a presumption of abuse.

b.　The median income by state and household size, as well as the expense amounts that the individual debtor must use for the means test are found at the ***Means Testing Information*** link on the Department of Justice United States Trustee program website, ***available at https://www.justice.gov/ust/means-testing***

c.　In determining whether a ***married debtor who files alone*** is an above- or below-median income debtor, the income of the non-filing spouse is included in the calculation unless the ***couple is separated under applicable nonbankruptcy law*** *or* the couple is ***living apart*** and the debtor files a ***statement under penalty of perjury*** that attests to the fact the couple ***lives apart*** and that ***discloses payments*** from the non-filing spouse attributable to the ***filing spouse's current monthly income.*** [B.C. § 707(b)(7)(B)]

> **Example:** Donald earns $40,000 per year. His wife Delia earns $30,000 per year. Donald and Delia live together. The median income for a family of two in the state in which Donald and Delia reside is $60,000. Only Donald plans to file for relief under Chapter 7. Donald is an above-median income debtor, because his and Delia's income combined is $70,000, which exceeds the state median.

6. Above-Median Income Debtors and the Chapter 7 Means Test

To determine whether there is a presumption of abuse, the above-median income debtor subtracts her ***monthly expenses*** from her ***current monthly income.*** The debtor then multiplies the ***difference by 60*** and compares the ***product*** with the following numbers.

a.　**$9,075:** If the ***product is less than $9,075,*** then the debtor's filing for relief under Chapter 7 ***does not create*** a ***presumption of abuse.*** [B.C. § 707(b)(2)(A)(i)(I)]

> **Example:** David is single and earns $50,400 per year. He lives in a state with a median income of $45,000 for single people. David's current monthly income is $4200, but his monthly means test expenses are $4,100, which leaves $100 per month for his unsecured creditors. Over 60 months, David has $6,000, which is less than $9,075. Therefore, there is no presumption of abuse.

b.　**$15,150:** If the ***product is greater than $15,150,*** then there is a ***presumption of abuse.*** [B.C. § 707(b)(2)(A)(i)(II)] Unless the debtor can rebut the presumption, the debtor cannot file for relief under Chapter 7.

> **Example:** Debi is single, earns $48,000 per year, and lives in a state with a median income of $45,000 for single people. Debi's current monthly income is $4,000, and her monthly expenses are $3,725. The difference of $275 when multiplied by 60 months equals $16,500, which exceeds $15,150. Therefore, the presumption of abuse arises and unless Debi is able to rebut it, she may not file for relief under Chapter 7.

c.　**$9,075 ≥ product ≤ $15,150:** If the ***product is greater than or equal to $9,075 but also less than or equal to $15,150,*** then the debtor must conduct the ***secondary abuse test.***

a. The Secondary Abuse Test

The *secondary abuse test* requires the debtor to compare the product *with* 25% of the debtor's non-priority unsecured claims. [B.C. § 707(b)(2)(A)(i)(I)] If the product is *equal to or greater than 25%* of the debtor's non-priority unsecured claims, then the presumption of abuse arises. If the product is *less than 25%* of the debtor's non-priority unsecured claims, then the presumption of abuse does not arise.

Example: Danielle is an above-median income debtor with current monthly income of $4,000 and means test monthly expenses of $3,800, leaving $200 per month. Because $200 x 60 months is $12,000, which falls between $9,075 and $15,150, the secondary abuse test applies. If Danielle's non-priority unsecured debt equals $28,000, then 25% of that amount is $7,000. The presumption of abuse arises, because $12,000 > $7,000. Unless Danielle can rebut the presumption, she cannot file for relief under Chapter 7.

Example: Same facts as in the example above, except Danielle's non-priority unsecured claims equal $60,000; 25% of those claims equal $15,000. The presumption of abuse does not arise, because $12,000 < $15,000.

(i) Rationale

The *rationale of the secondary abuse test* is that if the debtor has enough money left over after paying monthly expenses to pay at least 25% of her unsecured claims, then the debtor should file for Chapter 13 (or Chapter 11) and make such payments over time to the debtor's non-priority unsecured creditors.

b. Means Test Expenses

(i) The Standards

The means test allows the debtor to deduct certain expenses based on *applicable national and local standards.* [B.C. § 707(b)(2)(A)(ii)(I)] Thus, regardless of the debtor's *actual* expense, the standard expense figure governs.

Example: Donna owns her home and spends approximately $400 per month for homeowners' insurance, maintenance, and home utilities. The local standards provide $450 for such expenses. Donna may deduct $450 from her current monthly income even though she actually pays only $400 per month.

Example: Duane owns his home and spends approximately $490 per month for homeowners' insurance, maintenance, and home utilities. The local standards provide $450 for such expenses. Duane may only deduct $450 from his current monthly income even though he actually pays $490 per month.

But, a debtor *may not deduct* the amount provided by the national or local standards if the debtor *does not incur* the expense covered by the standard.

Example: Daria owns a car that she paid off two years ago. The local standards provide for a standard ownership expense to cover loan or lease payments, and a standard operating expense to cover gas, insurance, and maintenance. Daria may deduct the standard operating expense from her current monthly income. However, she may not deduct the standard ownership expense, because she no longer makes loan payments on the car. [**Ransom v. FIA Card Services,** 562 U.S. 61 (2011)]

(ii) Secured Debt

The means test allows a debtor to deduct the ***actual amount*** that she pays on her ***secured debt*** *even if* the applicable national or local standard provides a smaller deduction. [B.C. § 707(b)(2)(A)(iii)] As a result, a debtor with high secured debt fares better under the means test than a similarly situated debtor who has been more cautious in her spending.

e.g. **Example:** Dahlia and Denise are both above-median income debtors with current monthly income of $4,500 per month. Dahlia lives in a large home with a monthly mortgage payment of $1,850. Denise's home is more modest; her monthly mortgage payment is only $1,500. Dahlia and Denise each have other monthly expenses of $2,600. Dahlia's means test expenses total to $4,450 ($2,600 + home ownership expense of $1,850). Thus, Dahlia passes the means test, because $50 x 60 months = $3,000, which is less than $9,075. Denise, on the other hand, fails the "means test," because her monthly expenses are only $4,100 ($2,600 + home ownership expense of $1,500), leaving her with $400 per month or $24,000 over 60 months, which far exceeds the $15,150 figure that triggers a presumption of abuse.

(iii) Other Necessary Expenses

A debtor also may deduct the ***actual cost*** of ***other necessary expenses,*** including amounts paid for ***federal, state,*** and ***local taxes, life insurance, alimony, child support,*** and ***child care.*** [B.C. § 707(b)(2)(A)(ii)(I); *see* Official Form 122A-2, lines 16–24]

(iv) Charitable Contributions

A debtor's monthly expenses may include ***charitable contributions to any qualified religious or charitable entity or organization.*** [B.C. § 707(b)(1); § 548(d)(3) & (4)]

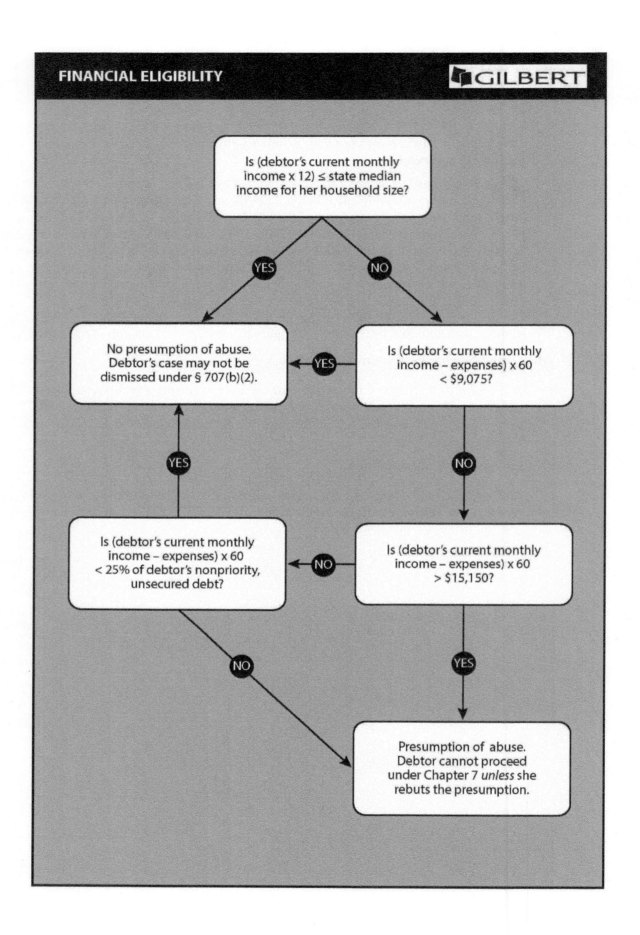

C. Distribution of Property of the Estate

1. Order of Payment

Claimants in a Chapter 7 case receive distribution according to the order prescribed by the Code.

a. Secured Creditors

If the Chapter 7 trustee has sold collateral that secures a claim, the secured creditor is paid from the sale proceeds before there is any distribution to priority or general unsecured creditors. The Chapter 7 trustee, however, does not work for the benefit of secured creditors. If the value of the secured claim exceeds that of the collateral, the trustee may abandon the property under § 554. The bankruptcy court also may have lifted the stay to allow a secured creditor to foreclose on the collateral. If property subject to a lien is not disposed of during the Chapter 7 case, such as by sale, abandonment, or allowing foreclosure by lifting the automatic stay, § 725 authorizes the bankruptcy court to dispose of the collateral by "return[ing] it to the proper secured creditor." [B.C. § 725; H.R. Rep. No. 95–595, at 382 (1977)] Thus, it is possible that the Chapter 7 trustee may sell no collateral during the case, even though there are secured creditors in debtor's case.

b. Priority Claims

Unsecured claims entitled to priority under § 507 are paid before any distribution to the general unsecured creditors and are paid in the order of priority provided by the Code. [*See* B.C. § 507; *see supra* Chapter Seven, § E] Timely filed claims or late-filed claims that are filed *on or before the earlier of* the date on which the trustee begins *final distribution or* the date that is *10 days after mailing of the trustee's final report* are the first unsecured claims paid out of any distribution made by the Chapter 7 trustee. [B.C. § 726(a)(1)] Such claims are paid in the following order:

(i) *administrative expenses of a trustee* to the extent that the trustee administers assets available for payment of *domestic support obligations* [B.C. § 507(a)(1)(C)];

(ii) *domestic support obligations* [B.C. § 507(a)(1)(A), (B)];

(iii) *administrative expenses* [B.C. § 507(a)(2)];

Note: A tardy claim for administrative expenses requires *court approval,* for cause, to be filed [B.C. § 503(a)].

(iv) *involuntary case gap claims* [B.C. § 507(a)(3)];

(v) *wages, salaries, or commissions* [B.C. § 507(a)(4)];

(vi) *contributions to employee benefit plans* [B.C. § 507(a)(5)];

(vii) *claims of grain farmers and United States fishermen* [B.C. § 507(a)(6)];

(viii) *consumer layaway claims* [B.C. § 507(a)(7)];

(ix) *unsecured pre-petition taxes* [B.C. § 507(a)(8)];

(x) *capital requirements of insured depository institutions* [B.C. § 507(a)(9)]; and

(xi) *claims for death or personal injury resulting from debtor's unlawful operation of a motor vehicle or vessel due to intoxication.* [B.C. § 507(a)(10)]

c. General Unsecured Claims

After satisfying all priority unsecured claims, the Chapter 7 trustee pays allowed unsecured claims that are **timely filed** and **justifiably late-filed** claims. [B.C. § 726(a)(2)] A late-filed claim will be paid second in the distribution scheme under § 726 if the creditor had **neither notice nor actual knowledge** of the case in time to file a claim on time and the creditor filed its claims in time to permit payment on the claim. [B.C. § 726(a)(2)(C)]

d. Unexcused Tardy Claims

Allowed claims filed late without justification are paid after all timely filed and justifiably late-filed claims. [B.C. § 726(a)(3)]

e. Penalty Claims

Next in the order of distribution are allowed unsecured or secured claims for **punitive, exemplary, or multiple damages,** or for **fines, penalties, or forfeitures** that do not constitute compensation for actual pecuniary loss. [B.C. § 726(a)(4)]

f. Interest

If there are sufficient funds to pay all of the allowed claims above, then the Chapter 7 trustee will pay interest, at the legal rate, that accrued from the date that the petition was filed on all priority and general unsecured claims paid pursuant to § 726(a)(1)–(4). [B.C. § 726(a)(5)]

g. Payment to Debtor

If there is any property of the estate left after payment of post-petition interest on the unsecured claims, it is distributed to the debtor. [B.C. § 726(a)(6)]

2. Pro Rata Payment

The general rule is that priority creditors **within a class** share equally in any distribution. Thus, within a priority class, there is no payment hierarchy.

e.g. **Example:** Debtor Corporation files a voluntary Chapter 7 petition. There are no secured creditors, and the general unsecured claims total $30,000. Administrative expenses are $5,000, and each of 10 employees of Debtor Corporation holds a fourth priority wage claim in the amount of $1,000. Unsecured pre-petition tax claims, with eighth priority status, total $20,000. If the amount available for distribution is $10,000, the administrative expenses will be paid in full ($5,000), and the 10 employees will receive $500 each. ($10,000 available − $5,000 administrative claims = $5,000/$10,000 wage claims = 50%; each creditor gets 50% of its $1,000 claim or $500.) The holders of the priority tax claims and the general unsecured claims will receive nothing. [B.C. § 726(b)]

a. Exceptions

There are several exceptions, however, to this general rule.

(i) Domestic Support Obligations

There is a hierarchy of payment among first priority domestic support obligation claims. The trustee, if she administers assets to pay a domestic support obligation, is paid first, then a spouse, former spouse, or child of the debtor with a domestic support obligation claim, and finally, a governmental unit with a domestic support obligation assigned to it by a spouse, former spouse, or child of the debtor. [B.C. § 507(a)(1)(A)–(C); *see supra* Chapter Seven, § E.2.a]

(ii) Conversion to Chapter 7

If a case is converted from Chapter 11, 12, or 13 to a case under Chapter 7, the administrative expense claims in the Chapter 7 case *after conversion* have priority over the administrative expenses incurred prior to conversion. [B.C. § 726(b)]

(iii) Super-Priority: Inadequately Protected Secured Creditor

If adequate protection is furnished under §§ 362, 363, or 364 to a creditor whose claim is secured by a lien on the debtor's property, but the adequate protection ultimately proves to be deficient, the creditor will receive an administrative expense claim with *priority over all other administrative expenses* allowed against the debtor's estate. [B.C. § 507(b)]

(iv) Super Super-Priority: Post-Petition Credit

If the trustee or the debtor in possession is unable to obtain unsecured post-petition credit by means of an administrative expense priority, the court may approve new credit or debt with priority over all other administrative expense claims, *including* any super-priority claims arising from the failure of adequate protection. [B.C. § 364(c)(1)]

3. Community Property

If any property of the estate constitutes community property or its proceeds, such property or proceeds must be segregated from other property of the estate. Special rules for distribution apply. For example, allowed claims for administrative expenses are to be paid either from the community property or from other property of the estate, as the interest of justice requires. [B.C. §§ 726(c), 541(a)(2)]

4. Exception: Subordination of Claims

The Chapter 7 payment hierarchy is subject to the Bankruptcy Code's provisions on subordination. Thus, a claim may be subordinated to a lower rank in the distribution if, for example, there is a subordination agreement or the principles of equitable subordination apply. [B.C. §§ 726(a), 510]

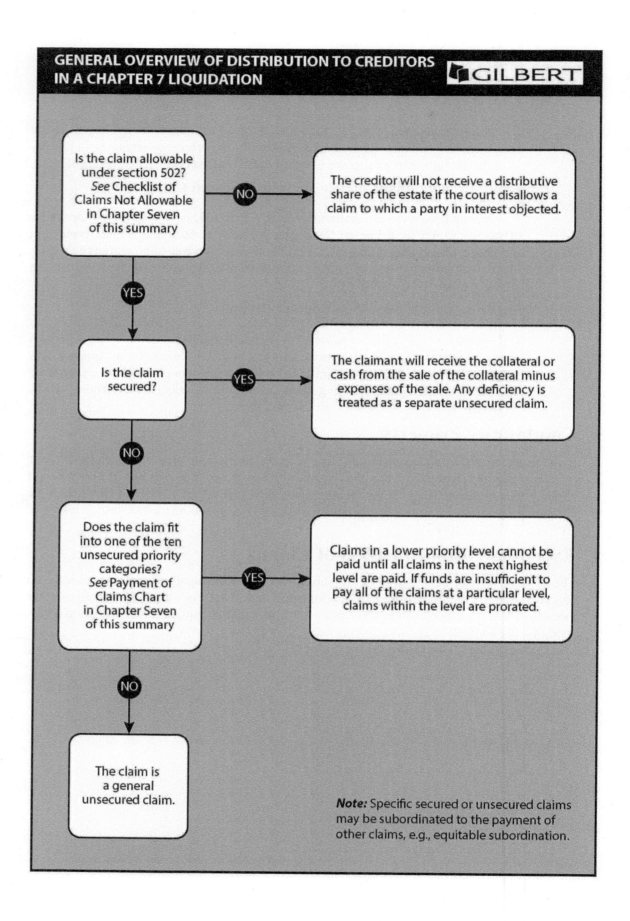

GENERAL OVERVIEW OF DISTRIBUTION TO CREDITORS IN A CHAPTER 7 LIQUIDATION

GILBERT

Is the claim allowable under section 502? *See* Checklist of Claims Not Allowable in Chapter Seven of this summary

NO → The creditor will not receive a distributive share of the estate if the court disallows a claim to which a party in interest objected.

YES ↓

Is the claim secured?

YES → The claimant will receive the collateral or cash from the sale of the collateral minus expenses of the sale. Any deficiency is treated as a separate unsecured claim.

NO ↓

Does the claim fit into one of the ten unsecured priority categories? *See* Payment of Claims Chart in Chapter Seven of this summary

YES → Claims in a lower priority level cannot be paid until all claims in the next highest level are paid. If funds are insufficient to pay all of the claims at a particular level, claims within the level are prorated.

NO ↓

The claim is a general unsecured claim.

Note: Specific secured or unsecured claims may be subordinated to the payment of other claims, e.g., equitable subordination.

D. Treatment of Certain Liens in a Chapter 7 Case

1. Avoidance of Liens Securing Penalties

The trustee may avoid a lien securing the type of claim described in § 726(a)(4) for a fine, penalty, or forfeiture, or for punitive, multiple, or exemplary damages that do not constitute compensation for actual pecuniary loss. [B.C. § 724(a)] "The purpose of § 724(a) is to protect unsecured creditors from the debtor's wrongdoing." [**Gill v. Kirresh (*In re* Gill),** 574 B.R. 709 (B.A.P. 9th Cir. 2017)] Paying a creditor that holds a lien on estate property for a penalty or fine does little to punish the debtor; instead, it is unsecured creditors, normally at the bottom of the distribution scheme, that will not be paid and, thus, bear the cost of the penalty or fine.

e.g. **Example:** Debtor files for relief under Chapter 7. Debtor's home is valued at $500,000. Bank has a first lien on the home and has filed a secured proof of claim for $370,000. The IRS has a second lien on the home in the amount of $161,000, of which $50,000 constitutes tax penalties. The Chapter 7 trustee sells the residence and pays off the first lien. The trustee, pursuant to § 724(a), avoids the penalty portion of the IRS lien; § 551 gives the trustee the right to preserve the avoided lien for the benefit of the unsecured creditors. [*See In re* **Gill,** *supra*]

2. Subordination of Tax Liens

The Code provides for the subordination of certain allowed tax claims that are secured by nonavoidable liens, e.g., a perfected tax lien, on estate property. [B.C. § 724(b)]

a. Exception for Ad Valorem Taxes

In 2005, Congress created an exception to § 724's subordination of tax liens for *ad valorem* tax liens. Section 724 adversely affected local governments' efforts to collect taxes. For example, "[m]any school boards obtain liens on real property to ensure collection of unpaid *ad valorem* taxes," but § 724's subordination rules meant that local governments, at times, could not collect the taxes, notwithstanding the presence of a lien. [H.R. Rep. No. 109–31, at 100 (2005)] Thus, the *general rule* is that the trustee cannot subordinate properly perfected unavoidable tax liens arising in connection with *ad valorem taxes.*

Congress, however, created an *exception to this exception for ad valorem taxes* at § 724(f). Thus, *ad valorem taxes can be subordinated* to pay for the following type of priority claims:

(i) wages, salaries, and commissions under § 507(a)(4); and

(ii) contributions to an employee benefit plan under § 507(a)(5).

[B.C. § 724(f)]

b. Exhaustion Requirement

In 2005, Congress added § 724(e) to ensure that the trustee exhausts other sources of funds to pay priority claimants *before* subordinating a tax lien. Therefore, before subordinating a tax lien, the *trustee must*

(i) exhaust the estate's *unencumbered assets;* and

(ii) consistent with § 506(c), recover from the property securing an allowed secured claim, the ***reasonable, necessary costs and expenses*** of preserving or disposing of the property.

[B.C. § 724(e)]

c. Distribution Scheme

Section 724 (b) does ***not*** apply if the tax lien can be avoided, for example as a preference. But if the tax lien is not avoidable, then § 724(b) provides that proceeds from sale of the property must be distributed in the following order:

(i) ***first,*** to any holder of an allowed claim ***secured by a nonavoidable lien*** on the property that is ***senior to the tax lien*** [B.C. § 724(b)(1)];

(ii) ***second,*** to ***the holders of any priority claims*** under § 507(a)(1)–(7), but the total distributions to the priority claimants ***must not exceed*** the amount of the allowed secured tax claim [B.C. § 724(b)(2)];

Note: The priority claimants entitled to distribution under § 724(b)(2) ***do not include*** eighth priority unsecured tax claims, ninth priority claims owed to federal depository institutions regulatory agencies, or tenth priority claims for death or personal injury resulting from intoxicated operation of a motor vehicle or vessel. [B.C. § 507(a)(8), (9) & (10)]

Exception: With one exception, of the priority claims for the administrative expenses of the trustee under § 507(a)(1)(C) or for administrative claims under § 507(a)(2), only those administrative claims incurred ***post-conversion to Chapter 7 from Chapter 11*** are included in this distribution. Thus, with the ***exception of post-petition, pre-conversion administrative claims for wages, salaries, or commissions***, the administrative expenses incurred in the Chapter 11 case prior to conversion do not participate in this distribution. [B.C. § 724(b)]

(iii) ***third,*** to ***the tax lienholder, but only*** to the extent that its allowed secured tax claim is ***greater*** than the total of all distributions made under § 724(b)(2) to priority claimants [B.C. § 724(b)(3)];

(iv) ***fourth,*** to the holder of an allowed claim secured by a nonavoidable lien on the property that is ***junior to the tax lien*** [B.C. § 724(b)(4)];

(v) ***fifth,*** to ***the tax lienholder*** to the extent that its allowed secured tax claim was ***not fully paid*** under § 724(b)(3). [B.C. § 724(b)(5)]; *and*

(vi) ***finally,*** to the ***Chapter 7 estate.*** [B.C. § 724(b)(6)]

e.g. **Example:** The Chapter 7 trustee sells nonexempt property and nets $50,000 in proceeds. The property is encumbered by the following nonavoidable liens: (1) an $8,000 first mortgage, senior to the tax lien; (2) a $14,000 tax lien; and (3) a $25,000 second mortgage. Priority claims for purposes of § 724(b)(2) total $13,000. (Assume the case was not converted from Chapter 11 to Chapter 7.) The proceeds will be distributed as follows:

(i) $8,000 to the first mortgage, leaving $42,000 of the original $50,000 in proceeds [B.C. § 724(b)(1)];

(ii) $13,000 to the unsecured priority creditors, leaving $29,000 [B.C. § 724(b)(2)];

(iii) $1,000 to the tax lienholder, leaving $28,000 [B.C. § 724(b)(3)];

Note: Section 724(b)(3) provides for distribution to the extent the tax lienholder's claim exceeds the distribution to priority claimants. The distribution to priority claimants was $13,000, and the tax lienholder's claim of $14,000 exceeds that amount by $1,000.

(iv) $25,000 to the second mortgage holder, leaving $3,000 [B.C. § 724(b)(4)]; and

(v) the remaining $3,000 to the tax lienholder. [B.C. § 724(b)(5)]

The other $10,000 of the $14,000 tax claim becomes an unsecured claim, which may be entitled to eighth priority status under § 507(a)(8). [Example modified from 6 Collier ¶ 724.03(5)(b)]

3. Multiple Claimants

Payment to more than one claimant within any particular level of distribution under § 724(b) is made in the order required under the Code outside of the provisions for the treatment of tax liens. [B.C. § 724(c)]

4. Similar Statutory Liens

Any statutory lien, e.g., an ERISA lien, whose priority is determined by the same method as that prescribed under 26 U.S.C. § 6323 for the priority of a tax lien, is treated under § 724(b) exactly like a tax lien, and is subordinated accordingly. [B.C. § 724(d); *see* H.R. Rep. No. 95–595, at 382 (1977) (stating that an example of such a lien "is the ERISA lien.")]

E. Partnership Trustee's Claim Against General Partners

1. Deficiency of Partnership Property

If the estate of a *Chapter 7 partnership debtor* lacks sufficient property to fully satisfy all claims against the partnership, the *trustee* is entitled to a claim for the *deficiency* against any general partner who is personally liable, but only to the extent that the general partner is personally liable under applicable nonbankruptcy law. [B.C. § 723(a)]

a. Nondebtor General Partners

In attempting to recover the deficiency, if practicable, the trustee must *first* pursue any general partner who is *not a debtor* in a bankruptcy case. Until the amount of the deficiency is determined, the court may require the partner to supply indemnity for or assurance of payment of any deficiency, or may enjoin the partner from disposing of property. [B.C. § 723(b)]

b. General Partners Who Are Debtors

The trustee has a claim against the *estate of each general partner who is a debtor* in a bankruptcy case *for the full amount of all claims* against the *partnership debtor.* The trustee's claim is entitled to distribution under § 726(a) the same as any other creditor of the general partner. [B.C. §§ 723(c), 726(c)]

(i) Disallowance of Claims of Partnership Creditors

A creditor's claim for which both the partnership debtor and a general partner are responsible will be *disallowed in the bankruptcy case of the general partner,* except to the extent that the claim is secured solely by the general partner's property and not by the partnership's assets. [B.C. § 723(c)]

2. Excess Recovery by Trustee

If the trustee in the partnership's bankruptcy case recovers from the general partners who are bankruptcy debtors an amount that *exceeds the deficiency* remaining after payment by the *nondebtor general partners under § 723(b)*, then the bankruptcy court, after notice and a hearing, must determine what is an *equitable distribution of the surplus* and the trustee must distribute the surplus to the bankruptcy estates of the general partners in the manner determined by the court. [B.C. § 723(d)]

F. Chapter 7 Discharge

1. In General

The bankruptcy court must grant the Chapter 7 debtor a discharge unless one of the 11 statutory grounds for denial of a Chapter 7 discharge applies. [B.C. § 727(a)] The statute contains a twelfth ground that appears to merely delay, not deny, the discharge. [B.C. § 727(a)(12)] The effect of the discharge is to discharge the debtor's personal liability on all debts that arose prior to the order for relief under Chapter 7, as well as from all debts that, under § 502, are treated as pre-petition debts. [B.C. §§ 727(b), 524(a)]

a. Exception: Nondischargeable Debts

The discharge does not include particular debts that are nondischargeable under § 523. [B.C. § 727(b)] It is important to distinguish between *a global denial of discharge* under § 727 and a determination under § 523 that a *specific debt is nondischargeable.* A *global denial of discharge* allows *all creditors* to pursue their claims post-bankruptcy. If a discharge is granted, however, only those creditors who are owed debts found to be nondischargeable under § 523 will be free to collect their claims post-bankruptcy.

2. Objection to Discharge

The Chapter 7 trustee, United States trustee, or a creditor may object to the debtor's discharge. [B.C. § 727(c)(1)] If a party in interest makes the request, the bankruptcy court may order the trustee to investigate the debtor's conduct to determine whether there is a basis for denying the discharge. [B.C. § 727(c)(2)]

3. Grounds for Denial of Discharge

The bankruptcy court may deny a discharge to a Chapter 7 debtor for any of the following reasons. [B.C. § 727(a)(1)–(12)]

a. Debtor Not an Individual

Under Chapter 7, only an individual may receive a discharge. Therefore, other persons, e.g., corporations and partnerships, are not granted a discharge. [B.C. § 727(a)(1)] The reason for the rule is to "avoid trafficking in corporate shells and in bankruptcy partnerships." [H.R. Rep. No. 95–595, at 384 (1977)] As a practical matter, however, if a corporation liquidates, there is no entity to pursue after liquidation of the firm in Chapter 7. In addition, the firm's owners generally are not responsible for the firm's pre-petition debts, unless they guaranteed or were co-signers on corporate obligations, or a creditor successfully pierces the corporate veil.

b. Transfer of Property with Intent to Hinder, Delay, or Defraud Creditors

The debtor will be denied a discharge if with the *intent to hinder, delay, or defraud* a creditor or an officer of the estate entitled to possession of the property, she transferred, removed, concealed, mutilated, or destroyed *property of the debtor,* within *one year* before the filing of the petition, or *property of the estate,* after the petition was filed. [B.C. § 727(a)(2)]

(i) Conversion of Nonexempt to Exempt Property on Eve of Bankruptcy

When Congress passed the Bankruptcy Reform Act of 1978, it made clear that pre-bankruptcy planning involving the conversion of non-exempt to exempt property "is not fraudulent as to creditors, and permits the debtor to make full use of the exemptions to which he is entitled under the law." [H.R. Rep. No. 95–595, at 380 (1977); S. Rep. No. 95–989, at 76 (1978)] Absent extrinsic evidence of fraud, the mere conversion of non-exempt to exempt property is not fraudulent. The question, however, is what constitutes extrinsic evidence of fraud. As the following two cases—handed down on the same day by the same Circuit—indicate, it is difficult to determine the line between acceptable pre-bankruptcy planning and improper conversion of assets that amounts to an intent to hinder, delay, or defraud creditors.

Example: Prior to filing for bankruptcy, Kenneth and Lucille Hanson ("Debtors") sold various pieces of non-exempt personal property. They undertook this course of action after having consulted an attorney. Debtors sold various vehicles to their son for fair market value. The son stored the vehicles on the Debtors' property while he lived with them. Debtors also sold household goods and furnishings to Kenneth's brother for fair market value. The brother stored these possessions at Debtors' home for some time because he lived out of state at the time of the sale. Debtors used the money from these sales to buy life insurance policies, which were exempt, and to prepay their mortgage, which they exempted as their homestead. In response to a creditor's objection to Debtors' exemptions, the bankruptcy court held that the Debtors' actions did not constitute extrinsic evidence of fraud. The district court affirmed and the Eighth Circuit affirmed, concluding that the bankruptcy court's decision to allow Debtors to claim their full exemptions was not clearly erroneous. The Eighth Circuit rejected creditor's argument that storage of the sold property at Debtors' home was a "badge of fraud." The court observed that the items were sold for fair market value and were not gifts. The court also noted that Debtors' son took out a loan to buy the vehicles, and subsequently sold one of them and kept the money for himself. [**Hanson v. First National Bank,** 848 F.2d 866 (8th Cir. 1988)]

Example: At the time that Dr. Tveten ("Debtor") filed for bankruptcy, he owed $19 million to several creditors because he had guaranteed debt for various real estate investments that had failed. Prior to filing for bankruptcy, Debtor sold almost all his non-exempt property for fair market value, and converted it into exempt property worth about $700,000. Debtor did so after having consulted with an attorney. Creditors objected to Debtor's discharge. The bankruptcy court denied Debtor a discharge, and the district court affirmed. The Eighth Circuit affirmed and held that the bankruptcy court's inference of fraudulent intent on Dr. Tveten's part was not clearly erroneous. The Eighth Circuit acknowledged that the standard governing the permissibility of exemptions and the standard for denial of discharge were the same—whether there is extrinsic evidence of fraud. The court noted, however, that in Dr. Tveten's case the state exemption was unlimited "with the potential for unlimited abuse." The court said that Dr. Tveten had liquidated almost all his property and converted it into exempt assets while owing his creditors $19 million. Doing so, according to the court, went "well beyond the purpose for which exemptions are permitted." The court acknowledged that Dr. Tveten was entitled to retain the property he had exempted, because state law governed the permissibility of his exemptions. But, federal law governed the question of whether he was entitled to a discharge. Allowing Dr. Tveten, "who earns over $60,000 annually, to convert all his major non-exempt assets into sheltered property on the eve of bankruptcy with actual intent to defraud his creditors 'would constitute a perversion of the purposes of the Bankruptcy Code.' " The court concluded by distinguishing the result in *Hanson* on the basis that the bankruptcy court in *Hanson* had found no extrinsic evidence of fraud. [**Norwest Bank Nebraska v. Tveten,** 848 F.2d 871 (8th Cir. 1988)]

Judge Arnold dissented in *Tveten* and wrote a concurring opinion in *Hanson* that criticized the court's deference to bankruptcy court findings premised on the amount of money involved. Judge Arnold noted that three things distinguished *Hanson* from *Tveten:* (1) Dr. Tveten was a doctor while the Hansons were farmers; (2) Dr. Tveten exempted $700,000 in property while the Hansons exempted $31,000; and (3) the state exemption Dr. Tveten used had no dollar limit while the state exemption used by the Hansons did. Judge Arnold noted that the Bankruptcy Code allows debtors to exempt property under state law without regard to whether the state exemption contains a monetary cap. Moreover, according to Judge Arnold, the amount of money at issue was irrelevant, because the state exemption statute had "no dollar limit, and for judges to set one involve[d] essentially a legislative decision not suitable for the judicial branch." [**Hanson v. First National Bank,** *supra*]

(ii) Bankruptcy Crimes

Bankruptcy fraud also may result in the conviction of a federal crime, the penalty for which is a fine, imprisonment for a maximum of five years, or both. [18 U.S.C. § 157]

c. Destruction or Concealment of Books or Records

The court may deny the debtor a discharge if she concealed, destroyed, mutilated, falsified, or failed to keep or preserve any recorded information, including books, records, documents, and papers from which her business transactions or financial state might be determined, unless the debtor's conduct or failure to act was *justified under the circumstances*. [B.C. § 727(a)(3)] Debtors do not have to keep books and records in any particular form, so long as the Chapter 7 trustee and creditors can figure out the reason for debtor's bankruptcy and understand debtor's financial condition. What is expected of a large corporation is not expected of a small business. The inquiry is a fact-intensive one. [6 Collier ¶ 727.03(3)]

d. Perjury, Bribery, Extortion, and Other Fraudulent Acts

The bankruptcy court also will deny a Chapter 7 debtor a discharge if she *knowingly and fraudulently* in or in connection with the bankruptcy case does any of the following:

(i) makes a false oath or account [B.C. § 727(a)(4)(A)];

(ii) submits or uses a false claim [B.C. § 727(a)(4)(B)];

(iii) gives, offers, receives, or attempts to obtain money, property, or advantage, or a promise of money, property or advantage for acting or forbearing to act, i.e., extortion or bribery [B.C. § 727(a)(4)(C)]; or

(iv) withholds from an officer of the estate entitled to possession any recorded information, including books, records, and papers, related to the debtor's property or financial affairs. [B.C. § 727(a)(4)(D)]

e. Failure to Account for Loss of Assets

Another basis for denial of the debtor's discharge is her failure to adequately explain any loss of assets or deficiency of assets to meet her liabilities. [B.C. § 727(a)(5)]

Example: Debtor settled a wrongful death suit with Creditors for $100,000. When Debtor subsequently filed for relief under Chapter 7, Creditors filed an adversary proceeding that, among other things, sought to deny Debtor a discharge under § 727(a)(5). As the basis for their § 727(a)(5) claim, Creditors argued that there was an "intentional and unexplained loss of value" in Debtor's residence, which Debtor valued at $390,000 in his bankruptcy schedules but which was worth $500,000, according to a valuation done four years earlier. The bankruptcy court granted summary judgment in favor of Debtor. The court concluded that there was "no evidence in the record that an actual loss occurred (requiring an explanation from the Debtor)." The court explained that a drop in value is not a " 'loss' of a tangible asset." [**Thomas v. Roberson (*In re Roberson*),** 2017 WL 2125807 (Bankr. D. V.I. 2017)]

f. Violation of Court Order or Refusal to Respond to Material Question

The court will deny the debtor a discharge if she refuses:

(i) to obey a valid court order, other than one directing the debtor to testify or to answer a material question [B.C. § 727(a)(6)(A)];

(ii) for a reason other than the Fifth Amendment privilege against self-incrimination, to testify or to answer a material question that the bankruptcy judge has approved [B.C. § 727(a)(6)(C)]; or

(iii) on the basis of the privilege against self-incrimination, to testify or to answer a judicially approved material question *after she has been granted immunity* regarding the matter on which privilege was invoked. [B.C. § 727(a)(6)(B)]

Example: State probate court appointed Debtor the guardian of various veterans' estates, and Creditor Corporation issued surety bonds in connection with the appointments. Debtor subsequently resigned as guardian when discrepancies were found in the guardianship accounts. The new guardians filed claims against Debtor, who then filed for relief under Chapter 7 with his wife. Creditor Corporation filed an adversary proceeding in Debtors' Chapter 7 case seeking a determination that the debts arising from the surety bonds were not dischargeable. While the adversary proceeding was pending, Debtors were indicted on various criminal charges stemming from the guardianships. Creditor Corporation then filed a motion to compel depositions, and Debtors responded with a motion to quash and for a protective order. The bankruptcy court directed Debtors to sit for the depositions, and Debtors invoked their privilege against self-incrimination. Debtors then filed an appeal of the bankruptcy court's decision and argued, in part, that the bankruptcy court had created a "Hobson's choice" of either having to invoke their Fifth Amendment right against self-incrimination or "suffer[ ] the effects of having an adverse inference drawn against them in the bankruptcy court." The district court, on appeal, affirmed the decision of the bankruptcy court. The district court explained that there was no error "in drawing an adverse inference against a civil litigant for invoking the right to remain silent" because the Fifth Amendment applies to criminal, not civil, proceedings. The bankruptcy court did not compel Debtors to testify, and Debtors invoked their Fifth Amendment right not to testify during the depositions. Thus, there was no risk that their testimony would be used against them in a future criminal proceeding. [**Phillips v. First National Insurance Co.,** 2011 WL 2447954 (S.D. Tex. 2011)]

g. **Acts Committed in Insider Case**

The bankruptcy court may deny the Chapter 7 debtor a discharge if the debtor commits any act described in § 727(a)(2)–(6), either during her bankruptcy case or within one year before the petition was filed, in connection with a separate bankruptcy case regarding an insider. [B.C. §§ 727(a)(7), 101(31)]

h. **Prior Discharge Obtained Under Chapter 7 or Chapter 11**

The bankruptcy court will deny a Chapter 7 debtor a discharge in her *current case* if she previously received a discharge in a Chapter 7 or a Chapter 11 case that was *commenced within eight years* before the date that the petition was filed in the current case. [B.C. § 727(a)(8)]

e.g. **Example:** Debtor filed for relief under Chapter 7 on June 3, 2010, and received a discharge on November 10, 2010. Debtor filed another Chapter 7 case on October 10, 2018. The court may not deny Debtor a discharge under § 727(a)(8), because she filed her *current* bankruptcy case more than eight years from the filing of her 2010 Chapter 7 case.

e.g. **Example:** Debtor filed for relief under Chapter 7 on October 10, 2017, and the bankruptcy court dismissed her case on November 15, 2017. The court did not dismiss Debtor's case under § 707(b). Debtor then filed another Chapter 7 case on December 15, 2017. Section 727(a)(8) does not apply, because Debtor did not receive a discharge in her prior case. Instead, the case was dismissed. But, Debtor may have problems with the automatic stay in her second Chapter 7 case. [B.C. § 362(c)(3)]

i. **Prior Discharge Obtained Under Chapter 12 or Chapter 13**

Similarly, the bankruptcy court will deny a Chapter 7 debtor a discharge if she previously was granted a discharge in a Chapter 12 or a Chapter 13 case that was *commenced within six years* before the date of the filing of the petition in the *current case, unless:*

(i) all of the allowed unsecured claims in the earlier case were *paid in full* [B.C. § 727(a)(9)(A)]; *or*

(ii) payments under the plan in the earlier case totaled *at least 70%* of the allowed unsecured claims, and the debtor's plan was *proposed in good faith and represented her best effort.* [B.C. § 727(a)(9)(B)]

EXAM TIP   **GILBERT**

It is important to remember that the six- or eight-year bar to discharge is measured from the date of the *bankruptcy petition,* not from the date of discharge, in the prior case to the date that the *petition* was filed in the current case.

---

j. **Waiver**

The debtor will not receive a discharge if the court approves a *written waiver of discharge* that she executes *after* the Chapter 7 order for relief. [B.C. § 727(a)(10)]

k. Failure to Complete Instructional Course

The debtor will be denied a discharge if post-petition she fails to complete an instructional course on personal financial management. [B.C. §§ 727(a)(11), 111] The failure to complete such a course is *not grounds* for denial of a discharge in *two situations*. The first is if the court determines, after notice and a hearing, that the debtor cannot complete such a course due to the debtor's *incapacity, disability, or active military service* in a military combat zone. [B.C. §§ 727(a)(11), 109(h)(4)] The second exception applies to debtors who live in a district for which the United States trustee or bankruptcy administrator, if applicable, has determined that the *approved courses are inadequate* to service the individuals who are required to take such courses. [B.C. § 727(a)(11)] BAPCPA added this ground for denial of discharge.

4. Delaying Entry of the Discharge

In 2005, Congress added a provision to the Code that says that the bankruptcy court shall not grant a Chapter 7 debtor a discharge if the court finds, after notice and a hearing held *no more than 10 days* before the entry of the discharge, that *reasonable cause* exists to believe either that *§ 522(q)(1) may apply* to the debtor's case *or* that there is a proceeding pending in which the debtor may be found guilty of a *felony listed in § 522(q)(1)(A)* or liable for a *debt described in § 522(q)(1)(B)*. [B.C. § 727(a)(12)] While the new provision is situated in the Code's denial-of-discharge section, the section appears to merely *delay, not deny, the debtor's discharge*. [*See* Bankruptcy Rule 4004(c)(1)(I) (the court may not grant a discharge if "a motion to delay or postpone the discharge under § 727(a)(12) is pending")]

🏳 GILBERT

CHECKLIST OF GROUNDS FOR DENYING A DISCHARGE IN A CHAPTER 7 CASE

THE FOLLOWING ARE GROUNDS FOR DENYING A DISCHARGE IN A CHAPTER 7 CASE:

- ☑ The debtor is *not an individual*

- ☑ The debtor *transferred, removed, concealed, mutilated, or destroyed his property* within a year before the petition, *or estate property* after the petition, with the *intent* to hinder, delay, or defraud a creditor or an officer of the estate

- ☑ The debtor *destroyed, concealed, mutilated, falsified, or failed to keep or preserve records or documents* concerning his business transactions and financial status, unless such conduct was justified

- ☑ The debtor knowingly and fraudulently, in or in connection with the case, made a *false oath or account* about a material issue, submitted a *false claim*, committed or attempted to commit *bribery or extortion*, or *withheld records or documents* pertinent to the debtor's property or financial affairs from an officer of the estate

- ☑ The debtor *failed to adequately explain any loss of assets* or deficiency of assets to meet liabilities

- ☑ The debtor *refused to obey a valid judicial order, or to testify* or answer a material question approved by the court other than on legitimate Fifth Amendment self-incrimination grounds

- ☑ The debtor *refused to testify or answer a material question* approved by the court on the ground of privilege against self-incrimination *after being granted immunity* with regard to the matter on which she invoked the privilege

☑ The debtor *committed any of the above acts in connection with a separate bankruptcy case regarding an insider* during or within a year before the debtor's case

☑ The debtor received a *discharge in a prior Chapter 7 or Chapter 11 case commenced within eight years before the date the petition was filed* in the present case

☑ Subject to two exceptions, the debtor received a *discharge in a prior Chapter 12 or Chapter 13 case commenced within six years before the date the petition was filed* in the present case

☑ The debtor executed a *court-approved written waiver* of discharge *after* the Chapter 7 order for relief

☑ Subject to two exceptions, the debtor *failed to complete a post-petition instruction course on personal financial management*

5. Revocation of Discharge

The bankruptcy court, upon request of a creditor, the Chapter 7 trustee, or the United States trustee and after notice and a hearing, must *revoke the debtor's discharge* if the debtor:

a. *obtained the discharge fraudulently,* and the party seeking revocation did not know of the fraud until after the discharge was granted [B.C. § 727(d)(1)];

b. *acquired property* that is property of the estate *or became entitled to acquire property* that would constitute property of the estate, and she *knowingly and fraudulently* failed to disclose this fact or to turn over the property to the trustee [B.C. § 727(d)(2)];

c. *committed one of the acts* described in § 727(a)(6) [B.C. § 727(d)(3)]; or

d. *failed to satisfactorily explain* (i) *a material misstatement* in an *audit* referred to in 28 U.S.C. § 586(f) *or* (ii) a *failure to make available for inspection* accounts, documents, financial records, papers, files and all other papers, things, or property belonging to the debtor that are requested for *the audit* referred to in 28 U.S.C. § 586(f). [B.C. § 727(d)(4)] Congress added this subsection to the Code in 2005.

6. Limitations Period for Discharge Revocation

The Chapter 7 trustee, a creditor, or the United States trustee must request revocation of the debtor's discharge under § 727(d)(1) within *one year* after the granting of the discharge. [B.C. § 727(e)(1)] A request under § 727(d)(2) or (d)(3) must be filed within *one year* after granting of the discharge or prior to the date that the *case is closed*, whichever is later. [B.C. § 727(e)(2)] BAPCPA added another ground for revocation of the debtor's discharge based on the debtor's failure to satisfactorily explain either (i) material misstatements in an audit or (ii) the debtor's failure to make various records available for inspection for an audit. [B.C. § 727(d)(4); 28 U.S.C. § 586(f)] Congress, however, did not amend § 727(e) to provide a limitations period for bringing a revocation of discharge proceeding under § 727(d)(4). As a result, there is no limitations period in the Code for bringing revocation of discharge proceedings related to the new audit language contained at § 727(d)(4).

G. Conversion

1. Voluntary Conversion

If a Chapter 7 case has not been converted from Chapter 11, 12, or 13, the debtor may convert the case from Chapter 7 to any of such other chapters at any time. [B.C. § 706(a)] The Supreme

Court in **Marrama v. Citizens Bank,** 549 U.S. 365 (2007) concluded that a Chapter 7 debtor who engages in fraudulent conduct does not have an absolute right to convert to Chapter 13.

Example: Debtor filed for relief under Chapter 7. Seven months prior to filing for bankruptcy, Debtor transferred a house in Maine, his principal asset, into a trust, for no consideration, in an effort to protect the property from his creditors. Debtor also made a number of "misleading or inaccurate" statements about the Maine home in his schedules. After the § 341 meeting, the Chapter 7 trustee informed Debtor's counsel that he intended to recover the property in Maine as an estate asset. Debtor then moved to convert his case to Chapter 13. The trustee objected, claiming that Debtor had tried to conceal the Maine property from creditors and that Debtor's motion to convert was made in bad faith. The bankruptcy court denied Debtor's request to convert. Both the First Circuit's Bankruptcy Appellate Panel and the First Circuit affirmed, while rejecting Debtor's argument that he had an absolute right to convert his case from Chapter 7 to Chapter 13. The Supreme Court affirmed the judgment of the First Circuit. The Court explained that the vast majority of "honest but unfortunate debtors [ ] possess an absolute right to convert their cases from Chapter 7 to Chapter 13." But nothing in § 706's text limits the bankruptcy court's authority to take appropriate action to address a debtor's fraudulent conduct. In dictum, the Court explained that a bankruptcy court's "broad authority" under § 105 to take any action to "prevent an abuse of process" was certainly "adequate to authorize an immediate denial of a motion to convert under § 706 in lieu of a conversion order that merely postpones the allowance of equivalent relief and may provide the debtor with an opportunity to take action prejudicial to creditors." [**Marrama**, *supra; see also supra* Chapter Two, § B.1 on § 105, *Marrama,* and the Supreme Court's later decision in *Law v. Siegel*]

2. Involuntary Conversion

Unless the debtor requests or consents to conversion, the court may ***not*** convert a Chapter 7 case to one under Chapter 12 or 13. [B.C. § 706(c)] However, the court may convert a Chapter 7 case to one under Chapter 11, upon a request by a party in interest, after notice and a hearing. [B.C. § 706(b)]

3. Eligibility

Conversion of a Chapter 7 case to another chapter of the Code requires that the debtor be eligible for relief under the particular chapter to which the case is being converted. [B.C. § 706(d)]

4. Means Test

If an ***individual Chapter 7 debtor with primarily consumer debts*** fails the "means test," then a presumption of abuse arises. In such a case, after notice and a hearing, the court, on its own motion or a motion by the Chapter 7 trustee, the United States trustee, the Bankruptcy Administrator in North Carolina or Alabama cases, or any party in interest, may dismiss or convert the debtor's case. The court may only convert the case to Chapter 11 or 13 with the debtor's consent. [B.C. § 707(b)(1)]

H. Dismissal

1. For Cause

After notice and a hearing, the court may dismiss a Chapter 7 case for ***cause,*** which includes the following circumstances:

a. ***the debtor is responsible for an unreasonable delay that is prejudicial to creditors*** [B.C. § 707(a)(1)];

b. ***the debtor has not paid fees or charges*** prescribed by chapter 123 of title 28 [B.C. § 707(a)(2)]; or

c. ***the debtor in a voluntary case has not filed a list of creditors and all schedules and statements*** required under § 521(a)(1) within ***15 days,*** or any extension granted by the court, after the petition was filed. [B.C. § 707(a)(3)]

Note: Only the United States trustee may move for dismissal under § 707(a)(3).

2. Abuse of Chapter 7

a. Means Test

If an ***individual Chapter 7 debtor with primarily consumer debts*** fails the "means test," then a presumption of abuse arises. In such a case, after notice and a hearing, the court, on its own motion or a motion by the Chapter 7 trustee, the United States trustee, the Bankruptcy Administrator in North Carolina or Alabama cases, or any party in interest, may dismiss the debtor's case or, with the debtor's consent, convert the case to Chapter 11 or Chapter 13. [B.C. § 707(b)(1), (2)]

b. Bad Faith or Totality of the Circumstances

In determining whether the filing of a Chapter 7 case ***by an individual debtor with primarily consumer debts*** in which the presumption of abuse either does not arise or is rebutted ***nonetheless constitutes abuse***, the court must consider:

(i) whether the debtor ***filed*** the petition in ***bad faith; or***

(ii) whether the ***totality of the circumstances of debtor's financial situation*** demonstrates abuse. The Code specifically includes as part of the evaluation of debtor's circumstances whether debtor plans to reject a personal services contract and the financial need for such rejection. [B.C. § 707(b)(3)]

Important: Section 707(b)(3) applies to cases in which the ***presumption of abuse*** does not arise, e.g., below-median income debtor, or has been ***rebutted.***

(i) Criteria: Totality of the Circumstances

Courts use a number of criteria to determine whether the individual debtor's filing for relief under Chapter 7 is an abuse. Courts examine some of the following factors in evaluating whether debtor's filing was an abuse under the totality of the circumstances:

(1) the debtor's ***reason for filing*** the Chapter 7 petition, e.g., because of ***unemployment, medical expenses, disability, or other misfortune;***

(2) the ***excessiveness or extravagance*** of the debtor's ***anticipated family budget;***

(3) the extent to which the debtor's ***statements and schedules accurately represent*** her actual financial condition;

(4) debtor's efforts to ***repay her debts or negotiate with creditors;***

(5) the availability of ***nonbankruptcy remedies;***

(6) whether debtor is ***eligible to file for relief under Chapter 13;*** and

(7) whether debtor's ***expenses*** can be ***reduced significantly without depriving*** her or her dependents of ***necessities.***

[*See, e.g.,* **DeAngelis v. Gearhart (*In re* Gearhart),** 2010 WL 4866179 (Bankr. M.D. Penn. 2010); *In re* **Cribbs,** 387 B.R. 324 (Bankr. S.D. Ga. 2008)]

c.   **Charitable Contributions**

In making its determination whether to dismiss a Chapter 7 case for abuse, the bankruptcy court *may not consider* the debtor's *charitable contributions* to any qualified religious or charitable entity or organization. [B.C. §§ 707(b)(1), 548(d)(3), (4)]

3. Crimes of Violence

The bankruptcy court may dismiss the case of an individual Chapter 7 debtor who has been convicted of a crime of violence or a drug trafficking crime if the victim of such crime moves for dismissal and the court determines that dismissal is in the best interest of the crime victim. Dismissal may occur only after notice and a hearing. [B.C. § 707(c)(2)] The court may not dismiss the case, however, if filing is necessary to satisfy a domestic support obligation. [B.C. § 707(c)(3)] A "crime of violence" is defined at 18 U.S.C. § 16, and a "drug trafficking crime" is defined at 18 U.S.C. § 924(c)(2). [B.C. § 707(c)(1); 18 U.S.C. §§ 16, 924(c)(2)] Congress added this provision to the Code in 2005 with the passage of BAPCPA.

Chapter Thirteen

Bankruptcy Code Chapter 11: Reorganization

CONTENTS

Chapter Approach

Chapter 11 is thought of as the *business reorganization* chapter, but it is limited to neither businesses nor reorganization. The Supreme Court has held that individual consumer debtors may file for relief under Chapter 11. In addition, a business may use Chapter 11 to liquidate instead of reorganize. Instead of filing a plan of reorganization, the debtor files a liquidating plan. In order to correctly answer an exam question about Chapter 11, you first must determine the *type of debtor* involved. Is the Chapter 11 debtor an *individual*? A *small business debtor*? Did the debtor *elect to proceed under subchapter V*? Or, is the Chapter 11 debtor an artificial entity that is not a small business debtor and did not elect subchapter V? Identifying the type of debtor is critical, because the Code's rules on appointment of a trustee, creation of an official unsecured creditors' committee, the existence and length of the debtor's exclusivity period, the need for the debtor to file a disclosure statement, and the rules on plan confirmation, including cram down, depend on the nature of the entity that filed for relief under Chapter 11. *See* the table immediately below for a summary of key differences among the types of debtors.

In Chapter 11, the debtor continues to manage its business as a *debtor in possession* and, with the *exception of a subchapter V* case, there is *no trustee*. The bankruptcy court may appoint a trustee in a non-subchapter V case for *cause,* such as the misconduct or incompetence of management, or because appointment is in the interests of creditors, equity security holders, and the estate. In a *small business case* and a *subchapter V case,* an official committee of unsecured creditors is not appointed unless the court for cause orders otherwise.

If your professor asks you to evaluate a *reorganization plan,* pay careful attention to the manner in which *claims are classified.* Make sure that the proposed plan includes the Code's *mandatory provisions.* A plan proponent may, but is not required to, include any number of the Code's *discretionary* provisions, tailoring the plan to the debtor's needs. Pay attention to the debtor's *exclusivity period* and any *"drop dead" dates* by which a plan must be proposed and/or confirmed. These time periods vary based on the type of Chapter 11 debtor involved. *See* the table below.

In evaluating whether the bankruptcy court can confirm a proposed plan of reorganization, start with the Code's *requirements for confirmation of a consent plan.* Doing so requires you to understand which classes of claims or interests must vote on the plan, what constitutes *impairment* of a class of claims or interests, and the votes necessary for an impaired class to *accept or reject* the plan. Pay attention to whether the case involves an *individual debtor* because there is an additional requirement for a consent plan if an *unsecured creditor* objects to plan confirmation. You also must understand how to apply the Code's *cram down* provisions, including the *absolute priority rule.* Keep in mind that the courts disagree about how the *absolute priority rule* operates in *individual* Chapter 11 cases. Understand how the *narrow and broad* interpretations of the rule work in such cases. Pay attention to whether the exam question involves a *subchapter V case* because the Code's normal *cram down rules do not apply.* Instead, *subchapter V* has its own rules on when the bankruptcy court can confirm a plan in which an *impaired class* (or classes) has rejected the plan, and the absolute priority rule does not apply.

A unique feature of Chapter 11 is the *§ 1111(b) election.* An undersecured creditor may *elect to have her entire claim treated as secured,* but at the cost of forfeiting an unsecured claim for a deficiency. The election is available in any Chapter 11 case. Your professor may ask you to evaluate whether a creditor should invoke the § 1111(b) election. In answering the question, consider: (i) the dividend the plan proposes to pay to the *unsecured creditors,* (ii) whether the plan proposes to *cash out* the secured creditor at the value of her collateral, (iii) whether confirmation will involve application of the Code's *cram down* provisions with respect to the secured creditor, and (iv) whether her *collateral is likely to appreciate or depreciate* in value.

As of the writing of this guide, there are *three groups of Chapter 11 debtors:* (1) *non-small business debtors*; (2) *small business debtors* that do *not elect subchapter V*; and (3) debtors that *elect subchapter V,* including small business debtors that make the election. Keep in mind that an *individual debtor* may fall into any one of these three categories.

Note: The debt limit for subchapter V cases currently is $7.5 million. The $7.5 million debt limit is in effect, as of the writing of this guide, until *June 21, 2024,* at which point, if Congress fails to act, the definition of a debtor under subchapter V will *revert to the definition of a small business debtor at § 101(51D).* In other words, subchapter V then will be open *only* to small business debtors.

The following table summarizes some of the differences among the *three groups* of Chapter 11 debtors:

CHAPTER 11 DEBTORS			GILBERT
	COLUMN I: **NON-SMALL BUSINESS** **AND NON-SUBCHAPTER** **V DEBTOR**	**COLUMN II:** **SMALL BUSINESS** **DEBTOR DOES NOT** **ELECT SUBCHAPTER V**	**COLUMN III:** **SUBCHAPTER V** **DEBTOR**
ELIGIBILITY: **DEBT LIMITS**	None	Aggregate noncontingent liquidated debts of $3,024,725 or less	Aggregate noncontingent liquidated debts of $7,500,000 or less **Note:** $7.5M until June 21, 2024
TRUSTEE	Normally, no trustee	Normally, no trustee	Yes
OFFICIAL COMMITTEE **OF UNSECURED** **CREDITORS**	Yes	Only if court for cause orders appointment	Only if court for cause orders appointment
DISCLOSURE **STATEMENT**	Yes	Depends on rules at § 1125(f)	Only if court for cause orders and then § 1125(f) applies
WHO MAY FILE PLAN?	Debtor has *exclusive* right to file plan for 120 days from order for relief	Debtor has *exclusive* right to file plan for 180 days from order for relief	Only the debtor
WHEN MUST PLAN BE **FILED?**	No particular time limit	No later than 300 days after order for relief	No later than 90 days after order for relief
ABSOLUTE PRIORITY **RULE (APR)**	Applies, but if debtor is an individual there is narrow and broad interpretation of APR	Applies, but if debtor is an individual there is a narrow and broad interpretation of APR	Does not apply

A. Eligibility for Relief

1. In General

Relief under Chapter 11 is available to *any person*—individual, corporation, or partnership—who *qualifies to be a debtor under Chapter 7,* except for a stockbroker or a commodity broker.

In addition, *railroads are eligible* for relief under special provisions of Chapter 11. [B.C. § 109(d)] Railroad reorganization, however, is a topic beyond the scope of this book.

2. Business or Consumer Debtors

Chapter 11 is designed primarily for *business reorganizations.* However, the Supreme Court has held that a consumer debtor, i.e., an individual not engaged in business, may qualify for relief under this chapter. [**Toibb v. Radloff,** 501 U.S. 157 (1991)]

B. Administration of Chapter 11 Case

1. Creditors' Committees

The Bankruptcy Code provides that shortly after the order for relief, the United States trustee shall appoint a committee of unsecured creditors, usually consisting of those *persons,* willing to serve, that hold the *seven largest unsecured claims* against the debtor. [B.C. § 1102(a)(1), (b)(1)] While the Code uses the term "shall," it is not unusual for the United States trustee to be unable to find creditors willing to serve on the unsecured creditors' committee. Thus, in many Chapter 11 cases, there is no official committee of unsecured creditors.

Note: Unless the bankruptcy court for cause orders otherwise, an official committee of unsecured creditors is *not appointed* in a *small business case or a subchapter V case.* [B.C. § 1102(a)(3)]

a. List of Creditors

The debtor is required to file a list of the creditors holding the 20 largest unsecured claims, excluding insiders. In a voluntary case, the list must be filed with the petition; in an involuntary case, it must be filed within two days after the entry of the order for relief. [Bankruptcy Rule 1007(d); Official Forms 104 (individuals), 204 (non-individuals)]

b. Membership on Creditors' Committee

Membership on a creditors' committee is not limited to individuals; other persons holding large unsecured claims may be appointed.

(i) Certain Governmental Units

Generally, governmental units are excluded from the definition of the term *person.* [*See* B.C. § 101(41)] For purposes of eligibility to serve on a Chapter 11 creditors' committee, however, "person" includes a governmental unit that:

(1) acquires an asset as a result of a loan guarantee agreement, or as a receiver or liquidating agent of a person, such as the FDIC or Resolution Trust Corporation [B.C. § 101(41)(A)];

(2) is a *guarantor* of pension benefits, e.g., the Pension Benefit Guaranty Corporation, payable by or for the debtor or an affiliate [B.C. § 101(41)(B)]; or

(3) is the *legal or beneficial owner of an asset* of (i) an employee pension plan that is a governmental plan, such as a state employee pension fund, or (ii) an eligible deferred compensation plan. [B.C. § 101(41)(C)]

(ii) Pre-Petition Committee

A creditors' committee may consist of the members of a committee created before the petition was filed if the committee was *fairly chosen* and exemplifies the types of claims to be represented. [B.C. § 1102(b)(1); Bankruptcy Rule 2007(b)]

c.   Additional Committees

The bankruptcy court, upon the request of a party in interest, may order the appointment of additional committees of creditors or equity security holders. The United States trustee appoints the committee. [B.C. § 1102(a)(2)] If the United States trustee deems it appropriate, she also may appoint additional committees of creditors or equity security holders to ensure adequate representation. [B.C. § 1102(a)(1)]

(i) Equity Security Holders

If a committee of equity security holders is appointed, it usually will consist of the seven largest holders, in amount, of the type of equity securities represented by the committee. [B.C. § 1102(b)(2)] Unless the court orders otherwise, the debtor must file a list of equity security holders of each class of equity security holders *within 14 days* after the entry of the order for relief. [Bankruptcy Rule 1007(a)(3)]

d.   Change in Committee Composition

Upon the request of a party in interest and after notice and a hearing, the bankruptcy court may order the United States trustee to *change the composition* of a creditors' or equity security holders' committee, because the court has determined that a change is needed in order to *ensure adequate representation.* The court may order the United States trustee to increase the size of a committee in order *to add a creditor that is a small business debtor,* as that term is defined in the Small Business Act. [15 U.S.C. § 632(a)(1)] The court may order the addition of a small business debtor to a committee if such debtor holds claims of the kind represented by the committee and the *aggregate amount of those claims is disproportionately large in relation to the annual gross revenue of the small business.* [B.C. § 1102(a)(4)] Congress added this provision to the Code in 2005 with the passage of BAPCPA.

e.   Mandatory Duties

A creditors' committee or equity security holders' committee must provide *access to information* to creditors who are not appointed to the committee but who hold claims of the type represented by the committee. [B.C. § 1102(b)(3)(A)] The committee also must *solicit and receive comments* from such creditors, and is subject to a court order compelling the committee to make any *additional report or disclosure* to such creditors. [B.C. § 1102(b)(3)(B), (C)] Congress added these duties to the Code in 2005.

f.   Powers and Discretionary Duties

A creditors' committee or an equity security holders' committee may engage in any of the following activities during a Chapter 11 case:

(i)   *consult with the debtor in possession* or with the trustee, if one has been appointed [B.C. § 1103(c)(1)];

(ii) *investigate the debtor's conduct, financial condition, assets and liabilities, business operations,* the *desirability of continuing* the debtor's business, and other matters pertinent to the case and to formulation of a plan [B.C. § 1103(c)(2)];

(iii) *participate in the preparation of a reorganization plan* [B.C. § 1103(c)(3)];

(iv) *advise the creditors or equity security holders* it represents of the committee's judgment or conclusions concerning any plan formulated [B.C. § 1103(c)(3)];

(v) *collect and file acceptances or rejections of a plan* [B.C. § 1103(c)(3)];

(vi) *if appropriate, request the appointment of a trustee or an examiner* [B.C. § 1103(c)(4)]; and

(vii) *render any other services* for the benefit of the creditors or equity security holders represented by the committee. [B.C. § 1103(c)(5)]

g. Employment of Attorneys or Accountants

A creditors' committee or an equity security holders' committee may hire attorneys, accountants, or other professionals to represent or perform services for the committee. The committee's hiring decision must be made at a scheduled meeting attended by a *majority of the committee members* and *court approval* is required. [B.C. § 1103(a)]

(i) Limitation: No Adverse Interest

An attorney or an accountant hired by a creditors' committee or an equity security holders' committee is prohibited from representing, during the period of her employment, any entity possessing an adverse interest in connection with the case. The representation of a creditor of the same class as the committee represents is not automatically deemed representation of an adverse interest. [B.C. § 1103(b)]

(ii) Prior Approval

It is important that a lawyer or an accountant employed by a creditors' committee or an equity security holders' committee make certain that she obtains court approval *before* rendering services, because, in many jurisdictions, a court will not retroactively grant approval absent extraordinary or exceptional circumstances.

2. Debtor in Possession

In a non-subchapter V case, unless a trustee is appointed in the case, the debtor in possession remains in possession of the property of the estate and continues to operate its business. The debtor in possession has all of the rights, powers, and duties of a trustee, *except* the right to compensation and the duty to investigate the debtor. [B.C. §§ 1101(1), 1107(a)] While there is a trustee in a *subchapter V case*, the debtor nonetheless is a *debtor in possession*. [B.C. § 1182(2)] Unless removed by the court as a debtor in possession, the subchapter V debtor continues to operate the business and has all of the rights, powers, and duties of a trustee, *except* the right to compensation and the duty to investigate the debtor. [B.C. §§ 1184, 1185]

a. Business Judgment

Because the debtor is familiar with its business and the industry, the courts will defer to the exercise of the debtor in possession's business judgment absent a showing that the decision is so manifestly unreasonable that the debtor in possession was not exercising sound business judgment but instead was acting in bad faith or on a whim. [*See, e.g., In re* **9 Houston LLC,** 578 B.R. 600 (Bankr. S.D. Tex. 2017) (in context of dispute over whether a part of the estate's sole asset should be sold pursuant to the debtor in possession's emergency motion or pursuant to a plan of reorganization); *In re* **SW Boston Hotel Venture, LLC,** 2010 WL 3396863 (Bankr. D. Mass. 2010) (in context of motion by debtor in possession under § 363 to approve the lease of condo units owned by debtor)]

b. Employment of Professionals

Any attorney, accountant, or other professional employed by the debtor in possession must be a **_disinterested_** person and cannot hold or represent any interest that is **_adverse_** to the estate. [B.C. §§ 101(14), 327(a)] A professional person is not disqualified from employment **_solely_** because she was employed by or represented the debtor prior to commencement of the bankruptcy case. [B.C. § 1107(b)] **_Section 1107_** of the Code does **_not apply to a subchapter V_** case. Instead, **_§ 1195_** of the Code provides the relevant rule. A person is not disqualified for employment under § 327 by a debtor that **_elects subchapter V solely_** because that person holds a pre-petition **_claim of less than $10,000_**. [B.C. § 1195]

3. Appointment of Trustee

The rules on appointment of a trustee differ for **_subchapter V versus non-subchapter V_** cases. In **_subchapter V,_** a trustee is appointed. [B.C. § 1183] Nonetheless, the debtor is a debtor in possession. [B.C. § 1182(2)] As debtor in possession, the subchapter V debtor continues to **_operate its business_** after filing of the petition. [B.C. § 1184] On request of a party in interest and after notice and hearing, the bankruptcy court may remove the debtor as debtor in possession. [B.C. § 1185] *See infra* § H of this Chapter on subchapter V.

Note: The remainder of this subsection 3 Appointment of Trustee provides the rules for cases **_not filed_** under **_subchapter V_**.

The debtor in possession usually is considered the most appropriate person to operate its business. Thus, it is well settled that appointment of a trustee is the exception, not the rule. [**_In re_ Eurospark Industries,** 424 B.R. 621 (Bankr. E.D. N.Y. 2010)] In fact, there is a presumption that the debtor should be allowed to remain in possession unless the need for a trustee is shown. [**_In re_ China Fishery Group, Ltd.,** 2016 WL 6875903 (Bankr. S.D. N.Y. 2016)] Nonetheless, after the filing of the petition and prior to confirmation of a plan, a party in interest or the United States trustee may request the appointment of a trustee. The bankruptcy court, after notice and a hearing, may order the appointment of a trustee (i) **_for cause,_** (ii) if the appointment is in the interests of creditors, equity security holders, and other interests of the estate, or (iii) if the bankruptcy court determines it is in the **_best interests_** of the creditors and the estate to appoint a trustee rather than **_convert or dismiss_** the case. [B.C. §§ 1104(a), 1112(b)] The party requesting appointment of a trustee has the burden of proving grounds for such appointment. Many courts require that the party requesting appointment of a trustee prove by **_clear and convincing evidence_** that cause exists under § 1104(a)(1) or the need for a trustee under § 1104(a)(2). *See, e.g.,* **_In re_ Ashley River Consulting, LLC,** 2015 WL 1540941 (Bankr. S.D. N.Y. 2015); **_In re_ LHC, LLC,** 497 B.R. 281 (Bankr. N.D. Ill. 2013); **_In re_ Adelphia Communications Corp.,** 336 B.R. 610 (Bankr. S.D. N.Y. 2006), *aff'd,* 342 B.R. 122 (S.D. N.Y. 2006). Some courts, however, use a preponderance of the evidence standard. *See, e.g.,* **_In re_ Costa Bonita Beach Resort,** 479 B.R. 14 (Bankr. D. P.R. 2012).

a. Cause for Appointment

Cause for appointment of a Chapter 11 trustee includes **_fraud, dishonesty, incompetence, or gross mismanagement,_** by current management, either before or after the filing of the bankruptcy case. [B.C. § 1104(a)(1)] The court, however, is not limited to fraud, dishonesty, incompetence, or gross mismanagement in establishing cause. While there is no one definitive list, courts have examined some of the following additional factors in making the "cause" determination:

(i) whether the debtor treated **_insiders and affiliates better or worse_** than its **_customers and creditors;_**

(ii) whether management's *conflicts of interest* interfered with its ability to satisfy its fiduciary obligations to the debtor;

(iii) whether management *misused or squandered assets and funds;*

(iv) whether management *lacked credibility* and had *lost creditor confidence*; and

(v) whether the misconduct alleged was *material.*

[*See, e.g., In re* **Ashley River Consulting, LLC,** *supra; In re* **LHC, LLC,** *supra*]

b.   Interests of the Estate

The Code provides that the court shall appoint a trustee if appointment is in the interests of creditors, equity security holders, and other interests of the estate. [B.C. § 1104(a)(2)] Some of the factors that courts examine in making a decision whether to appoint a trustee pursuant to § 1104(a)(2) include the following:

(i)   debtor's *trustworthiness;*

(ii) the *past and current performance* of the debtor;

(iii) the *prospects* for debtor's reorganization;

(iv) the business community's and creditors' *confidence in current management;* and

(v) the *benefits* of appointing a trustee weighed against the *costs* of doing so.

[*See, e.g., In re* **Ashley River Consulting, LLC,** *supra; In re* **Celeritas Technologies, LLC,** 446 B.R. 514 (Bankr. D. Kan. 2011)]

c.   Alternative to Conversion or Dismissal

If cause exists to dismiss the case or to convert it to Chapter 7, a bankruptcy court may appoint a Chapter 11 trustee or examiner instead, if doing so is in the *best interests of creditors and the estate.* [B.C. § 1112(b)(1)]

d.   Mandatory Motion by United States Trustee

The United States trustee must move for the appointment of a Chapter 11 trustee if there are *reasonable grounds to suspect* that current members of the governing body of the debtor, e.g., the board of directors, the chief executive officer, or the chief financial officer, or members of the governing body who selected the CEO or CFO participated in *actual fraud, dishonesty, or criminal conduct* in managing the debtor or the debtor's public financial reporting. [B.C. § 1104(e)] While the United States trustee must file a motion for appointment under such circumstances, the bankruptcy court is not required to appoint a Chapter 11 trustee.

e.   Choosing a Trustee

If the court orders the appointment of a trustee, generally the United States trustee consults with parties in interest and then *appoints* a *disinterested person*, other than himself, subject to the court's approval. [B.C. § 1104(d)] Alternatively, in cases other than railroad reorganizations, the Code provides for *election* of the trustee if a party in interest requests an election within *30 days after the court orders appointment* of a trustee. The election is held at a meeting of creditors convened by the United States trustee and is conducted in the same manner as the election of a trustee under Chapter 7. [B.C. §§ 1104(b)(1), 702] If an eligible, disinterested person is elected at a meeting of creditors, then the United States trustee must file a report certifying the election.[B.C. § 1104(b)(2)(A)] In cases in which an eligible, disinterested person is elected to serve as trustee after the United States trustee has appointed a trustee through consultation, the

United States trustee's filing of the report certifying the election terminates the service of the trustee appointed by the United States trustee. [B.C. § 1104(b)(2)(B); *see* Bankruptcy Rule 2007.1]

f. Duties of Trustee

The duties of a Chapter 11 trustee include many of the same duties performed by a Chapter 7 trustee, as well as several additional obligations. The Chapter 11 trustee's duties include the following:

(i) *to account for all property received* [B.C. §§ 1106(a)(1), 704(a)(2)];

(ii) *to examine proofs of claims* and object to the allowance of any improper ones [B.C. §§ 1106(a)(1), 704(a)(5)];

(iii) *to provide information requested by parties in interest* about the estate and the administration of the estate [B.C. §§ 1106(a)(1), 704(a)(7)];

(iv) *to file periodic financial reports,* including a statement of receipts and disbursements, with the court, the United States trustee, and the appropriate taxing authorities [B.C. §§ 1106(a)(1), 704(a)(8)];

(v) *to prepare and file* with the court and with the United States trustee *a final report and account* concerning the case [B.C. §§ 1106(a)(1), 704(a)(9)];

(vi) *to provide* the notice required by § 704(c) for creditors holding *domestic support obligation claims* [B.C. §§ 1106(a)(1), (8), 704(a)(10)];

(vii) *to continue to perform* the obligations of an administrator of an *employee benefit plan,* if at the start of the Chapter 11 case the debtor or an entity designated by the debtor served that function [B.C. §§ 1106(a)(1), 704(a)(11); 29 U.S.C. § 1002];

(viii) *to use reasonable and best efforts* to transfer patients to an appropriate health care business if the debtor is a *health care business* in the process of closing [B.C. §§ 1106(a)(1), 704(a)(12)];

(ix) *to file any document required* under § 521(a)(1), e.g., list of creditors, schedule of assets and liabilities, that the debtor has not filed [B.C. §§ 1106(a)(2), 521(a)(1)];

(x) *to investigate the debtor's conduct, financial condition, and business operations,* as well as *the advisability of continuing the debtor's business* [B.C. § 1106(a)(3)];

(xi) *to file a report of the investigation* conducted under § 1106(a)(3), relating any facts evidencing fraud, dishonesty, incompetence, misconduct, mismanagement, or irregularity in the management of the debtor's affairs, and to send a *copy of the findings* to any creditors' committee, equity security holders' committee, indenture trustee, or any other entity designated by the bankruptcy court [B.C. § 1106(a)(4)];

(xii) as soon as practicable, *to file a Chapter 11 plan, file a report* as to why the trustee will not file a plan, or *recommend conversion or dismissal* of the case [B.C. § 1106(a)(5)];

(xiii) *to provide available information to the taxing authorities* concerning any year for which the debtor failed to file a return [B.C. § 1106(a)(6)]; and

(xiv) *after a plan has been confirmed, to file any necessary or court-ordered reports.* [B.C. § 1106(a)(7)]

g. Authority to Operate Business

A trustee who is appointed in a Chapter 11 case is authorized to manage the debtor's business, unless the court rules otherwise. [B.C. § 1108] "If a trustee is appointed, the management is completely ousted, although occasionally a trustee hires former management to handle day-to-day operations." [H.R. Rep. No. 95–595, at 220 (1977)] As a consequence, the trustee replaces the debtor's directors, and they must surrender the corporation's property to the trustee. [*See* **Commodity Futures Trading Commission v. Weintraub,** 471 U.S. 343 (1985)]

h. Termination of Trustee's Appointment

The bankruptcy court may terminate the trustee's appointment at any time before a plan is confirmed. Any party in interest or the United States trustee may make such a request. If the bankruptcy court terminates the Chapter 11 trustee's appointment, after notice and a hearing, the court restores the debtor to possession and management of the estate property and of the operation of the debtor's business. [B.C. § 1105]

4. Appointment of Examiner

In a Chapter 11 case in which the court has not ordered the appointment of a trustee, the court sometimes will order the appointment of an examiner, prior to confirmation of a plan, *to investigate* any charges of fraud, dishonesty, incompetence, misconduct, mismanagement, or irregularity in managing the debtor's affairs by the debtor's present or former management. The appointment is made by the United States trustee, who selects a disinterested person other than himself. The debtor in possession, however, retains the estate property and continues to operate the business. [B.C. § 1104(c), (d)] The Code's provisions on appointment and duties of an examiner do *not apply* in a *subchapter V case*.

a. Reasons for Appointment

When the appointment of an examiner is requested by a party in interest or the United States trustee, the court, after notice and a hearing, *must order* that an examiner be appointed if the debtor's fixed, liquidated, unsecured debts exceed $5 million, excluding debts for goods, services, or taxes, and any debts owed to an insider. [B.C. § 1104(c)(2); **Loral Stockholders Protective Committee v. Loral Space & Communications, Ltd.** (*In re* **Loral Space & Communications, Ltd.**), 2004 WL 2979785 (S.D. N.Y. 2004) (stating that § 1104(c)(2) "mandates the appointment of an examiner where a party in interest moves for an examiner and the debtor has $5,000,000 of qualifying debt")] The purpose of § 1104(c)(2) is to give the shareholders of public firms "extra protection" by providing a mechanism for oversight by an independent person. [*See In re* **Loral,** *supra*] The court will also order the appointment of an examiner if the appointment is in the *best interests* of creditors, any equity security holders, and other interests of the estate. [B.C. § 1104(c)(1)]

b. Duties of Examiner

An examiner's duties include the following:

- **(i)** *to investigate the debtor's conduct, financial condition, assets and liabilities, and business operations, the advisability of continuing the debtor's business,* and other matters pertinent to the case and to formulation of a plan [B.C. § 1106(b), (a)(3)];

- **(ii)** *to file a report of the investigation,* relating any facts evidencing fraud, dishonesty, incompetence, misconduct, mismanagement, or irregularity in the management of debtor's affairs, and to send a *copy of the findings* to any creditors' committee, equity security holders' committee, indenture trustee, or other entities designated by the court [B.C. § 1106(b), (a)(4)]; and

(iii) to perform *any other responsibilities of a trustee* that the judge directs the debtor in possession not to perform. [B.C. § 1106(b)]

5. Right to Be Heard

The *Securities and Exchange Commission* may raise, and may appear and be heard on, any issue in a Chapter 11 case. The SEC, however, may not appeal from any judgment, order, or decree entered in the case. [B.C. § 1109(a)] While the Commission may not initiate an appeal, it may join or participate in one brought by a true party in interest. [H.R. Rep. No. 95–595, at 404 (1977)] A *party in interest* also may appear and be heard on any issue in a Chapter 11 case. A party in interest includes but is not limited to the debtor, the trustee, a creditors' committee, an equity security holders' committee, or an indenture trustee. Others asserting the status of a party in interest are determined on a case-by-case basis. [B.C. § 1109(b); **Seraphin v. Morris Publishing Group LLC (*In re* Morris Publishing Group LLC),** 2010 WL 599393 (Bankr. S.D. Ga. 2010) (denying motion of newspaper readers and subscribers to intervene and object to confirmation of plan of debtor newspaper group, because readers and subscribers had "no standing to object as parties in interest" and failed to show cause to allow them to intervene)]

a. Intervention in Adversary Proceeding

There is a split of authority as to whether a party in interest, which includes an unsecured creditors' committee, may intervene as of right in an adversary proceeding. [Bankruptcy Rule 7024] Some courts hold that a party in interest has an absolute right to intervene, because § 1109(b) provides the right to be heard "on any issue" in a Chapter 11 case. [5 Norton § 100.3; B.C. § 1109(b)] Other courts examine various factors, including whether existing parties can adequately represent the interest of the party seeking intervention, in ruling on a motion to intervene in an adversary proceeding. [*See, e.g.,* **United Methodist Publishing House Inc. v. Family Christian LLC (*In re* Family Christian LLC),** 530 B.R. 417 (Bankr. W.D. Mich. 2015) (denying motion of official creditors' committee to intervene as of right, after analyzing four-element test established by the Sixth Circuit); *see also* 5 Norton § 100.3 (distinguishing between "Bankruptcy Rule 2018 [which] deals only with general matters within a 'case' [and] 'adversary proceedings [which] are separately governed under Bankruptcy Rule 7024")]

6. Claims and Interests

The filing of proofs of claims or interests and the allowance of secured claims are accorded special treatment in a Chapter 11 case. [B.C. § 1111]

a. Proofs of Claims or Interests

In a Chapter 11 case, the court fixes and sends notice of a *bar date* that operates as a deadline for filing proofs of claims or interests. A claim or interest that is listed in the schedules filed by the debtor is deemed filed, for the scheduled amount, unless it is scheduled as disputed, contingent, or unliquidated. [B.C. § 1111(a); Bankruptcy Rule 3003(b), (c)] Therefore, in a Chapter 11 case, the holder of a correctly scheduled, undisputed, noncontingent, liquidated claim or interest is not required to file a proof of claim or a proof of interest.

b. Secured Claims

In a Chapter 11 case, both recourse and nonrecourse secured claims are treated as recourse claims for the purpose of allowance. [B.C. § 1111(b)(1)(A)] Thus, while an undersecured creditor holding a nonrecourse claim, either under an agreement or under applicable nonbankruptcy law, ordinarily cannot assert a deficiency claim for the portion of her claim exceeding the value of the collateral, the creditor is given recourse status under Chapter 11, with the effect being that the unsecured part of the claim will not be disallowed under Bankruptcy Code § 502(b)(1). [**Bank of America National Trust & Savings Association v. 203 N. LaSalle St. Partnership,** 526 U.S. 434 (1999) (stating in a footnote that § 1111(b) "provides that nonrecourse secured creditors who are undersecured must be treated in Chapter 11 as if they had recourse")]

Note: Outside of bankruptcy, if a claim is recourse, the creditor has a right to seek a personal judgment against the debtor for any deficiency; if a claim is nonrecourse, there is no such right. [*See* **203 N. LaSalle,** *supra* (stating in a footnote that "[a] nonrecourse loan requires the [creditor] to look only to the Debtor's collateral for payment")]

e.g. **Example:** Creditor holds a $500,000 claim secured by a first mortgage on Blackacre, which is valued at $400,000. The agreement between Creditor and Debtor provides that Creditor's claim is nonrecourse. Debtor files a Chapter 11 bankruptcy petition. Under § 1111(b)(1)(A), Creditor's claim is treated as if it were a recourse claim, and, thus, the $100,000 deficiency is allowed as a general unsecured claim. Of course, Creditor also holds an allowed secured claim in the amount of $400,000. [B.C. § 506(a)]

Note: Absent this provision, the unsecured portion of Creditor's claim would not be allowable under § 502(b)(1) because of its nonrecourse character. [*See In re* **Greenland Vistas, Inc.,** 33 B.R. 366 (Bankr. E.D. Mich. 1983) (stating that "an undersecured nonrecourse creditor may assert a deficiency claim under the Bankruptcy Code" unless it makes the § 1111(b)(2) election or the property is sold under § 363 or under the plan)]

(i) Exceptions to Conversion of Non-Recourse into Recourse Claims

There are a few situations in which a claim is *not* treated as if the holder has recourse, thus barring any unsecured claim for a deficiency:

(1) *if the creditor does not have recourse* and the *property is sold* either under Bankruptcy Code § 363 or under the plan of reorganization [B.C. § 1111(b)(1)(A)(ii)];

(2) *if the creditor does not have recourse* and, during the case (i) the *collateral is abandoned or is returned* to the secured creditor, or (ii) the *secured party forecloses* on the property after having been granted relief from the automatic stay [*See, e.g.,* **Mastan v. Salamon (*In re* Salamon),** 854 F.3d 632 (9th Cir. 2017) (holding that junior non-recourse lien was eliminated as a result of non-judicial foreclosure sale and, thus, § 1111(b) did not apply); *In re* **Union Meeting Partners,** 160 B.R. 757 (Bankr. E.D. Penn. 1993) (holding that because non-recourse creditor received property securing its lien, it received benefit of its bargain with debtor and, thus, was not "entitled to an unsecured deficiency claim under § 1111(b) in addition")]; or

Note: Section 1111(b)(1)(A)(ii) does not include abandonment, return of the property, or foreclosure after a lift of the stay, but these situations are similar to a § 363 sale. "In each of these cases, the secured creditor receives what it bargained for: the collateral if the debtor does not pay the debt." [7 Collier ¶ 1111.03(2)(a)]

(3) ***if the class to which the claim belongs makes the § 1111(b) election*** by at least two-thirds in amount and more than half in number of allowed claims in the class. [B.C. § 1111(b)(1)(A)(i)] ***Note:*** Usually, each secured claim is placed alone in a separate class.

c. Section 1111(b) Election

A partially secured creditor may elect to have her claim in a Chapter 11 case treated as ***secured to the full extent that the claim is allowed,*** even though under § 506(a) it otherwise would be considered secured only up to the value of the collateral. [B.C. § 1111(b)(2)] The 1111(b) election protects both the recourse and non-recourse secured creditor. It provides two benefits to the undersecured creditor whose property the debtor decides to retain, not sell. First, if the property is not sold, then any valuation "is speculative since the property will not have been exposed to the market." [5 Norton § 102:2] Second, the creditor, not the debtor, "capture[s] any future appreciation of the property securing the creditor's claim." [5 Norton § 102:2] Thus, the election protects the undersecured creditor from being "cashed out" at a time when real property prices are depressed.

Example #1: Debtor owes $500,000 to Creditor pursuant to a nonrecourse loan secured by a first mortgage on Blackacre, which has a fair market value of $400,000. Creditor's claim is classified in a separate class from the other claims in the case, and Creditor makes the election, under § 1111(b), to have her entire $500,000 claim treated as secured. Subsequently, Debtor defaults on payments to Creditor under the confirmed reorganization plan at a time when Blackacre has *appreciated in value* to $500,000. In this instance, the effect of the election will be to enable Creditor to recover the full amount of her claim.

Example #2: Assume the same facts as above, except that Creditor does ***not*** make the § 1111(b) election. Following Debtor's default, a third-party bidder pays $500,000 for Blackacre at the foreclosure sale. Since Creditor's allowed secured claim was $400,000, the surplus of $100,000 will go to Debtor's estate. Creditor's recovery will be limited to $400,000, plus whatever percentage she is entitled to under the plan on her unsecured claim for a deficiency.

(i) Exceptions: Creditor Cannot Make § 1111(b) Election

Creditors cannot make the § 1111(b) election under either of the following circumstances:

(1) ***if the creditor's interest in the property is of inconsequential value,*** as in the case of a low priority junior lien that would bring minimal or zero recovery at foreclosure [B.C. § 1111(b)(1)(B)(i)]; or

(2) ***if the creditor has recourse and the collateral is sold*** under § 363 or under the plan. [B.C. § 1111(b)(1)(B)(ii)] As with the exception for sales pursuant to § 363 or the plan for non-recourse claims, the sale permits the creditor to credit bid under § 363(k), for example, and thereby preserve the benefit of its bargain with the debtor. [7 Collier ¶ 1111.03(2)(a), (3)(b); *see **In re* Red Mountain Machinery Company,** 451 B.R. 897 (Bankr. D. Ariz. 2011) (stating that purpose of § 1111(b) "to protect an undersecured creditor's interest in future appreciation of the collateral is unnecessary where the creditor has already purchased the collateral by a credit bid")]

(ii) Waiver of Deficiency Claim

If the § 1111(b) election is made, the secured party forfeits her unsecured claim for any deficiency and also loses the opportunity to affect the decision of the unsecured class to accept or reject the reorganization plan. [B.C. § 1111(b)(2); *see* Bankruptcy Rule 3018(d) (stating that a creditor "whose claim has been allowed in part as a secured claim and in part as an unsecured claim shall be entitled to accept or reject a plan in both capacities")]

(iii) Preventing a Cash out

An undersecured creditor may make the § 1111(b) election when the debtor's plan proposes no payment to the unsecured creditors and the electing creditor wants to prevent a cash out for the value of her collateral. The creditor who elects § 1111(b) has her claim treated as a secured claim to the extent it is allowed. In other words, when the creditor elects § 1111(b), "the total amount owed is the allowed claim." *In re* **Griffiths**, 27 B.R. 873 (Bankr. D. Kan. 1983). Thus, paying the under-secured creditor who elects § 1111(b) *the value of her collateral* deprives that creditor of the total amount of her claim and the benefit of the § 1111(b) election. [B.C. § 1111(b)(2); *see, e.g., In re* **Griffiths**, *supra*]

(iv) Cram down

If a secured creditor making the § 1111(b) election rejects the proposed Chapter 11 plan, confirmation can be obtained under the Code's "cram down" provisions if the plan, in addition to providing for the creditor's retention of her lien, proposes to pay the electing creditor deferred cash payments that equal at least the *full dollar amount* of her allowed claim and that have a *present value,* as of the effective date of the plan, of at least the value of the collateral. [B.C. § 1129(b)(2)(A)(i)]

e.g. **Example:** Creditor loans Debtor $500,000, secured by a first mortgage on Blackacre, which at the time of the loan had a value of $600,000. Debtor defaults and then files a Chapter 11 petition. Blackacre has depreciated and is worth $400,000, and Creditor makes the § 1111(b) election. The proposed plan provides for Creditor to retain her lien on Blackacre and to receive deferred cash payments on her claim. Creditor rejects the plan. For the plan to be confirmed over Creditor's rejection, the proposed payments must total (face amount) at least $500,000 and must have a present value, as of the effective date of the plan, of at least $400,000. [B.C. § 1129(b)(2)(A)(i)]

(v) Time of Election

A creditor may make the § 1111(b) election at any time before the *end of the hearing on the disclosure statement* or within a later time set by the court. [Bankruptcy Rule 3014] If the court conditionally approves but does not conduct a final hearing on the disclosure statement, the creditor must make the § 1111(b) election *no later than the time set for filing objections to the disclosure statement* or some other time set by the bankruptcy court. [Bankruptcy Rules 3014, 3017.1(a)(2)] In a *subchapter V* case in which there is no disclosure statement, the bankruptcy court sets the date by which the creditor must make the § 1111(b) election. [Bankruptcy Rule 3014]

If your exam question involves an undersecured creditor, it is important to remember the **§ 1111(b) election,** which is unique to Chapter 11, whereby the creditor may elect to have her claim treated as **fully secured,** instead of being bifurcated into two claims—a secured claim up to the value of the collateral, and an unsecured claim for the balance. This election may prove beneficial to the creditor if the collateral is appreciating in value. The tradeoff is that the creditor forfeits her unsecured claim for any deficiency, e.g., if the collateral does not increase in value, and her corresponding vote in the relevant unsecured class.

7. Conversion or Dismissal

In appropriate circumstances, the bankruptcy court may order dismissal or conversion to another chapter of a Chapter 11 case. The debtor must be eligible to file for relief under the chapter to which her Chapter 11 case is converted. [B.C. § 1112] In BAPCPA, Congress made substantial changes to the Code's rules on conversion or dismissal of a Chapter 11 case.

a. Voluntary Conversion to Chapter 7

The debtor may convert a Chapter 11 case to Chapter 7 *unless*

(i) the debtor is *not* a debtor in possession [B.C. § 1112(a)(1)];

(ii) the case began with the filing of an involuntary Chapter 11 petition [B.C. § 1112(a)(2)]; or

(iii) the case was involuntarily converted to Chapter 11, i.e., on the request of an entity other than the debtor. [B.C. § 1112(a)(3)]

b. Mandatory Conversion to Chapter 7 or Dismissal

With certain exceptions, the bankruptcy court, upon request of a party in interest, must dismiss a Chapter 11 case or convert it to Chapter 7, whichever is *in the best interests of* creditors and the estate, if the party in interest *establishes "cause"* for dismissal or conversion. Notice and a hearing are required. [B.C. § 1112(b)(1)] Prior to the passage of BAPCPA, dismissal or conversion was within the court's discretion. In 2005, however, Congress changed the language of § 1112(b) from "may" to "shall," thereby making dismissal or conversion mandatory, absent some exception, upon a party in interest establishing cause.

(i) "Cause" for Dismissal or Conversion

If a party in interest establishes cause for dismissal or conversion of a Chapter 11 case and none of the relevant exceptions are satisfied, then the bankruptcy court must dismiss the case or convert it to Chapter 7. The Code lists *16 reasons*—a substantial expansion post-BAPCPA—as *cause* for dismissal or conversion. The list, however, is not exhaustive and a party in interest may raise and the court may find other cause to dismiss or convert the debtor's Chapter 11 case. The following are the 16 reasons that Congress provided in § 1112(b)(4):

(1) *substantial or continuing loss to or diminution of the estate* and the absence of a *reasonable likelihood of rehabilitation* [B.C. § 1112(b)(4)(A)];

(2) *gross mismanagement of the estate* [B.C. § 1112(b)(4)(B)];

(3) *failure to maintain appropriate insurance* that poses a *risk to the estate or to the public* [B.C. § 1112(b)(4)(C)];

(4) *unauthorized use of cash collateral* that *substantially harms* one or more creditors [B.C. § 1112(b)(4)(D)];

(5) *failure to comply with a court order* [B.C. § 1112(b)(4)(E)];

(6) *unexcused failure* to satisfy in a timely fashion any *filing or reporting requirement* [B.C. § 1112(b)(4)(F)];

(7) *failure* of the debtor without good cause to *attend the § 341 meeting* or a *Rule 2004 examination* [B.C. § 1112(b)(4)(G)];

(8) *failure of the debtor to provide information in a timely fashion or to attend meetings* reasonably requested by the United States trustee or bankruptcy administrator [B.C. § 1112(b)(4)(H)];

(9) *failure to timely pay taxes or to file tax returns* owed or due after the order for relief [B.C. § 1112(b)(4)(I)];

(10) *failure to file a disclosure statement, or to file or confirm a plan* within the time provided by the Bankruptcy Code or order of the bankruptcy court [B.C. § 1112(b)(4)(J)];

(11) *failure to pay any necessary fees or charges* imposed under chapter 123 of title 28 [B.C. § 1112(b)(4)(K)];

(12) *revocation of an order of confirmation* [B.C. § 1112(b)(4)(L)];

(13) *inability to substantially consummate a confirmed plan* [B.C. § 1112(b)(4)(M)];

(14) *material default* by the debtor with regard to *a confirmed plan* [B.C. § 1112(b)(4)(N)];

(15) *termination of a plan by reason of a condition contained in the plan* [B.C. § 1112(b)(4)(O)]; or

(16) *failure* of the debtor to *pay any domestic support obligation* that first becomes payable after filing of the petition. [B.C. § 1112(b)(4)(P)]

(1) Note on Language

Section 1112(b)(4) uses the word "includes;" thus, the list of reasons provided is not exhaustive. [B.C. § 102(3)] For example, in a voluntary case and upon request of the United States trustee, the court may dismiss or convert a Chapter 11 case to a case under Chapter 7 because of the *debtor's failure to file the information* required by § 521(a)(1), including a list of the creditors holding the 20 largest unsecured claims with their amounts, within *15 days* after the filing of the Chapter 11 petition. [B.C. § 1112(e)]

(ii) Exceptions to Mandatory Dismissal or Conversion

If the party in interest moving for dismissal or conversion of a Chapter 11 case establishes cause, the bankruptcy court is not required to dismiss or convert in certain situations.

(1) Unusual Circumstances

The court may not dismiss or convert the Chapter 11 case if it specifically identifies *unusual circumstances* that establish that dismissal or conversion is *not in the best interests of creditors and the estate* and the debtor or other party in interest establishes *all of the following*:

(a) there is a *reasonable likelihood* that a plan of reorganization will be *confirmed* for a *small business case* within the time frames established §§ 1121(e) and 1129(e), or *within a reasonable time period* if those sections do not apply to the case [B.C. §§ 1112(b)(2)(A), 1121(e), 1129(e)];

(b) "cause" for dismissal or conversion is an act or omission *other than substantial or continuing loss to or diminution of the estate and absence of a reasonable likelihood of rehabilitation* [B.C. § 1112(b)(2)(B), 1112(b)(4)(A)]; *and*

(c) there is a *reasonable justification* for the debtor's act or omission and that act or omission will be *cured within a reasonable period of time established by the court.* [B.C. § 1112(b)(2)(B)(i), (ii)]

Congress did not define what constitutes "unusual circumstances," but some courts have found that the term means " 'conditions that are not common in most chapter 11 cases.' " [*In re* **Wallace**, 2010 WL 378351 (Bankr. D. Idaho 2010), *aff'd*, 2011 WL 1230535 (D. Idaho 2011)]

e.g. **Example:** Debtor filed for relief under Chapter 11 and filed a plan of reorganization, dependent upon a significant infusion of capital, to pay all creditors in full on the plan's effective date. Creditors filed a motion to dismiss or convert Debtor's Chapter 11 case, and the bankruptcy court found that cause existed to dismiss or convert. The bankruptcy court held, however, that neither dismissal nor conversion was in the best interests of creditors and the estate. The court concluded that a plan that would pay creditors in full on the plan's effective date was "an unusual circumstance sufficient to deny conversion or dismissal even in the face of demonstrated cause." [*In re* **Orbit Petroleum, Inc.,** 395 B.R. 145 (Bankr. D. N.M. 2008)]

c. Farmers and Nonbusiness Corporations

If the debtor is a farmer or a nonbusiness corporation, the bankruptcy court may not convert the case to Chapter 7 unless the debtor requests the conversion. [B.C. § 1112(b)(1), (c)]

d. Appointment of Chapter 11 Trustee or Examiner

Even if grounds exist to dismiss or convert a Chapter 11 case, the bankruptcy court may determine that it is in the *best interests of creditors and the estate* to order the appointment of a trustee or examiner rather than order the dismissal or conversion of the case. [B.C. §§ 1112(b)(1), 1104(a)(2)]

e. Structured Dismissals

A structured dismissal is a *"hybrid dismissal and confirmation order"* in which the bankruptcy court dismisses the Chapter 11 case "while, among other things, approving certain distributions to creditors, granting certain third party releases, enjoining certain conduct by creditors, and not necessarily vacating orders or unwinding transactions undertaken during the case." [American Bankruptcy Institute Commission to Study the Reform of Chapter 11, 2012–2014 Final Report and Recommendations 270 (2014)] There is nothing in the Bankruptcy Code that specifically authorizes a structured dismissal, yet they are not uncommon. In **Czyzewski v. Jevic Holding Corporation,** 580 U.S. 451 (2017), the Supreme Court imposed a limitation on the use of structured dismissals. The Court held that without the consent of the affected parties, a bankruptcy court, as part of its dismissal order, cannot authorize a distribution scheme that "deviate[s] from the basic priority rules that apply under the primary mechanisms the Code establishes for final distributions of estate value in business bankruptcies."

f. Conversion to Chapter 12 or 13

The court may convert a Chapter 11 case to a Chapter 12 or 13 case *only if:*

(i) *the debtor requests the conversion* [B.C. § 1112(d)(1)];

(ii) *the debtor has not received a Chapter 11 discharge* [B.C. §§ 1112(d)(2), 1141(d)]; *and*

(iii) if the debtor requests *conversion to Chapter 12,* the court finds that conversion is *equitable.* [B.C. § 1112(d)(3)]

C. Rejection of Collective Bargaining Agreements

1. Introduction

Congress added § 1113 on rejection of collective bargaining agreements to the Code with the passage of the Bankruptcy Amendments and Federal Judgeship Act of 1984. Section 1113 is a response to the Supreme Court's decision in **National Labor Relations Board v. Bildisco & Bildisco,** 465 U.S. 513 (1984). A debtor in possession or Chapter 11 trustee that wants to reject a collective bargaining agreement must follow the requirements set forth at § 1113, not those governing rejection of executory contracts under § 365. [B.C. § 1113(a)]

2. Prerequisites for Rejection

Court approval of an application to reject a collective bargaining agreement requires satisfaction of a number of statutory conditions. *After filing* of the Chapter 11 petition and *before* the filing of the application to reject, the debtor must satisfy all of the following requirements.

a. The debtor must make a *proposal to the union to modify* the collective bargaining agreement. [B.C. § 1113(b)(1)(A)]

b. The proposal must be *based on the most complete and reliable information* available at the time of the proposal. [B.C. § 1113(b)(1)(A)]

c. The proposed *modifications must be necessary* to permit the reorganization of the debtor. [B.C. § 1113(b)(1)(A)]

d. The proposed modifications must treat *all of the affected parties fairly and equitably.* [B.C. § 1113(b)(1)(A)]

e. The debtor must *provide to the union such relevant information as is necessary to evaluate* the proposal. [B.C. § 1113(b)(1)(B)]

After making the proposal and *before the hearing* on the application to reject the collective bargaining agreement, the *debtor must meet at reasonable times with the union* and *negotiate in good faith* in an effort to reach mutually satisfactory modifications of the collective bargaining agreement. [B.C. § 1113(b)(2)]

The bankruptcy court will approve the *application to reject* the collective bargaining agreement *only* if it finds that the proposal satisfies the requirements listed in a-e above *and*

a. The union *refused to accept the proposal without good cause; and*

b. The balance of the equities *clearly favors rejection* of the collective bargaining agreement.

[B.C. § 1113(c)]

3. Hearing

The bankruptcy court must schedule a hearing on an application to reject a collective bargaining agreement within *14 days* after the application is filed. The court may extend for *7 days* the start of the hearing on the rejection application if the *circumstances* of the case coupled with the *interests of justice* require an extension. The debtor and union representative must agree to any further time extensions. [B.C. § 1113(d)(1)] The court must rule on the issue within *30 days* after the commencement of the hearing, unless the debtor and the union representative agree to an extension of such time period. [B.C. § 1113(d)(2)]

4. Protective Orders

The bankruptcy court may issue protective orders as are needed to prevent disclosure of the information provided to the union representative if disclosure of such information could *compromise the debtor's position* in relation to its *industry competitors.* [B.C. § 1113(d)(3)]

5. Interim Changes

The court may permit the debtor to make temporary interim modifications in the terms, conditions, wages, benefits, or work rules of a collective bargaining agreement if such changes are necessary to *continue the debtor's business* or to *avoid irreparable harm* to the estate. Notice and a hearing are required. [B.C. § 1113(e); *In re* **Evans Products Co.,** 55 B.R. 231 (Bankr. S.D. Fla. 1985) (granting debtor leave to implement interim changes to collective bargaining agreement, noting that debtor could not continue to operate its foundry due to "present negative cash flow")]

6. Unilateral Action Prohibited

The debtor may not unilaterally terminate or modify any terms of a collective bargaining agreement before compliance with the provisions set forth in § 1113. [B.C. § 1113(f)]

D. Retiree Benefits

1. Introduction

The Code provides procedural and substantive protections against a Chapter 11 company's modification of retiree benefits. [B.C. § 1114] The Code's provisions cover both union and non-union employees. [*See* B.C. § 1114(b)(1)] The Code's rules on modification of retiree benefits are complex. This summary provides only a brief overview.

a. Exception

Section 1114 does not apply to a retiree or the spouse or any dependent of the retiree if the retiree's *gross income* for the 12 months prior to the bankruptcy filing equals or exceeds *$250,000.* [B.C. § 1114(m)] However, if such a retiree can demonstrate to the court's satisfaction that she cannot obtain health, medical, life, and disability coverage comparable to that provided by the employer on the day before the filing of the Chapter 11 petition, then the protections of § 1114 apply to such retiree.

2. Definition of Retiree Benefits

The Code defines "retiree benefits" as payments to any entity or person for the purpose of providing or reimbursing payments for *retirees and their spouses and dependents* for *medical, surgical, or hospital care,* or *benefits* in the event of *sickness, accident, disability, or death* under a plan, fund, or program maintained or established by the debtor prior to the debtor's bankruptcy filing. [B.C. § 1114(a)]

3. Payment Obligation

The debtor in possession (or Chapter 11 trustee) must *timely pay* retiree benefits, unless an appropriate modification to such benefits has been put into place. [B.C. § 1114(e)] Any payment required to be made prior to plan confirmation has the status of an *allowed administrative expense.* [B.C. §§ 1114(e)(2), 503] Section 502(b)(7)'s limitation on allowable claims for damages for termination of an employment contract *do not apply* to claims for retiree benefits. [B.C. § 1114(j)]

4. Modification of Benefits

There are two basic paths to modify retiree benefits. First, the debtor in possession (or trustee) and the retirees' authorized representative may agree to a modification. [B.C. § 1114(e)(1)(B)] Second, if the debtor in possession and authorized representative cannot agree, then the court, acting on the motion of the trustee or authorized representative and after notice and a hearing, may order modification. [B.C. § 1114(e)(1)(A), (g), (h)]

a. Authorized Representative

In the case of retirees receiving benefits covered by a collective bargaining agreement, the *labor union* is the retirees' authorized representative *unless* the union *elects not to serve* as the authorized representative *or* the court, upon motion by a party in interest and after notice and a hearing decides that *different representation is appropriate*. [B.C. § 1114(b)(1), (c)(1)] If the union elects to not serve or the court determines different representation is appropriate, then the court, upon motion of any party in interest and after notice and a hearing, must order the *appointment of a committee of retired employees* to serve as the retirees' authorized representative. [B.C. § 1114(c)(2)]

For non-union retirees, the court, upon motion of any party in interest and after notice and a hearing, must order the *appointment of a committee of retired employees* to serve as the retirees' authorized representative. The United States trustee appoints the committee. [B.C. § 1114(d)]

b. Modification Proposal

Before filing an application to modify retiree benefits, the debtor in possession (or Chapter 11 trustee) first must make a *proposal to the retirees' authorized representative.* The requirements for the proposal are similar to those for a debtor's rejection of a collective bargaining agreement.

(i) The proposal must be based on the *most complete and reliable information* available. [B.C. § 1114(f)(1)(A)]

(ii) The proposal must treat all of the affected parties *fairly and equitably.* [B.C. § 1114(f)(1)(A)]

(iii) Modifications must be *necessary for the debtor's reorganization.* [B.C. § 1114(f)(1)(A)]

(iv) The debtor in possession (or Chapter 11 trustee), subject to any protective orders, must provide the authorized representative with the information necessary to evaluate the proposal. [B.C. § 1114(f)(1)(B), (k)(3)]

After making the proposal but prior to the hearing on the proposal, the debtor in possession (or Chapter 11 trustee) must *meet at reasonable times* with the authorized representative, *confer in good faith,* and attempt to reach *mutually satisfactory modifications* of the retiree benefits. [B.C. § 1114(f)(2)]

c. Hearing

The bankruptcy court must schedule a hearing on an application for modifying retiree benefits within *14 days* after the application is filed. The court may extend for *7 days* the start of the hearing on the modification application if the *circumstances* of the case coupled with the *interests of justice* require an extension. The debtor and union representative must agree to any further time extensions. [B.C. § 1114(k)(1)] The court must rule on the issue within *90 days* after the commencement of the hearing, unless the debtor and the union representative agree to an extension of such time period. [B.C. § 1114(k)(2)]

d. Protective Orders

The bankruptcy court may issue protective orders as are needed to prevent disclosure of the information provided to the union representative if disclosure of such information could *compromise the debtor's position* in relation to its *industry competitors.* [B.C. § 1114(k)(3)]

e. Failure to Agree: Final Order

With one exception, the bankruptcy court must enter a final order modifying retiree benefits if the court finds that *all of the following requirements* are satisfied.

(i) The debtor in possession (or Chapter 11 trustee) *complied with the requirements for making a modification proposal.* [B.C. § 1114(g)(1)]

(ii) The retirees' authorized representative *refused to accept the proposal without good cause.* [B.C. § 1114(g)(2)]

(iii) The modification is *necessary* to permit the *debtor's reorganization.* [B.C. § 1114(g)(3)]

(iv) All affected parties are treated *fairly and equitably.* [B.C. § 1114(g)(3)]

(v) The modification is clearly favored by the *balance of the equities.* [B.C. § 1114(g)(3)]

(i) Exception

The court cannot enter an order providing for a modification of benefits *at a level lower* than what the debtor in possession (or trustee) proposed if the debtor in possession (or trustee) satisfied the requirements stated above for Modification Proposal. [B.C. § 1114(f), (g)]

f. Interim Modifications

Prior to entering a final order on modification, the court may authorize, after notice and a hearing, an interim modification in retiree benefits if such interim modification is *essential to continuation of the debtor's business* or necessary to *avoid irreparable harm to the estate.* [B.C. § 1114(h)(1)] The motion to modify retiree benefits is not rendered moot by the implementation of interim changes. [B.C. § 1114(h)(3)]

g. Pre-Bankruptcy Modifications

If the debtor, during the *180 days* prior to filing for bankruptcy, *modified retiree benefits while insolvent,* then the court, on the motion of a party in interest and after notice and a hearing, must issue an order *reinstating as of the date of the modification* the benefits in effect immediately before the modification, *unless* the court finds that the *balance of the equities clearly favors such modification.* [B.C. § 1114(*l*)] Congress added this provision to the Code in 2005.

E. The Disclosure Statement and Chapter 11 Plan

1. The Disclosure Statement

a. Overview

After filing of the petition, the debtor or other plan proponent may not solicit acceptances or rejections of the plan unless they first have provided a plan (or plan summary) and a *written court-approved disclosure statement* containing *adequate information* to the holders of the claims or interests whose acceptances or rejections are being sought. [B.C. § 1125(b)] After the debtor or plan proponent files the disclosure statement, the bankruptcy court holds a hearing to consider the disclosure statement and any objections or modifications to the disclosure statement. With the exception of a conditionally approved disclosure statement, the court must provide at least *28 days' notice* of the hearing to the debtor, creditors, equity security holders, and other parties in interest. [Bankruptcy Rule 3017(a), 3017.1(b)]

Exceptions: BAPCPA added special rules for disclosure statements in small business cases. [B.C. § 1125(f), Bankruptcy Rule 3017.1; *see infra* § G] In a case in which subchapter V is elected, the debtor normally *does not file* a disclosure statement. [B.C. § 1181(b); *see infra* § H]

b. Adequate Information

Because the purpose of the disclosure statement is to provide information to creditors and equity security holders adequate to evaluate the plan, the Code requires that the disclosure statement contain sufficient information, under the circumstances, to enable a *hypothetical investor* typical of holders of claims or interests of the relevant class to make an *informed decision* to accept or reject the plan. [B.C. § 1125(a)(1)]

(i) Impact of BAPCPA

Congress amended the definition of *adequate information* in BAPCPA to provide that the disclosure statement should include "a discussion of the potential material Federal tax consequences of the plan to the debtor, any successor to the debtor, and a hypothetical investor typical of the holder of claims or interests in the case." [B.C. § 1125(a)(1)] In addition, the bankruptcy court also must consider the *complexity of the case,* the *benefit of additional information* to parties in interest, and *the cost of providing additional information* when evaluating the adequacy of information provided by the disclosure statement. [B.C. § 1125(a)(1)]

(ii) *Metrocraft* Factors

Deciding whether the disclosure statement provides adequate information is a fact-intensive inquiry. Some courts have adopted the factors set forth in *In re* **Metrocraft Publishing Services, Inc.,** 39 B.R. 567 (Bankr. N.D. Ga. 1984). [*See, e.g., In re* **Divine Ripe, L.L.C.,** 554 B.R. 395 (Bankr. S.D. Tex. 2016)] Those factors include:

(1) *the events leading to the filing* of the bankruptcy petition;

(2) *a description of the available assets and their value;*

(3) *the anticipated future of the company;*

(4) *the source of the information* stated in the disclosure statement;

(5) *a disclaimer;*

(6) *the present condition of the debtor* while in Chapter 11;

(7) *the scheduled claims;*

(8) *the estimated return to creditors* under a Chapter 7 liquidation;

(9) *the accounting method* used to produce financial information and the *names of the accountants* responsible for such information;

(10) *the future management* of the debtor;

(11) *the Chapter 11 plan* or a summary thereof;

(12) *the estimated administrative expenses,* including attorneys' and accountants' fees;

(13) *the collectibility of accounts receivable;*

(14) *financial information, data, valuations, or projections* relevant to the creditors' decision to accept or reject the Chapter 11 plan;

(15) *information relevant to the risks* posed to creditors under the plan;

(16) *the actual or projected realizable value from recovery of preferential or otherwise voidable transfers;*

(17) whether *litigation is likely to arise* in a nonbankruptcy context;

(18) *tax attributes* of the debtor; and

(19) *the relationship of the debtor with affiliates.*

c. Distribution of Disclosure Statement

Because the information needed by separate classes of claims or interests may vary in kind and detail, different disclosure statements may be sent to different classes. However, the holders of the claims or interests of the same class must receive the identical disclosure statement. [B.C. § 1125(c)]

d. Nonbankruptcy Securities Laws, Rules, and Regulations

The adequacy of the information contained in a post-petition disclosure statement is determined without regard to any nonbankruptcy law, rule, or regulation that otherwise would apply. Any agency, e.g., the Securities and Exchange Commission, or official responsible for administering or enforcing such non-bankruptcy law, rule, or regulation may appear and be heard on the issue of the adequacy of the disclosure statement. [B.C. § 1125(d)] Also, Chapter 11 includes a *safe harbor provision,* insulating from liability for violation of any applicable securities law, rule, or regulation, a person who in *good faith* and in compliance with the provisions of the Bankruptcy Code solicits acceptances or rejections of a plan, or participates in the offer, issuance, purchase, or sale of a security under a plan. [B.C. § 1125(e)]

e.   Distinguish Pre-Petition Solicitation

Acceptances or rejections of a plan may be solicited before the filing of a Chapter 11 petition only if the solicitation meets the disclosure requirements of any applicable securities or other nonbankruptcy law or regulation, or in the absence of any such law or regulation, is preceded by the disclosure of adequate information, as defined in Bankruptcy Code § 1125(a). [B.C. § 1126(b)] Section 1126(b) is valuable in cases involving pre-packaged Chapter 11 plans because after filing the petition the debtor that satisfies § 1126(b) can move quickly to the plan confirmation hearing.

2.   Filing a Plan

In a voluntary non-subchapter V case, the debtor may file a plan of reorganization with the Chapter 11 petition or at any other time. In an involuntary case, the debtor may file a plan at any time. [B.C. § 1121(a)]

a.   Exclusivity Period

Unless a trustee has been appointed in the case, the **debtor** has the exclusive right to file a plan for the first *120 days after* the order for relief. [B.C. § 1121(b), (c)(1)] A small business debtor has the exclusive right to file a plan for the first *180 days after* the order for relief. [B.C. § 1121(e)] There is *no exclusivity period* in a subchapter V case because *only* the debtor may file a plan. [B.C. § 1189(a)] Thus, *§ 1121* of the Code *does not apply* in a subchapter V case. [B.C. § 1181(a)] The subchapter V debtor must file its plan no later than *90 days after* the order for relief. [B.C. § 1189(b)]

b.   Extension or Reduction of Exclusivity Period

(i)   Neither a Small Business nor a Subchapter V Case

A party in interest may request, within the relevant exclusivity period, and the court, after notice and hearing, may grant a request to extend or reduce the debtor's exclusivity period. [B.C. § 1121(d)(1)] The Bankruptcy Code, however, places outer limits on the time to which the court may extend the exclusivity period. Thus, the court may not extend the *120-day exclusivity* period beyond *18 months* after the order for relief. [B.C. § 1121(d)(2)(A)]

(ii)   Small Business Non-Subchapter V Case

The bankruptcy court may extend the *180-day exclusivity* period, after notice and a hearing, if the following requirements are met: (1) the debtor provides *notice* to parties in interest, including the United States trustee; (2) the debtor shows *by a preponderance of the evidence* that it is more likely than not that the court will confirm a plan *within a reasonable time;* (3) the court imposes a new deadline when it grants the extension; and (4) the court signs the extension order *before* the *180-day period expires.* [B.C. § 1121(e)(1)(A), (e)(3)]

(iii) Subchapter V Case

There is no exclusivity period in a *subchapter V case* but the court may extend the 90-day period within which the debtor is to file its plan if the need for the extension is *attributable to circumstances* for which the *debtor should not justly be held accountable.* [B.C. § 1189(b)]

c. Other Proponents

In a Chapter 11 case that is neither a small business nor a subchapter V case, any party in interest, including a creditor, a creditors' committee, an equity security holder, an equity security holders' committee, or an indenture trustee, but *not the United States trustee* [B.C. § 307], may file a plan *but only if:*

(i) *a Chapter 11 trustee has been appointed* [B.C. § 1121(c)(1)];

(ii) *the debtor has not filed a plan within 120 days* after the order for relief [B.C. § 1121(c)(2)]; *or*

(iii) *the debtor has not filed a plan and obtained the acceptances* of every impaired class of claims or interests within *180 days* after the order for relief. [B.C. § 1121(c)(3)]

In a *small business case*, unless the bankruptcy court extends the *180-day* exclusivity period, any party in interest may file a plan after the exclusivity period ends. *Section 1121* of the Code *does not apply* in a subchapter V case. [B.C. § 1181(a)] *Only the debtor* may file a plan in a *subchapter V case*.

3. The Plan's Classification of Claims or Interests

With the exception of administrative, gap, and tax claims, the Bankruptcy Code requires that a Chapter 11 plan classify the claims and the equity interests in the case. [B.C. § 1123(a)(1)] However, the statutory provisions regarding the manner of classification are relatively brief, and much case law has developed in this area. [B.C. § 1122]

a. "Substantially Similar" Claims or Interests

A claim or interest may be placed in a particular class only if it is substantially similar to the other claims or interests included in that class. [B.C. § 1122(a)] The Code, however, does *not require* that all substantially similar claims be placed in the same class.

(i) Majority View

Most courts have held that § 1122(a) does not compel the classification of all substantially similar claims together in one class. Thus, a plan proponent can separately classify substantially similar claims if there is a reasonable or rational justification for the separate classification. [*In re* **LightSquared, Inc.,** 513 B.R. 56 (Bankr. S.D. N.Y. 2014)] Separate classification is proper if the creditors in the two classes have different legal rights or different interests in the plan, or if the plan proponent has a legitimate business reason for the separate classification. [*See In re* **STC, Inc.,** 2016 WL 3884799 (Bankr. S.D. Ill. 2016)]

> **e.g.** **Example:** Debtor Corporation filed for relief under Chapter 11 after Creditor, a long-time competitor, was awarded more than $5 million in damages in a patent infringement lawsuit. Creditor objected to Debtor's plan, which placed Creditor's claim in a separate class from the class of unsecured trade creditors. The bankruptcy court concluded that separate classification was proper. The court first noted that the trade creditors had different legal rights from Creditor. As a judgment creditor, Creditor had a "myriad of remedies to pursue, including execution, garnishment, citations, and the creation of a judgment lien." Unlike the trade creditors, Creditor also could pursue recovery against other, non-debtor defendants. The court also noted that Debtor had a legitimate business reason for the separate classification of trade creditors, which were critical to Debtor's successful reorganization. Finally, the bankruptcy court found that as a "direct and strong

competitor" of Debtor, Creditor had a "substantially different interest" in the plan from the trade creditors. Failure of Debtor's plan would mean "the elimination of [Debtor] as a significant competitor" and a substantial improvement in Creditor's market position. Creditor's "non-creditor interest" in the plan meant that separate classification was proper. [*In re* **STC. Inc.**, *supra*]

(ii) Minority View

A few courts follow what has been identified as the "strict approach" to separate classification of general unsecured creditors. This approach requires that similar claims be classified together, unless the legal character and status of the separately classified claim differs from the legal character and status of other general unsecured creditors. [B.C. § 1122(a); *see, e.g.,* **Granada Wines, Inc. v. New England Teamsters & Trucking Industry Pension Fund,** 748 F.2d 42 (1st Cir. 1984); *In re* **River Valley Fitness One L.P.,** 2003 WL 22298573 (Bankr. D. N.H. 2003)]

(iii) Gerrymandering

While most courts generally allow separate classification of similar claims, there is an important exception: a plan proponent may not separately classify similar claims in an attempt to gerrymander the plan confirmation vote. [**Mineral Technologies, Inc. v. Novinda Corp. (*In re* Novinda Corp.),** 585 B.R. 145 (B.A.P. 10th Cir. 2018)] If the sole reason for separate classification is to create an impaired class that will accept the plan, then separate classification is not allowed. [B.C. §§ 1122(a), 1129(a)(10); *see, e.g., In re* **STC, Inc.,** *supra*]

e.g. **Example:** Debtor proposes a plan with four classes. Classes 1 and 2 each contain one secured creditor and are unimpaired. Creditor has a large enough unsecured claim that if she votes with the general unsecured creditors, the plan cannot be confirmed. Creditor plans to vote against the plan, but without Creditor in the general unsecured class the class will vote in favor of the plan. Debtor puts Creditor into Class 3, and the remaining general unsecured creditors into Class 4. Both Class 3 and 4 are impaired. Creditor votes against the plan, but Class 4 votes in favor. Creditor objects to Debtor's plan. The bankruptcy court will not confirm the plan, because Debtor gerrymandered the unsecured classes in order to obtain an impaired class that would vote in favor of plan confirmation. [B.C. §§ 1126(c), 1129(a)(10), 1129(b)(2)(B)]

(iv) Administrative Convenience Claims

A plan proponent may create a separate class of *unsecured claims* with a value less than or reduced to an amount that the court approves as reasonable and necessary for *administrative convenience.* [B.C. § 1122(b)] Generally, such claims are paid in full in cash, and the estate benefits by the reduction of administrative expenses associated with "the cost of sending disclosure statements, soliciting votes from the *de minimis* creditors, and making fractional distributions." [*In re* **Autterson,** 547 B.R. 372 (Bankr. D. Colo. 2016); B.C. § 1122(b); 7 Collier ¶ 1122.03(4)]

e.g. **Example:** Debtor Corporation proposes a Chapter 11 plan with 2 classes of unsecured claims: an administrative convenience class and the class of general unsecured creditors. The administrative convenience class contains general unsecured claims of $500 or less, or claims of those creditors willing to reduce their claims to $500. The plan proposes to pay the administrative convenience claimants in full in cash on the plan's effective date. This type of separation of substantially similar claims into separate classes generally does not pose a problem for plan confirmation.

b. Specific Types of Claims or Interests

(i) Secured Claims

Usually, if secured creditors' liens are in different property or are entitled to different priorities in the same property, each secured claim should be placed alone in a separate class. [*See* 6 Norton § 109:2 ("Each secured claim is treated as a separate class unless there is another secured claimholder having identical and equal rights in the same collateral")]

(ii) Certain Priority Claims

Administrative expenses, involuntary case gap claims, and unsecured priority tax claims are *excepted* from the requirement of classification because the standards for confirmation require that the plan provide for such claims on an individual, as opposed to a class, basis. [B.C. §§ 1123(a)(1), 1129(a)(9)(A), (C)]

(iii) Administrative Convenience Class

The Code permits the plan to designate a separate class of small claims comprised of all unsecured claims that are less than, or by consent decreased to, an amount approved by the court as *reasonable and necessary.*

(iv) Interests

Equity interests in a sole proprietorship, a partnership, or a corporation must be classified separately from creditors' claims. Furthermore, common stock and preferred stock interests should be placed in different classes. [B.C. § 1122(a)]

4. Contents of Plan: Mandatory Provisions

All Chapter 11 plans must do the following:

a. *classify all claims and interests,* other than priority claims for administrative expenses, involuntary case gap claims, or eighth priority taxes [B.C. §§ 1123(a)(1), 507(a)(2), (3), (8)];

b. *specify any class that is not impaired* [B.C. § 1123(a)(2)];

c. *describe the treatment* to be accorded *any impaired class* [B.C. § 1123(a)(3)];

d. *treat every claim or interest within a particular class identically,* unless a holder consents to less favorable treatment [B.C. § 1123(a)(4)];

e. *establish adequate ways to implement the plan,* such as by [B.C. § 1123(a)(5)(A)–(J)]:

    (i)   *the debtor's retention* of estate property;

    (ii)   *the transfer of estate property* to another entity;

    (iii)   *merger or consolidation* of the debtor with other persons;

    (iv)   *the sale of estate property either subject to or free and clear of liens,* or the *distribution of estate property to the holders* of any interests in the property;

    (v)   *the satisfaction or modification of a lien;*

    (vi)   *the cancellation or modification of an indenture;*

    (vii)   *curing or waiving a default;*

(viii) *extending the maturity date,* or altering the interest rate or other terms of outstanding securities;

(ix) *amending the debtor's charter;* or

(x) *issuing securities of the debtor* or a successor to the debtor, or of an entity with whom the debtor has merged or has been consolidated for cash, property, existing securities, in exchange for claims or interests, or for any other proper purpose;

f. *include, in the charter of a corporate debtor or successor,* or any corporation with which debtor *merged or was consolidated, a provision prohibiting the issuance of nonvoting stock,* and complying with certain other requirements concerning voting powers [B.C. § 1123(a)(6)];

g. *provide for the selection of officers and directors* in a manner consistent with the interests of creditors and equity security holders and that does not violate public policy [B.C. § 1123(a)(7)]; and

h. *provide for payment,* in an *individual Chapter 11 case,* of debtor's post-petition earnings or future income sufficient to execute the plan. [B.C. § 1123(a)(8)]

Note: This requirement *does not apply* in a subchapter V case. [B.C. § 1181(a)]

5. Contents of Plan: Permissive Provisions

In addition to the mandatory items described above, a plan *may:*

a. *impair or leave unimpaired* any class of claims or interests [B.C. § 1123(b)(1)];

b. *assume, reject, or assign executory contracts or unexpired leases* [B.C. § 1123(b)(2)];

c. *settle or adjust any claim or interest* held by the debtor or the estate, or provide for the retention and enforcement of the claim or interest by the debtor, Chapter 11 trustee, or an appointed representative of the estate [B.C. § 1123(b)(3)];

d. *sell all or substantially all of the estate property,* and distribute the proceeds among claim and interest holders [B.C. § 1123(b)(4)];

e. *modify the rights of secured creditors or unsecured creditors, unless* the creditor's claim is secured *solely* by a security interest in real property constituting the debtor's principal residence [B.C. § 1123(b)(5)]; and

Note: The prohibition against modification of home mortgages applies to an individual Chapter 11 debtor. It prevents an individual Chapter 11 debtor from *stripping down* an undersecured mortgage on his principal residence to the fair market value of the residence. [*See* **Nobelman v. American Savings Bank,** 508 U.S. 324 (1993) (construing language in § 1322(b)(2), which is identical to that in § 1123(b)(5), and holding that anti-modification language precluded a Chapter 13 debtor from reducing outstanding mortgage principal to the fair market value of debtor's principal residence)]

See infra § H.6.c(ii) for subchapter V variation on § 1123(b)(5).

f. *include any other appropriate measure* that is consistent with the provisions of the Bankruptcy Code. [B.C. § 1123(b)(6)] For example, the Supreme Court has held that a bankruptcy court has the authority to order the IRS to allocate a Chapter 11 corporate debtor's tax payments first to *trust fund taxes,* before being applied to non-trust fund tax liabilities, if *necessary for the success of the debtor's reorganization.* [**United States v. Energy Resources Co.,** 495 U.S. 545 (1990)]

6. Contents of Plan: Exempt Property

If the *debtor is an individual*, any plan proposed by another entity may not include a provision to use, sell, or lease exempt property without the consent of the debtor. [B.C. § 1123(c)] Section 1123(c) *does not apply* to a subchapter V case. [B.C. § 1181(a)]

7. Contents of Plan: Interest on Arrearages

If the plan proposes to cure a default, the Code addresses the issue of interest on interest, e.g., interest on mortgage arrearages that include interest. The amount necessary to cure the default is determined by looking to the underlying contract and applicable nonbankruptcy law. [B.C. § 1123(d)] Congress added § 1123(d) in 1994 in order to "overrul[e] the decision of the Supreme Court in *Rake v. Wade,* 113 S. Ct. 2187 (1993) . . . [and] limit the secured creditor to the benefit of the initial bargain with no court contrived windfall." [H.R. Rep. No. 103–835, at 55 (1994)] If the parties' agreement and relevant nonbankruptcy law allow, the debtor also must pay the agreed-upon default rate of interest when curing a default. [**JPMCC 2006-LDP7 Miami Beach Lodging, LLC v. Sagamore Partners, Ltd. (*In re* Sagamore Partners, Ltd.),** 620 F. App'x 864 (11th Cir. 2015)]

8. Modifying a Plan

Prior to confirmation, a plan may be modified only by its proponent. [B.C. § 1127(a)] After confirmation and before substantial consummation of a plan, it may be modified, if warranted, by the proponent *or* by the reorganized debtor. [B.C. § 1127(b)] Notice and a hearing are required. Any modification must satisfy the statutory requirements concerning classification of claims or interests [B.C. § 1122], contents of the plan [B.C. § 1123], disclosure statement [B.C. § 1125], and the requirements for confirmation. [B.C. § 1129] An acceptance or a rejection of a plan before modification will be deemed to apply to the plan as modified unless the vote is changed within the deadline set by the court. [B.C. § 1127(d)]

BAPCPA added special rules for plan modification for *individual Chapter 11 debtors*. The individual debtor, United States trustee, trustee, or holder of an allowed unsecured claim may request modification of the individual debtor's plan at any time *after confirmation* but *before plan payments are complete,* regardless of whether the plan has been substantially consummated. [B.C. § 1127(e)] The modification request may involve any of the following:

a.   an *increase or decrease* in plan payments on claims of a particular class;

b.   an *extension or reduction* in the time period for such payments; or

c.   an *alteration of the amount of the plan's distribution* to a creditor to account for payments made on the creditor's claim other than under the plan.

Section 1127 *does not apply in subchapter V.* [B.C. § 1181(a)] *See infra* § H for modification rules for subchapter V cases.

F.   Confirmation of Plan

1. Confirmation Hearing

After proper notice, the court conducts a hearing to determine whether a proposed plan satisfies the elements necessary for confirmation. Any party in interest may file an objection to confirmation. [B.C. § 1128; Bankruptcy Rule 3020(b)]

2. Requirements for Confirmation of a Consent Plan

Confirmation of a consensual Chapter 11 plan requires that the plan proponent satisfy all of the following statutory requirements. [B.C. § 1129(a)]

a. Plan Complies with Code Provisions

The plan must comply with the applicable provisions of the Bankruptcy Code, such as the requirements for classification of claims and the mandatory contents of a Chapter 11 plan. [B.C. § 1129(a)(1)]

b. Proponent Complies with Code Provisions

The proponent of the plan must comply with the applicable provisions of the Code, such as those requiring disclosure of adequate information and solicitation of acceptances. [B.C. § 1129(a)(2)]

c. Plan Filed in Good Faith

The plan must be proposed in good faith and not by any means forbidden by law. [B.C. § 1129(a)(3)] [*See In re* **American Capital Equipment, LLC,** 688 F.3d 145 (3d Cir. 2012) ("[a] plan is proposed in good faith only if it will 'fairly achieve a result consistent with the objectives and purposes of the Bankruptcy Code' "); *In re* **Art & Architecture Books of the 21st Century,** 2016 WL 1118743 (Bankr. C.D. Cal. 2016) (" 'the important point of inquiry is the plan itself and whether such plan will fairly achieve a result consistent with the objectives and purposes of the Bankruptcy Code.' ")

Note: A determination that the debtor filed its chapter 11 petition in good faith *does not* mean that the debtor also satisfies § 1129(a)(3). It is possible for a debtor to file its *petition* in good faith but not file its *plan* in good faith.

d. Payment for Services or Expenses Approved

The court must approve as reasonable all payments made by the plan's proponent, the debtor, or a person issuing securities or receiving property under the plan for services or expenses in or in connection with the Chapter 11 case or related to the plan, e.g., attorneys' fees. [B.C. § 1129(a)(4)]

e. Officers, Directors, Insiders Disclosed

The plan must disclose the names and affiliations of all individuals who, after plan confirmation, will serve as officers, directors, or voting trustees of the debtor, a successor to the debtor, or a debtor affiliate participating in a joint plan with the debtor. [B.C. § 1129(a)(5)(A)(i)] Appointment of these individuals or their continuation as officers, directors, or voting trustees must be consistent with the interests of creditors, equity security holders, and public policy. [B.C. § 1129(a)(5)(A)(ii)] The plan proponent must also disclose the names and proposed compensation of all insiders who will be employed or retained by the reorganized debtor. [B.C. § 1129(a)(5)(B)]

f. Rate Change Approved

If the debtor's rates are regulated by a governmental commission, that commission must approve any rate change proposed by the plan, or the proposed rate change must be expressly conditioned on such approval. [B.C. § 1129(a)(6)]

g. "Best Interests of Creditors Test" Met

Each holder of a claim or interest of an *impaired class* either must (i) *accept* the plan *or* (ii) *receive* or retain under the plan property having a *present value,* as of the effective date of the plan, of *not less than the amount* that the holder would receive in a *Chapter 7 liquidation.* This element of confirmation usually is called the "best interests of creditors test." [B.C. § 1129(a)(7)(A)] Unlike other confirmation requirements, which apply to the *class* of creditors, the "best interests of creditors test" applies to *each creditor,* even if the creditor objecting to the plan on the basis of the test is part of a class that has voted to accept the plan.

Example: Debtor Company filed for relief under Chapter 11 and proposed a plan. Creditor voted against the plan and objected to confirmation on several grounds, including the plan's failure to satisfy the best interests test. While Debtor contended that it did not have substantial assets to liquidate, it failed to provide a persuasive liquidation analysis. Debtor also did not provide sufficient financial information for the bankruptcy court to conduct a "best interests of creditors" analysis. Finally, while the plan proposed making payments to creditors from future profits, the court concluded that the payment stream for these payments was "highly speculative." Thus, the bankruptcy court held that the Debtor had not established by a preponderance of the evidence that the plan satisfied the "best interest of creditors" test. [*In re* **Premiere Network Services,** 2005 Bankr. LEXIS 2298 (Bankr. N.D. Tex. 2005)]

Exception: If a holder has made the *election under § 1111(b),* the plan must provide that she receive property having a present value, as of the effective date of the plan, of at least the value of the collateral securing her claim. [B.C. § 1129(a)(7)(B)]

h. All Impaired Classes Accept Plan

Each class of claims or interests must have *accepted* the plan *or be unimpaired* under the plan. [B.C. § 1129(a)(8)] If this element is not satisfied, the plan cannot be confirmed under § 1129(a) as a *consent plan.* The plan proponent, however, may move for confirmation under the Code's *cram down* provisions at § 1129(b).

Note: Section 1129(b) *does not apply to a subchapter V case. See infra* § H.

(i) What Is Impairment?

A class is *deemed impaired unless* the plan provides for all claims or interests of that class to be treated in accordance with either of the following two methods. [B.C. § 1124]

(1) Rights Unmodified

A class is considered *unimpaired* if the plan does *not alter* the legal, equitable, or contractual rights of the holders of the claims or interests. Any change in a holder's rights, *even a favorable change,* constitutes impairment. [B.C. § 1124(1); *see In re* **L & J Anaheim Associates,** 995 F.2d 940 (9th Cir. 1993) (stating a claim is impaired if the claim holder's rights are changed, regardless of the kind or degree of change)]

(2) Deemed Unimpaired

Section 1124(2) provides that a class is deemed *unimpaired* if the plan proposes, regardless of any contractual or other legal right to accelerate payment on default, to:

(a) *cure any default,* other than one related to an *ipso facto* provision or of a kind that § 365(b)(2) does not require to be cured [B.C. § 1124(2)(A)];

(b) *reinstate the original maturity date* of the claim or interest [B.C. § 1124(2)(B)];

(c) *pay for any damages* caused by the claimant's or the interest holder's *reasonable reliance* on the right to accelerate [B.C. § 1124(2)(C)];

(d) *pay for any damages* caused by the debtor's failure to *perform a nonmonetary obligation,* other than a default arising from a failure to operate a nonresidential real property lease subject to § 365(b)(1)(A) [B.C. § 1124(2)(D)]; *and*

(e) *not otherwise alter* the legal, equitable, or contractual rights of the holder of the claim or interest. [B.C. § 1124(2)(E)]

(a) Cure and Deceleration

If the Chapter 11 debtor has defaulted on a payment obligation, the contract with the creditor may provide for accelerated payment on the creditor's claim, which means the creditor is entitled to full payment of the obligation upon default. If the debtor files for relief under Chapter 11 and proposes to cure any default and reinstate the terms of the parties' agreement, the creditor could argue that the debtor has impaired the creditor's claim, which was entitled to full payment based on the contract's acceleration clause. But, under § 1124 "a claim or interest is unimpaired by curing the effect of a default and reinstating the original terms of an obligation when maturity was brought on or accelerated by the default. . . . The holder of a claim or interest who under the plan is restored to his original position, when others receive less or get nothing at all, is fortunate indeed and has no cause to complain." [S. Rep. No. 95–989, at 120 (1978)]

(b) Foreclosure Judgments and Cure

If state law does not provide for the merger of a mortgage and foreclosure judgment, the debtor usually is permitted to cure the default and reinstate the obligation at any time *prior to a foreclosure sale.* [*In re* **Madison Hotel Associates,** 749 F.2d 410 (7th Cir. 1984)] But if the mortgage merges into the foreclosure judgment under state law, some courts have held that there is nothing to cure and reinstate. Other courts, however, have concluded that merger is irrelevant, because § 1124(2) evidences Congress's intent to permit deacceleration. [7 Collier ¶ 1124.04(6)]

(ii) What Constitutes Acceptance by a Class?

Any creditor or equity security holder whose claim or interest has been allowed may accept or reject a Chapter 11 plan by a signed writing identifying the plan and conforming to the appropriate Official Form. [B.C. § 1126(a); Bankruptcy Rule 3018(c); Official Form 314]

(1) Classes of Claims

Acceptance of a plan by a class of claims requires acceptance by creditors holding at least *two-thirds in amount and more than half in number* of the allowed claims actually being voted. [B.C. § 1126(c)]

Example: The debtor Ajax Corporation proposes a plan, if confirmed, that will pay Class 5, its general unsecured creditors, 30 cents on the dollar. There are 50 unsecured creditors in Class 5 with claims totaling $500,000. Of those 50 unsecured creditors, 25 creditors with claims totaling $250,000 cast ballots to accept or reject the plan. If 20 creditors (more than half in number of claims voting) with claims totaling $200,000 (80% in amount of claims voting) vote in favor of the plan, then Class 5 votes to accept the plan.

Example: The debtor Ajax Corporation proposes a plan, if confirmed, that will pay Class 5, its general unsecured creditors, 30 cents on the dollar. There are 50 unsecured creditors in Class 5 with claims totaling $500,000. Of those 50 unsecured creditors, 25 creditors with claims totaling $250,000 cast ballots to accept or reject the plan. If 12 creditors with claims of $170,000 vote in favor of the plan, then Class 5 has voted to reject the plan. While more than two-thirds in amount of claims voted in favor of the plan ($170,000/$250,000 = 68%), less than half in number of claims (12/25 = 48%) voted "yes" on the plan. The Code requires *both* two-thirds in amount of claims *and* more than half in number of claims to vote to accept the plan.

(2) Classes of Interests

Acceptance of a plan by a class of interests requires acceptance by equity security holders having at least *two-thirds in amount* of the allowed interests actually being voted. [B.C. § 1126(d)]

(3) Bad Faith Votes

Upon request of a party in interest and after notice and a hearing, the court may disqualify any acceptance or rejection *not made in good faith* or that was *not solicited in good faith* or in compliance with the provisions of the Code. [B.C. § 1126(e)]

Example: The debtor Gamma Company proposes a plan, if confirmed, that will pay Class 6, its general unsecured creditors, 40 cents on the dollar. Thirty of Gamma's unsecured creditors holding claims worth $600,000 vote on the plan. Kappa, Inc., one of Gamma's largest unsecured creditors with a claim of $325,000, votes in favor of the plan. Twenty of Gamma's other unsecured creditors holding claims of $100,000 also vote in favor of the plan, while $175,000 cast ballots rejecting the plan. If the bankruptcy court determines that Kappa's vote was not made or solicited in good faith or in compliance with the Code, then Kappa's vote will not count toward plan confirmation. In such a case, Class 6 will not have voted to approve the plan. Only 36% of the remaining claims ($100,000 "yes"/$275,000 claims remaining after disqualifying Kappa's claim) voted in favor of the plan.

(iii) Unimpaired Classes

If a particular class is not impaired under a plan, there is a conclusive presumption that the plan has been accepted by the class and by the holder of each claim or interest in the class. Consequently, it will be unnecessary for the proponent of the plan to solicit their acceptances. [B.C. § 1126(f)]

(iv) Classes Receiving No Property

A class that receives or retains no property under a plan is deemed to have rejected the plan. [B.C. § 1126(g)]

(v) Pre-Petition Acceptance or Rejection

If the acceptance or rejection occurs before commencement of the case, it is valid only if:

(1) it was solicited in accordance with any applicable nonbankruptcy law, rule, or regulation on the adequacy of disclosure; *or*

(2) if there is no such nonbankruptcy law, rule, or regulation, then the solicitation complied with the Code's requirements for disclosure of adequate information. [B.C. § 1126(b)]

In order for a pre-petition rejection or acceptance of a plan to count, the plan proponent must have sent the plan to substantially all creditors and equity security holders of the same class and within a reasonable time for them to accept or reject the plan. [Bankruptcy Rule 3018(b)]

In addition, if the claim of the creditor or equity security holder is based on a *security of record*, a pre-petition acceptance or rejection is valid *only if* the creditor or equity security holder was the holder of record of the security on the date specified in the solicitation. [Bankruptcy Rule 3018(b)]

i. Administrative Expenses and Involuntary Gap Claims

The plan must provide for *payment in full in cash* on the effective date of the plan for each claim that is entitled to priority as an administrative expense or as an involuntary case gap claim, unless the holder of the claim consents to different treatment. [B.C. §§ 1129(a)(9)(A), 507(a)(2), (3)]

j. First, Fourth, Fifth, Sixth, and Seventh Priority Claims

Unless the holder of a particular claim consents to different treatment, the plan must provide the following treatment to *each holder* of a domestic support obligation claim, wage or commission claim, claim for contributions to an employee benefit plan, claim by a grain farmer or United States fisherman, or a claim for a consumer layaway. [B.C. §§ 1129(a)(9)(B), 507(a)(1), (4)–(7)]

(i) *If the class has accepted the plan,* each claimant is entitled to receive deferred cash payments having a present value, as of the effective date of the plan, equal to the allowed amount of her claim. [B.C. § 1129(a)(9)(B)(i)]

(ii) *If the class has rejected the plan,* each claimant must receive total payment of her claim, in cash, on the effective date of the plan. [B.C. § 1129(a)(9)(B)(ii)]

k. Eighth Priority Tax Claims

In BAPCPA, Congress changed the treatment required under the plan for unsecured priority tax claims. Unless it consents to different treatment, each tax claimant entitled to eighth priority must receive *regular installment payments in cash:*

(i) having a present value, as of the effective date of the plan, equal to the allowed amount of the claim [B.C. § 1129(a)(9)(C)(i)];

(ii) over a period of time that ends *no later than 5 years from the order for relief* [B.C. § 1129(a)(9)(C)(ii)]; and

(iii) in a manner *no less favorable* than the plan's treatment—with the exception of a class of creditors under § 1122(b)—of the *most favored non-priority unsecured claim.* [B.C. § 1129(a)(9)(C)(iii)]

(i) Note: Secured Tax Claim

A secured tax claim that but for its secured status would qualify as an unsecured tax claim of a governmental unit entitled to priority under § 507(a)(8) is entitled to cash payments in the same manner and over the same time period as required for other priority tax claims. [B.C. § 1129(a)(9)(D)] Congress added this subsection to § 1129 in BAPCPA.

l. Ninth and Tenth Priority Claims

Section 1129 provides no special rules for the treatment of ninth or tenth priority claims. [*See* B.C. § 507(a)(9), (10)]

m. At Least One Impaired Class of Claims Accepts Plan

If the plan *impairs any class of claims,* then the plan must be accepted by *at least one class of claims* that is impaired, excluding any acceptances by insiders of the consenting class. [B.C. § 1129(a)(10)] The purpose of this requirement is to prevent a cram down, i.e., confirmation under § 1129(b), under circumstances in which none of the impaired classes of claims has accepted the plan.

Note: This requirement *does not* apply to cram down of a *subchapter V plan.* [B.C. § 1191(b); *see infra* § H.6.d(ii) of this Chapter]

n. Plan Is Feasible

The plan must be feasible, which means that confirmation of the plan is *not likely* to be followed by the debtor's liquidation or the need for further financial reorganization. [B.C. § 1129(a)(11)] The Code's feasibility test does not require guaranteed success, but the plan must propose a " 'realistic and workable framework.' " [*In re* **American Capital Equipment, LLC,** 688 F.3d 145 (3d Cir. 2012)]

Example: Married debtors filed for relief under Chapter 11. Husband was a solo practitioner, and Wife provided secretarial and clerical help to Husband in his law practice. Debtors proposed a plan that contemplated Husband, who was 68, working for thirty more years at his law practice. The court found that Husband, given his age, could not be expected to practice law full time for another thirty years and that fact "alone doom[ed] the plan as infeasible." [**United States v. Haas (***In re* **Haas),** 162 F.3d 1087 (11th Cir. 1998); *see also* **Jager v. InFirst Bank (***In re* **Jager),** 609 B.R. 156 (Bankr. W.D. Penn. 2019) (denying debtors' recusal request based on the bankruptcy judge's questions to counsel about debtors' ages, and citing to *Haas* and noting that the age and health problems of debtors in their 70s was a "relevant and appropriate consideration in determining plan feasibility" for a thirty-year Chapter 11 plan)]

o. Bankruptcy Fees Paid

All bankruptcy fees required under 28 U.S.C. § 1930 were paid prior to the confirmation hearing, or the plan must provide that they will be paid on the effective date of the plan. [B.C. § 1129(a)(12)]

p. Retiree Insurance Benefits Protected

The plan must provide for the continued payment of all retiree benefits at the level originally provided by the debtor unless (i) the debtor or trustee, if one is appointed, and the authorized representative of the recipients agree to a modification or (ii) the court orders the payments to be modified in accordance with § 1114. The plan must provide for the payment of retiree benefits for the time period that the debtor has obligated itself to provide such benefits. [B.C. § 1129(a)(13)]

q. Domestic Support Obligations

In an individual Chapter 11 case, the debtor must have paid all *post-petition domestic support obligations* required by judicial or administrative order, or by statute. [B.C. §§ 1129(a)(14), 101(14A)] Congress added this subsection to § 1129 in 2005. *Pre-petition domestic support obligations* are first-priority claims and, thus, are paid under the plan according to the requirements of § 1129(a)(9)(B). [B.C. §§ 507(a)(1), 101(14A)]

r. Disposable Income Requirement: Individual Cases

In 2005, Congress added to the requirements for confirmation of a consent plan a *disposable income test* for cases involving *individual Chapter 11 debtors.* The test is similar, but not identical, to Chapter 13's disposable income test. [*Compare* B.C. § 1129(a)(15) *with* § 1325(b)] If the holder of an *allowed unsecured claim objects* to confirmation of the individual debtor's plan, the bankruptcy court cannot confirm the plan unless it provides for one of the following two alternatives:

(i) payment of the *present value,* as of the plan's effective date, of such claim [B.C. § 1129(a)(15)(A)]; or

(ii) payment of the debtor's *projected disposable income* for the *longer* of two time periods: (a) the five-year period starting when the plan's first payment is due or (b) the period of time during which payments are made under the plan. [B.C. §§ 1129(a)(15)(B), 1325(b)(2)]

e.g. **Example:** David files for relief under Chapter 11, and proposes a five-year plan that impairs the class of general unsecured creditors. Craig is a general unsecured creditor, and votes against the plan. The class of general unsecured creditors, however, accepts the plan. Craig may object to plan confirmation. The language of § 1129(a)(15) is like that of § 1129(a)(7); it gives an individual creditor the right to object to plan confirmation even if the class of creditors to which he belongs has voted in favor of the plan under § 1129(a)(8). Therefore, the bankruptcy court cannot confirm David's plan unless the plan provides for payment *in full* of the general unsecured claims *or* devotes an *amount of money equal* to David's *five-year projected disposable income.*

Note: Section 1129(a)(15) does not *require* that the plan last for five years. There is no applicable commitment period as in Chapter 13. Thus, if an individual Chapter 11 debtor proposes a three-year plan that pays the equivalent of five years of projected disposable income, the debtor should not run afoul of § 1129(a)(15).

Note: Section 1129(a)(15) does not apply to a *subchapter V case.* [B.C. §§ 1181(a), 1191(a)]

s. Property Transfers

Any transfer of property by a non-profit corporation or trust under the plan must be made in accordance with applicable nonbankruptcy law. [B.C. § 1129(a)(16)] Congress added this subsection in 2005 in order to "restrict the authority of a trustee to use, sell, or lease property by a nonprofit corporation or trust." [H.R. No. 109–31, at 145 (2005)]

3. Cram down

Section 1129's cram down provisions *do not apply in subchapter V.* [B.C. § 1181(a); *see infra* § H.6.d(ii) of this Chapter] The cram down discussion *infra* applies *only to non-subchapter V cases.*

A bankruptcy court can confirm a plan if all the requirements of § 1129(a) are met *except* § 1129(a)(8), which requires every class of claims or interests to accept the plan or be unimpaired under the plan. Thus, on request by the proponent of a plan, the court will confirm the plan, despite the rejection by one or more impaired classes, if the plan *does not unfairly discriminate* and *is fair and equitable* with respect to any dissenting impaired classes. [B.C. § 1129(b)(1)]

a. Unfair Discrimination

The Code does not define "unfair discrimination" and provides no statutory guidance, as it does with the "fair and equitable" requirement. [*See* B.C. § 1129(b)(2)] The Code's legislative history makes clear that the "criterion of unfair discrimination is not derived from the fair and equitable rule or from the best interests of creditors test [but] [r]ather preserves just treatment of a dissenting class from the class's own perspective." [H.R. No. 95–595, at 417 (1977)] That language, however, provides little substantive guidance as to the contours of the statutory requirement. As a result, courts have grappled with how to determine what constitutes unfair discrimination. There are various tests for unfair discrimination, but most courts "tend to look at the disparity of treatment proposed in the plan, and whether such disparity can be justified under the Code." [7 Collier ¶ 1129.03(3)(a)]

Example: Debtor Corporation files a Chapter 11 plan that separately classifies a large tort claim (Class V) from the remaining general unsecured claims (Class VI), most of which are owed to trade creditors that will continue to supply goods to the reorganized debtor. The plan provides for the same percentage payment over time for Class V and Class VI, but Class VI claims are to be paid before payments are made to Class V. The reason for doing so is the size of the tort claim; pro rata payments to *all* unsecured creditors—trade and tort claimants—would result in very small payments to trade creditors due to the size of the tort claim. Because many of the general unsecured creditors will continue to supply goods to the reorganized debtor, it makes sense to pay them before making payments on the large tort claim. If the plan is feasible, however, both sets of creditors will receive the same percentage payout on their claims over time. Therefore, while the plan does discriminate between these two classes of creditors, the discrimination is not unfair. [*See* 7 Collier ¶ 1129.03(3)(b)(i)]

Note: It is important to remember that § 1129(b) prohibits unfair discrimination *only* " 'among creditors who have the same level of priority.' " [*In re* **Greate Bay Hotel & Casino, Inc.,** 251 B.R. 213 (Bankr. D. N.J. 2000) (overruling unfair discrimination objection of intercompany note holders because subordination agreements between debtor and such noteholders "changed the level of priority" of such noteholders)]

b. Fair and Equitable

The Code provides specific guidelines for determining whether a plan is fair and equitable with respect to a particular class. These tests differ according to whether the class comprises secured claims, unsecured claims, or equity interests. [B.C. § 1129(b)(2)]

(i) Secured Claims

If a class of secured creditors is *impaired and does not accept the plan,* then the plan's treatment of that class *must be fair and equitable.* (Remember that usually each secured claim is classified in a separate class if the liens are in different property or are entitled to different priorities in the same property.) As to any such impaired class, the plan is fair and equitable if it satisfies *one of the following three conditions.*

(1) Secured Party Retains Lien and Receives Deferred Cash Payments

The plan satisfies the Code's "fair and equitable" requirement if it provides for the creditor to retain her lien on the collateral for the allowed amount of the secured claim, and also to receive payment in deferred *cash* installments that total at least the allowed amount of the secured claim and that have a *present value,* as of the effective date of the plan, of at least the value of the collateral. [B.C. § 1129(b)(2)(A)(i)]

Example: Debtor files for relief under Chapter 11 and proposes a plan that places Creditor into Class 2 by itself. Creditor's claim is for $10,000 and is secured by collateral of the Debtor that is valued at $12,000. Debtor proposes to pay the Class 2 claim $2,000 per year over the course of five years at the market interest rate for such loans. The plan also provides that Creditor will retain its lien to the extent of the allowed amount of its claim. Creditor's claim is impaired, and Creditor votes against Debtor's plan and argues that the plan's treatment of Class 2 is not fair and equitable. The bankruptcy court will rule against Creditor on this ground. First, the plan provides that Creditor retains its lien to the extent of its allowed claim, as required by § 1129(b)(2)(A)(i)(I). Second, Creditor will receive deferred cash payments that equal the allowed amount of the claim ($2,000 per year × 5 years = $10,000). Third, Creditor's interest in the property is $10,000, which is the amount of its claim, and by paying the market interest rate on the claim the plan ensures that Creditor is receiving the present value of its $10,000 claim.

(a) Section 1111(b) Election

Recall that if a partially secured creditor elects, under § 1111(b), to have her entire claim treated as secured, then the deferred cash payments in a cram down must equal the full dollar amount of her allowed claim and must have a present value of at least the value of the collateral.

Example: Debtor files for relief under Chapter 11 and proposes a plan that places Creditor into Class 2 by itself. Creditor's claim is for $12,000 and is secured by collateral of the Debtor that is valued at $10,000. Creditor makes the § 1111(b) election. For the plan's treatment of Creditor to be *fair and equitable*, it must provide all of the following:

1. Creditor's *retention of its lien* on the property to the extent of the allowed amount of Creditor's claim, or $12,000.

2. The payment of deferred cash payments to Creditor with a *present value* of $10,000, which is the value of the collateral.

3. The payment of deferred cash payments to Creditor *totaling at least* the allowed amount of Creditor's claim, or $12,000.

[*See* **General Electric Credit Equities, Inc. v. Brice Road Developments, LLC (***In re* **Brice Road Developments, LLC),** 392 B.R. 274 (B.A.P. 6th Cir. 2008)]

(b) Interest Rate

The Supreme Court, in a plurality opinion, held that the interest rate to use in a Chapter 13 cram down is *prime plus.* The Court explained that the starting point is the *national prime rate,* which the bankruptcy court *adjusts for risk* based on factors such as the length and feasibility of the plan and the nature of the creditor's security. While the plurality did not determine what constitutes a proper risk adjustment, it did note that courts generally had approved 1% to 3% adjustments to the prime rate. *Till* was a Chapter 13 case, but the plurality noted that a number of provisions in the Code, including portions of § 1129(b), required discounting of a stream of payments to present value. Thus, the plurality concluded that Congress likely "intended bankruptcy judges and trustees to follow essentially the same approach when choosing an appropriate interest rate" under any of these other provisions of the Code. [**Till v. SCS Credit Corp.,** 541 U.S. 465 (2004)] Most bankruptcy courts have applied the prime-plus formula from the plurality's opinion in *Till* in Chapter 11 cram down cases. [*See* **Wells Fargo Bank v. Texas Grand Prairie Hotel Realty, LLC (*In re* Texas Grand Prairie Hotel Realty, LLC),** 710 F.3d 324 (5th Cir. 2013) (holding that it would not "tie bankruptcy courts to a specific methodology as they assess the appropriate Chapter 11 cramdown rate of interest," but noting that the "vast majority of bankruptcy courts" used *Till's* prime-plus formula in Chapter 11 cases)]

(2) Secured Party Receives Indubitable Equivalent

The plan satisfies the "fair and equitable" requirement if it provides the creditor with the *indubitable equivalent* of her secured claim. [B.C. § 1129(b)(2)(A)(iii)]

e.g. **Example:** Prior to bankruptcy, Creditor sold Debtor 79 tracts of land for $65 million. Debtor paid $9 million and financed the remainder through Creditor. While Debtor eventually paid Creditor over $60 million for the properties, Debtor failed to repay the debt in full by the maturity date of the loan. Debtor filed for relief under Chapter 11 and proposed a partial dirt-for-debt plan. (In a partial dirt-for-debt plan, the debtor transfers part of the collateral to the secured creditor in satisfaction of the creditor's claim.) The plan impaired Creditor's claim and Creditor voted against it, thereby triggering a cram down. After conducting valuation hearings, the bankruptcy court concluded that the Debtor's conveyance of 8 of the 79 tracts to Creditor and the payment of cash totaling about $1 million constituted the indubitable equivalent of Creditor's claim. On appeal, the Fourth Circuit rejected Creditor's argument that the uncertainties associated with property valuation make it impossible for *any* partial dirt-for-debt plan to satisfy the indubitable equivalent standard. The court noted that such a holding would "eviscerate" the standard because uncertainty inheres in all disputed valuations. The court affirmed the bankruptcy court's decision and "decline[d] to hold that a partial dirt-for-debt plan can never provide the indubitable equivalent of a secured creditor's claim, as a matter of law." [**Bate Land Co. LP v. Bate Land Timber LLC,** 877 F.3d 188 (4th Cir. 2017)]

(3) Collateral Sold and Lien Attaches to Proceeds

The third statutory method for satisfying the "fair and equitable" requirement for secured claims is for the plan to provide for the collateral to be sold free and clear of the creditor's lien, with the lien attaching to the proceeds of the sale. The lien on the sale proceeds must be treated in a manner described in (1) (deferred cash payments) or (2) (indubitable equivalent) above. For example, the debtor may turn over the sale proceeds to the secured creditor, which satisfies the secured creditor's claim. The secured creditor realizes the indubitable equivalent of its claim, and the debtor satisfies the Code's "fair and equitable" requirement.

Note: The sale is subject to the creditor's right, under § 363(k), to bid at the sale, purchase the property, and offset her claim against the purchase price. [B.C. § 1129(b)(2)(A)(ii)]

(ii) Unsecured Claims

If a class of unsecured creditors is *impaired and does not accept the plan,* then the plan's treatment of that class *must be fair and equitable.* As to any such impaired class, the plan is fair and equitable if it satisfies *one of the following two conditions.*

(1) Each Creditor Receives Property Equal to Allowed Claim

The first statutory method for satisfying the "fair and equitable" requirement for a class of unsecured creditors is for the plan to provide that each creditor in the class receive property, e.g., cash notes, stock, or other property of the debtor, having a *present value,* as of the effective date of the plan, equal to the allowed amount of her unsecured claim. [B.C. § 1129(b)(2)(B)(i)]

(2) Senior Classes Fully Paid Before Junior Classes

In many cases, the Chapter 11 debtor will not be able to pay its unsecured creditors in full. Thus, the Code provides the *absolute priority rule* as an alternative method for satisfying the "fair and equitable" requirement if a class of unsecured creditors is impaired and does not vote to approve the plan. The *absolute priority rule* requires that no holder of a claim or an interest that is junior to the impaired unsecured class receive or retain any property on account of the junior claim or interest. In other words, if an impaired unsecured class does not vote to approve the plan and the plan does not pay those claims in full, then the plan may not provide that the debtor's current equity holders retain their interests in the reorganized entity. [B.C. § 1129(b)(2)(B)(ii)]

(a) "New Value Exception"

The courts are split concerning the continuing validity of a pre-Code, judicially created exception allowing equity security holders to retain an interest in cases in which they make a (i) *fresh contribution,* (ii) *in money or money's worth,* that is (iii) *reasonably equivalent to the interest received or retained,* and (iv) *necessary for a successful reorganization.* [*See* **Case v. Los Angeles Lumber Products Co.,** 308 U.S. 106 (1939); *see, e.g., In re* **Civic Partners Sioux City, LLC,** 2013 WL 5534743 (Bankr. N.D. Iowa 2013) (holding that $150,000 new value proposal was insufficient while noting that court did not have to "definitely decide the application of the 'new value' exception"] In two opinions, the Supreme Court has dodged the issue of whether there is a "new value" exception to the absolute priority rule. [*See* **Bank of America National Trust and Savings Association v. 203 North LaSalle Street Partnership,** 526 U.S. 434 (1999) (without ruling on whether the new value exception survived enactment of the Bankruptcy Code, holding that plan giving pre-bankruptcy equity holders the sole right to contribute new capital and keep their equity, without consideration of alternatives, could not constitute new value); **Norwest Bank Worthington v. Ahlers,** 485 U.S. 197 (1988) (holding that debtors' promise of future "labor, experience and expertise" did not constitute "money or money's worth" and, thus, was not new value)]

(b) The Absolute Priority Rule in Individual Cases

In BAPCPA, Congress added an exception to the language of § 1129(b)(2)(B)(ii) for *individual debtors.* That *exception provides* that if the debtor is an individual, she may "retain property included in the estate under section 1115," subject to the Code's requirement for domestic support obligations. [B.C. § 1129(b)(2)(B)(ii), 1129(a)(14)] Congress also added § 1115, which defines property of the estate in an individual Chapter 11 case to include all property under § 541, all property acquired post-petition of the kind described in § 541, and all of the debtor's post-petition earnings. [B.C. § 1115] The courts have split on whether Congress intended, through these changes to the Code, to repeal the absolute priority rule for cases involving individual Chapter 11 debtors.

1. Narrow View

Most courts have adopted the *narrow* interpretation of the *absolute priority rule* for *individual* Chapter 11 debtors. Courts adopting the narrow view hold that the *exception excludes* from the operation of the absolute priority rule *only* the debtor's post-petition earnings and acquisitions of property.

Example: Debtor filed for relief under Chapter 13, but his case was converted to Chapter 11, because his debts exceeded the Chapter 13 debt limits. Debtor proposed that he retain valuable, non-exempt, pre-petition assets while paying a small dividend to his unsecured creditors, a majority of which voted to reject his plan. The bankruptcy court denied confirmation on the basis of the absolute priority rule. The Fifth Circuit affirmed. The court explained that with BAPCPA Congress amended § 1129(b)(2)(B)(ii) and added § 1115 in order to coordinate the rules for individuals in Chapter 11 to avoid having more favorable terms for individual debtors in Chapter 11 than in Chapter 13. By including the debtor's post-petition earnings and property in the new definition of estate property at § 1115, however, Congress also "had to modify the absolute priority rule so that a debtor would not be saddled with committing all post-petition property to satisfy creditors' claims." Thus, the court held that Congress did not repeal the absolute priority rule, but instead modified and refined it in order to protect an individual debtor's post-petition earnings and acquisitions of property. [*In re* **Lively,** 717 F.3d 406 (5th Cir. 2013)]

2. Broad View

A minority of courts has adopted the broad view of the absolute priority rule. Courts following the broad view do not apply the absolute priority rule to individual Chapter 11 debtors. They reason that the "except" clause in § 1129(b)(2)(B)(ii) speaks in terms of property under § 1115, and is not limited to post-petition property. Thus, the plain meaning of the statutory provisions leads to the conclusion that "the absolute priority rule no longer applies to prevent individual Chapter 11 debtors from retaining pre- or post-petition property over an unsecured creditor's objection." [**SPCP Group, LLC v. Biggins,** 465 B.R. 316 (M.D. Fla. 2011)]

EXAM TIP

Remember that if an impaired class of **unsecured claims** has rejected the plan, the *"fair and equitable"* element of a cram down is determined as follows: The plan is fair and equitable with respect to the class if (i) the plan proposes to pay each creditor in the class the full amount of her allowed unsecured claim on a present value basis, or (ii) no holder of a claim or interest that is junior to the class will receive or retain any property, on account of the junior claim or interest, under the plan. The rule stated in (ii) is known as **the absolute priority rule.** On an exam, make sure to note that some courts recognize a **new value exception to the absolute priority rule** if the plan provides for a class of equity security holders to receive or retain an interest in the reorganized debtor, on account of their junior interests, in exchange for a fresh contribution to the reorganized debtor in money or money's worth that is reasonably equivalent to the interest received or retained and necessary for the reorganization. Your professor also may test you on whether the absolute priority rule applies to an individual Chapter 11 debtor. It is important to understand how the courts have construed the statutory language in the cram down and estate property sections of the Code in order to arrive at the **narrow and broad interpretations** of the absolute priority rule.

DETERMINING WHETHER A CRAM DOWN IS FAIR AND EQUITABLE		GILBERT
TO BE FAIR AND EQUITABLE, THE PLAN MUST PROPOSE ONE OF THE ACCEPTABLE TREATMENTS FOR EACH CLASS OF CLAIMS OR INTERESTS THAT IS IMPAIRED AND HAS REJECTED THE PLAN.		
SECURED CLASSES*	**UNSECURED CLASSES**	**CLASSES OF EQUITY INTERESTS**
Creditor retains her lien on the collateral for the allowed amount of the secured claim, and receives deferred **cash** payments totaling at least the allowed amount of her secured claim and having a **present value** of at least the value of the collateral *or* Creditor realizes the **indubitable equivalent** of her secured claim *or* Collateral is **sold free and clear** of creditor's lien, with the lien attaching to the proceeds and treated in one of the ways above	Each creditor of the class receives property (not necessarily cash) having a **present value** equal to the allowed amount of her unsecured claim *or* No creditor or interest holder junior to the class receives or retains any property on account of the junior claim or interest (**absolute priority rule**)	Each interest holder receives or retains property having a **present value** equal to the allowed amount of any fixed liquidation preference or fixed redemption price to which the holder is entitled, or the value of her equity interest, whichever is the **greatest** *or* No interest holder junior to the class receives or retains any property on account of the junior interest
* Note that usually each secured claim is classified in a separate class.		

(iii) Equity Interests

With respect to a class of interests, the plan must propose one of the two following methods of treatment for such interests in order to satisfy the "fair and equitable" requirement.

(1) Holder Receives or Retains Property Equal to Any Applicable Fixed Liquidation Preference or Fixed Redemption Price, or Value of Equity Interest

Treatment of an impaired class of interests is fair and equitable, notwithstanding the class's vote against the plan, if the plan provides that each interest holder *receive or retain property* having a *present value,* as of the effective date of the plan, equal to the allowed amount of any fixed liquidation preference or fixed redemption price to which the holder is entitled, or the value of her equity interest, *whichever is the greatest.* [B.C. § 1129(b)(2)(C)(i)]

(2) Senior Classes Fully Paid Before Junior Classes

An alternative method of satisfying the "fair and equitable" requirement is if no interest holder that is junior to the class receives or retains any property on account of the junior interest. [B.C. § 1129(b)(2)(C)(ii)]

4. Denial of Confirmation

On the request of a governmental unit that is a party in interest, the court must deny confirmation of a plan if it finds that the *plan's principal purpose* is to *avoid taxes* or *registration under § 5 of the Securities Act of 1933.* In any hearing on this issue the governmental unit bears the burden of proof on the issue of avoidance. [B.C. § 1129(d)]

G. Small Business Debtors

1. Introduction

Prior to the passage of BAPCPA, the Bankruptcy Code permitted a debtor to elect treatment as a small business debtor. BAPCPA eliminated the election and made the small business provisions of the Bankruptcy Code mandatory for any debtor that satisfied the Code's definition of a small business debtor. The *debtor must designate* its status as either a small or not a small business by *checking the appropriate box* on the voluntary petition. [Official Forms 101, 201] In an involuntary case, the debtor must file a statement within 14 days of the order for relief as to whether it is a small business. [Bankruptcy Rule 1020(a)] The United States trustee or a party in interest may *object* to the debtor's designation within *30 days of the conclusion of the § 341 meeting* or within *30 days of any amendment* to the debtor's designation, whichever is later. [Bankruptcy Rule 1020(b)] The debtor's designation stands unless and until the court enters an order finding that the debtor's designation is incorrect. [Bankruptcy Rule 1020(a); *see In re* **Moore Properties of Person County, LLC,** 2020 WL 995544 (Bankr. M.D. N.C. 2020) (stating that a debtor's original designation as a small or non-small business "controls unless and until the court enters an order finding that a debtor's election is incorrect and such 'review is triggered by an objection to the designation.' ")]

The SBRA created *subchapter V* of chapter 11 of the Bankruptcy Code. A *small business case* is one in which the debtor qualifies as a *small business debtor* but *does not elect* to proceed under *subchapter V.* [B.C. § 101(51C)] A *small business debtor,* however, may *elect* to proceed under *subchapter V* of chapter 11. If the small business debtor elects subchapter

V, then the debtor's case is *not a small business case,* as the Code defines that term, and the subchapter V rules and procedures apply. [*See infra* § H of this Chapter]

2. Definition of a Small Business Debtor

The SBRA amended the Code's definition of a small business debtor. A *small business debtor* is any person *engaged in commercial or business activities,* including any affiliated debtor, whose aggregate *noncontingent liquidated secured and unsecured debts,* on the petition filing date or the date of the order for relief, are *$3,024,725 or less,* excluding debts owed to *affiliates or insiders.*

A debtor does not qualify as a small business debtor if its *primary activity* is the business of owning *single asset real estate.* [*See* B.C. § 101(51B) for definition of single asset real estate.] To qualify as a *small business debtor*, at least *50 percent* of the debtor's liabilities must arise from its *commercial or business activities*. [B.C. § 101(51D)]

The Code's definition of a *small business debtor does not include*:

a. *any member* of a group of affiliated debtors that has *aggregate noncontingent liquidated secured and unsecured liabilities greater than $3,024,725,* excluding debts owed to insiders and affiliates [B.C. § 101(51D)(B)(i)];

b. any corporate debtor subject to the reporting requirements of *§§ 13 or 15(d) of the Securities Exchange Act of 1934* [B.C. § 101(51D)(B)(ii)]; or

c. any debtor that is *an affiliate of a corporation* described above in clause b. [B.C. § 101(51D)(B)(iii)]

e.g. **Example:** Denzel works as an accountant for a large accountancy firm. Denzel also owns two houses. He lives in one house and rents out the other to a family. The rental house is a single residential unit. Denzel's annual gross income is $100,000: $85,000 from his accountancy job and $15,000 from his rental property. Denzel has assets of $500,000 and liabilities of $750,000. Of the $750,000 in liabilities, $250,000 is from his rental property business. Denzel files for relief under Chapter 11. Denzel does not qualify as a small business debtor. His liabilities are well below the $3,024,725 limit, but only one third of those liabilities arose from his business or commercial activities. [B.C. § 101(51D)(A)]

Note: While Denzel owns real property that he rents, he is not in the business of owning single asset real estate. First, the definition of single asset real estate contains an exception for "residential real property with fewer than 4 residential units." Denzel owns and rents only a single residential unit. Second, his rental income is only 15% of his gross; thus, the rental property does not generate substantially all of his gross income. [B.C. § 101(51B)]

e.g. **Example:** Dinah is the sole owner of *Atlas, Inc., Bella Corp.,* and *Calypso Company. Atlas, Bella,* and *Calypso* file for relief under Chapter 11 on the same day. Each firm's total liabilities range between $1 and $2 million, but the three firms' aggregate noncontingent liquidated liabilities equal $4 million. None of the three firms has insider or affiliate debt. *Atlas, Bella,* and *Calypso* are not small business debtors, because the aggregate of the three affiliated firms' liabilities exceeds $3,024,725. [*See In re* **CCT Communications, Inc.,** 420 B.R. 160 (Bankr. S.D. N.Y. 2009) ("affiliated debtors aggregate their non-insider, non-affiliate liquidated non-contingent debts" and if the aggregated amount exceeds the small business debt limit, then none of the debtors "is considered a small business debtor even though each debtor might be if treated separately")]

e.g. **Example:** Dinah is the sole owner and president of *Atlas, Inc., Bella Corp.,* and *Calypso Company. Atlas, Bella,* and *Calypso* file for relief under Chapter 11 on the same day. None of the firms qualifies as a single asset real estate business. *Atlas* has $1 million in liabilities, but $500,000 of that amount is a guarantee of a loan owed by *Bella. Bella* is current on the loan, which means that $500,000 of *Atlas's* debt is contingent. On the petition date, *Bella* and *Calypso* each have $1.5 million in liabilities. Pre-petition, Dinah had loaned $400,000 to *Bella* and $600,000 to *Calypso.* As the president of both firms, Dinah is an insider, which means that in computing liabilities for purposes of the small business debtor definition the $1 million in loans from Dinah to *Bella* and *Calypso* do not count toward the firms' liability totals. While *Atlas, Bella,* and *Calypso* qualify as a group of affiliated debtors, their aggregate noncontingent liquidated liabilities are $2.5 million ($500,000 for *Atlas* and $2 million for *Bella* and *Calypso* combined). Therefore, *Atlas, Bella,* and *Calypso* are small business debtors.

3. Official Committee of Unsecured Creditors

Unless the court for cause orders otherwise, an official committee of unsecured creditors is *not appointed* in a small business case. [B.C. § 1102(a)(3)] Prior to enactment of the SBRA, a debtor did not qualify as a small business debtor if the United States Trustee appointed an official committee of unsecured creditors. That no longer is the case. Normally, a committee will not be appointed in a small business case but if the court orders the appointment of a committee, the debtor still qualifies as a small business debtor.

4. Duties of Debtor in Possession or Trustee in Small Business Case

In small business cases, the Bankruptcy Code imposes on the debtor in possession or the Chapter 11 trustee, if one is appointed, additional obligations not applicable to a non-small business case. [B.C. §§ 308, 1116; Bankruptcy Rule 2015(a)(6); Official Form 425C] The *small business debtor* must:

a. file its *most recent balance sheet, statement of operations, cash-flow statement, and Federal income tax return* with the petition in a voluntary case or within seven days of the order for relief in an involuntary case, or file a *statement* made under *penalty of perjury* that such documents do not exist;

b. *attend all meetings* scheduled by the court or United States Trustee, including *an initial debtor interview* with the United States trustee prior to the § 341 meeting;

c. *file monthly operating reports* that include:

   (i)   the *debtor's profitability;*

   (ii) reasonable approximations of the *debtor's projected cash receipts and cash disbursements;*

   (iii) a comparison of *actual cash receipts and disbursements* with *prior projections;*

   (iv) whether the debtor is *complying with the requirements* imposed by the *Bankruptcy Code and the Federal Rules of Bankruptcy Procedure;*

   (v)   whether the debtor is *filing tax returns* and other required government filings in a *timely fashion;*

   (vi) whether debtor is *paying taxes and administrative expenses when due;*

   (vii) the *steps that debtor intends to make to remedy* any failure to comply with the requirements of the Bankruptcy Code or Rules, to file tax returns or other government reporting documents, or to pay taxes or other administrative expenses; and

   (viii) any other matter that is in the *best interests of the debtor and creditors,* and in the *public's interest in fair and efficient administration* of the bankruptcy laws;

d. *timely file all schedules and statements of financial affairs,* unless the court, after notice and hearing, grants an extension, which extension, absent compelling and extraordinary circumstances, shall not extend beyond 30 days after the order for relief;

e. *file all post-petition financial and other reports* required by the Federal Rules of Bankruptcy Procedure or by local bankruptcy rules;

f. subject to § 363(c)(2)'s rules on use, sale, or lease of cash collateral, *maintain insurance* that is customary and appropriate to the industry;

g. *timely file all tax returns and other required government filings;*

h. subject to § 363(c)(2)'s rules on use, sale, or lease of cash collateral, *timely pay all taxes entitled to administrative expense priority,* except taxes contested in appropriate proceedings being diligently prosecuted; and

i. allow the *United States trustee to inspect the debtor's business premises, books, and records* at reasonable times, after reasonable prior written notice, unless the debtor waives notice.

5. United States Trustee Duties in Small Business Case

a. The United States trustee has additional oversight obligations in small business cases. [28 U.S.C. § 586(a)(7)] The United States trustee must:

   (i)   conduct an *initial interview with the debtor* as soon as practicable after the order for relief but *before the date set for the § 341 meeting;*

   (ii) if appropriate and advisable, *visit the debtor's business premises,* ascertain the *state of the debtor's books and records,* and verify that the debtor has *filed its tax returns;* and

   (iii) *review and monitor the debtor's activities* in order to determine as soon as possible whether debtor will be *unable to confirm a plan.*

b. At the *initial debtor interview,* the United States trustee shall:

   (i)   begin to *investigate the debtor's viability;*

   (ii) ask about the *debtor's business plan;*

   (iii) explain the debtor's obligation to *file monthly operating reports* and other *required reports;*

   (iv) try to develop an *agreed scheduling order;* and

   (v)   *inform* the debtor of other *obligations.*

6. The Small Business Debtor's Disclosure Statement and Plan

a. **Disclosure Statement**

   If the court determines that a disclosure statement must be filed, then it must be filed *no later than 300 days after* the order for relief. [B.C. § 1121(e)(2)] The Bankruptcy Code does not provide a deadline for filing the disclosure statement in non-small business cases. Otherwise, the Bankruptcy Code's disclosure-statement requirements are more flexible for small compared with non-small business cases.

   (i)   The bankruptcy court may determine that a disclosure statement is not needed because the *plan provides adequate information.* [B.C. § 1125(f)(1)]

   (ii) The bankruptcy court also may approve a disclosure statement submitted on *standard forms.* [B.C. § 1125(f)(2); Official Form 425B]

(iii) The bankruptcy court may *conditionally approve* the disclosure statement subject to final approval at a hearing after notice. [B.C. § 1125(f)(3)(A)] The debtor may solicit votes on the plan based on a conditionally approved disclosure statement, but the debtor must mail the disclosure statement *no later than 25 days before* the plan confirmation hearing. [B.C. § 1125(f)(3)(B)] The court may combine the final hearing on the disclosure statement with the hearing on plan confirmation. [B.C. § 1125(f)(3)(C)]

b. Exclusivity Period

Unless the court grants an extension or for cause orders otherwise, the *small business debtor* has the exclusive right to file a plan for the first *180 days after* the order for relief. [B.C. § 1121(e)(1)]

c. "Drop Dead" Date

Unless the court grants an extension, the plan and disclosure statement, if any, must be filed no later than *300 days after* the order for relief. [B.C. § 1121(e)(2)] Courts have struggled with how to interpret the 300-day deadline language that BAPCPA added to the Code.

(i) Non-Debtors and the 300-Day Deadline

The Bankruptcy Code does not specifically state that the "debtor" must file a plan and disclosure statement, if any, within 300 days. Thus, the question has arisen whether the 300-day plan-filing deadline applies to debtors and non-debtors alike. The few courts that have addressed the issue generally have held that the 300-day time limit applies only to the debtor, not to other parties in interest that want to file a plan. [*See, e.g., In re* **Simbaki, Ltd.,** 522 B.R. 917 (Bankr. S.D. Tex. 2014) (holding that 300-day deadline does not apply to non-debtor plan proponents); *In re* **Florida Coastal Airlines, Inc.,** 361 B.R. 286 (Bankr. S.D. Fla. 2007) (holding that the 300-day plan proposal period in § 1121(e)(2) "applies only to plans filed by the debtor and that there is no statutory deadline for the filing of such a reorganization plan by any party in interest other than the debtor")]

(ii) Plan Amendments Outside the 300 Days

It is unclear whether the Bankruptcy Code only requires the filing of a plan within 300 days or whether all amendments to the plan also must be filed within the 300-day period. There is very little case law on the issue, but those few courts that have considered the question appear to focus on whether an amendment outside the 300 days is simply a cleaned-up version of the first-filed plan or a fundamentally different plan from the originally filed plan. [*See, e.g., In re* **Castle Horizon Real Estate, LLC,** 2010 WL 3636160 (Bankr. E.D. N.C. 2010) (holding that the 300-day deadline applied to a plan that was not a " 'cleaned up' version of the original"); *In re* **Florida Coastal Airlines, Inc.,** *supra* (holding that debtor's amended plan, which was filed more than 300 days after the order for relief, related back to original plan filed within the 300-day period because the amended plan was "fundamentally a cleaned-up version of [debtor's] original plan")]

(iii) Debtor Incorrectly Identifies Itself as *Not* a Small Business Debtor

The small business debtor must identify itself as such on the voluntary petition or must file a statement indicating its status in an involuntary case. If the court later determines that the debtor is a small business, even though debtor had identified as a non-small business, the question arises whether the 300-day deadline for filing a plan runs from the order for relief or from the court's subsequent determination that the debtor is a small business. The few cases that have addressed the issue have held that the 300-day deadline runs from the order for relief.

Example: Debtor filed for relief under Chapter 11 and checked the box on the petition stating that it was not a small business debtor. Two months later, the United States trustee objected to the debtor's designation on the petition. More than four months after the debtor had filed its voluntary petition, the bankruptcy court determined that the debtor's designation on the petition was incorrect and that the debtor indeed was a small business debtor. The court held that the 300-day plan-proposal deadline ran from the debtor's filing of the petition, leaving the debtor with six, as opposed to ten, months to file a plan. [*In re* **Display Group,** 2010 WL 4777550 (Bankr. E.D. N.Y. 2010)]

(iv) Debtor Incorrectly Identifies Itself as a Small Business Debtor

If a debtor initially checks the small business debtor box on the petition and does not elect subchapter V, then the debtor's Chapter 11 case proceeds as a small business case. [Bankruptcy Rule 1020(a)] If the debtor later seeks to change its designation to a non-small business, the question that arises is whether the debtor may avoid the consequences of not satisfying the Code's small-business deadlines *before* the change of status to a non-small business. There are few cases specifically on the issue of the 300-day deadline. [*See In re* **Swartville, LLC,** 483 B.R. 453 (Bankr. E.D. N.C. 2012) (approving debtor's amended petition stating that debtor was *not* a small business debtor and holding that the debtor's failure to file its second amended plan within the 300-day deadline was excusable and not grounds for dismissal because the debtor had mistakenly and in "good faith" checked the wrong box on the petition and that mistaken designation neither benefitted debtor nor prejudiced creditors)]

(v) Case Converted to Chapter 11

What happens if the debtor originally files under another chapter of the Bankruptcy Code and later converts her case? Does the 300-day deadline run from the original bankruptcy filing or from the date of conversion to Chapter 11? There is very little case law on the issue.

Example: Debtor originally filed for relief under Chapter 13 in August of 2011. In December of 2012, the bankruptcy court granted her motion to convert her case to Chapter 11. Debtor filed her Chapter 11 plan approximately four months later and a confirmation hearing was scheduled for June of 2013. When the debtor sought an extension of the confirmation hearing date, the United States trustee objected on the ground that debtor had filed her plan more than 300 days from the order for relief, which was the date that she commenced her bankruptcy case under Chapter 13. The bankruptcy court agreed with the interpretation of the Code advanced by the United States trustee and cited to the language of § 348(a), which provides that conversion to another chapter does not change the date of the order for relief. Because the debtor filed her Chapter 11 plan about 20 months from the commencement of her Chapter 13 case, she failed to satisfy the Code's requirement that a Chapter 11 small business debtor file the plan within 300 days of the order for relief. [*In re* **Rivera,** 2013 WL 3367100 (Bankr. D. P.R. 2013)]

d. Plan Confirmation

The bankruptcy court must confirm the small business debtor's plan *no later than 45 days after* the plan is filed, unless the time for confirmation is extended. [B.C. §§ 1129(e), 1121(e)(3)]

e. Time Extensions

The court may extend the small business debtor's (1) *exclusivity period,* (2) *300-day deadline* for filing a plan and disclosure statement, and (3) *45-day period* for plan confirmation, but only if several conditions are satisfied [B.C. § 1121(e)(3)]:

(i) the *small business debtor* provides *notice* to parties in interest, including the United States trustee;

(ii) the *small business debtor* demonstrates by a *preponderance of the evidence* that it is *more likely than not* that the court will *confirm a plan within a reasonable period of time;*

(iii) the court imposes a *new deadline* when it grants the extension; and

(iv) the court *signs the order* extending the deadline *before the existing deadline expires.*

Example: Debtor filed for relief under Chapter 11 and checked the box on the petition stating it was a small business debtor. On the 299th day after filing its petition, Debtor filed a motion to extend the 300-day deadline for filing its plan. But, § 1121(e)(3) requires that the order extending the deadline be signed prior to the expiration of the 300-day deadline. The court explained that because a hearing was needed before extending the deadline, "no order *could have been* signed before that deadline expired" and, in fact, no order was signed before the deadline expired. Thus, the bankruptcy court denied Debtor's motion to extend the 300-day deadline for filing its plan of reorganization. [*In re* **Veridia, LLC,** 2016 WL 3049655 (Bankr. S.D. W.Va. 2016)]

H. Subchapter V

1. Introduction

Congress enacted the SBRA on August 23, 2019, and the law went into effect 180 days later on February 19, 2020. [Pub. L. No. 116–54 § 5 (2019)] The SBRA created *subchapter V* of chapter 11 of the Bankruptcy Code.

In a voluntary case, the debtor must check the box on the petition indicating it *chooses to proceed under subchapter V.* [Official Forms 101, 201] In an involuntary case, the debtor must file a statement within 14 days of the order for relief as to whether it is a small business debtor and, if so, whether it elects to proceed under subchapter V. [Bankruptcy Rule 1020(a)] The United States trustee or a party in interest may *object* to the debtor's election within *30 days of the conclusion of the § 341 meeting* or within *30 days of any amendment* to the debtor's election, whichever is later. [Bankruptcy Rule 1020(b)] The debtor's election stands unless and until the court enters an order finding that the debtor's election is incorrect. [Bankruptcy Rule 1020(a)]

2. Differences from Other Chapter 11 Cases

There are a number of ways in which a subchapter V case differs from other Chapter 11 cases, including small business cases. [*See infra* § 4 for a table showing the Chapter 11 sections not applicable in subchapter V.] With the SBRA, Congress sought to "streamline the bankruptcy process by which small business debtors reorganize and rehabilitate their financial affairs." [H.R. Rep. No. 116–171, at 1 (2019)] The SBRA's changes to the Code were an effort to expedite the Chapter 11 process and make it more cost-effective for subchapter V debtors. In *In re* **Seven Stars on the Hudson Corporation,** 618 B.R. 333 (Bankr. S.D. Fla. 2020), Judge Grossman listed the following benefits available in a subchapter V case:

a. *eliminating* the *absolute priority rule*;

b. *eliminating the requirement* that an *official committee* of unsecured creditors be appointed;

c. *eliminating the requirement* that debtor file a *disclosure statement*;

d. "appointment of a *Subchapter V trustee* to assist [the debtor] in developing a consensual plan";

e. allowing *only the debtor to file a plan*;

f. allowing the debtor "to *modify a claim secured only by a security interest in the debtor's principal residence*," but only if the new value the debtor received from granting the security interest "was used primarily in connection with the debtor's business and not primarily to acquire the property";

g. allowing confirmation of a plan even if all classes of claims and interests reject the plan;

h. allowing the debtor to pay *administrative expenses over time*;

i. *modifying § 327(a)'s requirement of disinterestedness* so that a professional person is not disqualified for employment solely because that person holds a pre-petition claim of less than $10,000; and

j. *eliminating* the "requirement to pay *quarterly U.S. Trustee fees*."

3. Definition of a Subchapter V Debtor

a. Impact of COVID Acts and BTATCA

As originally enacted, the SBRA defined "debtor" as a *small business debtor.* [Pub. L. No. 116–54 (2019)] Thus, the Code's small business debtor definition applied to both small business cases and subchapter V cases. But, in COVID-related legislation, Congress temporarily amended subchapter V's definition of debtor to increase *the debt limit* for subchapter V to *$7,500,000*. [CARES Act § 1113(a)(1) , COVID Extension Act § 2(a)(1)] The temporary amendment to subchapter V's debtor definition sunsetted on March 27, 2022. But, in the BTATCA, Congress, once again, increased the debt limit for subchapter V to $7.5 million. [BTATCA § 2d)] The BTATCA change sunsets on *June 21, 2024.* Therefore, as of the writing of this guide, *either* of the following type of debtor may elect to proceed under subchapter V:

(i) a *small business debtor,* as defined by § 101(51D); *or*

(ii) a debtor whose liabilities are *greater than $3,024,725 but less than or equal to $7,500,000,* and that satisfies the other requirements of § 1182(1)'s definition of "debtor."

If a *small business debtor elects* to proceed under subchapter V, then the bankruptcy case is *no longer a small business case.* [B.C. § 101(51C)] Subchapter V's provisions at §§ 1181–1195 govern the case. If the small business debtor *does not elect* subchapter V, then chapter 11's rules, including its special provisions for small business cases, govern.

b. Current Definition

The *current definition of a subchapter V debtor* is any person *engaged in commercial or business activities,* including any affiliated debtor, whose aggregate *noncontingent liquidated secured and unsecured debts,* on the petition filing date or the date of the order for relief, are *$7,500,000 or less,* excluding debts owed to *affiliates or insiders.* [B.C. § 1182(1)(A)] To qualify as a *subchapter V debtor,* at least *50 percent* of the debtor's liabilities must arise from its *commercial or business activities.* [B.C. § 1182(1)(A)] A debtor does not qualify as a subchapter V debtor if its *primary activity* is the business of owning *single asset real estate.* [*See* B.C. § 101(51B) for definition of single asset real estate.]

(i) Engaged in Commercial or Business Activities

There is limited subchapter V case law on the question of what it means for a debtor to be "engaged in commercial or business activities." The courts are in agreement that "engaged in" means at the time of the bankruptcy petition. [*See, e.g., In re* **Offer Space, LLC,** 629 B.R. 299 (Bankr. D. Utah 2021) ("to be eligible for Subchapter V, a debtor must be presently 'engaged in commercial or business activities' on the date of filing the petition for relief' "); *In re* **Johnson,** 2021 WL 825156 (Bankr. N.D. Tex. 2021) ("the 'engaged in' inquiry is inherently contemporary in focus instead of retrospective, requiring the assessment of the debtor's current state of affairs as of the filing of the bankruptcy petition")] \

Courts are divided, however, on whether the debtor's business must be operational at the time of bankruptcy and also on how broadly to read the phrase "commercial or business activities."

Example: Married debtors filed for relief under Chapter 7 and sought to convert their case to a subchapter V Chapter 11 case. Prior to filing for bankruptcy, Husband had owned and managed several oil and gas companies but at the time of the petition the companies were defunct. Because the defunct firms were not carrying out any commercial or business activities at the time of the bankruptcy petition, Husband did not qualify for relief under subchapter V of Chapter 11. The bankruptcy court also rejected Debtors' arguments that Husband's current job as an officer in a firm solely owned by his mother (Mother) meant that he was engaged in commercial or business activities and that Wife was an affiliate of Husband. The court explained that Husband was nothing more than an employee "with heightened obligations" of Mother's firm. The court noted that Debtors confused the definition of "insider" with that for an "affiliate." Neither Husband nor Wife owned an interest in Mother's firm, which was not the debtor in bankruptcy. Thus, the court held that neither Husband nor Wife qualified for relief under subchapter V, and denied Debtors' motion to convert. [*In re* **Johnson,** *supra*]

Example: Debtor, an individual, filed for relief under Chapter 11 and elected subchapter V. Prior to filing for bankruptcy, Debtor had worked as a manager for Hailco. Debtor was the sole owner of JMI, a limited liability company, and JMI owned 30% of Hailco. Hailco failed financially and ceased operations prior to Debtor's bankruptcy case. Because Hailco had failed, Debtor took a job with an insurance brokerage firm. Debtor had no equity interest in the insurance firm; he was a W-2 wage earner. The bankruptcy court explained that the phrase "commercial or business activities" has a "broad and expansive meaning." Thus, the court concluded that Debtor's work for JMI and his wind down work for Hailco counted as commercial or business activity. The court also concluded that Debtor's work "as a wage earner" for the insurance firm constituted "commercial or business activities" because he sold "a product in the private marketplace in order to make money for himself and his employer." Recognizing the "seemingly radical nature" of its conclusion about Debtor's work for the insurance firm, the bankruptcy court explained that not "every private sector wage earner is eligible for relief under Subchapter V" because the Code also requires that at least 50% of the debtor's liabilities arise from the debtor's commercial or business activities. [*In re* **Ikalowych,** 629 B.R. 261 (Bankr. D. Colo. 2021)]

(ii) Business of Owning Single Asset Real Estate

A debtor does not qualify as a subchapter V debtor if its *primary activity* is the business of owning *single asset real estate.* [*See* B.C. § 101(51B)]

Example: Debtor, which owned and operated a 79-room hotel, filed for relief under Chapter 11 and elected to proceed under subchapter V. Debtor's liabilities fell below the debt limits for subchapter V, and all its liabilities arose from its business activities. Creditor, however, claimed that Debtor was not eligible for subchapter V because Debtor's primary activity was owning single asset real estate. The bankruptcy court held that the hotel was not a single asset real estate project because Debtor provided "services *other* than those incidental to renting hotel rooms." Unlike the owner of vacant land or an apartment complex, the owner of a hotel provides daily cleaning services, daily check-in service, which requires a 24-hour reception desk, repair and maintenance services for hotel rooms, and often "additional amenities", such as business services, wi/fi, conference rooms, swimming pools, gym facilities, and even guest laundry services. The court explained that even a hotel that provides fewer amenities still "require[s] more staff, more cost, and more effort than companies managing vacant land or even an apartment complex where tenants sign a one-year lease and require little additional assistance." Creditor also argued that the hotel was a single asset real estate project *unless* the additional amenities offered by Debtor generated additional income. The bankruptcy court rejected this argument by noting that the Code contained no such requirement. The court concluded that the hotel was not single asset real estate and, thus, Debtor was eligible for relief under subchapter V. *In re* **ENKOGS1, LLC,** 626 B.R. 860 (Bankr. M.D. Fla. 2021).

(iii) Exclusions

Subchapter V's definition of *debtor does not include*:

(1) *any member* of a group of affiliated debtors that has *aggregate noncontingent liquidated secured and unsecured liabilities greater than $7,500,000,* excluding debts owed to insiders and affiliates [B.C. § 1182(1)(B)(i)];

(2) any corporate debtor subject to the reporting requirements of *§§ 13 or 15(d) of the Securities Exchange Act of 1934* [B.C. § 1182(1)(B)(ii)]; or

(3) any debtor that is *an affiliate of a corporation* described in clause (2) above. [B.C. § 1182(1)(B)(iii)]

4. Code Sections That Do Not Apply in Subchapter V

Certain Code provisions do not apply to a subchapter V case. [B.C. § 1181] Many of these exclusions involve either *small business cases*, as defined at § 101(51D), or *individual cases.* The third column of the table notes the *exception* when the Code section *would apply* to a *subchapter V* case. [B.C. § 1181(b)] If Column III is blank for any Code section in the table, then that particular section (or subsection) of the Code *never applies in subchapter V.*

COLUMN I: CODE SECTION	COLUMN II: BRIEF EXPLANATION	COLUMN III: WHEN SECTION MAY APPLY
§ 105(d)	Status conferences	
§ 1101(1)	Definition of debtor in possession	
§ 1102(a)(1), (2) & (4)	Creation of official committee of unsecured creditors; creation of additional committees or equity holders' committee	If the bankruptcy court for cause so orders
§ 1102(b)	Committee composition	If the bankruptcy court for cause so orders and a committee is created under § 1102(a)
§ 1103	Committee powers and duties	If the bankruptcy court for cause so orders and a committee is created under § 1102(a)
§§ 1104, 1105, 1106	Appointment and duties of trustee or examiner; termination of trustee appointment	
§§ 1107 & 1108	Rights and duties of debtor in possession; authorization to operate business	
§ 1115	Property of the estate	
§ 1116	Small business cases: trustee or DIP duties	
§ 1121	Who may file a plan	
§ 1123(a)(8) & (c)	Plan contents: cases in which debtor is an individual	
§ 1125	Postpetition disclosure and solicitation	If the bankruptcy court for cause so orders
§ 1127	Plan modification	
§ 1129(a)(15)	Plan confirmation: cases in which debtor is an individual	
§ 1129(b)	Requirements for confirmation under cram down	
§ 1129(c)	Court can confirm only one plan	
§ 1129(e)	Small business cases: timeline for confirmation	
§ 1141(d)(5)	Effect of confirmation: cases in which debtor is an individual	

There also is a *special discharge rule* applicable to *certain subchapter V cases*. If the bankruptcy court confirms a subchapter V debtor's plan pursuant to § 1191(b), then chapter

11's rule on discharge at *§ 1141(d) only applies to the extent provided by § 1192.* *See infra* § H.7 for a more detailed explanation.

5. Administration of a Subchapter V Case

a. Property of the Estate

In a *subchapter V* case, including individual cases, § 541 defines what constitutes property of the estate, *unless* the debtor's plan is confirmed pursuant to § 1191(b). [*See* § 1181(a) (excluding operation of § 1115)] If a subchapter V debtor's plan is confirmed under § 1191(b) (cram down), then property of the estate includes:

(i) property specified in § 541 [B.C. § 1186(a)];

(ii) *property* of the kind specified in § 541 that *the debtor acquired after bankruptcy* but *before* closing, dismissal, or conversion of the case, whichever occurs first [B.C. § 1186(a)(1)]; and

(iii) *earnings* from *services performed by the debtor after bankruptcy* but *before* closing, dismissal, or conversion of the case, whichever occurs first. [B.C. § 1186(a)(2)]

(i) Comparison with Non-Subchapter V Case

In a non-subchapter V Chapter 11 case in which the debtor is *not an individual,* § 541 defines what constitutes property of the estate. In an *individual chapter 11 case, property of the estate* also includes *all property acquired by the debtor* and *all earnings from services* performed by the debtor *after bankruptcy* but *before* closing, dismissal, or conversion of the case, whichever occurs first. [B.C. § 1115]

b. Subchapter V Trustee

Section 1183, not §§ 1104–1106, provides the rules for appointment of a trustee in subchapter V. [B.C. § 1181(a)] A *trustee is appointed* in *every subchapter V case.*

(i) Trustee Appointment

If the number of subchapter V cases in a particular region warrants it, the United States trustee for that region may appoint *a standing trustee* to serve in subchapter V cases. Such appointment is subject to the approval of the United States Attorney General. [B.C. § 1183(a); 28 U.S.C. § 586(b)] If there is no standing trustee appointed, then the United States trustee must appoint *one disinterested person* to serve as the trustee in a subchapter V case. [B.C. § 1183(a)] Within *seven days after selection* as a trustee and *before beginning official duties,* the trustee must *post a bond* in favor of the United States, conditioned on *faithful performance of her official duties.* [B.C. §§ 322(a), 1183(a)]

(ii) Duties of Subchapter V Trustee

The trustee has the following duties in a subchapter V case:

(1) *account* for all property received [B.C. §§ 704(a)(2), 1183(b)(1)];

(2) if a purpose would be served, *examine proofs of claim* and *object* to allowance of improper claims [B.C. §§ 704(a)(5), 1183(b)(1)];

(3) if advisable, *oppose the debtor's discharge* [B.C. §§ 704(a)(6), 1183(b)(1)];

(4) unless the court orders otherwise, *furnish information* about the estate and its administration as requested by a party in interest [B.C. §§ 704(a)(7), 1183(b)(1)];

(5) make a *final report and file a final account* of the estate's administration with the court and United States trustee [B.C. §§ 704(a)(9), 1183(b)(1)];

(6) if the court *for cause* so orders upon request of a party in interest, the trustee, or the United States trustee, perform certain duties of a Chapter 11 trustee, including *investigating and reporting* on the debtor's business, financial condition, and advisability of continuing the business, and *filing* such *post-confirmation reports* as are necessary or are ordered by the court [B.C. §§ 1106(a)(3), (4) & (7), 1183(b)(2)];

(7) appear and be heard at the *status conference* required by § 1183 and at *any hearing* about (1) *value of property* subject to a *lien*; (2) *plan confirmation*; (3) *post-confirmation modification* of plan; or (4) *sale of property of the estate* [B.C. § 1183(b)(3)];

(8) make sure the debtor starts making *timely payments* required by a confirmed plan [B.C. § 1183(b)(4)];

(9) if the debtor is *removed as debtor in possession*, perform the remaining duties prescribed by § 704(a), *except* those described at § 704(a)(1), (3) & (4), file the *lists, schedules, and statements* required by § 521(a)(1), if the debtor has not already filed them, and for any year for which the debtor has not filed a tax return *provide information required by the taxing authority* to the extent it is available [B.C. §§ 704(a)(2), (5), (7)–(12), 1106(a)(1), (2) & (6), 1183(a)(5)];

(10) if there is a *domestic support obligation claim*, perform the duties required by § 704(c) [B.C. § 1183(b)(6)]; and

(11) facilitate development of a *consensual plan.* [B.C. § 1183(b)(7)]

(iii) Termination of Trustee Service

If the debtor obtains confirmation of a *consensual plan of reorganization* under § 1191(a), then the subchapter V's service is terminated when the plan is *substantially consummated.* [B.C. § 1183(c)(1)] No later than *14 days after* the plan is substantially consummated, the debtor must *file notice with the court* of the plan's substantial consummation and serve that notice on the subchapter V trustee, the United States trustee, and all parties in interest. [B.C. § 1183(c)(2)] After termination of the subchapter V trustee's service, the United States trustee may *reappoint a trustee* as needed to perform duties under a confirmed plan *after removal of the debtor as debtor in possession* or to appear and be heard at a hearing on *post-confirmation modification* of the subchapter V plan. [B.C. §§ 1183(b)(3)(C), 1183(c)(1), 1185(a)]

c. Debtor in Possession

Even though a trustee is appointed in subchapter V, the debtor remains a *debtor in possession* and *continues to manage its business*. The debtor in possession has all the *rights of a Chapter 11 trustee*, *except* the right to compensation under § 330 of the Code, and all the *duties of a Chapter 11 trustee*, *except* the duties listed at § 1106(a)(2)–(4). [B.C. § 1184] The duties and reporting requirements of a subchapter V debtor are essentially the same as those for small business debtors. [B.C. § 1187(a), (b); *see supra* § G.4 of this Chapter]

The bankruptcy court, after notice and a hearing and upon request of a party in interest, can remove a subchapter V debtor as a debtor in possession for *failing to perform* its obligations under a confirmed plan, or *for cause,* including fraud, dishonesty, incompetence, or gross mismanagement of the debtor's affairs, whether pre- or post-petition. [B.C. § 1185(a)] The bankruptcy court may *reinstate* the debtor as debtor in possession on request of a party in interest, and after notice and a hearing. [B.C. § 1185(b)]

d. Examiner

There is no Code provision for appointment of an examiner in a subchapter V case. Section 1104 on appointment of an examiner and § 1106, which describes the duties of an examiner in a Chapter 11 case, *do not apply to subchapter V.* [B.C. § 1181(a)]

e. Official Committee of Unsecured Creditors

Unless the court for cause orders otherwise, an official committee of unsecured creditors is *not appointed* in a subchapter V case. [B.C. § 1102(a)(3)]

f. Employment of Professional Persons

Section 327 applies in a subchapter V case, but § 1195 modifies § 327's requirement of *disinterestedness.* In subchapter V, a person is not disqualified under § 327(a) for employment by the debtor *solely* because that person holds a *pre-petition claim of less than $10,000.* [B.C. § 1195]

g. Status Conference

No later than *60 days after* the order for relief, the bankruptcy court must hold a *status conference* to further the *expeditious and economical resolution* of the subchapter V case. [B.C. § 1188(a)] The bankruptcy court may extend the time for the status conference if the extension is *attributable to circumstances* for which the *debtor should not justly be held accountable.* [B.C. § 1188(b)] No later than *14 days before* the status conference, the debtor must file a report with the court that describes the debtor's efforts to achieve a *consensual plan of reorganization.* The debtor must serve this report on the *trustee and all parties in interest.* [B.C. § 1188(c)]

6. Disclosure Statement and Plan

a. Disclosure Statement

Unless the bankruptcy court orders otherwise, the subchapter V debtor *does not file* a disclosure statement. [B.C. § 1181(b)] If the court orders the debtor to file a disclosure statement, then the disclosure statement rules applicable to a small business case apply. [B.C. §§ 1125(f), 1187(c); *see supra* § G.6.a of this Chapter]

b. Filing the Plan

Only the subchapter V debtor may file a plan. [B.C. § 1189(a)] The debtor must file the plan no later than *90 days after* the order for relief although the bankruptcy court may extend the 90-day period if the extension is *attributable to circumstances* for which the *debtor should not justly be held accountable*. [B.C. § 1189(b)] The debtor may submit its plan using Official Form 425A.

(i) The 90-Day Requirement

What happens if a debtor files for relief under another chapter of the Bankruptcy Code and seeks to convert the case to Chapter 11 and elect subchapter V *after* the plan filing deadline already has expired? The courts have split on the question.

Example: Debtor filed for relief under Chapter 13 about seven months after the SBRA's effective date. Debtor submitted his Chapter 13 plan, filed tax returns, and objected to proofs of claim. Two months after the bankruptcy filing, the IRS filed a proof of claim that resulted in Debtor's liabilities exceeding the debt limits for Chapter 13. At his plan confirmation hearing, Debtor informed the court that he intended to convert to Chapter 11 and elect subchapter V because he no longer qualified for Chapter 13. The subchapter V deadlines had elapsed by the time Debtor sought to convert his case. The bankruptcy court held that Debtor could convert his case to one under subchapter V and granted Debtor's motion to extend the relevant subchapter V deadlines. The court noted that Debtor's liabilities fell within Chapter 13's debt limits when he filed for bankruptcy. The court also pointed out that Debtor had been diligent: he had timely filed his plan and also had filed his taxes. The court explained that while Debtor knew that he owed taxes, he "had no specific knowledge of what the IRS's claim would be and had no premonition that it might throw a proverbial wrench into his Chapter 13 case." Thus, the bankruptcy court found that the need for an extension of the subchapter V deadlines was attributable to circumstances for which the debtor should not justly be held accountable. [*In re* **Keffer,** 628 B.R. 897 (Bankr. S.D. W. Va. 2021)]

Example: In 2019, prior to passage of the SBRA, Debtor filed for relief under Chapter 11 as a small business debtor. A year later and several months after the SBRA's effective date, Debtor filed an amended petition to elect to proceed under subchapter V. By that time, the 60-day deadline to hold the subchapter V status conference and the 90-day deadline for the debtor to file its plan had long passed. The bankruptcy court noted that it had the power to extend these deadlines if the need for the extension was "attributable to circumstances for which the debtor should not justly be held accountable." The court explained that the statute looks at *circumstances* beyond the debtor's control, *not* whether the debtor is responsible for failing to meet the subchapter V deadlines. The court noted that the fact the SBRA was not in effect when a debtor filed for bankruptcy was not "a circumstance beyond the debtor's control" justifying an extension. The court concluded that "[i]t was the debtor that made the decision to elect into Subchapter V after expiration" of the deadlines and "[n]o circumstances beyond the debtor's control caused the debtor to make that decision." The court explained that the SBRA provided a balance between the rights of debtors and creditors. The decision by a debtor to elect subchapter V after its deadlines had expired "should not foist upon creditors all of the added powers of a Subchapter V debtor without one of the most significant protections afforded to creditors under the SBRA—that the case proceed expeditiously." The bankruptcy court held that dismissal of Debtor's case under § 1112(b)(4)(J) was proper, because without an extension of the 90-day filing deadline, Debtor had failed to file a plan within the time fixed by the Code. [*In re* **Seven Stars on the Hudson Corporation,** 618 B.R. 333 (Bankr. S.D. Fla. 2020)]

c. Plan Contents

(i) Mandatory Plan Provisions

The subchapter V plan *must* satisfy all the requirements of § 1123(a), *except* § 1123(a)(8), which provides that in an individual Chapter 11 case the debtor must provide for all or such portion of her post-petition personal service earnings as needed for execution of the plan. [B.C. § 1181(a); *see supra* § F.2 of this Chapter] Instead, subchapter V requires that *all debtors,* not just individual debtors, commit to payment of such *future earnings or income* as necessary to execute the plan.

The subchapter V plan *must provide*:

(1) a *brief history* of the debtor's business operations [B.C. § 1190(1)(A)];

(2) a *liquidation analysis* [B.C. § 1190(1)(B)];

(3) *projections* about the debtor's ability to make *plan payments* [B.C. § 1190(1)(C)]; and

(4) for the *submission* of all or such portion of the *debtor's future earnings or income* to the *trustee's supervision and control* as is needed to execute the plan. [B.C. § 1190(2)]

(ii) Permissive Plan Provisions

The subchapter V debtor's plan *may* include any of the provisions allowed by § 1123(b), although subchapter V modifies the exception contained at § 1123(b)(5). Section 1123(b)(5) provides that a Chapter 11 debtor's plan may modify the rights of holders of secured claims *other than* a claim secured only by the debtor's principal residence.

A subchapter V plan, however, *may* modify a claim secured only by the *debtor's principal residence if new value* received in connection with granting of the security interest

(1) was *not used primarily* to acquire the real property [B.C. § 1190(3)(A)]; and

(2) was *used primarily* in connection with the debtor's *small business.* [B.C. § 1190(3)(B)]

Example: Debra owns a house, which is her principal residence. Bank One holds the mortgage on the house, which is currently valued at $125,000. The mortgage balance is currently $100,000. Two years ago, Debra took out a second mortgage on her home through Bank Two and used the loan proceeds to buy new equipment for her small business. The Bank Two mortgage balance is currently $35,000. Debra has filed for relief under Chapter 11 and elected subchapter V. In her plan, Debra may modify Bank Two's claim even though it is secured only by her principal residence. The proceeds of the Bank Two loan were *not* used to buy Debra's home; they were used to buy equipment for her business and, thus, were used primarily in connection with her small business. Bank Two will have a secured claim of $25,000 ($125,000 value of home minus Bank One's secured claim of $100,000) and an unsecured claim for the remainder of the $10,000 owed on the mortgage to Bank Two.

Note: Debra cannot used § 1190(3) to modify Bank One's mortgage because she used the proceeds to buy her home, which is her principal residence.

d. Plan Confirmation Requirements

(i) Consensual Plan

If the plan satisfies all the requirements of § 1129(a) *except* (a)(15), then the bankruptcy court must confirm the plan. [B.C. § 1191(a)] Section 1129(a)(15) provides a *disposable income requirement for individual debtors.* Subchapter V has a disposable income requirement for *all debtors* in the case of confirmation by cram down. [B.C. § 1191(c)(2)]

Important difference: Section 1129(a)(15) provides that a *single unsecured creditor* may object to plan confirmation on the basis of the *disposable income requirement.* Therefore, even if the unsecured creditor belongs to a class of unsecured creditors that voted to accept the plan, that creditor still may object to confirmation if the plan does not satisfy the disposable income requirement in an individual debtor case. By comparison, subchapter V's disposable income requirement *only applies* to determine whether the subchapter V plan is *fair and equitable* with regard to a *class of claims or interests* when the plan is crammed down. [B.C. § 1191(b), (c)]

(ii) Subchapter V Cram down

Section 1129(b)'s cram down rules do not apply in subchapter V. [B.C. § 1181(a)] Thus, subchapter V has eliminated the *absolute priority rule.*

Subchapter V has its own rules for confirmation in cases in which an impaired class or classes votes to reject the debtor's plan. In fact, subchapter V's cram down rules allow for confirmation of a plan even if *no impaired class* has voted to accept the plan. [B.C. § 1191(b)] The court may confirm such a plan if with regard to *each dissenting impaired class* the plan (1) *does not discriminate unfairly* and (2) is *fair and equitable.* [B.C. § 1191(b)] Subchapter V's cram down provisions also contain a *special rule* for payment of *administrative and gap creditor claims*. [B.C. § 1191(e)]

(1) Not Discriminate Unfairly

The new subchapter V provisions do not define what constitutes unfair discrimination. Therefore, the existing Chapter 11 case law that has developed on § 1129(b)(1)'s requirement that the plan not discriminate unfairly likely will apply in subchapter V cases under § 1191(b). [*See supra* § F.3.a of this Chapter]

(2) Fair and Equitable

Section 1191(c) contains three *rules of construction* for determining whether a nonconsensual plan is *fair and equitable.* The first is directed specifically to a class of *secured claims*. [B.C. § 1191(c)(1)]. The second is a *disposable income* requirement. [B.C. § 1191(c)(2)] The third is a *heightened feasibility requirement* coupled, in some cases, with a requirement that the plan contain *appropriate remedies* when the debtor fails to make plan payments. [B.C. § 1191(c)(3)]

Important: Because the language of the *disposable income* and *heightened feasibility* provisions is *not* limited to unsecured creditors, it is unclear whether those requirements also apply to a case involving *only* a dissenting class (or classes) of secured creditors.

(a) Class of Secured Claims

A plan is *fair and equitable* with regard to a *dissenting impaired class* of secured creditors if the plan satisfies the requirements of § 1129(b)(2)(A). [B.C. § 1191(c)(1); *see supra* § F.3.b(i) for § 1129(b)(2)(A)'s requirements] While a plan rejected by an impaired class of secured creditors must satisfy § 1129(b)(2)(A), it is not clear whether it also must satisfy the *disposable income* and *heightened feasibility* provisions if *only* secured creditors vote to reject the plan. [*See, e.g.,* **In re Pearl Resources LLC,** 622 B.R. 236 (Bankr. S.D. Tex. 2020) (confirming debtors' jointly administered subchapter V plan—rejected *only* by three classes of impaired *secured* creditors—and, without discussing whether the disposable income and heightened feasibility requirements apply to a case involving only rejecting classes of secured creditors, finding that the plan satisfied those subchapter V cram down provisions]

(b) Disposable Income Requirements

A plan is *fair and equitable* with regard to a *dissenting impaired class* of claims or interests if the plan satisfies *either of the following requirements:*

1. the plan provides that all of the debtor's *projected disposable income* for the *three-year period* starting on the date the first plan payment is due will be applied to make payments under the plan [B.C. § 1191(c)(2)(A)]; *or*

2. the *value of property* to be distributed under the plan for the *three-year period* starting on the date the first plan distribution is due is *not less than* the debtor's *projected disposable income* [B.C. § 1191(c)(2)(B)]

   Note: The bankruptcy court may *extend the three-year period* but not beyond *five years* from the date on which the first plan payment is due or the first plan distribution is due. [B.C. § 1191(c)(2)(A), (B)]

3. *Disposable income* is income that the debtor receives *minus* expenses that are *reasonably necessary* for

   a. *maintenance or support* of the debtor or the debtor's dependents [B.C. § 1191(d)(1)(A)];

   b. a *domestic support obligation* that first becomes due *after* filing of the petition [B.C. § 1191(d)(1)(B)]; *or*

   c. the *continuation, preservation, or operation* of the *debtor's business.* [B.C. § 1191(d)(2)]

   Example: Elderly married debtors filed for relief under Chapter 11 and elected to proceed under subchapter V. Debtors proposed a plan funded by the sale of real property; it included no payments from the debtors. Debtors had *no disposable income* because Husband was retired and Wife planned to retire. The bankruptcy court concluded that the plan was not fair and equitable because it failed the disposable income test. For this and other reasons, the court denied confirmation of debtors' subchapter V plan. [**In re Young,** 2021 WL 1191621 (Bankr. D. N.M. 2021)]

(c) Feasibility and Remedies for Default

Cram down under subchapter V also requires that the plan satisfy a *heightened feasibility standard* and that it provide, in certain cases, *appropriate remedies* in the event that the debtor fails to make plan payments.

1. Feasibility

The bankruptcy court must determine that the debtor (i) is able to *make all plan payments or* (ii) there is a *reasonable likelihood* that the debtor will be able to make all plan payments. [B.C. § 1191(c)(3)(A), (B)(i)] This requirement creates a *heightened feasibility finding* compared with that under § 1129(a)(11). Section 1129(a)(11) only requires that liquidation or further financial reorganization is *not likely* to follow confirmation. Subchapter V's feasibility standard "requires a showing that the debtor can realistically carry out its plan . . . and that the reorganized debtor can stand on its own two feet." [*In re* **Pearl Resources LLC,** 622 B.R. 236 (Bankr. S.D. Tex. 2020)]

A crammed down subchapter V plan must satisfy *both* § 1129(a)(11)'s and § 1191(c)(3)(A)'s feasibility requirements.

2. Appropriate Remedies

If the bankruptcy court's feasibility determination rests on the "reasonable likelihood" test for feasibility, then the subchapter V plan also must provide *appropriate remedies,* such as liquidation of nonexempt assets, in the event that the debtor fails to make payments under the plan. [B.C. § 1191(c)(3)(B)(i), (ii); *see* ***In re* Pearl Resources LLC,** *supra* (finding that plan satisfied § 1191(c)(3)(B) because it provided for the sale of sufficient assets in the event debtors could not pay allowed claims)]

(3) Administrative and Gap Creditor Claims

In a non-subchapter V case, the plan must provide for payment of *administrative claims* and, in an involuntary case, *gap creditor claims in full, in cash* on the plan's effective date. [B.C. § 1129(a)(9)(A)] That is true regardless of whether the non-subchapter V plan is a *consent plan* or one confirmed under § 1129(b)'s *cram down provisions*.

In *subchapter V,* however, the requirement that administrative and gap creditor claims be paid in full, in cash on the effective date of the plan *only applies* to a *consensual plan*. [B.C. § 1191(a)] If the plan is confirmed under subchapter V's *cram down* provisions, then the plan may provide for payment of *administrative and gap creditor claims* over time *through the plan*. [B.C. § 1191(e)]

(a) Unexpired Lease of Nonresidential Real Property

The CAA amended § 365(d)(3) of the Code to provide the bankruptcy court in a subchapter V case with the power to extend beyond 60 days from the order for relief the time within which a debtor must perform its obligations under an unexpired lease of nonresidential real property. [*See supra* Chapter Eleven, § D.8.a(i) for discussion of the change] An obligation of the debtor's for which such an extension is granted is treated as ***an administrative expense.*** [CAA § 1001(f)(1)] The CAA's amendment to § 365(d)(3) ***expired*** on ***December 27, 2022.*** [CAA § 1001(f)(2)] But a debtor that commenced its subchapter V case ***before December 27, 2022,*** may avail itself of the CAA's amendments to § 365(d)(3). [CAA § 1001(f)(2)(B)] Thus, in a case commenced before the CAA's sunset date, the debtor in a subchapter V plan that is crammed down may pay unpaid post-petition rent over time under the plan, instead of in full in cash on the plan's effective date. [*Compare* B.C. § 1191(e) *with* § 1129(a)(9)(A)]

1. Cases Filed After December 27, 2022

After the expiration of the CAA, it is unclear whether unpaid post-petition rent will be treated as an administrative expense subject to § 1191(e)'s special payment rules. In a subchapter V case decided ***prior to the enactment of the CAA,*** the bankruptcy court concluded that § 1191(e) "does not apply to administrative rent." The court explained that § 1191(e) refers to administrative claims under § 507(a)(2), and § 507(a)(2), in turn, refers to administrative expenses under § 503(b). But the court noted that "a debtor's obligation to pay post-petition rent is governed solely by ***Section 365,*** not by *Section 503(b)."* [***In re* Seven Stars on the Hudson Corporation,** 618 B.R. 333 (Bankr. S.D. Fla. 2020)]

(b) Small Business Act Loans

The CAA added a ***temporary*** § 1191(f) that provides that the subchapter V plan that is crammed down may propose to repay a § 503(b)(10) claim when payment is "due under the terms of the loan giving rise to such claim." [*Compare* CAA § 320(c) *with* § 1129(a)(9)(A)] ***Recall*** that the CAA added a ***temporary*** § 503(b)(10), which grants administrative expense status to debts incurred under § 364(g)(1). [CAA § 320(b); *see supra* Chapter Eleven, § C.9 on § 364(g)(1)] Section 364(g)(1) is itself a ***temporary amendment*** to the Code that provides that the bankruptcy court, after notice and a hearing, may authorize a trustee or debtor in possession in a Chapter 11 subchapter V case to obtain a ***loan under the Small Business Act.*** If the loan is not forgiven pursuant to the provisions of the Small Business Act, then the debt has ***super-super priority.*** [CAA § 320(a); B.C. §§ 364(c)(1), 1183, 1184; 15 U.S.C. § 636(a)]

1. CAA's Sunset Clause

While the changes to §§ 364, 503(b), and 1191 sunsetted on ***December 27, 2022,*** they apply to any case begun ***before December 27, 2022.*** [CAA § 320(f)(2)(B)]

7. Discharge

a. Consent Plans

If the subchapter V plan is a consent plan, then with the exception of the rules for ***individual debtors*** spelled out at § 1141(d)(5), the discharge provisions of § 1141 apply. [B.C. § 1181; *see infra* I.1 on Post-Confirmation Matters] In a non-subchapter V case, the *individual* Chapter 11 debtor does not receive a discharge until *all plan payments are completed.* [B.C. § 1141(d)(5)] Section 1141(d)(5) does not apply to a subchapter V consent plan; therefore, an individual debtor receives her discharge upon *plan confirmation.*

b. Cram down

If the plan is confirmed under subchapter V's cram down provisions, then the debtor does *not receive a discharge upon plan confirmation*. Instead, the court grants the debtor a discharge *as soon as practicable* after the debtor completes all payments due *within the first three years of the plan* or such longer period of time, *not to exceed five years,* fixed by the bankruptcy court. [B.C. § 1192]

(i) Debts Discharged

Regardless of whether (i) a proof of claim was filed, (ii) the claim was allowed, or (iii) the holder accepted the plan, the debtor is discharged from *all pre-confirmation debts* and from *all debts arising from:*

(1) the *rejection of executory contracts or unexpired leases* not assumed by the trustee or debtor in possession;

(2) the *recovery of property* under §§ 522, 550, or 553; and

(3) *eighth priority tax claims* that arose post-petition.

[B.C. §§ 1141(d)(1)(A), 502(g)–(i)] The debtor also is discharged from all debts for *administrative expense* claims *allowed under § 503* and provided for in the plan. [B.C. § 1192]

(ii) Debts Not Discharged

The debtor is *not discharged* from any debt:

(1) on which the last payment is due *after the plan's first three years* or such longer period, *not to exceed five years,* fixed by the court. [B.C. § 1192(1)]; or

(2) of the kind listed in *§ 523(a)*. [B.C. § 1192(2)]

(1) Debtor or Only Individual Debtor?

Section 1192 uses the term "debtor," not individual debtor. Yet, § 523(a) provides that a discharge under § 1192 does not discharge an *individual* debtor from the debts listed. In **Gaske v. Satellite Restaurants Inc. (*In re* Satellite Restaurants Inc.),** 626 B.R. 871 (Bankr. D. Md. 2021), the bankruptcy court held that the exceptions to discharge at § 523(a) "apply only to individual Subchapter V debtors." [*See also* **Cantell-Cleary Co. v. Cleary Packaging LLC (*In re* Cleary Packaging LLC),** 630 B.R. 466 (Bankr. D. Md. 2021) (citing favorably to *Gaske* and holding that "the section 523(a) exceptions to discharge do not apply to the discharge of a Subchapter V entity debtor")] There is contrary authority in Chapter 12 cases interpreting language at § 1228 quite similar to that at § 1192. [*See infra* Chapter Fourteen, § E.5.b(ii)] Thus, it is unclear whether the discharge of an artificial entity, such as a corporation, under § 1192 *excludes* the debts listed under § 523(a).

I. Post-Confirmation Matters

1. Effects of Confirmation

The provisions of a confirmed Chapter 11 plan are binding on all creditors and equity security holders, the debtor, any general partner in the debtor, and any entity that issues securities or acquires property under the plan. The fact that the claim or interest of a creditor, equity security holder, or general partner is impaired under the plan and that such creditor, equity security holder, or general partner did not accept the plan is irrelevant; they still are bound by the terms of the plan. [B.C. § 1141(a); *see* **Browning v. Levy,** 283 F.3d 761 (6th Cir. 2002) (discussing res judicata effect of confirmation order)]

a. On Property

Unless the plan or the confirmation order provides otherwise, confirmation causes all property of the estate to vest in the debtor. [B.C. § 1141(b)] In addition, unless the plan or confirmation order provides otherwise and with certain limited exceptions, after confirmation, all property that is dealt with by the plan is free and clear of all claims and interests of creditors, equity security holders, and general partners in the debtor. [B.C. § 1141(c), (d)(2), (d)(3); *see infra* § I.1.b(iii) for exceptions]

(i) Secured Creditors

The general rule is that liens pass through bankruptcy unaffected. Section 1141(c), however, is an exception to this general rule. In interpreting § 1141(c)'s "free and clear" language, a number of courts have held that "under section 1141(c), the confirmation of a Chapter 11 plan voids liens on property dealt with by the plan unless they are specifically preserved, if the lien holder participates in the reorganization." [**Elixir Industries v. City Bank & Trust (*In re* Ahern Enterprises),** 507 F.3d 817 (5th Cir. 2007); *see also* **Airadigm Communications, Inc. v. FCC (*In re* Airadigm Communications, Inc.),** 519 F.3d 640 (7th Cir. 2008) (stating that if a "secured creditor participates in the debtor's bankruptcy and the ultimate plan does not preserve the creditor's interest, the interest is gone")]

(1) "Dealt with" by the Plan

Courts have reached different conclusions on what it means for the lien to be "dealt with" by the plan. Some courts have concluded that the lien itself must be dealt with by the plan. [*See, e.g.,* **In re Penrod,** 50 F.3d 459 (7th Cir. 1995) ("unless the plan of reorganization, or the order confirming the plan, says that a lien is preserved, it is extinguished by the confirmation" so long as the lien holder participated in the bankruptcy case)] Others have held that it is the property subject to the lien that must be deal with by the plan. [*See, e.g.,* **Elixir Industries,** *supra;* **In re Regional Building Systems, Inc.,** 251 B.R. 274 (Bankr. D. Md. 2000) (stating that "[i]t is entirely sensible the Congress would have focused lien extinguishment in chapter 11 on whether the property subject to the lien has been dealt with by the plan, not on whether the lien was specifically provided for by the plan")]

(2) Amount of Creditor Participation

Courts also have reached different conclusions on the amount of creditor participation needed to extinguish a lien under the plan. [*In re* **Northern New England Telephone Operations, LLC,** 504 B.R. 372 (Bankr. S.D. N.Y. 2014) (stating that "[c]ourts are divided over the precise level of participation that is required for a creditor's lien to be extinguished under a Plan")] Does notice of the plan with the opportunity to object suffice? [*See, e.g.,* ***Regional Building Systems,*** *supra* (§ 1141(c) requires nothing more than the lien holder "having been given notice of the proposed plan's terms and the opportunity to object to confirmation of the plan")] Or is more active participation, e.g., filing a proof of claim, needed? [*See, e.g.,* ***Penrod,*** *supra* (holding that if the creditor files a proof of claim, and the reorganization plan provides for payment of the claim but is silent concerning the lien, confirmation extinguishes the lien, because the creditor participated in the case.

b. Discharge of Debts

Unless the plan or the confirmation order provides otherwise, confirmation discharges the debtor from ***all pre-confirmation debts,*** as well as from debts arising from (i) the rejection of executory contracts or unexpired leases not assumed by the trustee or debtor in possession; (ii) the recovery of property under §§ 522, 550, or 553; and (iii) eighth priority tax claims that arose post-petition. [B.C. §§ 1141(d)(1)(A), 502(g)–(i)] These debts are discharged regardless of whether (i) a proof of claim was filed, (ii) the claim was allowed, or (iii) the holder accepted the plan.

(i) Discharge Not Restricted to Individuals

A Chapter 11 discharge is not restricted to individual debtors, as in Chapter 7; thus, ***artificial persons***, such as ***corporations and partnerships,*** may be discharged as well. [B.C. § 1141(d)(1)(A)] Confirmation terminates all rights and interests of general partners and equity security holders who are dealt with by the plan. [B.C. § 1141(d)(1)(B)]

(ii) When Does Discharge Occur?

(1) Not Subchapter V

In a non-subchapter V Chapter 11 case, the time the discharge occurs differs for ***individual*** versus non-individual cases. In a case not involving an individual, ***confirmation of the plan*** discharges the debtor. In an ***individual case,*** the debtor does not receive a discharge for any debt provided for by the plan until the bankruptcy court grants a discharge upon the debtor's ***completion of all payments under the plan.*** [B.C. § 1141(d)(5)(A)]

(a) Exception to Completion-of-Payments Requirement

After confirmation of the plan and after notice and a hearing, a bankruptcy court may grant a discharge to an ***individual debtor*** who has ***not completed her plan payments*** if all of the following conditions are satisfied:

1. the ***present value*** as of the plan's effective date of property distributed to unsecured creditors is equal to or greater than what those creditors would have received in a ***Chapter 7 liquidation*** [B.C. § 1141(d)(5)(B)(i)];

2. ***modification*** of the plan under § 1127 is ***not practicable.*** [B.C. § 1141(d)(5)(B)(ii)]; and

3. the exemption limits under § 522(q) do not apply. [B.C. § 1141(d)(5)(B)(iii)]

(b) Exemption Limits Under § 522(q)

The court may not grant the *individual debtor* a discharge unless it determines, after notice and a hearing held *no more than 10 days before* the entry of the discharge order, that there is *no reasonable cause to believe* that:

1. *§ 522(q)(1)* may apply to the debtor [B.C. § 1141(d)(5)(C)(i)]; and

2. there is a *proceeding pending* in which the debtor may be found guilty of a felony described in *§ 522(q)(1)(A)* or liable for a debt described in *§ 522(q)(1)(B).* [B.C. § 1141(d)(5)(C)(ii)]

It is unclear whether this provision results in a *denial of discharge* or merely a *delay in entry of the discharge.*

(2) Subchapter V

In subchapter V, the time the debtor is discharged depends on whether the plan is a *consent plan* or was confirmed under subchapter V's cram down provisions. If a consent plan, *confirmation of that plan* discharges the debtor, whether the debtor is an individual or an artificial entity. [B.C. § 1181(a), stating § 1141(d)(5) not applicable] If the plan was crammed down, then the debtor is discharged as soon as practicable after the *debtor completes all payments* due within the plan's first *three years*, or such longer period, not to exceed five years, that the court fixes. [B.C. § 1192] The cram down discharge rule applies regardless of whether the debtor is an individual or an artificial entity.

(iii) Exceptions to Discharge Applicable to All Chapter 11 Cases

(1) Individual's Nondischargeable Debts

If the debtor is an individual, a Chapter 11 discharge *does not include* any debts that are nondischargeable under § 523, e.g., certain taxes, domestic support obligations, educational loans. [B.C. §§ 1141(d)(2), 1181(a), 1192(2)]

(2) Liquidating Plan

The debtor will not receive a discharge if:

(a) the confirmed plan provides for the liquidation of all or substantially all of the estate property [B.C. § 1141(d)(3)(A)];

(b) the debtor does not engage in business after the plan is consummated [B.C. § 1141(d)(3)(B)]; and

(c) the debtor would not be granted a discharge under § 727(a) in a Chapter 7 case. [B.C. § 1141(d)(3)(C)]

(3) Corporate Debtors

In BAPCPA, Congress created several *exceptions* to the discharge received by a *corporate debtor.* Confirmation of a plan does not discharge a corporate debtor from any of the following debts:

(a) debts for *fraud* under § 523(a)(2)(A) or (B) that are owed to a *domestic governmental unit* [B.C. § 1141(d)(6)(A)];

(b) debts owed to a person as a result of an action filed against the United States government under *31 U.S.C. § 3721 et seq.* or any similar State statute [B.C. § 1142(d)(6)(A)]; or

(c) any *tax or customs duty* for which the debtor made a *fraudulent return or willfully attempted to evade or defeat* such tax or customs duty. [B.C. § 1141(d)(6)(B)]

(4) Officers and Directors; Co-Debtors

Confirmation of a Chapter 11 plan discharges only the debtor. Discharge of the debtor does not affect the liability of any other entity for such debt. [B.C. § 524(e)] Thus, unless the Chapter 11 plan provides for the release of non-debtor parties, confirmation of the plan does *not discharge co-debtors* or *co-obligors,* e.g., a non-debtor jointly obligated on a default judgment. [*See, e.g.,* **Ramco-Remodel America Corporation v. Wallis (*In re* Ramco-Remodel America Corporation),** 536 B.R. 206 (Bankr. W.D. Tenn. 2015) ("discharge of a debtor does not similarly provide for an automatic discharge of co-debtors or co-obligors")]

(5) Failure to Give Notice

If the debtor knows of a creditor's claim but fails to schedule it, and the creditor does not receive notice of the bankruptcy proceedings, the principle of due process should prevail over the Code's discharge provisions, and so the debt should not be discharged. But a creditor may not sleep on its rights. Thus, if a creditor that filed a claim in the debtor's bankruptcy case and had actual notice of the debtor's plan, its contents, and the confirmation hearing but failed to object, the creditor cannot complain of an erroneous ruling that it had a "full and fair opportunity to litigate." [**United Student Aid Funds, Inc. v. Espinosa,** 559 U.S. 260 (2010)]

c. Termination of Automatic Stay

Generally, confirmation of a Chapter 11 plan terminates the automatic stay, because property that vests in the debtor is no longer property of the estate and confirmation of a reorganization plan usually discharges the debtor. [B.C. § 362(c)(1), (c)(2)(C)] For individual non-subchapter V plans and subchapter V plans confirmed by cram down, confirmation does not discharge the debtor. [B.C. §§ 1141(d)(5), 1192] Section 362(c) provides that the stay of any act other than an act against estate property, e.g. an act against the debtor, does not terminate until the earliest of the closing of the case or its dismissal, or entry of or denial of a discharge. [B.C. § 362(c)(2)(A)–(C)]

2. Implementation of Plan

Notwithstanding any nonbankruptcy law concerning financial condition, the Bankruptcy Code requires that the debtor and any successor implement the plan and comply with all court orders. Furthermore, the court is authorized to order the debtor and any other necessary party to execute or deliver any instrument required for the transfer of property under the plan and to perform whatever else is needed to consummate the plan. [B.C. § 1142]

3. Distribution

If the plan conditions an entity's participation in distribution on the entity's surrender or presentment of a security or on the doing of some other act, the entity must perform accordingly within *five years* after the date of the *entry of the confirmation order* or it will forfeit the right to share in distribution under the plan. [B.C. § 1143]

4. Revocation of Confirmation Order

Within *180 days* after the entry of the order confirming the Chapter 11 plan, a party in interest may request that the order be revoked, but only on the ground that it was *procured by fraud.* If, after notice and a hearing, the confirmation order is revoked, the court must provide protection for any rights that have been acquired by an entity's good faith reliance on the confirmation order, and it also must revoke the debtor's discharge. [B.C. § 1144; *see* **Tenn-Fla Partners v. First Union National Bank (*In re* Tenn-Fla Partners),** 226 F.3d 746 (6th Cir. 2000)]

5. Exemption from Securities Laws

Generally, securities offered or sold by the debtor or its successor under a Chapter 11 plan in exchange for claims against or interests in the debtor or for administrative expense claims are exempt from the registration requirements of § 5 of the 1933 Securities Act and from registration requirements in any state or local securities law. [B.C. § 1145(a)] Furthermore, such an issuance is deemed to be a public offering, thereby escaping the restrictions imposed by Rule 144 of the Securities and Exchange Commission concerning the resale of securities that are part of a private placement. [B.C. § 1145(c)] Congress created this exemption to facilitate reorganizations. At the time that Congress enacted the Code, there was "great uncertainty" about the ability of creditors that received securities in a debtor's reorganization to sell those securities without running afoul of the federal securities laws. "This uncertainty act[ed] as a retarding force on the flexibility of the reorganization process." [H.R. Rep. No. 95–595, at 237 (1977)]

a. Underwriter

At the time that Congress created the securities exemption, the SEC considered any creditors that received 1% of a distribution of securities under a debtor's reorganization plan to be an underwriter. Congress was concerned with the ability of such creditors to resell their shares in the public market without filing a registration statement. "Thus, the resale provisions allow resale by creditors that are not real underwriters. . . . The technical statutory underwriter is excluded because of the restrictive impact on bankruptcy plans." [H.R. No. 95–595, at 238 (1977)]

Thus, a creditor or an equity security holder receiving securities under a Chapter 11 plan normally may resell them, unless she really is an "underwriter," a term which the Code defines in great detail. [B.C. § 1145(b)] An underwriter includes, for example, an entity that purchases a claim against or an interest in the debtor, or an administrative expense claim, with the *intention of distributing securities* that it will acquire under a Chapter 11 plan in exchange for the claim or interest. Similarly, the definition includes an entity that offers to sell securities on behalf of those receiving securities under a plan, or that offers to buy such securities from them for the purpose of resale pursuant to an agreement related to the plan. While the bankruptcy definition of an underwriter also covers an issuer, as used in § 2(11) of the Securities Act of 1933, neither the debtor nor its successor are considered "issuers." [*See* **In re Standard Oil & Exploration, Inc.,** 136 B.R. 141 (Bankr. W.D. Mich. 1992) (concluding debtor was not an issuer, agreeing with cases that hold that the term "issuer" for purposes of § 1145(b)(1)(D) should be read narrowly to include only "control persons," and explaining that if § 1145(b)(1)(D) were construed broadly "no debtor in possession or trustee would ever be able to issue exempt securities as envisioned by the Bankruptcy Code")] An issuer does include a controlling person, i.e., a creditor holding 10% or more of the debtor's securities. [H.R. No. 95–595, at 238

(1977)] Any party considered to be an underwriter must comply with the registration requirements and any resale restrictions of the securities laws.

6. Special Tax Provisions

The issuance, transfer, or exchange of a security *or* the making or delivery of an instrument of transfer under a confirmed plan may not be taxed under any law imposing a stamp tax or similar tax. [B.C. § 1146(a)] The Supreme Court held that this exemption "does not apply to transfers made before a plan is confirmed under Chapter 11." [**Florida Department of Revenue v. Piccadilly Cafeterias, Inc.,** 554 U.S. 33 (2008)]

The court may authorize a plan proponent to request a determination, from a State or local governmental unit responsible for collecting or determining income tax, of the plan's tax effects. The request must be limited to *questions of law.* [B.C. §§ 1146(b), 346] In the event of an *actual controversy,* the court may declare such effects after the *earlier of* (i) the *date on which the governmental unit responds* to the request or (ii) *270 days after such request* is made. [B.C. § 1146(b)]

J. *Manville*-Type Trust/ Injunction

1. Used in Chapter 11 Asbestos-Related Cases

Section 524(g) of the Bankruptcy Code authorizes the bankruptcy court to order the type of trust/injunction used in the *Johns-Manville* case. [**Kane v. Johns-Manville Corp.,** 843 F.2d 636 (2d Cir. 1988)] Section 524(g) applies only to cases in Chapter 11 involving *asbestos-related liabilities* of the debtor when an indeterminable number of substantial future demands for payment necessitate use of the trust in order to deal equitably with claims and future demands. [B.C. § 524(g)]

Note: Section 542(g) is a complex and detailed provision. This study guide provides only a quick summary of what the injunction is designed to accomplish. Please consult a Chapter 11 practitioner's guide for details on the injunction.

2. Actions Against Debtor Enjoined

This provision permits the court, after notice and a hearing, to enjoin suits against (i) the debtor; (ii) officers, directors, affiliates, and insurance companies of the debtor; (iii) successors to the debtor; and (iv) any other entity directly or indirectly liable for claims or demands against the debtor. [B.C. § 524(g)(4)] Instead of suits being brought against the debtor, or such other entities, *present and future claims and demands will be brought against the trust,* which will be established under the plan of reorganization and will be funded by securities of the debtor and future payments to be made by the debtor. [B.C. § 524(g)(2)(B)]

3. Note: Rule of Construction

The Bankruptcy Reform Act of 1994, which amended the Code to authorize use of the *Manville-type* trust/injunction, also contains the following rule of construction: "Nothing in [Code section 524(g)] shall be construed to modify, impair, or supersede any other authority the court has to issue injunctions in connection with an order confirming a plan of reorganization." [Bankruptcy Reform Act of 1994, § 111(b), 108 Stat. at 4117]

Chapter Fourteen

Bankruptcy Code Chapter 12: Family Farmer or Fisherman with Regular Annual Income

CONTENTS	PAGE

Chapter Approach

If your exam question involves a farming or fishing operation, consider whether Chapter 12 will apply and, if so, its advantages for the debtor. Study carefully the Bankruptcy Code's definition of a *family farmer* or *family fisherman* [B.C. § 101(18) & (19A)], and note that corporations and partnerships, as well as individuals and their spouses may qualify for Chapter 12 relief. Recall that Chapter 12 gives the family farmer or family fisherman access to the bankruptcy court through a speedier, simpler, and less expensive procedure than under Chapter 11, and with higher debt limitations, in particular for family farmers, than those of Chapter 13. In situations in which farmland has depreciated greatly in value, Chapter 12 may offer a good alternative for the family farmer debtor.

Your professor may ask you to decide under which reorganization chapter of the Code the debtor should file for relief. Therefore, it is important to understand how Chapter 12 is similar to and different from other reorganization filing chapters. Although many of the provisions of Chapter 12 are very similar, or identical, to their counterparts found in Chapter 13, there are some important differences. For example, a *standard discharge* under Chapter 12 differs substantially from a Chapter 13 standard discharge. For an individual debtor, this means that *all* debts that are nondischargeable under § 523(a) are not discharged in a Chapter 12 case. Under a Chapter 13 standard discharge, the debts that are nondischargeable are specified in Code § 1328(a) and include some but not all of the nondischargeable debts described in § 523(a).

As for Chapter 11, an earlier edition of this study guide listed only *differences* between Chapters 11 and 12. The Small Business Reorganization Act of 2019, however, created subchapter V and amended some of the rules applicable to small business cases. As a result, there now are some similarities between the two chapters, although almost all those similarities are between cases filed under subchapter V of Chapter 11 and cases filed under Chapter 12. For example, in both subchapter V and Chapter 12, only the debtor may propose a plan and, unless the same limited exception applies, the debtor must propose its plan within 90 days of the order for relief. Nonetheless, there still are many differences between Chapters 11 and 12. For example, the § 1111(b) election for secured creditors applies only to Chapter 11 cases and, thus, is *not* available in Chapter 12.

Finally, note that very few debtors file for relief under Chapter 12. For example, in 2020, there were only 560 Chapter 12 cases filed in all 94 U.S. judicial districts. The numbers were similar in prior years: 498 in 2018 and 599 in 2019. Across the United States, Chapter 12 cases were less than 1% of all bankruptcy cases filed in calendar years 2018, 2019, and 2020.

A. Eligibility for Relief

1. In General

Chapter 12 relief is available only to a family farmer or family fisherman with regular annual income. [B.C. § 109(f)]

2. Definitions

a. Family Farmer or Family Fisherman with Regular Annual Income

A family farmer or family fisherman with regular annual income is an individual, corporation, or partnership with annual income that is *sufficiently stable and regular* to permit the family farmer or family fisherman to make payments under a Chapter 12 plan. [B.C. § 101(19), (19B)]

b. Family Farmer

The Code's definition of a family farmer includes *individuals,* or individuals and their spouses, and *corporations or partnerships.* The definition varies depending on the nature of the entity. [B.C. § 101(18)]

(i) Individuals

If an individual (or an individual and spouse) satisfies all of the following five requirements, then she is considered a family farmer [B.C. § 101(18)(A)]:

(1) the individual (or individual and spouse) is *engaged in a farming operation;* and

(2) on the date that the Chapter 12 case is filed:

  (a) the individual's (or individual's and spouse's) *total debts do not exceed $11,097,350;*

  Note: Congress substantially increased the debt limit with the *Family Farmer Relief Act of 2019.* [Pub. L. No. 116–51 (2019)]

  (b) at least *50% of the individual (or individual's and spouse's) total noncontingent, liquidated debts comes from a farming operation* owned or operated by the individual (or individual and spouse); *and*

  Note: This 50% figure does *not* include any debt for the individual's (or individual's and spouse's) principal residence, *unless* the debt arises from a farming operation.

  (c) the individual (or individual and spouse) receive from the farming operation *more than 50% of gross income* for *either* of the following time periods:

   1. the taxable year before the taxable year in which the bankruptcy case is commenced *or*

   2. each of the second and third taxable years before the taxable year in which the bankruptcy case is commenced.

   Example: Debtor owned and operated a rice farm until 2010, when he became disabled. Debtor filed a Chapter 12 case in late 2013. On his 2012 tax return, Debtor listed two sources of income: (1) $20,362.80 from Social Security; and (2) $30,688 from a class action settlement related to crop losses for the years 2006–2008. The Chapter 12 trustee moved to dismiss the case and argued, among other things, that Debtor had not received more than 50% of his gross income from farming operations in 2012, because the settlement money related to farming activities from 2008 and 2009. The bankruptcy court disagreed and looked to the Internal Revenue Code, which treats settlement proceeds as income in the year in which they are received. The court explained that the Bankruptcy Code only requires that the debtor *receive* the income during the relevant time frame; it does not require that the debtor *earn* the income during that time frame. Thus, the court held that Debtor had received more than 50% of his gross income from a farming operation in 2012, which was the taxable year preceding the taxable year (2013) in which the Debtor filed for relief under Chapter 12. (The bankruptcy court nonetheless held that Debtor was ineligible for Chapter 12 relief because he failed to satisfy another part of the family farmer definition.) [***In re McLawchlin,*** 511 B.R. 422 (Bankr. S.D. Tex. 2014)]

c. Corporations and Partnerships

A corporation or a partnership that satisfies *all of the following requirements* is considered a family farmer. [B.C. § 101(18)(B)]

(i) If the entity is a corporation, its *stock is not publicly traded.*

(ii) *One family* (or one family and its relatives) *holds more than 50% of the outstanding stock or equity* in the corporation or the partnership.

(iii) The *family or the relatives conduct the farming operation.*

(iv) *More than 80% of the value of the corporate or partnership assets concerns the farming operation.*

(v) On the date that the Chapter 12 petition is filed:

  (1) the *total debts* of the corporation or the partnership *do not exceed $11,097,350;* and

  Note: Congress substantially increased the debt limit with the *Family Farmer Relief Act of 2019.* [Pub. L. No. 116–51 (2019)]

  (2) *at least 50% of the total noncontingent, liquidated debts* of the corporation or the partnership *come from a farming operation* that it owns or operates.

  Note: This 50% figure does *not* include any debt for a home that the corporation or partnership owns and that constitutes the principal residence of a shareholder or a partner, unless the debt arises from a farming operation.

d. "Farming Operation"

A farming operation "includes farming, tillage of the soil, dairy farming, ranching, production or raising of crops, poultry, or livestock, and production of poultry or livestock products in an unmanufactured state." [B.C. § 101(21)] In determining whether a debtor is engaged in a "farming operation," a majority of courts follow the "totality of the circumstances" test, which examines whether the debtor, at the time of the Chapter 12 filing, "intend[ed] to continue to engage in a 'farming operation.' " *In re McLawchlin, supra* (holding that debtor was not eligible for relief under Chapter 12 because he had failed to show that he either "intended to salvage his previous rice farming operation or that he otherwise intended to engage in a farming operation in the future")]

e. Family Fisherman

The Code's definition of a family fisherman includes (i) individuals, or individuals and their spouses, and (ii) corporations or partnerships. The definition varies depending on the nature of the entity. [B.C. § 101(19A)]

(i) Individuals

If an individual (or an individual and spouse) satisfies *all of the following requirements,* then she is considered a family fisherman. [B.C. § 101(19A)(A)]

  (1) On the date that the Chapter 12 case is filed:

  (a) the individual's (or individual's and spouse's) *total debts do not exceed $2,268,550;* and

     (b) at least *80% of the individual (or individual's and spouse's) total noncontingent, liquidated debts come from a commercial fishing operation* owned or operated by the individual (or individual and spouse); and

     Note: This 80% figure does *not* include any debt for the individual's (or individual's and spouse's) principal residence, *unless* the debt arises from a commercial fishing operation.

     (c) the individual (or individual and spouse) receives from the commercial fishing operation *more than 50% of gross income* for the taxable year before the taxable year in which the bankruptcy case is filed.

f. Corporations and Partnerships

A corporation or a partnership that satisfies *all of the following requirements* is considered a family fisherman. [B.C. § 101(19A)(B)]

(1) If the entity is a corporation, its *stock is not publicly traded.*

(2) *One family* (or one family and the family's relatives) *holds more than 50% of the outstanding stock or equity* in the corporation or the partnership.

(3) The *one family or the one family and its relatives conduct the commercial fishing operation.*

(4) *More than 80% of the value of the corporate or partnership assets* relate to the *commercial fishing operation.*

(5) On the date that the Chapter 12 petition is filed:

     (a) the *total debts* of the corporation or the partnership *do not exceed $2,268,550;* and

     (b) *at least 80% of the total noncontingent, liquidated debts* of the corporation or the partnership *come from a commercial fishing operation* that it owns or operates.

     Note: This 80% figure does *not* include any debt for a home that the corporation or partnership owns and that constitutes the principal residence of a shareholder or a partner, *unless* the debt arises from a commercial fishing operation.

EXAM TIP   **GILBERT**

It is important to remember that only an individual with regular income is eligible for Chapter 13 relief, but that an individual, a partnership, *or* a corporation can be eligible for Chapter 12 relief if qualified as a *family farmer or family fisherman* with regular *annual* income under Code § 101(18), (19), (19A), and (19B).

---

3. Voluntary Petition

A case under Chapter 12 may be commenced only by the filing of a voluntary bankruptcy petition. [B.C. §§ 301, 303(a)]

4. 180-Day Bar

A family farmer is *ineligible* for relief under Chapter 12 if the family farmer was a debtor in a case that was *pending* in the *preceding 180 days* (i) because of the family farmer's willful failure to obey court orders or to appear before the court in proper prosecution of the case, or

(ii) as a result of the family farmer's request for a voluntary dismissal of the case following a party's request for relief from the automatic stay. [B.C. § 109(g)]

Note: In 2005, with the passage of BAPCPA, Congress added family fishermen as eligible debtors under Chapter 12. Congress, however, did not amend § 109(g). Thus, § 109(g)'s prohibition does not apply to family fishermen.

B. Similarities to and Differences from Chapter 13

1. Introduction

Pre-BAPCPA, many of the rules and procedures governing Chapter 12 cases paralleled those governing Chapter 13 cases. With BAPCPA, however, Congress changed a number of provisions applicable to both Chapter 12 and Chapter 13 cases. While there are still similarities between the two chapters, there now are fewer than there were before BAPCPA's passage. The similarities and differences set forth below relate primarily to the pre-plan period. *See infra* § D of this chapter for similarities and differences in the requirements for confirmation for Chapter 12 versus Chapter 13 plans.

2. Similarities to Chapter 13

a. Filing the Petition

As mentioned previously, the Chapter 12 case may be commenced only by the filing of a *voluntary* petition. This is also true of a Chapter 13 case. [B.C. §§ 301, 303(a)]

b. Co-Debtor Stay

In both Chapter 12 and Chapter 13, in addition to the automatic stay of § 362(a), there is a stay against individuals who are liable with the debtor on consumer debts or who have secured consumer debts of the debtor. [B.C. §§ 1201, 1301]

c. Trustee

The appointment of a trustee, either a standing trustee or one for the particular case, is mandatory, and the trustee's duties in Chapter 12 and Chapter 13 are very similar as long as the debtor continues to be a debtor in possession. [B.C. §§ 1202(a), (b)(1)–(4), 1302] However, if a Chapter 12 debtor is removed from possession, the trustee is charged with several of the duties of a Chapter 11 trustee and also with operation of the debtor's farm or commercial fishing operation. [B.C. §§ 1202(b)(5), 1203] With the enactment of BAPCPA, Congress created new duties for the Chapter 12 trustee in cases in which the debtor owes a *domestic support obligation.* [B.C. § 1202(b)(6), (c)] Those duties are the same as the ones imposed on Chapter 13 trustees. [B.C. § 1302(b)(6), (d)]

d. Property of the Estate

Estate property is the same in a Chapter 12 case as in a Chapter 13 case. [B.C. §§ 1207(a), 1306(a)] Ordinarily, a Chapter 12 debtor remains in possession of property of the estate unless otherwise directed by (i) a court order removing the debtor from possession, (ii) a provision in a confirmed plan, or (iii) the confirmation order. [B.C. § 1207(b); *cf.* § 1306(b)] Furthermore, the Code expressly provides for a *Chapter 12 debtor in possession to continue to operate the farm or commercial fishing operation.* [B.C. §§ 1203, 1304(b)]

(i) Removal

The bankruptcy court may remove the debtor as debtor in possession for *cause,* including "fraud, dishonesty, incompetence, or gross mismanagement" of the debtor's affairs either prior to or after filing of the Chapter 12 case. [B.C. § 1204(a)] The Code defines *cause* for appointment of a trustee or examiner in a Chapter 11 case in the same way. [*See* B.C. § 1104(a)(1)]

e. No Disclosure Statement

Creditors in Chapter 12 and Chapter 13 cases have no right to vote on the plan, and the debtor does not file a disclosure statement.

f. Who May File a Plan?

In both Chapter 12 and Chapter 13, *only the debtor* may file a plan. [B.C. §§ 1221, 1321]

g. Pre-Confirmation Modification

The Chapter 12 debtor may modify the plan at any time prior to confirmation as long as the modified plan satisfies the requirements for confirmation. [B.C. § 1223(a)] The rule is the same in Chapter 13. [B.C. § 1323]

3. Differences from Chapter 13

a. Eligibility for Relief

The debt ceiling for eligibility under Chapter 12 is $2,268,550 for family fishermen and $11,097,350 for family farmers. To file for Chapter 13, an individual's debts must be less than $2,750,000. [B.C. § 101(18), (19A), 109(e)]

b. Debtor's Rights and Duties

In addition to permitting the debtor to continue to operate his farm or commercial fishing operation, Chapter 12 confers on a debtor in possession *all of the rights and duties of a Chapter 11 trustee,* except the right to compensation and the duty to investigate the debtor. [B.C. § 1203; *cf.* B.C. §§ 1303, 1304]

c. Commencement of Payments

In Chapter 13, the debtor must begin making payments by the *earlier* of *30 days* after the *filing of the plan* or the *start of the Chapter 13* case. [B.C. § 1326(a)(1)] The Code provides no specific period in which a Chapter 12 debtor must begin making payments. [B.C. § 1226]

d. Time for Filing the Plan

The Chapter 12 debtor must file a plan *within 90 days* of the order for relief. [B.C. § 1221] A *Chapter 13 debtor* may file a plan with the petition but must file a plan *within 14 days after* the filing of the petition (or within 14 days after a case is converted to Chapter 13). [Bankruptcy Rule 3015(b)]

e. Adequate Protection

The Code expressly states that *§ 361* on adequate protection *does not apply in Chapter 12 cases.* [B.C. § 1205(a)] Instead, Congress created § 1205 to address adequate protection in the context of Chapter 12 cases. Section 1205 provides that adequate protection is designed to protect against a decline in the value of the *property* securing a claim or of an *entity's ownership interest* in the property. [B.C. §§ 1205(b)(1), (2), (4); *compare* **United Savings Association of Texas v. Timbers of Inwood Forest Associates, Ltd.,** 484 U.S. 365 (1988)]

The statute sets forth the following nonexclusive methods of providing adequate protection in a Chapter 12 case:

(i) a *cash payment* or *periodic cash payments* [B.C. § 1205(b)(1)];

(ii) an *additional or replacement lien* [B.C. § 1205(b)(2)];

(iii) paying for the use of farmland the *reasonable rent customary* in the community where the land is located based on the rental value, net income, and earning capacity of the land [B.C. § 1205(b)(3)]; or

(iv) *other relief* that will provide adequate protection. Other relief does not include granting an administrative expense claim. [B.C. § 1205(b)(4)]

Note: Section 361 *does not include* the "reasonable rent" provision of § 1205(b)(3).

f. Sale Free and Clear

The *Chapter 12 trustee,* with the court's authorization after notice and a hearing, may sell farmland, farm equipment, or property used to carry out a commercial fishing operation, including a commercial fishing vessel, *free and clear* of the interest of an entity other than the estate in such property. [B.C. § 1206] Section 1206 does not replace § 363(f). Rather, it "modifies section 363(f) to allow family farmers or fishermen to sell assets not needed for the reorganization prior to confirmation without the consent of the secured creditors." [8 Collier on Bankruptcy § 1206.01(1)] The secured creditor's lien attaches to the proceeds of the sale.

Chapter 13 has no such provision.

C. Similarities to and Differences from Chapter 11

1. Introduction

In the prior edition of this study guide, this section listed only differences from Chapter 11. The SBRA, however, created subchapter V and amended certain provisions of the Code applicable to small business debtors. Those changes resulted in similarities between Chapter 12 and *some* Chapter 11 cases. The similarities and differences set forth below between Chapter 12 and Chapter 11 relate primarily to the pre-plan period. *See infra* § D of this Chapter for similarities and differences in the requirements for plan confirmation for Chapter 12 versus Chapter 11 plans.

2. Similarities

a. Trustee and Debtor in Possession

A *Chapter 12 trustee* (either a standing trustee or one appointed for the particular case) serves in the case even if the family farmer or family fisherman remains a debtor in possession. [B.C. § 1202] The same is true in a subchapter V case. A *subchapter V trustee* is appointed but the debtor remains a debtor in possession unless removed by the bankruptcy court. [B.C. §§ 1182(2), 1183, 1185] The debtor in possession in both Chapter 12 and subchapter V cases has *all of the rights and duties of a Chapter 11 trustee,* except the right to compensation and the duty to investigate the debtor. [B.C. §§ 1184, 1203]

b. No Creditors' Committees

There is no provision in Chapter 12 for the appointment of creditors' committees or equity security holders' committees. [*Cf.* B.C. § 1102] Unless the bankruptcy court for cause orders otherwise, a committee of creditors is *not appointed* in a *subchapter V* or a *small business case*. [B.C. § 1102(a)(3)] In addition, unless the bankruptcy court for cause orders otherwise, Chapter 11's provisions on appointment and powers of creditors' and equity security holders' committees *do not apply* in subchapter V. [B.C. §§ 1181(b), 1102, 1103]

c. Disclosure Statement

The Chapter 12 debtor does not file a disclosure statement. The debtor in a *subchapter V* case generally does not file a disclosure statement. [B.C. § 1181(b)]

d. Who May File a Plan?

Only the Chapter 12 debtor may file a plan. [B.C. § 1221] The same is true for *subchapter V cases*—only the debtor may file a plan. [B.C. § 1189(a)]

e. Time for Filing the Plan

The Chapter 12 debtor and the *subchapter V* debtor must file the plan no later than *90 days after* the order for relief. The bankruptcy court may extend the 90-day period only if the need for the extension is *attributable to circumstances* for which the debtor *should not justly be held accountable.* [B.C. §§ 1189(b), 1221]

f. Pre-Confirmation Modification

The Chapter 12 debtor may modify the plan at any time prior to confirmation as long as the modified plan satisfies the requirements for confirmation. [B.C. § 1223(a)] The rule is substantially the same in Chapter 11. [B.C. §§ 1127, 1193(a)]

3. Differences

a. Voluntary Petition Only

Unlike a Chapter 11 case, a Chapter 12 case can be commenced only by the filing of a voluntary petition. [B.C. §§ 301, 303(a)]

b. Co-Debtor Stay

Chapter 12 has a co-debtor stay; Chapter 11 does not. [B.C. § 1201]

c. Adequate Protection

Under Chapter 12, adequate protection is determined by Code § 1205, rather than under § 361 as in a Chapter 11 case. [*See supra* Part B.3.e for more about § 1205]

d. § 1111(b) Election

Partially secured creditors cannot elect to have their claims treated as fully secured under Chapter 12. This election is a unique feature of Chapter 11. [B.C. § 1111(b)]

e. Sale Free and Clear

The *Chapter 12 trustee,* with the court's authorization after notice and a hearing, may sell farmland, farm equipment, or property used to carry out a commercial fishing operation, including a commercial fishing vessel, *free and clear* of the interest of an entity other than the estate in such property. [B.C. § 1206; *see supra* Part B.3.f for more about § 1206] *Chapter 11* contains no provision comparable to § 1206.

D. Plan Confirmation

1. Confirmation Hearing

Except for cause, the confirmation hearing must be concluded no later than *45 days after* the plan is filed. Any party in interest, including the Chapter 12 trustee or the United States trustee, may object to plan confirmation. [B.C. § 1224] Bankruptcy Rule 3015(f) provides the rules on objecting to plan confirmation.

a. Comparison with Chapter 13

In a *Chapter 13 case*, the confirmation hearing must be held *no earlier than 20* and *no later than 45 days* after the *§ 341 meeting*, unless the court determines that it would be in the *best interests of creditors and the estate* to hold the confirmation hearing at an *earlier date* and there is *no objection* to doing so. [B.C. § 1324(b)]

b. Comparison with Chapter 11 Small Business Case

In a Chapter 11 small business case, the bankruptcy court must confirm the plan *no later than 45 days after* the plan is filed, unless the court extends the time under § 1121(e)(3). [B.C. § 1129(e)]

2. Confirmation Requirements

The bankruptcy court cannot confirm a Chapter 12 plan unless it satisfies *all of the following requirements.* [B.C. §§ 1222, 1225]

a. Plan Complies with Code Provisions

The plan must comply with the provisions of Chapter 12, as well as with the Code's other applicable provisions. [B.C. § 1225(a)(1)]

(i) Sufficient Income for Plan Execution

The Chapter 12 plan must provide for the *submission* of all or such portion of the debtor's *future earnings or other future income* to the *trustee's supervision and control* as needed for plan execution. [B.C. § 1222(a)(1)]

(1) Comparison with Chapters 11 and 13

Subchapter V and Chapter 13 have the same rule. [B.C. §§ 1190(2), 1322(a)(1)]

(ii) Full Payment of Priority Claims

With one exception, the Chapter 12 plan must provide for payment in *full, in deferred cash payments*, of all *priority claims* under § 507, unless the holder of a particular claims agrees to different treatment. [B.C. § 1222(a)(2)]

(1) Comparison with Chapter 13

Chapter 13 has the same rule and the same exception described below. [B.C. § 1322(a)(2)]

(2) Exception to Full Payment

The plan may provide for less than full payment of **domestic support obligations** that as of the filing of the petition had been assigned to a **governmental unit** or were owed directly to or recoverable by a governmental unit so long as the plan provides that all of the **debtor's projected disposable income** is applied to make plan payments for the **five-year period** starting when the first plan payment is due. [B.C. §§ 1222(a)(4), 507(a)(1)(B)]

(3) Temporary Amendment

The CAA **temporarily** added a new subsection (d) to § 1225. It provides that the debtor may pay a § 503(b)(10) claim "when due under the terms of the loan giving rise to such claim." [CAA § 320(d)] Section 503(b)(10), another **temporary amendment**, grants administrative expense status to debts incurred under § 364(g)(1). [CAA § 320(a), (b); *see supra* Chapter Eleven, § C.9 on § 364(g)(1)] Section 364(g)(1) also is a **temporary amendment** to the Code that provides that the bankruptcy court, after notice and a hearing, may authorize a debtor in possession or trustee authorized to operate the business in a Chapter 12 case to obtain a **loan under the Small Business Act**. If the loan is not forgiven pursuant to the provisions of the Small Business Act, then the loan is treated as a debt with **super-super priority.** [CAA § 320(a); B.C. §§ 364(c)(1), 1203, 1204; 15 U.S.C. § 636(a)]

While the changes to §§ 1225, 503(b), and 364 sunsetted on **December 27, 2022,** they apply to any case begun **before December 27, 2022.** [CAA § 320(f)(2)]

(iii) Same Treatment for Claims or Interests of a Class

If the plan classifies claim and interests, then it must provide the **same treatment for claims or interests in the same class**, unless the holder of a particular claim or interest agrees to a less favorable treatment. [B.C. § 1222(a)(3)]

(1) Comparison with Chapters 11 and 13

The rule is much the same in Chapter 11. [B.C. § 1123(a)(4)] Chapter 13 has a provision similar to § 1222(a)(3), except that there is no exception permitting the holder of a particular claim or interest to consent to less favorable treatment than others of the same class. [B.C. § 1322(a)(3)]

(iv) Claim of Governmental Unit—Farming Operation

The Chapter 12 plan must provide for the payment of any claim, either pre- or post-petition, owed to a **governmental unit** arising out of the **sale, transfer, exchange, or other disposition** of any property used in the **debtor's farming operation**, with the claim treated as unsecured and not entitled to priority. [B.C. §§ 1222(a)(5), 1232(a)] Note that this requirement applies to "any property used in the debtor's farming operation." There is no mention of assets used in commercial fishing operations.

(v) Duration of Plan

With the exception of payments on certain long-term debts, payments under the Chapter 12 plan may not extend beyond *three years,* unless the court for cause approves a longer time period. The court, however, may not approve a plan period that is longer than *five years.* [B.C. § 1222(c)]

(1) Comparison with Chapter 13

Pre-BAPCPA, the Code's rules on plan duration were similar for Chapter 12 and Chapter 13 cases. Post-BAPCPA, however, the rules governing plan duration for *Chapter 13 cases* turn on the debtor's status as an *above-median or below-median income debtor.* [B.C. § 1322(d); *see infra* Chapter Fifteen, § D.3]

b. Fees Paid

All fees, charges, or amounts required by chapter 123 of title 28 to be paid prior to confirmation have been paid. [B.C. § 1225(a)(2)]

c. Plan Proposed in Good Faith

The plan must be proposed in good faith and not by any means forbidden by law. [B.C. § 1225(a)(3)]

(i) Comparison with Chapters 11 and 13

Both Chapter 11 and Chapter 13 contain similar requirements. [B.C. §§ 1129(a)(3), 1325(a)(3). Chapter 13, however, also requires for plan confirmation that the *petition* was *filed in good faith.* [B.C. § 1325(a)(7)]

d. Plan Is Feasible

The plan must be *feasible,* which means that the bankruptcy court must find that the debtor will be able to make all plan payments. [B.C. § 1225(a)(6)]

(i) Comparison with Chapter 13

Chapter 13 has an identical requirement. [B.C. § 1325(a)(6)]

e. Domestic Support Obligations

The debtor must pay all *domestic support obligations* required by judicial or administrative order, or by statute, that came *due after filing* of the petition. [B.C. §§ 101(14A), 1225(a)(7)]

(i) Comparison with Chapter 13

Chapter 13 has an identical requirement. [B.C. § 1325(a)(8)]

f. Treatment of Secured Creditors

The bankruptcy court cannot confirm the debtor's plan unless as to *each allowed secured claim:*

(i) the secured creditor *accepts the plan* [B.C. § 1225(a)(5)(A)];

(ii) *the debtor surrenders the collateral* to the secured creditor [B.C. § 1225(a)(5)(C)]; *or*

(iii) the plan (1) provides that the creditor *retains the lien* securing its claim and (2) provides for the distribution of *cash or other property* having a present value, on the effective date of the plan, of at least the amount of the creditor's allowed secured claim. [B.C. § 1225(a)(5)(B)]

(i) Comparison with Chapter 13

Chapter 13 has requirements for treatment of secured claims that Chapter 12 does not contain. First, if the Chapter 13 plan proposes *periodic payments* for a secured creditor, those payments must be in *equal monthly amounts,* unless the creditor has accepted the plan. [B.C. § 1325(a)(5)(B)(iii)(I)] If the secured creditor's collateral is *personal property*, then the amount of the payments must suffice to provide adequate protection to the creditor over the course of the plan, unless the creditor has accepted the plan. [B.C. § 1325(a)(5)(B)(iii)(II)] Chapter 13 also has the *hanging paragraph.* [B.C. § 1325(a)(9)] There is no comparable provision in Chapter 12.

g. Treatment of Unsecured Creditors

(i) Best Interests of Creditors

The Chapter 12 plan must provide that *each unsecured creditor* holding an allowed claim will receive property having a *present value,* as of the effective date of the plan, that is not less than the amount she would receive for her claim in a case under Chapter 7 if the estate were liquidated on that date. [B.C. § 1225(a)(4)]

(1) Comparison with Chapter 13

Chapter 13 has the same "best interests" test. [B.C. § 1325(a)(4)]

(2) Comparison with Chapter 11

In Chapter 11, the plan must satisfy the "best interests" test for *each* holder of a claim in an *impaired class* if the holder did not consent to the plan. [B.C. § 1129(a)(7)(A)]

(ii) Best Efforts

If an unsecured creditor or the Chapter 12 trustee objects to confirmation of a plan, the bankruptcy court may not confirm the plan unless *one of the following three conditions* is met.

(1) The plan provides for 100% payment of the unsecured creditor's claim. [B.C. § 1225(b)(1)(A)]

(2) The debtor commits all of his *"projected disposable income"* to plan payments for three years or for any longer plan period approved by the court not exceeding five years. [B.C. §§ 1225(b)(1)(B), 1222(c)]

(3) The plan proposes to distribute *property whose present value* is equal to or greater than the debtor's *projected disposable income* for the relevant plan period. [B.C. § 1225(b)(1)(C)]

(iii) Disposable Income

In Chapter 12, disposable income is that portion of the debtor's income that is *not reasonably necessary* to (1) *maintain or support* the debtor or her dependents, (2) pay post-petition *domestic support obligations*, or (3) pay the expenses required for the *continuation, operation, and preservation of the debtor's business.* [B.C. § 1225(b)(2)]

(1) Comparison with Subchapter V

With the exception of the 100% payment alternative under § 1225(b)(1)(A), *Subchapter V's* cram down provisions are the same as Chapter 12's requirements for plan confirmation when the trustee or an unsecured creditor objects to the plan. [*Compare* § 1191(c)(2)(A) & (B) *with* § 1225(b)(1)(B) & (C). Also, subchapter V defines "disposable income" for purposes of its cram down provisions the same as does Chapter 12. [*Compare* B.C. § 1191(d) *with* § 1225(b)(2)]

(2) Comparison with Chapter 13

Chapter 13 also has a disposable income test that applies when the plan does not provide for full repayment of allowed unsecured claims and an unsecured creditor or the trustee objects to confirmation. [B.C. § 1325(b)] The definition of *disposable income* in Chapter 13 cases differs from that in Chapter 12 cases in several respects.

(a) Chapter 12 does not use the term *current monthly income.* Instead, the Code simply says income received by the debtor. [*Compare* B.C. § 1225(b)(2) *with* B.C. § 1325(b)(2)]

(b) Unlike Chapter 13, Chapter 12 has no express exclusion from disposable income for a debtor's *charitable contributions.* [*Compare* B.C. § 1225(b)(2) *with* § 1325(b)(2)(A)(ii)]

(c) The amount of the Chapter 13 debtor's *reasonably necessary expenses* depend on whether the debtor's income is *above or below the median* for the state in which she filed her bankruptcy petition. [B.C. § 1325(b)(2), (3)] That is not the case for the Chapter 12 debtor.

3. Permissive Plan Provisions

The provisions at § 1222(b)(1)–(12) that a Chapter 12 debtor *may* include in its plan are similar, but not identical, to those for Chapter 13 plans. [B.C. § 1322(b)(1)–(11); *see* Chapter Fifteen, Part D.4. a–e, g–k] There are several differences, however, between the Code's permissive provisions for Chapter 12 versus Chapter 13 cases.

a. Modifying Rights

The Chapter 12 plan may modify the rights of holders of secured or unsecured claims. [B.C. § 1222(b)(2)] There is no exception for claims secured solely by the debtor's principal residence.

(i) Comparison with Chapter 13

A Chapter 13 plan modify the rights of holders of secured or unsecured claims *except* modification of a *claim secured solely by a security interest in real property constituting the principal residence of the debtor* is prohibited. [*Compare* B.C. § 1222(b)(2) *with* § 1322(b)(2)]

(ii) Comparison with Subchapter V

Subchapter V, like Chapter 12, allows the modification of a claim secured only by the debtor's principal residence. Subchapter V, unlike Chapter 12, places a *new value* condition on when the debtor may avail itself of this right to modification. [B.C. § 1190(3); *see supra* Chapter Thirteen, § H.6.c(ii)]

b. Post-Petition Taxes and Certain Consumer Debts

A Chapter 13 plan may provide for the payment of all or part of a claim for *post-petition taxes* or a *post-petition consumer debt* for property or services needed for the debtor's performance under the plan. [B.C. §§ 1305, 1322(b)(6)] Chapter 12 has no comparable provision.

c. Sale or Distribution of Property

A Chapter 12 plan may propose to sell all or any part of estate property or distribute all or any part of estate property among entities having an interest in the property. [B.C. § 1222(b)(8)] Chapter 13 has no such provision.

d. Payment of Secured Claims

A Chapter 12 plan may provide for secured creditors to be paid over a longer period than the three or five years referred to in § 1222(c). However, any such provision must conform to the requirement for confirmation contained in § 1225(a)(5). [B.C. § 1222(b)(9)]

> **e.g.** **Example:** Debtor borrows $1.7 million from Bank, at 8% interest, secured by a 30-year first mortgage on Debtor's farm, which is valued at $2 million. Several years later, Debtor files a Chapter 12 bankruptcy petition. The market value of the farm has decreased to $1 million. Debtor's plan provides for Bank to retain its lien on the farm, and for Bank's claim to be modified by reducing the principal of its allowed secured claim to $1 million (the value of the collateral). The plan also proposes payments, having a present value of $1 million, over 30 years at a discount rate of 7%. The provision satisfies the applicable requirement for confirmation and should be permissible if the terms are found to be reasonable. [B.C. §§ 1222(b), 1225(a)(5)(B)] Note that if Bank's total claim is $1.7 million, the claim has been bifurcated; Bank now holds an unsecured claim in the amount of $700,000. [B.C. § 506(a); *see, e.g.,* **Travelers Insurance Company v. Bullington,** 878 F.2d 354 (11th Cir. 1989) (affirming bankruptcy court decision confirming Chapter 12 plan and finding that debtors' plan providing for payment of creditor's secured claim over 30 years did not violate § 1225 because § 1222(b)(9) is an "express exception to the section 1222(c) five-year limit")]

E. Post-Confirmation Matters

1. Trustee Pays Creditors

Ordinarily, the trustee disburses the payments to creditors under a *Chapter 12 plan.* [B.C. § 1226(c)]

2. Effects of Confirmation

With certain exceptions related to the debtor's discharge, the terms of a confirmed Chapter 12 plan *bind the debtor, each creditor, each equity security holder, and each of the debtor's general partners,* regardless of whether the plan provides for their claims and regardless of whether these parties objected to, accepted, or rejected the plan. [B.C. § 1227(a)] Except as the plan or plan confirmation order provides, confirmation *vests all estate property* in the *debtor.* [B.C. § 1227(b)] With certain exceptions related to the debtor's discharge and except as the plan or plan confirmation order provides, the property vested in the debtor is *free and clear* of any claim or interest provided for in the plan. [B.C. § 1227(c)]

3. Modification of the Plan

a. In General

After confirmation but before completion of plan payments, the debtor, Chapter 12 trustee, or the holder of an allowed unsecured claim may request modification to:

(i) *increase or decrease payments* to a particular class of claims [B.C. § 1229(a)(1)];

(ii) *extend or reduce the time* for such payments [B.C. § 1229(a)(2)];

(iii) *change the amount of distribution* to be paid to a creditor to take account of payments the creditor receives outside the plan [B.C. § 1229(a)(3)]; or

(iv) provide for payment of a *post-petition claim by a governmental unit* for disposition of property used in debtor's farming operation. [B.C. §§ 1229(a)(4), 1232(a)]

The Code imposes an *outer time limit* on the modified plan. The modified plan cannot provide for payments to *exceed three years* from the time that the first payment was due under the original plan, unless, *for cause*, the court extends the time period. The bankruptcy court cannot extend the time beyond *five years* from the date that the original plan's first payment was due. [B.C. § 1229(c)]

b. Debtor Modification Request

Only the debtor may request a modification in the following two situations:

(i) based on an *increase in the debtor's disposable income*, a modification to *increase payments to unsecured creditors* for a particular month such that the aggregate of those payments exceeds the debtor's disposable income for that month. [B.C. § 1229(d)(1)]

(ii) in the plan's final year, a modification such that payments under the plan would leave the debtor with *insufficient funds* to carry on its *farming operation* after completion of the plan. [B.C. § 1229(d)(2)]

Both restrictions protect the Chapter 12 debtor from creditors seeking to increase plan payments based on increases in the debtor's disposable income or from increases that would undermine the debtor's ability to continue its farming operation post-bankruptcy.

4. Revocation of the Confirmation Order

The bankruptcy court within *180 days* of the confirmation order and after notice and a hearing may revoke the order of confirmation if the order was *procured by fraud*. [B.C. § 1230(a)] If the court revokes the confirmation order, it may *convert or dismiss* the Chapter 12 case unless, within the time the court fixes, the debtor obtains confirmation of a modified plan. [B.C. § 1230(b)]

a. Comparison with Chapters 11 and 13

Both Chapter 11 and Chapter 13 contain provisions on revocation of the confirmation order for fraud similar to those of Chapter 12. [B.C. §§ 1144, 1330]

5. The Discharge

Confirmation of the Chapter 12 plan does *not constitute a discharge.* The Chapter 12 debtor receives a discharge upon *completing all plan payments* and, if the debtor is required to pay a *domestic support obligation,* after certifying that the amounts due for that obligation have been made. [B.C. § 1228(a)]

a. Comparison with Chapters 11 and 13

Both the *individual Chapter 11* debtor and the *Chapter 13 debtor* receive a discharge upon completion of plan payments. [B.C. §§ 1141(d)(5), 1328(a)] A *subchapter V debtor*—individual or artificial entity—whose plan is confirmed under subchapter V's cram down provisions receives a discharge as soon as practicable after completing all plan payments due within the first 3 years of the plan or such longer time, not to exceed 5 years, as the court may fix. [B.C. § 1192] In any other Chapter 11 case, confirmation of the debtor's plan operates as a discharge. [B.C. § 1141(d)(1)]

b. Debts That Are Not Discharged

(i) Long-Term Debts

If the Chapter 12 plan provides for curing a default within a reasonable time and maintaining payments during the case on *any secured or unsecured claim* on which *the final payment is due after the last plan payment*, then that debt is *nondischargeable.* [B.C. §§ 1228(a)(1), 1222(b)(5)]. If the plan provides for paying an allowed *secured claim,* consistent with the Code's confirmation requirements, over a period in excess of the *three or five years* allowed by the Code, then that debt is *nondischargeable.* [B.C. §§ 1228(a)(1), 1222(b)(9), 1222(c), 1225(a)(5)]

(1) Comparison with Chapter 13

Chapter 13 has the same nondischargeability rule if the Chapter 13 plan provides for curing a default within a reasonable time and maintaining payments during the case on *any secured or unsecured claim* on which *the final payment is due after the last plan payment*. [B.C. §§ 1328(a)(1), 1322(b)(5)]

(ii) Section 523

Any debt that is not dischargeable under § 523 of the Code *is not discharged* in Chapter 12. A debt owed to a *governmental unit* related to disposition of assets used by the Chapter 12 debtor in its *farming operation* is *not* considered a nondischargeable debt under § 523(a)(1). [B.C. §§ 1228(a)(2), 1232]

Does the exception to discharge for debts enumerated under § 523 apply to individual and artificial entities? While § 523 states that a discharge under § 1228 does not discharge an *individual* debtor from various enumerated debts, § 1228 provides that the *debtor* is granted a discharge except for debts *of the kind* specified in § 523. There is very limited case law on the question. The courts that have decided the question have ruled that in Chapter 12, the debts enumerated under § 523 are excepted from discharge in cases filed by *individuals and artificial entities,* e.g., corporations. [*See, e.g.,* **Southwest Georgia Farm Credit v. Breezy Ridge Farms, Inc. (*In re* Breezy Ridge Farms, Inc.),** 2009 WL 1514671 (Bankr. M.D. Ga. 2009); **New Venture Partnership v. JRB Consolidated (*In re* JRB Consolidated),** 188 B.R. 373 (Bankr. W.D. Tex. 1995)]

(1) Comparison with Chapter 13

The debts that are nondischargeable in *Chapter 13* are specified in Code § 1328(a) and include some but not all of the nondischargeable debts described in § 523(a).

(2) Comparison with Subchapter V

Subchapter V's discharge rule for crammed down plans contains exception-to-discharge language similar to § 1228(a)(2) and, thus, the same question has arisen: are the § 523 debts excepted from discharge in cases filed by artificial entities? There are few published cases, but the courts have reached contrary conclusions. [*See supra* Chapter Thirteen, § H.7.b(ii)(2)(a)]

(iii) The *Enron* Exemption Exception

BAPCPA added a provision to the denial-of-discharge section for *individual Chapter 12 debtors;* the provision is tied to the so-called *Enron* exemption exception at § 522(q). The Code provides that the bankruptcy court may not grant a discharge to an individual Chapter 12 debtor unless it has found *no reasonable cause to believe* that: (1) *§ 522(q)(1) may apply* to the debtor *and* (2) there is a proceeding pending in which the debtor may be found guilty of a felony described in *§ 522(q)(1)(A)* or liable for a debt described in *§ 522(q)(1)(B).* [B.C. §§ 1228(f), 522(q)] The court's finding must come after *notice and a hearing* held no more than *10 days* before *entry of the discharge order.* It is unclear whether this provision results in a *denial of discharge* or merely a *delay in entry of the discharge.*

c. Hardship Discharge

Chapter 12 provides for a hardship discharge of all *unsecured debts* except the *long-term debts* provided for under § 1222(b)(5) and (9), and debts that are *nondischargeable* under § 523(a). [B.C. § 1228(c)] The bankruptcy court may grant a hardship discharge to a Chapter 12 debtor that has not complete all plan payments if all the following requirements are met.

(i) the debtor's failure to make all play payments is due to *circumstances for which the debtor should not justly be held accountable* [B.C. § 1228(b)(1)];

(ii) the present value of property to be distributed under the plan for each allowed *unsecured claim* is *not less than* the amount that would have been paid in a *Chapter 7 liquidation* [B.C. § 1228(b)(2)]; and

(iii) plan modification is *not practicable.* [B.C. § 1228(b)(3)]

CHECKLIST OF NONDISCHARGEABLE DEBTS UNDER CHAPTER 12   GILBERT

THE FOLLOWING IS A CHECKLIST OF THE DEBTS THAT ARE NOT DISCHARGEABLE UNDER CHAPTER 12:

☑ *Long-term secured or unsecured debts* with the final payment due after the last payment under the plan if the Chapter 12 plan provides for curing a default within a reasonable time and maintaining payments during the case

☑ *Debts for secured claims that the Chapter 12 plan has provided to pay over a longer period* than the three or five years referred to in § 1222(c) and in a manner consistent with § 1225(a)(5)'s requirement for confirmation

☑ All debts that are nondischargeable under § 523(a)

F. Conversion or Dismissal

1. Voluntary Conversion to Chapter 7

The debtor has an absolute right to convert the case to Chapter 7, and this right cannot be waived. [B.C. § 1208(a)]

2. Voluntary Dismissal

The debtor also has the nonwaivable right to dismiss the case if it has not been converted earlier from Chapter 7 or Chapter 11. [B.C. § 1208(b)]

3. Discretionary Dismissal or Conversion to Chapter 7

The court may dismiss the case or convert it to Chapter 7, on the request of a party in interest, if the debtor has committed *fraud* in connection with the case. Notice and a hearing are required. [B.C. § 1208(d)]

4. For Cause Dismissal

On the request of a party in interest, the court may dismiss the case *for cause*. Notice and a hearing are required. [B.C. § 1208(c)]

a. "Cause"

The Code lists 10 reasons that constitute cause for dismissal. [B.C. § 1208(c)] Section 1208, however, uses the word "including." Therefore, a bankruptcy court may dismiss for reasons other than those specifically listed in the statute. [B.C. § 102(3) ("includes" and "including" are not limiting)] The statutory reasons for which a Chapter 12 case may be dismissed for cause include:

(i)   *gross mismanagement or unreasonable delay by the debtor* that is prejudicial to creditors [B.C. § 1208(c)(1)];

(ii)   *failure to pay any necessary fees* or charges imposed under chapter 123 of title 28 [B.C. § 1208(c)(2)];

(iii)   *failure to file a plan within 90 days* after the filing of the petition, or within any period of extension granted by the court [B.C. §§ 1208(c)(3), 1221];

(iv)   *failure to begin making timely payments* under a confirmed plan [B.C. § 1208(c)(4)];

(v)   *denial of confirmation* of the debtor's plan, and denial of a request for an extension of time to file another plan or to modify the plan [B.C. § 1208(c)(5)];

(vi)   *a material default by the debtor* concerning a provision of a confirmed plan [B.C. § 1208(c)(6)];

(vii)   *revocation of a confirmation order that was procured by fraud,* and the court's refusal to confirm a modified plan [B.C. §§ 1208(c)(7), 1230];

(viii) *termination of a confirmed plan because of the happening of a condition* contained in the plan [B.C. § 1208(c)(8)];

(ix)   *continuing loss* to or *diminution of* the Chapter 12 estate, and the *absence of a reasonable likelihood of rehabilitation* [B.C. § 1208(c)(9)]; or

(x)   debtor's failure to pay any post-petition *domestic support obligation.* [B.C. § 1208(c)(10)]

Chapter Fifteen

Bankruptcy Code Chapter 13: Individual with Regular Income

Chapter Approach

Chapter 13 is designed for an *individual debtor,* including a debtor engaged in business, who has a regular source of income and who desires to repay all or a percentage of her debts pursuant to a plan that she has the *exclusive right* to propose. Post-BAPCPA, however, a debtor who fails the "means test" may have little choice but to file for relief under Chapter 13, because Chapter 7 is unavailable to her and Chapter 11 is too complex and expensive. Keep in mind that a case under Chapter 13 is very different from a Chapter 7 liquidation case, and that BAPCPA's changes to the Bankruptcy Code account for some of those differences.

The following table summarizes some of the differences between a Chapter 7 and a Chapter 13 case for an individual debtor:

INDIVIDUAL DEBTORS: COMPARISON OF CHAPTER 7 AND CHAPTER 13		GILBERT
	CHAPTER 7	**CHAPTER 13**
ELIGIBILITY	1) Below-median income debtor *or* 2) Pass the "means" test	1) Individual with 2) Regular income *and* 3) Debts < $2,750,000
TYPE OF CASE	Voluntary or involuntary	Only voluntary
ESTATE PROPERTY	***Excludes*** debtor's post-petition earnings	***Includes*** debtor's post-petition earnings
AUTOMATIC STAY	No co-debtor stay	Applies, with limited exceptions, to co-debtors on ***consumer*** debt
TIME IN BANKRUPTCY	Varies based on complexity of case	1) 3-year plan for below-median income debtor 2) 5-year plan for above-median income debtor
VALUATION OF CLAIMS SECURED BY PERSONAL PROPERTY	1) ***Replacement value*** 2) If acquired for ***personal, family, household*** purposes, then replacement = ***retail value***	Same as Chapter 7, ***except*** claim = ***amount of debt*** *if*: 1) ***PMSI*** in ***motor vehicle*** acquired for ***personal use*** within ***910 days*** of bankruptcy *or* 2) ***PMSI*** in any other personal property acquired within ***one year*** of filing for bankruptcy
HOW CREDITORS ARE PAID	From liquidation of debtor's non-exempt assets	According to terms of debtor's 3- or 5-year plan based on debtor's ***projected disposable income***
WHEN DEBTOR RECEIVES DISCHARGE	Varies, depending on length of Chapter 7 case, but no requirement that debtor pay a particular amount over a certain time period as in Chapter 13	Normally, only upon completion of plan payments

A. Eligibility for Relief

1. In General

Chapter 13 relief is available to an *individual* (i) who has *regular income,* and (ii) whose *debts* total less than $2,750,000. The indebtedness must be noncontingent and liquidated, determined as of the date of the filing of the petition. [B.C. § 109(e)] The BTATCA eliminated the separate secured and unsecured debt limits previously in effect instead establishing an aggregate debt limit of less than $2.75 million for Chapter 13 eligibility. The BTATCA's amendment to § 109(e) sunsets on *June 21, 2024.* If Congress fails to act before June 21, 2024, to make permanent or to extend the $2.75 million total debt limit for Chapter 13 cases, then the secured and unsecured debt limits for Chapter 13 eligibility in effect on the date before the BTATCA's enactment or June 20, 2022, will go into effect. [BTATCA § 2(i)]

a. Individual with Regular Income

The Code defines an "individual with regular income" as an "individual whose income is sufficiently stable and regular to enable such individual to make payments under a plan under Chapter 13 . . ., other than a stockbroker or a commodity broker." [B.C. § 101(30)] In most cases, a Chapter 13 debtor's regular income is generated from her wages or salary, but it may be derived from almost any legitimate source, such as interest income, rental income, a business, a pension, a trust, or even welfare, if it is regular enough to fund the debtor's plan of repayment. The courts have reached different conclusions on whether to consider Social Security benefits as part of a debtor's regular income.

cf. **Compare: Santiago-Monteverde v. Pereira (*In re* Santiago-Monteverde),** 512 B.R. 432 (S.D. N.Y. 2014) ("Social Security income may not be considered in a Chapter 13 eligibility determination.") *with **In re** Patrick,* 2013 WL 168222 (Bankr. S.D. Miss. Jan. 16, 2013) ("[I]t is well settled that chapter 13 relief is available even to an individual who receives only Social Security benefits.")

Remember: The Bankruptcy Code specifically excludes Social Security benefits from the calculation of *current monthly income.* [B.C. § 101(10A)(B)]

b. Voluntary Petition Only

A Chapter 13 case may be commenced only by the filing of a voluntary petition. [B.C. §§ 301, 303(a)]

c. Joint Case

An individual with regular income and her spouse may file a joint petition, in which case the debt limitation of $2,750,000 applies to their *aggregate* indebtedness. [B.C. §§ 302(a), 109(e)]

2. Individuals Ineligible for Chapter 13 Relief

Stockbrokers and commodity brokers are not eligible for relief under Chapter 13. [B.C. § 109(e)] Also, an individual debtor in a case that was *pending in the preceding 180 days* and *dismissed* is not eligible if the dismissal was due to the debtor's willful failure to obey court orders or appear before the court to prosecute her case, or was a result of the debtor's request for a voluntary dismissal of the case following a party's request for relief from the automatic stay. [B.C. § 109(g)]

B. Co-Debtor Stay

1. Stay in Favor of Certain Individuals

The filing of a Chapter 13 petition operates not only as a stay of actions against the debtor under § 362, but also as a stay against any civil action or other act by a creditor to collect a *consumer debt from an individual who secured that debt* or who is otherwise *liable on that consumer debt with the debtor.* [B.C. § 1301(a)]

2. Consumer Debt

The Code defines a consumer debt as one "incurred by an individual primarily for a *personal, family, or household purpose."* [B.C. § 101(8)]

3. Exceptions to Co-Debtor Stay

The co-debtor stay does not apply in two situations:

a. the Chapter 13 case has been closed, dismissed, or converted to Chapter 7 or 11; or

b. the co-debtor became liable on or secured the debt in the *ordinary course of his business.*

[B.C. § 1301(a)(1), (2)]

4. Grounds for Relief from Stay

After notice and a hearing, the bankruptcy court must grant relief from the co-debtor stay in any of the following circumstances. [B.C. § 1301(c)]

a. Co-Debtor Received Consideration

To the extent that the co-debtor, not the Chapter 13 debtor, was the actual recipient of the consideration for the claim, the creditor may be granted relief from the stay. [B.C. § 1301(c)(1)] If the Chapter 13 debtor is nothing more than a co-signer or guarantor of an obligation, then it is the co-debtor who received the benefit and the creditor should be able to recover from the co-debtor. The court should not lift the co-debtor stay, however, if the debtor also received some consideration for the creditor's claim. [8 Collier ¶ 1301.03(2)(a)]

e.g. **Example:** Nancy, T.J., and Katherine purchased property together. They borrowed money from Bank for the purchase, and signed a promissory note payable to Bank. The note was secured by a deed of trust on the real property. Bank assigned the note and deed of trust to Third Party. Nancy, T.J., and Katherine lived on the property until Third Party foreclosed on the property. Nancy filed for relief under Chapter 13, and Third Party moved to lift the stay against T.J. and Katherine. The bankruptcy court noted that Debtor received some of the consideration for the loan because she had lived in the home with non-debtors T.J. and Katherine. In other words, Nancy was not a mere co-signer with the consideration flowing only to non-debtors T.J. and Katherine. The court in *dicta* stated that in such a case, Third Party would fail to meet its burden to lift the co-debtor stay against T.J. and Katherine. [*See In re* **Williams,** 374 B.R. 713 (W.D. Mo. 2007); B.C. § 1301(c)(1)]

b. Creditor's Claim Unpaid Under Plan

To the extent that the debtor's Chapter 13 plan proposes not to pay the creditor's claim, the creditor may receive relief from the stay. [B.C. § 1301(c)(2)] The Code says "to the extent that." Thus, "[i]f the debtor proposes not to pay a portion of the debt" under her plan, "then the stay is lifted to that extent." [H.R. Rep. No. 95–595, at 122 (1977)] If the plan proposes to pay a creditor but the creditor receives no dividend because the creditor failed to file a proof of claim, then the creditor is not entitled to relief from the co-debtor stay. [8 Collier ¶ 1301.03(2)(b)]

Example: Arbors of Oregon ("Arbors") provided care to Diann Grace at its residential nursing facility. Willie, Diann's husband, signed a promissory note related to Diann's care from Arbors of Oregon. Willie subsequently filed for relief under Chapter 13 and proposed a plan that would pay 24.5% of Arbors' claim for the cost of Diann's care. Arbors of Oregon moved to lift the co-debtor stay in order to pursue Diann Grace, because Debtor's plan failed to pay Arbors in full for its claim. The bankruptcy court ruled to lift the stay to allow Arbors to pursue Diann for the debt. The court noted, that the statutory language "to the extent" limited Arbors to collect from Diann only what was not paid to Arbors in Debtor's Chapter 13 case. [***In re* Grace**, 2015 WL 912532 (Bankr. N.D. Ohio 2015); B.C. § 1301(c)(2)]

(i) Note

If a creditor moves to lift the co-debtor stay on this basis, the stay automatically terminates with respect to the creditor *20 days after filing of the motion unless* the debtor or any individual liable on the debt with the debtor files and serves a written objection on the creditor. [B.C. § 1301(d)]

c. Irreparable Harm to Creditor

The bankruptcy court must grant relief from the co-debtor stay to the extent that the creditor's interest will be *irreparably harmed* if the stay remains in effect. [B.C. § 1301(c)(3)] Congress provided examples of irreparable harm in the legislative history: "where the codebtor is deteriorating financially, by loss of his job, or where the codebtor is about to leave the jurisdiction, and would no longer be available to make good on the debt if the debtor were unable to complete payments under the plan." [H.R. Rep. No. 95–595, at 122 (1977)]

Example: Debtor borrows $3,000 from Credit Union and executes a consumer promissory note, which Friend co-signs as a favor. Subsequently, Debtor files a Chapter 13 petition and a proposed plan. Friend purchases a one-way ticket to Switzerland with the stated intention of permanently residing there beginning next week. Credit Union is justified in making a prompt request for relief from the co-debtor stay under § 1301(c)(3).

C. Administration of Chapter 13 Case

1. Appointment of Chapter 13 Trustee

In regions where many Chapter 13 cases are filed, the United States trustee ordinarily appoints a qualified individual to serve as a *standing trustee.* Otherwise, the United States trustee appoints a disinterested person as the trustee for a particular case, or the United States trustee may serve as the trustee in the case. [B.C. § 1302(a); 28 U.S.C. § 586(b)]

a. Duties of Trustee

The duties of a Chapter 13 trustee include the following:

(i) *to account for all property received* [B.C. §§ 1302(b)(1), 704(a)(2)];

(ii) *to make sure that the debtor performs* her intention regarding debts secured by estate property [B.C. §§ 1302(b)(1), 704(a)(3), 521(a)(2)(B)];

(iii) *to investigate* the debtor's financial affairs [B.C. §§ 1302(b)(1), 704(a)(4)];

(iv) *to examine proofs of claims* and object to the allowance of any improper ones [B.C. §§ 1302(b)(1), 704(a)(5)];

(v) *if circumstances warrant,* to *object to* the debtor's discharge [B.C. §§ 1302(b)(1), 704(a)(6)];

(vi) *to provide information requested by parties in interest* about the estate and the administration of the estate [B.C. §§ 1302(b)(1), 704(a)(7)];

(vii) *to prepare and file* with the court and with the United States trustee a *final report and account* concerning the case [B.C. §§ 1302(b)(1), 704(a)(9)];

(viii) *to appear and be heard at any hearing* regarding (i) valuation of property on which there is a lien, (ii) confirmation of a Chapter 13 plan, or (iii) post-confirmation modification of a plan [B.C. § 1302(b)(2)];

(ix) *to furnish nonlegal advice and assistance* to the debtor in implementing the plan [B.C. § 1302(b)(4)];

(x) *to ensure that the debtor begins making the payments* proposed by the plan within the *earlier of 30 days* from filing of the Chapter 13 petition or filing of the Chapter 13 plan [B.C. §§ 1302(b)(5), 1326(a)(1)];

(xi) if there is a *domestic support obligation claim, to provide the notice* required by § 1302(d) [B.C. § 1302(b)(6), (d)];

(xii) *if the debtor is engaged in business*:

(1) *to investigate* the debtor's conduct, financial condition, and business operations, as well as the *advisability of continuing* the debtor's business [B.C. §§ 1302(c), 1106(a)(3)]; and

(2) *to file a report* of the investigation that states whether:

(a) there are any facts evidencing fraud, dishonesty, incompetence, misconduct, mismanagement, or irregularity in management of debtor's affairs [B.C. §§ 1302(c), 1106(a)(4)]; or

(b) any causes of action are available to the estate [B.C. §§ 1302(c), 1106(a)(4)]; and

(xiii) if the debtor owes a *domestic support obligation:*

(1) *to provide written notice* to the holder of *the domestic support obligation* of the right to use the services of the State child support enforcement agency for the State in which the claim holder resides to help with *collecting child support* during and after the Chapter 13 case. [B.C. § 1302(d)(1)(A)(i); 42 U.S.C. §§ 664, 666] The written notice must include the State agency's address and phone number. [B.C. § 1302(a)(1)(A)(ii)];

(2) *to provide written notice* to the relevant *State child support enforcement agency* that includes the name, address, and phone number of the holder of the domestic support obligation claim [B.C. § 1302(d)(1)(B)]; and

(3) if the court grants the *debtor a discharge* under § 1328, to *provide written notice* to both the holder of the domestic support obligation claim and the relevant State child support enforcement agency of [B.C. § 1302(d)(1)(C)]:

      (a) the debtor's discharge;

      (b) the debtor's most recent address;

      (c) the name and address of the debtor's most recent employer; and

      (d) the name of each creditor holding nondischargeable claims under § 523(a)(2) or (4), or holding claims that the debtor reaffirmed under § 524(c); and

(xiv) unless the plan or plan confirmation order provides to the contrary, *to disburse the payments* to creditors under the confirmed plan. [B.C. § 1326(c)]

Note: Duties (i) through (vii) are also duties of a Chapter 7 trustee.

2. Rights and Powers of Debtor

In a Chapter 13 case, the *debtor has the exclusive right* to use, sell, or lease estate property under § 363(b), (d), (e), (f), or (*l*). Thus, for example, a debtor may use, sell, or lease property out of the ordinary course of business, in accordance with § 363(b). [B.C. § 1303]

a. Debtor Engaged in Business

A debtor engaged in business is a *self-employed individual* who incurs trade credit in producing income from her business, which she is *entitled to operate unless the court orders otherwise.* [B.C. § 1304] A Chapter 13 debtor engaged in business has the exclusive right to use, sell, or lease property in the ordinary course of business [B.C. § 363(c)] and to obtain credit. [B.C. § 364] However, these rights are subject to any limitations specified in those sections, as well as to any restrictions or conditions imposed by the court. [B.C. § 1304(a), (b)]

(i) Duties

A debtor engaged in business must file periodic financial reports, including a statement of receipts and disbursements, with the court, the United States trustee, and the appropriate taxing authorities. [B.C. §§ 1304(c), 704(a)(8)]

3. Post-Petition Claims

Certain kinds of post-petition claims may be filed in a Chapter 13 case. One is for *taxes* that become due during the pendency of the case, and another is for *consumer debts* incurred by the debtor after the order for relief for property or services that the debtor needs to carry out the plan. [B.C. § 1305(a)]

a. Allowance

Post-petition claims for such taxes and necessary consumer debts are treated as pre-petition claims for the purpose of allowance, but they are determined as of the date that they arise. [B.C. § 1305(b)]

b. Exception: Failure to Obtain Approval

A post-petition claim for necessary consumer debts will be disallowed if the claimant knew or should have known that prior approval of the debt by the trustee was practicable and was not obtained. [B.C. § 1305(c)]

4. Property of Estate

The Chapter 13 estate consists of (i) all property specified in § 541; (ii) all § 541 property acquired by the debtor post-petition, but before the *earliest* of the closing, dismissal, or conversion of the case; and (iii) all of the debtor's earnings from services performed post-petition, but before the *earliest* of the closing, dismissal, or conversion of the case. [B.C. § 1306(a)] The *debtor retains possession* of all property of the Chapter 13 estate *unless a confirmed plan or confirmation order provides otherwise.* [B.C. § 1306(b)]

5. Conversion or Dismissal

In appropriate circumstances, a Chapter 13 case may be dismissed or converted to another chapter of the Bankruptcy Code under which the debtor is eligible. [B.C. § 1307]

a. Voluntary Conversion to Chapter 7

The debtor has an absolute right to convert the case to Chapter 7, and this right cannot be waived. [B.C. § 1307(a)]

b. Voluntary Dismissal

The debtor also has the nonwaivable right to dismiss the case if it has not been converted earlier from Chapter 7, 11, or 12. [B.C. § 1307(b)] There is a long-standing split of authority as to whether the debtor's right to dismiss is absolute or subject to a bad faith or fraud exception. Some courts have concluded that the Supreme Court's decision in **Marrama v. Citizens Bank** 549 U.S. 365 (2007) resolved the issue in favor a recognizing a bad faith exception. [*See, e.g.,* **Jacobsen v. Moser (*In re* Jacobsen),** 609 F.3d 647 (5th Cir. 2010) ("[p]roceeding from the propositions in *Marrama* that an apparently unqualified right is subject to an exception for bad faith . . . we conclude that § 1307(b) is subject to a similar exception, at least when the debtor's request for dismissal is made in response to a motion to convert under § 1307(c)"); *see supra* Chapter 12, § G.1 for discussion of *Marrama*] Other courts, however, have held that the Chapter 13 debtor has an absolute right to dismissal under § 1307(b) and that the Supreme Court in **Law v. Siegel,** 571 U.S. 415 (2014) rejected *Marrama's* dictum on which other courts have relied in finding a bad-faith exception. [*See, e.g.,* **Smith v. U.S. Bank (*In re* Smith),** 999 F.3d 452 (6th Cir. 2021) (holding that the language of § 1307(b) is "mandatory"—"the court 'shall dismiss' a Chapter 13 case"—and noting that the Supreme Court in *Law v. Siegel* had "flatly rejected the idea that § 105(a) vests in the bankruptcy courts equitable power to disregard the Code's provisions when they lead to results that seem unfair")]

c. Discretionary Dismissal or Conversion to Chapter 7

Upon a request by a party in interest or the United States trustee, the court, *for cause,* may dismiss the case or convert it to Chapter 7, whichever is in the *best interests of creditors and the estate*. Even if one or more grounds exist, however, conversion or dismissal of the case is within the court's discretion and not a matter of right. Notice and a hearing are required. [B.C. § 1307(c)]

(i) "Cause"

Reasons for dismissal of the case or conversion to Chapter 7 include the following:

(1) *unreasonable delay* by the debtor that *prejudices creditors* [B.C. § 1307(c)(1)];

(2) *failure to pay any necessary fees or charges* imposed under chapter 123 of title 28 [B.C. § 1307(c)(2)];

(3) *failure to file a plan* within 14 days after the filing of the petition (or within 14 days after conversion to Chapter 13), unless an extension is granted for cause [B.C. § 1307(c)(3); Bankruptcy Rule 3015(b)];

(4) **failure to begin making payments** under the proposed plan within **the earlier of 30 days** of filing the plan or filing the Chapter 13 petition [B.C. §§ 1307(c)(4), 1326(a)(1)];

(5) **denial of confirmation of the debtor's plan,** and denial of a request for an extension of time to file another plan or to modify the plan [B.C. § 1307(c)(5)];

(6) **a material default** by the debtor concerning a provision of a confirmed plan [B.C. § 1307(c)(6)];

(7) **revocation of a confirmation order procured by fraud,** and denial of confirmation of a modified plan [B.C. §§ 1307(c)(7), 1330];

(8) **termination of a confirmed plan because of the happening of a condition contained in the plan,** other than completing all payments [B.C. § 1307(c)(8)];

(9) **failure to file** within 15 days (or any court-ordered extension) after the filing of the petition the following information [B.C. §§ 1307(c)(9), 521(a)(1)]:

    (a) a list of creditors;

    (b) a schedule of assets and liabilities;

    (c) a schedule of current income and current expenditures;

    (d) a statement of the debtor's financial affairs;

    (e) a certificate signed by the debtor's attorney or by the debtor if not represented by an attorney that the debtor received the notices required by § 342(b), but only if the debtor's liabilities are primarily consumer in nature;

    (f) all payment advices received by the debtor from any employer within 60 days before filing the petition;

    (g) a statement of monthly net income itemized to show how such income was calculated; and

    (h) a statement disclosing any reasonably anticipated increase in income or expenditures over the 12-month period following the filing of the petition;

But note: Only the United States trustee may request conversion or dismissal for the debtor's failure to file the above information.

(10) **failure to timely file the statement of intention** required by § 521(a)(2) [B.C. § 1307(c)(10)];

But note: Only the United States trustee may request conversion or dismissal for the debtor's failure to file the statement of intention.

(11) **failure by the debtor to pay any domestic support obligation** that first becomes payable after filing of the petition [B.C. § 1307(c)(11)]; or

(12) **lack of good faith** in filing the Chapter 13 petition.

(ii) Pre-Petition Tax Returns

If the debtor fails to file her pre-petition tax returns, as required by § 1308, the bankruptcy court, upon a request by a party in interest or the United States trustee, must dismiss the case or convert it to Chapter 7, whichever is in the **best interests of creditors and the estate.** [B.C. § 1307(e)]

d. Conversion to Chapter 11 or 12

Before a Chapter 13 plan is confirmed, the court may convert the case to Chapter 11 or 12 upon a request by a party in interest or the United States trustee, but only if the debtor is eligible for relief under that chapter. Notice and a hearing are required. [B.C. § 1307(d), (g)]

e. Exception for Farmers

If the debtor is a farmer, a Chapter 13 case cannot be converted to Chapter 7, 11, or 12 *unless* the debtor requests conversion. [B.C. § 1307(f)]

f. Property of Estate in Converted Case

If a case is converted from Chapter 13 to another chapter of the Code, property of the estate in the converted case consists of property of the estate on the *date of the Chapter 13 filing* that remains in the possession or control of the debtor on the date of conversion. [B.C. § 348(f)(1)(A)] The Supreme Court, in a unanimous opinion, held that if the debtor converts the case to Chapter 7 after confirmation of her plan, any post-petition wages that the Chapter 13 trustee has received but not yet disbursed to creditors must be returned to the debtor. [**Harris v. Viegalahn,** 575 U.S. 510 (2015)]

If the debtor converts the case in *bad faith*, property of the estate in the converted case will consist of the estate property on the date of conversion. [B.C. § 348(f)(2)]

6. Filing Pre-Petition Tax Returns

If the debtor has not filed *tax returns* for any taxable period ending during the *four years prior to filing of the petition,* the debtor must file those returns with the appropriate tax authorities no later than the day before the *date first scheduled for the § 341 meeting.* [B.C. § 1308(a)]

a. Time Extension—Chapter 13 Trustee

If the debtor *fails to file her tax returns* by the day before the date first scheduled for the § 341 meeting, the Chapter 13 trustee may hold open that meeting for an additional period of time to allow the debtor to file her returns. [B.C. § 1308(b)(1)] With the limited exception for an extension by court order, the *additional time period* cannot extend:

(i) *beyond 120 days after the § 341* **meeting** if the debtor's return was past due on the petition filing date [B.C. § 1308(b)(1)(A)]; *or*

(ii) beyond the *later of 120 days after the § 341 mee*ting *or* the *date on which the return is due* under the last automatic extension requested by the debtor if the debtor's return was not past due on the petition filing date. [B.C. § 1308(b)(1)(B)]

b. Time Extension—Court Order

The bankruptcy court may *extend the time period* for the debtor to file her returns if the debtor demonstrates by a preponderance of the evidence that the failure to file is attributable to *circumstances beyond the debtor's control.* The court may only do so after notice and a hearing and by an order entered prior to expiration of the time period described above. The court may extend the time period established by the trustee but not for

(i) *more than 30 days* for returns that were past due on the petition filing date [B.C. § 1308(b)(2)(A)]; *or*

(ii) a period beyond the applicable extended due date for returns that were not past due on the petition filing date. [B.C. § 1308(b)(2)(B)]

D. Chapter 13 Plan: Contents and Confirmation

1. Filing a Plan

Only the *debtor* may file a Chapter 13 plan. [B.C. § 1321] She must file the plan with the *petition or within 14 days thereafter* (or within 14 days after conversion to Chapter 13), unless the court grants an extension for cause. [Bankruptcy Rule 3015(b)]

2. Confirmation Hearing

After proper notice, the court conducts a hearing to determine whether a proposed plan satisfies the elements necessary for confirmation. Any party in interest may file an objection to the plan. [B.C. § 1324(a)] The confirmation hearing may be held *no earlier than 20 days nor later than 45 days* after the date set for the § 341 meeting, unless the court determines that it is in the best interests of the creditors and the estate to hold the confirmation hearing at an earlier date and no party objects to doing so. [B.C. § 1324(b)] Unless the court orders otherwise, *objections* must be filed at *least seven days before the confirmation hearing.* [Bankruptcy Rule 3015(f)] If there are no timely objections to the plan, then the bankruptcy court may determine that the plan was proposed in good faith and not by any means forbidden by law without receiving evidence on these issues. [Bankruptcy Rule 3015(f); B.C. § 1325(a)(3)]

3. Requirements for Plan Confirmation

The bankruptcy court can confirm a Chapter 13 plan *only* if the plan satisfies *all of the following requirements.* [B.C. §§ 1322(a), 1325]

a. Plan Complies with Code Provisions

The plan must comply with the provisions of Chapter 13, as well as with the other applicable provisions of the Code. [B.C. § 1325(a)(1)] For example, the court may not confirm a plan for an individual debtor who is ineligible for relief under Chapter 13. A plan filed by an individual who was a debtor in a case that was pending in the preceding 180 days and dismissed because of the debtor's willful failure to obey court orders cannot be confirmed. [*In re* **Smith,** 286 B.R. 104 (Bankr. W.D. Ark. 2002); B.C. § 109(g)] Moreover, a Chapter 13 plan *must* include or abide by the following Code requirements. [B.C. § 1322(a), (d)]

(i) Sufficient Income to Be Turned over to Trustee

The plan must provide for the *submission* of all or such part of the debtor's *future earnings or other future income* to the supervision and control of the *Chapter 13 trustee* as is needed for implementation of the plan. [B.C. § 1322(a)(1)]

(ii) Same Treatment for Claims of a Class

If the plan designates classes of claims, it must provide identical treatment for all claims within any one class. [B.C. § 1322(a)(3)]

(iii) Full Payment of Priority Claims

With one exception, the plan must provide that all priority claims will be paid in full in deferred cash payments, unless a particular creditor consents to different treatment. [B.C. § 1322(a)(2); **United States v. Monahan (*In re* Monahan)**, 497 B.R. 642 (B.A.P. 1st Cir. 2013)]

(1) Exception

The plan may provide for less than full payment of *domestic support obligations* that as of the filing of the petition had been assigned to a *governmental unit* or were owed directly to or recoverable by a governmental unit so long as the plan provides that all of the *debtor's projected disposable income* is applied to make plan payments for the *five-year period* starting when the first plan payment is due. [B.C. §§ 1322(a)(4), 507(a)(1)(B)]

(2) Interest on Priority Claims

While priority claimants in a Chapter 13 case are entitled to receive payments totaling the full amount of their claims, the payments need not equal the *present value* of their claims. The one *exception* is a priority unsecured debt for a *domestic support obligation.* The Code's definition of a *domestic support obligation* specifically includes interest accruing on the underlying debt under applicable nonbankruptcy law. [B.C. § 101(14A)] The Code does permit the payment of interest on priority unsecured claims that are *not dischargeable* but only in the rare case in which the debtor otherwise has *disposable income* sufficient to pay *all allowed claims in full.* [B.C. § 1322(b)(10); *In re Monahan, supra*]

(3) Temporary Amendment

The CAA *temporarily* added a new subsection (d) to § 1325. It provides that the debtor may pay a § 503(b)(10) claim "when due under the terms of the loan giving rise to such claim." [CAA § 320(e)] Section 503(b)(10), another *temporary amendment* by the CAA, grants administrative expense status to debts incurred under § 364(g)(1). [CAA § 320(a), (b); *see supra* Chapter Eleven, § C.9 on § 364(g)(1)] Section 364(g)(1) also is a *temporary amendment* to the Code that provides that the bankruptcy court, after notice and a hearing, may authorize a debtor engaged in business or a trustee authorized to operate the debtor's business to obtain a *loan under the Small Business Act*. If the loan is not forgiven pursuant to the provisions of the Small Business Act, then the loan is treated as a debt with *super-super priority.* [CAA § 320(a); B.C. §§ 364(c)(1), 1304; 15 U.S.C. § 636(a)]

While the changes to §§ 1325, 503(b), and 364 sunsetted on *December 27, 2022,* they apply to any case begun *before December 27, 2022.* [CAA § 320(f)(2)]

(iv) No Material Alteration of Certain Retirement Fund Loans

The plan may *not materially alter* the terms of a loan taken by the debtor from any of the following *retirement plans:* (1) a plan under § 408(b)(1) of the Employee Retirement Income Security Act ("ERISA"); (2) a plan subject to § 72(p) of the Internal Revenue Code; or (3) a thrift savings plan in the Federal Employee's Retirement System that meets the requirements of 5 U.S.C. § 8422(g). [B.C. §§ 1322(f), 362(b)(19); *see* 3 Collier ¶ 362.05(18)]

(v) Plan Length

The time period during which the debtor must make payments under her plan varies depending on whether she is an **above- or below-median income debtor.** For a debtor whose income is **at or above the median** for her state, plan payments may not extend beyond **five years.** [B.C. § 1322(d)(1)] For below-median income debtors, plan payments may not extend beyond **three years** unless the court finds cause to approve a longer time period that does not exceed five years. [B.C. § 1322(d)(2)]

(1) When Does the Plan's Term Begin?

The Chapter 13 debtor files the plan either with the petition or within 14 days thereafter. The Code requires the debtor to start making **plan payments** no later than **30 days after filing the plan** or the **order for relief,** whichever comes first. [B.C. § 1326(a)(1)] Some courts hold that this first payment, which occurs prior to plan confirmation, starts the five-year period for plan payments. [**In re Humes,** 579 B.R. 557 (Bankr. D. Colo. 2018)] Other courts start the plan-payments clock with the first payment made post-confirmation. [**In re Morris,** 2014 WL 3818947 (Bankr. E.D. N.C. 2014)]

Example: Darren is an above-median income debtor. On March 5, 2018, he filed his Chapter 13 plan at the same time that he filed his petition for relief under Chapter 13. Darren makes his first plan payment in April of 2018. [B.C. § 1326(a)(1); Bankruptcy Rule 9006(a)(1)] His plan is confirmed and Darren makes his first post-confirmation payment in June of 2018. In a jurisdiction that follows the rule used in *In re Humes,* Darren would make his final plan payment in April of 2023. In a jurisdiction that follows the rule in *In re Morris,* Darren would make his final plan payment in June of 2023.

b. Fees Paid

All fees, e.g., the filing fee, charges, or amounts required to be paid prior to confirmation by chapter 123 of title 28, or by the plan, must have been paid. [B.C. § 1325(a)(2)]

c. Plan Filed in Good Faith

The plan must be proposed in **good faith** and not by any means forbidden by law. [B.C. § 1325(a)(3)] The test for good faith is fact-intensive and a majority of courts take a " 'case-by-case' approach" in evaluating whether the plan was proposed in good faith. [**In re Banks,** 545 B.R. 241 (Bankr. N.D. Ill. 2016)] Absent "serious debtor misconduct or abuse," a Chapter 13 plan should satisfy the good faith test. [8 Collier ¶ 1325.04(1)] If no objection to confirmation is filed, the court may determine that the plan was proposed in good faith and not by any means forbidden by law without receiving evidence on these issues. [Bankruptcy Rule 3015(f)]

(i) Comparison of Plan Versus Petition

The consequences of a finding that the plan was not filed in good faith under § 1325(a)(3) may differ from those of a finding that the debtor did not file the petition in good faith under § 1325(a)(7). If the debtor did not file the petition in good faith, the court likely will dismiss the case. A bankruptcy court, however, may give the debtor another opportunity to file a plan if the court concludes that the debtor did not propose her original plan in good faith. [*See In re McCreary,* 2009 WL 5215587 (Bankr. C.D. Ill. 2009)]

d. Best Interests of the Creditors

Each unsecured creditor must receive *property whose present value*, as of the plan's effective date, at least equals what the creditor would receive in a *Chapter 7 liquidation* case. [B.C. § 1325(a)(4)]

e. Plan Is Feasible

The plan must be *feasible*, which means that the bankruptcy court must find that the debtor will be able to make all plan payments. The debtor need not prove that the plan is guaranteed to be successful, but she must show that the plan has a *reasonable chance of success.* [B.C. § 1325(a)(6); *In re* Ewing, 583 B.R. 252 (Bankr. D. Mont. 2018); *In re* Merhi, 518 B.R. 705 (Bankr. E.D. N.Y. 2014)]

f. Debtor Filed for Bankruptcy in Good Faith

The debtor must have filed the *Chapter 13 petition in good faith.* [B.C. § 1325(a)(7)]

g. Domestic Support Obligations

Debtor must pay all *domestic support obligations* required by judicial or administrative order, or by statute, that came *due after filing* of the petition. [B.C. §§ 101(14A), 1325(a)(8)]

h. Tax Returns

Debtor must have filed all *pre-petition* federal, state, and local *tax returns,* as required by § 1308. [B.C. §§ 1308, 1325(a)(9)]

i. Treatment of Secured Creditors' Claims

The plan must satisfy *one of the following three* requirements for *each allowed secured claim:* (1) the secured creditor *accepted the plan;* (2) the debtor *surrendered the collateral;* or (3) the debtor *complied* with the Code's *cram down requirements.* [B.C. § 1325(a)(5)]

(i) Plan Acceptance

A secured creditor may *accept its treatment* under the plan. [B.C. § 1325(a)(5)(A)] A secured creditor's failure to object to the treatment of its claim in the plan may constitute acceptance of the plan. [**Flynn v. Bankowski (*In re* Flynn),** 402 B.R. 437 (B.A.P. 1st Cir. 2009)]

(ii) Surrender

The debtor may *surrender the collateral* to the secured creditor. [B.C. § 1325(a)(5)(C)] Surrender of the collateral does not extinguish the creditor's unsecured claim for any deficiency resulting from sale of the surrendered collateral. [**AmeriCredit Fin. Servs. v. Tompkins,** 604 F.3d 753 (2d Cir. 2010)]

(iii) Cram down

The debtor may *cram down* a non-consenting secured creditor's claim so long as the plan *preserves the creditor's lien* on the collateral and distributes to the creditor *cash or other property* with a *present value,* on the plan's effective date, of at least the *amount of the creditor's allowed secured claim.* [B.C. § 1325(a)(5)(B)]

Cram down means that the debtor has modified the secured creditor's rights over its objection. [**DaimlerChrysler Servs. N. Am. LLC v. Taranto (*In re* Taranto),** 365 B.R. 85 (B.A.P. 6th Cir. 2007)]

(1) Lien

The plan must preserve the creditor's lien until the *earlier* of payment of the *underlying debt* or *discharge.* The Chapter 13 debtor's discharge, however, does not include the discharge of a debt on which the plan provides to cure a default and maintain payments during the case, and for which the last payment is due *after* the last payment under the plan is due. [B.C. §§ 1322(b)(5), 1328(a)(1)] If the Chapter 13 case is dismissed or converted before the plan is completed, then the lien holder retains the lien to the extent nonbankruptcy law allows. [B.C. § 1325(a)(5)(B)(i)(II)]

e.g. **Example:** Darlene purchased a vacation home five years ago. Fifteen years remain on the mortgage held by Bank3, which is in default. The balance on the mortgage is $100,000. Darlene's plan proposes to cure the default within a reasonable time and maintain payments on the mortgage. Bank3's mortgage on Darlene's vacation home remains even after Darlene completes her plan payments and obtains a discharge, because Darlene did not pay off the mortgage during her plan and the Bankruptcy Code excepts from discharge such long-term debts in which the final payment on the secured loan is due after the final plan payment. [B.C. §§ 1322(b)(5), 1328(a)(1)]

(2) Present Value

The plan must pay secured creditors the *present value* of their secured claims. That means that the plan must provide for the payment of interest on secured claims over the course of the debtor's three- or five-year plan. The interest rate is the *Till* rate, which the Supreme Court defined as the *national prime rate adjusted for risk.* The Supreme Court in *Till* did not decide the proper risk adjustment but did note that courts had "generally approved adjustments of 1% to 3%." [**Till v. SCS Credit Corporation,** 541 U.S. 465 (2004)]

(3) Valuing the Secured Creditor's Claim

A claim is secured to the extent of the creditor's interest in the collateral. The bankruptcy court should determine the value "in light of the purpose of the valuation" and "the proposed disposition or use" of the collateral. [B.C. § 506(a)(1)] In a Chapter 13 case, the value of *personal property* is *replacement value.* [**Associates Commercial Corp. v. Rash,** 520 U.S. 953 (1997); B.C. § 506(a)(2)] *Replacement value,* however, varies depending on the *purpose* for which the debtor acquired the property.

(a) Personal, Family, Household Purposes

If the debtor acquired the property for *personal, family, or household purposes,* then *replacement value* is the *retail price* considering the age and condition of the property at the time of valuation. [B.C. § 506(a)(2)]

e.g. **Example:** Delilah purchased a minivan for her family on August 5, 2014. She financed the vehicle through *Carz 'R Us.* Delilah filed for relief under Chapter 13 on September 2, 2017. Delilah still owes $15,000 on the minivan. Retail price for a three-year-old van of that condition is $12,000; wholesale price is $10,500. Even though *Carz 'R Us* has a purchase-money security interest in a motor vehicle acquired for personal use, the hanging paragraph does not apply because Delilah purchased the minivan more than 910 days prior to filing for bankruptcy. Because Delilah acquired the minivan for family purposes, the van's value is $12,000, which is the retail price. *Carz 'R Us* has a secured claim for $12,000, and an unsecured claim for $3,000.

(b) Not for Personal, Family, Household Purposes

If the debtor did not acquire the property for *personal, family, or household purposes,* then the value is *replacement value without deduction for costs of sale or marketing.* [B.C. § 506(a)(2)] Section 506(a)(2) does not specify what figure to use for replacement value when the collateral was not acquired for personal, family, or household use. But, § 506(a) supposedly codified the Supreme Court's decision in *Rash.* In *Rash,* the Supreme Court described replacement value as "the cost the debtor would incur to obtain a like asset for the same 'proposed . . . use,' " and it indicated that ascertaining such value would "depend on the type of debtor and the nature of the property." [**Rash,** *supra*]

(4) Cram down Exception: The Hanging Paragraph

With BAPCPA, Congress added an unnumbered paragraph, which courts have labeled the "hanging paragraph," to the end of § 1325(a). Most courts have held that if the hanging paragraph applies to a secured creditor's claim, then the debtor may not bifurcate the creditor's claim into a secured and an unsecured claim. [*See, e.g.,* **Nuvell Credit Co., LLC v. Dean (*In re* Dean),** 537 F.3d 1315 (11 Cir. 2008); **Wachovia Dealer Servs. v. Jones (*In re* Jones),** 530 F.3d 1284 (10th Cir. 2008); **DaimlerChrysler,** *supra*] If the hanging paragraph applies, the creditor's *secured claim equals the amount that the debtor owes the secured creditor,* regardless of the actual value of the collateral. The hanging paragraph applies in two situations.

(a) Creditor has a *purchase-money security interest* in a *motor vehicle* that the debtor *acquired for personal use* within *910 days* of filing for bankruptcy. [B.C. § 1325(a)(9) hanging paragraph]

> **e.g.** **Example:** On May 1, 2016, Darren purchased a car on credit from *Cal's Cars* for personal use. *Cal's Cars* has a purchase-money security interest in the vehicle. Darren filed for relief under chapter 13 on July 1, 2017. Darren owes $25,000 on the car, which is worth $20,000. Without the hanging paragraph, *Cal's Cars* would have a secured claim for $20,000, and an unsecured claim for $5,000. Because the hanging paragraph applies, however, *Cal's Cars* has a secured claim for $25,000, which is the amount of Darren's indebtedness.

(b) Creditor has a *purchase-money security interest* in *any other thing of value* if the debt was incurred *within one year of the bankruptcy filing.* [B.C. § 1325(a)(9) hanging paragraph] Most courts have held that the one-year provision does *not* apply to motor vehicles because the hanging paragraph creates two categories of collateral—motor vehicles and any *other* thing of value.

> **e.g.** **Example:** Debtor acquired a motor vehicle for business use within one year of filing for relief under Chapter 13. DaimlerChrysler has a purchase-money security interest in the car. At the time that he filed for

bankruptcy, Debtor owed more than $43,000 on the car, which was worth $22,000. Because debtor acquired and used the vehicle for business, not personal, use, the 910-day provision in the hanging paragraph did not apply. The one-year provision in the hanging paragraph also did not apply because that provision was limited to "anything of value *other than a motor vehicle.*" [*In re* **Horton,** 398 B.R. 73 (Bankr. S.D. Fla. 2008); *but see In re* **Littlefield,** 388 B.R. 1 (Bankr. D. Me. 2008) (holding that one-year provision in the hanging paragraph applied to purchase-money security interest in motor vehicle acquired for business use within one year of bankruptcy)]

(5) Cram down Exception: Debtor's Principal Residence

(a) Bifurcation of Home Mortgage

Bankruptcy Code § 1322(b)(2) *prohibits* a Chapter 13 debtor from *stripping down* an undersecured mortgage on the *debtor's principal residence* to the fair market value of the home, notwithstanding § 506(a), if the last payment on the secured creditor's claim is due after the final plan payment. [**Nobelman v. American Savings Bank,** 508 U.S. 324 (1993); B.C. § 1322(b)(2); *but see* **Hammond v. Commonwealth Mortgage Corp. (*In re* Hammond),** 27 F.3d 52 (3d Cir. 1994) (allowing bifurcation of a home mortgage that also created security interests in *personal property*)]

e.g. **Example:** Dannie purchased his home seven years ago. The home is Dannie's principal residence. Dannie obtained financing from Local Bank, which holds the 30-year mortgage. The balance on the home loan is $150,000, but Dannie's home is worth only $110,000. The Code's anti-modification provision does not allow bifurcation of Local Bank's claim into a $110,000 secured claim and a $40,000 unsecured claim. Instead, Dannie must pay Local Bank according to the terms of the original loan agreement with the bank.

(b) Permissible Modification of Home Mortgage Payments

If the final payment on a debt secured solely by a security interest in real property constituting the debtor's principal residence is due *before* the last payment under the plan, it is permissible for the plan to modify payment of the debt in accordance with Code § 1325(a)(5). [B.C. § 1322(c)(2)]

(c) "Unsecured" Junior Mortgage

Although there is a split of authority, the majority view holds that a junior mortgage that is *wholly unsecured* is not protected from modification and, therefore, can be "stripped off" and treated as a general unsecured claim. [*See, e.g.,* **Branigan v. Davis (*In re* Davis),** 716 F.3d 331 (4th Cir. 2013) (explaining that under § 506(a) valueless liens are unsecured claims and finding that "the Bankruptcy Code permits the stripping off of valueless liens in Chapter 13 proceedings"); *but see In re* **Frame,** 2009 WL 8725111 (Bankr. D. Minn. 2009) (finding that debtor cannot strip off valueless lien on debtor's principal residence)]

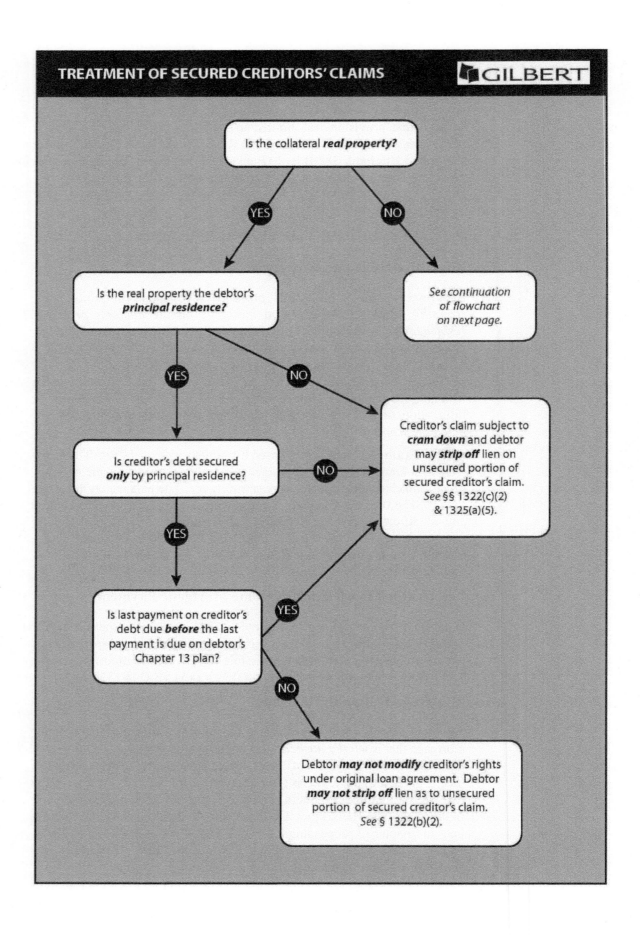

TREATMENT OF SECURED CREDITORS' CLAIMS　　■GILBERT

Is the collateral *real property?*

YES　　　NO

Is the real property the debtor's *principal residence?*

See continuation of flowchart on next page.

YES　　　NO

Is creditor's debt secured *only* by principal residence?

NO

Creditor's claim subject to *cram down* and debtor may *strip off* lien on unsecured portion of secured creditor's claim. *See* §§ 1322(c)(2) & 1325(a)(5).

YES

Is last payment on creditor's debt due *before* the last payment is due on debtor's Chapter 13 plan?

YES

NO

Debtor *may not modify* creditor's rights under original loan agreement. Debtor *may not strip off* lien as to unsecured portion of secured creditor's claim. *See* § 1322(b)(2).

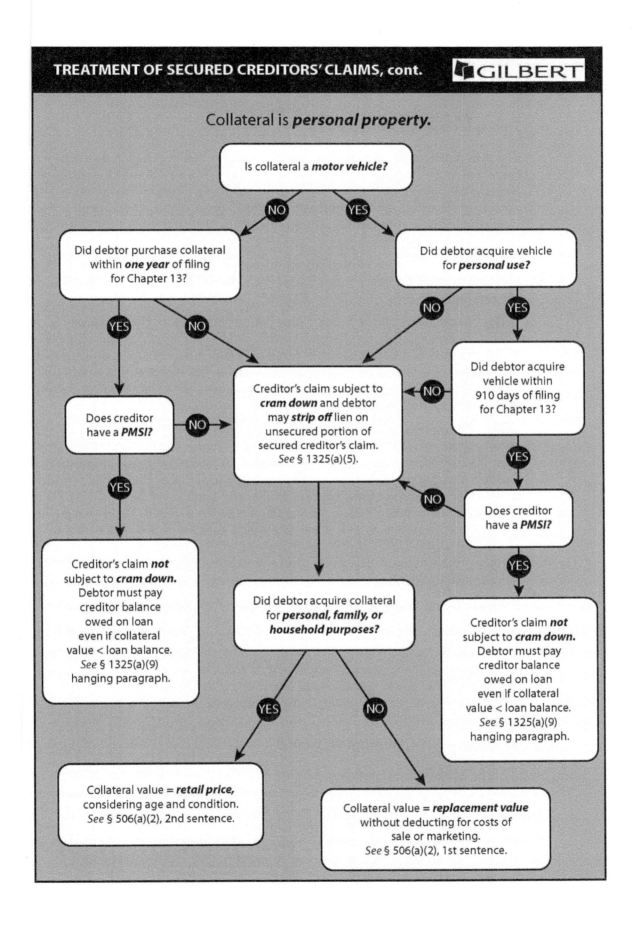

Collateral is **personal property.**

Is collateral a **motor vehicle?**

NO → Did debtor purchase collateral within **one year** of filing for Chapter 13?

YES → Did debtor acquire vehicle for **personal use?**

Did debtor purchase collateral within one year:
- YES → Does creditor have a **PMSI?**
- NO → Creditor's claim subject to **cram down** and debtor may **strip off** lien on unsecured portion of secured creditor's claim. See § 1325(a)(5).

Did debtor acquire vehicle for personal use?
- NO → Creditor's claim subject to cram down...
- YES → Did debtor acquire vehicle within 910 days of filing for Chapter 13?

Does creditor have a **PMSI?**
- NO → Creditor's claim subject to cram down...
- YES → Creditor's claim **not** subject to **cram down.** Debtor must pay creditor balance owed on loan even if collateral value < loan balance. See § 1325(a)(9) hanging paragraph.

Did debtor acquire vehicle within 910 days of filing for Chapter 13?
- YES → Does creditor have a **PMSI?**
- NO → Creditor's claim subject to cram down...

Does creditor have a **PMSI?**
- YES → Creditor's claim **not** subject to **cram down.** Debtor must pay creditor balance owed on loan even if collateral value < loan balance. See § 1325(a)(9) hanging paragraph.
- NO → Creditor's claim subject to cram down...

Creditor's claim subject to cram down → Did debtor acquire collateral for **personal, family, or household purposes?**
- YES → Collateral value = **retail price,** considering age and condition. See § 506(a)(2), 2nd sentence.
- NO → Collateral value = **replacement value** without deducting for costs of sale or marketing. See § 506(a)(2), 1st sentence.

j. Treatment of Unsecured Creditors' Claims

The debtor's plan must satisfy the *best interests of the creditors* test and, if the trustee or an unsecured creditor objects to plan confirmation, the *projected disposable income* test.

(i) Best Interests of Creditors Test

The plan must provide that *each unsecured creditor* holding an allowed claim will receive property having a *present value,* as of the effective date of the plan, of *not less* than the amount he would *receive* for his claim in a *Chapter 7* case on that date, taking into account the exemptions that would be available to the debtor. This element of confirmation usually is referred to as the "best interests of creditors test." [B.C. § 1325(a)(4)]

Note: The present value of plan payments must equal or exceed "the hypothetical distribution under Chapter 7", *not* the present value of the creditor's allowed claim. [*In re* Young, 61 B.R. 150 (Bankr. S.D. Ind. 1986)]

e.g. **Example:** Debi is a below-median-income debtor. Her three-year plan proposes to pay her unsecured creditors $100 per month, which amounts to a 10% dividend to Debi's unsecured creditors. Debi, however, has a valuable non-exempt asset, which if liquidated, would provide her unsecured creditors in a Chapter 7 case with a 15% dividend. Debi's plan does not satisfy the best interests of creditors test and, thus, the bankruptcy court cannot confirm the plan.

e.g. **Example:** Dell owes his unsecured creditors $30,000 and his plan proposes to pay those creditors in full by paying $500 per month over the 60-month plan. Had Dell filed for relief under Chapter 7, he would have paid his unsecured creditors $30,000 from his non-exempt assets. The bankruptcy court cannot confirm Dell's plan, because the Code requires Dell to pay the *present value* of $30,000 to his unsecured creditors. Without paying interest on the $30,000, Dell is not paying his unsecured creditors at least what they would have recovered under Chapter 7. [*See In re* Hardy, 755 F.2d 75 (6th Cir. 1985) ("When liquidation will result in full payment of all allowed unsecured claims, a debtor cannot defer payment of the claims without providing interest payments to the creditors")]

(ii) Projected Disposable Income Test

If the *trustee* or an *unsecured creditor* objects to the plan, then the bankruptcy court cannot confirm the plan unless as of the plan's effective date the plan *either* (a) pays the unsecured creditor the *present value of its claim or* (b) provides that the debtor applies all of her *projected disposable income* during the *applicable commitment period,* starting on the date of the first plan payment, to making plan payments to her unsecured creditors. [B.C. § 1325(b)(1)]

(1) Applicable Commitment Period

The *applicable commitment period* is the length of time that the debtor must make payments under her plan and depends on whether the debtor's annual income is above or below the median for the state in which the debtor resides at the time of bankruptcy. The applicable commitment period for *above-median-income debtors* is *five years or 60 months*, and for *below-median-income debtors* it is *three years or 36 months.* [B.C. § 1325(b)(4)(A)]

Exception: The applicable commitment period may be less than three or five years, whichever time period is applicable, but *only if* the debtor's plan pays all unsecured claims in full over the shorter time period. [B.C. § 1325(b)(4)(B)]

Example: Denise is an above-median-income debtor and, therefore, the applicable commitment period for her plan is five years or 60 months. Denise may propose and the bankruptcy court may approve a plan with an applicable commitment period of four years or 48 months if the plan provides for payment in full to all of Denise's unsecured creditors over the plan's 48-month period.

(2) Disposable Income

Disposable income is *current monthly income* minus *reasonably necessary expenses.* Disposable income excludes child support payments, foster care payments, and disability payments for a dependent child to the extent reasonably necessary to be expended for such child. [B.C. § 1325(b)(2)] It also excludes amounts to repay certain *pension loans.* [B.C. § 1322(f)]

(3) Reasonably Necessary Expenses

Reasonably necessary expenses are amounts reasonably necessary to be expended for (i) the *maintenance or support* of the debtor or a dependent of the debtor; (ii) a *domestic support obligation* that first becomes payable post-petition; (iii) certain *charitable contributions*; and (iv) the *continuation, preservation, and operation of a business*, if the debtor is engaged in business. [B.C. § 1325(b)(2)] For *above-median* income debtors, reasonably necessary expenses are the *"means test"* expense amounts. [B.C. § 1325(b)(3)] For *below-median* income debtors, the bankruptcy court determines the reasonableness of the debtor's expenses.

(a) Charitable Contributions

The debtor may deduct from her current monthly income *charitable contributions* to a *qualified religious or charitable entity or organization* in an amount not to exceed *15%* of the debtor's *gross income* for the year in which the contributions are made. [B.C. §§ 1325(b)(2)(A)(ii), 548(d)(3), (4)] The Code defines a *qualified religious or charitable entity or organization* as an entity described in § 170(c)(1) or an entity or organization described in § 170(c)(2) of the Internal Revenue Code. [B.C. § 548(d)(4), 26 U.S.C. § 170(c)(1), (2)]

Example: Diane has current monthly income of $4,000, and is an above-median income debtor. Her $3,900 of monthly expenses includes $400 that Diane tithes each month to her church. Diane's charitable contributions are 10% of her gross income; therefore, she may include them in the calculation of her disposable income.

(4) Certain Retirement Plan Loans

Amounts that the debtor is required to repay certain retirement plan loans are not considered part of the debtor's disposable income. [B.C. §§ 1322(f), 362(b)(19)]

(5) Projected Disposable Income

The Bankruptcy Code defines *disposable income* but not *projected disposable income.* Because the calculation of *current monthly income* is backward looking—at the six months prior to filing for bankruptcy—a debtor whose financial circumstances change prior to bankruptcy may have less (or more) actual income to commit to a Chapter 13 plan than the disposable income calculation shows. The Supreme Court has held that in determining a debtor's *projected disposable income,* the bankruptcy court "may account for changes in the debtor's income or expenses that are known or virtually certain at the time of confirmation." [**Hamilton v. Lanning,** 560 U.S. 505 (2010)]

e.g. **Example:** During the six months prior to filing for bankruptcy, Dominique, a single person, received a one-time buyout from her employer, which significantly increased her gross income for several months. As a result, Dominique's current monthly income is $5,000 (making her an above-median income debtor) and her disposable income is $1,200 per month. But, Dominique cannot afford to pay her unsecured creditors $1,200 per month, because the actual income from her new job is only $2,000 per month. Her actual monthly expenses are $1,830, leaving her $170 per month in actual disposable income. The bankruptcy court may take account of the known changes to Dominique's income and confirm a plan in which she pays $155 per month to her unsecured creditors.

Note: A debtor may commit less than her full disposable income to plan payments to her unsecured creditors. The reason is to provide the debtor with a cushion or reserve to take account of unexpected changes in monthly expenses. [8 Collier ¶ 1325.11(4)(c)(ii)]

4. Permissive Provisions

A Chapter 13 plan *may include* any of the following provisions. [B.C. § 1322(b)]

a. Classification of Claims

The plan may specify various *classes of unsecured claims* in accordance with Bankruptcy Code § 1122, provided that it does not discriminate unfairly against any particular class. [B.C. § 1322(b)(1)] In 1984, Congress amended § 1322(b)(1) to allow a Chapter 13 plan to provide different treatment for a consumer debt on which an individual co-debtor is also liable than for other unsecured claims. [B.C. § 1322(b)(1)] The amendment, which courts call the "however clause," has been the subject of much debate. Some courts hold that the "however clause" creates an exception to the unfair discrimination requirement for co-debtor consumer claims and, thus, there is no unfair discrimination analysis for plans treating co-debtor consumer claims differently from other unsecured claims. The majority of courts, however, hold that the clause qualifies the unfair discrimination analysis although the courts struggle with the degree of qualification. [*See* **Meyer v. Renteria (*In re* Renteria),** 470 B.R. 838 (B.A.P. 9th Cir. 2012) (describing the various positions taken by courts)]

(i) "Unfair Discrimination"

The courts have developed a number of tests for determining unfair discrimination, including The Balance Approach, The Bright-line Approach, and the Reasonableness Approach. [*In re* **Engen,** 561 B.R. 523 (Bankr. D. Kan. 2016) (summarizing the multitude of tests)] In determining whether discrimination against a class is fair, many courts use the following four-part test:

(1) whether there is a *reasonable basis* for the discriminatory treatment;

(2) whether the plan could be implemented *without* the discrimination;

(3) the presence or absence of *good faith;* and

(4) whether the degree of discrimination is directly related to the basis or rationale for the discrimination.

[*In re* **Engen,** *supra*]

 Example: Married debtors filed for relief under Chapter 13 and proposed a plan that separately classified their delinquent tax debts, some of which were non-dischargeable. The proposed plan would have resulted in full payment of the nondischargeable tax debt with no payment for the remaining unsecured non-priority creditors. The Chapter 13 trustee objected to the plan, and the debtors amended it to delete the special classification for their tax creditors. Subsequently, however, debtors objected to their own amended plan and claimed that the Bankruptcy Code allowed them to prefer their tax creditors in the plan. The bankruptcy court overruled the objection and confirmed the plan without special treatment for the tax creditors. The debtors appealed and the Eighth Circuit affirmed the bankruptcy court's decision. The Eighth Circuit found that the debtors had failed to satisfy the four-part test for unfair discrimination. For example, the court concluded that the "plan lack[ed] good faith" because the debtors "propose[d] to 'protect' those creditors least in need of protection, at the expense of the most vulnerable." [**Copeland v. Fink (***In re* **Copeland),** 742 F.3d 811 (8th Cir. 2014)]

 Example: Debtor filed for relief under Chapter 13. At the § 341 meeting, she stated her intention to pay the unsecured part of Car Company's claim in full to prevent Car Company from seeking relief from the co-debtor stay and pursuing co-debtor for payment. Debtor, however, failed to amend her Chapter 13 plan to so provide, and Car Company objected to confirmation of the plan because it failed to give Car Company preferential treatment of its unsecured claim. The Chapter 13 trustee opposed preferential treatment for Car Company's unsecured claim. The bankruptcy court held that "the language of § 1322(b)(1) creates an exception to the unfair discrimination test in cases involving co-signed debt" and that "Congress intended to permit debtors to specially classify co-debtor claims without convincing a court that the classification is not unfairly discriminatory." Thus, as long as Debtor satisfied the other requirements for confirmation of her Chapter 13 plan, preferential treatment of Car Company's unsecured claim compared with other unsecured claims would not preclude confirmation of the plan. [*In re* **Monroe,** 281 B.R. 398 (Bankr. N.D. Ga. 2002)]

b. Modification of Creditors' Rights

With one exception, the plan may modify the rights of secured creditors or unsecured creditors, e.g., by changing the size and timing of installment payments.

(i) Exception: Principal Residence

The plan *may not modify* the rights of a creditor whose claim is secured *solely* by a security interest in real property constituting the *debtor's principal residence.* [B.C. § 1322(b)(2)] The Code defines a security interest as a *lien created by an agreement.* [B.C. § 101(51)] Thus, § 1322(b)(2)'s anti-modification provision prevents the debtor from doing such things as reducing the amount of the loan's monthly payments, converting a variable to a fixed interest rate, or extending the term of the loan. [*See* **Anderson v. Hancock,** 820 F.3d 670 (4th Cir. 2016)] A majority of courts use the petition date as the date for determining debtor's principal residence. [*In re* **Brinkley,** 505 B.R. 207 (Bankr. E.D. Mich. 2013)]

 Example: Debtor filed for relief under Chapter 13, and listed a doublewide mobile home on her Schedule B of personal property. Debtor listed no real property on Schedule A. In her Chapter 13 plan, Debtor proposed to modify the rights of Green Tree, which held the security interest in her mobile home. Green Tree argued that because Debtor used the mobile home as her principal residence, § 1322(b)(2) precluded her from modifying its rights. The bankruptcy court disagreed. The court held that while the mobile home was Debtor's principal residence, it was personal, not real, property under Alabama law. As a result, § 1322(b)(2) did not apply. [***In re* Manning**, 2007 WL 2220454 (Bankr. N.D. Ala. 2007)]

(ii) Hybrid Properties

Most courts use one of three tests to decide whether § 1322(b)(2) applies to real property that serves not only as the debtor's principal residence but also as the location for some commercial activity. Courts using the ***case-by-case approach*** look to the ***totality of the circumstances*** to determine whether the parties' predominant intent was to enter into a primarily residential or commercial transaction. Courts using the ***bright-line test,*** by comparison, do not apply § 1322(b)(2) if the real property serves any other function besides the debtor's principal residence. Finally, courts using the ***third approach*** focus on the fact that the word "only" in § 1322(b)(2) does not modify "debtor's principal residence;" it modifies the word "secured." These courts apply § 1322(b)(2) to real property that serves as the *only* security for the debt so long as the debtor "principally resides in *some portion* of the real property." [***In re* Hutsler,** 2016 WL 7984348 (Bankr. W.D. Mo. 2016)]

Example: Debtors filed for relief under Chapter 13. Prior to bankruptcy, they had purchased three tracts of land on which sat two houses. The Debtors lived on the residence on one tract of land; the father of one of the debtors ("Father") lived in the second home on one of the other three tracts of land. Father also farmed some of the acreage. The Debtors financed the purchase through WFO Investments. The purchase-money note provided for $1,500 monthly payments and bore a 10% annual interest rate. The note had a balloon payment due approximately one year after Debtors filed for bankruptcy. The Debtors' plan provided for payment to WFO of $2,000 per month for 48 months, at 4.55% interest, with the balloon payment due at the end of the 48-month payment period. WFO objected to the Debtors' plan on the basis of § 1322(b)(2). Debtors argued that only one of the three tracts of land contained *their* principal residence, and that Father farmed some of the other land. Thus, they argued that § 1322(b)(2) did not apply, because WFO's claim was secured *not only* by real property that was a principal residence. The court applied each of the three tests used by most courts in cases involving hybrid use of the real property on which sits the debtor's principal residence. The court found that under any of the three tests, WFO's claim was secured by real property that was the debtor's principal residence. Thus, the court held that Debtors could not modify WFO's rights under the loan documents. [***In re* Hutsler,** *supra*]

c. Cure or Waiver of Default

The plan may cure or waive any default. [B.C. § 1322(b)(3)]

d. Order of Payments

The plan may provide for any general unsecured claim to be paid concurrently with any secured claim or with any unsecured priority claim. [B.C. § 1322(b)(4)]

e. Long-Term Debts

Sometimes a debtor has a long-term debt for which the last payment is due after the due date of the final payment required by the Chapter 13 plan. If such a debt is in default—whether secured or unsecured—the Chapter 13 plan may provide for *curing the default* within a reasonable time and *maintaining payments* while the case is pending. [B.C. § 1322(b)(5)] This section, by specific statutory authorization, frequently is applied with respect to claims secured solely by real property constituting the principal residence of the debtor, notwithstanding the exception contained in § 1322(b)(2) concerning non-modification of home mortgages. Cure, however, does not permit the debtor to modify the rights of a creditor whose claim is secured by real property that is the debtor's principal residence.

EXAM TIP

If your professor asks you to determine whether Chapter 7 or Chapter 13 would provide optimal relief for the debtor, often an important factor will be the debtor's desire to keep her home. Section 1322(b)(3) allows the Chapter 13 plan to include a provision to cure any default. But suppose that the final mortgage payment will be due after the due date of the last payment required by the Chapter 13 plan. Under these circumstances, the debtor may use § 1322(b)(5) to include a provision in the plan to *cure the default within a reasonable time* and *maintain the payments* while the case is pending, with the balance of the mortgage payments to be made after completion of the payments under the plan. In this way, the debtor can retain her home, but the long-term mortgage debt will not be discharged in the debtor's Chapter 13 bankruptcy case. You might note in your answer that if keeping her home is the debtor's main goal, Chapter 7 probably will not be as attractive an option, because many mortgagees require the debtor to get current before reaffirming. In Chapter 13, the debtor has a reasonable time to cure.

(i) Cure

If the debtor seeks to cure a default with respect to a lien on her principal residence, cure is permitted until a foreclosure sale conducted according to applicable nonbankruptcy law has occurred. [B.C. § 1322(c)(1)] Cure focuses on the debtor's ability to "decelerate and continue paying a loan, thereby avoiding foreclosure." [**Anderson v. Hancock,** 820 F.3d 670 (4th Cir. 2016)]

(ii) "Reasonable Time"

What constitutes a reasonable time to cure a default depends on the circumstances of the particular case. Courts examine various factors in making the "reasonable time" determination but "give primary consideration to whether the cure period is the debtor's best effort and is the most that the debtor can reasonably be expected to pay considering his income." [**Hence v. Indian Cave P'ship (*In re* Hence),** 2007 WL 1176787 (S.D. Tex. 2007), *aff'd,* 255 Fed. App'x 28 (5th Cir. 2007)]

(iii) Interest on Arrearages

If the plan proposes to cure a default, the amount necessary to cure the default is determined by looking to the underlying contract and applicable nonbankruptcy law. [B.C. § 1322(e)] Therefore, a creditor will be entitled to interest on interest only if it was agreed to by the parties and is permissible under state law, or alternatively if it is required by state law.

f. Post-Petition Tax Claims or Necessary Consumer Debts

The plan may provide for the payment of any allowed post-petition claims for taxes that become due during the pendency of the case, or for certain necessary consumer debts incurred after the order for relief. [B.C. §§ 1322(b)(6), 1305]

g. Assumption or Rejection of Executory Contracts or Unexpired Leases

The plan may provide for any previously unrejected executory contract or unexpired lease to be assumed, rejected, or assigned in accordance with § 365. [B.C. § 1322(b)(7)]

h. Property Used to Pay Claims

The plan may provide for particular claims to be paid from property of the estate or from the debtor's property. [B.C. § 1322(b)(8)]

i. Vesting of Property

The plan may provide for property of the estate to vest in the debtor or in another entity when the plan is confirmed or at a subsequent time. [B.C. § 1322(b)(9)]

j. Interest on Nondischargeable Debts

The plan may provide for the payment of interest accruing post-petition on unsecured nondischargeable debts *but only if* the debtor has disposable income available to pay interest after providing for full payment of all allowed claims. [B.C. §§ 1322(b)(10), 1328(a)]

k. Miscellaneous Provisions

The plan also may contain any other provisions that are appropriate and consistent with the Bankruptcy Code. [B.C. § 1322(b)(11)]

5. Modification of Plan

The debtor has the *exclusive right* to modify a plan *prior to confirmation.* The modified plan must satisfy the requirements of § 1322. [B.C. § 1323]

E. Payments

1. Commencement of Payments

Unless the court orders otherwise, the debtor must begin making payments under a proposed plan no later than *30 days* after the *earlier* of the order for relief or the date that the plan is filed. [B.C. § 1326(a)(1)]

2. To Whom Are Payments Made?

The debtor must remit *plan payments* to the trustee. [B.C. § 1326(a)(1)(A)] In the following two situations, however, the debtor's payment goes directly to the creditor.

a. Personal Property Lease

The debtor directly pays the lessor for scheduled post-petition payments on a lease of personal property. [B.C. § 1326(a)(1)(B)]

b. Adequate Protection

The debtor makes *adequate protection* payments directly to a creditor with a *purchase money security interest in personal property* but only with respect to the amount that comes due post-petition. [B.C. § 1326(a)(1)(C)]

(i) Effect on Payments to Trustee

The debtor reduces the amount owed to the trustee by the amounts paid directly to the personal property lessor and to the creditor for adequate protection payments described above. The debtor must provide the *trustee* with *evidence of the payment,* including the amount and date of the payment. [B.C. § 1326(a)(1)(B), (C)]

(ii) Insurance

No later than *60 days* after filing the petition, the debtor who retains *personal property* must provide to the *lessor* of such property or to a creditor with a *purchase money security interest* in such property evidence that the debtor is maintaining required *insurance coverage* on the property. The debtor's obligation continues as long as the debtor retains possession of the property. [B.C. § 1326(a)(4)]

3. Pre-Confirmation Payments to Trustee

Prior to confirmation and subject to § 363, the court, after notice and hearing, may increase or decrease the payments required of the debtor. [B.C. § 1326(a)(3)] The trustee retains any payment made before confirmation until the confirmation hearing. If the plan is confirmed, the trustee makes distributions as provided for by the plan as soon as practicable. However, if confirmation is denied, the money must be returned to the debtor, less any unpaid administrative expenses that have been allowed. [B.C. § 1326(a)(2)]

4. Payment Orders

After plan confirmation, the court may order the debtor's employer, or any other entity providing income to the debtor, to make direct payments to the Chapter 13 trustee. [B.C. § 1325(c)] The bankruptcy court cannot order the Social Security Administration to make payments directly to the trustee. [8 Collier ¶ 1325.12(2)]

5. Distribution

Ordinarily, the payments under a confirmed plan are sent to creditors *by the trustee* unless the plan or the confirmation order provides otherwise, such as where a debtor engaged in business is allowed to perform this function. [B.C. § 1326(c)]

6. Administrative Expenses

Prior to or concurrent with each payment to creditors under a Chapter 13 plan, the trustee is required to pay any unpaid administrative expenses or bankruptcy fees or charges, as well as the percentage fee set for a standing trustee, if one has been appointed. [B.C. § 1326(b)(1), (2)] In addition, BAPCPA amended the Bankruptcy Code to provide for the payment of compensation owed to a Chapter 7 trustee in a debtor's *subsequent* Chapter 13 case. The trustee must have been allowed compensation, which remained unpaid, due to the conversion or dismissal of the debtor's *prior case* pursuant to the § 707(b) abuse test. [B.C. § 1326(b)(3)] In such a case, the plan must provide for *monthly* payments to the Chapter 7 trustee by *pro rating* the amount owed over the *term of the Chapter 13 plan.* [B.C. § 1326(b)(3)(A); *In re Kuhn,* 337 B.R. 668 (Bankr. N.D. Ind. 2006)] The *monthly payment cannot exceed* the *greater of $25 or* the *total amount payable to the general unsecured creditors* over the term of the plan *multiplied by 5%* and then *divided by the number of months* in the plan. [B.C. § 1326(b)(3)(B)]

7. Filing Fee

The debtor may apply to pay the Chapter 13 filing fee in installments. [Bankruptcy Rule 1006(b)(1); Official Form 103A] The deadline for paying the entire Chapter 13 filing fee is the time of the first payment to creditors under the plan. [8 Collier ¶ 1326.03(1)]

F. Post-Confirmation Matters

1. Effects of Confirmation

A confirmed plan *binds the debtor and every creditor,* regardless of whether a creditor has accepted or rejected the plan or has objected to confirmation of the plan, or whether the creditor's claim is provided for by the plan. [B.C. § 1327(a)]

Example: Debtor filed for relief under Chapter 13, and proposed a plan that provided for payment of only the principal of his outstanding student loans and discharge of that debt once he paid off the principal through the plan. Debtor owed United Student Aid Funds ("United") $17,832.15, which represented both the principal and interest on his student loans. United filed a proof of claim and received a copy of Debtor's plan but failed to object to the plan. The bankruptcy court confirmed the plan, even though Debtor had filed no adversary proceeding to determine dischargeability of the debt and the court had made no findings on undue hardship. After completing plan payments on the principal on his student loans, Debtor obtained a discharge on the interest due on the loans. When collection efforts were undertaken for the loan interest, Debtor filed a motion with the bankruptcy court asking for enforcement of the earlier discharge order. United opposed the motion and filed a cross-motion under Federal Rule of Civil Procedure 60(b)(4) to set aside as void the bankruptcy court's order confirming Debtor's plan. The bankruptcy court denied United's cross-motion and ordered that collection activities stop. The district court reversed the bankruptcy court, but the Tenth Circuit reversed the district court's order. The United States Supreme Court affirmed the decision of the Tenth Circuit and held that Rule 60(b)(4) did not provide United with a basis for voiding the bankruptcy court's confirmation order. Thus, the bankruptcy court's confirmation order stood. While affirming the Tenth Circuit's decision, the Supreme Court faulted the Tenth Circuit for concluding that unless a creditor timely objects to confirmation a bankruptcy court *must* confirm the plan, even if the plan provides for the discharge of student loan debt without an undue hardship determination. The Supreme Court noted that the Bankruptcy Code "makes plain that bankruptcy courts have the authority—indeed, the obligation—to direct a debtor to conform his plan to the requirements of §§ 1328(a)(2) and 523(a)(8)." [**United Student Aid Funds, Inc. v. Espinosa,** 559 U.S. 260 (2010)]

a. Property

Unless the Chapter 13 plan or the confirmation order provides otherwise, confirmation causes all property of the estate to vest in the debtor "free and clear of any claim or interest of any creditor provided for by the plan." [B.C. § 1327(b), (c)] The debtor may request in the plan a determination of the amount of a creditor's secured claim. With the exception of a secured claim held by a governmental unit, any determination in the plan about the amount of a secured claim binds the holder of that claim, even if the holder files a contrary proof of claim or the debtor schedules the claim, or a claim objection was filed. [Bankruptcy Rules 3015(g), 3012] In order to bind the secured claim holder, however, the plan containing a request to determine the amount of the secured claim must be served on the holder of that claim and any other party designated by the bankruptcy court in the manner required for service of a summons and complaint. [Bankruptcy Rules 3012(b), 7004] Therefore, notice to the secured creditor is critical. If the creditor receives proper notice of the valuation of its claim in the plan and fails to object, then it is bound by confirmation of the Chapter 13 plan.

Example: Debtor owns a vehicle that is not subject to the hanging paragraph following § 1325(a)(9). The car is worth $9,500 but Debtor still owes Car Company $16,000 for the vehicle. Debtor filed for relief under Chapter 13 and filed a plan that proposed stripping off Car Company's lien once Debtor completed plan payments on Car Company's $9,500 secured claim. Car Company received proper notice of Debtor's plan, but failed to object to the lien-stripping provision in the plan. The bankruptcy court confirmed Debtor's plan. Car Company is bound by the terms of the plan. Therefore, when Debtor completes plan payments on the $9,500 secured claim, Car Company no longer has a lien on Debtor's vehicle. [For a pre-BAPCPA case with similar facts, *see In re* **Harvey,** 213 F.3d 318 (7th Cir. 2000)]

(i) Note on Notice

Official Form 113—the Chapter 13 Plan—contains a check box on the first page of the plan to inform secured creditors whether the plan places a "limit on the amount of the secured claim, [ ] which may result in a partial payment or no payment at all to the secured creditor." [Official Form 113 § 1.1] If a district uses its own Local Form Chapter 13 Plan, then the Local Form must include an initial paragraph that includes a statement as to whether the plan "limit[s] the amount of a secured claim based on a valuation of the collateral for the claim." [Bankruptcy Rules 3015(c), 3015.1(c)(2)]

b. Debts

In a Chapter 13 case, confirmation does *not* operate as a discharge of the debtor's debts. [B.C. § 1328; *see infra* § G of this Chapter]

2. Post-Confirmation Modification

The debtor, the trustee, or an unsecured creditor may request a modification of a plan at any time after it has been confirmed but before all payments have been made. Generally, a request for post-confirmation modification of a plan occurs under circumstances in which the income or expenses of the debtor have *changed materially and unexpectedly.* [B.C. § 1329(a); 8 Collier ¶ 1329.03]

a. Reasons for Seeking Modification

The debtor, the trustee, or an unsecured creditor may request a modification of the plan for any of the following reasons:

(i) to *increase or reduce the amount of payments* to a particular class [B.C. § 1329(a)(1)];

(ii) to provide for a *longer or shorter payout* period [B.C. § 1329(a)(2)];

(iii) to change the amount to be paid to a creditor to *adjust for any payment* the creditor received on its claim outside of the plan [B.C. § 1329(a)(3)]; or

(iv) to *reduce amounts* to be paid under the plan by the *actual amount spent for health insurance* for the debtor and any dependent not covered by health insurance. [B.C. § 1329(a)(4)] The debtor must document the cost of the insurance and show the following:

(1) the expenses are *reasonable and necessary;*

(2) for a debtor who previously paid for health insurance, the amount is *not materially larger* than what it *previously cost* the debtor for health insurance or to maintain the lapsed policy;

(3) for a debtor who did not previously have health insurance, the amount is *not materially larger* than the cost for a *similarly situated debtor;*

(4) the amount is *not otherwise accounted for in determining disposable income* under § 1325(b); and

(5) if any party in interest requests proof that insurance was purchased, the debtor will file such proof.

e.g. **Example:** Married debtors filed for relief under Chapter 13. The bankruptcy court confirmed debtors' plan. Three years later, the Chapter 13 trustee moved to modify the plan under § 1329 to increase debtors' monthly payments by $746. The trustee showed that the debtors' income had increased by $50,000 since plan confirmation. Both the bankruptcy court and the district court concluded that they lacked authority to grant the trustee's motion because § 1329 did not specifically provide for modifications to the plan based on post-confirmation increases in debtors' income. The Seventh Circuit noted that the trustee's proposed modification satisfied the requirements of § 1329 but that § 1329 did not "contain an explicit standard" for deciding when the court should approve such a modification. The court explained that both the purposes of Chapter 13—to allow debtors a fresh start without the need to liquidate assets and to ensure that debtors devoted all disposable income to repaying creditors—and the legislative history of the 1984 amendments, which provided that the trustee or unsecured creditors, not simply the debtor, could seek a post-confirmation modification of the plan supported the trustee's position. The Seventh Circuit held that a bankruptcy court may permit a post-confirmation modification to increase plan payments if the court determines that debtors can afford the increase in payments. [**Germeraad v. Powers,** 826 F.3d 962 (7th Cir. 2016)]

3. Revocation of Confirmation Order

Within *180 days after an order confirming* a Chapter 13 plan has been entered, a party in interest may request that the order be revoked on the ground that it was *procured by fraud.* Revocation is discretionary. If after notice and a hearing the confirmation order is revoked, the court may grant the debtor time to propose and obtain confirmation of a modified plan. Otherwise, the court must convert or dismiss the case under § 1307. [B.C. § 1330]

4. Debtor's Failure to Make Payments

If the debtor fails to make all payments under the plan, a party in interest or the United States trustee may move for dismissal of the case or conversion to Chapter 7. [B.C. § 1307] Alternatively, the debtor may request a hardship discharge if the circumstances warrant.

G. Discharge

1. Overview of the Chapter 13 Discharge

The Bankruptcy Code, as originally enacted, provided the Chapter 13 debtor with a broader discharge of debts than the Chapter 7 debtor. While the Chapter 13 discharge is still broader than that for Chapter 7, Congress, most recently with the enactment of BAPCPA, has increased the number of nondischargeable debts in Chapter 13 cases.

With the exceptions listed below, a standard Chapter 13 discharge includes all debts that are provided for by the plan or that have been disallowed by the court under § 502. Unless the debtor has executed a court-approved written waiver of discharge subsequent to the order for relief, the debtor will be granted a discharge as soon as practicable after she has:

a. made *all payments* under the plan; and

b. *certified* that she has *paid all domestic support obligations* required by *judicial or administrative order, or by statute* and due prior to the date of the certification.

[B.C. § 1328(a)]

2. Cases to Which Discharge Does Not Apply

The Code provides that the Chapter 13 debtor will not receive a discharge in certain situations. Make sure to distinguish between this *global denial of discharge* and the nondischargeability of specific debts discussed below.

a. Instructional Course

A Chapter 13 debtor will not receive a discharge if she fails to complete post-petition the *instructional course on personal financial management* mandated by § 111 of the Bankruptcy Code. [B.C. §§ 1328(g), 111]

(i) Exception #1: Incapacity, Disability, Active Military Duty

A debtor need not complete the instructional course if she is unable to do so due to *incapacity, disability,* or *active military duty in a military combat zone.* [B.C. §§ 1328(g)(2), 109(h)(4)]

(ii) Exception #2: Inadequate Service

A debtor need not complete the instructional course if the United States trustee or Bankruptcy Administrator determines that the instructional courses in the *district in which she resides* are *inadequate* to service individuals in need of such services. [B.C. § 1328(g)(2)]

b. Prior Bankruptcy Cases

The debtor will not receive a discharge in her current Chapter 13 case if she has received a discharge within a certain time period in a prior bankruptcy case. The time between the filing of the earlier case and the current Chapter 13 case varies depending on the chapter under which the debtor filed her prior case.

(i) Prior Chapter 7, 11, or 12 Case

The debtor will not receive a discharge in her current Chapter 13 case if she received a discharge in a case filed under *Chapters 7, 11, or 12* during the *four years prior to the filing* of her current Chapter 13 case. [B.C. § 1328(f)(1)] The time period runs from the *filing date* of the prior case to the *filing date* of the current Chapter 13 case.

Example: Debtor filed for relief under Chapter 7 on July 29, 2002; he received a discharge on February 5, 2003. Debtor filed for relief under Chapter 13 on January 5, 2007. Because Debtor filed his Chapter 7 case more than four years before his later Chapter 13 case, he is entitled to a discharge in the later Chapter 13 case. The four-year time period runs from the *filing date* of the prior Chapter 7 case, not the date on which Debtor received his discharge. [**Carroll v. Sanders (*In re* Sanders),** 551 F.3d 397 (6th Cir. 2008)]

(ii) Prior Chapter 13 Case

The debtor will not receive a discharge in her current Chapter 13 case if she received a discharge in a case filed under *Chapter 13* during the *two years* prior to the filing of her current Chapter 13 case. [B.C. § 1328(f)(2)] The time period runs from the *filing date* of the prior case to the *filing date* of the current Chapter 13 case.

c. Exemption Issue Under § 522(q)

The bankruptcy court may not grant a discharge unless it has determined, after notice and a hearing held *no more than 10 days* before the discharge order, that there is *no reasonable cause to believe* that:

(i) the Bankruptcy Code's limitation on state-law exemption rights pursuant to § 522(q)(1) may apply to the debtor [B.C. §§ 1328(h)(1), 522(q)(1)]; *and*

(ii) there is a pending proceeding in which the debtor may be found guilty of one of the *felonies listed in § 522(q)(1)(A) or* liable for a *debt described in § 522(q)(1)(B).* [B.C. §§ 1328(h)(2), 522(q)(1)]

This provision of the Code should operate to *delay* rather than *permanently deny* the debtor a discharge. The reason for the delay is to allow time to determine whether the debtor's homestead exemption should be limited under § 522(q). "Once that determination is made, and the nonbankruptcy proceeding is no longer pending, the chapter 13 discharge can be granted." [8 Collier ¶ 1328.09]

3. Nondischargeable Debts

The standard Chapter 13 discharge does not include the following *debts.*

a. Long-Term Debts

If the plan provides for curing any default within a reasonable time and maintaining payments while the case is pending on any debt for which the last payment is due *after* the final plan payment, then that debt is not dischargeable. [B.C. §§ 1328(a)(1), 1322(b)(5); *see In re* **Russell**, 458 B.R. 731 (Bankr. E.D. Va. 2010) (stating that "[l]ong-term debts treated under the cure-and-maintain provisions of § 1322(b)(5) are excluded from the discharge")]

b. Certain Taxes

The following types of taxes are not dischargeable:

(i) *trust fund taxes* [B.C. §§ 1328(a)(2), 507(a)(8)(C)];

(ii) a tax for which a *return, or equivalent report or notice,* if required, was *not filed or given or* was filed or given but *after the date on which it was due and* within the *two year-period prior to filing* of the bankruptcy petition [B.C. §§ 1328(a)(2), 523(a)(1)(B)]; and

(iii) a tax for which the debtor either made a *fraudulent return or willfully attempted* to *evade or defeat* the tax. [B.C. §§ 1328(a)(2), 523(a)(1)(C)]

c. Fraud

Debts for money, property, services, or an extension, renewal, or refinancing of credit obtained by *fraud, consumer debts* exceeding *$800* incurred within *90 days* of bankruptcy for *luxury goods,* or *cash advances* exceeding *$1,100* obtained within *70 days* of bankruptcy are not dischargeable. [B.C. §§ 1328(a)(2), 523(a)(2)]

d. Unscheduled Debts

Debts that the debtor did not *list or schedule* in time for the creditor to *timely file a proof of claim* are not dischargeable, unless the creditor had *notice or actual knowledge* in time to make a timely filing. [B.C. § 523(a)(3)(A)]

e. Section 523(a)(2) or (4)

Debts that are potentially nondischargeable under *§ 523(a)(2) or (4),* and that the debtor neither *listed nor scheduled* in time for the creditor to *timely file a proof of claim* and *timely request a determination of dischargeability* are not dischargeable, unless the creditor had *notice or actual knowledge* in time to make a timely filing. [B.C. § 523(a)(3)(B)]

Note: Section 523(a)(3)(B) also applies to § 523(a)(6) debts, but § 1328's exceptions to discharge do not include § 523(a)(6).

f. Embezzlement

Debts owed for *embezzlement, larceny,* or *fraud or defalcation in a fiduciary capacity* are not dischargeable. [B.C. § 523(a)(4)]

g. Domestic Support Obligations

Domestic support obligations are not dischargeable. [B.C. §§ 1328(a)(2), 523(a)(5)] *Debts for support* owed under state law to a *state or municipality* that are enforceable under the Child Support Enforcement Act are not dischargeable. [42 U.S.C. § 656(b)]

h. Student Loans

Unless excepting the debt from discharge will constitute an *undue hardship* on the debtor and her dependents, *student loan debt* is nondischargeable. [B.C. §§ 1328(a)(2), 523(a)(8)] *Health Education Assistance Loans* ("HEAL"), in cases in which the three conditions for discharge required by the applicable federal nonbankruptcy statute have not been satisfied, also are not dischargeable. [42 U.S.C. § 292f(g); **United States v. Beams,** 2008 WL 1774423 (S.D. Ind. 2008) (noting that discharge of a HEAL loan is even more difficult than for general student loans because the debtor must satisfy "the more stringent standard of unconscionability")]

i. Certain Personal Injury Debts

A debt for *death or personal injury* caused by the debtor's operation of a *motor vehicle, vessel, or aircraft* while *intoxicated* from using *alcohol, drugs, or another substance* is not dischargeable. [B.C. §§ 1328(a)(2), 523(a)(9)]

j. Restitution

A debt for *restitution,* or a *criminal fine,* that is included in the debtor's sentence for *conviction of a crime* is not dischargeable. [B.C. § 1328(a)(3)] A debt for *restitution* or *damages awarded in a civil action* against the debtor as a result of *willful* or *malicious injury* that caused *death or personal injury* also is nondischargeable. [B.C. § 1328(a)(4)]

k. Certain Consumer Debts

Post-petition consumer debts for property or services necessary for the debtor to perform the plan are not dischargeable, if the corresponding claims were allowed, and if the trustee's prior approval to incur the debt was practicable but was not obtained. [B.C. §§ 1328(d), 1305(a)(2), (c)]

If you encounter an exam question that asks you to decide whether the debtor should file for relief under Chapter 7 or Chapter 13, one factor to consider is the difference in the *kinds of debts that can be discharged* under each chapter.

4. Hardship Discharge

a. Requirements

If the debtor has not made all payments under the plan, the court, after notice and a hearing, may award a hardship discharge if the following three conditions exist:

(i) the *debtor's failure* to complete payments under the plan is due to *circumstances* for which she should not *justly be held accountable* [B.C. § 1328(b)(1)];

(ii) *each unsecured creditor holding an allowed claim has received property* under the plan, having a present value as of the effective date of the plan, of not less than the amount that he would have received for his claim in a Chapter 7 [B.C. § 1328(b)(2)]; and

(iii) *modification* of the plan is *not practicable.* [B.C. § 1328(b)(3)]

b. Debts Discharged in Hardship Case

A hardship discharge discharges the debtor from all unsecured debts provided for by the plan or disallowed under § 502 *except* the following:

(i) debts that are *nondischargeable under § 523(a)* [B.C. § 1328(c)(2)];

(ii) *Health Education Assistance Loans ("HEAL")* not meeting the three conditions for discharge under the applicable federal nonbankruptcy statute [42 U.S.C. § 292f(g)];

(iii) *long-term debts* provided for under the *cure provision of Code § 1322(b)(5)* [B.C. § 1328(c)(1)]; and

(iv) *post-petition consumer debts for property or services necessary for the debtor to perform the plan,* if the corresponding claims were allowed, and if the trustee's prior approval to incur the debt was practicable but was not obtained. [B.C. §§ 1328(d), 1305(a)(2), (c)]

5. Revocation of Discharge

The court may revoke a Chapter 13 discharge that was *obtained by the debtor's fraud* if the party in interest seeking the revocation *did not know* of the fraud until *after the discharge* was awarded. The party seeking revocation must make its request for revocation no later than *one year* from the *date the discharge was granted.* Notice and a hearing are required. [B.C. § 1328(e)]

THE FOLLOWING IS A CHECKLIST OF THE DEBTS THAT ARE NOT DISCHARGEABLE UNDER CHAPTER 13:

STANDARD DISCHARGE

- ☑ *Long-term debts* if the plan provides for curing any default within a reasonable time and maintaining payments during the case, and the final payment on the debt is due after the final plan payment

- ☑ *Trust fund taxes*

- ☑ A *tax* for which a *return, or equivalent report or notice,* if required, was *not filed or given* or was filed or given but *after the date on which it was due* and within the *two year-period prior to filing for bankruptcy*

- ☑ A *tax* for which the debtor either made a *fraudulent return or willfully attempted to evade or defeat* the tax

- ☑ Debts for money, property, services, or an extension, renewals or refinancing of credit obtained by *fraud, consumer debts* exceeding *$800* incurred within *90 days* of bankruptcy for *luxury goods,* or *cash advances* exceeding *$1,100* obtained within *70 days* of bankruptcy

- ☑ Debts that the debtor did not *list or schedule* in time for the creditor to *timely file a proof of claim,* unless the creditor had *notice or actual knowledge* in time to make a timely filing

- ☑ Debts that are potentially nondischargeable pursuant to *§ 523(a)(2) or (4)* that the debtor neither *listed nor scheduled* in time for the creditor to *timely file a proof of claim* and *timely request a determination of dischargeability,* unless the creditor had *notice or actual knowledge* in time to make a timely filing

- ☑ Debts owed for *embezzlement, larceny,* or *fraud or defalcation in a fiduciary capacity*

- ☑ *Domestic support obligations* and *debts for support* owed under state law to a state or municipality that are enforceable under the Child Support Enforcement Act

- ☑ *Student loans* absent undue hardship for the debtor and her dependents

- ☑ *Health Education Assistance Loans* ("HEAL") for which debtor fails to satisfy the discharge requirements of 42 U.S.C. § 292f(g)

- ☑ Debts *for death or personal injury* caused by the debtor's operation of a *motor vehicle, vessel, or aircraft* while *intoxicated* from using *alcohol, drugs, or another substance*

- ☑ *Restitution or a criminal fine* that is included in the debtor's sentence upon conviction of a crime

- ☑ *Restitution* or *damages awarded in a civil action* against the debtor as a result of *willful* or *malicious injury* that caused *death or personal injury*

- ☑ *Post-petition consumer debts for property or services necessary for the debtor to perform the plan,* if the corresponding claims were allowed, and if the trustee's prior approval to incur the debt was practicable but was not obtained

HARDSHIP DISCHARGE

- ☑ *Long-term debts* if the plan provides for curing any default within a reasonable time and maintaining payments during the case, and the final payment on the debt is due after the final plan payment

- ☑ All debts that are *nondischargeable under § 523(a)*

- ☑ *Health Education Assistance Loans* ("HEAL") for which debtor fails to satisfy the discharge requirements of 42 U.S.C. § 292f(g)

- ☑ *Post-petition consumer debts for property or services necessary for the debtor to perform the plan,* if the corresponding claims were allowed, and if the trustee's prior approval to incur the debt was practicable but was not obtained

Review Questions and Answers

Review Questions: Short Answer

CHAPTER ONE. INTRODUCTION

1. Debtor files for relief under Chapter 7. Prior to bankruptcy, Acme performed services for Debtor, but Debtor has not yet paid Acme. Debtor claims that Acme did not perform according to the terms of the parties' contract and, thus, Debtor does not owe Acme for its work. Does Acme have a claim in Debtor's Chapter 7 case?

2. Does the United States trustee program operate in all 94 judicial districts in the United States?

3. Can a bankruptcy petition preparer offer a potential debtor legal advice?

4. On February 1, Donna borrowed $1,000 from Friend and promised to pay Friend back with interest by July 1. On June 15, Donna filed for bankruptcy. Does Friend have a secured claim in Donna's bankruptcy case?

5. A debtor must be insolvent in order to file for relief under Chapter 7. TRUE or FALSE?

CHAPTER TWO. JURISDICTION AND PROCEDURE; SOVEREIGN IMMUNITY

6. Do bankruptcy judges have lifetime tenure?

7. Acme Company files for relief under Chapter 11. The same day, Zed Corporation, an affiliate of Acme's, also files a Chapter 11 petition. The bankruptcy court grants Acme's motion for joint administration of its case with Zed Corporation. Does the order for joint administration mean that Acme's and Zed's assets, debts, and causes of action are pooled?

8. Does the United States district court have original and exclusive jurisdiction over bankruptcy cases?

9. Can the bankruptcy court enter a final judgment or order in a core proceeding?

10. Debtor files for relief under Chapter 11 and Creditor files an adversary proceeding complaint to determine the priority of certain security interests in a commercial building owned by Debtor. Creditor's complaint included claims against Debtor and the County Clerk, whom Creditor alleged had improperly indexed Creditor's deed of trust. After the bankruptcy court dismissed several counts of Creditor's complaint, Creditor moved to sever and withdraw the reference of its claims against County Clerk. Must the reference be withdrawn?

_____

11. Debtor obtained a divorce and the state court ordered him to pay alimony to his wife. Debtor failed to make the payments, and the state court eventually awarded Debtor's ex-wife more than $1 million in past-due payments and interest. Debtor then filed for bankruptcy. The bankruptcy court dismissed Debtor's bankruptcy case, concluding that it was simply a two-party dispute between Debtor and his ex-wife and served no bankruptcy purpose. The bankruptcy court found that the state court was the more appropriate forum for resolving family law issues, such as those presented in the case. Is the bankruptcy court's decision correct?

_____

12. Debtor operates his law practice in Kansas City, Missouri, which is in Missouri's Western District, but Debtor maintains his residence and is domiciled in the State of Kansas. Debtor filed for bankruptcy in the Western District of Missouri. Debtor's principal assets are located in Kansas, but his principal place of business (his law practice) is located in the Western District of Missouri. Creditor files a motion to dismiss the case for improper venue. Will the bankruptcy court grant Creditor's motion?

_____

13. If a bankruptcy court denies a creditor's motion to lift the stay, can the creditor appeal that decision?

_____

14. Debtor filed for relief under Chapter 13 and proposed a plan that provided for payment of Creditor's claim. Creditor objected to its treatment under Debtor's plan. The bankruptcy court denied confirmation of the plan and ordered Debtor to propose a new plan. Can the Debtor immediately appeal the bankruptcy court's order denying confirmation of her plan?

_____

CHAPTER THREE. COMMENCEMENT AND ADMINISTRATION

15. Debtor, an individual, filed for relief under Chapter 7. Two weeks prior to filing for bankruptcy, Debtor obtained credit counseling over the phone from one of the nonprofit budget and credit counseling services on the list approved by the United States trustee. Has the Debtor satisfied the Code's credit counseling requirement?

_____

16. In January, Debtor, an individual, files a Chapter 13 petition, which is dismissed in March because of Debtor's intentional failure to obey certain orders of the bankruptcy court. In June, Debtor seeks to file another Chapter 13 petition. Is she eligible? _____

17. Debtor is a consumer. She files for relief under Chapter 11. Is Debtor eligible for relief under Chapter 11? _____

18. Debtor, who is an accountant, inherited his family's farm several years ago when his parents passed away. Debtor's aggregate noncontingent, liquidated debts are $1 million. Debtor does weekend farming so only 10–20% of his gross income each year comes from his weekend farming operation. Is Debtor eligible to file for relief under Chapter 12? _____

19. Debtor is employed and earns $3,000 per week. She owes $600,000 in unsecured debts and $600,000 in secured debts. Is she eligible for relief under Chapter 13? _____

20. Debtor owes $90,000 in unsecured debts, owes no secured debts, and earns a salary of $2,000 per week. Three creditors file an involuntary Chapter 13 petition against Debtor. If Debtor is generally not paying his debts as they become due, will an order for relief be entered? _____

21. Chapter 7 Debtor owes a $10,000 consumer loan that is secured by her car. Creditor wants to know whether Debtor plans to retain the car or surrender it. Is Debtor required to disclose her intention? _____

22. May the bankruptcy court waive a debtor's attendance at the § 341 meeting? _____

23. Debtor files for relief under Chapter 7. Debtor converts her case to Chapter 13. Must Debtor file her Chapter 13 plan within 14 days of conversion to Chapter 13? _____

24. Debtor files for relief under Chapter 13. She files some of her schedules, but fails to file (i) copies of all her pay stubs for the 60-day period prior to bankruptcy, (ii) a statement of financial affairs, and (iii) a statement of her monthly income. On Day 46 of her bankruptcy case, is Debtor's bankruptcy case automatically dismissed? _____

CHAPTER FOUR. CASE ADMINISTRATION: OFFICERS OF THE ESTATE

25. Can the United States trustee serve as a trustee in a Chapter 11 case? _____

26. Is a trustee normally appointed in a Chapter 11 case? _____

27. Acme Corporation files for relief under Chapter 11. There are reasonable grounds to suspect that current members of Acme's board and the CEO have engaged in actual fraud in managing Acme. Must the United States trustee move for appointment of a Chapter 11 trustee?

_____

28. Same facts as Question 27. The United States trustee moves for and the bankruptcy court orders appointment of a Chapter 11 trustee. Does the trustee have the authority to waive Debtor Corporation's attorney-client privilege concerning communications made by the former officers and directors to Debtor Corporation's attorney prior to bankruptcy?

_____

29. Debtor files for relief under Chapter 7. The Chapter 7 trustee sells estate property to Buyer. After sale to Buyer, the trustee discovers that Debtor was not the sole owner of the property. Buyer sues the trustee. Is the trustee personally liable for breach of her duties?

_____

30. Debtor files a voluntary Chapter 11 petition. There is no Chapter 11 trustee in the case. Debtor's fixed, liquidated, unsecured debts are $10 million, not counting debts for goods, service, taxes, or debts owed to Debtor's insiders. Creditor, long before the plan confirmation hearing, requests appointment of an examiner. Must the bankruptcy court order appointment of an examiner?

_____

31. Husband and Wife file a voluntary Chapter 13 petition. A month after the filing, Wife is in a car accident with Son. Wife hires Attorney to represent her and Son, both of whom sustained personal injuries in the car accident. About six months later, Debtor's Bankruptcy Attorney learns that Wife was injured in the auto accident. Bankruptcy Attorney was under the mistaken impression that only Son was harmed. Bankruptcy Attorney then filed an application under § 327 for Special Counsel. Can the bankruptcy court issue a *nunc pro tunc* retention order?

_____

32. Acme Health Care Company operates an assisted living facility for the elderly. Acme files for relief under Chapter 11. Must the bankruptcy court order the appointment of a patient care ombudsman?

_____

33. Debtor is an individual and hires Lawyer to file her Chapter 7 petition. Is Lawyer entitled to have her fees paid from Debtor's Chapter 7 estate?

_____

34.   Law Firm performed services for Chapter 11 Debtor. Law Firm obtained court authorization for employment and subsequently submitted its fee application requesting the bankruptcy court to award compensation for its professional services. Creditor challenged Law Firm's fees and the bankruptcy court held a hearing on the matter. Law Firm then submitted a request to the court to award compensation for the fees Law Firm incurred in defending its fee application. Will the bankruptcy court award Law Firm compensation for the fees it incurred defending its fee application?

_____

CHAPTER FIVE. THE BANKRUPTCY ESTATE

35.   Debtor, an individual, files for bankruptcy. Are Debtor's post-petition wages included in property of the estate?

_____

36.   Debtor files for relief under Chapter 7 in October. In November, her father dies suddenly. Debtor inherits $10,000. Debtor claims that the $10,000 is not property of the estate because she inherited the money after her bankruptcy filing. Is Debtor correct?

_____

37.   Debtor files for relief under Chapter 7. She has worked for Acme Company for 25 years and has vested in the company's ERISA-qualified pension plan. Are the monies in Debtor's pension plan part of her bankruptcy estate?

_____

38.   Debtor files for relief under Chapter 13. Shortly before bankruptcy, Big Bank lawfully repossessed Debtor's car. Big Bank had a perfected security interest in the vehicle, and Debtor had missed several monthly payments on the car. Debtor's attorney notified Big Bank of Debtor's bankruptcy filing, but Big Bank did not return the vehicle; it retained it. Does Big Bank's retention of Debtor's car violate the automatic stay?

_____

39.   Debtor files for relief under Chapter 7. Debtor owns a pedigree dog that has puppies a month after the Chapter 7 filing. Are the puppies property of the bankruptcy estate?

_____

40.   Does property of the estate include exempt property?

_____

CHAPTER SIX. THE BANKRUPTCY ESTATE: THE TRUSTEE'S AVOIDING POWERS

41.   On June 1, Debtor Acme Corporation purchases office equipment on credit from Xanadu Company. Acme takes delivery of the equipment on June 2. Acme grants Xanadu a security interest in the equipment. Acme files for bankruptcy on June 10 and Xanadu files a UCC–1 in the proper state office on June 12. Can Trustee avoid Xanadu's security interest in the equipment?

_____

42. On November 1, 2018, BankTwo made a $15,000 unsecured loan to Debtor. On March 1, 2019, Debtor transferred real property, valued at $60,000, to Niece for no consideration and with the intention of defrauding Debtor's creditors. On September 1, 2021, Debtor files for bankruptcy. Debtor has not repaid BankTwo. Under State law, BankTwo could avoid the transfer to Niece. Can the trustee avoid the transfer of the real property to Niece? _____

43. Debtor, an individual, got a new job that paid more money but he needed a vehicle to get to work. In May, Debtor's Neighbor put a placard on the windshield of his old car saying that the car was for sale. The car was 12 years old but in good condition. Debtor and Neighbor negotiated over the price, and Debtor paid Neighbor $1,500 in cash for the car on May 15. On July 10, Debtor filed for relief under Chapter 7. Can the Chapter 7 trustee avoid the transfer of the $1,500 to Neighbor as a preference? _____

44. On February 1, Bank loans Acme $250,000, and Acme grants Bank a security interest in its equipment. The parties sign a valid security agreement on February 1. On March 15, Bank files a UCC–1 on Acme's equipment in the proper state office. On June 1, Acme files for bankruptcy. _____

   a. Can the trustee avoid Bank's security interest as a preference? _____

   b. If Acme files for bankruptcy on August 5, can the trustee avoid Bank's security interest as a preference? _____

45. Debtor purchases goods on credit from Seller and is insolvent when she receives the merchandise on June 1. The sale was in the ordinary course of the Seller's business. On June 2, Debtor files a voluntary bankruptcy petition. Can Seller reclaim the goods from Debtor? _____

46. A year prior to bankruptcy, Debtor borrowed $20,000 from Friend. As Debtor's financial situation deteriorated, he realized that he had to file for bankruptcy. Prior to filing, Debtor scraped together $1,000 and paid Friend $1,000 of the $20,000 that he still owed Friend. Debtor then filed for relief under Chapter 7. Debtor's unsecured creditors will receive a 5% dividend in the bankruptcy case. Is the payment to Friend a preference? _____

47. A month before filing for bankruptcy, Debtor, who is insolvent, transfers property to Amy for less than reasonably equivalent value. Amy sells the property to Ben, who takes in good faith, pays fair value for the property, and is unaware of the transaction between Amy and Debtor. Debtor files for bankruptcy. Can the trustee recover the property from Ben? _____

48. Acme Company filed for relief under Chapter 11. At the time of bankruptcy filing, Bank had an account at Big Bank with a balance of $50,000. Prior to bankruptcy, Trade Creditor had performed services for Acme worth $40,000. Acme failed to pay Trade Creditor. Two months prior to Acme's bankruptcy filing Big Bank purchased Trade Creditor's claim for $25,000. Does Big Bank have a right of setoff against Acme?

_____

49. Debtor Company filed for relief under Chapter 11. Big Bank is one of Debtor's secured creditors. A year ago, Big Bank made a working capital loan to Debtor, and Debtor granted Big Bank a security interest in its inventory, whether now owned or hereafter acquired. Big Bank properly perfected its security interest. After filing for bankruptcy, Debtor purchased new inventory for its business. Does Big Bank's security interest attach to the new inventory?

_____

CHAPTER SEVEN. CLAIMS OF CREDITORS

50. Debtor files a Chapter 7 petition. Prior to bankruptcy, Creditor rendered services to Debtor for a fee of $12,000. The parties' contract provided for interest for late payment. At the time of bankruptcy, interest amounted to $500. Creditor files a claim for $12,500 and Debtor objects, arguing that unsecured creditors, like Creditor, are not entitled to interest in bankruptcy. Is Debtor correct?

_____

51. Debtor files a Chapter 7 petition. Debtor owns a home subject to Bank One's properly recorded mortgage of $100,000.

a. Debtor's home is valued at $75,000. Can Debtor strip down Bank's lien to the value of her home?

_____

b. Bank Two holds a junior mortgage on Debtor's home; the balance on the loan is $25,000. Can Debtor strip off Bank Two's lien because it is completely underwater?

_____

52. Ernest Employee is Debtor Corporation's Vice-President of Sales. Debtor has fallen on hard times and not paid its executives for the past two months. Debtor files a Chapter 11 petition in an attempt to reorganize its business. At the time of bankruptcy, Debtor Corporation owes Employee $20,000. Does Employee have a priority claim for $20,000?

_____

53. Debtor files for bankruptcy. Debtor owes Creditor $1,000 on an unsecured consumer debt. Debtor files a motion with the bankruptcy court to reduce Creditor's claim to $800. Can the bankruptcy court grant Debtor such relief?

_____

54. Debtor files a Chapter 7 petition. Debtor has $8,000 in assets to pay her unsecured priority and general unsecured creditors. Administrative expenses are $4,000. Debtor owes property taxes of $2,000 for the year prior to the date of filing her bankruptcy petition. She also owes $6,000 in federal income taxes for the two years prior to filing her bankruptcy petition. Unsecured creditors' claims total $30,000. Will the unsecured creditors receive a dividend in Debtor's bankruptcy case? _____

55. Debtor files for relief under Chapter 7. Debtor owes Creditor $100,000, which is secured by a security interest on $110,000 worth of Debtor's property.

    a. Must Creditor file a proof of claim in order to have an allowed claim? _____

    b. Would the answer change if Debtor had filed for relief under Chapter 11? _____

56. If Creditor in Question 55 above fails to file a proof of claim in Debtor's Chapter 7 case, is Creditor's security interest on Debtor's property void? _____

57. Acme Company signed a five-year lease with Landlord at a monthly rental of $8,000. Acme repudiates the lease and immediately files for bankruptcy. At the time of bankruptcy filing, there are four years remaining on the lease, and Acme is current on rent. Landlord is able to re-rent the property but for only $5,000 per month. Landlord files a claim for $144,000 (48 months x $3,000 monthly rent differential). Will Landlord's claim be allowed for $144,000? _____

58. Debtor Corporation files for relief under Chapter 11 but the case is converted to Chapter 7. If Debtor Corporation's assets are insufficient to pay all administrative expenses, do the Chapter 11 pre-conversion administrative claimants and the Chapter 7 administrative claimants share *pro rata* in any distribution? _____

CHAPTER EIGHT. DEBTOR'S EXEMPTIONS

59. Debtor files for Chapter 7. She owns her home valued at $100,000. The balance on her mortgage loan with BigBank is $100,000. Debtor takes the federal exemptions. Can Debtor use § 522(d)(1) to exempt some of the value of her home? _____

60. Debtor files a Chapter 7 petition in a state that has opted out of the federal exemptions. Can Debtor choose the federal exemptions? _____

61. Debtor files a Chapter 7 petition. Prior to bankruptcy, Debtor had purchased a home financed by Bank Two, which holds the mortgage on the property. Can Debtor avoid Bank Two's mortgage, under Bankruptcy Code § 522(f), to the extent that it impairs an exemption? _____

62. Husband and Wife ("Debtors") file a joint petition for relief under Chapter 7. Debtors own a home valued at $150,000. Debtors borrowed the money to purchase the home from Big Bank, which holds the mortgage. The outstanding balance on the loan is $110,000. If Debtors use the federal exemptions, can they exempt all the equity in their home? _____

63. Debtor files for relief under Chapter 7 on February 1, 2021, in the Eastern District of Michigan. Debtor grew up in Toledo, Ohio, but changed his domicile to Novi, Michigan, on June 30, 2020. Do Michigan's exemptions apply in Debtor's Chapter 7 case? _____

64. Does the "mansion loophole" exception to exemptions in § 522(p) and (q) apply to debtors in opt-out states? _____

65. Debtor files for relief under Chapter 7. Prior to filing for bankruptcy, Debtor inherited her mother's Roth IRA. Debtor wants to exempt the monies in the Roth IRA under § 522(b)(3)(C). Can she do so? _____

66. Debtor, an individual, files for relief under Chapter 7. Debtor owns a small plot of land worth about $10,000. Pre-petition, Debtor took out a small loan of $3,000 from Bank in order to do some work on the land before building a small home on the plot. Can Debtor redeem the property from Bank's lien by paying Bank $3,000? _____

67. Debtor files for relief under Chapter 7 and receives a discharge. Can Creditor with a pre-petition, nondischargeable domestic support obligation proceed against Debtor's exempt property to collect on her domestic support obligation? _____

CHAPTER NINE. DISCHARGE OF INDEBTEDNESS

68. Debtor files for bankruptcy. Answer TRUE or FALSE to the following statements about Debtor's discharge.

   a. Debtor is a corporation and files for relief under Chapter 7. At the end of the Chapter 7 case, the bankruptcy court will grant Debtor a discharge. _____

   b. Debtor files for relief under Chapter 13 and after completing payments under her plan receives a standard discharge. Creditor's $100,000 pre-petition debt against Debtor for willful or malicious injury to Creditor's property is nondischargeable. _____

c. Debtor Corporation files for relief under Chapter 11. Prior to bankruptcy, Debtor Corporation filed a fraudulent tax return. The debt for taxes covered by the fraudulent return is not dischargeable.

    _____

d. Debtor files for relief under Chapter 7. Debtor scheduled Creditor's claim for $10,000 for fraud respecting the debtor's financial condition. Creditor does not file an adversary proceeding in Debtor's Chapter 7 case requesting that the bankruptcy court declare Creditor's debt nondischargeable. The bankruptcy court grants Debtor a discharge. Creditor's debt for $10,000 is discharged.

    _____

e. Debtor files for relief under Chapter 7. Creditor holds a claim against Debtor for $10,000 for fraud respecting the debtor's financial condition. Debtor did not schedule Creditor's claim, and Creditor had neither notice nor knowledge of Debtor's bankruptcy case. The bankruptcy court grants Debtor a discharge. Creditor's debt for $10,000 is discharged.

    _____

69. Debtor files for relief under Chapter 7. During her bankruptcy case and before the court grants Debtor a discharge, she negotiates a reaffirmation agreement with Creditor. Creditor provided Debtor with the § 524(k) disclosures prior to Debtor signing the agreement. The agreement was filed with the court a month ago. Debtor, however, is having second thoughts. If she rescinds the reaffirmation agreement, is it unenforceable?

    _____

70. If a debtor is represented by an attorney when she negotiates a reaffirmation agreement, must the bankruptcy court hold a discharge hearing?

    _____

71. Debtor files for relief under Chapter 13 and the following year applies for a job with Private Employer. Private Employer offers Debtor the job contingent on the results of her background check. When the background check reveals Debtor's Chapter 13 bankruptcy case, Private Employer rescinds its offer. Has Private Employer violated the anti-discrimination prohibition contained at § 525(b)?

    _____

72. Is post-petition interest on a nondischargeable tax debt also not dischargeable?

    _____

73. Debtor files for relief under Chapter 7. If Creditor mails Debtor a letter proposing an agreement under which Debtor would reaffirm its debt to Creditor, does Creditor violate the automatic stay?

    _____

74.   Debtor filed for relief under Chapter 11. Prior to bankruptcy, Creditor had obtained a fraud judgment against Debtor. Creditor filed an adversary proceeding in Debtor's bankruptcy case and alleged that its claim against Debtor for fraud was not dischargeable under § 523(a). Debtor argued that collateral estoppel did not apply to the adversary proceeding, because the standard of proof in the state court trial was preponderance of the evidence while § 523 required proof by clear and convincing evidence. Is Debtor correct?

_____

75.   Debtor borrowed $10,000 from Bank. Mother signed as guarantor on the loan. Debtor filed for relief under Chapter 7 and obtained a discharge of her debts, including the $10,000 debt owed to Bank. Is Mother's debt to Bank also discharged?

_____

CHAPTER TEN. ADMINISTRATIVE POWERS: THE AUTOMATIC STAY

76.   Debtor files a voluntary Chapter 7 petition. Would the following post-petition actions be enjoined by the automatic stay? Assume that the non-debtor party has received notice of Debtor's bankruptcy filing.

_____

    a.   Debtor is a corporation. A year prior to Debtor's filing for bankruptcy, Bank loaned Debtor $200,000 and Debtor granted Bank a security interest in all of Debtor's equipment. After learning of Debtor's bankruptcy, Bank files a UCC–1 on the equipment in the proper state office. Does Bank's filing violate the automatic stay?

_____

    b.   Debtor is an individual. After the filing of Debtor's Chapter 7 case, Girlfriend files a paternity action in state court to establish that Debtor is the father of her child. Does Girlfriend's action violate the automatic stay?

_____

    c.   Debtor Corporation has $10,000 in a corporate account at Bank One. Debtor owes Bank One $50,000 on an unsecured pre-petition loan. After Debtor Corporation files for bankruptcy, Bank One sets off the $10,000 debt it owes to Debtor against the $50,000 claim it has against Debtor. Does Bank's setoff violate the automatic stay?

_____

77.   Debtor files a Chapter 7 petition and desires to retain possession of her car, which has a fair market value of $5,000. The car was financed by Bank, which holds a purchase-money security interest in the car. The debt owed to Bank is $7,000. Debtor is current on her car payments. Can Debtor retain possession of the car without redeeming it or reaffirming the debt?

_____

78.   TRUE or FALSE? A creditor must demonstrate cause in order to succeed on a lift-of-stay motion.

_____

79. Debtor filed for relief under Chapter 13. The IRS filed a proof of claim in Debtor's case for $20,000 that Debtor owed in pre-petition federal income taxes. Debtor was entitled to a $2,000 tax refund for the prior, pre-petition tax year, but the IRS set off that refund against Debtor's $20,000 pre-petition tax liability. Debtor claims that the IRS violated the automatic stay. Is he correct? _____

80. Debtor files a Chapter 7 petition. Before filing for bankruptcy, Debtor passed a bad check and the local prosecutor had begun criminal proceedings against Debtor. Can the state court criminal proceeding on the bad check charge continue post-petition? _____

81. Debtor filed for relief under Chapter 7. Prior to bankruptcy, Landlord had obtained a judgment of possession against Debtor for her failure to pay rent. Debtor filed for bankruptcy before the actual eviction and currently resides in the residential apartment. State law gives Debtor the right to cure the entire monetary default. When Debtor filed for bankruptcy, she also filed a certification under penalty of perjury that she had the right to cure the default and deposited with the court clerk the rent due for the 30 days following the date she filed her bankruptcy petition. Debtor served the certification on Landlord. Can Landlord proceed with eviction of Debtor? _____

82. Debtor, a small business, files for relief under Chapter 11. This is Debtor's second bankruptcy filing. Debtor's prior Chapter 11 small business case was filed two years ago and dismissed one year ago. Does the automatic stay apply in Debtor's current small business case? _____

CHAPTER ELEVEN. ADMINISTRATIVE POWERS: §§ 363–366

83. a. Is OverSecured Creditor entitled to adequate protection to prevent the accrual of post-petition interest from shrinking its equity cushion? _____

    b. Is UnderSecured Creditor entitled to interest on its claim because the automatic stay delays Creditor from foreclosing on its collateral? _____

84. Must the bankruptcy court hold a hearing if Debtor wants to sell property of the estate out of the ordinary course of business? _____

85. Debtor files a Chapter 11 petition and has $10,000 on deposit in a checking account at Bank. Prior to bankruptcy, Bank extended a small business loan to Debtor; as of bankruptcy, the balance on the loan stands at $30,000. Can Debtor use the money in the account to pay expenses incurred in the ordinary course of its business? _____

86. Debtor files for relief under Chapter 11. Debtor owns a piece of land worth $200,000. Debtor borrowed against the land and owes $250,000 to various banks; Debtor used the land as collateral for the loans. Bank1 is first in line, and is owed $100,000. Bank2 has a second mortgage on the property, and is owed $75,000. Bank3 has a third mortgage on the land, and also is owed $75,000. Bank1 files a motion to lift the automatic stay for cause under § 362(d)(1), claiming that its interest in the land is not adequately protected. Will the court grant Bank1's motion?

_____

87. Debtor files for relief under Chapter 7. Debtor co-owns a piece of property (Property) as a tenant in common with Friend. The property is valued at $100,000. Property is used for recreation only, and it is impracticable to partition Property between Debtor and Friend. The Chapter 7 trustee wants to sell the interests of both Debtor and Friend. Can the Chapter 7 trustee do so?

_____

88. Acme Company files for relief under Chapter 11. Acme's customer list is valuable property that contains personally identifiable information, e.g., names, mailing and e-mail addresses, social security numbers. At the time of bankruptcy, Acme had in place a policy prohibiting the transfer of such personally identifiable information to anyone not affiliated with Acme Company. Acme, as debtor in possession, wants to sell the list, but the sale is not consistent with Acme's policy. Can Acme do so?

_____

89. Debtor Corporation files for relief under Chapter 11. Debtor wants to reject its collective bargaining agreement with Union. Does § 365 govern rejection of the agreement?

_____

90. Debtor files for bankruptcy. Prior to bankruptcy, Debtor signed a lease agreement with Car Creditor for a vehicle. The purchase price was $25,000. The vehicle has an economic life of 12 years. The term is for 5 years or 60 months, and Debtor has no right to terminate the agreement. At the end of 60 months, the vehicle is projected to have a fair market value of $6,500. The agreement provides Debtor with an option to buy the vehicle at the end of 60 months for one additional payment of $10. Can Debtor assume the agreement?

_____

91. Debtor files for relief under Chapter 11 on June 1. Debtor leases its office equipment from OfficeCo. The lease term is five years with three years remaining at the time of bankruptcy. It is now September 15, and OfficeCo claims that its lease with Debtor is deemed rejected because Debtor failed to assume the lease within 60 days of its bankruptcy filing. Is OfficeCo correct?

_____

92. Debtor files for relief under Chapter 11. Prior to bankruptcy, Debtor entered into a trademark licensing agreement with Acme. Debtor is the licensor. In its Chapter 11 case, Debtor rejected the trademark licensing agreement. Does Acme have the right to use the trademark even though § 365(n) does not include trademarks?

_____

CHAPTER TWELVE. CHAPTER 7—LIQUIDATION

93. Debtor files for relief under Chapter 7 on February 1, 2021. Debtor's monthly income varies, because she works on commission. Debtor's gross income in 2020 was $34,000. Debtor earned $3,000 in August and September of 2020, $2,500 in October, $3,500 in November, $4,000 in December of 2020, and $2,000 in January of 2021. Is Debtor's current monthly income $2,833.33?

_____

94. Debtor files a voluntary Chapter 7 petition on July 1. Debtor works several jobs, so her monthly income varies. For the months of January and February, Debtor earned $2,500 each month. In March, Debtor earned $2,700, while in April and May she earned $2,000 each month. In June, Debtor earned $3,500. Debtor resides in a state with an annual median income of $30,000. Is Debtor an above-median income debtor?

_____

95. Debtor files a voluntary Chapter 7 petition. She earns $24,000 per year; the median annual income in her state is $40,000. Does Debtor qualify for relief under Chapter 7?

_____

96. Same facts as Question 95 above, except Debtor now earns $48,000 per year. Does Debtor's filing for relief under Chapter 7 create a presumption of abuse?

_____

97. Debtor files a voluntary Chapter 7 petition. She earns $4,000 each month and has done so for the past two years. The median state income is $40,000 per year. Debtor's monthly means test expenses total $3,900. Does Debtor's filing for relief under Chapter 7 create a presumption of abuse?

_____

98. Same facts as Question 97 above, except Debtor's monthly means test expenses total $3,800, and her total unsecured debt equals $40,000. Does Debtor's filing for relief under Chapter 7 create a presumption of abuse?

_____

99. Debtor files a voluntary Chapter 7 petition in the bankruptcy court for the Eastern District of Michigan. Debtor is an above-median income debtor. She owns a 2012 Honda Accord that is paid off. Can Debtor include the national standard for owning a vehicle in her monthly means test expenses?

_____

100.   Creditor is a general unsecured creditor of Debtor, who recently filed for relief under Chapter 7. After payment is made to priority unsecured creditors, $5,000 remains for Debtor's general unsecured creditors. Even though Creditor had notice in time to file a claim, Creditor tardily filed its claim for $5,000. General unsecured creditors (including Creditor's $5,000 claim) hold claims worth $50,000 in Debtor's Chapter 7 case. Will Creditor receive $500 in Debtor's Chapter 7 case?   _____

101.   Debtor files for relief under Chapter 7. There is $6,000 available for distribution to unsecured creditors. Administrative expenses equal $2,000. Debtor has no other priority creditors. General unsecured creditors hold allowed claims that equal $40,000. Creditor A has a claim for $1,000. Will Creditor A receive $400 in Debtor's Chapter 7 case?   _____

102.   Debtor files a voluntary Chapter 7 petition on January 10, 2018. This is not Debtor's first bankruptcy filing. On March 20, 2010, Debtor received a discharge in a Chapter 7 case that she had filed on December 15, 2009. Is Debtor eligible for a discharge in her current Chapter 7 case?   _____

103.   About six months prior to filing for bankruptcy, Debtor transfers his home, his only asset with any significant value, to his sister for $100, in an attempt to protect his home from his creditors. Debtor owns the home free and clear; it is worth approximately $100,000. Debtor files a voluntary Chapter 7 petition. Will Debtor receive a discharge in his Chapter 7 case?   _____

104.   Debtor files a voluntary Chapter 7 petition. She is an above-median income debtor and fails the "means" test. Must the bankruptcy court dismiss Debtor's Chapter 7 case?   _____

CHAPTER THIRTEEN. CHAPTER 11—REORGANIZATION

105.   Debtor files for relief under Chapter 11. Debtor is not a small business and does not qualify for subchapter V. If there is insufficient interest among Debtor's unsecured creditors, must the United States trustee still appoint an official committee of unsecured creditors?   _____

106.   Debtor Company files for relief under Chapter 11. Debtor is engaged in business activities and has total liabilities of $2 million, all of which derive from Debtor's business activities. Debtor's business does not involve single asset real estate. Must the United States trustee appoint an official committee of unsecured creditors?   _____

107. Debtor, an individual, files for relief under Chapter 11. Debtor is engaged in business activities and has liabilities of $2.5 million, 75% of which derive from Debtor's business activities. Assume Debtor is not in the business of owning single asset real estate. Does Debtor have the option of electing to be treated as a small business debtor? _____

108. Debtor Corporation files for relief under Chapter 11. Must Debtor Corporation's plan pay administrative creditors in full in cash on the plan's effective date? _____

109. Acme Company files for relief under Chapter 11. Creditor files a motion to convert or dismiss Acme's Chapter 11 case. After notice and a hearing, the bankruptcy court determines that cause exists to convert the case to Chapter 7. Can the bankruptcy court order the appointment of a Chapter 11 trustee instead of granting Creditor's motion to convert? _____

110. Farmer files for relief under Chapter 11. Creditor files a motion to convert Farmer's case to Chapter 7. Farmer objects to conversion. Can the bankruptcy court convert Farmer's Chapter 11 case to Chapter 7? _____

111. *Diner, Inc.* is a small restaurant with assets of approximately $1 million and liabilities of approximately $1.5 million. All of *Diner's* liabilities arise from its business activities. On February 1, *Diner* files for relief under Chapter 11.

    a. If *Diner* does not elect subchapter V, may Creditor file a proposed plan on June 2? _____

    b. If *Diner* does elect subchapter V, may Creditor file a proposed plan on May 2? _____

112. Debtor files a Chapter 11 petition and elects to proceed under subchapter V. Debtor files its subchapter V plan but not a disclosure statement. May Debtor begin to solicit acceptances from the various classes on its plan? _____

113. Debtor files a Chapter 11 petition and subsequently files a plan that proposes to pay Debtor's general unsecured creditors 10 cents on the dollar. Debtor has 10 general unsecured creditors, 9 of which hold claims of $5,000. Creditor X holds a $55,000 claim. All 10 creditors cast ballots on Creditor's plan; 9 of the 10 creditors vote in favor but Creditor X casts a "no" vote on the plan. Ignoring the possibility of confirmation by cram down, can Debtor obtain confirmation of its plan? _____

114. Debtor Corporation files for relief under Chapter 11. Debtor does not elect to proceed under subchapter V. Debtor Corporation files a proposed plan of reorganization that is accepted by all classes and confirmed by the court. Does confirmation operate as a discharge with respect to Debtor Corporation? _____

115. Acme Corporation files a voluntary Chapter 11 petition. Acme does not elect subchapter V. Acme owes $10,000 in pre-petition tax claims to the IRS; the claims are entitled to eighth priority. The IRS has not agreed to any treatment that differs from the Code's requirements. Acme proposes a Chapter 11 plan that pays the IRS regular cash installments that equal the present value of its claim over five years from the plan's effective date. Can the bankruptcy court confirm Acme's plan?

    _____

116. Debtor, an individual, files for relief under Chapter 11 and does not elect subchapter V. Debtor proposes a five-year plan under which his general unsecured creditors will receive approximately 25% of the face value of their claims. Debtor is devoting his projected disposable income to plan payments over the plan's five-year period. While the class of general unsecured creditors votes to approve Debtor's plan, Creditor X objects to the plan. If Debtor otherwise satisfies the requirements of § 1129(a) for plan confirmation, will Debtor obtain confirmation of his plan?

    _____

117. Debtor, an individual, files for relief under Chapter 11 and does not elect subchapter V. Debtor proposes a plan that proposes to pay the class of general unsecured creditors approximately 25% of the face value of their claims. The class of general unsecured creditors votes to reject Debtor's plan. Under the plan, Debtor proposes to retain valuable, non-exempt, pre-petition assets. If Debtor's plan otherwise satisfies the other requirements for confirmation under § 1129(a), can the bankruptcy court confirm the plan?

    _____

118. Debtor Corporation files for relief under Chapter 11. Creditor A and Creditor B are both unsecured creditors. Debtor proposes a plan in which Creditor A is placed in a separate class from Creditor B whose claim is included in the class of general unsecured creditors. Creditor A objects to confirmation of Debtor Corporation's plan. Is the separate classification of Creditor A proper?

    _____

CHAPTER FOURTEEN. CHAPTER 12—FAMILY FARMERS AND FAMILY FISHERMEN

119. Fisherman, an individual, has total debts of $5 million, 90% of which come from his commercial fishing operation. All of Fisherman's gross income for the past decade is from his commercial fishing operation. Does Fisherman qualify for relief under Chapter 12?

    _____

120. Farmer files for relief under Chapter 12 but then decides that he should have filed for relief under Chapter 7. Creditor objects to conversion to Chapter 7, but Farmer claims that he has an absolute right to convert. Is Farmer correct?

    _____

121. Indicate whether the following statements are TRUE or FALSE.

    a. A Chapter 12 case may be commenced by the filing of a voluntary or an involuntary petition for relief.

      _____

    b. Only the Chapter 12 debtor may file a plan.

      _____

    c. Once a trustee is appointed in Chapter 12, the debtor is removed as debtor in possession.

      _____

    d. The Chapter 12 debtor receives a discharge upon confirmation of the Chapter 12 plan.

      _____

122. Farmer's Chapter 12 plan is confirmed and after making all payments under the plan, she is granted a standard Chapter 12 discharge. Will a pre-petition debt for Debtor's fraud while acting in a fiduciary capacity be discharged if it was provided for in Debtor's plan?

      _____

CHAPTER FIFTEEN. CHAPTER 13—INDIVIDUAL WITH REGULAR INCOME

123. Debtor is an individual with regular income. Debtor has two secured debts—on her home and car, and owes a total of $60,000 to two unsecured creditors. Debtor has fallen on hard times financially, and struggles to pay her monthly bills. Creditor is Debtor's largest unsecured creditor. Can Creditor file an involuntary Chapter 13 petition against Debtor?

      _____

124. Indicate whether the following statements are TRUE or FALSE.

    a. Only an individual debtor with consumer debts may file for relief under Chapter 13.

      _____

    b. The filing of a Chapter 13 petition operates to stay any action by a creditor seeking to collect from a co-debtor a debt on which the Chapter 13 debtor also is liable.

      _____

    c. With certain exceptions for nondischargeable debts, confirmation of a Chapter 13 plan discharges the debtor from personal liability on pre-petition debts.

      _____

125. Debtor filed for relief under Chapter 13, but now wants to dismiss her case. Does she have an absolute right to do so?

      _____

126. Debtor files a Chapter 13 petition accompanied by a plan that proposes to pay her unsecured creditors all of her projected disposable income for 36 months or three years. Debtor's plan does not result in unsecured creditors being paid in full. Debtor earns a steady $3,500 per month and has done so for the past two years. The annual median income in the state in which Debtor resides is $40,000. Unsecured Creditor objects to confirmation. Does Debtor's proposed plan comply with the Code's requirements for confirmation?

      _____

127.	Debtor files a Chapter 13 petition accompanied by a plan that proposes to pay Car Creditor the present value of $20,000 over the five-year duration of the plan. (Debtor is an above-median income Debtor.) A year before filing for relief under Chapter 13, Debtor purchased the car that Car Creditor financed. Debtor bought the car for personal use. The car is valued at $20,000, but Debtor owes Car Creditor $25,000 on the vehicle. Does Debtor's proposed plan comply with the Code's requirements for confirmation?

_____

128.	Debtor files a Chapter 13 petition. Bank holds the mortgage on Debtor's condo, which is her principal residence. The condo is valued at $75,000. Debtor owes Bank $90,000 on the mortgage loan. There are 20 years remaining on the mortgage. Debtor's plan proposes to make payments under the mortgage contract on $75,000, and treat the remaining $15,000 on the loan as an unsecured claim. Can the bankruptcy court confirm the plan?

_____

129.	Debtor's Chapter 13 plan is confirmed and after making all payments under the plan, she is granted a standard Chapter 13 discharge. Will a pre-petition debt for Debtor's willful (but not malicious) injury to Neighbor's property be discharged if it was provided for in Debtor's plan?

_____

130.	Debtor files for relief under Chapter 13, and files a Chapter 13 plan with her petition. She is an above-median income debtor. Debtor makes her first plan payment to the Chapter 13 trustee on March 1, 2021, which is within 30 days of her filing for bankruptcy. Does the five-year period of payments under her plan begin on March 1?

_____

131.	Debtor files for relief under Chapter 13 and files her plan with her petition. Debtor is an above-median income debtor. Debtor proposes a five-year plan that pays Car Creditor, which holds a perfected security interest in a car that Debtor purchased three years ago, the remaining principal balance on the car loan in equal monthly installments. Car Creditor objects, claiming it is entitled to interest. Debtor says that Car Creditor is not entitled to interest on its plan payments, because Car Creditor is undersecured. Is Debtor correct?

_____

Answers to Short-Answer Review Questions

1. **YES** — A claim is a right to payment, even if it is unliquidated, unmatured, disputed, or contingent. Even though Debtor disputes Acme's right to payment, Acme has a claim. Having a claim does *not* mean that Acme will be paid out of the Chapter 7 estate. Only allowed claims are paid, and Debtor likely will object to Acme's claim. [B.C. § 502]

2. **NO** — The United States trustee program does not operate in the six judicial districts in Alabama and North Carolina. In those districts, the bankruptcy administrator performs many of the same functions performed by the United States trustee.

3. **NO** — A bankruptcy petition preparer cannot offer legal advice, including the appropriate chapter under which the debtor should file for relief, whether debts will be discharged, and whether debtor will be able to keep her home, car, or other property. A bankruptcy petition preparer cannot use the word "legal" or any similar word in advertising its services and cannot advertise under any category that includes the word "legal" or any similar term.

4. **NO** — Friend is an unsecured creditor. Donna promised to pay Friend back, but there is no collateral securing Donna's promise.

5. **FALSE** — The Bankruptcy Code does not require that a debtor be insolvent to file for relief under Chapter 7, or under Chapters 11, 12, or 13.

6. **NO** — Bankruptcy judges do not have lifetime tenure, because they are not Article III judges. They serve for 14-year terms as judicial officers of the United States district court. [28 U.S.C. § 152]

7. **NO** — Joint administration or procedural consolidation allows the use of a single docket for administrative matters. Thus, if Acme is designated the "lead" case, the court clerk would docket on Acme's docket rather than docketing the same matter twice—once on Acme's and once on Zed's case docket. Had the court granted a motion for substantive consolidation, Acme's and Zed's assets, debts, and causes of action would be pooled. Substantive consolidation is far less common than procedural consolidation or joint administration.

8. **YES** — The district courts have original and exclusive jurisdiction over bankruptcy cases and are vested with exclusive jurisdiction over all of the debtor's property, regardless of its location, as of the filing of the bankruptcy petition. The district courts also have exclusive jurisdiction over all property of the estate. [28 U.S.C. § 1334(a), (e)]

9. **DEPENDS**   If the core proceeding is not a *Stern* claim, then the bankruptcy court may enter a final judgment or order. If the core proceeding is a *Stern* claim, then the bankruptcy court may enter a final judgment or order only with the parties' consent. If the core proceeding is a *Stern* claim but the parties do not consent to the bankruptcy court entering a final order or judgment, then the bankruptcy court must submit proposed findings of fact and conclusions of law to the district court to review *de novo*.

10. **NO**   The district court must withdraw a proceeding from the bankruptcy court if resolution of the proceeding requires substantial and material consideration of a nonbankruptcy federal statute and that statute has more than a *de minimis* impact on interstate commerce. Mandatory withdrawal, however, is not implicated if the dispute requires resolution only of state, not nonbankruptcy federal, law. Creditor's claims involve a determination of the validity and priority of liens under state law. The claims do not involve nonbankruptcy federal law and, therefore, mandatory withdrawal is not applicable. [28 U.S.C. § 157(d)]

Note: The district court may exercise its discretion to grant permissive withdrawal under 28 U.S.C. § 157(d).

11. **YES**   A bankruptcy court may abstain from hearing a case by dismissing the entire case or suspending all proceedings in the case if the interests of creditors and the debtor are better served by dismissal or suspension. [B.C. § 305(a)(1)] A significant factor weighing in favor of dismissal under § 305(a)(1) is the absence of a true bankruptcy purpose, especially in a case that is little more than a dispute between the debtor and a single creditor. Because Debtor's bankruptcy case was nothing more than the continuation of his dispute over alimony payments to his ex-wife, no bankruptcy purpose was served. State court was a better forum for resolving such state law issues.

12. **NO**   A debtor may file for bankruptcy in any district in which his domicile, residence, principal assets, or principal place of business is located. [28 U.S.C. § 1408(1)] The venue statute provides four alternative bases for venue. Because Debtor's principal place of business is located in the Western District of Missouri, venue is proper there and the bankruptcy court will deny Creditor's motion.

13. **YES**   In **Ritzen Group, Inc. v. Jackson Masonry, LLC,** 140 S. Ct. 582 (2020), the Supreme Court, in a unanimous opinion, held that a bankruptcy court's ruling on a motion for relief from the automatic stay "forms a discrete procedural unit" in the bankruptcy case and "[t]hat unit yields a final, appealable order when the bankruptcy court unreservedly grants or denies relief."

14.	NO	The Supreme Court has held that the relevant proceeding from which an immediate appeal may be taken in the context of consideration of a Chapter 13 plan is "the process of attempting to arrive at an approved plan that would allow the bankruptcy to move forward." Because Debtor is free to propose a revised plan, the bankruptcy court's order denying confirmation did not terminate the relevant proceeding. Thus, Debtor may not immediately appeal the bankruptcy court's order. [**Bullard v. Blue Hills Bank**, 575 U.S. 496 (2015)]
15.	YES	The Code requires Debtor to obtain credit counseling services within 180 days of filing for bankruptcy. Debtor received credit counseling two weeks before filing for relief under Chapter 7. She received counseling from a service approved by the United States trustee. Credit counseling may occur over the phone, in person, or on the Internet, and may be done in individual or group sessions. [B.C. § 109(h)]
16.	NO	Debtor is ineligible for relief because she was a debtor in a case that was pending in the preceding 180 days and dismissed due to her willful failure to obey the court's orders. [B.C. § 109(g)(1)]
17.	YES	While Chapter 11 is often referred to as the business reorganization chapter, the Supreme Court has held that an individual consumer debtor may file for relief under Chapter 11. [**Toibb v. Radloff,** 501 U.S. 157 (1991)]
18.	NO	Only a family farmer or family fisherman with regular income may file for relief under Chapter 12. [B.C. § 109(f)] The Code defines a family farmer as an individual whose aggregate noncontingent, liquidated debts do not exceed $11,097,350 and who receives more than 50% of his gross income for the tax year preceding bankruptcy or each of the second and third years prior to bankruptcy from his farming operation. [B.C. § 101(18)] Debtor's debts fall below the debt limit, but he does not earn more than 50% of his gross income from farming. If he wishes to reorganize, Debtor must file for relief under Chapter 11 or 13.
19.	YES	Debtor has $1.2 million in debts, which is far below the Chapter 13 debt ceiling of $2,750,000. The $2.75 million debt limit is in effect until June 31, 2024, at which point, if Congress fails to act, the separate secured and unsecured debt limits in effect on June 20, 2022 will govern a debtor's eligibility for relief under Chapter 13. [B.C. § 109(e); BTATCA § 2(i)(2)]
20.	NO	A Chapter 13 case may be commenced only by the filing of a voluntary petition. Therefore, the involuntary petition against Debtor will be dismissed. [B.C. § 303]

21.	**YES**	In a Chapter 7 case, an individual debtor with property subject to a security interest must within the earlier of 30 days from the petition or on or before the § 341 meeting state her intention to (1) surrender the property; (2) redeem the property; or (3) reaffirm the debt that the property secures. [B.C. § 521(a)(2)(A); Official Form 108] Within 30 days of the date set for the § 341 meeting, the debtor must perform her intention with regard to the property as to which she filed her statement of intention. [B.C. § 521(a)(2)(B)]
22.	**DEPENDS**	The courts are divided about whether a bankruptcy court has the discretion under § 343 to waive the debtor's attendance at the § 341 meeting. A majority of courts, however, waive *physical* attendance at the § 341 meeting for good cause.
23.	**YES**	Debtor must file her Chapter 13 plan within 14 days of conversion of her case to Chapter 13. The 14-day period may only be extended for cause and on notice as the bankruptcy court directs. [Bankruptcy Rule 3015(b)]
24.	**YES**	If an individual in a voluntary Chapter 7 or Chapter 13 case fails to file all the information required by § 521(a)(1) within 45 days of filing her petition, then her case is automatically dismissed on Day 46. [B.C. § 521(i)(1)] Debtor failed to file the documents required by § 521(a)(1)(B)(iii)–(v); therefore, the Code provides for automatic dismissal of the case. It is unclear, however, how that happens, and it is possible, notwithstanding the "automatic dismissal" language that a court order is needed.
25.	**DEPENDS**	The United States trustee may serve as the trustee in a subchapter V case but not in a non-subchapter V Chapter 11 case. [B.C. §§ 1104(d), 1183]
26.	**DEPENDS**	A trustee is appointed in a subchapter V Chapter 11 case but the debtor remains in possession. [B.C. §§ 1182(2), 1183] In a non-subchapter V case, the bankruptcy court may appoint a trustee, but such appointment is the exception to the rule. The debtor normally stays in possession of estate property and continues to manage its business.
27.	**YES**	Congress amended the Bankruptcy Code in 2005 to require the United States trustee to file a motion for appointment of a Chapter 11 trustee under certain circumstances. Because reasonable grounds exist to suspect that Acme's board and its CEO have engaged in actual fraud in managing Acme, the United States trustee must file a motion for appointment of a trustee. [B.C. § 1104(e)]
28.	**YES**	On appointment, the trustee effectively becomes Debtor Corporation's new management and, therefore, the corporate attorney-client privilege passes from former management to the trustee. Thus, the trustee has the power to waive Debtor Corporation's attorney-client privilege concerning communications made by former officers and directors to Debtor Corporation's attorney before bankruptcy. [**Commodity Futures Trading Commission v. Weintraub**, 471 U.S. 343 (1985)]

29. **DEPENDS**   The Circuits are split on the type of conduct that gives rise to liability on the part of the trustee. Some courts hold trustees personally liable for *either* intentional or negligent violations of their fiduciary duties, while others impose personal liability only for intentional violations of the trustee's duties.

30. **YES**   The Code requires the bankruptcy court to appoint an examiner if a party in interest requests such appointment prior to plan confirmation and the debtor's fixed, liquidated unsecured debts exceed $5 million, excluding debts for goods, services, taxes, or debts owed to insiders. Notice and a hearing are required. [B.C. § 1104(c)(2)]

31. **UNCLEAR**   In its decision in **Roman Catholic Archdiocese of San Juan v. Acevado Feliciano,** 140 S. Ct. 696 (2020), the Supreme Court explained that *nunc pro tunc* orders cannot be used to create facts that never actually occurred. In the short time since the Supreme Court's decision, several bankruptcy courts have held that it no longer is appropriate to issue *nunc pro tunc* retention orders. Eliminating such orders does not necessarily mean that a bankruptcy court will not compensate a professional person who provided beneficial services without first obtaining the court's approval of her employment. While the Code requires court approval of employment for an award of compensation, it does not require authorization *prior* to the performance of services. [*See, e.g.,* **In re Roberts,** 618 B.R. 213 (Bankr. S.D. Ohio 2020)] Nonetheless, a professional person should file an application for authorization of employment before performing professional services.

32. **YES**   An assisted living facility is a long-term care facility, and a long-term care facility is a health care business. [B.C. § 101(27A)(B)] In the Chapter 7, 9, or 11 bankruptcy case of a health care business, the court must order the appointment of a patient care ombudsman unless the court decides that such appointment is not necessary for patient protection. This requirement is new to the Code with the passage of BAPCPA. The court must order the appointment within 30 days of the commencement of the case. The ombudsman monitors the quality of patient care and represents patients' interests. [B.C. § 333]

33. **NO**   The Supreme Court has held that § 330(a)(1) does not authorize payment of estate funds to the debtor's Chapter 7 lawyer for the lawyer's work representing the debtor in debtor's bankruptcy case. Therefore, Lawyer must obtain her fee upfront from Debtor and not rely on compensation from estate funds under § 330(a)(1). [**Lamie v. United States Trustee,** 540 U.S. 526 (2004)]

34. **NO**   In **Baker Botts LLP v. ASARCO LLC,** 576 U.S. 121 (2015), the Supreme Court held that § 330(a)(1) does not authorize bankruptcy courts to award compensation to attorneys for work defending their fee applications.

35.	**DEPENDS**	The answer depends on the chapter of the Bankruptcy Code under which the debtor files for relief. Section 541(a)(6) excludes from estate property the individual debtor's post-petition earnings. But in a non-subchapter V Chapter 11 case, and in Chapter 12 and 13 cases, an individual debtor's post-petition wages are part of the bankruptcy estate. [B.C. §§ 1115(a)(2), 1207(a)(2), 1306(a)(2)] In a Chapter 11 case in which the *individual debtor* elects to proceed under *subchapter V*, the *debtor's earnings* for services rendered *after* the filing of the petition but *before* the Chapter 11 case is closed, dismissed, or converted to Chapter 7, 12, or 13, whichever first occurs, are *not* included in property of the estate *unless* the debtor's plan is confirmed under § 1191(b). [B.C. § 1186(a)(2); *see* § 1181(a)(1) (excluding § 1115)]
36.	**NO**	An interest that a debtor acquires or becomes entitled to through inheritance within *180 days* of her bankruptcy filing constitutes property of the estate. [B.C. § 541(a)(5)(A)] Debtor became entitled to the money upon her father's death and that occurred within a month of her bankruptcy filing. Thus, the $10,000 is part of her bankruptcy estate.
37.	**NO**	Section 541(c)(2) of the Code provides that a restriction on the transfer of the debtor's beneficial interest in a trust is enforceable in bankruptcy if that restriction is enforceable under applicable nonbankruptcy law. The Supreme Court has held that § 541(c)(2) covers ERISA-qualified pension plans. [**Patterson v. Shumate,** 504 U.S. 753 (1992)] Therefore, Debtor's interest in the trust of her ERISA plan is excluded from property of her bankruptcy estate.
38.	**NO**	In **City of Chicago v. Fulton,** 141 S. Ct. 585 (2021), the Supreme Court resolved a split of authority as to whether a creditor that does not turn over property of the estate, but merely continues to hold it, violates the automatic stay provision found in § 362(a)(3), which stays not only "any act to obtain possession of property of the estate," but also an act "to exercise control over property of the estate." The Supreme Court held that "mere retention of estate property after the filing of a bankruptcy petition does not violate § 362(a)(3) of the Bankruptcy Code."
39.	**YES**	Debtor owned the dog at the start of her bankruptcy case and, thus, the dog is property of the estate. The puppies are offspring of estate property and, therefore, also are property of the estate under § 541(a)(6).
40.	**YES**	Be careful not to confuse exclusions from property of the estate with exemptions. If property is excluded from the estate under § 541(b), it means that the property never comes into the bankruptcy estate. Therefore, there is no need to exempt it. By comparison, property that is exempt comes into the bankruptcy estate. The debtor may exempt it, thereby removing the possibility, if the full value is exempted, of the trustee selling the property to distribute the proceeds to unsecured creditors.

41. **NO** The example falls within the exception under § 9–317(e) for purchase money security interests. Xanadu has a purchase money security interest because Acme used the funds extended through credit to buy the office equipment in which it granted a security interest. The trustee's powers under § 544 are subject to retroactive perfection allowable under applicable nonbankruptcy law. [B.C. § 546(b)] Section 9–317 is applicable nonbankruptcy law, and it provides that the creditor takes priority over a lien creditor whose rights arise between attachment and filing of a UCC–1 so long as the creditor files its financing statement within *20 days* of the *debtor taking delivery* of the collateral. Acme took delivery on June 2. The trustee became a hypothetical lien creditor on June 10 when Acme filed for bankruptcy. Xanadu filed its financing statement on June 12, within 20 days of June 2. Therefore, while ordinarily the trustee would be able to avoid the security interest, it cannot do so here because it is a purchase money security interest, the trustee became a lien creditor between attachment and filing of the financing statement, and the creditor perfected by filing its financing statement within 20 days of the debtor taking delivery of the equipment.

Note: Xanadu did not violate the automatic stay by filing its UCC–1 after the start of the bankruptcy case. *See* B.C. §§ 362(b)(3), 546(b).

42. **YES** The trustee cannot avoid Debtor's fraudulent transfer of the property under Bankruptcy Code § 548(a) because it occurred more than two years prior to bankruptcy. But BankTwo is an actual unsecured creditor that extended credit before the transfer, has an allowable claim in Debtor's bankruptcy case, and can avoid the transaction under State law. Therefore, the trustee can avoid the entire transfer under § 544(b) even though the value of the transferred property exceeds the amount of BankTwo's claim. The trustee's recovery is for the benefit of all creditors, even those that extended credit *after* the transaction sought to be avoided. [**Moore v. Bay,** 284 U.S. 4 (1931)]

43. **NO** The trustee must establish all the elements of a preference under § 547(b). One element is that the transfer is on account of an antecedent debt. [B.C. § 547(b)(2)] There is no transfer on account of an antecedent debt in this example. Debtor paid $1,500 to Neighbor in cash at the time that Neighbor transferred the vehicle to Debtor. Debtor incurred no debt in buying the car. Thus, there is no preference.

44.a. **YES** Section 547(e)(2)(A) provides that if a creditor perfects its interest within 30 days of the transfer, then the transfer is made at the time that it takes effect between the debtor and creditor. The transfer is the grant of the security interest. Bank perfected on March 15, which is more than 30 days from the grant of the security interest. When perfection happens outside the 30-day window, § 547(e)(2)(B) provides that the transfer is deemed to occur on the day of perfection. That means that the transfer to Bank is on account of an antecedent debt (debt arose on February 1) and is within 90 days of bankruptcy filing (March 15 to June 2) when the Debtor is presumed insolvent. Bank improves its position as a secured creditor. All the elements of a preference are satisfied, which means that the trustee can avoid the security interest. Bank is unsecured in Debtor's bankruptcy case.

44.b.	**NO**	The transfer still occurs on March 15, but bankruptcy was filed more than 90 days after the transfer. [B.C. § 547(b)(3), (4)] Thus, there is no preference.
45.	**YES**	With certain exceptions not relevant to this fact pattern, Seller can reclaim the goods from Debtor if she makes a proper reclamation demand, because the (i) the sale was in the ordinary course of Seller's business; (ii) Debtor received the goods while insolvent; and (iii) Debtor received the goods within 45 days of the bankruptcy filing. A proper demand for reclamation must be in writing and done (i) no later than 45 days after Debtor received the goods; or (ii) no later than 20 days after the start of the bankruptcy case, if the 45-day period has expired. If Seller cannot reclaim, Seller still may be able to assert an administrative expense claim for the goods sold. [B.C. §§ 503(b)(9), 546(c)(2)]
46.	**YES**	The $1,000 payment is a transfer to Friend, an unsecured creditor, within 90 days of bankruptcy when Debtor is presumed insolvent, and Friend obtains more than she would obtain had the transfer not occurred. Without the transfer, Friend would have received $1,000 (5% of $20,000) from Debtor's bankruptcy case. With the transfer, however, Debtor receives $1,950: $1,000 plus another $950 (5% of $19,000 remaining on the debt).
47.	**NO**	The transfer to Amy was a fraudulent transfer. It was made for less than reasonably equivalent value while Debtor was insolvent. Thus, the trustee may avoid the transfer under § 548(a)(1)(B)(i), (ii)(I). But, the trustee may not recover the property from Ben, because Ben is not the initial transferee and, thus, has a defense to a recovery action. Because Ben took in good faith, without knowledge of the voidability of the transfer, and paid value, the trustee may not recover from Ben. [B.C. § 550(b)(1)] The trustee may recover the value of the property from Amy, however, because she was the initial transferee. [B.C. § 550(a)(1)]
48.	**NO**	Trade Creditor transferred the claim to Big Bank during the 90 days prior to Acme's bankruptcy filing and Acme was presumed insolvent for that 90-day period. Therefore, Big Bank has no right of setoff. [B.C. § 553(a)(2), (c)]
49.	**DEPENDS**	The general rule is that an after-acquired property clause in a pre-petition security agreement is not effective to create a security interest in property acquired by the debtor or the estate after the bankruptcy filing. [B.C. § 552(a)] But if the parties' security agreement extends to pre-petition collateral and its proceeds, profits, products, and offspring, then the creditor's security interest attaches to post-petition collateral that constitutes the proceeds, profits, products, or offspring that are traceable to pre-petition collateral. [B.C. § 552(b)(1)]

50.	**NO**	Debtor is confusing pre-petition interest on an unsecured claim with post-petition interest on such a claim. Creditor is entitled to include the $500 as part of his claim, because the parties' contract provides for interest. But, unless the estate is solvent, holders of unsecured claims are not entitled to post-petition interest. [B.C. § 506; **United Savings Association of Texas v. Timbers of Inwood Forest Associates**, 484 U.S. 365 (1988) (stating that the "substantive effect" of § 506 is to deny "undersecured creditors post-petition interest on their claims")] Therefore, Creditor has an unsecured claim for $12,500 but receives no post-petition interest on the claim in Debtor's Chapter 7 case.
51.a.	**NO**	The Debtor may not strip down Bank's lien to the value of the property. [**Dewsnup v. Timm**, 502 U.S. 410 (1992)]
51.b.	**NO**	Bank Two is completely underwater because the home is worth $100,000 and Bank One's claim is $100,000. Thus, there is no value left to cover Bank Two's claim. But, Debtor may not strip off Bank Two's lien on the property. If the property appreciates in value post-petition, Bank Two will receive the benefit of that appreciation, not the Debtor. [**Bank of America v. Caulkett**, 575 U.S. 790 (2015) (declining to limit *Dewsnup* to "partially—as opposed to wholly—underwater liens")]
52.	**NO**	Pre-petition wages for the 180-day period prior to bankruptcy are fourth priority unsecured claims but have priority for only $15,150. Therefore, Employee has a fourth priority claim for $15,150 and a general unsecured claim for $4,850. [B.C. § 507(a)(4)]
53.	**DEPENDS**	BAPCPA added § 502(k) to the Code, which allows a debtor to move to reduce by no more than 20% the amount of a claim for an unsecured consumer debt. The problem is that the Code requires the debtor to satisfy all of the following requirements: (1) the claim is for an unsecured consumer debt; (2) creditor unreasonably refused to negotiate an alternative repayment schedule that an approved nonprofit and credit counseling agency under § 111 proposed on the debtor's behalf; (3) the debtor's offer was made at least 60 days prior to bankruptcy; (4) the offer provided for payment of at least 60% of the debt over a period not to exceed the loan's repayment period, or a reasonable extension of that period; and (5) no portion of the debt under the alternative repayment schedule is nondischargeable. [B.C. § 502(k)] In addition, the debtor must prove by clear and convincing evidence that (1) the creditor unreasonably refused to consider the debtor's proposal *and* (2) the proposal was made before the expiration of the 60-day period. Debtor satisfies the first requirement—Creditor's claim is for an unsecured consumer debt. If Debtor can satisfy all the remaining requirements, then the bankruptcy court, after a hearing, may reduce the $1,000 claim to $800. But the Code's requirements are substantial and it is quite likely that Debtor will be unable to satisfy all the requirements for relief under § 502(k).

54.	**NO**	In Chapter 7, priority claimants are paid in the order of priority in the Code. Administrative expenses are second priority claims; therefore, they are paid before tax claims and, in this example, are paid in full. After paying the administrative claims, there is $4,000 left to pay the $8,000 in tax claims. Tax claimants share *pro rata* in remaining funds, if there are insufficient funds to pay them in full. The federal taxing authorities are 75% of the remaining tax claims ($6,000 of $8,000), which means that they get 75% of the $4,000 remaining or $3,000. The property tax claimant gets $1,000 or 25% of the $4,000 remaining. After paying the tax claimants, there is no money available to pay a dividend to the general unsecured creditors.
55.a.	**YES**	In a Chapter 7, 12, or 13 case, a secured creditor must file a proof of claim in order to have an allowed claim. [Bankruptcy Rule 3002(a)]
55.b.	**DEPENDS**	In a Chapter 11 case, however, the secured creditor need not file a proof of claim form if the debtor correctly schedules the creditor's debt and does not list the debt as contingent, unliquidated, or disputed. [Bankruptcy Rule 3003(c)(2)]
56.	**NO**	A secured creditor's lien is not void simply because the creditor fails to file a proof of claim. [Bankruptcy Rule 3002(a)]
57.	**NO**	The time remaining on the lease is less than 80 months, which means that Landlord's allowed claim is no more than one year's rental, which is $96,000. Landlord's claim for the remaining $48,000 ($144,000 − $96,000) is disallowed. [B.C. § 502(b)(6)]
58.	**NO**	If a case is converted from Chapter 11 to Chapter 7, the administrative expenses claims in the Chapter 7 case have priority of payment over the administrative expenses claims incurred prior to conversion.
59.	**NO**	Debtor has no equity in the property. Debtor can only exempt up to the value of her equity in the property.
60.	**NO**	An opt-out state restricts debtors domiciled in the state to exemptions allowed under state law and federal nonbankruptcy law.
61.	**NO**	Section 522(f)(1) allows avoidance of judicial liens and nonpossessory, nonpurchase-money security interests in household furnishings, household goods, wearing apparel, appliances, books, animals, crops, musical instruments, or jewelry. A mortgage is a consensual lien; a judicial lien is not. *Compare* B.C. § 101(36) (judicial lien) *with* B.C. § 101(37) (lien). A mortgage is a consensual lien on real property, and not in one of the categories of property listed in § 522(f)(1)(B).
62.	**YES**	Husband and Wife each can take the homestead exemption in § 522(d)(1), which means that each can exempt $27,900 in value, or a total of $55,800. [B.C. § 522(m)] Debtors have $40,000 in equity in their home; therefore, they can exempt all of the home's equity.

63.	**NO**	Debtor has not been domiciled in Michigan for the 730 days prior to filing his bankruptcy petition in the Eastern District of Michigan. Therefore, Debtor must use the exemptions for the State where he was domiciled for the longer portion of the 180 days *prior* to the 730 days before his bankruptcy filing. Two and a half years ago, Debtor was domiciled in Ohio; therefore, Ohio's exemption law applies to his Chapter 7 case. [B.C. § 522(b)(3)(A)]
64.	**DEPENDS BUT LIKELY YES**	Section 522(p) and (q) apply "as a result of [the debtor's] electing" the state law exemptions. The issue is whether these limitations on state law exemptions apply *only* to non-opt-out states, because only in non-opt-out states may debtors *elect* the state law exemptions. The majority rule is that § 522(p) and (q) apply in both opt-out and non-opt-out states.
65.	**NO**	In a unanimous opinion, the Supreme Court held that monies in an inherited IRA do not qualify for exemption under § 522(b)(3)(C), because the monies do not constitute retirement funds. [**Clark v. Rameker,** 573 U.S. 122 (2014)]
66.	**NO**	The individual debtor's right of redemption under Chapter 7 only applies to tangible personal property, not real property. Therefore, Debtor cannot redeem the land from Bank's lien. [B.C. § 722]
67.	**YES**	The general rule is that, unless the case is dismissed, property exempted by the debtor is not liable ***during or after the case*** for any pre-petition debt or any debt deemed under § 502 to have arisen before bankruptcy. [B.C. § 522(c)] One exception to this general rule, however, is for nondischargeable domestic support obligations. [B.C. §§ 522(c)(1), 523(a)(5)]
68.a.	**FALSE**	A corporate (or any non-individual) debtor does not receive a discharge in Chapter 7. [B.C. § 727(a)(1)]
68.b.	**FALSE**	A standard discharge in Chapter 13 excepts from discharge an award of damages for willful or malicious injury that caused personal injury or death. [B.C. § 1328(a)(4)] Unlike § 523(a)(6), it does ***not*** except from discharge an award of damages for injury caused to property.
68.c.	**TRUE**	A corporate Chapter 11 debtor is not discharged from a tax debt for which the corporation made a fraudulent return. [B.C. § 1141(d)(6)(B)(i)]
68.d.	**TRUE**	If a creditor fails to file an adversary proceeding requesting a nondischargeability determination from the bankruptcy court for a debt for fraud respecting the debtor's financial condition under § 523(a)(2), then the debt is discharged. [B.C. § 523(c), Bankruptcy Rule 7001(6)] The same is true for debts under § 523(a)(4) and (a)(6).
68.e.	**FALSE**	A creditor's debt for fraud is not discharged if the creditor's debt is not scheduled and the creditor had neither notice nor knowledge of the bankruptcy case in time to timely file a proof of claim and timely request a determination of dischargeability. [B.C. § 523(a)(3), (c)]

| 69. | **YES** | The Code provides that a reaffirmation agreement is not enforceable if the debtor rescinds the agreement prior to discharge or within 60 days after the agreement is filed with the court, whichever occurs later. It has only been 30 days since the agreement was filed and the bankruptcy court has not yet granted Debtor a discharge. Therefore, Debtor still has time to rescind the agreement and render it unenforceable. [B.C. § 524(c)(4)] |

| 70. | **NO** | If the debtor was represented by an attorney when the reaffirmation agreement was negotiated, then a discharge hearing is discretionary with the court. However, if the judge schedules a hearing, the debtor must attend. [B.C. §§ 524(d), 521(a)(5)] |

| 71. | **POSSIBLY NOT** | Some courts have noted the difference in language between § 525(b) on private employers and § 525(a) on governmental units. Section 525(a) prohibits a governmental unit from *denying,* terminating, or discriminating with respect to employment of a debtor. By comparison, § 525(b) only prohibits terminating or discriminating with respect to debtor's employment. Private Employer did not terminate or discriminate with respect to debtor's employment; it *denied* her employment because of her bankruptcy filing. Thus, Private Employer's action may not run afoul of the Code's anti-discrimination provisions. [*See, e.g.,* **Burnett v. Stewart Title, Inc. (In re Burnett),** 635 F.3d 169 (5th Cir. 2011); *see also* **Myers v. TooJay's Management Corp.,** 640 F.3d 1278 (11th Cir. 2011)] |

| 72. | **YES** | The great weight of authority is that post-petition interest on a nondischargeable tax debt also is not dischargeable. |

| 73. | **MOST LIKELY NO** | Most courts agree that a creditor does not violate the automatic stay by merely sending the debtor a letter proposing a reaffirmation agreement. |

| 74. | **NO** | The Supreme Court has held that the preponderance-of-the-evidence standard is the standard of proof for the discharge exceptions at § 523(a). [**Grogan v. Garner,** 498 U.S. 279 (1991)] |

| 75. | **NO** | With certain limited exceptions that do not apply to this fact pattern, the discharge of a debtor's debt does not affect the liability of other entities, such as sureties or guarantors. Thus, while Debtor's debt to Bank is discharged, Mother's is not. [B.C. § 524(e)] |

| 76.a. | **YES** | Bank has violated the automatic stay, because the equipment is property of the estate and Bank tried post-petition to perfect its lien against estate property. [B.C. § 362(a)(4)] The exception to the automatic stay at § 362(b)(3) does not apply. |

| 76.b. | **NO** | The Code provides an exception to the stay for the commencement or continuation of any civil action or proceeding to establish paternity. [B.C. § 362(b)(2)(A)(i)] |

| 76.c. | **YES** | The setoff of a debt owing to the debtor—the $10,000 in the pre-petition account—against a claim against the debtor—Bank's claim for $50,000 based on the prepetition loan—violates the stay. [B.C. |

§ 362(a)(7)] Had the Bank simply placed a temporary hold on Debtor's account while promptly seeking relief from the automatic stay, then there would not be a stay violation. [**Citizens Bank of Maryland v. Strumpf,** 516 U.S. 16 (1995)]

77.	**DEPENDS**	Prior to the passage of BAPCPA, some courts allowed the Debtor to ride through bankruptcy, so long as she was current on her car payments, without redeeming the vehicle or reaffirming the debt. The Code now contains a stay termination provision, which provides if an individual Chapter 7 debtor fails to reaffirm the debt or redeem the property securing the creditor's purchase-money interest within 45 days after the first meeting of creditors, then the automatic stay terminates and the property is no longer estate property. [B.C. § 521(a)(6)] Some jurisdictions do not allow repossession of a vehicle based solely on an *ipso facto* clause in the parties' contract. In these jurisdictions, if Debtor is current on her car payments, then termination of the automatic stay has no effect on her ability to retain possession of her vehicle.
78.	**FALSE**	Cause is one basis for lifting the stay but it is not the only way a creditor can succeed on a lift-of-stay motion. [B.C. § 362(d)(1)] The court will lift the stay of an act against property if the debtor has no equity in the property and the property is not necessary for an effective reorganization. [B.C. § 362(d)(2)] The Code also contains provisions related to lifting the stay in a single asset real estate case [B.C. § 362(d)(3)] and in a case in which a creditor's claim is secured by real property and the filing of bankruptcy is part of a scheme to hinder, delay, or defraud creditors. [B.C. § 362(d)(4)]
79.	**NO**	In 2005, Congress added an exception to the automatic stay to cover this fact scenario. A governmental unit may offset an income tax refund for a pre-petition taxable period against a pre-petition tax liability, if offset is allowed under nonbankruptcy law. Nonbankruptcy law (26 U.S.C. § 6402(a)) allows the IRS to set off tax liabilities against tax refunds. Debtor's tax liability and tax refund were for pre-petition taxable periods. Therefore, the IRS did not violate the automatic stay.
80.	**DEPENDS, BUT LIKELY**	The Bankruptcy Code provides an exception to the stay for the commencement or continuation of a criminal action against the debtor. [B.C. § 362(b)(2)] The courts are split as to whether this exception applies to a criminal proceeding for passing a bad check. The concern is that prosecution puts pressure on the debtor to pay a debt that is dischargeable; other creditors do not enjoy the benefit of the state as a collection agent. The majority of courts, however, have held that § 362(b)(2)'s plain language does not distinguish between criminal proceedings based on the prosecutor's motive; therefore, the automatic stay does not apply to the commencement or continuation of a prosecution against the debtor for passing a bad check.

81.   **NO**   The automatic stay is in effect for 30 days from the date of the petition, because Debtor filed and served the required certification, and deposited 30 days' worth of rent with the court clerk. [B.C. § 362(*l*)(1)] If during the 30 days following Debtor's filing of the petition, Debtor pays the past-due rental, and files with the court and serves on Landlord a further certification that she has cured the entire default that led to the judgment for possession, then the automatic stay applies and prevents Landlord from taking further action to evict Debtor from her apartment. [B.C. § 362(*l*)(2)]

82.   **NO**   Congress amended § 362 in 2005 in an effort to deal with what it considered abusive serial filings by small business debtors. Because Debtor's current case is a small business case and Debtor's prior Chapter 11 case was a small business case dismissed within two years of the filing of Debtor's current case, the automatic stay does not apply in Debtor's current case. [B.C. §§ 362(n)(1)(B), 101(51C), (51D)]

83.a.   **NO**   Adequate protection protects the secured creditor against a decrease in the collateral securing the creditor's loan. The accrual of post-petition interest increases Creditor's claim, which, in turn, shrinks any existing equity cushion. The shrinkage of the equity cushion, however, is not due to a decrease in the collateral value and should not trigger adequate protection. Therefore, a bankruptcy court should not provide adequate protection to a creditor in a case in which post-petition interest payments erode the equity cushion.

83.b.   **NO**   Adequate protection does not entitle an undersecured creditor to compensation (i.e., interest) for the delay in foreclosure on his collateral and reinvestment of the proceeds. The United States Supreme Court has held that adequate protection means protection against depreciation in "the value of the collateral," and not protection of "a secured party's right to immediate foreclosure." [**United Savings Association of Texas v. Timbers of Inwood Forest Associates, Ltd.**, 484 U.S. 365 (1988)]

84.   **DEPENDS**   The Code requires notice and a hearing to use, sell, or lease property of the estate other than in the ordinary course of business. [B.C. § 363(b)(1)] But if no party in interest timely requests a hearing, then the property may be sold without an actual hearing if proper notice was given. [B.C. § 102(1)(B)(i)]

85.   **NO**   The checking account is cash collateral. Bank has a right to set off its $30,000 claim against Debtor's checking account. Bank's claim is secured, by virtue of § 506(a). Therefore, even though Debtor is acting in the ordinary course of its business, it must obtain either Bank's consent to use of the cash collateral or court approval, after notice and a hearing. [B.C. § 363(a), (c)(2)]

86.	**NO**	Bank1 is adequately protected by the $100,000 equity cushion that it has in Debtor's land. In determining the equity cushion, the bankruptcy court will compare the value of the property ($200,000) to the amount of Bank1's secured claim and any other *senior* secured claims ($100,000). Therefore, Bank1 has a $100,000 equity cushion in the land.
87.	**DEPENDS**	Four requirements must be met before Friend's interest in Property can be sold along with Debtor's. If the trustee fails to satisfy even one of those four requirements, then the sale cannot go forward as planned. The facts in the scenario make clear that two of the four requirements are satisfied: it is impracticable to partition Property, and Property is not used to produce, transmit, or distribute for sale electric energy or natural or synthetic gas for heat, light, or power. But two requirements remain. The amount the trustee would realize from selling the estate's undivided interest in Property must be *substantially less* than what would be realized from selling Property free of Friend's interest. In addition, the benefit to the estate must outweigh the detriment to Friend. [B.C. § 363(h)]
88.	**DEPENDS**	Acme can sell the list, but only after appointment of a consumer privacy ombudsman and court approval, after notice and a hearing, of the sale. The bankruptcy court must take account of the facts, circumstances, and conditions of the sale and find that no showing was made that the sale would violate nonbankruptcy law. [B.C. § 363(b)(1)]
89.	**NO**	In Chapter 11, § 1113 governs rejection of collective bargaining agreements, not § 365. The debtor in possession "may assume or reject a collective bargaining agreement only in accordance" with the provisions of § 1113. [B.C. § 1113(a)] Section 1113 contains a number of conditions that the debtor in possession must satisfy in order to reject its collective bargaining agreement. For example, the Code mandates that before filing an application to reject the collective bargaining agreement, the debtor in possession must make a proposal to the union to modify the agreement. [B.C. § 1113(b)(1)(A)] Therefore, Acme cannot reject its collective bargaining agreement by using the rules under § 365 of the Code.
90.	**NO**	Section 365 does not apply because the agreement is a disguised sale, not a lease, of the vehicle. The "lease" cannot be terminated and Debtor has an option to buy the vehicle for nominal additional consideration $10. [U.C.C. § 1–203(b)] Thus, there is no lease to assume.

91.   **NO**   OfficeCo confuses the time for assumption or rejection in a Chapter 7 case with that in a Chapter 11 case. In Chapter 7, if a debtor does not assume or reject within 60 days of the order for relief an executory contract or an unexpired lease of personal property or residential real property, then the contract or lease is deemed rejected. [B.C. § 365(d)(1)] In Chapter 11, however, assumption or rejection of an executory contract or an unexpired lease of personal property or residential real property may occur at any time prior to the confirmation of a plan. However, OfficeCo may request that the court, in its discretion, direct the trustee or the debtor in possession to assume or reject within a fixed period of time. [B.C. § 365(d)(2)]

92.   **YES**   The Code's definition of intellectual property does not include trademarks, trade names, or service marks. [B.C. § 101(35A)] Thus, § 365(n) does not apply to trademarks. But in **Mission Product Holdings v. Tempnology, LLC,** 139 S. Ct. 1652 (2019), the Supreme Court held that a debtor-licensor's rejection of a trademark licensing agreement was a breach of that contract, not a rescission of it. Because rejection does not rescind rights previously granted to the licensee, the debtor-licensor's rejection does not "deprive[ ] the licensee of its rights to use the trademark." The Court's decision rested on § 365(g). The Court explained that Congress had done "nothing in adding Section 365(n) to alter the natural reading of Section 365(g)—that rejection and breach have the same results." Thus, the "debtor-licensor's rejection [did not] revoke the trademark license."

93.   **NO**   Current monthly income is the average monthly income from all sources that the debtor receives in the six-month period ending on the last day of the month immediately preceding the debtor's bankruptcy filing. Debtor filed for relief on February 1, 2021, which means that Debtor's current monthly income is $3,000. The income earned from August of 2020 through the end of January of 2021 is $18,000. That figure divided by six months results in a monthly average of $3,000. Debtor's gross annual income divided by 12 results in $2,8333.33. If the Debtor earns the exact same amount each month, then dividing annual gross income by 12 works. If the Debtor's income varies by month—because she works on commissions, her salary increases or decreases, or her work hours increase or decrease—using annual gross income results in an incorrect figure. You use current monthly income to determine the debtor's eligibility for Chapter 7; the figure also is important for determining the amount that the debtor must pay unsecured creditors under her Chapter 13 plan.

94.	**YES**	You determine whether a debtor is an above- or below-median income debtor by figuring out the debtor's current monthly income, multiplying that number by 12, and comparing it with the state's annual median income. Current monthly income is the average monthly income from all sources for the six-month period prior to the debtor's filing for bankruptcy. During the months of January through June, Debtor earned $5,000 (January and February) + $2,700 (March) + $4,000 (April and May) + $3,500 (June) *or* $15,200, which results in current monthly income of $2,533 ($15,200/6). The result, when annualized, is $30,400 (rounding up product of $2,533 × 12), which is $400 higher than the state median.
95.	**YES**	Debtor is a below-median income debtor; therefore, there is no presumption of abuse. [B.C. § 707(b)(2)] Her case may be dismissed only if it was filed in bad faith or the granting of relief would be an abuse of discretion under a totality of the circumstances. [B.C. § 707(b)]
96.	**DEPENDS**	The mere fact that Debtor's annual income exceeds the state's median income does *not* create a presumption of abuse. The "means test" determines whether Debtor's filing for relief under Chapter 7 creates a presumption of abuse.
97.	**NO**	Debtor is an above-median income debtor, whose current monthly income is $4,000. Her means test expenses are $3,900, leaving $100 per month disposable income. That means disposable income over 60 months (because Debtor is an above-median income debtor) of $6,000, which is below $9,075. Thus, there is no presumption of abuse. [B.C. § 707(b)(2)(A)(i)(I)]
98.	**YES**	Debtor is an above-median income debtor, whose current monthly income is $4,000. Her means test expenses are $3,800, leaving $200 per month disposable income. That means disposable income over 60 months (because Debtor is an above-median income debtor) of $12,000, which is between $9,075 and $15,150. Thus, Debtor must perform the secondary abuse test, which compares her disposable income over 60 months with 25% of her unsecured debt. Because $12,000 is greater than $10,000 (25% of Debtor's unsecured debt), there is a presumption of abuse. Debtor has sufficient disposable income to pay at least 25% of her unsecured debt in a Chapter 13 case. Unless Debtor can rebut the presumption of abuse, her Chapter 7 case will be dismissed.
99.	**NO**	Debtor owns her car free and clear, so she is not making any car payments. She may not deduct the national standard for a car ownership expense as a monthly means test expense. [**Ransom v. FIA Card Services**, 562 U.S. 61 (2011)]

100.	**NO**	Creditor filed its claim late and, therefore, is only paid *after* all the timely filed general unsecured claims. Because there is not enough money to pay all the timely filed claims (recovery is approximately 11% per creditor—$5,000 assets/$45,000 in claims), Creditor receives nothing in Debtor's Chapter 7 case. [B.C. §§ 726(a)(2), (3)]
101.	**NO**	Administrative expenses have second priority of payment and, therefore, are paid before any general unsecured creditors. [B.C. § 507(a)(2)] After paying the administrative expenses, there is $4,000 available to pay $40,000 worth of general unsecured claims. That means that each general unsecured creditor receives a 10% dividend ($4,000 assets/$40,000 claims). Ten percent of Creditor A's $1,000 claim is $100 (10% × $1,000), not $400.
102.	**YES**	An individual Chapter 7 debtor will not receive a discharge of her debts if she files her current Chapter 7 case within 8 years of having filed a prior Chapter 7 case. The dates run from filing, not from discharge. While Debtor received her discharge within the 8-year period, her earlier Chapter 7 case was filed more than 8 years ago. Therefore, Debtor is entitled to a discharge in her current Chapter 7 case. [B.C. § 727(a)(8)]
103.	**NO**	Debtor transferred valuable property—his home is worth $100,000— to his sister, an insider, for nominal consideration in an effort to hinder, delay, or defraud his creditors. He did so within one year of filing for bankruptcy. Thus, he will not receive a discharge in his Chapter 7 case. [B.C. § 727(a)(2)] In addition, the Chapter 7 trustee likely will file an adversary proceeding in the bankruptcy case to recover the home from Debtor's sister because it was a fraudulent transfer. [B.C. § 548(a)(1)(A)]
		Note: The time period for Chapter 7's denial-of-discharge provision is one year, while the time period for fraudulent conveyances is two years.
104.	**DEPENDS**	If Debtor consents, the bankruptcy court may convert the case to Chapter 11 or 13. [B.C. § 707(b)(1)] If Debtor does not consent to conversion, however, then the bankruptcy court will dismiss Debtor's Chapter 7 case.
105.	**NO**	The Bankruptcy Code provides that as soon as practicable after the order for relief, the United States trustee *shall* appoint an official committee of unsecured creditors. [B.C. § 1102(a)] It is not unusual, however, for the United States trustee to be unable to find creditors willing to serve on the unsecured creditors' committee. Thus, in many Chapter 11 cases, there is no official committee of unsecured creditors.
106.	**NO**	Debtor qualifies as a small business debtor and may elect subchapter V. [B.C. §§ 101(51D), 1182(1)] The answer to this question does not change, however, if Debtor does elect subchapter V. Unless the court for cause orders otherwise, a committee of creditors is not appointed in a small business or subchapter V case. [B.C. § 1102(a)(3)]

107.	**NO**	Debtor may elect subchapter V but the Code's small business provisions are mandatory (since the passage of BAPCPA) for any debtor that satisfies the small business debtor definition of § 101(51D). Debtor satisfies the definition: (a) engaged in business activities; (b) not in the business of single asset real estate; (c) debts under $3,024,725; and (d) more than 50% of those liabilities arose from the Debtor's business activities.
108.	**DEPENDS**	Debtor must pay administrative creditors in full in cash on the plan's effective date—unless the holder of a particular claim agrees otherwise—if the case is not a subchapter V case, regardless of whether the plan is a consent plan or confirmed under § 1129(b)'s cram down provisions. [B.C. § 1129(a)(9)(A)] If Debtor elected to proceed under subchapter V, the answer depends on whether the plan is a consent plan or is confirmed under subchapter V's cram down provisions. If a consent plan under subchapter V, then Debtor must pay administrative creditors in full in cash on the plan's effective date, unless the holder of a particular claim agrees to the contrary. [B.C. §§ 1191(a), 1129(a)(9)(A)] If the plan is confirmed under subchapter V's cram down provisions, then Debtor may pay administrative claimants over time under the plan. [B.C. § 1191(e)]
109.	**YES**	The bankruptcy court may order the appointment of a Chapter 11 trustee instead of converting the case if the court determines that appointment of a trustee is in the best interests of the estate and of creditors. [B.C. § 1112(b)(1)]
110.	**NO**	The Code does not permit a bankruptcy court to convert a farmer's Chapter 11 case to Chapter 7 if the farmer does not request conversion. [B.C. § 1112(c)] Therefore, the bankruptcy court cannot convert Farmer's case to Chapter 7, because Farmer objects to such conversion.
111.a.	**NO**	*Diner* is a small business debtor, because (i) it is engaged in business activities, (ii) its primary activity is not the business of owning single asset real estate, (iii) its liabilities are less than $3,024,725, and (iv) more than 50% of its liabilities arise from its business activities. [B.C. § 101(51D)(A)] The exclusivity period for a small business debtor is 180, not 120, days. [B.C. § 1121(e)] Therefore, Creditor may not file a plan within 120 days of *Diner's* bankruptcy filing.
111.b.	**NO**	While 90 days has elapsed, which is the time within which the subchapter V debtor is supposed to file its plan, the Code provides that *only* the subchapter V debtor can file a plan. [B.C. § 1189(a)]
112.	**YES**	Unless the bankruptcy court for cause orders otherwise, the subchapter V Chapter 11 debtor does not file a disclosure statement. [B.C. § 1181(b)]

113.	**NO**	The court will not confirm a consent plan unless each class of claims is either unimpaired or accepts the plan. [B.C. § 1129(a)(8)] The class of general unsecured creditors is impaired under the plan, because creditors are receiving less than full payment on their claims. [B.C. § 1124(1)] A class of claims accepts the plan if at least two-thirds in amount and more than half in number of claims vote in favor of the plan. [B.C. § 1126(c)] While 9 of 10 unsecured claimants voted "yes," thereby satisfying the "more than half in number" requirement, only 45% in amount voted in favor. Total claims = $100,000; 9 creditors with claims of $5,000 and a 10th creditor with a claim of $55,000. Because Creditor X holds such a large claim, its "no" vote meant that Debtor could not satisfy the two-thirds in amount requirement.

114. **YES**

In a Chapter 11 case, a discharge is not limited to an individual debtor as it is in Chapter 7. Unless the plan or the confirmation order provides otherwise, *confirmation* discharges Debtor Corporation from all pre-confirmation debts, as well as from certain other debts specified in § 1141(d)(1)(A).

Note: The result would differ if the confirmed plan were a liquidating plan and Debtor Corporation—which would be denied a discharge under Chapter 7—did not engage in business after consummation of the plan. [B.C. § 1141(d)(3)]

115. **NO**

The Code requires that an eighth priority tax creditor be paid regular cash installments that equal the present value of its claim over a period of time that does not exceed five years from the order of relief, not the plan's effective date. [B.C. § 1129(b)(9)(C)] The IRS has not agreed to different treatment, which means that the bankruptcy court cannot confirm Acme's plan.

Note: In a non-subchapter V case, there can be a significant gap in time between filing of the petition and the plan's effective date.

116. **YES**

If a general unsecured creditor objects to confirmation of an individual debtor's plan, the court cannot confirm the plan unless (i) the plan pays the present value, as of its effective date, of the creditor's claim; or (ii) the debtor pays at least his projected disposable income over five years from the first plan payment or the time during which plan payments are made, whichever time period is longer. [B.C. § 1129(a)(15)] Debtor is paying his projected disposable income over a five-year period, which also is the time during which plan payments are being made. Therefore, Debtor's plan satisfies § 1129(a)(15), and the bankruptcy court can confirm the plan.

117. **DEPENDS** If the court follows the narrow interpretation of the absolute priority rule, then the court cannot confirm Debtor's plan. The class of general unsecured creditors has voted to reject Debtor's plan, which means that the court cannot confirm as a consent plan because the unsecured creditors are impaired (receiving only 25% of their claims). [B.C. § 1129(a)(8)] The court could confirm using the Code's cram down rules, but the absolute priority rule is an issue. Courts following the majority narrow interpretation of the absolute priority rule hold that *only* the debtor's post-petition earnings and acquisitions of property are excluded from operation of the absolute priority rule. That means that Debtor cannot retain valuable, non-exempt pre-petition property that could be used to pay more than a 25% dividend to his general unsecured creditors. If the court follows the broad interpretation of the absolute priority rule, which is the minority position, then the court could confirm Debtor's plan.

118. **DEPENDS** The Code does not require that substantially similar claims be put into the same class. [*See* B.C. § 1122] Most courts have held that a plan may separately classify substantially similar claims if there is a reasonable or rational justification for the separate classification. If Debtor put Creditor A into a separate class in order to gerrymander the plan confirmation vote, however, the bankruptcy court will not confirm the plan.

119. **NO** Fisherman has $5 million in debt, which exceeds the $2,268,550 debt limit for family fishermen under Chapter 12. [B.C. § 101(19A)] Congress increased the debt limit for family farmers, but not family fishermen, to $10 million (now $11,097,350) with the Family Farmer Relief Act of 2019. [Pub. L. No. 116–51 (2019)]

120. **YES** A Chapter 12 debtor may convert the case to Chapter 7 at any time. [B.C. § 1208(a)]

121.a. **FALSE** A Chapter 12 case may be commenced only by the filing of a voluntary petition. [*See* B.C. § 303(a)]

121.b. **TRUE** Only the debtor may file a plan. [B.C. § 1221]

121.c. **FALSE** A Chapter 12 trustee (either a standing trustee or one appointed for the particular case) serves in the case even if the family farmer or family fisherman remains a debtor in possession. [B.C. § 1202]

121.d. **FALSE** Confirmation of the Chapter 12 plan does not constitute a discharge. The Chapter 12 debtor receives a discharge upon completing all plan payments and, if the debtor is required to pay a domestic support obligation, after certifying that the amounts due for that obligation have been made. [B.C. § 1228(a)]

122. **NO** The standard discharge in Chapter 12 does not discharge any debts of a kind specified in § 523(a). [B.C. § 1228(a)(2)] Section 523(a)(4) provides that a debt for fraud while acting in a fiduciary capacity is not dischargeable.

Note: A creditor with a claim under §§ 523(a)(2), (4), or (6) must initiate an adversary proceeding in the bankruptcy case for a determination of whether the creditor's claim is not dischargeable. If the creditor fails to do so, the creditor's claim will be discharged. [B.C. § 523(c)]

123. **NO** An involuntary petition may only be filed against an individual under Chapter 7 or Chapter 11 of the Code. [B.C. § 303(a)]

124.a. **FALSE** An individual debtor who is engaged in business may file for relief under Chapter 13. An individual who is self-employed and incurs trade credit in producing income from that employment is engaged in business. [B.C. § 1304(a)]

124.b. **FALSE** There is a co-debtor stay in Chapter 13, but it is limited to creditor actions to collect on a *consumer* debt of the debtor, not any debt of the debtor, from a co-debtor. [B.C. § 1301(a); *see* earlier answer on debtor engaged in business]

124.c. **FALSE** A Chapter 13 debtor receives a standard discharge after completing all plan payments and, if the debtor is required to pay a domestic support obligation, after certifying that the amounts due for that obligation have been made. [B.C. § 1328(a)]

125. **DEPENDS** There is a long-standing split of authority as to whether the debtor's right to dismiss is absolute or subject to a bad faith or fraud exception. Some courts have concluded that the Supreme Court's decision in **Marrama v. Citizens Bank,** 549 U.S. 365 (2007) resolved the issue in favor a recognizing a bad faith exception. Other courts have held that the Chapter 13 debtor has an absolute right to dismissal under § 1307(b) and that the Supreme Court in **Law v. Siegel,** 571 U.S. 415 (2014) rejected *Marrama's* dictum on which other courts have relied in finding a bad-faith exception.

126. **NO** Debtor is an above-median income debtor, because she earns $42,000 per year (current monthly income of $3,500 × 12) and the median income in her state is $40,000. Therefore, Debtor's plan must provide that she commit all of her projected disposable income for 60, not 36, months. [B.C. § 1325(b)(1), (4)]

127. **NO** Car Creditor has a purchase-money security interest in Debtor's vehicle, which was purchased for personal use within 910 days of Debtor's bankruptcy filing. Therefore, the hanging paragraph under § 1325(a)(9) applies, which means that Car Creditor's claim is not bifurcated into a secured ($20,000) and unsecured ($5,000) claim under § 1325(a)(5). Instead, Debtor must treat the entire $25,000 as a secured claim in order to satisfy the Code's requirements for confirmation.

128. **NO** A plan may modify the rights of holders of secured claims but cannot modify the rights of a holder of a claim secured only by the debtor's principal residence. [B.C. § 1322(b)(2)] Bank's claim is secured only by Debtor's principal residence. Therefore, Debtor's plan runs afoul of § 1322(b)(2)'s prohibition.

129. **YES** A standard Chapter 13 discharge excepts from discharge a debt for restitution or damages awarded against the debtor in a civil action because of the debtor's willful or malicious injury that caused personal injury to or death of an individual. [B.C. § 1328(a)] While Debtor's conduct was willful but not malicious, it resulted in property damage, not personal injury to an individual. Thus, the debt is dischargeable.

Note: Had Debtor filed for relief under Chapter 7, the debt also would have been discharged. While § 523(a)(6), which applies to Chapter 7 cases, covers injury to *both* persons and property, it requires a willful *and* malicious injury. Section 1328(a)(4) requires only a willful *or* malicious injury.

130. **DEPENDS** There is a split of authority on the question of when the five-year plan period begins. Some courts hold that the five-year period starts to run with the debtor's first plan payment, which normally occurs within 30 days of the filing of the petition. [B.C. § 1326(a)(1)] Other courts start the five-year period with the first payment that the debtor makes under the plan post-confirmation.

131. **NO** Debtor is incorrect and is confusing § 506(b)'s requirement of interest on an oversecured claim with § 1325(a)(5)'s requirement that a Chapter 13 plan pay secured creditors the present value of their claims. In order to give Car Creditor its present value, Debtor must pay interest on Car Creditor's claim. The interest rate paid on secured claims over the term of the plan is the *Till* rate, named after the Supreme Court's decision in **Till v. SCS Credit Corporation**, 541 U.S. 465 (2004). The Till rate is the national prime rate adjusted for risk; the risk adjustment generally means an additional 1–3% added to the national prime rate.

Essay Questions and Answers

QUESTION I

Apex, Inc., a small widget producer, filed for relief under chapter 11. Bell Bank is Apex's largest secured creditor. Several years ago, Bell made a loan to Apex. The balance on the loan is $1.2 million; the loan is secured by a mortgage on Apex's plant, which is valued at $1.5 million. Apex's second largest secured creditor is Crafty Financial, which extended Apex a loan whose outstanding balance is $500,000. Crafty has a perfected security interest in Apex's inventory and accounts receivable, which are valued at $450,000. Apex has 10 unsecured creditors; the ten include Crafty. Apex's three largest unsecured creditors (apart from Crafty) are Daft Company, Enigma Corporation, and Flighty, Inc. Apex owes Daft $60,000; Enigma $70,000; and Flighty $100,000. The remaining six unsecured creditors are owed claims of $2,000 or less. Total unsecured claims (Classes 3 ($280,000) & 4 ($10,00) below) equal $290,000. All of Apex's debts are noncontingent and liquidated, and arose from Apex's business activities.

Apex proposes the following plan:

1) Class #1: Bell. Apex continues to pay Bell according to the terms of the parties' original contract.

2) Class #2: Crafty. Apex proposes to extend the loan repayment period on Crafty's loan by five years.

3) Class #3: Unsecured claims of $2,000 or less or creditors with larger claims willing to reduce their claims to $2,000 will be paid in full in cash on the plan's effective date.

4) Class #4: Unsecured claims in excess of $2,000 will be paid in five annual installments with 5% interest; the first payment will be made on the effective date of the plan. Total payout over five years = 20% of creditor's claim.

5) The four family members who currently own the firm will retain their ownership interests in Apex.

Apex knows that Bell and Crafty will vote in favor of the plan. Crafty, Daft, Enigma, and Flighty do not intend to reduce their claims to $2,000 in order to participate in Class #3. The other six unsecured creditors in Class #3 will vote in favor of the plan. Apex also knows that Daft and Enigma will vote "yes" on the plan. Apex is unsure how Flighty will vote.

1. Assume that Apex does not elect to proceed under subchapter V. If Flighty votes "no" on the plan, can Apex obtain confirmation? Assume all creditors will cast votes.

2. Assume that Apex elects to proceed under subchapter V. If Flighty votes "no" on the plan, can Apex obtain confirmation? Assume all creditors will cast votes. Make sure your answer includes a discussion of whether Apex qualifies to elect subchapter V.

QUESTION II

Darlene has come to your law office for advice. She wants to file for bankruptcy, and you determine that she qualifies for relief under Chapter 7. While talking with Darlene, you discover the following facts:

- Darlene rents an apartment for $650 per month. Her landlord has obtained a judgment for possession of the apartment against her, which he likely is going to execute on within the next few days. Darlene wants to remain in her current apartment.

- Darlene purchased a car about a year ago. She financed the car through *Carl's Cars* ("CC"). The contract with CC contains an *ipso facto clause* that provides, among other things, that filing for bankruptcy is a default under the contract. Darlene needs the car to get back and forth to her job. She is current on her car payments and, in fact, always has made her car payment on time.

1. If Darlene files for bankruptcy before execution of the judgment for possession, will she be able to stay in the apartment during the pendency of the bankruptcy case? Assume that the jurisdiction in which Darlene lives allows apartment dwellers, after entry of the judgment for possession, to cure the monetary default that gave rise to the judgment for possession. Explain what needs to happen to keep Darlene in her apartment.

2. Darlene cannot afford to redeem her car and does not want to reaffirm the debt with CC. Explain to Darlene what happens if she fails to redeem or enter into a reaffirmation agreement, as provided for under § 521(a)(6) of the Bankruptcy Code? Assume that the jurisdiction in which Darlene lives does not honor *ipso facto clauses* if the debtor is making timely, regular payments on the collateral.

QUESTION III

Dorothy and Ed are in their late fifties and have been married for 25 years. They have come to your law office because creditors are hounding them "night and day" to pay delinquent medical and credit card bills. Dorothy and Ed want to jointly file for bankruptcy. They ask about Chapter 7 and tell you that their neighbor, who is a lawyer, told them that they do not qualify based on their income. You ask Dorothy and Ed some basic questions about their income and expenses, and they tell you the following:

Dorothy's and Ed's financial situation has been rocky for some time. Three years ago, Dorothy was in a serious car accident. Dorothy is covered by Ed's health insurance, but the plan has a high deductible and did not cover some of Dorothy's care. As a result, the couple has $87,000 in unpaid medical bills. Dorothy had to take an unpaid leave from her job, which put a further strain on the couple's finances. They maxed out their credit cards; the card balances are: (1) $25,000 on Master Card; (2) $30,000 on Visa; and (3) $15,000 on Discover.

Dorothy and Ed purchased their home fifteen years ago. *Local Bank* holds the mortgage on the home. The current balance on the home loan is $107,650, and there are fifteen years left on the loan. Dorothy and Ed recently had the home appraised, because they considered taking out an equity line to pay off their credit cards. The appraiser valued their home at $175,000. The home is not entireties property.

Dorothy's and Ed's household goods and clothes are valued at approximately $26,000; no item of clothing or household furnishings exceeds $700 in value. Ed owns a valuable watch worth about $1,700. Dorothy also has several pieces of fine jewelry worth approximately $1,700. Dorothy and Ed own two cars, both of which were purchased for personal use from (and financed by) *New Motors*. Dorothy owes $21,000 on her car, which is valued at $21,000 at retail. Ed owes $25,000 on his vehicle, which is valued at retail at approximately $22,000.

Ed has an ERISA-qualified pension plan currently valued at $150,000. Dorothy works but has no pension benefits through her job.

Dorothy and Ed gross $5,000 per month from their respective jobs. Median income for a two-person family in their state is $59,000. Their *actual* monthly expenses and deductions are $4,700. Their *means* test monthly expenses and deductions are $4,800.

1. After a few quick calculations, you realize that Dorothy's and Ed's neighbor was wrong; Dorothy and Ed do qualify for relief under Chapter 7. Explain to Dorothy and Ed *why* they qualify. Be specific.

2. Explain to Dorothy and Ed what property they can protect from their creditors and what property, if any, they cannot protect if they file for relief under Chapter 7. If they file, Dorothy and Ed will use the federal exemptions.

   Remember: Dorothy and Ed plan to file a joint petition.

QUESTION IV

The past few years have been hard on Darius. A few years ago, he was hospitalized due to complications from diabetes. Darius could not afford to pay the hospital bill, but had worked out an arrangement to pay in monthly installments. Unfortunately, Darius lost his well-paying job, stopped paying the hospital, and ignored the hospital's efforts to work out a payment plan. About a year ago, the hospital turned the $45,000 outstanding bill over to a collection agency. Around the same time, Darius gave his sister Jade a New England Tall Case Clock (circa 1820) that had been in their family for generations. The clock had been left to Darius by his grandfather who passed away 10 years ago. Darius gave Jade the clock for "safekeeping." She paid nothing for the clock, which is valued at $25,800.

Darius files for relief under Chapter 13. Darius has been insolvent for the past 18 months. Can the Chapter 13 trustee recover the New England Tall Case Clock from Jade? Explain why (or why not), and evaluate all relevant theories.

QUESTION V

Debi Duncan is an aspiring clothing designer who grew up in southeastern Illinois. Over the past few years, she has tried to jump start her career by auditioning for and, in some cases, appearing on several reality shows for new designers.

Duncan moved to New York City to attend design school. After graduating in April of 2016, Duncan moved to Los Angeles, where she appeared on *It's in the Bag,* a new reality show about fashion accessories. Duncan was eliminated in the early rounds of the competition, but earned a reputation as the "bad girl" on the show. Unable to find work in Los Angeles, Duncan moved to New York City in December of 2018, because she was offered a spot as the "design consultant" on *The Alarm,* an unconventional local morning television show. Unfortunately, in early 2020, Duncan received news that her mother was dying. Duncan gave up her job in New York City and on March 1, 2020, flew home to Illinois to care for her mother. Duncan's mother passed away in April of 2020, leaving Duncan a small inheritance. Duncan decided to open her own design business, and signed a ten-year lease at a rental of $5,000 per month for a large, commercial space in a fashionable neighborhood. Her timing, however, was bad. Public health restrictions due to COVID made it a struggle to get sufficient foot traffic to make the business a success. As debts mounted, Duncan decided to file for bankruptcy.

1. If Duncan was domiciled in Illinois since March 1, 2020, could she use the Illinois exemptions if she filed for bankruptcy on February 1, 2021? If not, what state exemptions must she take?

2. Before filing for bankruptcy, Duncan notified Landlord that she was vacating the premises and could no longer pay rent. The next day, she filed for relief under Chapter 7. At the time that she filed for bankruptcy, Duncan was up to date on her lease payments. Nine years remained on the lease. Landlord was able to re-let the premises but for only $4,000 per month. Landlord files a proof of claim in Duncan's Chapter 7 case for $108,000: 108 months (9 years) x $1,000 (the difference between Duncan's monthly rental and the new monthly rental rate). The Chapter 7 trustee objects to Landlord's proof of claim. What is the basis for the trustee's objection?

ANSWERS TO QUESTION I

1.   Classes #2 & #4 are impaired, because their contractual rights were changed. For Crafty, Apex changed the payment period while for the general unsecured creditors Apex agreed to pay only 20% of what was owed. In order to obtain confirmation under § 1129(a) as a consent plan, each class of claims must *either* be unimpaired (Classes 1 & 3) *or* accept the plan. Class #4 contains $280,000 in claims, including Crafty. The problem is that Flighty's claim is $100,000 of the total $280,000 in Class #4, or about 36% of the total amount of claims. In order for a class of claims to accept the plan, more than half in number (3 of the 4 will vote "yes") and at least two-thirds in amount must accept. *See* § 1126(c). Without Flighty's claim as a "yes," the two-thirds in amount requirement is not met. Thus, there can be no consent plan.

   But, if at least one impaired class votes "yes," Apex may proceed to cram down. Crafty is an impaired "yes" class, so § 1129(a)(10) is met and Apex may try unsecured creditor cram down. Section 1129(b)(2) requires that the plan not discriminate unfairly. The separation of the administrative convenience creditors into Class #3 is proper under § 1122(b). The plan also must be fair and equitable. For a plan to be fair and equitable with regard to a non-accepting unsecured class (§ 1129(b)(2)(B)), the plan either must pay the unsecured claims in full (which it does not do) *or* not allow any junior claimant to receive or retain property. This is the absolute priority rule, and the plan violates it by allowing the owners of the firm to retain their interests in the firm if Class #4 votes "no." (*Note:* There is no *new value* proposed in the plan.) Therefore, if Flighty votes "no," then Apex cannot confirm its proposed plan.

2.   First, Apex qualifies for subchapter V. It is engaged in commercial or business activities and its primary business activity is producing widgets, not owning single asset real estate. Apex's aggregate debts, all of which are not contingent and unliquidated, fall below the debt limit for subchapter V debtors. Finally, all of Apex's debts arose from its business activities. B.C. § 1182(1).

   The same analysis for Part 1 of the question applies to Apex not being able to obtain confirmation of a consent plan; Apex cannot satisfy § 1129(a)(8)'s requirement that all impaired classes vote to accept the plan. B.C. § 1191(a), (b). Subchapter V, however, has its own cram down provisions, which has no absolute priority rule. Therefore, the fact that the four family members will retain their ownership interests in Apex does not automatically preclude confirmation by cram down. Nonetheless, the plan must not unfairly discriminate (*see* analysis under Part 1 above) and must be fair and equitable. To be fair and equitable, the plan, as of its effective date, *either* must provide that (a) all of the debtor's projected disposable income to be received during the three-year period, or such longer time not to exceed five years that the court fixes, starting with the plan's first payment is applied to making plan payments *or* (b) the value of the property to be distributed during the three years (or maximum five years) starting on the date of the first plan distribution is not less than the debtor's projected disposable income. B.C. § 1191(c). Projected disposable income for a corporate entity, like Apex, means the income that Apex receives that is not reasonably necessary to pay expenses necessary for the continuation, preservation, or operation of its business. B.C. § 1191(d)(2). Without more facts, however, it is impossible to determine whether Apex satisfies the "fair and equitable" requirement and, thus, whether Apex can obtain confirmation of its subchapter V plan through cram down.

   Remember: The subchapter V plan also must satisfy the heightened feasibility requirement. Depending on the court's feasibility determination, the plan also may have to provide appropriate remedies in the event that plan payments are not made. B.C. § 1191(c)(3).

ANSWERS TO QUESTION II

1.   First, when Darlene files for bankruptcy she must deposit the next month's rent of $650 with the clerk of the court. Her state allows her to cure the default that gave rise to the judgment for

possession, so she must file a certification to that effect with the petition and serve the certification on the landlord. *See* § 362(*l*)(1). Second, Darlene must pay the past-due rental owed (cure) within 30 days of the filing of the petition. She also must file a certification that she has cured with the bankruptcy court and serve that certification on the landlord. If she does so, then the stay will not lift under § 362(b)(22). That means that the landlord cannot evict her because the stay would prohibit the landlord from doing so.

2. Section 521(a)(6) provides that the car will no longer be estate property and that the automatic stay will terminate as to the stay on day 45 after the § 341 meeting, unless Darlene either redeems or signs a reaffirmation agreement. Because the contract contains an *ipso facto* clause CC could argue that the bankruptcy filing was an event of default and that once the stay is gone CC may repossess the car. Darlene needs the car for work. Section 521(a)(6) states that the creditor may take action as allowed by "applicable nonbankruptcy law." But, state law here does not allow repossession when the debtor is paying on the vehicle. Therefore, if Darlene does nothing, the stay will lift but CC cannot repossess the car because Darlene is paying on the vehicle and, thus, there is no event of default apart from filing for bankruptcy, which this jurisdiction does not recognize as an event of default.

Note: State law varies on the legal effect of ipso facto clauses.

ANSWERS TO QUESTION III

1. Dorothy and Ed are above-median income debtors, because they earn $60,000 per year and median income is $59,000. Their means test expenses leave $200 per month, which multiplied by 60 equals $12,000. Because $12,000 is above $9,075 (no presumption of abuse) but below $15,150 (presumption of abuse), the secondary abuse test must be done. Dorothy and Ed have $160,000 in unsecured debt—$87,000 in medical bills, $70,000 in credit card debt, and $3,000 on Ed's car. [*New Motors'* secured claim is $22,000. Ed is an individual in a Chapter 7 case, so replacement value for property acquired for personal use is the price charged by a retail merchant. *See* § 506(a)(2)] Twenty-five percent of $160,000 = $40,000. Because the amount that they have left over each month x 60 = $12,000, which is significantly less than 25% of their unsecured debt, there is no presumption of abuse. Dorothy and Ed simply do not have the financial resources to pay even 25% of their unsecured creditors' claims. They may file for Chapter 7.

2. Because Dorothy and Ed are married and filing jointly, they can double the federal exemptions. § 522(m).

    1) Homestead: $27,900 × 2 = $55,800. The problem is that after taking account of the mortgage of $107,650, there is still $11,550 in equity.

    2) Vehicles: The value of the vehicles is determined by § 506(a)(2), because Dorothy and Ed are individuals contemplating a Chapter 7 case, and the cars were acquired for personal use. Thus, the values are $21,000 for Dorothy's and $22,000 for Ed's. Neither Dorothy nor Ed has any equity to exempt.

    3) Jewelry: Dorothy and Ed each may fully exempt their jewelry, because each has jewelry worth less than $1,875. *See* § 522(d)(4).

    4) Household goods: All may be exempted, because the total value of $26,000 is less than the maximum allowed for a married couple. § 522(d)(3). In addition, each item of clothing or household good is valued at $700 or less.

    5) Pension: an ERISA-qualified pension is not property of the estate under § 541(c)'s spendthrift trust clause.

    6) Wildcard: they have exhausted the homestead exemption, so they only have $2,950 left ($1,475 each), which they can apply to their home.

Conclusion: Dorothy and Ed can protect everything except all the equity in their home. After taking the homestead exemption and adding the $1,475 (2x) from the wildcard and taking account of the bank's mortgage, there still is $8,600 in equity for which there is no exemption. Calculation = $175,000 (home value) − $107,650 (mortgage on house) − $55,800 (homestead exemption) − $2,950 (wildcard exemption) = $8,600. Therefore, while they qualify for Chapter 7, it may not be a good choice for them. The trustee may sell the couple's home to get the nonexempt value for the benefit of the unsecured creditors.

ANSWERS TO QUESTION IV

The transfer of the clock is avoidable by the Chapter 13 trustee using either § 548 and/or § 544(b) with the Uniform Fraudulent Transfer Act (UFTA) or the Uniform Voidable Transactions Act (UVTA), whichever applies in the jurisdiction. The trustee can argue either constructive fraud, which is easier, or actual fraud.

On the constructive fraud issue under § 548(a)(1)(B)(i) & (ii)(I), Darius was insolvent on the date of the transfer (past 18 months and transfer happened a little over a year ago) and the transfer was for less than reasonably equivalent value as Jade paid nothing for it. The same is true under § 544(b)(1) using § 5 of the UFTA or UVTA. The only difference between § 548 and § 5 of both the UFTA and UVTA is that § 5 applies only to present creditors; the Bankruptcy Code does not distinguish between present and future creditors. In this case, however, the hospital was a present creditor at the time of the transfer. The statute of limitations has not run yet on either § 548 (2 years) or the UFTA or UVTA (4 years; *see* § 9 of UFTA, UVTA).

The Chapter 13 trustee also has a decent case for actual fraud under both § 548 and § 544 (pulling in § 4 of the UFTA or UVTA). There are several badges of fraud: (1) a transfer for less than reasonably equivalent; (2) to an insider—the sister Jade; (3) while debtor was insolvent; and (4) around the same time as the hospital turned over his case for collection.

In terms of recovery from Jade, the trustee would move under § 550. Jade does not have a defense here since she is the initial transferee. Section 548(c) does not help her with regard to a lien as she did not give value. The same is true for § 550(e)—she made no improvements. In fact, Jade has no claim at all since she was never a creditor—she paid nothing for the clock.

ANSWERS TO QUESTION V

1. No, Duncan may not use the Illinois exemptions. Under § 522(b)(3)(A) Duncan had to have been domiciled in Illinois for 730 days prior to filing for bankruptcy. She lived in Illinois for less than one year prior to filing, so the statute then requires an examination of the 6 months prior to that two-year period, which is August of 2018 through the end of January of 2019. Duncan lived in New York City and Los Angeles during that time period. She spent about 4 months in L.A. and 2 months in New York City. If the debtor is domiciled in more than one state during the 6-month period, the state in which debtor is domiciled for the "longer portion of the 180-day period than in any other place" is the state whose exemptions govern. Therefore, the California exemptions apply to Duncan's case.

2. Under § 502(b)(6), the claim of a lessor resulting from the termination of a lease of real property is rent reserved by the lease for the *greater* of one year *or* 15% of the remaining term, not to exceed three years, plus any unpaid rent on the petition filing date. One year's rent is $60,000 (12 months × $5,000). The term remaining on the lease is 9 years or 108 months; 15% of that remaining term is a little over 16 months for $81,000. (*Note:* The 15% cap does not exceed three years' rent.) Either way, Landlord does not recover $108,000. Instead, Landlord gets $81,000, because it is the *greater* of one year's rent *or* rent for 15% of the lease's remaining term.

   Note: If the term remaining on the lease is greater than 80 months but less than 240, then the Landlord recovers rent for 15% of the lease's remaining term.

Table of Cases

Table of Statutes

Table of Rules